Gower
Handbook
of Training
and Development

SECOND EDITION

GOWER
HANDBOOK
OF TRAINING
AND DEVELOPMENT

SECOND EDITION

Edited by
John Prior, MBE, FITD

Gower

**in association with
the Institute of Training Development**

First published 1991
Second edition published by
Gower Publishing Limited
Gower House
Croft Road
Aldershot
Hampshire GU11 3HR
England

Gower
Old Post Road
Brookfield
Vermont 05036
USA

Reprinted 1997

British Library Cataloguing in Publication Data
Development. – 2Rev.ed
  I. Prior, John
  658.3214
  ISBN 0–566–07446–X

Library of Congress Cataloguing-in-Publication Data

Gower handbook of training and development / edited by John Prior. –
  2nd ed.
    p.   cm.
    Includes index.
    ISBN 0–586–07446–X
    1. Employees – Training of – Handbooks, manuals, etc.   2. Personnel
  management – Handbooks, manuals, etc.   I. Prior, John, 1933–
  II. Title: Handbook of training and development.
  HF5549.5.T7G557   1994
  658.3′ 124–dc20   93–36857
                                                                         CIP

Typeset in 10 point Cheltenham by
Raven Typesetters, Ellesmere Port, S. Wirral
and printed in Great Britain by
Hartnolls Limited, Bodmin.

To Heather, Katie, Mandy and Jacquie,
with my love and thanks for their
patience and forebearance with a
trainer over so many years.

'I have a feeling that you can do a lot
if you've been properly trained. I hope
I have been.'

Her Majesty the Queen broadcasting from
Buckingham Palace in the BBC programme
Elizabeth R. on 6th February 1992.

Contents

and maintenance systems – training design – orientation and the psychological contract – problems, not symptoms – guidelines sales training function – research, development and design – off-the-job delivery – on-the-job follow-up – validation – reaction – knowledge – behaviour – the trainer

PART THREE   WAYS AND MEANS

– doing – internalized learning skills – blockages – motivation – contracts – styles – trainer-centred and group-centred approaches

PART FOUR TRAINING FOR SKILLS

PART FIVE MANAGEMENT TRAINING AND DEVELOPMENT

xiii

List of illustrations

Foreword by Sir James Munn, OBE FITD

President of the Institute of Training and Development 1989–92

This handbook appeared at an opportune time, as shown by the success of the first edition. I am very pleased that a second edition has been justified so soon and that it has been possible to revise the text substantially to take new developments into consideration.

Over recent years a new impetus has been given to training and development by the work of the National Training Task Force and the Training and Enterprise Councils. This impetus has increased with all the additional competitive pressures of the single European market. The larger organizations have for the most part recognized what is required: the volume of training has to be increased and its quality improved. Smaller companies are also realizing in increasing numbers that they too need training and development if they are to be successful and grow – perhaps even to survive.

To be effective, training must be properly planned and delivered, up-to-date and well based. That, in turn, requires a thorough grasp of the principles and practice of human resource development (HRD), and this handbook provides well-informed coverage of the whole field of HRD.

Compiled with the encouragement and support of the Institute of Training and Development, the handbook is an authoritative work that will prove most useful to students of training and development. However, its main function is as a source of reference for all who have a responsibility for planning or delivering training and development: T&D managers and directors; and also line managers, who *xvii* have a duty to ensure that their staff become as effective as possible. If training is to give a full return on investment, training managers need to be thoroughly professional in their approach. This publication should assist towards that end, for it contains much practical advice, as well as useful theory.

Edited for Gower by John Prior, the handbook has been carefully planned and structured. Contributions of individual authors are arranged in five parts to form a coherent whole, and there is a reading list at the end of most chapters.

The handbook is a most useful addition to the literature of training and development, and I am confident that it will continue to help both trainers and students for a considerable time to come.

Preface to the second edition

It has been widely recognized within the training and development profession that the first edition of this comprehensive handbook met a long-felt need by assembling a range of contributions that covered most aspects of the T & D field. This second edition has been revised throughout to reflect the many important changes that have taken place since. It also includes three completely new chapters: on culture and learning, how people learn and choosing resources.

For many years training and development managers have felt the need for guidance in fulfilling and improving their professional role in business. Directors and line managers must also have had an uneasy feeling from time to time that they were not adequately meeting their personal responsibility for developing the full potential of their staff. Admittedly, this may not be brought home to some of them until they miss being promoted because they have not trained one of their subordinates to take over!

There has been no shortage of books on the multifarious aspects of the trainer's job. It was felt, however, that it would be useful to have a number of views and advice, gathered from experts in the field, readily available in one volume. No fewer than 49 training and development professionals have pooled their knowledge and experience to produce a guide to the most important aspects of T & D, ranging from the environment in which it operates to detailed suggestions as to how it can be done.

The handbook is presented in five parts: the world of training and development; planning and managing it; methods, techniques and aids; training for skills; and some aspects of management development. Where appropriate, the chapters are illustrated by figures or diagrams. In addition to the many reading lists there are two glossaries: one on training terms at the end, and another on computer-based and interactive video terms, in Chapter 26.

The theme running through the book is professionalism leading to the highest quality, with which there can be no compromise.

xix

Training does not have to be trendy to be effective and profitable, so well-tried methods are included as well as the most modern. The common factor is that they must always be systematically planned and professionally carried out in the interest of the individual as well as of the organization. Sir John Harvey-Jones highlighted this in his excellent television review of a range of businesses, by analysing various aspects of what he so aptly called the current commercial revolution. He stressed the need for the total involvement, participation and training of all members of the organization.

Training and development must of course be related to actual business needs. It follows that training managers must understand how their organizations work, and be informed of future plans, so that they can provide appropriate training objectives. They must be taken into the confidence of their boards. It is pointless expecting them to produce the right answers if they have not been told in good time what is planned for the future in the line of corporate change. Similarly, senior management should be aware of, approve of, and be involved in, the training and development that is going on.

Over the past 25 years considerable strides have been made in T & D in the United Kingdom, but we have been overtaken by some of our overseas competitors. At this critical time, however, the situation is improving, as the boards of many more firms are belatedly realizing what they stand to lose if they do not make the most of all their resources. Training is particularly important at times of recession: without it we cannot take advantage of upturns when they do come.

Traditionally, staff were thrown into the deep end or left to work things out for themselves by trial and error. Sometimes the only advice consisted of being criticized when things were less than perfect. This was often accompanied by remarks to the effect that potential efficiency had ceased after the recruitment of the critic! Even now, the T & D function in many firms is not run on business lines, at times not even on a proper budgetary basis. Indeed, there are still a few organizations who consider poaching to be cheaper than training. It can be, of course, and is certainly easier, but only in the very short term.

One of the most encouraging recent developments has been the progress made in T & D by comparatively small firms. Some of these have received awards for their whole-hearted implementation of effective training, often in difficult circumstances. The National Training Awards scheme has undoubtedly encouraged practical programmes in a wide range of businesses that hitherto had not realized their potential for improvement. It would be difficult nowadays to find a progressive and successful business that did not offer an effective training and development programme to all its staff. When this is professionally implemented, the firm reaps further benefit. So, too, does the individual employee, whose personal development and potential are enhanced.

Vitally important as it is, however, T & D has to be taken in the context of the business as a whole. It exists to improve the organization's profitability and to help individuals grow to the limit of their potential. It is a means to an end, and should not be mistaken for an end in itself.

All managers are measured by the effectiveness of what they do, and T & D managers should not expect to be judged differently. It is hoped this book will help them to provide value for money. Deeds, not intentions, are what matter, so above all we must ask whether our programmes achieve what they set out to do. Constant evaluation is necessary as part of the continuous review process. What might have been adequate for yesterday's comparatively static situation is not enough in today's ever-changing climate – and will certainly be quite insufficient for the challenges of tomorrow.

Training is one of the most rewarding professions and yet it is encouraging that really good trainers are never fully satisfied with their efforts. One might say that anyone who is satisfied should be looking for another job. Perhaps trainers have underplayed their role far too much in the past. Had it not been for professional bodies such as the Institute of Training and Development and the Institute of Personnel Management, government, industry and commerce alike would be less aware of the necessity for T & D. But trainers themselves must live up to their agreed standards and prove their own value.

The contributors to this handbook have certainly proved themselves. They are busy people, as successful professionals tend to be; but, as we all know, the way to get something done promptly and well is to ask someone who is overworked already. I unashamedly applied that principle in recruiting a team for the book. Now, therefore, I should like to acknowledge with thanks their co-operation, and also the thorough way in which they have prepared their chapters with the object of helping other trainers and managers, by sharing their knowledge and experience. Their enthusiasm for this venture has been very stimulating, as has that of Sir James Munn who has kindly contributed a foreword again.

Our colleagues are not trying to sell you their wares as the only way of doing things effectively. Nevertheless, they are suggesting that it might be worth your while to look in more detail at some of the ideas and experiences that they have used successfully elsewhere.

I have not hesitated to use selected items from other publications where relevant. In particular, I have drawn on both the *Gower Handbook of Management Development* and their *Personnel Management Handbook*. In every case the original material has been reviewed by the authors before inclusion in this book.

Editing this handbook has been made easier because of the proven standing of our contributors in the world of T & D, and by their willingness as true professionals to adapt flexibly to our aims and the agreed synopsis in the interest of our readers. This does not necessarily mean we all agree on everything! Obviously no single volume can possibly cover any professional activity completely, but we hope this one will prove valuable to everyone concerned with the continuous training and development of 'human resources', our most important (and expensive!) resource.

John Prior

Notes on contributors

MICHAEL ABRAHAMS FIPM
(Choosing resources)

Michael Abrahams is a partner in a management development consultancy. Before setting up the consultancy he was head of Management Development and Training at Marks & Spencer, a post he held for 15 years. He is an academic advisor to the City University MBA programme, and has been a visiting lecturer at Templeton College, Oxford, Ashridge Management College, and Manchester Business School. Assignments within the commercial sector cover a variety of enterprises, including retailing, supermarkets, electronics, distribution, recruitment and fast foods.

CHRIS BELL BSc MEd PGCE
(Using training aids)

Chris Bell is currently head of Continuing Education and Development at the University of Plymouth. His department is responsible for industrial short courses, staff development, franchising of polytechnic courses into colleges in the south-west, European innovations and projects, and the Training, Enterprise and Education Directorate of the Employment Department's *Enterprise in Higher Education* project.

Previously, he was responsible for a wide range of staff-development activities within the University, including teaching about the use of media. Before joining the University, he worked in the School of Education at the University of Bath, where he was involved in evaluation and distance learning for a multinational oil company. Editor of the journal, *Educational and Training Technology International*, he is also the author and editor of several books, mainly on evaluation and assessment.   *xxiii*

ROGER BENNETT PhD MIMgt FITD MBPsS CEng
(Developing effective trainers; the effective trainer checklist)

Dr Roger Bennett has over twenty years' experience in training, management education, research and consulting. Having carried out much research into trainer effectiveness, he has conducted workshops, seminars and conferences on this subject around the world. He has worked in engineering and in several business schools, including the International Management Centre where he launched the United Kingdom's first Master's degree in T & D, and he has been a board director of two companies. Editor of the *Journal of European Industrial Training*, he was also series editor for the ITD's *Get in There* workbook and video package for training managers, and his published works include *Improving Trainer Effectiveness* (Gower, 1988). He now runs his own company called The Management Development Consultancy.

PETER BOWEN BA(Hons) MLitt FITD FIMgt
(The trainer as manager)

Peter Bowen is Managing Director of Management Performance Limited, and was previously Company Training Manager for W.H. Smith Limited. His career includes academic appointments as the Director of the Centre of Employment Policy Studies at the Henley Management College, and as Head of the Department of Behavioural Studies at Newcastle upon Tyne Polytechnic. Specializing in technical and management skills assessment and training, he is currently Professor of Management Training and Development at the International Management Centres, Buckingham.

ANNETTE BRADLEY
(Interpersonal skills training)

Annette Bradley specializes in counselling, team-building and interpersonal skills training. She has a particular interest in the application of Gestalt psychology in management development. Her earlier work experience included drug rehabilitation, sales, marketing and the theatre.

J.C. CARROLL CEng FIMechE FIMgt FITD
(Standards in the training context)

Chris Carroll is a chartered engineer who continues to bring the engineer's searching, analytical and constructively critical approach to the training function. He has been involved in industrial training for more than thirty years, in this country and abroad, and in 1988 was awarded the International Gold Medal of the Institute of Training and Development for services to international human resource development. He is involved actively with a wide range of bodies which influence the design of training and development policies and practices in the United Kingdom, and was until recently the director with responsibility for
xxiv the development and delivery of standards in engineering manufacture for the

Engineering Training Authority, the only authorized Industry Lead Body for the engineering manufacturing sector.

DAVID CASEY BSc Cert Ed
(Team-building)

David Casey started his working life as a teacher. From those early days, a deep interest in creating learning environments has been a continuing theme in his work. His interest in management began when he left teaching to manage the R&D laboratories of Berger Paints, and later the training function for part of Reed International. He then combined his managerial expertise with his initial teaching experience and started creating learning environments for managers. Since 1971 this work has widened to encompass full management teams and whole organizations in both the private and public sectors in the United Kingdom. As well as working independently, he is an associate at Ashridge.

DAVID CLUTTERBUCK BA(Hons)
(Using evaluation techniques)

David Clutterbuck is an entrepreneur and management author with more than 20 titles to his name, including *The Winning Streak, The Marketing Edge, Turnaround, Everyone Needs a Mentor, Making Customers Count* and *Raising the Profile* (of HR). Formally editor of *International Management*, he has founded numerous other management periodicals. He lectures and carries out management development projects internationally. Since 1982 he has been the chairman of The ITEM Group, a communications project-management company with special interests in training, corporate communications and in-company periodicals. He is also senior partner in Clutterbuck Associates, an editorial-based management company.

BILL CRITCHLEY MBA
(Team-building)

Bill Critchley is a business director of Ashridge Consulting Group, and an independent organization change agent and counsellor. He specializes in strategic change, with particular emphasis on the deep cultural level of organizations, and their underlying systemic nature. Much of his work is process consulting at various levels, working with groups to clarify their purpose, improve their interrelationships and facilitate the process of change.

He gained his MBA from Cranfield School of Management, and holds a Diploma in Organization Consulting (Gestalt) and a Diploma in Clinical Psychotherapy (Gestalt). Prior to joining Ashridge Consulting Group, he worked for Hay Management Consultants, Sheppard Moscow & Associates and Marketing Improvements Ltd. Before going to Cranfield, Bill worked as a marketing director within the C.T. Bowring Group, as a product manager at Lever Bros. & Associates, and as a retail area manager for K Shoes Ltd.

His published works are: *Second Thoughts on Team Building, Organizations get stuck too* and *Managing organizational change – is it just an illusion?*   *xxv*

IAN CUNNINGHAM BSc MA PhD FRSA FIMgt FInstD FITD FIPM
(Self-managed learning)

Dr Ian Cunningham is an independent consultant and a Visiting Fellow at Sheffield Business School. He is also on the board of the Centre for Self-managed Learning and of the Centre for the Study of Change. He was chief executive of Roffey Park from 1987–1992. He has been a Senior Research Fellow at Ashridge Management College; chairman and managing director of the consultancy Metacommunications Ltd; a divisional head in a regional management centre; a trainer in local government; a manager and a research chemist. From time to time he has also held visiting professorships in the United States and India.

He has published over 80 articles and papers on strategic management, leadership, management, learning, organizational change and cross-cultural management. He has recently completed a book on *Strategic Learning*.

STUART DALZIEL CIPM FITD
(Organizational training needs)

Stuart Dalziel is now retired. Following production experience, he had 30 years' involvement in training and personnel matters at local and national levels. A founder member of the IPM Training and Development Committee, he was vice-president for Training and Development from 1970 to 1972. As a member of the examination committee he chaired the group which designed and launched what is now the Institute's Certificate in Personnel Practice. Latterly he has been a consultant in education and training, and IPM examiner in vocational education and training.

A.I.S. DEBENHAM DFC AE MA FIMgt FITD
(Management games and case studies)

Ian Debenham graduated in Mechanical Sciences at Cambridge and joined the Asiatic Petroleum Company (Shell), spending a year in the United States with Shell Pipeline. There followed six years' service with the Royal Air Force, including two years' training pilots and two years' crew training; he was then Wing Commander Chief Instructor of an operational training unit.

Returning to Shell, and after experience in the Aviation, Supplies and Industrial Relations departments, he spent ten years in the Training department, where he was head of the Training Services Division.

He left to become an independent consultant, in which role he pioneered the Techniques of Training courses for BACIE and ran them in commercial and industrial companies in the United Kingdom and Hong Kong. He has also planned and run management development programmes, and has presented papers at the International Federation of Training and Development Organizations in Dublin, Calgary, Sydney and Madrid.

EUGENE DONNELLY MPhil CertEd DipECON and PolSc
(The need to market training)

Eugene Donnelly started his professional career as a Training Development Officer with the Industrial Training Service shortly after the passing of the Industrial Training Act in 1964, and this consultancy role was followed by a period in which he was actively engaged in the training of Training Officers to meet the requirements of the new legislation. He then moved on to a wider personnel function and was responsible for the personnel management courses at what is now Middlesex University. His research, consultancy and publication interests lie in two main areas, the training of trainers and the training of junior managers.

DAVID LOUIS FRANCIS BA DipEd DLitt MIPM FIOD
(Communication skills training)

Dr Dave Francis is a prolific writer on management topics and has an extensive teaching and consulting practice in Europe and the Far East. He specializes in team development, decision making processes and business strategy development. His books include: *The Top Team Audit, Improving Work Groups, Unblocking Organizational Communication* and *Step-by-Step Competitive Strategy*.

JOHN FRICKER BA DipEd MA FITD
(Training for change: an investment in people)

After a career in the Army involved in a wide range of training and development activities, **John Fricker** joined National Westminster Bank Group in 1979, where he became Director of Group Training, with responsibility for the co-ordination and direction of all training worldwide. He was chairman of the Institute of Training and Development, member of the Advisory Committee on Education and Training of the London Chamber of Commerce and Industry, national chairman of the Open University Steering Group on Enterprise in Higher Education and visiting Fellow at the Cranfield School of Management.

JOHN GILES MA DipSocSci CIPM FIMgt FITD FInstAM
(Learning how we learn)

John Giles was director of Roffey Park Management College and Institute from 1969 until he retired in 1987. He was Vice-President, Training and Development, Institute of Personnel Management (1975–77), Chairman of the British Association for Commercial and Industrial Education (BACIE) 1980–82, chairman of the Institute of Training and Development (1986–88) and President of the International Federation of Training and Development Organizations (1989). From early experience in the newspaper industry and public relations together with work in the Youth and Youth Employment services, he spent several years *xxvii* managing the Education and Training Departments of the Boots Company and, later, of the Co-operative Wholesale Society.

ADRIAN GREEN MITD AIMgt
(Practical approaches to culture and training)

Adrian Green has designed and implemented management of change and management development programmes for companies in the financial services sector and has spent many years working with organizations in both the public and private sectors to research and develop leading edge strategies and training programmes. He carries out training and research work with various universities and is also a consultant with the British Association for Commercial and Industrial Education (BACIE).

VALERIE HAMMOND BA FIMgt FRSA
(The learning organization)

Valerie Hammond is Chief Executive of Roffey Park Management Institute, having previously been at Ashridge. This followed a career in advertising, information technology and the oil industry. Current interests include management learning, cultural and organization change, the management of diversity leadership and women's development. She plays an active role in the European Foundation for Management Development, is a past president of the European Women's Management Development Network.

KEN HILL
(Training the sales force)

Ken Hill was, at the time of writing, manager of Sales Training for the Prudential Assurance Company, responsible for the sales and sales management training of Europe's largest employed sales force (c.12,000 staff). He joined Prudential in December 1984, with a brief to restructure sales training to enable the company to cope with the substantial changes it was undertaking in response to market and legislative pressures, and he managed a budget of around £17 million and some 140 training staff. Previously, he was Operations director of a consultancy practice, and provided training and consultancy services in various industries in the United Kingdom, Europe and South Africa. Since October 1992, he has 'practised what he preached' and moved to front line operations as a branch manager, responsible for around 100 sales and sales support staff, and a new business target of £2.5 millions.

VIVIEN HODGSON BSc PhD
(On-line education and development)

Dr Vivien Hodgson is a lecturer at the Centre for the Study of Management Learning at the University of Lancaster. She was awarded a New Blood Lectureship in 1986 to investigate the application of new technology for management education. Since then she has published several articles on this and the related topic of open and distance learning.

PETER HONEY BA(Psych) DLitt DipEd FIMC FITD
(Preferred learning skills)

Dr Peter Honey is a chartered psychologist who works as a management consultant. He worked for Ford Motor Company and British Airways before becoming a freelance in 1969. He specializes in anything to do with people's behaviour and its consequences, and divides his work between designing and running training programmes, consultancy assignments and writing. He has written widely on behavioural topics in over fifty publications. His books include *Face to Face Skills*, *The Manual of Learning Styles*, *Solving People-Problems*, *Improve Your People Skills*, *The Manual of Learning Opportunities* and *Problem People and How to Manage Them*. He has advised on the contents of many training films and written the accompanying booklets. He features in the Video Arts production *Talking about Behaviour*.

He is Professor of Managerial Learning at the International Management Centres; a Fellow of the Institute of Management Consultants and the Institute of Training and Development; a chartered psychologist with the British Psychological Society; and a member of the Association for Management Education and Development.

ROY JOHNSON BSc MBA
(Neuro-linguistic programming)

Roy Johnson is Managing Director of PACE and uses NLP to support companies and individuals in the process of performance improvement and change. He has developed and run programmes for senior managers, managers and sales people in blue chip companies, the public sector and smaller companies. Before setting up PACE in 1985, he was an officer in the Royal Navy, then spent 10 years in Rank Xerox, as a Regional Manager and Manager of Management Training. He is a highly experienced trainer and Master Practitioner of NLP.

IAN ALISTAIR JOHNSTON BSc PhD
(The changing environment)

Dr Ian Johnston, a graduate of Birmingham University, is Director General of the Training, Enterprise and Education Directorate of the Employment Department. He joined the Employment Department in 1969. Between 1971 and 1972 he was Private Secretary to the Permanent Secretary, Sir Denis Barnes; during *xxix*

1975–77 he was a First Secretary (Labour Attaché) to the British Embassy, Brussels and in 1978, he became an Assistant Secretary (Director, ACAS). He has worked for the Training, Enterprise and Education Directorate (and its predecessor organizations, the Manpower Services Commission and the Training Agency) since 1984.

ROBERT J. KELLY DipEd MIMgt MITD
(Glossary)

Robert Kelly directs HRD projects world-wide. He is acknowledged by governments and corporations as an effective agent of change. He drafts legislation and national development plans for governments and has directed industrial start-up projects as joint ventures for corporations and international agencies. His contribution to human resources development in the Third World has been acclaimed by the World Bank and certain United Nations specialized agencies.

CAROL LAW MA
(Individual and group learning)

Carol Law joined the Industrial Training Research Unit in 1981 and has worked on a wide range of projects, including the POISE project (Project on Instructor Style Effectiveness) which identified the techniques used by effective instructors. She was appointed a Director of the Unit in 1985. After leaving the Unit in 1990, she joined British Gas to work within the Training and Management Development function. On secondment, she now resides in Washington, DC, where she is manager of Coroporate Programs at the International Management and Development Institute, and also works on pre-school education issues in the United States for the Center for Strategic & International Studies. She has published widely in the field of training and development.

BOBBIE McCLELLAND
(The changing environment)

Bobbie McClelland is a Senior Executive Officer in the Training, Enterprise and Education Directorate of the Employment Department. She joined the Employment Department in 1977 and is currently Personal Assistant to Dr Ian Johnston, Director General of the Directorate.

DAVID McCONNELL BA DipEd PhD
(On-line education and development)

Dr David McConnell is a lecturer in the Centre for the Study of Management Learning at Lancaster University. He has worked at Murdoch University in educational development, and at the Open University where he was involved in the introduction and evaluation of the Cyclops shared screen technology and electronic bulletin boards and E-mail. More recently, he was a lecturer in the

School of Education at Bath University. His current interests include open and distance learning and the educational potential of electronic networking and communication.

IAN MacKAY BSc(Econ) DMS DML MPhil MCIM
(Business language training)

The late **Ian MacKay** was a Senior Lecturer in Management at Bournemouth Polytechnic now Bournemouth University. Before moving into education he worked in economic research and subsequently held personnel and training posts in a variety of industries. He was a consultant in human resource development and the author of many articles and books on management topics.

JUDI MARSHALL BA(Hons) PhD
(Developing women managers)

Dr Judi Marshall is a Reader in Organization Behaviour in the School of Management at the University of Bath. Early in her academic career she studied managerial job stress and published extensively on this topic. In the late 1970s she turned her attention to women in management and this has been one of her main areas of research, writing and consultancy ever since. She is also interested in organizational culture and change.

KEITH MARSHALL CEng MIEE
(Training records)

Keith Marshall is a chartered engineer and head of Product Design for EnTra, the current main tasks of which are to define the competences required in engineering manufacture, and to develop standards and qualifications that will be applicable to all users of engineering skills. He started with the EITB eight years ago, beginning in the Advanced Technology team and subsequently leading the New Developments Group.

ED MOORBY MPhil BSc(Econ) CEng FIMechE FIPM FIMgt FITD
(Mentoring and coaching)

Ed Moorby has over 25 years' experience of working in training and development with Ford Motor Company, the Engineering and then Air Transport and travel ITBs, the Prudential Corporation and, most recently, the TSB Retail Bank, latterly as director of Training and Development. He has a strong interest in Europe and was president of the European Institute for Vocational Training from 1988–1993.

Since 1990 he has written *How to Succeed in Employee Development*, published by McGraw-Hill, and been a self-employed consultant. A member of the Training and Development Lead Body since its inception, he was also *xxxi* appointed as chief examiner in Employee Development for the Institute of Personnel Management in 1991.

JOHN MORRIS BSc(Econ) PhD MBA FIMgt
(Action learning: the long haul)

Dr John Morris is Emeritus Professor of Management Development at Manchester Business School and a managing partner of The Development Consortium, a consultancy specializing in action learning and organizational change. He pioneered action-learning programmes at Manchester Business School, and was awarded the Burnham Medal of the British Institute of Management for contributions to management development. He has also worked on development assignments in many leading organizations, including Willis Faber, Thorn EMI, Yorkshire Water, and the National Health Service, and has served as a member of management studies panels of the University Grants Committee and the Council for National Academic Awards.

ALAN MUMFORD BA DLitt CIPM
(Effectiveness in management development)

Alan Mumford is an independent consultant and visiting Professor of Management Development at International Management Centres. He offers help on improving management performance through effective learning processes, and has worked with senior managers and directors in a variety of organizations, including Ford of Europe and Pilkington. His previous experience in management development included periods with John Laing & Sons, IPC Magazines and International Computers Limited and a spell as a deputy chief training adviser at the Department of Employment, while for six years he was Executive Resources Adviser to the Chloride Group. From 1971 to 1973 he was Vice President (Training and Development) of the Institute of Personnel Management, and he has published numerous articles and books on management development.

SIR JAMES MUNN OBE FITD
(Foreword)

Sir James Munn, who was President of the Institute of Training and Development from 1989 to 1992, served in the Indian Civil Service from 1941 to 1948, after which he taught modern languages in Glasgow and Falkirk before becoming Rector of Rutherglen Academy 1966–1970, and of Cathkin High School 1970–1983. A member of the Consultative Committee on the Curriculum from 1968 onwards, he was appointed chairman of that Committee between 1980 and 1987, and he also served for ten years as a member of the University Grants Committee. He held the position of chairman of the MSC Committee for Scotland for four years from 1984, during which period he was chairman of the MSC/Training Commission from 1987 to 1988, and he is currently a University
xxxii Commissioner.

HUGH PARRY FCII FITD MIMgt
(Training for quality)

Hugh Parry is an Enforcement Officer (Training and Competence) with the Life Insurance and Unit Trust Regulatory Organization (LAUTRO). Before taking up his present position, he had gained over 20 years' experience in insurance and training, both in the United Kingdom and abroad. He is a Chartered Insurance Practitioner and holds the ITD Diploma in Training Management. He is particularly interested in encouraging people to take greater responsibility for their own personal development, leading to greater individual commitment.

KERI PHILLIPS BA MA PGCE CTA
(Interpersonal skills training)

Keri Phillips is an independent consultant specializing in self-managed learning for managers. He has co-authored several books for trainers on interpersonal skills training and consultancy skills. His career includes being a tutor at a management training college, shop-floor worker, salesperson and team leader. He has degrees in politics and a qualification in humanistic psychology.

JOHN PRIOR MBE BA FITD MIPM MIL
(Preface)

John Prior had six years of active military service in the United Kingdom, Europe and the North-West frontier, leaving the army as a brigade staff captain in the Royal Artillery. He became deputy staff controller of the Prudential, then Training and Development manager, responsible for the training, career and management development of their 22,000 full-time UK staff. A member of various committees and former president of the Institute of Training and Development, he was awarded their gold medal in 1993. Chairman of the South-East Regional National Training Awards Judging Panel for 6 years, he has also been for many years chairman of the Board of Wycombe Royal Grammar School. He was honorary secretary of the Cystic Fibrosis Trust's Sussex Region for 22 years and is still active in their service.

W. LESLIE RAE MPhil FIMC FITD
(Job training needs)

Leslie Rae is an independent management and trainer training consultant with Ellray Associates, and has many years of personal training experience. Concentrating on in-company consultancy and training in a wide range of people skills, he has worked in a number of industries and has been a training officer, a training manager and internal consultant for the Training Agency. He is a regular contributor to the professional training press and has a number of publications on management and training skills to his name.

MARGARET ANNE REID MA DipSocSci CIPM FIMgt
(Approaches and strategies)

Margaret Anne Reid had experience in Personnel and Training Management in clothing and engineering before moving to Leeds Polytechnic and becoming Principal Lecturer, responsible for Training of Trainer programmes and post-graduate Diploma in Personnel Management. She was later appointed Principal Fellow and Director of the MBA programme at the University of Leeds, where, having recently retired, she currently holds an honorary appointment. An Honorary Life Companion of the Institute of Personnel Management, she was vice-president (Education) from 1981 to 1983.

GRAHAM ROBINSON BA FInstD
(Management development and organization development)

Graham Robinson is a founder director of Kennedy Robinson Business Development, a consultancy specializing in organization and management research and development. With the company he has specialized in advising its clients on the design and development of senior management organization structures, the development of interdisciplinary project teams and working with senior managers on their own development and that of the groups for which they have responsibility. He has worked at board level with organizations including the Standard Chartered Group, CMB, British Aerospace and Granada in the private sector and with the Employment Department, the States of Guernsey Civil Service, the International Atomic Energy Agency and the UK Civil Service College.

His career has been spent almost entirely in the field of management and organization research and development, at Ashridge Management College, as a personnel director in the compter industry and, most recently, as a consultant and adviser. He is author of a number of publications on business and management development.

ROB SIBTHORPE FCII FBIBA MIMgt MITD
(The benefits of training and development)

Rob Sibthorpe is Training and Development manager with a leading inter-national group. He designs and runs courses on management skills, communi-cations and insurance subjects. His lively, incisive style makes him a popular speaker on courses and at conferences. As well as running the training scheme for his company, he is heavily involved in overseas training. His current schedule of travels includes Cyprus, the Caribbean, South America and China.

ANDREW STEWART MA PhD CPsychol AFBPsS
(Performance appraisal)

Dr Andrew Stewart is managing director of Informed Choice, consulting industrial psychologists. Previously, he lectured at Aberdeen and Surrey universities, was Personnel and Management Development officer at IBM (UK) Limited and Senior Fellow at the Institute of Manpower Studies. He is co-author (with Valerie Stewart) of *Practical Performance Appraisal, Managing the Manager's Growth*, and *Managing the Poor Performer.*

HILARY TEMPLE BA FITD
(Flexible learning)

Hilary Temple is a director of Hilary Temple Associates, a consultancy specializing in organizational development through occupational competence, the implementation of flexible/open learning in organizations and the development of case studies and open learning materials. An increasing amount of their work is in contextualizing standards for small and medium enterprises. Her recent book *Open Learning in Industry* contains many examples of open learning in action. A Fellow of the Institute of Training and Development she is a member of the editorial boards of *Open Learning* and *Open Learning Systems News.*

LINDSAY WALLACE BSc MSc CPsychol AMITD
(Training records)

Lindsay Wallace is a chartered psychologist, with a degree in Psychology, and a Master's degree in Occupational Psychology from Hatfield Polytechnic. She specialized initially in advising colleagues and client companies on selection issues, carrying out research and development projects where appropriate, particularly on trainability testing. From 1983 to 1991 she worked for the Engineering Industry Training Board, and as project leader for assessment and quality assurance in the EITB's Standards Unit. She is now APL manager at Hopwood Hall College.

GEORGE WEBSTER FIMgt FIPM FITD
(The training and development profession)

George Webster, after an early career in electrical engineering and as a technical teacher, moved into industry first as a training manager for Standard Telephones and Cables Limited, and then became Group training manager for British Domestic Appliances Limited. When the Training Services Agency was established in 1974 he joined the Industry Division to assist ITBs with the development and funding of strategic plans. In 1979 he moved to take up the newly created post of Executive Director of the Institute of Training and Development. He is a founder member of the ITD, and was President of the Institute in 1977. He was elected Chairman of the newly formed European Training and Development Organization in March 1991.

EDGAR WILLE
(The learning organization)

Edgar Wille worked initially in farming and in the coal industry. He was appointed head of Training and Development for NCB Computer Services and then head of Management Development for British Coal. As an Ashridge associate, he has worked on managing change, employment law, business ethics, international management and UK management development practices. He has written widely on management development experience, and has worked in the United States, the Middle East and Pakistan. Currently, he is Ashridge's project manager in the Czech and Slovak Republics.

TERESA WILLIAMS BA FIPM MITD
(Practical approaches to culture and training)

Teresa Williams works as a consultant in the field of training trainers, management and personal development. She has written a number of publications including *50 Activities for Developing Management Skills, Vol. 2* (Gower, 1989) and *Debriefing – the Key to Learning* (BACIE, 1991). She works in many different sectors, sizes and types of organization, and with learners from different ethnic origins. It is this diversity which has provided her with many of the ideas for practical approaches to the implications of culture on the learning and development process.

MICHAEL WOODHALL BA MA
(Business language training)

Michael Woodhall is head of International Programmes at Dorset Business School
(Bournemouth University). International Programmes provides the local, national and international business community with a range of courses and consultancy services on language for effective business communication. A Germanist by training, he was head of Languages at one of France's leading business schools before setting up and running the Language Learning Centre at Manchester Business School. He is co-author (with Professor Marianne Howarth) of *Making Your Mark – Effective Business Communication in Germany* and *Hotel Europa – Deutschland – Business German for Beginners*.

PHILLIP WRIGHT PhD FITD
(The cultural mosaic)

Dr Phillip Wright holds a PhD in Industrial Training and Institutional Management from the Penn State University. For the past ten years he has served in a voluntary capacity as Academic Dean of the Canadian Institute of Management, where his duties have included policy and academic achievement for a management development programme with more than 2100 students in all ten Canadian provinces. At present, he is Associate Professor of Human Resources Management in the Faculty of Administration at the University of New Brunswick.

PETER WYNN ACII MITD
(Computer-based training)

Peter Wynn was until recently Open Learning manager, National Training – Design and Development at the Prudential Assurance Company. He set up a new Open Learning team supporting the Pru's office staff in 1986, following his previous experience as a manager in the Training and Development Division, and joined the National Training Design team in August 1991. He has been closely associated with the Chartered Insurance Institute, and has been both a committee member and chairman of the Training and Development Forum as well as serving on other CII committees. He has also spoken on computer-based training and interactive video at several conferences.

BERNARD WYNNE BA MSc MIPM FITD
(Using evaluation techniques)

Bernard Wynne is a director of the ITEM Group, based in Buckinghamshire. An experienced trainer and management development practitioner, and formerly head of Management Development for the Woolwich Building Society, he currently works with companies in all business sectors, advising on all aspects of training. He has special interest in the subjects of leadership, total quality and customer service.

Part One

THE WORLD OF TRAINING AND DEVELOPMENT

1   The changing environment[1]

Ian Johnston and Bobbie McClelland

Prosperity, enterprise and business growth in the 1990s demands a world-class workforce. For any nation to succeed in internationally competitive markets, the following requirements are essential:

1. companies need to invest fully in people;
2. individuals need to achieve their full potential;
3. enterprise and ideas must flourish; and
4. learning must be accessible, relevant and stimulating.

Throughout the world companies are realizing that the development of their human resources is the key not only to business survival, but also to business success.

CHALLENGES FOR THE FUTURE

Over the next decade all industrial countries face a period of rapid change and development which will pose problems. There will be ever-growing competition, not just from within the European Community, as the 'single market' becomes a reality, but from the emerging new economies of Eastern Europe, Japan and the fast developing nations of the Pacific rim. Indeed, the many new countries just starting out on industrialization will also prove serious economic rivals, especially in low-skill, low-value-added products.

There will also be substantial development in new technology, both in terms of new methods of production and goods produced, and, most importantly, in the skills required by the workforce. Environmental concerns are likely to accelerate the development of new processes and new products.

Demographic changes will have a considerable impact. In most European

[1] © Crown copyright 1991 and 1994. Reproduced with the permission of the Controller of Her Majesty's Stationery Office.

countries including the United Kingdom the labour force will grow only slowly, even if they use more effectively the untapped potential of their people. In Great Britain the labour force was projected to fall by 0.1m between mid-1992 and mid-1993 to 27.9m. By the year 2006, it is expected that the labour force will be 1.7m higher than at the mid-1992 level. Almost all of the projected increase is likely to be among women who are expected to make up 46 per cent of the workforce. About 76 per cent of those who will be in the labour force in the year 2006 are already of working age. In contrast, the developing world's population will be growing by nearly 50 per cent. So cheap labour in world markets will be in ample supply and the leading developed nations will need to concentrate even more on high-skill, high-value-added operations.

In addition, as people become better educated there will be an expectation, indeed, perhaps a demand, amongst the workforce that their employers concentrate more attention on their individual development both as employees and as citizens.

HOW TO MEET THE CHALLENGES

The challenges these issues pose mean that companies wanting to remain competitive in international, regional or even local markets must look towards developing a more highly skilled workforce, towards cultivating specialist skills in new areas and towards attaining a higher level of basic education and training in order to increase flexibility. It will mean upgrading and updating skills, improving management skills at all levels, and ensuring that all the skills individual members of the workforce possess are effectively utilized.

This implies a cultural and strategic change in how training, or human resource development, is viewed. Increasingly, training must be for the whole workforce and not just for the young new entrant. Individuals must be expected to take an active role in their own development. Line management and supervisors must add the responsibility of being trainers and mentors to their staff to their perception of key management functions. In-company training can often be veiled in secrecy or confusion or ignorance.

The need for urgent action is reinforced from a number of quarters. *Training in Britain* was a unique and wide-ranging study of vocational education and training. The study focused specifically on funding, activity and attitudes to training. It provides the most comprehensive survey findings available on training in Britain, and shows that although total training effort is considerable, the level of participation in training varies substantially. Over £18 billion, or approximately 6 per cent of the wage bill, was spent by employers in 1986/87. The level of employer investment is estimated to be rising and in 1992/93 was around £20 billion.

Despite this, one in three of the working population in Britain have no qualifications and one in three individuals had never had training. Perhaps the most significant issue exposed by the study was that for many individuals training is beyond or peripheral to their outlook. About one-third of the economically active 19- to 34-year-olds and about half of those aged 35 and over said they could not imagine any circumstances in which they would seek to undertake further education or training.

One in five employers reported conducting no training in the survey year concerned. On average employers reported that about half of their workforce had received some training. Apart from new recruits however, this was concentrated on training managers, skilled employees and others with high levels of existing skills. Few employers attempt to calculate the cost of training or to evaluate its benefits, or even to integrate planning of training with wider business or corporate plans.

In Britain this and other evidence has led to increasing concern amongst business leaders, culminating in the Confederation of British Industry (CBI) report *Towards a Skills Revolution*. Recognizing that individuals are now the only source of sustainable competitive advantage, the CBI found that skill levels are lower than those of competitor countries. The implication drawn is that to maintain and improve the position nothing short of a skills revolution is required. Efforts must be aimed at mobilizing employees' commitment and at encouraging self-development and lifetime learning. Future challenges can only be met, first, by providing better education and training that create economic, social and personal benefits, thus raising aspirations so that people expect and demand to receive education and training throughout their lifetime, and secondly, by making sure that opportunities for lifelong learning exist. The CBI concluded that there should be clear objectives for company training, and that these would be best defined by outputs in terms of nationally recognized vocational quali- fications. To this end, the CBI developed National Education and Training Targets designed to increase education attainment and skill levels, both for young people and the adult workforce. The targets have received widespread support.

European social charter

Within Europe some countries have legal minimum requirements for training by companies. In 1989 the European Commission promoted a Social Charter which stated: 'Every worker of the European Community must be able to have access to vocational training and to benefit therefrom throughout his working life.' This had been followed by a Commission proposal for a recommendation on access to continuing vocational training which is not binding on member states. Even so, leading companies will wish to develop their own strategies which are likely to be far more wide-ranging than any common-denominator or minimum legal requirements.

BRITISH GOVERNMENT ROLE

The British Goverment considers that companies should train to the extent needed to fulfil their business objectives and not to some bureaucratic external arbitrary 'minimum', and, under the Conservative administration, has preferred a voluntary approach. In December 1988, it published a White Paper, *Employment*

5

for the 1990s, which set out a new voluntary framework for training. This aimed to promote, in a new partnership with employers, the establishment of a training system which would be capable of contributing to Britain's international competitiveness.

Within this system, and indeed more generally, there are at least five levels of public support or intervention: national; sectoral; regional/local; company; and individual.

National

Most governments provide public support for basic further and higher education. Some legislate to set minimum standards for training. The British Government prefers a voluntary approach. It sees its role as setting the economic climate in which enterprise can flourish, and providing or encouraging the creation of supportive institutional arrangements in terms of education and training.

The British Government is keen that employers take the leading role in meeting the challenges faced. In 1989, a National Training Task Force (NTTF), an employer-led group, was established to advise the Government in carrying out its training responsibilities. This body has now been succeeded by the National Advisory Council for Education and Training Targets (NACETT). The Council has been formed to monitor progress towards the National Targets and advise the Government on performance and policies which influence progress towards them.

A key feature of Government policy in recent years has been the focus on establishing national training 'standards'. As part of the theme that training is necessary to fulfil business objectives, these standards are explicitly founded on the actual competences required to perform specific jobs. Such 'standards' of competence need careful expert definition, must be nationally recognized, must be set and owned by employers, and are relevant *de jure* to occupational needs.

These standards are fed into new National Vocational Qualifications. In September 1986 the National Council for Vocational Qualifications (NCVQ) was set up to take forward the introduction of a flexible qualification system. Employers were seen to have a unique role to play in identifying the standards required and in driving forward the work of the Council through their ability to define and monitor future skill requirements and training needs. About 160 employer-led 'lead industry bodies' are actively working on describing the standards required in their industries and all the main vocational examining and validating bodies are reforming and developing their awards to reflect the standards being determined by employers. There is now a comprehensive set of national vocational qualifications (NVQs) covering 80 per cent of the employed population up to degree level. Further work is being undertaken to complete the framework.

These new national qualifications are seen as crucial to efforts made to raise the quality and skills of the workforce. By setting out a defined ladder of achievement (through gaining modules or progressing through levels) they motivate as well as define competence levels. By concentrating on the end product or 'outcomes' of learning rather than on the training process itself, they provide much greater relevance to both the individual and employer, and also free companies, colleges and Training and Enterprise Councils (TECs) to use the most cost-effective routes to develop competence. They also represent a clear yardstick against which employers can assess competence levels within their workforce and make accurate judgements and plans for future training needs.

Because national vocational qualifications (NVQs) are located within a national framework, they can clearly identify the career paths people may follow through the qualification system. This offers individuals a clearer view of their future career development. Through giving credit for relevant competence NVQs in principle encourage career switches and multiskilling. They also enable employers to see how their workforce's competence can be extended and expanded to cope with ever-changing demands.

A national and comprehensive standards and qualifications system can therefore establish a clear framework for employers and providers to develop relevant and cost-effective training. It can help motivate individuals to add to skills through life by providing a clear ladder of progression.

In addition to these vocational qualifications, a new qualification, the General National Vocational Qualification (GNVQ), is being introduced in schools and colleges. GNVQs provide a broad-based vocational education involving the acquisition of basic skills and knowledge underpinning a vocational area and a range of core skills. This combination of vocational and core skills will provide a foundation from which students can progress to further and higher education or into employment and further training. The target is to build up to a framework of qualifications covering 14 broad subject areas up to the equivalent of A level standard by September 1995.

Sectoral

In most countries employers join together to act collectively in training matters, through Chambers of Commerce, other employer associations, or in associations for particular sectors of industry, which if they specialize in training matters are known as Industrial Training Organizations.

Industrial Training Organizations can provide a focal point for all training matters within a specific sector of the economy. Together with other lead bodies, they are responsible for defining the sector's current and future training needs, and for ensuring that action is taken to meet them. In Britain the sector level will have a central role to play in setting the occupational 'standards' by acting as the lead bodies bringing together employers and other interests. The network of Industrial Training Organizations at present in Britain covers around 85 per cent of the nation's workforce. There is no single model because each sector is different and requires different sectoral training.

In some countries, and in the past in Britain, sectoral or employer organizations were empowered to raise a financial levy on companies carrying out inadequate training. The Conservative Government in Britain, though, takes the

7

view that training to meet the needs of companies should take place on a voluntary basis, with companies free to choose the amount and nature of the investment made in training. In *Employment for the 1990s* the British Government therefore abolished all but three statutory training boards, but encouraged the setting up of employer-led Industrial Training Organizations on a voluntary basis.

Regional/local

Most countries have some form of regional/local state or employer organizations supporting or organizing training activity.

In Britain we now have Training and Enterprise Councils (TECs) in England and Wales and Local Enterprise Companies (LECs) in Scotland. They ensure that responsibility and power for state-funded training activity is developed to the local level, and give local top business executives the principal role, in partnership with other interests in the community. TECs are separate legal organizations with responsibility for spending public money in achieving training for young people and for unemployed people, and in stimulating enterprise and training by companies and small businesses. They are a forum for assessing economic and social needs, setting local priorities, and developing new ways of meeting the training needs of their area. Most importantly, they are taking the lead in encouraging local employers to develop training efforts which are of the scale and quality required to meet the challenges of the future.

There are 82 TECs in England and Wales, and 22 LECs in Scotland.

Companies

It is, however, at company level that the vast majority of training decisions are taken and the real opportunities are to be grasped.

The CBI report *Towards a Skills Revolution* acknowledges that in the 1990s and beyond, the future will belong to companies which compete on the basis of superior skills, responsiveness and innovative capability.

Technology can be purchased or copied, as can productive capacity and market access. Finance is rarely a constraint. In the absence of protectionist measures, ready access to raw materials or the advantages of geographic location will seldom compensate for competitive shortcomings. Teams of skilled, committed and experienced people do not just happen. They are planned, developed, and come about as a result of systematic long-term investment.

It is acknowledged that where employers have training as part of a broader 'people' strategy including careers planning, reward, and assessment practices, they rarely lose people and find it easier to recruit. Making training central to a company's operation therefore brings significant gains in business performance.

The greater rewards will come to companies which regard training as for everyone at every level in a company. The lead needs to be from the very top of the company at chairman or chief executive level and must pervade the whole workforce. This means that a company's training strategy must include management education, training and development. Directors and managers of large companies need to acquire international and strategic management skills and to give much greater emphasis to their own human-resource activities. In Britain lack of management skills and qualifications is itself regarded as a crucial problem. It is vital that Britain's managers take a leading role in and show their own absolute commitment to their personal training, development and qualifications.

The National Forum for Management Education and Development, an employer-led initiative, was set up because of the perception that Britain lagged behind its international competitors in the field of management development. The Forum aims to improve the quality of Britain's management and increase national competitive advantage. It provides a focus for debate at national and local levels by involving employers, individuals and education providers.

The Management Charter Initiative has been set up as the Forum's operating and marketing arm. Through the Management Charter Initiative, the Forum aims to increase employer awareness of management development. Any employing organization can join the Management Charter Initiative provided it signs up to the 'Charter' or Code of Practice. The Code expresses a commitment to introduce and sustain good management development practice.

'Investors in People'

A similar 'seal of approval' approach exists in Britain for company-wide training and development practice. Called 'Investors in People', it is aimed at enabling and encouraging all employers to raise their performance through the effective development of their workforce. The objective is a national standard for effective investment in people, based on actions taken by successful businesses. Companies are encouraged to meet this standard, and those which do so will be invited to seek recognition for their achievement.

The main parts of the standard are as follows:

- making a public commitment from the top to develop all employees to achieve business objectives;
- regularly reviewing the training and development needs of all employees;
- taking action to train and develop individuals on recruitment and throughout their employment; and
- evaluating investment in training and development to assess achievement and improve future effectiveness.

Although this may seem to be simple common sense or normal good practice, surprisingly few companies carry out every step systematically. So few firms meet the standard straight away and it may be seen as testing or a counsel of perfection by some. However, with CBI, TEC and Government support many firms are pledging to work towards applying the criteria in full. Such pledges to be effective need: to be open; to be from the top; to demonstrate analysis of

9

contributions to realizing plans, objectives or vision; and to make a commitment to introduce systems and set measurable targets.

'Investors in People' provides a framework for TECs to review and recognize the achievement of firms. The target is for at least half of all employers employing over 250 people to have achieved the 'Investors in People' standard by 1996.

Individuals

Training and development strategies will work best if the emphasis is on putting individuals first and providing opportunities whereby everyone can make maximum use of their potential, and if individuals are helped and motivated to make fullest use of their talents. Their horizons need to be broadened and their expectations of themselves raised.

Increasingly, the market for learning will point to the needs of the individual. This will be especially true of the growing market for adult employees who will be looking to continue their education and training.

Companies will need to develop training strategies which centre more on the individual. These strategies are likely to cover a range of practical measures, including company-wide training audits, the use of skills assessment, the development of individual action plans and the availability of guidance, coaching and monitoring. Some companies may wish to extend learning opportunities beyond the needs of workplace or career, as part of a wider education, welfare, commitment or remuneration strategy. In addition, companies will want to consider how pay, reward and assessment systems might provide incentives for improved skills and performance gained through training.

The development of action planning processes in companies will offer significant opportunities for improving existing training provision; by placing the individual at the centre of the decision concerning their future training, there should be an improved match between the individual's needs and the learning undertaken. It will also more readily identify what skills already exist among the labour force. By separating planning and provision it will be easier to highlight unnecessary barriers to learning opportunity. Finally, because the plan will seek targets and measurable output, it will focus training providers on methods of delivering learning which meet the needs of the individual more effectively.

Open and flexible learning

Learning methods which are open and flexible thus become much more important. They offer more effective and accessible routes to learning which should help make investment in training more cost-effective, especially when associated with flexible, modular accreditation systems which enable achievement to be recognized and rewarded continuously. Open and flexible learning allows the learner or trainee to undertake learning at a time, place, pace, quality and cost that suits them. As just stated, it links ideally with action planning and ongoing assessment.

New technologies as applied to the learning process (e.g. computer-based training, simulation and the application of artificial intelligence and expert systems) all allow training to be brought to the workplace or into the home in particularly powerful ways to attract individual trainees. The planner of company training and the counsellor of individual trainees now have a very wide range of methods and opportunities to meet a particular training need. Many are available in near tailor-made modules.

CONCLUSION

People are the key to the future success of any company or economy. Quality is the feature that sells goods and services, and it is competent people who assure quality. Training to recognized standards and qualifications is the route to quality performance and quality performance equals profit. For businesses to be successful they must train and motivate their main resource.

FURTHER READING

Training, Enterprise and Education Directorate of the Employment Department (1989), *Training in Britain, A Study of Funding, Activity and Attitudes*, HMSO.

Confederation of British Industry (1989), *Towards a Skills Revolution*.

Employment Department (1988), *Employment for the 1990s*, Cm540 HMSO.

European Community (1989), *European Social Charter*.

European Community (1993), 'Proposal for a Council recommendation on access to continuing vocational training', *Official Journal* of the European Communities, C23/8, 27 January.

2 The benefits of training and development

Rob Sibthorpe

The current fashion in the language of training is to call it an investment. The reasoning for this appears to be defensive. In times of economic difficulties, the training budget is often cut. By renaming training costs from an expense to an investment, training managers are hoping to protect their budgets (and, of course, their jobs).

This change of nomenclature is welcomed. If it leads to a healthy regard for the training effort, it will prove a successful ploy. However, there is a danger that the analogy may collapse under challenge. If that happens, any temporary gain made today may be difficult to sustain or recover; the world grows suspicious when old ideas are given new labels.

This chapter first examines how the investment label can be challenged. It then proposes a more exact label (within the paradigm of commerce). Finally, it details many of the benefits which, regardless of label, training offers to modern business.

Throughout this chapter the term 'business' is used in the widest sense. The same applies to related terms, like 'commerce'. It would perhaps be better to use a term like 'activity', but any word suffers from the reader's unique perspective and experience. The word 'business' suggests an activity with a productive purpose. That purpose may be to make a profit, to provide a service, to sell a machine; the 'business' may be financial, educational, manufacturing; the reader may be an engineer, a teacher, a salesman, an entrepreneur. All those who wish to pursue a purpose have many things in common. One of these things is the need for training and development.

TRAINING: IS IT AN INVESTMENT?

The *Shorter Oxford English Dictionary* defines 'investment' as 'an amount of money invested in some species of property'. The same work defines the verb thus: 'To employ (money) in the purchase of anything from which interest or profit is expected'. It is in this latter sense (incidentally dating from the early seventeenth century) that the modern label uses the term. The argument is that the costs of training produce profit. It may even be wise to spend more money to improve the quality of training – and so make more profit. Of course, this is an unassailable truth if the purpose of the business is to provide and run training programmes. For companies and consultants in this line, money spent on expanding the product can easily be seen as an investment. But the same may not be said of the buyers (which includes internal customers of an in-house training department).

For most people, an investment is something acquired because its value should increase. An oil painting, a diamond tiara, a house; while there may be occasional dips in the markets, these things usually increase in value. Of course, some elementary steps should be taken to protect the investment. An oil painting stored in a garden shed may become worthless; a diamond tiara might best be kept in the vaults of a bank; a house needs constant maintenance and repair. The extra costs of storage and care cannot be regarded as part of the investment value, because they do not affect the value proportionately. The tiara may rise from £10,000 to £15,000 irrespective of the banker's charges for storage. Repairs to the house roof may simply allow the house to keep its present value, with no addition equal to the contractor's invoice. These costs protect the investment, and allow it to achieve the increase of which it is capable.

Often, investment is made in an item which will not increase in value. It is doomed to depreciate. In future years, it may be worth no more than scrap. How can this be seen as an investment? The answer requires a shift of focus, from the intrinsic value of the item to its production value. For example, a machine is important for the value of the goods it produces. While the value of the machine itself may reduce sharply, the cost can still be regarded as an investment as related to the machine's productive value. This seems more in line with the costs of training: surely they can be related to the productive value of the persons who are trained?

Unfortunately, the analogy fails again. The cost of the machine equates to the cost of the person, not the cost of training. A machine, once installed, does not have to be developed in order to be productive. Training does not, of itself, make a person productive: it simply gives the person the opportunity to become more productive; it enables, but there is no inevitability about the result. In this view, training costs seem more closely related to maintenance costs which enable the machine to work at its optimum level.

TRAINING: A BETTER LABEL

This, then, is the true nature of training. It is a maintenance cost. The investment is the cost of people; but, to be most productive, people must be cared for and given the opportunity to perform. Training is one method which can be used to achieve this. It is not, of course, the only method. Most managers today are familiar with the theories of Maslow, Herzberg and other researchers in the field   *13* of leadership and motivation. Often, the investment in people can be protected by a form of motivation which encourages those people to work hard. Training is one of the options.

BENEFITS OF TRAINING AND DEVELOPMENT

There are many ways in which the modern business can benefit from training and development of the people it employs. These can be examined easily under the division proposed by John Adair in his model of 'action-centred leadership'. These three aims that Adair identified are: the task; the team; and the individual.

Benefits of training and development to the task

The first essential of any business is survival. All businesses need people who are skilled at something. It may require skilled carpenters or machine designers, or experts in law and accounting. It can, of course, buy these skills; but then it will need people who are skilled at selection, negotiation and organization. What no business can avoid is the conclusion that it must have people who have some skills in order to survive. A business which requires skilled carpenters but does not employ or hire skilled carpenters will be out of business.

The priority for survival is so obvious it seems hardly worth mentioning. However, it is easy for a business to recruit an employee and then devote little time to helping that employee achieve the skills that are necessary. In some organizations, it is not even clear what skills are important. This problem is increased if a company uses an ineffective method of selection. A survey in 1986 showed that 81 per cent of companies in the United Kingdom used the interview method; but evidence shows that interviewing (especially if unstructured) is the least effective method of staff selection (Open University, 1990). In their report, the Open University detail the effectiveness of four different methods:

Assessment centres	0.41
Cognitive aptitude tests	0.27
Personality tests	0.15
Unstructured interview	0.14

This does not mean that interviewing should be abandoned. Interviews have a place within a deeper process, and structured interviews can be effective. The *second* stage towards structuring is to prepare a job description and specification. The *first* stage is to realize the necessity (and that often requires a change of attitude).

Change

In addition to survival – or, maybe, as an adjunct – every business must change. Customers change; needs change; circumstances change; no business can remain static. Unfortunately, change is a state which is not often welcomed. People become comfortable with their life-style and the way they work, and many people view change with apprehension. Training is an essential method to help people with change. Change itself may be necessary for survival; but change can also lead to increased productivity or reduced costs.

Increased productivity

In order to stay in business in a competitive world, increased productivity is often critical. Sometimes this increase can be achieved by a change in working systems, or by automation. In both cases workers have to be trained in the use of the system or new equipment.

Increased productivity can also be achieved by making the workers themselves more skilful. Profits can be increased by reducing costs; but this is unlikely to be achieved unless workers are helped to realize what costs are incurred and how they can be saved. All the changes demanded in a business require training; but more than this, training is a way of producing change.

Task expertise

Quality is more than a buzz word. More than ever, businesses are realizing how important quality of product or service has become. Tom Peters may well be regarded as the leader of the campaign for quality in business, although he is by no means alone in his appeals to modern business to adopt quality standards.

But adopting standards does not in itself produce quality. Whatever the business of the company, quality can only be achieved if the employees work with quality in mind. Training can help to implement a quality approach, to promote discussions and a general attitude to seek quality, and to help employees improve their expertise and thus the quality of the service or product. Here, especially, the widest definition of 'business' applies. Quality is the aim, but it is the customer who decides if the quality is right. All businesses have customers of course; but not all are able to name them. There are obvious customers and others not so obvious (as Charles Handy notes in *The Age of Unreason* and his topical comments on management within schools). If a customer is defined as 'any person who looks to me for some service or product', then the list will include more than the names of those who pay the invoices.

Reduction of mistakes

When mistakes are made in business, the potential costs are threefold. First, there is the cost of rectifying the mistake. Second, there is the loss to the company's image or reputation. Third, there may be a claim for compensation if somebody has suffered injury or damage because of the mistake. Training can help to reduce the chance of mistakes, but also to instruct employees on the action they should take when a mistake comes to light. Often, the costs resulting from a mistake can be reduced if correct action is taken early.

Standardization

The final benefit to the task of the company which can come through training is the standardization of work. A training programme helps to ensure that all staff work in the same way, to the same standards. Also, where there is a turnover in staff figures, training can provide a continuity in the work standards.

This benefit not only comes from training courses; it can also be translated into training manuals. Many managers spend hours training new staff to do new jobs, only to find that staff leave and they must repeat the exercise. The modern training manager will help line managers draft instruction manuals and booklets, which not only helps achieve standardization but reduces the training workload on the line manager.

Benefits of training and development to the team

There are four main areas where the teamwork in a company can be improved through training and development

Recruitment

Whether the labour market is in excess supply or excess demand, training is an important factor.

In times of labour shortage (as predicted in the United Kingdom following demographic shift), prospective employees have the upper hand. They can demand better conditions, and can choose their employer. Salary levels and career prospects remain important; but a company that cannot offer an effective training and development programme may find it will not attract good employees.

In times of high unemployment, training programmes have a new challenge. The need for a job will encourage a greater number of applicants, and some of those will be less able and experienced than the usual level of recruit. This puts further pressure on the training programme to be effective. A company which has no structured training, or has relied on existing staff to pass on their learning without special training, will be at a serious disadvantage.

Exchange

One benefit of training courses which is not often realized is the ability for employees in different part of the company to exchange views and information. Many businesses today operate on a cost-centre or profit-centre basis, and this can produce parochial attitudes. It is not unknown for employees of the company to work for many years without knowing that they are fellow employees. The exchange of views and information helps promote a common identity in the company and social ties, and can generate new solutions to problems.

The Hawthorne effect

A training and development programme is one way of realizing the 'Hawthorne' effect first noted by Elton Mayo.

The Hawthorne effect occurs when employees feel they have been selected for special attention. Mayo found that employees who took part in experiments worked to higher productivity levels, despite the challenges thrown to them within the experimental project. The changes involved working hours, rest pauses, even diet. Favourable changes should have increased productivity; unfavourable changes should have the reverse effect. Instead, output increased steadily despite the changes.

This result – arising, it seems, from the special attention given to the selected employees – must not be taken out of context. Herzberg has shown that cosmetic improvements do not always motivate. In the Mayo experiments, the cosmetic changes fell within a selective programme. It is this that makes interesting comparison with training and development.

When employees are selected for a training programme, they may express reluctance. This is a common external result. However, the internal result – the psychological effect on the employees – is usually the reverse: employees feel pleased to be given the attention.

Ideas

Business thrives on ideas. Modern businesses, living in times of constant change, need to generate ideas as much as they need to generate the products and services they exist to provide. A business can no longer afford to wait for its competitors to lead the field with new ideas, and follow in their wake. Ideas must be generated internally.

Of course, there are consultants who are prepared to help generate ideas; and a business may decide to meet the fees of these consultants. An alternative, or parallel, method is to use the training and development of staff as a way of generating ideas.

Benefits of training and development to the individual

Many of the items discussed under the headings of task and team apply also to the individual. However, there are four main areas where it is worth singling out direct effects on the individual of a training and development programme.

Motivation

The Hawthorne effect (discussed earlier) was studied in the context of teams of workers. However, motivation can often be an individual force.

Stimulation

One problem for modern business is that it cannot afford to employ more people   *17* than necessary. The result of this is that the people who are employed have so much work to do, they have little time to think about this work. One thing which a training and development programme offers is the opportunity to be away from the daily pressures of work, and to take a wider perspective. This can help individuals realize their role in the organization. It can also lead to a change in the individual's perceptions of the business.

Presentation skills

Training and development programmes give an excellent opportunity for developing the skills of presentation. Through role plays, video recordings and syndicate work, employees can be exposed to the experience of making presentations in a friendly atmosphere.

Knowledge

The final main benefit to the individual from a training and development programme is the increase in knowledge. Experience is a great teacher; but people will only learn from experience the lessons which happen to emerge from daily life. This is reactive learning.

A training and development programme can equip people with knowledge before it is needed. This is proactive learning. The advantage is that employees will be better able to handle new problems because they have the knowledge they need to assess the situation.

TRAINING AND DEVELOPMENT: THE NEED FOR A LINK WITH THE CORPORATE OBJECTIVES

Finally, the modern training manager will ensure that the training and development programme is matched to the corporate objectives. Two examples (one general, the other specific) will help to demonstrate.

The challenge of language

Many businesses today are planning to expand into overseas markets. One of the earliest decisions the business must make relates to the language challenge: how many employees should they have who can speak French, Spanish, German, and so on? This decision should be part of the corporate plan.

After the decision is made, the company can set about acquiring language skills. Some of the supply of linguists may come through the personnel department's recruitment efforts. Some may come from the training and development programme for existing staff. In this guise, training and development is working for the future. People will be given language training although they do not need to speak a foreign language at the time the training is given. This is an important point to emphasize. So often, training needs are realized too late. The question asked of many training managers is: 'how will this training help my staff do their work today?' The question must be changed to: 'how will this training help my staff do the work we plan for them in the future?'

The challenge of change to new systems

The specific example comes from the London insurance market. This market, which traditionally has relied on a vast amount of human contact followed by a vast amount of paperwork, is changing rapidly. Computer systems have been installed at Lloyd's of London and throughout the London insurance market. These systems not only cut down the amount of paperwork, but also much of the work currently done face to face between the buyers (brokers) and the sellers (underwriters). Although some face-to-face contact will always be necessary, even more of the face-to-face work done today will not be done in five or six years' time.

The implications for employment are dramatic. Unless the volume of business coming to the London insurance market expands considerably, many of the people employed by brokers and underwriters will not be required. A company can respond to this challenge in two ways. It can wait until the staff are no longer needed, and make them redundant. This will be costly to the company, and damaging to the individuals.

The better plan is to begin a training and development programme now which will fit the present employees to do different work for the company in five or six years' time. There will certainly be vacancies in the company in other areas (which would otherwise have to be filled by new recruitment, and incur high recruitment costs). Again, training and development is seen here as being proactive, and as being related not to the present-day needs of the company, but to the planned future of the business.

CONCLUSION

This chapter has examined some of the advantages of training and development. It has by no means covered all the possibly advantages. Any training and development programme is concerned with humans, and humans are the most complex creatures on this planet.

It would be foolish to regard training and development as the only way of protecting the investment a business makes in its people. There are other ways of protecting that investment. Training and development can sometimes be the most effective way but it is by no means a panacea. What is essential is that the modern training manager links the training activity to the future requirements of the company, by giving the training and development which is needed to help the business achieve its corporate objectives.

FURTHER READING

Adair, J. (1983), *Effective Leadership*. Aldershot: Gower.
Handy, C. (1989), *The Age of Unreason*, London: Business Books.

Higgs, M. (1989), *Management I*, London: CII Tuition Service.

Maslow, A.H. (1987), *Motivation and Personality*, 3rd edn, New York: Harper & Row (first published 1954).

Onions, C.T. (ed.) (1973, reset 1986), *Shorter Oxford English Dictionary*, Oxford: Clarendon Press.

Open University (1990), *Personnel Selection*, TV broadcast.

Peters, T. and Austin, N. (1985), *A Passion for Excellence*, London: Collins.

3 Training for change: an investment in people

John Fricker

In the late 1970s the forecast for the 1980s was one of both recurring change and permanent change, exemplified by slower real growth, continuing inflation, rising expectations among employees, human rights demands, ethical considerations and increasing consumerism and environmentalism. Experience has proved that forecast to be remarkably accurate.

If such is the nature of change at a strategic level, the reality is often harsher at an organizational level. Most organizations, at some time, have to face significant and far-reaching change such as mergers, expansion, contraction, responses to competition, relocation, restructuring – to say nothing of changes to management style or organization culture which may in fact be either the cause or the effect of some of those very changes just mentioned.

An open mind on the future is, arguably, one of the most potent assets an organization can possess. As the pace of change increases, to be able to understand all the variables which bear upon the management of an organization is not enough of itself. This is the real enigma of the change process and promotes such fundamental questions as:

- What should our strategy be, and how and when will we know if we have got it right?
- How will we know when we should change our strategy – or even rethink our primary task?
- Should we be looking for faster and faster response times when, paradoxically, there has never been a greater need for strategic consistency which avoids the crisis management and short-termism which so often has bedevilled the effective management of organizations?

The problem is that too many businesses are still waiting for conditions to 21 return to 'normal' when, in fact, what we are seeing today is the 'new normal'. The good old days are gone. Businesses have a choice: they can adjust to these changes, make the most of them, find new opportunities and keep moving forward; or they can dig in, keep their heads down and wait. The first is not easy; the second is unthinkable.

On all sides the only constants seem to be complexity and contradiction. But in this welter of uncertainty a key ingredient for stability, and for successful coping with and managing change, is the contribution which properly organized and integrated training can make; by planning ahead, by making training congruent with corporate objectives and by investing in human resource development so that other business investments are enabled to pay off.

Speaking at the opening of the IPM/BACIE Conference on 'Improving performance – a partnership in learning' in April 1989, Lord Young of Graffham, then Secretary of State for Trade and Industry said:

> Training is not a virtue to be propagated by Government. It is something that industry must do for itself. It is not an end in itself and it does not exist for the sake of the trainers. It is something that must be relevant to industrial survival, progress and competitiveness.

The pace and demands of change are quickening very noticeably and timescales are becoming so compressed that even Harold Wilson's much quoted statement that 'a week in politics is a long time' seems very much out of date. In today's world a week in business can see a transformation from a reasonably predictable world on Monday, to a fundamental upheaval by Friday.

Perhaps the most recent model for change on a macro scale was Big Bang and its aftermath in the City. Although the initial turbulence and the many aftershocks which followed were significant and far-reaching by any standards, that event of itself was not as extensive as what seems to be occurring now and which looks like remaining with us for the foreseeable future.

In 1990 Professor Amin Rajan of the City University Business School, London, predicted that up to half the companies in Europe could disappear by the turn of the century because they lacked the skilled technical workers they needed to provide the right type of customized products and services. The case he argued was a 'lack of investment in education and training in the 1980s when the world went through fundamental structural changes' (Rajan, 1990). These comments reflect the short-term thinking of many employers during the last decade, when many were caught unawares by the sudden economic recovery of the mid-1980s. Seldom has there been a more poignant indication of training and human resource development being seen as an investment for tomorrow, rather than as a cost for today.

THE CHALLENGE FOR TRAINING

By the year 2000 the proportion of 16- to 19-year-olds ready to enter the UK market for employment will have changed very markedly. Demographic predictions reveal that by 1994 the number will have fallen from 3.35 million to 2.57

million. Thereafter, there will be a slow but slight rise, reaching only 2.78 million by the turn of the century.

At the same time that the total number of young people is falling, the educational standards and attainments of those leaving school are low. There are many who would argue that the history of British vocational training and education is largely a history of failure. Good intentions have never been translated into effective action. As a result, more than a century after concern was first voiced, Britain still possesses neither a network of high-quality technical schools, nor a flourishing industrial training system. Companies, schools and governments have all failed to address the needs of the average employee.

Despite a massive investment in education over the last 20 years, research findings have consistently revealed that Britain's workforce is under-educated, under-trained and under-qualified. Some 40 per cent of school-leavers have no useful qualifications and over 50 per cent of all employed people in Britain have no qualification at all which equates to the old GCE 'O' level.

However imaginative and forward-looking our latest educational reforms may be, they are likely to be threatened by a lack of qualified teachers. The same constraint applies in both youth and adult training; the difference is that it is almost certainly more severe. After decades of neglect and the near disappearance of traditional apprenticeships in many industries, the United Kingdom lacks the human resources required for a training revolution. It has nothing to compare with the West German *Meister*, who plays such an important part in the training of young recruits. If Britain truly wants to raise the standard of industrial training, it must invest resources in the training and certification of many more trainers.

In the last decade of this century there are tremendous challenges to be faced by all kinds of businesses and enterprises. Internally, there was no respite in the pace of continued technological advances, coupled with continuing and growing market pressure for sustained product sophistication, innovation and variety. Externally, competition has been increased and sustained, fuelled by the advent of the single European market and the growth of hi-tech, high-skill, high-quality and high-output economies in South East Asia and the Pacific Basin.

Another challenge which, paradoxically, compounds the challenge presented by low skills levels and a dearth of meaningful qualifications is that presented by a growing focus on the individual. Here, the most fundamental challenge will lie in the shift in the relationship between the individual and the company. Historically, employees have been treated on a collective basis, according to well-established and prescriptive rules and regulations. Individuals were dependent on the company for a variety of benefits, terms and conditions of service. Roles were clearly specified, enforced and segmented by the company – 'a fair day's pay for a fair day's work'. The company stood protectively between the individual and the external business environment which, by today's standards, was reasonably predictable – the steady state.

In future the individual, whether singly or, more likely, in teams, will be called upon to take more initiative, add value and contribute in previously untried ways, released from the constraints which applied before and empowered to take charge and better himself, at the same time as contributing to corporate *23* wellbeing and business success. The chief challenge emerging from this will be the overwhelming need to change the attitudes not only of the employer, but of the individual as well – and, in so doing, the fundamental challenge of training as a cost, or an investment, will have to be addressed.

THE CHALLENGE FOR MANAGEMENT

Clearly, many line managers, and the number is growing, recognize the importance of effective training and development. However, recognition is one thing; active and purposeful involvement is another. There are still far too many managers who only pay lip service to their key role in achieving results through the people they lead and for whose training and development they are ultimately responsible.

By definition, managers must meet this challenge with and through the efforts of others. but a further challenge which, by implication, relates to all the other challenges, is the changing nature of the workforce. For example, the average young member of staff today is more socially sophisticated, is more questioning, is more demanding and will generally seek and expect earlier responsibility than his or her counterpart in the past. Managers will therefore need to adapt to meet this challenge if the required results are to be achieved in all other areas. Training in general, and management training in particular, must consequently take this factor into account, by focusing sufficiently on the most appropriate ways in which managers can obtain the optimum contribution from all members of staff in achieving the required quality of service and level of productivity.

It is hardly surprising to find that many of the employees at the sharp end of businesses are weary of the endless debate on the well-worn subject of the changes being experienced and of the effects they are having on their daily routines. Indeed, some may be asking if it will ever stop; for the foreseeable future the answer is 'no'. But the constant which runs through this welter of ambiguity and paradox is the overwhelming importance of the role to be played by the people in the business. There is ample current empirical research data to support the thesis that organizations do succeed in managing change when they invest an appropriate level of resources in the change process – particularly the human resources.

A survey of emerging trends in training and development in the United Kingdom by Laurie International Limited (1990) stresses that top managers, as well as line managers, will need to adopt human resource development as a real priority. It says that training and development are top priorities now that speed and adaptability have become competitive weapons in an era of continuously changing markets.

Chairmen and chief executives need to recognize the value of learning as the primary force to facilitate and achieve change in their organizations. Their leadership role requires them to match their conviction with consistent, demonstrable commitment. The starting point is to agree and promulgate well-documented, comprehensive business strategies from which training needs can be derived. Senior executives must also ensure that line managers share their commitment to learning and insist on quality in all aspects of training and development.

To do this effectively managers will have to prepare their staff for the changes, both expected and unexpected, which undoubtedly lie ahead. They must ensure that their staff are given the knowledge and skills – and the confidence – to deal with inevitable pressures. The ways in which we react to and manage these pressures and the commitment we demonstrate to our people will have a considerable effect on our future success. Indeed, for those new to the market, possibly employing large numbers of inexperienced people and supporting considerable investment in the business, proper attention to staff and customer care is likely to be the difference between success and failure.

Enabling staff to accept change is one of the most valuable of the many skills of leadership. This means that managers at all levels must be flexible in approach, sympathetic in attitude and positive in style in order to provide this help.

Flexible So as to deal successfully with the practical effects of change in an open-minded manner.

Sympathetic So as to understand fully the anxieties caused by change to others.

Positive So as to give people confidence in the instructions and decisions passed down to them by someone who is clearly seen to have confidence in his or her own decisions – and confidence in the future.

It is no longer acceptable for line managers to abrogate responsibility for the training and development of their staff. They cannot hive it off to the training function by sending staff away to be 'processed' by the trainers and then returned to the real world of work to get on with the job. A three-way contract between line managers, trainers and students is essential. This will forge strong links between training programmes and corporate objectives, with the pre-occupation of success or failure being directly linked to improved competitive edge in the marketplace. Linking the investment of the training budget to the strategic plan does not seem a particularly novel idea, but it is quite remarkable how few companies actually apply this approach.

As part of their responsibility for the training and development of their staff, line managers must expect to be assessed on the extent to which they discharge this function as part of their normal role. If one separates the concepts of education and training, where the latter is decidedly job-specific, then it is quite possible to construct a legitimate argument for linking course performance evaluation into the overall performance appraisal plan. Indeed, it is evident that line managers, whose budgets pay for training, are much more anxious to experiment with this idea in order to improve their perceived return on investment.

In general, awareness of increasingly intense competition and the require-ment to retain costs has resulted in a greater understanding by senior line management of the importance and value of training. It is now seen as an   *25* investment for the future, rather than a cost on the present. Moreover, it is now regarded as short-sighted for line management to slash training budgets in an attempt to reduce operating costs. But it is certainly possible, with a greater degree of professionalism, to ensure higher added value from the training budget.

THE CHALLENGE FOR HUMAN RESOURCE MANAGEMENT

Human resource managers, until very recently known as personnel managers, are striving to make their mark – for many of them a very new mark – on the management of organizations. They will contend, and with justification, that they have a significant role to play in the organization, describing it as 'pivotal' and one which can add value. The argument presented to support this view is both reasonable and sensible. They contend that, unless an organization has a coherent approach to the management of its human resources, it is likely to be unable to meet its business objectives. Regrettably, such a view may be heard but not listened to, and, unless the pious words are matched with true professionalism in a markedly different role, there is a likelihood that it will be dismissed as special pleading.

A study by the Cranfield School of Management (1990) and the consulting group of Price Waterhouse attempted to discover what human resource practitioners believe to be the main issues confronting them. Some 6,000 companies and public sector bodies in the United Kingdom, West Germany, France, Spain and Sweden have been examined by drawing upon the resources of leading business research centres in the countries concerned.

The survey examined the responses of human resource professionals to a range of questions relating to human resource strategies, methods and attitudes towards recruitment, pay, benefits, employee relations, work patterns, training and development. As regards training and development, some important findings have emerged, notably as follows:

- Personnel responsibility is increasingly being delegated to line management, and in particular, as part of that function, the training and development of both shop-floor workers (or their equivalent) and managers.
- Organizations throughout the countries covered by the survey have increased significantly their investment in training, particularly with respect to managers and professional staff, although there is little evidence of the systematic evaluation of such training.
- Although the survey reveals that between 60 per cent and 90 per cent of the responding companies systematically analyse their training needs, it also shows up a lack of knowledge among human resource professionals of how much their companies are actually spending on the training and development of their staff.
- Managers are currently being trained across a wide spectrum of what can be called 'people management' skills and it is 'people management' which is expected to dominate in almost all of the countries surveyed.

- Apart from the traditional reaction responses of trainees and their line managers to particular training experiences, the validation and evaluation of training tends to be informal and unsystematic.

Of all the findings perhaps the two most telling are that, although the vast majority of organizations are increasing their investment in training and systematically identifying training needs, there is apparently no complementary system for evaluating the effectiveness of such training and assessing its value for money. In all too many cases training and development remain expensive acts of faith.

That there is no virtue in training for its own sake – only in terms of profitability and efficiency – has a certain grim logic. Training does not stand or fall in its own right and trainers delude themselves if they think otherwise. Nevertheless, the contribution which training and development can make towards the achievement of a company's corporate objectives, and thereby its greater profitability, is enormous, and the overwhelming majority of recent research shows that it is the companies which commit significant resources to training which are the successful ones.

The Laurie International Report (1990) identified as the most important and critical success factor for the successful management of training and development, that training and development objectives must be derived from business objectives. To promote this critical success factor it is essential that line managers are informed, committed to and actively involved in the training activity. Equally essential is that human resource professionals in general, and trainers in particular, become business literate and get involved. This can be achieved by moving trainers away from the traditional training role towards being internal consultants capable of contributing to organizational analyses, and it is a logical next step where attributes, performance and outcomes are inextricably linked with corporate competence and the achievement of organizational goals.

In such a way, the pay-off will not be to increase the trainers' workload, but dramatically to heighten their involvement, and commitment through involvement, in a true partnership with line management in the examination of the business objectives and the assessment, both short and long term, of the training implications. This is arguably the most effective means of ensuring that the training and development activities are truly congruent with corporate objectives.

At a more mundane, but no less important level, such a process of involvement and shared ownership of the training activity will close the gap between what happens when people receive training and what happens when they return to the workplace.

People re-entering from a training event often discover that the attitude in the workplace is not sympathetic to what they have just experienced, and that the work environment is out of tune with the training that is taking place. The inevitable assumption is that training has not been effective, whereas, in reality, although the learning may have been excellent, the opportunity to practise what was learned does not exist and so the training is (wrongly) condemned. Unless *27* people are genuinely able to practise the newly acquired knowledge and skills in a working environment which supports them, the training will always fail effectively to transfer and the investment in training will have been wasted.

THE CHALLENGE FOR TRAINERS

Few would dispute that training and development must be at the top of the agenda for all businesses, or that the most successful and competitive organizations are those which provide consistently high levels of effective and relevant training. The key test, by definition, therefore, in assessing the effectiveness of training is the extent to which it achieves the organization's objectives by being linked to its forward strategy and business plan.

On this basis it is important to agree on three basic assumptions about training. First, the purpose of training is to change behaviour so that individuals can perform a more purposeful, effective and valuable service for the company. Secondly, the effectiveness of the training must be quantifiable and measurable, however difficult this may be, in order to calculate the outcomes in terms of value for money and contribution to the bottom line. Thirdly, the true cost of training, including all the variables such as R&D, design, release costs, housekeeping costs, faculty, and external provision, must be calculated as soon as possible at the start of the development of the training plan. Only in this way can costs be judged as acceptable by the company and, as a result, be committed and controlled on a continuing basis.

Mention has been made several times already that training outcomes must be congruent with corporate strategy and that training planning must be locked into business planning. Only in this way will training be effective, efficient and relevant. But what if corporate objectives are not clearly articulated, or that there is no shared vision, or that the business planning as a result is no good? This poses not only a challenge, but also scope for genuine proactive involvement by the trainer in the company's affairs.

Effective business planning, although essential for market success or corporate survival, is not universally well done. Many companies still plan their business on the basis of overcoming short-term deficiencies, in market share, appropriately skilled staff, return on investment and so on. Others are taking a more forward-looking view by identifying what needs to be done differently in order to achieve the necessary changes; what will people need to learn in order to become involved in the change process and what contributions will training and development have to make and at what cost.

The really successful organizations – and they need not be huge multinationals performing on a worldwide scale – are those which take a strategic view of business planning. Very often they know what they have to do, but lack the organizational capacity to put it into action. They solve the problem by critically reviewing the capabilities the organization will need to acquire and the capabilities both individuals and groups will have to develop in order to carry the strategic plan through. This, in turn, dictates what the contribution from human resource development, the global role of training, should be. In time, the effectiveness of the training contribution can be assessed in the light of business achievements against plan, and adjustments, where necessary, can be made for the future.

It is in the strategic planning scenario that training and development people can collaborate with line managers to enable them to rethink their assessment of the future needs and direction of the organization, and thus their approach to business planning.

But the transition to such a new and dramatically different role will not be easy. Moreover not all top managements will be happy to see human resource and training professionals influential in this new way. In all too many organizations training has, in the past, been seen as a low-status activity, peripheral to the main thrust of the business. Senior executives still harbour deep-seated prejudices and unhappy memories of personnel and training managers as the custodians of much of the old-style central apparatus they are now seeking to get away from, or of training people put into that role because they were either failures in other, more important, operational assignments or had chosen to take a 'soft option'.

Trainers must now ask if they can really present themselves as convincing orchestrators of the new thinking, and if the ideas and tools they have as part of their stock-in-trade are good enough or relevant enough to undertake such a formidable task. Undoubtedly, the responsibilities will be awesome. Not all trainers by any means will either want, or have, the necessary consulting skills and abilities to break into such a radically different activity, and a heavy training investment in themselves will be essential. But what could be more challenging and exciting that actively contributing to decisions about organizational changes which are necessary to secure the future in a changing environment? Properly resourced and trained, they will be able to collaborate with line executives to assess the causes of the organization's performance in the present and help to chart its planned performance in the future.

Whatever the vision for the future, historically, much of the responsibility for making a success of training and development has rested not only with the trainers themselves, but with the line management of the organization at all levels. Without the visible and sustained commitment to training from the very top, the chairmen and chief executives no less, and without a culture in the organization which is supportive of training, many of the more go-ahead trainers face frustration and disillusionment. Despite having contacts with employees at all levels, and thus gaining a feel for and an understanding of the current and emerging problems within the organization, many trainers find themselves allowed little scope for applying themselves to provide solutions. Too often they are 'viewed as a service, rather than an integral part of management development policies' (Davies and Burgoyne, 1984).

Undoubtedly, there is a need for change in the status of the training and development function. Such a change cannot be brought about by exhortation. Trainers themselves must shoulder a large part of the burden of responsibility for bringing it about: by changing themselves, by being innovative, imaginative and forward-looking, by developing new learning strategies, by shedding many of the self-effacing tactics of the past – in effect, by being truly professional.

Essentially, the change in the status of training cannot be brought about if we do not regard and treat the providers of learning – whether they are teachers in schools, lecturers in higher education, faculties in universities, colleges and business schools or trainers in companies – as people engaged in work of high importance, whose responsibilities are often daunting, of whom equivalent respect and reward should be accorded. They have a prestigious and crucial role to play.

CONCLUSION

The culture which is frequently to be found in organizations, both large and small, that have been relatively sheltered, through regulation, from the full rigour of market competition, tends to stress correct form and procedure in all activities. Quality of service, customer care and risk control were based on the principles of rules of procedure, inspections and sanctions, with limited feedback provided to the staff. Supporting this, organizational structures have been typically hierarchical, with long chains of command reinforced by strict systems of reporting and accountability.

The challenge now is to develop a much more market-driven culture without losing reliability and meticulous attention to detail, underpinned by sound ethical principles, which remain essential to continued and sustained success. This is what lies at the heart of the change process which will guarantee survival and in which trainers must become deeply involved and committed.

There is now a growing acceptance that training and development must be driven by the strategy of the organization. This, in turn, has significant implications for trainers, where the emphasis will be on concentrating upon organizational needs, through developing individuals so as to arrive at an organization which devotes itself to long-term learning, rather than to short-term training. Such learning demands continuous and meaningful interaction between people and their working environment. An environment which is both supportive and stimulating will lead to considerable learning, and, through this, to individual and organizational growth. But for this to happen changes have to take place, particularly in the traditional rule-based organizations where structure, systems and procedures were designed to maintain stability at all costs by preserving the status quo and getting people to toe the line.

In the learning organization training is not an activity which is separate from day-to-day activities. Instead, it is an inherent part of the working environment. When people need to know or learn something, the information and the facilities to learn must be immediately available to them. By this means learning organizations learn from all sources and directions, so that change is not only accepted but is eagerly sought out and the challenges it brings are welcomed. Such a result reduces the impact of change and strengthens the organization's ability to cope successfully and to survive (Bentley, 1990).

Success, therefore, can be derived from a learning culture where training and development become demand-led, rather than supply-driven. With the genuine and enthusiastic commitment and backing of top management and the allocation of resources to match, training will work to ensure that organizations attract, train, develop and retain the people talent needed to guide them successfully through the current decade and into the next century. Participative leadership of a learning culture, supported by goal-oriented human resource development, means that organizations will generate better solutions from their own commitment, experience and creativity – and training for change will make it work.

FURTHER READING

Bentley, Trevor. (1990), 'A training consultant at work – a personal view', *Banking & Financial Training*, **6**, (2), June, 12–14.

Cranfield School of Management (1990), *The Price Waterhouse Cranfield Project on International Strategic Human Resource Management*, Bedford.

Davies, J. and J. Burgoyne, (1984), *Career Paths of Direct Trainers*, Sheffield: MSC.

IPM/BACIE Conference (1989), 'Improving performance – a partnership in learning', 25–27 April.

Laurie International Limited (1990), *Training and Development. Top Management Issues for the New Decade*, London.

Rajan, Amin. (1990), *A Zero Sum Game. Business Know-How and Training Challenges in an Integrated Europe*, London: The Industrial Society.

4 Training for quality

Hugh Parry

The *Shorter Oxford English Dictionary* defines quality over a large number of lines. What do trainers understand by the word when it is applied in a training situation? Is it perhaps a training course provided by a well-known institution with good publicity material? Is it a tried and tested programme which many have been through and therefore it must be good? If the product was of high quality and effectiveness once, is it still and will it remain so?

This chapter sets out to look at the notion of quality as it is applied to training and will probably pose more questions than it answers. If that is to be the case, then it will have been a worthwhile exercise, because all successful trainers have a desire to stretch the barriers of their learning and understanding.

The next question is 'does quality matter?' Well, since all individuals have their own concept of what quality is, it may be felt that the answer will depend on circumstances. What though would happen to the person having to undertake some serious medical treatment being faced with two doctors? The first one has trained at a top teaching hospital and exudes confidence. The other's origins are less certain, and to add to the concern a medical book is left open at the appropriate page on the bedside locker while treatment is being carried out.

Why then should there be double standards concerning when quality is or is not desirable? Poor quality training will lead to poor quality responses from trainees and the ultimate effect will be resistance to future programmes of training, irrespective of the quality of that subsequent training.

Some line managers have suggested that the higher the quality of training provided, the higher the cost, which in turn will lead to reduced profits. Quality is not mutually exclusive to profit, particularly when it is related to investment in that most important of resources – the human variety. If any proof were needed that this is in fact the case, the consistent success of organizations such as Marks & Spencer and Sainsbury should be conclusive. The benefits of quality training, quality merchandise, quality marketing and so on are apparent. The ability to continue to succeed while competitors react badly to economic cycles is also a valuable point to bear in mind for those who believe in putting quality first.

QUALITY – TURNING A COST INTO AN INVESTMENT

What is often referred to as the 'mud on the wall' technique of throwing training at individuals irrespective of need, is the antithesis of quality training. If one paints a house without the correct preparation, the results may appear good for a while, but where there is no primer, the paint will flake away. So with training: if the foundation is not there, then the superficial benefit will vanish fairly quickly.

The basis of quality training, 'Training Needs Analysis', will be covered later. In this section the concern is cost. Cost is being incurred, and logically it might be expected that benefit should arise. However, anyone who has managed the training function (and presumably the training budget) of an organization will be aware that training is one of those areas in which the term 'parasitic' is sometimes used; that is, riding on the backs of the money-making departments while contribution was not quantified, leading to attack when times were difficult.

The training manager can be at fault, at least partly. It is essential that in the eyes of the line managers, money put into training is seen as an investment rather than a cost. Training managers should insist on being judged on the contribution made to the business objectives of an organization via the business plan. It follows, therefore, that the training manager must be part of the process of agreeing those plans.

What has become a rather meaningless phrase (often heard from chairmen presenting annual reports) is, 'our people are our most valuable asset/resource'. In fact, in many organizations the staff are the least cared-for resource available to the manager. Training in the United Kingdom is, regrettably, often still seen as a necessary evil rather than a positive contribution to the future wellbeing and success of a business.

It is all very well identifying the problems, but what about solutions? The starting point is the business plan, as has already been mentioned. When the operational plan, be it for a product launch or the total operations for a year, is being prepared, a cost will be allocated to achieving those targets. It is possible that a new machine will have to be purchased. That will be viewed as an investment since the machine will still be there in the future. It may, therefore, be a transferable asset from this business plan to the next, and so on. If the same test is applied to training, the move begins towards quality, and regarding training as an investment rather than cost.

Trained skills must also be transferable. Too often they are seen as being of short-term benefit to an organization, since the long-term benefit might be gathered by other employers. This is a short-sighted view. Many problems have been caused in Britain by narrow training schemes which do not allow people to move from section to section within organizations. Redundancies have resulted in one part of an organization while there are unfilled vacancies elsewhere in quite similar areas in the same organization. For those who feel that staff will leave to go elsewhere, consider Germany where the practical framework for vocational training is well established and effective, and in some sectors, the staff turnover is under 1 per cent. People tend to leave not because of quality training, but because of the lack of it!

Quality training – proven quality, that is, which adds to the effectiveness of staff and thus to the bottom line – is the criterion for changing the methods by which training budgets are arrived at. The trend will be away from the traditional 'how much can be spared for training?' to 'what is the desired outcome to achieve our business objectives and how much will it cost?' By this method, it will be seen that the most hard-headed 'bottom liner' will see the benefits of training and the means will be found to make the investment rather than pay the cost.

FOCUSING TRAINING

Reference was made earlier to the 'mud on the wall' approach; that is, hitting everyone at apparently the same stage of development with the same training programme/course. It happens regardless of whether the training is to be of assistance to the individual, whether it is relevant to present or anticipated roles, or even whether it is needed. The individual may have arrived in the organization from school, or other educational institution, or from other employment. Logically, it does not seem appropriate to force people through a course to teach them what they may already know. However, because the system is established and agreed, it is not flexible enough to take account of variations. In this context, training is governed by input rather than desired outcome. Input in this sense follows a simple process – you have been here for so long, therefore it is time to go on such and such a course.

Desired outcome on the other hand revolves around the expectations of a given programme of training. These expectations will need balancing between the organization and the individual. This brings us back to the theme of quality. Which of the two methods outlined above are most likely to be seen as quality training leading to quality results? Which of the two methods outlined are likely to make individuals welcome further training because they know it will be relevant and lead to improved performance and improved rewards?

It is common practice today for people to be set specific objectives in the workplace, objectives which may be reviewed on a half-yearly basis. For each objective, key tasks will often be identified, and each key task will have criteria of performance. It is one thing to achieve a task, which, like playing the recorder, may be termed as quite easy. How well it is achieved is the province of the performance criteria. The task may be easy to do, but perhaps difficult to do well.

On the face of it, this has little if anything to do with training. However, if the key task and performance criteria taken together are outside the current ability of the individual, it can then be turned into a training objective. Consider the following example.

Key task   Process unsecured loan applications to laid down procedure.

Performance criteria   Three per hour within an error rating of 3 per cent.

34   *Training objective*   At the end of this programme of training the individual will be able to process unsecured loan applications to laid down procedures at the rate of three per hour and within an error rating of 3 per cent.

This may appear over-simplified. However, it is precise and related closely to the job in hand. Its very precision leads to clear expectations on all sides of the required outcome so thtat there can be no misunderstanding. Someone already operating at that standard will clearly not need the training. The definition of required outcome, clearly and without ambiguity, arises from questions being asked and answers given.

This is a reasonably simple method of assessing training needs (a process discussed in greater detail elsewhere). The main point to remember is that training needs can be assessed in a variety of ways; for example, observation, change of responsibilities and so on. In this case, we have focused the training by means of discussion with the individual, when responsibilities were expected and skills and knowledge had to be provided. It is a clear training solution to a clear training need and not an indiscriminate waste of resources.

QUANTITY v QUALITY AS MEASURES OF TRAINING EFFECTIVE-NESS

It is not only in the field of training that activity is judged to be a sign of effectiveness. For many years, and in some cases continuing today, appraisals, where they took place, set great store by the activity of employees. The terms 'hardworking', 'industrious' and 'head down' were all taken to be complimentary.

No one will disagree that hard work and correct mental attitude will often bring their just rewards, but only if supervisors or managers are doing their job correctly by ensuring that the hard work is channelled; that is, directed to what needs doing and how it needs to be done. In this way, hard work will bring its own reward, because it is directed towards getting the job done in the appropriate way and to the desired end.

The parallel with training is clear. When the training manager is called to account for the activity of the training department at the end of the year, what has been the method of reporting? It may well be that the following are familiar: 'we had more students than ever before'; we had a 50 per cent increase in courses run and 40 per cent increase in the total number of students attending'; 'we started to run eight new courses this year'. The list is not complete, but the point is made. The visual impact of training is the one which is stressed. Possibly because of a feeling of insecurity on their part, the trainers, who are used to being accused of being users, rather than providers, of wealth, have sheltered behind the high-visibility strategy of making sure training is seen to be happening. Hence, an overemphasis on formal courses. In reality, a very large amount of the training manager's resource may well be given to the development of line managers on what are the most effective solutions to the training needs of staff.

The revised approach, of tailoring training to individuals, has far better long-term results for the individual and the organization, although in the short term it   *35* makes for more difficult reporting. Fewer courses will be run because there will be more individual coaching and non-classroom learning. The tendency will be for fewer large gatherings due to the great increase in the use of technology, and also the provision of resource centres where students are able to work quietly through their own programme at their own pace, using a variety of methods but under the guidance of a tutor.

Other means of measuring effectiveness must be found, and other means of convincing the organization that training works. We come back to this word 'outcomes' which was discussed earlier. Measures of quality rather than quantity might include:

- Increased sales from the telephone sales unit.
- Fewer complaints from customers.
- Fewer rejects at quality inspection stage.
- Increased profit.

Increased profit as a measure of the quality of training? This may well be the final arbiter on the quality and effectiveness of training. However, an important point will have been gained on the way through. The trainees know quality when they experience it and will be enthusiastic towards training. With the old time-served course system, disenchantment over irrelevant material quickly sets in, as does derision of future training initiatives.

TRAINING THROUGHOUT LIFE OR FOR LIFE?

A great deal of publicity has been given to the various government initiatives on training over the past few years, and recently, further comment has been made over the assertion that 'there is no such thing as training for life'. Whether we accept such a general comment as absolutely true, without any exception, is not important. Few can object to the concept that one cannot be trained for one year (as an example) and that training should last for the next 40 years. In other words, we are seeing a move away from once-and-for-all training towards the continuous drip-feed of training and education. The barriers between training and further/higher education are coming down. Perhaps a good example of this removal of barriers is the increasing number of organizations who look upon MBA courses as an integral part of management training and development.

Coaching will be seen by many as little more than formalizing the system of imitation which has been in operation formally and informally since time began. Children imitate adults, as they learn to do things for themselves. It is interesting that for one of the most important jobs we will ever undertake, that of parent, there is little or no formal training available, let alone given. Could this be because subconsciously we are in a constant process of learning from adults around us?

Trainers should have experience and knowledge and should be able to demonstrate all those little tricks which make life in the workplace easier. However, have they been properly trained to pass on these gems? Will they engender enthusiasm in the trainee or simply act as demonstrators, who may eventually drive the new employee away from the job, and possibly the organization, because of a lacklustre attitude to the role?

One does not become a competent trainer/coach/mentor only by going on courses. It requires aptitude and a willingness to put oneself in the position of the trainee. It requires time to listen and appreciate, since that is the only way to be able to offer the assistance that the trainee requires.

If we look back at the example of parents and children, one of the popular phrases in current use is 'the allocation of prime or quality time' to one's children. Strip away the jargon and it means paying attention to or concentrating on the child. It means 100 per cent attention, and not part-time attention while some other activity is being undertaken. So it should be with the trainer. If training is ongoing – that is, constantly changing and revising – and responding to developments, and not a one-off burst at the beginning of working life, it is important to get it right. It might be assumed that future developmental training will rely on a satisfactory foundation. In that case it is essential to ensure the message goes in correctly and so the trainer's prime or quality time is needed. Perhaps a full-time instructor without a production target for example?

The development of Standards of Competence and the National Vocational Qualifications network will be an important spur to the concept of continuous training. It is interesting to note the increase in what might be described as self-motivated learning. The success of the Open University, Open College and various innovative Institutes of Further Education show a thirst for knowledge. If people are prepared to do this in their own time, is it not possible, given the opportunity, that they will want to do it in connection with their own occupation? By basing this system of National Qualifications on work based assessments, relevance is ensured. By recognizing acquired skills and recording them by means of a qualification, people will be encouraged to pursue their personal development and thus be more receptive to training programmes of all types. In short, such programmes will be seen to be relevant, and relevance is a cornerstone of quality.

CUSTOMER CARE AND TOTAL QUALITY MANAGEMENT

The frozen smile mouthing the words 'have a nice day' are calculated to ruin most people's days even if there is a slight hint of sincerity behind the words! The scene described has been the death of many customer-care programmes which have sought to bring home the notion to staff at all levels, from board level downwards, that any organization exists for its customers and not the other way round. Indeed, every individual within an organization is a customer of other individuals within that organization. Just as an organization's business plan must be built around its marketing strategy, then so must it be seen that identification of both the customer and the fact that that customer is at the end of the line of everything we do, good or bad, is paramount.

The fact that the process must be a continuous one, if it is to have any lasting effect, appears to have been lost on many people. Many programmes have been run with the best of intentions, only to founder because of insufficient attention to embedding the principles into the organization. Too often, all that can be remembered of the customer-care programme was that it was a pleasant few days!

It is difficult to believe that suppliers are deliberately rude, unkind or unhelpful to clients or customers, so why should such programmes be necessary at all? Too much time on training programmes has been devoted to the *process* without making people fully aware of the *content* of the training. Few people have avoided being in the situation where they have been in a state of frustration caused by organizational difficulties. The prime example is to be told 'it's not our company practice to ...'. Yet every so often someone comes forward who is able to cut through the red tape by having that wider vision that encompasses the customer.

Interestingly, the best customer-care programmes do not introduce anything new to the organization which would appear alien to the staff. Via intensive surveys of staff and customers, the suppliers of this training ascertain what are the best practices within the organization, what the customers really like, and then, via the programme, encourage others in the organization to adopt the same approaches. Earlier reference was made to the link between quality and the bottom line. Successful customer-care programmes have confirmed this link.

Total quality management (TQM) is different from customer-care programmes in so far as it cannot be a single event. It is a process which requires absolutely everyone in an organization to be included in a programme of *continuous* improvement. It requires a change in the culture in an organization, in its management and in its staff's attitude to quality. The ultimate objective of TQM is sustained competitive advantage via satisfied customers. TQM enables a company to maximize its investment in its human resources. By the time the process is going, it becomes impossible to remove the momentum, unlike customer-care programmes which are easily hijacked by a few people in key positions (not necessarily at the top) being obstructive.

INTERNATIONAL SIGNIFICANCE OF TRAINING FOR QUALITY

To say that quality is quality wherever it occurs is, perhaps, stating the obvious. But quality is related to appropriateness. Low-technology solutions for irrigation and sanitation projects in developing countries are quality. Thus, the training to carry out such projects must reach a degree of quality that is empathetic to its surroundings, even though it might be quick, cheap and easy to produce. This empathy must be seen in various contexts, some examples of which are as follows:

- Recognition of difficulties in understanding due to language.
- Reservations brought about by deep-seated suspicion of strangers.
- Using appropriate training methods to the environment.

38 It is easy to make such comments about the developing world. Most people would wish to see those in such obviously less fortunate circumstances succeed, by receiving the most effective training which would enable them to receive quality facilities at the end of it.

However, we are less sensitive to those closer to home. Have we, for example, taken the trouble to learn about our European neighbours? If we wish to develop trading and social relationships which are durable, our preparations should be detailed and appropriate as they would be in the case of the developing world. Do we make efforts to learn other languages or do we expect everyone to speak our language? Do we take the trouble to learn about how we should behave at meetings, at social events and particularly in other people's homes if invited?

The European Community's social charter proposals would touch the quality of life as they would the environment. As part of a multistate European community, agreement to changes in employment structures or industrial processes might well involve large new retraining programmes, as has the removal of barriers between East and West Europe. Training for quality (of life) will also mean addressing of traditional prejudices arising on grounds of race, nationality, sex, religion and any number of other restrictions to development. Earlier, customer care, and focusing attention on the end client, was mentioned. This in itself is breaking down barriers, and now, it has been widened to look at why it is necessary to break down barriers on an international basis. The proposals spell out very clearly the right to vocational training, and surely the most impressive feature of the Charter is the all-encompassing nature of the language: for example, 'throughout working lives'; 'no discrimination'; and 'continuing and permanent training systems'.

CONCLUSION

Quality in any sphere suggests the best. The best should always be celebrated and the development of the Government's 'Investors in People' initiative will be a valuable partner to National Training Awards, which have provided a tangible way of celebrating quality. By publicizing the reasons for the awards, other organizations are able to compare their own operations with those of the award winners and benefit from the confirmation that quality training works. The awards are so structured as to afford businesses and organizations of varying sizes the opportunity to spread their success story by illustrating their initial problem, how they went about dealing with it and then showing the successful outcome. One case of particular interest was of an organization which had to undertake some specific training to comply with new legislation. Not only was the training considered a success in its own right by achieving the specific objectives set, but it also achieved a significant improvement in sales.

Once again, we are faced with outcomes – the successful results – not necessarily the route to those outcomes, although quality input is more likely to lead to quality output. The same applies to Standards of Competence which are being developed. Training routes leading to competence at a certain level are the route to the end objective – the demonstration of that competence. Certification of quality is becoming increasingly common as a requirement for   *39* suppliers of goods and services (most commonly through BS5750 or ISO9000). Quality is no longer an option!

Throughout this chapter, there has been an attempt to look at the concept of quality. It often falls into the category of 'I know it when I see or experience it' – an intangible state with tangible results. Seen as an investment, rather than a cost or a drain on resources, enables training to be put in the context of part of the process of improving the bottom line.

Focusing where the training is to hit rather than adopting the scatter-gun approach leads easily into using quality, as opposed to quantity, as an appropriate measure of how effective the training has been – looking at outcomes rather than input. Training for life was also examined, and it should be noted that this cannot be seen as appropriate in a world which recognizes constant personal and organizational development. Customer care and, more particularly, total quality management are means of keeping people involved in that process.

As we enter the 1990s, there will be a greater recognition of the need to work closely with others, rather than in constant competition. However, competition will still exist, and perhaps become even stronger. Quality training will then be even more essential to ensure success.

Finally, the list of further reading which follows does not pretend to be complete, nor it is related specifically to training. Where quality is the prime goal of an organization, it is a reasonable assumption that quality training will play an important part in the attainment of that goal. The listed books, in part or in total, relate to success built on quality, express ideas on how quality will be achieved or lay down foundations which facilitate quality.

FURTHER READING

Blanchard, Kenneth and Spencer Johnson (1983), *The One Minute Manager*, London: Fontana.

Garratt, Bob (1987), *The Learning Organisation*, London: Fontana/Collins.

Kenney, John and Margaret Reid (1986), *Training Interventions*, London: Institute of Personnel Management.

Peters, Tom and Robert Waterman Jr (1982), *In Search of Excellence*, London: Harper & Row.

Seiff, Marcus (1986), *Don't Ask the Price*, Guild Publishing, Weidenfeld & Nicholson.

5 Standards in the training context
Chris Carroll

Following comparisons of the performance of the UK education and training system with the systems used in other countries, the need for a basis upon which to show improved education and training system performance arose as a political imperative. It gave new impetus to the idea of educating and training to meet specified standards and led to dramatically changed definitions of the roles of Industry Training Organizations and to the creation of the National Council for Vocational Qualifications. The start of the single European market led to the need for harmonization, or at least understandable comparability of employment competences and training standards across Europe. Much change is still occurring in this area and the chapter that follows attempts to update and clarify a wide range of 'standards' issues in the training context.

WHAT ARE STANDARDS?

The dictionary definition of a standard includes 'an exemplar; a basis for measurement; a criterion; an established or accepted model; a definite level of excellence or adequacy required, aimed at or possible'. In this chapter a standard means that which establishes the attainment required; whether this is in an industrial context where the attainment relates to the specification of a product or service, or in a human context where the standard relates to the behaviour or performance of a person. A standard may be implicit and very subjective, hence 'she is a well-behaved child', but is of most use in measurement and comparison when based upon some objective criterion and expressed explicitly. Standards may relate to outputs, that which is achieved, or they may relate to the process by which the output is attained. Both are important. If no clear standard exists for the output required it is impossible to know whether it is met. If no clear process standard exists, then getting the desired output will be something of a lottery. It may cost more in time and resource than is necessary. It is helpful, therefore, if the output standard required can be related readily to the process by which it is to be met.

Process standards

In the past, industry gave priority to the measurement of output standards. Products were inspected after the production process and rejects thrown away or reworked. Managements came to recognize that it is cost effective to concentrate resources upon improvement and control of process, so that defects reduce to zero and neither rejects nor rework are needed. In training and education, similar changes were occurring and the same attention was being given to the improvement and control of processes.

Thus the examination of training facilities concentrated upon the following aspects.

The quality of facilities   Was the environment right; did it mimic the environment in which the skills learned would be used? Was the equipment used of a standard that truly represented the equipment found in the workplace? Was the instructional equipment up to date and supplied in sufficient quantities? Was the provision of consumables adequate, and so on?

The quality of instructional staff   Did the instructional staff have appropriate skill and knowledge in the topics taught? Were they properly trained in the techniques of instruction? Were they competent to carry out assessment and to use the output from that assessment effectively, and so on?

The quality of programmes   Did the programmes of training properly reflect workplace needs? Did they provide a sound basis upon which to build further training and development? Were the instructional staff involved in their creation and did they therefore 'own' and believe in them? Were they appropriate for the kind of trainee involved and so on?

The quality of systems   Were there regular reviews of the training content? Were the needs of the trainees and their employers re-examined systematically? Did the staff have their training needs assessed regularly, and were those needs met consistently? Were the staff themselves properly engaged and involved in the review processes?

Assessment methodology   It was probably in the area of assessment that the greatest changes in training took place. The quality control lessons of industry and commerce apply equally to training. Measurement of the performance of the trainee allows judgement not only about the quality of the performance of the trainee, but also about the quality and effectiveness of the process that brought the trainee to that standard. Thus formative assessment invaded the training centre. Instructors learned to use the 'error' signals generated by the assessment of trainees to judge whether to change the instructional tactic, to add or subtract material from the programme, to repeat training exercises or to introduce new ones. Even in traditional summative assessment, where examinations of output skill were taking place to judge whether the trainee passed or failed, important changes of attitude and practice started to occur. The idea of a variable standard of quality with some performances being worth more 'marks' than others ended in favour of an all-or-nothing approach. Either the standard was met, or it was not. If grading was possible, the implication was that the standard was not properly set.

Quality control systems   Any proper examination of the training process sought effective quality control. It was important to ensure that formative assessment worked effectively to qualify and improve the training process, while summative assessment gave an objective view of whether the trainee did or did not meet the output standard required.

Process and output used jointly

The joint use of process and output standards results in a very effective methodology for trainees within a controlled programme. If the trainee is well selected and the programme and process are sound, there is a high probability that the required output standard will be met. The operation of a 'sampling' system to monitor those parts of the output standard that can be measured objectively further increases the likelihood of the achievement of the standard. But the system does not provide a method for measuring the competence of individuals who have not been through the process. Nor does it guarantee that all the competences required for industrial performance are tested or reached. Because the process allows valid inferences to be drawn about certain competences, they are not subject to an objective test. Summarizing, the system uses an organized training programme with a good process control and objective sampling of standards. It gives a high probability of success with optimal use of formal assessment.

Assessment independent of the training process

Open assessment is independent of the training process, and must allow for the assessment of individuals who have not passed through that process. Thus it is essential to define output standards more specifically and more comprehensively. Within those output standards it becomes necessary to define all the beneficial effects that would have been inferred but not measured within a training programme. The behaviour of a trainee in a commercial environment is observed during the training process. It is not normally remarked upon, except in the most general way, unless it falls outside the explicit or implicit norms for the organization. An individual who has not been through such a training process but who claims to have the competences that the training process develops, must be given the opportunity to show that the competences are present. Since there has been no opportunity to observe the individual in the commercial environment and to infer the required competence, other evidence of competence must be sought.

Typically, a training or development programme in industry or commerce   *43* provides opportunities at three levels to infer or measure competence. The least formal of these opportunities arises in the employment environment – the reaction of the trainee to that environment; the way in which the trainee develops relationships with other people; the way in which the trainee seizes opportunities to be constructive and to learn from the environment – each offers chances for formative and summative assessment. The second opportunity for assessment lies within the special training events and learning opportunities organized deliberately for the trainee. Reactions to these events and opportunities are a rich source of assessment data. Finally, at the most formal level, are the specific tests and assessments completed by the trainee to show that the necessary competences are there. These tests and assessments seek to show by adequate sampling that the processes used have been successful.

However, the performance criteria laid down for a person who has not been through an industrial or commercial training programme must provide effective alternatives to the evidence gained at all three levels within a training programme. It cannot be a 'sampling' mechanism since there is no process to sample. They must provide evidence that all the required competences are present. The issue of 'open assessment' therefore creates a need for entirely new disciplines in the definition of output standards. It leads into the wider idea of competence defined by the Employment Department, the National Council for Vocational Qualifications and the Scottish Vocational Education Council. The demand for formal assessment is greatly increased, and there is a danger that if it is wrongly applied to trainees in well-controlled training programmes, it will be wasteful.

Output standards

The Employment Department (ED), the National Council for Vocational Qualifications (NCVQ) and the Scottish Vocational Education Council (SCOTVEC) all advocate that the standard required from an individual should be defined in terms of an output. The implication is that the method of reaching the output is irrelevant to the objective measurement of the presence of the standard. If the goal is reached, the route to it does not matter! This allows a definition of competence, which is external to the individual. It is a useful approach in that it allows easier direct measurement of the effect sought. For example, if the standard required is that the individual 'drives a class A motor vehicle from X to Y without offending any of the tenets of the Highway Code', judgement can be made about this 'competence' by observing the vehicle as it travels from X to Y. To judge whether the driver is totally competent, the journey must include all the possible opportunities to offend against the Highway Code. This may mean a very long journey or many repetitions of a shorter one. Realistic simulation might be more effective.

The substitution of an 'output' standard alone for a standard based upon control of process and the selective use of 'output' measures requires the specific definition of all the implicit aspects of performance that the process generates and that have previously been dealt with by proper inference. There is little evidence yet to judge the extent to which this requirement can be met, and at the higher levels of qualification in particular, significant debate still continues as to both the learning and the economic effectiveness of the method.

Defining output standards

If output standards are to form the basis of a national system of qualifications, they must be agreed universally and have a wide range of acceptability to the customer.

There are many kinds of customers for occupational standards: professional trainers, educational institutions, training providers, publishers of educational material, and so forth. But these are only the middlemen and must not be allowed to control the shape and content of standards. The real customers are the trainees themselves and their current or potential employers, and standards must be defined and described in ways that are meaningful to these real customers.

This creates two dilemmas. First, the standard must be general enough to be widely useful, but specific enough to be helpful in real work. A standard liberally peppered with words like 'appropriate' and 'suitable' will not endear itself to the user looking for meaningful guidance. Second, it must use language and methodology sufficiently detailed and unambiguous that professionals can prepare standards, but which is not so dense and jargon-ridden that 'real' people cannot understand it. To the professional trainer the definition of an output is a difficult business susceptible to many nice, semantic arguments. There is a danger of becoming bogged down in these arguments. Is there a significant difference between 'can operate a photocopier' and 'can produce good copies of documents using a photocopier'? The latter is a clearer description of an output. The non-specialist may find the distinction difficult to see, however, since it will be assumed that the only reason to operate a photocopier will be to produce good copies. Such semantics will not help the credibility of the trainer, and so it is vital to involve the customers directly in the preparation of the standards and to recognize their authority in the choice of words used in them.

The output statement is very helpful in deciding whether an individual can perform a function, but it may say little about the human competences needed to perform that function. In the earlier example of the vehicle travelling from X to Y, the competences deployed will vary with several factors: the road conditions; the nature and characteristics of vehicle driven; the weather; the required journey time; the nature of the control system in the vehicle; the 'emergencies' encountered; the behaviour of other drivers; the behaviour of passengers in the driven vehicle; the physical capability of the driver, and so on. Output statements therefore need to define the range of working variables that will affect them by including a 'range statement'. Each variable above is an 'indicator' of a changeable factor needing to be covered in the assessment. The 'range statement' must be specific about the required range and it is very difficult to set specific ranges from some variables. Some variables will require an 'artificial' assessment process, either because they are so wide ranging that it would take *45* too long and be too expensive to test each of them practically, or because they are essentially knowledge based.

But apart from these working variables, it is highly likely that different drivers use different human characteristics to get similar effects. For example, some may use creative flair to find new and effective ways of dealing with situations. Others will learn and develop 'habitual' approaches. Both can be good enough to meet the performance requirements. In circumstances where a range of human competences may each lead equally to an effective realization of the output standard, the trainer will need to decide which of these competences to develop within a training programme. This will depend to a large extent upon the characteristics of the trainee, but other factors also will be important. A well-defined occupational standard will not define the training methodology or programme required to reach it. An occupational standard is independent of the training route and may be approached in various ways. The trainer will continue to have an important role in designing training approaches that allow achievement of the standard under varying circumstances.

The occupational standard of competence

An occupational standard demands the belief that the whole of a function or occupation can be described in terms of the outputs it creates. Some analytical work has already been done to prove this belief and at the lower levels of qualification there is increasing confidence about it. At higher levels, however, the premise remains largely untested. It is important to recognize that other methods of definition of performance are helpful and should be seen as complementary to occupational standards-based approaches. For example, the trainer will still wish to use behavioural profile approaches in improving performance, and will be helped in the measurement of performance, and of changes in it, when profiles are placed inside an output-based, occupational standard of competence. Since its early, hard-line, approach towards functional analysis as the only way forward, it is noticeable that the Employment Department has moderated its views, and consequently a number of reconciliations with other appropriate methodologies have occurred.

The Employment Department prefers an approach to occupational standards based upon analysis of function. The resulting occupational standard has three parts:

1. The competence statement – what the person can do.
2. Performance criteria – the criteria used to measure capability.
3. The range statement – the range of working variables within which capability must be maintained.

Functional analysis

Analysis of function starts with an agreed, succinct, definition of that function. Some authoritative group with expert knowledge of the function needs to be drawn together to create this initial definition since what follows is entirely dependent upon its effectiveness. As an example of an opening definition, the Training and Development Lead Body (TDLB) defines the training and development function as follows: 'Develop human potential to assist organizations and individuals to achieve their objectives'. This initial broad function is broken down – disaggregated is the technical term – into suitable component parts according to rules for this process agreed by the initial group.

For the TDLB, disaggregation follows the training cycle: that is, identifying training and development needs; designing and updating training and development strategies, plans and systems; providing learning opportunities, resources and support; evaluating the effectiveness of human resource development strategies, plans and systems; and establishing and maintaining effective communications and feedback systems. For engineering manufacture, analysis pursues the product life cycle: that is, research; development; design; manufacture; construction; installation; operation; maintenance; servicing; and dismantling.

Disaggregation continues at ever greater levels of detail until the individual standard elements emerge. These are the smallest disaggregated statements that will sensibly stand alone. Each of these elements is an occupational standard and must include not only the disaggregated statement of function, but also performance criteria and a range statement. These elements form the basis for the construction of units of competence.

The process of disaggregation will often reveal that the original functional definition is not well chosen, or that the disaggregation rules could be improved. In these circumstances it will be necessary to soften up and modify the higher-level structures already agreed. It is a process akin to annealing work-hardened metal to make it possible to change its shape, or like the well-known 'top down' approaches used in writing computer software. The whole process of functional analysis has many of the characteristics of computer software production, with the element equating to the single line of software that emerges at the heart of a series of nesting analyses. It will surely prove amenable to the use of the same sorts of software tools and environments as in software engineering, and some attempts have already been made to produce computerized systems of functional analysis and qualification design.

The annealing process is made more difficult by the division of labour at lower levels of disaggregation: that is, if the disaggregated functions are given to separate working groups to get them done speedily or because of the need for specialized knowledge at that level. It is therefore very worth while to take time to ensure that the initial function definition and the early stages of disaggregation are well founded and robust.

Codes of practice and seals of approval

Individual standards established for every function in an enterprise will prove invaluable in several ways, particularly in identifying training needs, in designing effective training, and in validating and evaluating the effectiveness of that *47* training. Individual standards are like bricks in a wall, they do not of themselves necessarily hang together very well or form a coherent training policy. Firms need well-defined policies for their use. They need to allocate scarce resources and ensure that the most important and urgent issues get priority. The requirements for firms to have policies and plans for training as part of their relationship with statutory training organizations have already largely disappeared. With only two exceptions, both in the construction field, they were dismantled entirely by July 1991. Instead, the growth of voluntary codes of practice operated by non-statutory industry training organizations may be seen. In particular the Code of Practice of the National Council for Industry Training Organizations has an increasing role, while the 'Investors in People' (IIP) programme is playing an important part in ensuring that organizations have effective overall strategies for the training and development of employees.

British Standard BS 5750

A possible alternative or complement to the IIP programme is wider adoption of British Standard BS 5750 (ISO 9000) as a basis for company training policy. Some suppliers of training are already approved to this standard. Many trainers see it as an over-formal approach and some have expressed difficulty in envisaging the trainee as a 'product', subject to the objective product quality control criteria which BS 5750 demands. Others are very enthusiastic about the prospect.

WHAT IS THE DIFFERENCE BETWEEN A 'STANDARD' AND A 'QUALIFICATION'?

Standards are not of themselves qualifications, but form a very effective basis for a vocational qualifications system. A vocational qualification is formed by adding an assessment to a standard. They are thus very similar and contain several common components.

Competence-based qualifications

Competence-based qualifications identify and recognize the occupational competences, as defined earlier, that an individual can deploy. They do not identify what an individual has done, nor what process of education and training that individual has experienced, except where those functions provide valid evidence of the occupational competences sought.

A system of competence-based occupational qualifications need not, and should not, be seen as an alternative to process-based systems. The benefits sought may be entirely different and both will have their valuable place in the total structure of education and training. A process-based system may be seen as contributing to the competences required to get a vocational qualification, but its total benefit may be much wider than that and it would be wrong to attempt to narrow the aims of process-based arrangements merely to make them congruent with those of competence-based vocational qualifications. Similarly, competence-based vocational qualifications must maintain a clear view of vocational and occupational needs and should express their objectives in these terms. Their principles must not be softened or generalized merely for the sake of making it easier for process-based qualifications to be included in the structure.

Assessing competence

A competence-based qualification results from adding a requirement for assessment to the unit of competence created from a group of occupational standards or elements: that is, there must be some method of assessing whether the individual meets the standard for the qualification. The definition of the units within the qualification will therefore usually look very similar to those within the standard, with the addition only of requirements for assessment. Because the assessment depends upon the ability to perform a function rather than a task, it may be especially helpful in opening qualifications (and, more importantly, employment) to individuals with special needs; those with a hearing impairment for example, or another disability that would disbar them from consideration for a requirement expressed in task terms.

In adding requirements for assessment, the need arises to deal with aspects of underpinning knowledge and understanding not mentioned explicitly in the standard itself. The standard is in output terms and the performance criteria will enable judgement to be made whether that output is met. There is the issue of the range statement to remember. Can a practical assessment method be devised which will allow measurement of output against all the variables in the range statement? If not, it will be necessary to conduct an 'artificial' assessment that supports the primary assessment and allows a judgement of competence to be made in a valid and economic way. The primary requirement is to prove competence in action. Other assessment methods provide support and additional evidence; they do not substitute for the primary demonstration. It follows from this that most assessments of competence will take place in the working environment or in a simulated environment indistinguishable from it.

Underpinning knowledge and understanding

These items represent a significant challenge in the definition of vocational qualifications. At the lower levels there is little difficulty. Often it will be unnecessary to define underpinning knowledge and understanding, since the primary demonstration of competence will prove beyond doubt that they are there to the extent required. At higher levels, however, it becomes very difficult and this is an area where the competence premiss has yet to be totally proven.

The issue can be looked at from two standpoints. First, the 'essential' knowledge. What is the essential knowledge required by an engineering designer, for example? Is it the whole of the content of an engineering degree course? Is it a good deal more than that? How can the presence of this knowledge be assessed, given that it is forbidden to specify an education and *49* training route and that a self-taught designer is not totally unknown? Even in relation to 'essential' knowledge the problem is likely to prove intractable. Second, what is the 'other' knowledge that designers use? What was the extra ingredient that prompted Issigonis to design the 'mini'? What subtle combination of life's experiences brought him to the magic moment of creation? How can those things be defined and described in a way that enables them to be included in a specification for competence? Can it ever be done? Perhaps not, but it should not prevent the effort, nor the inclusion of that about which certainty exists.

It is particularly important that it should be attempted at the higher levels, for technology and for management. These are the areas where, comparatively speaking, the greatest gains are to be made. The boundary of the map of certainty can be driven outwards to cover a wider area, but a start must be made with that which can be done now. Not to attempt to map this ground is to ensure that it remains forbidden territory and that competence-based approaches remain limited by existing prejudices.

Units of competence

The qualification will contain several units of competence – not a fixed number, but the number necessary to put together a qualification that makes sense to the people performing the function described. It implies a practical approach based upon consultation with the customers rather than a tidy theoretical approach aimed at educational parity and courses of a size to fit neatly into timetables.

Elements of competence

Further, within each unit, and exactly as with the occupational standard, there are the elements of competence that are the assessed components of the qualification. Each of these elements must have at least one performance criterion and the qualification is not complete until all the performance criteria, for all the elements, are met.

Summarizing, a vocational qualification comprises a number of units of competence. A unit of competence is the lowest level at which any part of a qualification will be certified for credit accumulation. It consists of a collection of elements meaningful in an employment context and is made up as follows:

- Several elements of competence (what the holder can do).
- At least one performance criterion for each of these elements (specifying how the presence of the competence, including any necessary underpinning knowledge and understanding, is to be proved).
- A range statement (making clear the variables over which the competence must maintain).

COMPETENCE IN THE INDIVIDUAL

The definition of competence used by the Employment Department, the National Council for Vocational Qualifications and the Scottish Vocational Education Council needs careful understanding. It adopts a view of competence that is outside the individual. Also, it equates an output with a competence, whereas the everyday use of the term 'competence' implies something inside the individual that produces the output. Competence within the individual is made up of a mixture of innate ability and acquired skills, natural traits and learned behaviours. There is every reason to suppose that each individual, set the task of producing precisely the same output (supposing it were possible), would do so by using different combinations of ability and skill, traits and behaviours. Output and competence cannot therefore be directly equated, but it is not unreasonable to infer certain competences from consistently repeated output standards. Remember carefully when referring to a unit of competence in an occupational standard using the ED definition, or a vocational qualification using the NCVQ/ SCOTVEC definition, that it does not refer to a unit of internalized human competence (whatever that might conceivably be), but to an output standard from which to infer human competence.

These distinctions will be of only limited interest to an employer who is assessing a candidate for the ability to perform a function, for example: to design aeroplanes; to fill supermarket shelves; to wait at table; to supervise a team; to drive a public service vehicle; to make engineering press tools; to manage an insurance company. They are still very important to the trainer who has to decide, in the absence of the ability of an individual to perform one of these functions, whether that individual can be trained so to do.

TRAINING FOR COMPETENCE

The trainer must still design and deliver training. The introduction of output-based standards offers no absolution from this task. It follows that the trainer must analyse training needs at a level inside the element of competence, because there will be various routes to the required output standard and it may be a waste to service the learning of any more than the best of them. (How many of the several effective methods of long division do you know? Who said 'what's long division'?)

Not only that, but the training strategy chosen will relate strongly to the characteristics of the trainee. 'Chalk and talk' can work well for the motivated, intelligent, hungry-for-data trainee. But what of the rest? It cannot be over-emphasized that learning strategies still have to be chosen. Having a well-defined output standard will not necessarily make the choice of learning strategy any easier and will not get rid of the need.

THE ROLE OF THE EMPLOYMENT DEPARTMENT

In all the current discussion of occupational standards, the role of the Employ-   *51* ment Department is crucial. It continues to give a strong lead, but many believe that recent reorganization has led to a weakening of the resources available. The Department has an extremely difficult task. Changes of the nature and magnitude that it advocates really deserve careful long-term research and comparative analysis against existing systems. The performance problems of the nation do not allow such a careful approach and the Department is hurrying along what must surely be recognized by all as a high-risk experiment without the benefit of a safety net. Trainers owe it to them to do their best to make it work, but that includes challenging hard when the wrong direction is taken.

Strategic direction

Under its Chairman Sir Brian Wolfson, the National Training Task Force (NTTF) had the primary responsibility for the new initiatives dealing with the introduction of standards-based approaches. This body was wound up at the end of 1992 and the Secretary of State has since created a Strategy Group under the chairmanship of the Employment Department to continue the work of NTTF. It is for trainers from industry and commerce to ensure that this new body receives accurate intelligence on which to base its strategies. It must be ensured that it concerns itself not only with unemployment-oriented programmes at the lower employment levels, but with the whole structure of continuing training and career development to secure the effective management and technological competences that are essential for the future of the nation.

Lead bodies

Many lead bodies have been created to give specific direction to the creation of standards and qualifications. Some of these lead bodies have a functional base like the Training Development Lead Body or the Management Lead Body and cross all industrial and commercial sectors. Others, like the National Retail Training Council have a sectoral remit. Both functional and sectoral bodies are required but it is difficult to see any coherent strategy behind the creation of lead bodies in such large numbers (there are already about 150) and there is a danger that their proliferation will, like the unnecessary proliferation of statutory training boards in the 1960s, bring them into disrepute and, in so doing, drag down the essential ones. The Employment Department has indicated clearly its awareness of this problem and is attempting rationalization through the creation of Occupational Standards Councils.

The Training and Development Lead Body (TDLB)

Among the most important of the lead bodies, and of particular concern to trainers, is that for training and development (TDLB), which has set and published the standards and the qualifications structure that trainers will work within. It is important because its approaches and its methodologies are examined critically by trainers and will be used by them to make up their minds whether occupational standards, vocational qualifications, functional analysis and so forth really do work, or whether we are simply being over-credulous. Several Awarding Bodies have been identified to offer National Vocational Qualifications based upon the TDLB standards, and initial uptake of the qualifications is beginning. The National Council for Vocational Qualifications and the Scottish Vocational Education Council have established mechanisms for the separate accreditation of the TDLB units relating to assessment and verification, so that Awarding Bodies other than those offering full TDLB qualifications can offer the units and thus increase dramatically the number of assessors and verifiers qualified to operated NVQ systems.

Youth Training and training for the adult unemployed

Among those most likely to benefit from the introduction of occupational standards and vocational qualifications are trainees in Youth Training (YT) and in programmes for the adult unemployed. Care must be taken that in its anxiety to introduce standards for these schemes, important as they are politically for youth and other unemployment, the Employment Department does not cause a distortion nor compromise the proper needs for occupational standards and vocational qualifications in the whole environment of industry and commerce. A scheme designed wholly or mainly to meet the needs of the unemployed is most unlikely to be right for industry and commerce as a whole. It is important that the whole structure is coherent. The tendency to create a 'low end' system based upon YT, the adult unemployed and the sixteen-year-old school leaver and a separate, elitist 'high end' system for those progressing from the eighteen-year-old leaving into polytechnics and universities must be resisted. The real differences in the cost of doing different kinds of standards-based training must be recognized and accounted for. If open access is to work properly, the system must be seen to be seamless, to offer opportunities for those with ability and will to move from the bottom to the top of the competence structure without discontinuity and to serve the employment needs of individuals and firms for the benefit of the nation. The introduction of General National Vocational Qualifications into the secondary and tertiary education system, so as to offer a vocationally based, general education alternative to traditional academic courses is very helpful in this regard, but the possibility of confusion between NVQs and GNVQs is very real and there is a strong argument for a change of name of the GNVQ to separate the two very clearly.

TRAINING AND ENTERPRISE COUNCILS (LOCAL ENTERPRISE COMPANIES IN SCOTLAND)

In Youth Training and training for the adult unemployed, the new Training and Enterprise Councils (Local Enterprise Companies in Scotland) have an immediate key part to play. They have insisted quite properly that nationally based occupational standards and vocational qualifications are used within their grant-funded schemes. They are the key agencies for the promulgation of the   *53*

'Investors in People' programme and must ensure a clear connection between this programme and NVQs. Like the Employment Department, they must ensure that their priorities are not distorted by unemployment issues; that they give proper attention to securing continuing training and development through to the highest levels of management; and that they serve well the long-term needs of key industries.

THE NATIONAL COUNCIL FOR VOCATIONAL QUALIFICATIONS (NCVQ)

From its inception in 1986 the Council has had an extremely complex and difficult task. Its initial target of making qualifications available to 80 per cent of the population by the end of 1992 was achieved and it deserves great credit for this. The management of the process of creation of NVQs has, however, been a wasteful and inefficient one and must be improved considerably during 1993 and 1994 when virtually all of the existing qualifications are due for review and reformation. Implementation of qualifications has become a higher priority but the Council's position on marketing still appears to many to be equivocal. Finding the right balance of resources to deal both with implementation and reformation during 1993/94 will be a considerable problem. It is clear that the Government will wish to reduce and eventually remove its funding from NCVQ and it seems inevitable that as a consequence NCVQ will be forced to adopt stances more sensitive to the market for qualifications than it has hitherto.

THE ROLE OF PROFESSIONAL BODIES

As NCVQ moves to introduce National Vocational Qualifications above Level IV, its relationships with the senior professional institutions (essentially the chartered bodies) has been given considerable attention. In particular, the introduction of Occupational Standards Councils was driven extensively by the interests of professional bodies. The need to take account of the requirements of these professional bodies is very important. The less well-established professional bodies are likely to welcome NVQs. They offer an opportunity for increased credibility. But no National Vocational Qualification at higher level will be accepted broadly if it does not offer an acceptable route to recognition by the chartered bodies. The roles of professional bodies vary greatly from sector to sector. In some areas they enjoy true regulatory rights. It is impossible to practise as a professional in those areas without the appropriate membership qualification. In other areas, membership of a professional body shows a high level of education, training and experience, but the absence of membership does not inhibit employment and does not show absence of competence. In these areas many senior and well-qualified personnel do not belong to professional bodies. While, therefore, it is most important to have the co-operation and involvement of professional bodies, it is also vital to deal with the needs of employees working at higher levels who are not in membership of such bodies.

54   Some chartered bodies feel threatened by the prospect of NVQs above Level

IV. Their concerns may arise from the judgement that firms and individuals will see an NVQ as an alternative to membership of a professional body. This is a very real concern, since many employers do not see professional membership by itself as a good indicator of specific competence and may welcome a qualification that offers more direct evidence in this regard.

Professional bodies may also be wary of methods of analysis that challenge traditional occupational boundaries and result in descriptions of competence that do not fit tidily onto the current institutional map. This wariness cannot be allowed to prevent analysis, since the existing institutional structure may inhibit change. The structure is likely, in the longer term, to benefit from processes that engender critical examination and allow for new aggregations of competences.

It cannot be assumed that there is congruence between the requirements for membership set by an institution and the requirements for competence dictated by particular roles and tasks in industry. Both are important and must fit into a successful system of NVQs above Level IV.

An answer may lie in persuading the institutions to give more weight to evidence of competence and in using NVQs as a basis for judging the suitability of candidates for membership. Continuing efforts must be made to persuade professional bodies that NVQs are not a threat and can be very helpful to them in increasing their membership and in bringing their entry requirements more closely into alignment with the needs of employers. Competence-based approaches, using work-based training and credit accumulation, have the potential to bring many more individuals to the state of competence where they can prove that they warrant membership of a professional body.

Because of the very real and proper concerns of professional bodies, it is important that NCVQ maintains good, co-operative relationships with them. It is important to avoid giving the impression that professional groups are somehow different from others in terms of the criteria and the rigour which NCVQ will apply to them. NCVQ must not compromise its tenets, nor set criteria for professional bodies that are different in principle from those insisted upon for other organizations.

FURTHER EDUCATION

The role of further education (FE) organizations changes markedly with the introduction of occupational standards and vocational qualifications. It is important that they continue to offer coherent educational programmes in their own right, but also that they are prepared to show how components of these programmes contribute to the achievement of occupational standards and vocational qualifications. The lead bodies, in laying down standards, will be wise to bear in mind the vital part played by the FE sector in the generation of industrial and commercial competence. They must make it as easy as possible for the FE sector to respond to industry's needs, and they will achieve this by explaining what those needs are, by involving FE staff directly in the analysis of those needs and by providing as much up-to-date information as they can on the changes that are occurring. At the same time, they must bear in mind how much *55* change is occurring and the extent to which the control of that change is moving from educational syllabus designers to industrial and commercial staff.

THE ROLE OF EMPLOYERS

Employers have a huge role in the definition and use of occupational standards and vocational qualifications. They are real potential gainers from a system that can enable them to specify directly the competences that they need and to measure more directly than ever before the effectiveness of training in their own firms. Further, the system has the potential to bring into competent availability many thousands of individuals who could otherwise be lost to employment entirely or might be employed at levels and in tasks that did not use their competences. None of this can be done if employers are unwilling to devote time to the definition and testing of the standards or will not bear the cost of setting up and maintaining the system. The cost will not be trifling but it will be small in comparison to the benefits.

THE ROLE OF THE INDIVIDUAL

In all this, the most important player is the individual. Occupational standards and vocational qualifications offer an open door to qualifications that industry wants and can use. They create opportunities for personal development unfettered by the rigidities of past systems; they reduce possibilities of redundancy through personal obsolescence; they increase the chances of promotion; they expand opportunities for employment; they enable the individual to plan a pattern of self-development keyed to known industrial and commercial needs. Moreover they offer an opportunity to become part of a workforce committed to self-development in an industrial and commercial environment where the needs and the opportunities are made plain. It has to be good for the individual and it has to be even better for the organization.

FURTHER READING

Bookhouse Training Centre (1990), *What is all this NVQ Business? – A blueprint for discussion.*

Burke, John W. (ed.), *Competency based education and training*, The Falmer Press.

Careers and Occupational Information Centre (undated), *Knowledge and Competence – Current issues in training and education.*

HMSO (undated), *Employment for the 1990s.*

HMSO, *Working Together – Education and Training.*

Scottish Vocational Education Council (undated), *Insufficient Evidence? – The final report of the competency testing project.*

National Council for Vocational Qualifications, *National Vocational Qualifications: Criteria and procedures – March 1989.*

National Council for Vocational Qualifications (undated), *The National Council for Vocational Qualifications – Its purposes and aims.*

National Council for Vocational Qualifications (1990), *The NCVQ Database.*

National Council for Vocational Qualifications, *National Vocational Qualifications and Special Needs.*

National Council for Vocational Qualifications, (undated), *NCVQ Information Notes* (various) (undated).

National Council for Vocational Qualifications (1989), *Extension of the NVQ framework above Level IV – a consultative document.*

National Council for Vocational Qualifications and the Further Education Unit (1988), *National Vocational Qualifications – initial criteria and guidelines for staff development in further and higher education.*

The Training, Enterprise and Education Directorate of the Employment Department, *Competence and Assessment*, the quarterly bulletin of the Standards Methodology Unit (Occasional papers).

The Training, Enterprise and Education Directorate of the Employment Department, *National Vocational Qualifications – A guide for training providers.*

The Training, Enterprise and Education Directorate of the Employment Department (1991), *Training and Development Standards – The occupational standards of the Training and Development Lead Body.*

The Training, Enterprise and Education Directorate of the Employment Department. *Technical Advisory Group Guides – Development of Assessable Standards for National Certification – Guidance Notes 1–8.*

The Training, Enterprise and Education Directorate of the Employment Department and the Information Technology Lead Body, *A guide to developing standards of competence in the constructive use of IT.*

6 The training and development profession

George Webster

As society progresses new occupations arise and may, with the passage of time, become defined, structured and regulated through the formation and activities of professional bodies. Training and development is one such occupation, currently passing through its gestation period, to emerge as a significant profession for those engaged in human resource development, and an influence on society and the national economy.

AN HISTORICAL PERSPECTIVE

The effective communication of knowledge and skill to aid learning emerges from pre-history as an essential support activity to survival. The training function was initially an intuitive and subsequently a planned activity to assist prowess, task competence and work organization. The progress of mankind is irrevocably linked with the processes employed to develop knowledge, skills and values of individuals and facilitate the effective working of groups to achieve specific objectives.

History has been shaped by success in training, never more so than when it has been employed to secure advances in military activities, construction, transport, communication and public administration. Civilization, created through social and technological development, has advanced by the transfer of knowledge, skills, beliefs and values, and is the product of generations of people who have passed on their craft, technical and managerial skills, and ethical values to others, allowing them to build and continue to add to an existing skill base.

It is not surprising that there was an early conceptual division between 'education' – the process of helping people acquire, store, relate and transmit knowledge – and 'training' – the process of helping people gain and apply knowledge, in conjunction with the use of senses, to perform an activity to a specified standard. 'Thinking' and 'doing' have in the past frequently been seen to be unrelated functions – even to the extent, in some people's eyes, of one being counterproductive to the other!

This phenomenon has been particularly true in the case of labour-intensive industries, where Pavlovian responses and concepts of 'human machines' have predominated. The trainer's role in these cases has in general been equally downgraded to match the concept. This is exemplified by the Industrial Revolution and the transfer of work from domestic workshops to factories filled with low-skilled workers. Responsibility for training moved from the respected master craftsmen, heavily involved in skill transfer, to supervisors with little or no need for training skills in order to manage large numbers of low-skill operatives.

The age of technical innovation saw the return of master craftsmen to train people to reach new levels of manual skill. However, the growing demand for scientific knowledge to underpin this advance was left largely unanswered until enlightened public benefactors commenced the process of establishing 'mechanics' institutes in the larger towns. These were later to become the public institutions forming the Further Education system. Although this filled the middle ground between academia and training it did little to advance the role of trainers employed within industry, or to advance their place and status within their organizations, where they were generally employed as instructors.

The move towards 'scientific management' presented the next opportunity for advances within the training occupation. However, emphasis on course attendance rather than skill development proved limiting both to the effectiveness of training and to the trainer who, in the majority of cases, took on the role of course broker or booking agent and perhaps operated a very subjective form of evaluation largely based on student satisfaction. The training role was often being filled by someone whose limits had been overreached in other occupations.

The United Kingdom's struggle to achieve economic recovery in the postwar years highlighted the need for an effective and flexible national workforce, capable of meeting the demands of changing world markets and escalating technological change as industry re-equipped and transferred from war production to peacetime products. The quality and quantity of training undertaken by a voluntary system, even with the stimulus of an Industrial Training Council, was seen to be inadequate to address the problems and, in particular, incapable of taking advantage of the demographic 'bulge' of school leavers in the mid-1950s to mid-1960s. Thus, following the failure of attempts to promote employer interest and commitment, legislation was brought into being to impose financial penalties for employers in key industrial sectors who did not train their employees.

Coincident, and not unrelated to this new environment, was the awakening of trainers to the realization they should do more to control their own destiny. Opportunities to do this through existing bodies were explored but failed to give assurance that the trainers' objectives would be achieved. The situation left little alternative but for the trainers to establish a new national body and progress to full professional recognition, with all that this step entails.

THE ESTABLISHMENT OF A PROFESSIONAL BODY

The model for UK professional bodies has been long established, arising initially to meet the needs of those engaged in occupations in the medical, legal and maritime fields, all characterized by factors such as status, responsibility and trust, and operating across a wide field of public interest. Accountancy, scientific, technological, management and many more occupations have progressively added to the list in never-ending succession.

Expectations of a professional body are that it will essentially be self-regulating and have all, or most, of the following features:

1. Be firmly based on a body of theoretical or scientific knowledge.
2. Establish standards of competence attested by examination and practice.
3. Provide means for the recognition of competence (usually via post-nominal letters).
4. Undertake research to advance the body of knowledge and practice of the profession.
5. Provide information for members and the public benefit.
6. Provide members with services and a means for continuing professional development.
7. Establish codes of ethical behaviour and good practice.
8. Represent the interests of the profession and its members.

By definition a 'professional person' is one who meets and applies the standards and codes of the appropriate body. The need for public protection has, in extreme circumstances, required statutory action and registration to enforce membership of a professional body. This has occurred in a relatively small number of occupations. Most professional bodies rely on public recognition and trust in the purpose and standing of the body, and the integrity of the self-regulation that is applied. In particular, this recognition must come from stake holders, that is, those engaged in the profession, their employers and the clients served by the profession. In many occupations, including training, this level of recognition is hard-earned and is still being built. However, the demands for professional competence which can be nationally or internationally accredited is growing in training and many other occupations. Employers are increasingly becoming more discerning in the employment of training staff, seeking 'fully rounded' trainers able to work at all levels in the organization and be sensitive to and cope with changing business requirements, organization structures and human resource development needs. Trainers who are able to involve and use change management in the training and development function are able to adapt to or adopt new approaches and take advantage of new technology in the training field. For the trainer, working in an environment of accelerating change and complexity, the need for personal accreditation, together with the need for continuous professional development and access to information and other services, is increasing to a point where membership of a professional body is becoming more and more of a necessity.

NATIONAL INFLUENCE

The infrastructure for training and development in the United Kingdom has itself been subject to a succession of changes and the case for having a professional body to represent the interest of trainers is as strong, if not stronger, than ever. While it is true that political will, and the power struggle between public and private funding issues, hold the central arena, there is a growing awareness that the professional trainer's focus on quality standards, learner-centred approaches and the relationship which has been established between business achievement and the creation of learning cultures and learning environments, is a matter for consideration and is having a growing influence. For the first time, the professional trainer has the potential to capture public attention and direct it to support actions and initiatives leading to good practice and social development.

The Institute of Training and Development (ITD), responsible for reviving and firmly establishing the HRD (human resource development) concept within the United Kingdom, has achieved a significant advance in bridging the conventional barrier between 'Education' and 'Training'. It has led the country into a new era in which education and training are seen to be complementary, offering a lifelong continuity of development, which, to quote ITD's definition of HRD, 'is the process by which people achieve their full potential in life and work'. Truly a significant influence on the part of a professional body and one that will produce continuing benefit for many years to come.

THE PROFESSIONAL TRAINER

All studies of the training occupation soon lead to the conclusion that there is no single training role or standard occupational model of a trainer. Trainer roles vary according to a variety of factors which include: the level of managerial responsibility; the degree of active involvement in the analysis and interpretation of social, cultural, business or organization needs; the degree of active involvement in analysis and counselling associated with the training and development of individuals and groups; and the extent of required specialism within the design, delivery and evaluation aspects of the training function.

Some studies have identified key role definitions which enable distinctions to be made in the work trainers do. An example of this can be seen in the results of a study undertaken by Dr Roger Bennett and Tad Leduchowicz (see also chapter 16) which classifies the following roles:

Trainer A role primarily concerned with the actual direct delivery of training and helping people to learn.

Provider A role primarily concerned with the design, maintenance and delivery of training programmes.

Consultant A role primarily concerned with analysing business problems, recommending or advising on training conclusions, and working with managers, trainers and providers to advise on goals, policies, evaluation and so on.

61

Innovator A role primarily concerned with helping organizations to manage change and solve performance problems.

Training Manager A role primarily concerned with planning, organizing, controlling and developing the total training function.

As roles vary, so do the tasks involved and the knowledge and skill required to perform them. A useful inventory of these tasks was researched by Terry Morgan and Martin Costello of the Air and Travel Industry Training Board and published jointly by the Manpower Services Commission (MSC) and ITD, under the title of *Trainer Task Inventory*. However, the general expectation held of 'professional trainers' is that they all will have acquired a core of knowledge and skills with sufficient breadth and depth to support skill transfer and movement across a relatively wide range of roles. This gives a requirement for professional development programmes that extend from tactical, operational level to strategic, management level and integrate both the management and the training function.

The acquisition of the broad compendium of knowledge and skill required by the trainer is increasingly achieved through systematic training and development programmes, which are themselves progressively designed to provide ladders of progression, accreditation, credit accumulation and credit transfer within a national system, and provide a basis for international equivalence within the single European market and other areas of the world.

TRAINER QUALIFICATIONS

In order to achieve the widest range of recognition, trainer qualifications have followed accepted levels of national accreditation and are provided at three main levels: Certificate, a foundation programme which is essential task oriented; Diploma, which is oriented towards higher levels of operation and the management of the function; and Master's degree level programmes which are either specialist-oriented or centre on higher levels of training strategy, organizational development and business economics.

The Government's initiative in the late 1980s, designed to revolutionize vocational training in the United Kingdom through the introduction of nationally accredited competence-based qualifications for all occupations, resulted in the creation of a 'Lead Body' with specific responsibility for the development of Training and Development competency standards. The Training and Development Lead Body (TDLB) produced 132 national standards to meet a wide range of occupational roles and as a basis for the construction of appropriate National Vocational Qualifications (NVQs) and Scottish Vocational Qualifications (SVQs) in Scotland.

TDLB also published a framework of standards for use by Awarding Bodies. This framework has the standards arranged over three levels (out of a five-level system used nationally to give comparisons across all occupational sectors), with descriptors for each of the three levels as follows:

Level 3 Statement of Competence Deliver training specified and designed by others, assess the outcomes of that training and design training and, from identified learning needs, design training which facilitates learning and meets objectives at operational level.

Level 4 Statement of Competence Design, deliver, manage and evaluate training and development programmes and learning experiences to meet individual and organizational objectives.

Level 5 Statement of Competence (draft) Contribute to the formulation of strategic objectives and the identification of future capability requirements; design and implement HRD systems to meet those objectives; and design and operate procedures for the evaluation of outcomes.

The Institute of Training and Development (ITD) was the first body to pilot and award Training and Development NVQs. However, this organization believed the TDLB standards were insufficiently comprehensive to meet the needs of professional trainers and it therefore offers a series of enhanced qualifications, using a wider range of TDLB standards plus the addition of selected Management Lead Body standards. These provide an ITD recommended 'Professional Pathway' as an added option to the basic NVQ qualifications. ITD has retained the 'Certificate' and 'Diploma' titles to distinguish them from NVQ Level 3, 4 and 5 qualifications.

Extensive piloting by ITD has led to academic recognition of the competency-based approach in respect of Master's degree programmes and an increasing number of universities are giving credit towards a Master's degree in

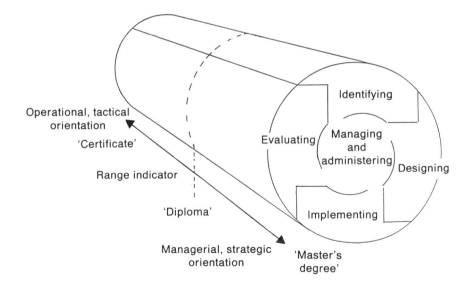

Figure 6.1   Training cycle – an expanded model

human resource development for Level 4 and 5 NVQ qualifications. The significantly increasing demand for trainer qualifications, particularly the demand for Diploma and Master's degree qualifications, is a clear indication of the rapid growth of professionalism within the training occupation.

A model (see Figure 6.1), extrapolated from the well-known and established training cycle (identification of training needs, design, delivery and evaluation), depicts the relationship of many of these factors and has been devised by the author for use as a framework for the development of ITD's qualification structure.

The following three central assumptions are contained in the model.

Holistic characteristic

The elements making up the training function are deliberately shown open-ended and interconnecting to depict the holistic characteristic of the function, which requires knowledge of the whole cycle in order to perform adequately in any one of the parts. Kenny and Reid (1986) have highlighted the essential need for evaluation to take place within each segment, and Donnelly (1987) has argued a case for pre-entry requirements to be satisfied in the move between one element and the next. However, the model shown above goes beyond this in terms of the underpinning knowledge and skill required to perform successfully in any sector of the cycle. This assumption has significant implications for unit accreditation of competencies based on functional analysis.

Related managerial and administrative skills.

These run as a thread of variable dimension throughout the training function, changing according to role and responsibility. This area of the model is again left open to illustrate the integration of the management and training functions.

Normally, administration is a relatively high feature and management a relatively low feature at one end of the range, and this relationship progressively changes the further one moves along the range. Generally all trainers have administrative responsibilities concerned with managing or facilitating learning, whether it be arranging the provision of training or the creation and maintenance of training environments or recording progress, achievement and so on. The management role can vary between supervisory management, with responsibility for health and safety, welfare and security, to important managerial responsibilities for human resource development strategy at the highest level in the organization. There is a corresponding growing 'risk' element as the trainer becomes more involved in organizational intervention and enters the sensitive field of power politics.

Range indicators

The range of responsibility, and levels of authority, complexity, sensitivity, knowledge and skill, vary considerably depending on the role and the nature of the organization and the perceptions of those involved. While recognizing these factors, those designing a qualification framework have little alternative but to make arbitrary divisions based on levels of comparability with national academic and competence standards used across a general range of professional occupations, and the marketability of qualification, that is, cost value and credibility to members of the profession and employers. The range indicator in the model stops short of the Master's degree, which extends into creative use of the subject (for example, in comparative studies or intervention strategies), or relates to other disciplines in order to develop highly specialized competencies (for example, learning and technology).

CODE OF PROFESSIONAL PRACTICE

In terms of ethics, the professional trainer's most serious responsibility is in relation to the learner. This can reflect in many ways; for example, in terms of loyalty and trust, which may revolve around the fulfilment of a 'learning contract' established between the learner, the trainer and the organization, where promises and commitment are in danger of not being honoured. It may revolve around a question of confidentiality, concerning the learner's progress or attainment; it can relate to the use of a methodology which has potential to damage the learner's mental or physical health; or it might revolve around a difference between the objectives of the organization and the interests and objectives of the individual, which could lead to exploitation of the learner. Unable to legislate for all eventualities, the code can only point the way for trainers to follow.

There are, of course, other ethical considerations, which are personal to the trainer: for example, accepting commitments which are beyond one's capabilities, plagiarizing work, or not giving due credit. ITD's code of professional practice endeavours to embrace all these issues and establish a framework of good practice relating, first, to those one is responsible to – employer, client, colleagues and the peer group – and, secondly, to those one is responsible for – the learners. It also reminds professional trainers of the continuing need for self-development. The code is detailed in Figure 6.2, and is commended to all those practising in the field of human resource development.

PROFESSIONAL LEADERSHIP

ITD believes that the first urgent step towards proactive professional leadership, is the creation of a policy framework that can:

- Guide the Institute's own members and give them a rationale they can follow and promote in their dealings with their own and other managements and which can encourage and stimulate action.
- Enable the Institute to work with other bodies and organizations, take initiatives and, where appropriate, make approaches to Government, employers, trades unions and the educational world; to redress negative attitudes to training and development and formulate and promote *65*

1. INTRODUCTION

    The Institute's mission is to:

    - Lead in the development of a learning world
    - Serve the professional interests of members (individuals and organizations)
    - Uphold the highest ideals in Human Resource Development

    The term Human Resource Development embraces that process whereby people develop their full potential in life and work.

2. OBJECTIVE

    The Code lays down standards of practice for all members of the Institute to follow in respect of their behaviour, personal development and their professional relations with their employers, clients, fellow practitioners, trainees, students, and the general public. Whilst the Code is prescribed primarily for members of the Institute, it is hoped that all engaged in training and Human Resource Development will adopt these precepts.

3. THE CODE OF PROFESSIONAL PRACTICE

    The Code of Professional Practice relates to five aspects of members' behaviour, namely:
    Behaviour and Personal development
    Equal opportunities
    Relations with individuals for whose training, development or guidance members are responsible
    Relations with the employing or client organization and its employees or trainees
    Relations with other organizations

4. BEHAVIOUR AND PERSONAL DEVELOPMENT

    Members shall:

    4.1   Work to the highest standards complying not only with the law (including the law on copyright) but also with published codes of practice and generally accepted best practice as it affects training and development.
    4.2   Conduct their work based activities with a high standard of courtesy and integrity and respect the dignity and privacy of individuals.
    4.3   Accept responsibility for their own work and the effective use of the resources entrusted to them; demonstrate by personal example and ordered approach the self-discipline and conduct expected of the professional. Accept assignments within their own competence or when required seek appropriate expertise from properly qualified individuals.
    4.4   Strive to enhance the good standing of the Institute and its members and of the HRD profession at large.
    4.5   Maintain a personal programme of Continuous Professional Development (CPD) and keep abreast of changes and developments relevant to the profession.

5. EQUAL OPPORTUNITIES

Members shall:

5.1 Be aware of relevant legislation, statutory codes and recommendations.
5.2 Promote good practice and the elimination of unlawful or unfair discrimination on the grounds of gender, race, age, disability, sexuality, colour, ethnic and national origin and religion.
5.3 Accept personal responsibility for assisting under represented groups to develop in the profession.

6. RELATIONS WITH INDIVIDUALS FOR WHOSE TRAINING, DEVELOPMENT OR GUIDANCE MEMBERS ARE RESPONSIBLE

Members shall:
6.1 Establish and maintain relationships with individuals to ensure that effective learning and development takes place.
6.2 Establish realistic plans to meet stated learning objectives and defined standards of competence.
6.3 Ensure the safety and well-being of those personnel within their responsibility or sphere of influence by adhering to both legislation and relevant advisory codes at all times.

7. RELATIONS WITH EMPLOYING OR CLIENT ORGANIZATION EMPLOYEES

Members shall:

7.1 Respect the confidentiality of information gained in the course of work and refrain from using such confidential information for personal benefit or in a way that may be damaging to any employing or client organization.
7.2 Inform the client or employing organization immediately of any personal interest which may conflict with the employer's interests.
7.3 Act honestly and loyally in carrying out the lawful policy and directions of the employing or client organization and refrain from damaging its image or reputation.

8. RELATIONS WITH OTHER ORGANIZATIONS

Members shall:

8.1 Make clear in any public statement whether they are acting in a personal capacity or representing the Institute or any other organization.
8.2 Be ready to share the results of research, new knowledge and skills; to acknowledge the work of others and to give professional assistance in public affairs insofar as commercial confidentiality allows.
8.3 Comply with and be subject to the Articles of Association of the Institute and the regulations from time to time in force.
8.4 Co-operate with investigations conducted by the ad hoc sub-committee of the Professional Standards Committee of the Institute, arising from complaints against members who may have infringed the Code.

Figure 6.2 The ITD Code of Professional Practice

professionally sound, effective, training and development strategies and policies at all levels.
- Provide a framework for swift and authoritative responses to the initiatives of Government and others.

This framework has been developed and published under the title *Towards Professional Leadership*. It makes definitive statements on key issues and provides the following guidelines for the parties involved.

The case for human resource development

Business and organizational effectiveness in the current conditions of rapidly accelerating technological, economic, social and political change, essentially depends upon the personal effectiveness of the individuals and groups who make up organizations in industry, commerce, the public sector or anywhere else. More than ever before, individuals and groups need effective training and development, and continuous updating and retraining, to equip them with the knowledge, skills and attitudes they require in order to deal successfully with the impact upon them of technological, economic and social change. People need, above all, to learn how to learn in order to gain the confidence and the motivation to seek and accept learning and development opportunities throughout their lives.

Awareness of the importance of human resource development at board and management level has been low in the United Kingdom. As a consequence, investment of money, time and effort has been reluctant and low. Perhaps not surprisingly, employees also have tended to underrate its value. A primary task, therefore, for professional training and development practitioners is to change attitudes to training and development of both employers and employees alike.

The planning and direction of the management of money and material resources have long been accepted as key functions of management by boards of directors and their executive managers in successful organizations in industry, commerce, the public sector or elsewhere. The management of learning within an organization, however, has not been accorded similar priority at board or executive management level, except in a very few organizations. Human resource development has tended to be regarded as an optional extra, outside the mainstream of business or commercial planning and direction. The continuance of these attitudes in the future will be dangerous, perhaps critically so, for business and organizational prosperity.

In essence, the main purpose of human resource development is no less than to facilitate continuous organizational flexibility, change and development and to create appropriate conditions for success.

The nature of training

Training is the management of the learning process. More specifically it is an oriented process of development the knowledge, skills and attitudes of individuals and groups to enable them to perform effectively or to improve performance in a job, occupation or role. The job or role will normally be in a business employment situation in industry, commerce or public sector organization, but it may also be in another context such as sport or voluntary associations.

Training is directed towards behaviour change resulting in performance improvement which is readily measurable. Training, unlike education, is a means to an end, not an end in itself. It is usually sponsored by an organization and, therefore, is generally related to identified organizational needs. However, it is unlikely to succeed to a reasonable level unless it also meets the identified learning needs of the individuals involved.

To be effective, training needs to be learner-oriented as opposed to trainer-oriented. Its aim is to stimulate and help learners to learn rather than to impose upon them the knowledge, skills, attitudes or value systems of the trainer.

Who needs training?

Training and development should be regarded by employers as well as by individuals as an integral part of employment, throughout a lifetime, whether in one or many different employments. Training needs should be regularly reviewed and training and development plans prepared and implemented. Training should not be regarded as a once-and-for-all investment confined to young people only, but should be seen as a lifelong process of personal development.

Learning opportunities should be available for individuals and groups within organizations in industry, commerce or the public sector wherever and whenever training and development needs are identified. Training should also be available to individuals not in employment who wish to prepare themselves for employment by acquiring appropriate knowledge, skills or attitudes.

Responsibility for training

All the parties involved share responsibility for training and development in the following ways.

Individuals

Unless individuals are willing to invest their time, effort, readiness to change behaviour and sometimes their cash, little training can take place. They carry a prime responsibility for training. They should be entitled to expect returns in terms of new or improved knowledge, skills and attitudes necessary for getting or creating employment, maintaining job security, changing employment, improving earnings, promotion, or simply personal satisfaction.

Employers and other sponsoring bodies

Boards of directors and similar groups carry a main strategic responsibility: for   *69* placing training among their key planning policies; for allocating adequate funds for it to be carried out; and for requiring managers to fulfil their responsibilities for training. Training begins in the boardroom and, unless it is recognized as a strategic priority there, is unlikely to be pursued by those responsible elsewhere in the organization. Boards are entitled to expect returns on their investment in the form of continually improved organizational performance and development.

Managers

A substantial responsibility for the implementation of training rests with managers at all levels. They should be expected to include training among the key activities of managing. They are responsible: for identifying the training and development needs of employees at all levels; for designing and managing the learning process; and for creating conditions conducive to learning by individuals and groups. Managers also have responsibility for evaluating the results of training and development by monitoring progress and modifying provisions accordingly, and they are entitled to expect improved levels of competence and performance.

Government

Government has responsibility on behalf of the community at large for maintaining and developing the economic and social health and strength of the country as a whole. It should contribute by providing legislation to create conditions conducive to the steady development of training, including measures to stimulate, facilitate and regulate the responsibilities of the other parties involved in training. This may include funding, especially at the initial stages. Government should also be expected to provide training, directly or through agencies, to fill gaps unlikely to be filled by other providers or sponsors.

Professional bodies

The responsibility for continuously monitoring and developing expertise falls mainly upon the professional bodies. They should be expected to guide other responsible parties as well as lead their membership towards continuous improvement of professional performance.

Examining and awarding bodies

Standards of excellence are the chief responsibility of examining and awarding bodies, such as the Lead Body. They should provide methods of measuring competence and should continually review standards to keep abreast of technological and social change.

Trainer provider institutions and organizations

These are responsible for developing and improving their programmes as the result of continuing evaluation and dialogue with users and clients. They should maintain close liaison with users and clients to ensure that programmes are in line with changing development needs as well as learning design.

Human resource development professionals

Their prime responsibility should be for helping managers to manage the learning in their organizations. They should be catalysts, interventionists and facilitators rather than teachers. They should be responsible for stimulating positive attitudes to training and development among managers. To achieve this, they need to understand and be integrated with the main objectives and technologies of their organizations: they have responsibility for making their contributions to the BUSINESS, not just to the expertise of training and development. Above all, they have responsibility for establishing and maintaining the credibility of training and of themselves.

National infrastructure

A comprehensive national infrastructure, in which all the responsible parties can participate in a co-ordinated and dynamic way, is essential. ITD believes that the success of human resource development depends upon:

- Professional and credible leadership.
- Positive investment of funds, managerial effort and support from industry, commerce and public sector employers, and all employer and employee representative bodies.
- Legislative arrangements supported, if necessary, by enforcement powers vested in Government.

A professionally led national infrastructure backed by legislation is both essential and feasible.

DEVELOPING A LEARNING SOCIETY

Towards Professional Leadership is a blueprint for building a learning society. A society with a new culture in which self-development is an accepted concept, and is facilitated and supported as a matter of course by all those concerned. It portrays a culture in which organizations recognize and value their human resources and create 'learning environments', providing encouragement and help at all levels, with the active participation of managers and others, to assist employees to realize their full potential. It calls on the active involvement of all to commit to a life-long process of self-development. It requires the creation of a national infrastructure that is proactive and supportive, with a national policy *71* framework that is discerning of both local and national needs, and able to co-ordinate, research and provide guidance and practical support – with the aid of statutory powers if necessary – to keep human resource development at the 'leading edge' and so develop the national economy and enhance the wellbeing of the country.

It is this context of the future that underlies the mission statement of ITD:

- To LEAD in the development of a learning world.
- To SERVE the professional interests of members.
- To UPHOLD the highest ideals in human resource development.

FURTHER READING

Perry, P.J.C. (1976), *The Evolution of British Manpower Policies,* BACIE.
Bennett, Roger (1988), *Improving Trainer Effectiveness*, Aldershot: Gower.
Morgan, Terry and Martin Costello (1984), *Trainer Task Inventory*, ITD.
Kenney, John and Margaret Reid (1986), *Training Interventions*, IPM.
Donnelly, Eugene (1987), *The Training Model: Time for a change?*, ICT.
Policy Studies Institute (1990), *The Training and Development of Trainers*, Training, Enterprise and Education Directorate of the Employment Department.

7 The need to market training

Eugene Donnelly

In the past we have always tended to think of training in the context of a service transmitted to potential customers by the use of a 'selling' process: we continually discuss the 'need to sell training' and in so doing radically undersell the potential of the training activity as a medium for the development of human resources within an organization. The function of the training specialist in this context conjures up views of selling a product or service to management through the medium of persuasive techniques aimed at short-term targets, such as maximizing the use of existing training resources through course attendance. The increasing complexity of business and extension of professionalism in training has made this, essentially short-sighted, viewpoint redundant. We must now envisage the selling function within training as part of a much wider activity related to the deeper goals of the marketing activity.

MARKETING AND TRAINING

There are a wide diversity of definitions as to the nature and content of marketing but wide agreement on the main elements. The Institute of Marketing (quoted in Donnelly and Prior (1987)) stresses the managerial and profit-related concepts and states that marketing is 'the management process responsible for identifying, anticipating and satisfying customer requirements profitably'. This definition reminds us that, at the end of the day, we must meet budget requirements, a useful counterpoint to the traditional assumption that training in itself is somehow necessarily a good thing. The theme of marketing as a process for determining demand has a long history in the literature of marketing and is illustrated in the definition of Brech (1953) who argued that 'Marketing is the process of determining consumer demand for a product or service, motivating its sale and distributing it into ultimate consumption at a profit'.

A wider definition, and one which serves to underline the distinction between the narrowness of the purely limited selling function and that of the much broader, and more complex area of marketing, is that of Kotler who states:

Marketing is the business function that identifies current unfilled needs and wants, defines and measures their magnitude, determines which target markets the organisation can best serve, and decides on appropriate products, services, and programmes to serve these markets. Marketing serves as the link between a society's needs and its pattern of industrial response. (Kotler, 1984)

If we think of training as a service function within an organization, which it is, then the effectiveness of the content and evaluation of that service can only be measured by the extent to which it relates to predefined corporate goals. This approach is far removed from the traditional selling approach which, as Donnelly and Prior (1987) pointed out 'was usually piecemeal and often consisted of "pushing" individual courses, the justification for which tended to emanate from the training department, possibly with a view to meeting assumed or loosely defined general needs'. One starting point in the marketing of training must therefore be to ensure that training policies emanate from the manpower policy of the organization. In simple terms, we must relate the projected product to the defined market environment, ensuring that training priorities are similar to organizational priorities. Credibility in both marketing and training comes from the capacity to meet perceived customer needs.

BUDGETS AND PRICING POLICY

These customer needs, and consequent training activities, must also be defined within the constraints of available budgets. In marketing our training product, we must therefore make a realistic assessment of projected costs and expected benefits. This will entail decision in, for example, the area of opportunity costing. Would the projected costs of a particular training activity justify the expenditure, or would it be more economic to spend the budget in an alternative activity? Would it be cheaper to employ newly qualified accountants rather than developing our own? What are the short- and long-term implications of such a policy? Consideration must also be given to training 'mix': would it be cheaper to carry out the training on the organization's premises, using existing staff, or utilize external training resources on the trainer's premises? In such situations, we must combine training decision with those related to cost minimizing, as the long-term effect of repeatedly using external resources may lead to relatively sophisticated training which is unrelated to either the requirements or, possibly more important, the cultural expectations of the organization.

Pricing is also determined by the extent to which you may be willing to subsidize a loss leader in order to generate future training activities. The potential size of your training market will also help determine the amount of resources invested in training; large repeat orders will often justify high initial expenditure. But it should be noted that training programmes, like any other product, have a limited shelf life.

DEMAND FACTOR

74   We must distinguish between latent demand and potential demand in the

development of our training market. Latent demand arises from a vague want by potential customers, in which case it is a necessary function of the trainer to make an objective analysis of the situation. Turrell (1980) makes the point that most changes in technology, legislation, manpower composition and markets will generate a need for training. An important factor in this context is the ability of a trainer to gauge the competence and capacity for change on the part of the employees in the organization. Pettigrew *et al.* (1982) underline the necessity for 'cultural congruence' in training activities, otherwise the training may be extremely effective pedagogically but have results which are unacceptable within the organization. For example, a democratic approach to learning may lead to conflict in a highly autocratic organization.

Potential demand is demand which is clear-cut and backed by the necessary budget, but which will require interpretation by the trainer in terms of feasibility and methodology. Any demand for training will require the definition of behavioural objectives and a definitive statement of the training target. This requires the analyses of factors such as: age and status of potential trainees; skill category; and expected rates of retention and comprehension. We must also be sensitive to the effect that training is likely to have on our potential customers. Will they be highly motivated or reluctant, and consequently feel threatened? Will they view training as a spur to promotion, as an activity associated with success or as an indication of inadequacy? Demand is largely based on perception. However, we often see what we want to see, and such perceptions may be formed from the climate of opinion within the organization and the attitudes transmitted by the opinion leaders within the management team.

A demand for training may also stem from legislation, for example safety training. Or it may be a natural by-product of the trainer's industry: the market for training in the computer industry, with its fast changing technology, is likely to be more dynamic than that in heavy engineering.

DECISION FACTORS DETERMINING THE PURCHASE OF TRAINING

Considerable research has been done on the factors determining the purchase of the products. It is helpful to restate some of these factors in the context of training. Baker (1985) quotes Gordon Brand who proposed an eight-step model, which may be summarized in the training context as follows:

1. Recognition that the problem has a training solution. It should be noted that training is one of a series of strategies for the solution of organizational problems. Other possibly options include: reorganization; changes in technology; review of recruitment and selection policies.
2. The characteristics of the training need (trainee category, learning media, on- or off-job, etc.).
3. Potential applications of the training. Trainers should show originality in this context and develop beyond the classroom-type orientation of training. We must see our organizational environment as a media for learning.
4. Potential suppliers (in-company and external).

5. Evaluation of learning resources and their potential for application. To what extent are we utilizing the management team as a training resource? What are our current strengths?
6. Selection of trainer. What criteria are we using? Is it mainly job experience? Are we using 'failed' managers as a soft option? Do we apply the training criteria used for new managers to new trainers (e.g. do we analyse developmental needs)?
7. Development of delivery system.
8. Evaluation of training. What types of evaluation methodology do we use? When are they applied? What is the source of our evaluation criteria? Does training meet pre-defined objectives?

MARKET RESEARCH AND PRODUCT POLICY

It is essential that projected training activities result from objective research, if only to help ensure that our products, and the policies from which they are derived, are rooted in perceived and accepted reality. We must be prepared to use analytical techniques such as: effectively designed questionnaires; attitude surveys; job training analyses; sampling techniques; and material generated by specialists in organization and job design.

In determining product policy, we must get the organization to ask and answer fundamental, if obvious, questions. The starting point is an accurate definition of corporate strategy, which should answer such questions as: What business are we in? Where do we want to go? What part of the business life cycle is the organization in (growth–maturity–decline)? What is the capacity of the organization in the context of handling change? In relation to current training policies and training activities: what is the expected life span of current policies and training activities? Is there a perceived demand for new training policies and training programmes? What are the projected safe areas and those of high risk? Do current policies and activities meet organizational objectives and do they relate to the cultural expectations of the organization? Are current training activities operating within budgetary constraints? Are these budgets based on pre-analysed manpower requirements or simply on a historical percentage of overall budgets? What are the areas of high throughput and those where high consumer resistance is likely? What are the costs of not training (e.g. failure to meet European Community directives)?

We must also consider the extent to which proposed training programmes fit into the current training activities. Do they complement them or are they in a completely different category, or at a different level? To what extent, if any, can existing facilities be utilized? Is there a cost-benefit argument for the extension of the present training programmes (e.g. economies of scale)? Apart from possible economies of scale likely to emerge from the development of existing training expertise, do projected changes derive from current organizational policies and objectives, or can they be justified on the basis of projected developments in external markets, or strategic changes in product policies? We must be clear on one point: what will the proposed changes in policies, and subsequent training activities achieve in terms of existing policies?

The fact that a need has been isolated and agreed upon does not excuse the common failure to test the market with the subsequent training product, even if only on a limited scale. This will normally require the establishment of briefing meetings for relevant managers and possibly the inclusion of potential trainees in the pre-training sessions. Pre-training briefing should be followed by a pilot course in which both course members and their managers supply feedback. Flexibility is the key requirement at this stage in the development of the training programme. While it is important that feedback sessions are provided on any training activity, it is doubly important that they are made available at the pilot stage. This stage in the marketing process can only be successful if behavioural objectives have been accurately defined, and a willingness shown on the part of the trainer to make changes where they have been shown to be necessary.

PRICING POLICY

The successful marketing of training depends to a large extent on the ability of trainers to distinguish between the cost of their product and the price which it can realistically expect to command within the organization. Cost relates to such factors as: overheads; preparation time (including research); opportunity cost (likely returns from the alternative use of resources); publicity; training handouts; trainer's time; and visual aids.

The actual price which a trainer can charge to the budgets of his or her clients will largely relate to what the market will bear. If the trainers are in a monopoly position, without comparative competitors, they will obviously have some leeway in their charging arrangements, although there is likely to be a point where external competitors will emerge in a highly profitable market. It may also be unwise to be apparently using a monopoly advantage when you may need the active co-operation of colleagues at a later stage in the training cycle! At this stage trainers will need to differentiate their produce from those of actual or potential competitors. This will not usually be difficult if they have a high level of acceptability within their organization.

However, trainers must be sensitive to the distinction between short- and long-term pricing policies. They may wish to lower their initial price in order to develop demand, with a view to increasing the price at a later date when the training has attained a measure of acceptability and obvious worth. A possible problem with this context is the tendency of some managers to equate value with price: the greater the price, the greater the assumed value. A paramount feature in this area is that of relating cost procedures to the internal budget system. All budgets are likely to be historical rather than training-determined. In an ideal world the senior managers within an organization would derive their training budgets from manpower budgets and calculate their training budget from accurately costed, pre-defined, training needs. But in reality the training budget is more likely to be determined on a 'last year plus inflation' basis. Trainers must therefore be cost effective within the limitations of their organization environment.

Cost effectiveness can be achieved only by ensuring that there is an effective mix in the use of limited training resources. We must, therefore, be aware of external and internal training resources, relevant cost comparisons, and the reasons for and against using internal and external training resources.

External resources supply a potentially wide and diverse reservoir of knowledge, skill and experience and are of particular use in the one-off context; for example, in industrial relations training or training requiring a high capital outlay, such as fork-lift truck training. It may also be useful as a medium for the introduction of new ideas or fresh perspectives. Nevertheless, we must note the limitations of external training resources. An obvious disadvantage is that of cost, although this may have the effect of generating the assumption that there is a positive relationship between cost and effectiveness. A serious limitation of external training is what may be termed the culture gap.

MARKETING AND THE ORGANIZATIONAL CULTURE

The culture of an organization comprises the norms, values and social expectations which are unique to each organization, and is extremely difficult to both extricate and define. We are only conscious of the uniqueness of an organization's cultural values and expectations when we leave it and enter another organization. A culture is much more than the sum of job descriptions in the organization. If we cannot understand and relate to an organization's cultural norms we are unlikely to be able to change them through the training process or market the function with any degree of success. A useful starting point in the context is the use of attitude surveys as a means of determining the extent to which the assumed norms and expectations of the organization relate, or are out of line with, those of the training function. Traditionally, trainers have tended to confuse what they perceive as the training priorities of the organization with those as perceived by senior management. In marketing terms, they have designed a product without having accurately researched either the product or its intended customers. This results in a lack of support from potential customers with a resultant loss of acceptability and credibility by trainers. Trainers' reactions to this situation range from a feeling of being grossly misunderstood to that of being a purely reactive functionary concerned with highly formalized training programmes of an off-the-shelf variety. But it could be argued, with some considerable justification, that the skill of training practitioners lies in their ability to understand and use the cultural values of their organizations. This far outweighs any other single factor in terms of their potential for relevance within the organizational environment. There is often a tendency among trainers to assume that, because they are the 'experts' in training, they therefore know better than their prospective customers what they should be doing in the areas of both training policy and the implementation of training.

We must always distinguish between what is required within an organizational culture on purely training criteria and what is likely to be acceptable in practice. Bennett and Leduchowicz bring out this point in their distinction between 'overall' and 'interim' training officers:

'Overall' trainer effectiveness is the relationship between the correct identification of organizational needs, the selection of those needs that can be satisfied through training, the translation of these into training objectives, engaging in training activities that are in line with the organizational culture and achieving outcomes that contribute to the organizational goals. 'Interim' effectiveness relates to the attainment of intermediate or short-term goals. (Bennett and Leduchowicz, 1983).

Our product must always be customer- rather than product-directed. We, as professionals, may disagree with this sentiment and feel that we are selling our profession short. In the end, however, we must, like our medical colleagues, realize that our function at the policy end is to advise, and, where relevant, spell out the implications of taking certain courses of action and suggest alternatives. Success in this activity rests largely on our ability to influence events through the manipulation of relationships within our organization. Our power base rests on our capacity to develop relationships. Pettigrew *et al.* (1983) underlined this important point when they argued that cultural identification was more important than technical competence. They defined cultural identification as: 'the capacity of a person to understand, empathise and use his knowledge of the values, beliefs, patterns of behaviour, language and other symbols of a culture other than his own in order to influence that other culture.'

THE TRAINER'S ROLE

It should not be assumed that the trainer has a merely reactive role in the development of the training product. Our professional expertise as trainers puts us in a powerful position to contribute to and help develop both training policy and its implementation. At the policy level we can assist in the interpretation of the policies into training objectives and help interpret their content, so that it is effectively communicated to our potential training market: the target population. We must minimize the use of training jargon and use arguments which are acceptable to the target population. In practice, this means targeting perceived problems and gaining the acceptance of potential customers by illustrating a knowledge of their current concerns.

There are a variety of ways in which this initial marketing activity can be carried out. Meetings can be arranged at which the trainer can determine and distinguish the acceptable from the actual training requirements, and gauge the relative acceptability of projected policies and activities. These requirements will vary considerably between both categories of trainee and sections of the organization. Managers may view training as a signal suggesting promotion at a future date or interpret it as a slight on their competence. The sales department is likely to see training as a prerequisite for effective sales development and a medium for maintenance of the sales team. But a newly computerized accounting department may not relish the training needed to update them on the latest accountancy packages, particularly if the current software is apparently acceptable for their present requirements.

Communicating the message of training in our organizational training market   *79* also gives the trainer an opportunity to consider the available range of training resources. Are we matching our accommodation to the level of our trainee categories? If we run management courses in an hotel, is the service at a level which senior managers expect, or have time and continual usage blunted the motivation and competence of suppliers? Do our training materials reflect the changes continually taking place within the organization, or are they getting dog-eared and irrelevant? Are we using training material which is unadventurous and crudely presented? Can we usefully extend our channels of communications to help ensure that our potential customers are aware of our product with a sufficient lead time to allow decisions on training to be made within the normal constraints of time and budget?

There is often little relationship between the time and effort that trainers expend on the establishment of training policies and their implementation on the one hand, and the effort dedicated to effectively communicating the resulting product on the other. We tend to rely on the intuitive feeling that a good product necessarily sells itself in the organizational marketplace. Nothing could be further from the truth, as we can see from the multi-million budgets used by well-known brand names in the continuing espousal of their products. Having determined the nature of our product, we must ensure that our potential customers at all levels of the organization are aware of its existence; and having effectively presented our case for training, we must also ensure that our potential customers are persuaded to use the product. This can be done through the medium of management presentations, remembering that the 'medium is often the message'. Every presentation, no matter how apparently innocuous or trivial, can either reinforce, or destroy, our credibility as trainers.

PRESENTING THE CASE

There is an assumption in some organizations that the definition of training requirements is necessarily followed by their implementation. The reality is often quite different, for one main reason: lack of effective presentation to management. An in-company training presentation must meet six basic requirements, as follows:

1. There must be a clear statement of the problem, or problems, being addressed. This initial statement should be short, sharp and entirely relevant to the problems as perceived by the organization's management team.
2. This should be followed by an analysis of the factors causing the problem and the effects that the problem is having on the operation of the organization, or is likely to have in the future.
3. The training solutions proposed should then be presented, illustrating priorities and sequence of implementation, within a time scale; that is, immediate, short term, middle term and long term. In each instance there must be an explanation of the implications of taking the proposed course of action and the likely results of inaction.

4. Agreement should be obtained on managers' projected areas of responsibility for the implementation of policies and programmes.
5. Broad agreement should be reached regarding evaluation activities; that is, criteria, type, timing and responsibility.
6. Budgetary implications must, where possible, be defined.

It is often useful to try out suggested presentation material on those who will be potentially involved in its application. This is helpful for two main reasons: first, it forewarns of their possible involvement and therefore limits the element of threat; and secondly, the presenter is given an opportunity to try out his material and receive immediate feedback without loss of face. An important feature of this presentation activity is that we are gauging the potential capacity of the management team to accept and implement change. If we attempt to move too fast we can easily neutralize any success already achieved. Underestimating the managing team's ability to assimilate new training activities and experiences can easily lead to serious underutilization of manpower potential, with serious consequences for the future of the organization. It is obviously vital that we make a professional presentation; we are marketing our services in a major context – possibly more important, we are also selling ourselves.

DETERMINANTS OF CREDIBILITY

Given the importance of credibility in the marketing structure of the trainer, how can we set about extending our credibility? A leading factor in the area of credibility is that of our powers of persuasion. We can only persuade if we are ourselves convinced of the rightness of a particular course of action: it must be consistent with our beliefs and values and the beliefs and values of potential customers. A large and important element in the ability of trainers to persuade will depend on their technical competence, particularly on the selling factors of the training function. Why should organizations and their employees train? Kenney and Reid (1986) outlined the most important justifications for training. These include:

- Effective learning reduces training costs and speeds.
- The profitable employment of new trainees.
- Staff efficiency can be enhanced and updated by ongoing training, ensuring both job and organization performance standards are being met.
- The volume and quality of work can be attained and possibly extended through the more effective use of existing resources and a resultant decrease in faulty work.
- Labour turnover can be reduced.
- Training can be used to help ensure the development of new skills, knowledge and attitudes.
- Reduced accident levels.

81

- Enhanced morale through the development of latent employee potential.
- Greater capacity to handle change.

There are a series of factors which can help extend our competence in the area of persuasion. These are noted by writers, such as DeLozier (1976), in the general context of the marketing communication process, and include such pointers as:

- Effective persuasion develops through enhanced credibility.
- Credibility increases with the perception on the part of the customer of increased gain.
- Retention of selling material increases with repetition.
- Arguments against our apparent self-interest are more likely to be acceptable.
- We must identify with the expectations and perceptions of our potential customers.
- We must be positive.
- Power and influence are closely related.

The central feature in the development of our capacity for persuasion is the ability to illustrate the existence of potential gain for the participant in the training process. Such gains are obviously easier to sell if they can be stated in terms of cost savings. However, we must be conscious of the difficulties inherent in any investment within the sphere of human resource development, particularly in the short term. This applies to any form of investment: a fact which is often overlooked by those hostile to training.

ADVERTISING AND PROMOTION

The main function of advertising is to increase awareness of our training product, although it will also have an information element. There are a series of arguments which must be considered in justification of the use of advertising media in the marketing of training. It is an important weapon in the continuing need effectively to utilize scarce training resources by ensuring that all our potential customers are aware of what is on offer. It also helps us gain support for highly specific training, possibly in the form of courses mounted to meet projected, or possibly even reactive requirements. There may be a market beyond the immediate demand area that we have isolated. For example, we may find that a training programme developed for specialist computer staff will meet the requirements of other employees in the organization, if suitably modified.

Similarly, it may be possibly to adapt a presentation designed for senior managers so that it can supply an information base for other employees in the organization. This also has the advantage that it gives the hallmark of senior management support to the product, and, in doing so, supplies an important marketing requirement: the acceptability and subsequent credibility which normally stems from product consumption by market leaders. Acceptability at this level also helps to ensure that the product is in line with current market expectations – an essential ingredient in successful marketing.

Effective advertising tends to sharpen our critical faculties in the area of image building. What type of image should we project to potential customers? We must resist the temptation to project a format which is heavily reliant on sophisticated training technology and beyond the competence of the organization either to understand or utilize. There is little point in leading the world if the world is either unable or unwilling to follow! Publicity material does not necessarily have to follow the often tired and jaded format of the organization. We must use clear, readable prose, and a professional layout. The tendency in many organizations is to cover old ground by ignoring the existence of specialists in the design of selling material within our own selling and marketing sections. We would expect them to use our training expertise. Why should we not be willing to utilize theirs?

Irrelevant training jargon should be avoided in advertising materials. This is normally interpreted by managers as a screen for self-justification and the development of spurious and irrelevant superiority. But we must not be afraid to use our technical terms and methodologies. For example, both managers and potential trainees must understand the requirement for clear behavioural objectives and the uses and limitations of evaluation techniques. We must also be aware of using currently popular terminology in our advertising copy. Managers are generally sensitive to anything that sounds remotely like sociological jargon. To give two extreme but actual examples: 'to develop a meaningful interface between production and sales'; and 'to expedite congruent relationships in the management team'.

Advertising media should follow the conventional routes for information within the organization, but realists will be aware of what happens to much of the material circulating between managers and departments. We have all seen the long, boring lists which pour forth from training departments in a seemingly endless repetitive stream, straying out to irrelevant parts of the organization and lacking any measure of user-friendly content. We must aim training advertising at specific markets within the organization. Managers will have quite different expectations from technicians or accountancy specialists and our approach to training advertising materials must reflect this difference.

Such material should contain three main features. First, it must clearly define the target population. Second, the behavioural objectives should be stated, with the possible insertion of what the training activity does not cover. Third, it should contain an outline syllabus of each activity and spell out the training methods used.

There is a growing realization among trainers, especially those in larger organizations, that there is likely to exist a series of common elements in their training programmes which could possibly be shared with other organizations, either in their industry or within their geographic area. Obvious examples are common-denominator themes, such as safety training, supervisory training and basic clerical training. However, it is necessary to ensure that a common demand does actually exist and that it is not being superimposed for reasons of cost or administrative convenience. Where an organization is in the market to share its training facilities (and its costs), the advertising process can be simplified by using a ring-binder format which allows for flexibility in the advertising process. The external marketing of training requires an extension of the advertising process to investigate the projected training requirements of prospective customers, and the widening of the distribution network to encompass such organizations as local Chambers of Commerce, local authorities, trade organizations and possibly the local press. One obvious limitation to the sharing process is that of confidentiality, but in reality this is seldom relevant in this context.

Promotional campaigns aimed at developing and extending the training market must take as their starting point the definition of their prospective market area. This can range from the highly specific training requirements of individual managers, met within the organizational environment, to the very generalized training needs of craft trainees. The latter category will possibly be trained on the premises, in a specialist training centre, and at a technical college. As the needs vary, so must the type of promotional material.

The starting point for all promotional material is the justification of the product in terms suitable for, and acceptable to, the potential customer. In the case of managers, we will want to underline the potential for development of the individual to meet the challenge of change, with the added inducement of status-related training at a level consonant with their expectations. We must also illustrate a sensitivity to their problems, and target the proposed training to help alleviate these problems. Training techniques used will also have to reflect the expectations of potential customers: problem-centred work groups with other members of the peer group and minimal theory inputs can usefully be promoted when selling management training in promotional campaigns. Craft trainees will expect to have both a workshop and a college-based theory element. Promotional material will, therefore, be aimed at potential school-leavers and should be couched in language acceptable to the aspirations of this target population. Actual promotion in this context will largely be by word of mouth, or through school careers officers, the local press, and the possible use of display material for recruitment in the organization.

While we must consider the above factors, what we can actually do in the context of promotional campaigns will largely depend on budgets. It is useful to develop a series of promotional campaigns: comparing likely outcomes on a pound-for-pound basis. Experienced salesmen will point out that 50 per cent of the money used in advertising is wasted, but you can never tell which 50 per cent. This does not absolve us of the responsibility for ensuring that promotion campaigns come within acceptable budget levels and constitute a realistic part of the overall training budget. The tendency is to assume that good training sells itself and any promotional activity is simply icing on the cake. The reality is that scarce training resources used on the development of training requirements can easily be wasted through our inability or unwillingness to use promotional material.

CONCLUSION

The central function of marketing in the context of training is to ensure we have the right product in the right place at the right time. These requirements can be met only if the organization has:

- Defined its objectives.
- Developed training policies related to these objectives.
- Based training design on pre-defined behavioural objectives.
- Effectively targeted the potential training population.
- Professionally marketed the training product, within cultural and budgetary constraints.
- Realistically evaluated results in terms of expected outcomes.

FURTHER READING

Baker, M.J. (1985), *Marketing: an introductory text*, Macmillan Education.

Bennett, R. and T. Leduchowicz (1983), *What makes an effective trainer?* Bradford: MCB University Press.

Brech, E.F.L. (1953), *Principles of management*, Longmans.

DeLozier, M. Wayne (1976), *The marketing communication process*, Tokyo: McGraw-Hill.

Donnelly, E.L. and J.K. Prior (1987). 'The marketing of training and development', *Training and Development*, **6**, (1).

Kenney, J., and M. Reid (1986), *Training interventions*, Institute of Personnel Management.

Kotler, P. (1984), *Marketing management: analysis, planning and control*, Englewood Cliffs, NJ: Prentice Hall.

Pettigrew, A.M., G.R. Jones and P.W. Reason (1982), *Training and development roles in their organisational setting*, Sheffield: Manpower Services Commission.

Turrell, M. (1980), *Training analysis: a guide to recognizing training needs*, Macdonald and Evans.

Part Two

PLANNING AND MANAGING TRAINING AND DEVELOPMENT

8　The learning organization

Valerie Hammond and Edgar Wille

There are short-lived schemes and there are fundamental ideas. The learning organization is a fundamental idea, one that enters into everything that is thought and said and done in an organization. Even if the phrase gives way to something else, the idea will not. It is one of those concepts which, once grasped and put into practice, means that life will never be quite the same again, either for the individual or for the organization which in turn is comprised of individuals. Yet, like most profound ideas, it is only a simple way of looking at what goes on, anyway. The only reason for talking about it is that when you know about it you can set about creating conditions favourable to its growth, instead of it just happening accidentally.

WHAT IS A LEARNING ORGANIZATION?

The phrase 'the learning organization' is being used to describe the bringing together of people to achieve some objective, great or small, in conditions where they are all searching, all the time, for ways of doing whatever needs to be done in a better way. In learning organizations people are alert all the time for signals which show whether or not they are on the path to success in achieving their objectives. Learning organizations are continuously looking at the detail of their actions in the light of the whole, informed by a vision which they share with each other.

Feedback is crucial to the learning organization because it needs to know whether what is being attempted is working out. Accounts, reports, spread sheets, salespeople's sense of customer opinion, shop-floor workers, perceptions of how practical a new system is – all are monitored and seriously considered. No one's view, no feedback, is ignored, because such organizations learn and succeed only by listening. The ideal of the learning organization, obviously easier to state than to achieve, is never to take anything for granted, to expose everything to keen examination, and to respect everyone's view, even where it is not decided to follow it. In such organizations, openness prevails and trust develops, because without these approaches the best ideas will not surface and productive dialogue will be stillborn.

No doubt all this sounds too good to be possible. Indeed, it does need careful examination and more study than one chapter in a book can offer. Nevertheless, if this chapter can whet the appetite of the reader to carry out this examination, and, perhaps, in his or her own local environment, experiment to see if the idea can begin to work, then our purpose in writing it will have been met.

ROOTED IN THE LEARNING ORGANISM

The learning organization is not a technique on which a manual can be written entitled, '50 ways to create a learning organization', or, worse still, 'How to create a learning organization in 50 days'. It is rooted in the very nature of what it is to be human. Human beings are not static creatures; neither are any animals or plants. All are living; and the true nature of being alive is development and change. The only difference about human beings is that they know that this is so, though they will vary in the extent of their awareness.

From the moment of birth, the human being is set on a path of change, of development. Within every seven years each molecule of the physical body will have undergone complete transformation. Every microsecond of life yields new learning in the mind and spirit, from infancy even to extreme old age. It is never possible for a human being to say 'I have arrived, I am now totally what I will always be'. In fact perhaps our terminology is wrong and we should speak of ourselves as 'human becomings'. Life is a journey and we are always on the move, that is what makes human life such an adventure. Of course, the cynic will say, quite rightly, that the movement can be backward as well as forward, but that is a challenge and one over which we have some control.

This is about the individual, about the learning organism. Our subject is the learning organization, which is an expansion of the idea of the individual learning organism. When individuals work in concert, they constitute a learning organization. Whether they recognize it or not, they will learn together, even if they do not make as much use of the fact as they might.

However, there is a difference. Individuals can think and talk and act. Organizations cannot, and are therefore, in one sense, abstractions. Peter Senge (1990) has written: 'Organizations learn only through individuals who learn. Individual learning does not guarantee organizational learning. But without it no organizational learning occurs.'

SYNERGY

Organizational learning is not merely the sum total of what the individuals have learned, just as an organization is not just the sum total of the people working in it. Between the people who comprise an organization there are magic connections – relationships – which cause the whole to be greater than the mere sum of the parts (or, the cynic may say, less). Relationships create synergy, which is often defined simply as $1 + 1 = 3$ or more. When two people work together they can add an ingredient to each other's contribution that would not have existed if they had contemplated in isolation. Even the solitary thinker will draw on what has been read, seen or experienced in the past. The contribution of others is still central, for the lone philosopher has a mind peopled by a great multitude and concentrates on bringing order to the diversity.

The school of thought known as 'symbolic interactionism', first expressed by George Mead (1934) in *Mind, Self and Society*, involves the idea that, whenever we have any sort of communication with another person, we go from the encounter a different person, however slight the change. A new 'I' is continually being constructed. This supports the idea that change and learning are of the essence whenever people get together, so that organizations do think, have attitudes, and do learn, in and through the interaction of the people who compose them. In fact, the very language we use of organizations treats them as living entities. We speak of them as having a heart, a soul, a spirit, thought, vision, values. We do not simply mean the spirit, soul, heart, or vision of the chief executive, or of the members of the organization as individuals: we are envisaging it as a living organism in its own right.

The learning organization at its best involves the deliberate creation of this synergy. The role of the leaders in such organizations is to create frameworks and conditions in which the necessary co-operation and also constructive conflict can be undertaken. This became apparent to Ashridge Management Research Group (AMRG) as international companies were studied during the *Management for the Future* project (Barham *et al.*, 1988). This was built upon in the research carried out by AMRG for the Training, Enterprise and Education Directorate of the Employment Department in some 150 companies during 1989/ 90 (Wille, 1990). This project enquired into how far people development is the key to improved business performance.

RELEASING ENERGY AND POTENTIAL

Some of the most successful companies said that the real job of their managers was to release the energies and skills of their staff in order to enable them to learn to learn, to accept responsibility for continuous improvement in everything they did. Managers are there to coach, counsel the employees and facilitate their ability to contribute. So said Colin O'Neill, who was largely responsible for implementing this policy at Rothmans. He added that he had never yet met anyone who in their heart did not want to contribute, but people had to be trained to release this potential.

Such an approach transforms the management and organizational style. It puts Taylorism into reverse, however much it may be claimed that Taylor improved the material lot of the workers of his day. He proceeded on the basis that there were thinkers and there were doers, and the two functions had to be separated in the interest of productivity. So management did the thinking; jol s were broken down into a form where they could be carried out with minimum thought and maximum speed, and the workers parked their brains at the factory gate and just did as they were told. This was the exact opposite of the learning organization, even though Taylor secured a better financial deal for the doers.

SAS, the Scandinavian airline, insists that it is essential to move from the position where only a few managers are active and most employees are passive. They want everyone active. None can be passive in a service organization. And managers have to learn to cope with the risks involved. The learning organization is not elitist, and it asks for and values everybody's contribution.

LEARNING TEAMS

At Nissan Motors in the North-East, the workers, like those at Rothmans and a number of other companies we visited, are organized into self-managing teams with a leader to facilitate their self-management. They look after their own target-setting and target-meeting. They have all the information on objectives and progress publicly displayed and are trained to understand and use it. This is the feedback element of the learning organization in practice. It gives the lie to the distinction between thinkers and doers, when shopfloor workers at the daily team meeting will raise points about statistical process control in which they have all been trained. Nissan, from the first day of appointment, get their employees to learn about their three key principles of *flexibility, quality* and *teamwork*. The departure from elitism is manifest in the way in which everyone is treated as a partner in the enterprise. They see themselves as a chain of producers in which the next person in line is a customer whose needs must be satisfied. This chain is linked by communication, and the aim is to work with each other to learn how to do things better. The full story is told by Peter Wickens (1987) in *The Road to Nissan*. Doug Lorraine, the Training Manager, summed up the approach: 'If we must talk about managers, then managers are those who manage people and the people manage the task. The manager trains and develops the people, so that they become aware of the power and energy they possess.'

David Cox (1988), former managing director of Ind Coope Burton Brewery, says in his book, *By GIBB and GABB*, that it is not enough for managers to manage the resources of a company; they have to manage the relationships too. This is just what we did in the five years during which the brewery transformed itself. Learning and communications were of the essence in the process. Another example of a company which learned how to transform itself is IBC Vehicles who, as Bedford Vans, had been losing badly for a decade. They changed their work style and organized the workforce of 1,750 people into 130 teams, with a lot of self-control, which implies learning. Within two years they were making a profit, and in place of conflict there was a sense of involvement and ownership around the works.

ORGANIZATIONAL STYLE

The approach expressed in these examples means a complete change in organizational relationships. In place of rigid hierarchies there is a sense of being more like colleagues. Some companies, like Mars, actually call all their employees 'associates'. An increasing number of companies are doing away with the old privileges which divided the management from the rest of the employees. Single-status working, or more accurately common conditions of employment, is now the norm in these organizations, with all staff having the same eating and parking places and the same pensions and hospital insurance schemes. You could have a learning organization without this, but the collegian spirit is necessary to sharing insights and to have everyone respecting all colleagues as fellow learners and fellow workers.

Another aspect of the organizational style implicit in a learning organization is the reduction of dependency which is associated with pushing down responsibility as close as possible to the final action point. People are treated as being capable of learning, of having the ability to decide for themselves how to solve immediate problems. It comes as a shock at first to realize that this freedom is available. From birth we are brought up to be dependent upon experts. First, it is parents who know best, then teachers tell us what we need to know and often stifle our natural curiosity in the process, so that by the time we come to work we expect the boss to tell us what to do and how to do it. We fail to realize our latent power, that we have the capacity to make a difference. And when perhaps a new boss wants to free us to learn and act, we may at first be quite dismayed.

THE LEARNING CYCLE

Another model of the learning organization can be built upon the learning cycle particularly associated with the name of David Kolb (1984) of Case Western Reserve University. This cycle starts off with a person having experiences. These may be particular experiences or the whole stream of experience which never ceases for any of us until we die. We do, however, learn from experience as such. Learning starts when we reflect upon it. So stage two of the cycle is to observe what has happened to us as if we were outside ourselves and to reflect upon what we see. As we reflect, certain principles and concepts become clear. They are capable of being generalized into new situations. So Kolb calls this third stage of the learning cycle 'abstract conceptualization'. But in the world of practical affairs, such as business, abstract concepts are just that – abstract – and business is about action. So the fourth stage is to test out the principles we have arrived at by reflecting on our experiences, either by replicating the experience or by trying out the principle in new circumstances. If it works (or even if it does not), we then have a new experience to reflect upon and so on and on. Learning never stops.

What happens in the experience of the individual happens within the organization. The only proviso is the same as for the individual, that reflection must take place. In creating a learning organization the key is to provide proper frameworks, as in some of the organizations we have mentioned, so that what Norman Evans (1985), Director of the Learning from Experience Trust, has called 'systematic reflection' may take place. Opportunities, permissions, facilities to reflect together must be provided. This systematic reflection is well expressed by David Bohm (1965), writing on relativity, and quoted by Senge, in the word *dialogue*, which in its original Greek form expressed the idea of 'meaning passing or moving through' people 'a free flow of meaning between people, in the sense of a stream that flows between two banks'. In dialogue, a group accesses a larger 'pool of common meaning' than can be assessed individually.

TOTAL QUALITY AS LEARNING EXPERIENCE

It has become increasingly clear that when companies establish total quality management (TQM) as a way of life, they are in fact establishing a learning organization.

It is generally recognized that 'total quality' is not a technological issue. It is a people issue. The aim is to get everybody in the company at all levels to take pride in ensuring that the customers, including the internal customers – the next in the chain – get what they want and expect. In *Out of the Crisis*, Dr W. Edwards Deming (1986), the guru of the quality movement, gives 14 points as the key to getting to total quality. Eleven of them are to do with people and their attitudes.

He puts responsibility for quality back with all the employees by proposing that they should no longer depend on inspection. He asks them to improve, constantly and forever, every process for planning, production and service. This expresses the idea behind the Japanese word *kaizen*, which conveys the idea of continuous improvement in a most thorough and permanent manner. Where else could such a comprehensive approach be undertaken other than an organization where everyone is learning all the time to do everything better? And it is not just the responsibility of the managers. He wants 'everyone in the company to work to accomplish the transformation'. This approach is evident in a number of the companies visited by AMRG, and they are not only of Japanese parentage.

Another signal point from Deming is 'Drive out fear'. This means that people have permission to make mistakes and learn from them. If you live in fear, you will never take risks and gain the learning that flows from doing so, whether those risks succeed or not. You will not innovate. You will not be open and share with your colleagues, for fear that they will 'get one up on you'. You will not admit to mistakes if you are in a climate of 'management by blame'. In Nissan, when someone makes a mistake, it is not seen as his or her fault. It is seen as caused by inadequate training or supervision, or the use of wrong materials. The person owns and tags the mistake, points it out and gets it rectified. That is the learning organization in action.

The Deming way requires common conditions of service for all. 'Break down barriers between staff areas' and 'Remove barriers that rob people of pride of workmanship'. He proposes that 'slogans, exhortations and targets for the workforce' be eliminated. In a real learning organization people learn to set their own targets, to exhort themselves, and to grow into a deeper awareness of what is needed than slogans could ever provide. They do not need to be harangued and harassed. They are party to what needs to be done. As Senge (1990) says, they do not 'buy into' other people's vision; they help create the corporate vision. This may all seem rather idealistic, but it is happening, and it will ultimately be the only way to overcome the age-old conflict between 'them' and 'us' – the managers and owners on the one side and the workers on the other.

Total quality places great emphasis on training, but really as a means of enabling people to become learners, to give them the tools to play their part in the learning and improvement process. This is the first time we have mentioned training in this chapter! This emphasizes the point that being a learning organization is not about doing a lot of training as a separate activity. Learning organizations will do a lot of training, but that is not the core of the concept. Deming urges companies to institute training on the job and to 'institute a vigorous program of education and self-improvement for everyone'.

Ford in the United Kingdom have now followed their American parent in offering support for any kind of learning, irrespective of whether it relates to the job. This is to enhance the self-image of people and to help them to learn to learn, so that it may become part of their way of life and work. This does not make Ford a learning organization, but it will help its employees to play their part in creating one.

The way in which TQM is a channel for the creation of the learning organization is further illustrated by Stanbridge Precision Turned Parts Limited, a company employing some 60 people. Bob Knox, the owner-manager, has agreed to accept the rigorous quality standards as one of his clients as important to the company's long-term future. In so doing, he has agreed to involve all his employees in the process and to provide them with the training necessary to enable them to play their part in learning how to grow the company further.

McKechnie Metals have adopted TQM in accordance with their business policy statement, continuously to improve operating performance 'by the combined efforts and involvement of everybody in the business'. All management and shop-floor staff are being given the necessary training so that they can be so involved. An intriguing aspect of this, which very much fits in with the concept of the learning organization, is that some 12 middle managers, supervisors and shop-floor workers have been trained to act as facilitators to the learning of their 70 colleagues. It illustrates how TQM does break down barriers and involve everyone in the development of new approaches, which is another way of describing learning.

COMMUNICATION AND CULTURE CHANGE

TQM is an example of culture change, but there are many other ways in which culture is changed. There is, in fact, a burgeoning literature on the subject, for example Williams *et al.* 1989. The popular definition of culture is 'the way things are done round here'. To change such ways, which have often become deep-rooted over a long period of time is a fundamental learning experience. Any organization which succeeds in culture change will have established itself as a learning organization in order to achieve the desired changes. Culture change is a matter of getting people to adopt new attitudes, with a new behaviour flowing from new perspectives. If the new perspectives are imposed, they are unlikely to stick, so there must be a joining together of all employees in identifying and understanding what needs to be done. This involves sharing of vision from the top of the organization, and a willingness on the part of senior management to learn from what everybody has to say and to seek consensus in a shared vision.

Some companies which could not be described as learning organizations are at least taking the first steps in that direction by taking on board the Industrial Society team-briefing approach. Information is shared, though initially this tends to be done in a top-down way. Some companies make a point of sharing the main outcomes of their management committee meetings and monthly results as soon as they are available. They do this both by a series of meetings to spread the knowledge downward and by written communication; but this does not create learning organizations because it is not sufficiently a matter of true dialogue.

Another learning approach which some companies have adopted is to have a series of workshops to involve everyone in producing a company mission statement. This is closer to the idea of the learning organization, because they are together learning what business they are in and agreeing about values, standards and objectives. In Harcros Chemicals managing director Peter Savage (1987), author of *Who Cares, Wins*, has written to all staff with an accompanying video. The tone is of one colleague talking to another. The theme is 'growing together' and it aims to 'release the untapped potential in all 3,500 of us'. This is then followed by a series of meetings and workshops in which it is intended that 'active listening to people's ideas and opinions at all levels will become the norm'.

There are a variety of other methods whereby culture, customer care and competitive advantage are addressed in companies, some of which can contribute to organizations becoming learning organizations when the effort is sufficiently disseminated. Amongst these are teams of people working together on special live projects and the widespread use of task forces, as for example, employed by Lucas, who have had as many as 70 managers at a time working full-time on them as developmental experiences and as a means of identifying needed change. This of itself does not constitute a learning organization, but, when extended more widely, can do so. Lucas have in fact made moves in this direction, as, for example, in what they call 'the cell approach'.

LEARNING *THROUGH* THE JOB

Another move in the direction of the learning organization occurs when management and people development is seen as not being restricted to 'off-the-job' training. Sending people on courses has an important contribution to make, but, on its own, according to the Wharton School in Philadelphia, it accounts for only 7 per cent of the learning of people who attend such programmes (Wille, 1990). They therefore stress the importance of ensuring that best use is made of their 7 per cent. But if off-the-job training is not the only way what else is there? 'On-the-job' is the usual alternative, but the phrase is too redolent of learning only by imitation, being thrown in at the deep end, being left to flounder until light begins to dawn or someone takes pity on you.

The phrase 'through the job' has a more active and purposeful ring about it. The job to which one is appointed is being planned in a way which ensures that it will yield learning to enable the acceptance of further responsibility, and with it further learning. Learning through the job, when fully implemented in a company, is still not quite the same as a learning organization because it relates to the individual essentially as an individual. Nevertheless, if everyone is learning through the job it is likely that they will be learning collectively through the interrelationships of their jobs and of their personal contacts. It is also likely that a company that takes learning through the job seriously will also be concerned with organizational learning.

A whole range of contributions can be made to use the job as a learning medium. Team leading, with its implications for organizational learning, is one of them. Adding variety to jobs is another, or switching emphasis. There is nothing better than getting out to listen to the customers to identify what the job really should be, and to gain ideas on how to set about doing it more effectively. Listening to other stakeholders, such as suppliers, the community, government bodies and professional institutions can all contribute.

Above all learning through the job must mean asking all the time 'What have I learned today?' A good mentor will help people to do this. A good boss will coach staff to take practical steps, like keeping work diaries of what has been learned. The job itself is seen all the time as yielding lessons to be applied immediately. The Kolb learning cycle comes alive. The experiences of the job are reflected upon, and principles drawn and tried out. If everyone is doing this within a framework of organizational learning, where not only the individual learns through the job, but also all the colleagues learn together at the interfaces of their jobs, then you have the learning organization.

Learning off the job can then be linked with the learning through the job, both personally and collectively. providers of skills training and knowledge sharing, together with providers of special learning experiences, can design these in conjunction with clients to ensure that maximum transferability occurs back on the job. This is a challenge to business schools, development specialists, managers and learners to ensure that what is needed is what is provided.

INNOVATION

Much of this chapter has indirectly addressed the issue of innovation. Learning is about understanding and doing something new. You do not learn what you already know, and you do not learn to do what you already can, though you might learn to do it better. So, learning is about new things or innovation, and innovation is the secret of competitive success. A better quality product; a lower price; better service – these are the areas where the learning organization concentrates its efforts. It is about providing customers or clients with something more suitable for their purposes in effectiveness and price than they can get anywhere else. Continuous improvement is the way to this, and the route to such improvement is by continuous learning, not only as individuals on our own, but as individuals in concert and in relationship with each other.

In a report to the Club of Rome, called *No Limits to Learning*, James Botkin (1979) and his colleagues make the distinction between what they call maintenance learning and innovative learning. maintenance learning is shock learning, where you have to react to the unexpected, without real preparation, or where you have to learn as you go along just to survive. The purpose of the learning organization is to avoid this reactive kind of learning, usually in crisis situations, and, instead, to engage in innovative learning 'which is the necessary means of preparing individuals and societies to act in concert in new situations'. Innovative learning has to be participative, according to these writers, because 'it is an attitude characterized by co-operation, dialogue and empathy'. They continue: 'It means not only keeping communications open, but also constantly testing one's operating rules and values, retaining those that are relevant and rejecting those that have become obsolescent.'

OUR BUSINESS IS LEARNING

Pedler, Boydell and Burgoyne (1988) define the learning company as: 'an organization which facilitates the learning of all its members *and* continuously transforms itself'. You have to have both parts of the statement and the purpose is the continuous transformation. That is what learning does.

IBM have said: 'Our business is learning and we sell the by-products of that learning.' That just about sums up the whole theme of the learning organization. It says in effect, that, whatever your job, when you are working, both on your own and even more with others, the whole purpose is to learn. This involves changing your understanding and approach in concert with your colleagues, and on that basis producing goods or services acceptable to the customers. As Bob Garratt has put it, 'learning is the key developable and tradeable commodity'. A final note of caution from Peter Senge (1990): As lifelong learners 'you never arrive ... You can never say "We are a learning organization" any more than you can say "I am an enlightened person".'

FURTHER READING

Attwood, M. and N. Beer (1988), 'Development of a Learning Organization', *MEAD*, 19, (3), autumn.

Barham, K., J. Fraser and L. Heath (1988), *Management for the Future*, Berkhamsted: Ashridge Management Research Group.

Bohm, D. (1965), *The Special Theory of Relativity*, New York: W.A. Benjamin.

Botkin, J.W., M. Elmandjra and M. Malitza (1979), *No Limits to Learning*, Oxford: Pergamon Press.

Cox, D. (1988), *By GIBB and by GABB*, Lichfield: David L. Cox.

De Geus, A.P. (1988), 'Planning as Learning', *Harvard Business Review*, March/April.

Deming, W.E. (1986), *Out of the Crisis*, Cambridge University Press.

Evans, N. (1985), *Post Education Society*, London: Croom Helm.

Garratt, B. (1989), *The Learning Organization*, London: Fontana.

Hayes, R.H., S.C. Wheelwright and K.B. Clark (1988), *Dynamic Manufacturing: Creating the Learning Organization*, New York: Free Press.

Imai, K. (1986), *Kaizen*, New York: Random House.

Kolb, D. (1984), *Experiential Learning*, Englewood Cliffs: Prentice Hall.

Mead, G.H. (1934), *Mind, Self and Society*, University of Chicago Press.

Mintzberg, H. (1987), 'Crafting Strategy', *Harvard Business Review*, July/August.

Pedler, M., T. Boydell and Burgoyne J. (1988), *Learning Company Project Report*, Sheffield: Training, Enterprise and Education Directorate of the Employment Department.

Quinn, J.B. (1989) 'Strategic Change, Logical Incrementalism', *Sloan Management Review*, summer.

Savage, P. (1987), *Who Cares, Wins*, London: Mercury Books.

Senge, P.M. (1990), *The Fifth Discipline*, New York: Doubleday.

State, R. (1989), 'Organizational Learning – the Key to Management Innovation', *Sloan Management Review*, spring.

Wickens, P. (1987), *The Road to Nissan*, London: Macmillan.

Wille, E. (1990), *European Guide to American Executive Programmes*, Berkhamsted: Ashridge Consultancy Group.

Wille, E. (1990), *People Development and Improved Business Performance*, Berkhamsted: Ashridge Management Research Group.

Williams, A., P. Dobson and M. Walters (1989), *Changing Culture*, London: Institute of Personnel Management.

9 Approaches and strategies

Margaret Anne Reid

The expression 'flavour of the month', (that is, the current popular choice), must surely be used more frequently to describe approaches to training and development than to any other area of management. It seems not unreasonable to ask why yesterday's strategies and techniques appear to be discarded with the same rapidity as last year's fashions in clothes, or why a training approach adopted successfully by one organization turns out to be a hopeless failure in another. To find an answer it is necessary to consider what has been happening to organizations over the past two decades.

The organization environment has moved from one of stability and certainty to frequent and often unpredictable change. The situation requires a flexible workforce, able to update skills and attitudes, as well as change from job to job with relative ease. Not only have jobs been restructured, but also organizations, with subsequent changes in their culture. These and other factors have had their effect on the type and characteristics of the training and development required and consequently upon the skills of those responsible for this function.

Deciding upon the most appropriate way of achieving learning/training objectives can involve choices at three different levels:

- Determining a general approach (for example, the analytical approach).
- Choosing an appropriate training strategy (for example, a formal training course led by an instructor).
- Selecting a particular training/learning method (for example, role playing).

This chapter is concerned with decisions at the first and second of these levels. It is not suggested that any one of the approaches or strategies is intrinsically better or worse than any of the others, but rather that the skill lies in finding the 'best fit' in all the circumstances.

DETERMINING THE GENERAL APPROACH

The number of general approaches which have gradually evolved to meet different situations may be regarded as falling on a continuum ranging from trainer-directed at one end to trainee-centred at the other. They are, however, not necessarily mutually exclusive and at times may be used to complement each other. The most suitable approach will be contingent upon a number of factors: the leadership style, commitment and philosophy of top management; the objectives, culture, structure and history of the organization; and the stability and turbulence of the environment.

The following six approaches will be reviewed:

- The analytical approach.
- The competency/competence approach.
- The problem-solving approach.
- The continuous development approach.
- The learning organization.
- Strategic human-resource management.

The second section of the chapter will consider the relevant criteria in choosing a particular type of strategy.

The analytical approach

Historically this has been associated with a careful survey of organizational training needs, followed by detailed analysis of knowledge, skills and attitudes required for each job. An appraisal of each employee's performance can then be made against the analysis, and the 'training gap' identified. The job characteristics determine the detail of the analysis, ranging from a list of responsibilities and related knowledge, skills and attitudes to the minutiae of hand/eye movements necessary to carry out intricate operator skills.

The planning process then involves determining the training techniques most appropriate to achieve the desired objectives and drawing up a suitable programme. Evaluation of the results feeds back into the first stage of assessing needs and recommences the cycle.

This approach is logical and particularly applicable in situations where what has to be done can be closely defined and is likely to remain constant over a sufficiently long period, or concerns a sufficient number of people to justify the expense of the analysis. Handy (1985) described a 'role culture' as a bureaucratic institution where each employee is expected to conform to a written job description and where it may be considered dysfunctional to carry out duties or assume responsibilities outside one's prescribed role. Such organizations thrive in a 'steady state' and conditions that enable them to reap the benefits of economies of scale. Here, this 'systematic model' and the attendant analysis is highly relevant and totally congruent with the organization culture.

The model is appropriate in some circumstances today. It is at its most useful *101* for jobs which can be closely defined, and least applicable to positions of senior management, where an important part of the incumbent's responsibility may be to determine exactly what the job should involve at different times. It is not, however, inherently a prescription for change, does not specifically address organization problems, and, unless teamwork is highlighted as a result of the job analysis, it is concerned with the employee on an individual basis. It also presupposes a 'trainer' who, with the help of others, will carry out the analysis, plan and implement the training, evaluate the results, and ensure that everything goes according to a predetermined plan.

The competency/competence approach

Until comparatively recent times, these terms were used fairly loosely. Current developments, however, have brought about the need for more careful definition, and an important distinction must be made between:

- the attributes, traits or skills that the job holder needs to bring to the job to perform competently; and
- the parts or 'functions' of the job which must be competently carried out.

The former might be regarded as required 'input' and are normally termed 'competencies', whilst the latter relate to 'output' and are associated with the word 'competences'.

Competencies applied to managerial roles

A number of researchers, for example Boyatzis (1982), Mintzberg (1980), Andrew and Valerie Stewart (1981), have suggested lists and clusters of characteristics, attributes and skills possessed by successful managers. These can be defined as competencies, and used as a basis for management development. This approach fits very well with the concept of assessment centres, where individual managers can be tested so that personal development plans can be formulated. The centres are used for diagnosing potential and identifying current weaknesses, as well as for compiling an inventory of skills as a basis for manpower planning. It is an attractive approach in that it relates management development activities directly to effectiveness. The term 'development' suggests the importance of learning to play to strengths as well as overcoming weaknesses, and in increasing self-awareness of both factors, experience at the assessment centre becomes part of the learning process.

The effectiveness of this approach is wholly dependent upon success in identifying the vital competencies. Critics suggest that these are likely to change not only with managers' own career progression, but also as organizations change their structures and culture in response to a rapidly changing environment. For instance, an organization operating as a role culture with a bureaucratic style of management may expand and become a task culture, where the skills or competencies of leading or partaking in project teams may be very different from those required previously. The prescription and predictability of the role culture emphasize the need for planning, controlling and monitoring, whilst in the task culture, the skills of working with a variety of teams and the abilities of creativity and innovation may be paramount. It can be argued that the competencies necessary for managerial effectiveness can be specific to a given organization at a particular time. These same competencies could actually impede organizational change, if managers were to refuse, or be unable, to change their style.

The question of how to determine the competencies necessary for effectiveness then arises. One method, adopted by Klemp and McLelland (1986), consists of identifying top and average performers and determining by means of analysis, the characteristics which distinguished the outstanding from the average performers. After a number of years' experience in using this job competency assessment, it became apparent that certain competencies were generic – that is they appeared in all top performers of jobs of the same general type. This is an important discovery, if it enables the compilation of a set of competencies relevant to the senior manager in any type of organization.

Mintzberg defined ten roles common to the work of all managers, grouped under three headings:

1. Interpersonal roles: figurehead, leader, liaison.
2. Informational roles: monitor, disseminator, spokesman.
3. Divisional roles: entrepreneur, disturbance handler, resource allocator, negotiator.

From the study of these roles he suggested eight sets of basic managerial skills which might be regarded as competencies.

- Peer skills.
- Leadership skills.
- Conflict resolution skills.
- Information-processing skills.
- Skills in decision-making.
- Resource-allocation skills.
- Entrepreneurial skills.
- Skills of introspection.

A third method is to determine what are seen by senior management to be the attributes of effective managers within an organization, using techniques such as critical incident, questionnaires, or repertory grid. This has the merit of ensuring that the competencies so defined are appropriate to the specific circumstances, but is open to the danger of cloning in that the views of senior managers may be influenced by past history and current culture, thus perpetuating conditions which may not be appropriate in a changing environment.

Competences

These are frequently derived from Functional Analysis (see Chapter 5). The National Council for Vocational Qualifications is basing its awards on competences which can be assessed in the workplace. The Council defines competence as 'the ability to perform work activities to the standard required in employment'. The emphasis is not merely upon what an individual needs to be able to do, but also upon *performance standards* which will be understood by both employers and employee. One of the obvious differences between the competence approach and job analysis is that the latter usually relates to the requirements of a specific job in a particular situation, whilst a main principle of the competences concept is that they are underlying abilities that relate to many different situations. The approach therefore has special application in companies where there are trainees who are not actual employees, but are on secondment from schools or colleges as a learning experience, or participating in government training schemes.

The Management Charter Initiative (MCI) has also compiled a list of standards based on functional analysis. This comprises units and elements which specify national standards of managerial competence. This list is used as a basis for a three-stage system of qualification (certificate, diploma, MBA).

The problem-solving approach

A different starting point places emphasis on the main problems and issues facing the organization, and training may be viewed as a tool to equip employees to overcome the difficulties being experienced. This type of approach will be found at the self-development end of the continuum described above. Discussion of problems frequently results in heightened self-awareness of shortcomings or learning needs, and because most problems are multifaceted, solution frequently involves group activity. This approach can vary from the formation of permanent or temporary problem-solving groups, sometimes more in the nature of quality circles, or of action learning.

A more detailed account of action learning is the subject of Chapter 38; suffice it here to say that the main features are that groups of people (learning sets) meet together as 'comrades in adversity' (Revans, 1983) to help each other solve their problems. The key is to recognize one's own ignorance and by posing relevant questions to identify what is preventing the solution of the problem, and what steps it is necessary to take. The emphasis is upon action; the learning is encapsulated in the implementation and in the reflection and questioning thereupon. Instead of being directed by a trainer, each stage is under the control of a 'set' and has become embodied in the learning process itself. If a set advisor exists, the role is to assist the members to become a part of a working team, not to give directions. This approach is essentially one of team work, and is particularly appropriate in what Handy (1985) describes as a 'task culture', which has a matrix structure so that multidisciplinary project teams work together on
104 either a temporary or permanent basis.

It can also be a suitable approach for the power culture (Handy, 1985). Where roles cannot be rigidly defined, there must be some overlap of jobs; employees must be able to deputize for each other and work as a team. The set can assess their training needs, and plan and implement the training, seeking help when required. An important aspect is to reflect upon the results of action taken, thus making the evaluation part of the learning process. In this context, the approach is a prescription for participation; it will not flourish, but merely create discontent and disillusionment where the management style is dogmatic, and senior management are determined to go their own way regardless of suggestions from their teams.

The continuous development approach

Development can be continuous only if it is self-directed, because it necessitates the ability to learn from everyday experience as well as from any formal training provided. There has been a gradual, but rapidly accelerating, change of emphasis from training (which implies dependence upon an outside agency, such as a trainer), to learning, which is achieved by the individual. The concepts of self-development, self-managed learning and learning to learn, are increasingly influencing the design of training programmes.

The Institute of Personnel Management has produced a statement, *Continuous Development: people and work* which defines continuous development as 'learning from real experience at work' and 'learning throughout working life, not confined to useful but occasional injections of training'. The statement emphasizes a number of important conditions including:

- Spelling out the implications of the organization's strategic plan in terms of the knowledge and skills of relevant employees.
- Integration of learning at work: encouragement must be given to all employees to learn from the problems and challenges of their day-to-day activities.
- The impetus for continuous development must come from the chief executive and members of the top management team.

The ultimate aim is that investment in the continuous development of personnel is seen to be as important as investment in research and development or in new equipment, and that the practice of continuous development is fully integrated into the working environment. In such a situation, development is not 'an extra thing for us to do – it's about doing all the things we have to do in a developmental way' (NHS Training Authority, 1985).

The learning organization

It has been argued (Reid *et al.* 1992) that organizations are powerful learning environments: people within them are adapting their attitudes and altering their behaviour towards each other as a result of their interactions. Subordinates' *105* conduct is affected by that of their boss, by what they perceive will bring rewards, such as salary increases or praise, and by the organization culture. Without doubt, an organization's training philosophy and approach is most clearly demonstrated by the day-to-day behaviour of its managers. Increasing attention is being paid to the concept of a learning organization, which is seen as one which not only facilitates the learning and development of its employees, but is itself in a constant process of transition and change. Characteristics of the learning organization include (Beck, 1989):

- A recognition of personal effort and achievement.
- Designated periods in timetables and work schedules where the focus deliberately turns away from business requirements towards a consideration of team relationships and individual needs.
- Encouragement of teams to look wider than the single work unit and to expand their horizons by networking.
- The absolute commitment and open style of top management.

More comprehensive treatment of this topic will be found in Chapter 8.

Strategic human resources management

This concept involves linking the management of human resources directly with organization efficiency and competitiveness. Training and development is not a determinant of strategy, but a tool to be used in the effort to obtain maximum organizational performance. Manpower planning and training and development are integrated into the business plan and the responsibility for implementing it rests with management. The focus is firmly on outcomes. The concept is not really new; in 1973, John Humble was describing management development as 'an important by-product of running a business efficiently' (Humble, 1973).

This approach is not incompatible with those described above; it may, however, raise questions regarding time horizons and evaluation. When attempting to evaluate training for long-term objectives or outcomes it is notoriously difficult to establish cause and effect, or indeed at times to predict what the actual outcome of the training or development might be. It would seem that some training initiatives, such as activities directed towards flexibility of attitudes, are always going to require an element of faith. Furthermore, in times of financial difficulty there can be a conflict between short-term aims of economy and longer-term training aims on which the future well-being of the organization might depend. Whilst the direct connection with organization performance is indisputably necessary, top management requires a philosophy which recognizes the need for flexibility, continuous development and long-term as well as short-term aims.

At the beginning of this chapter, it was suggested that the different approaches do not necessarily exclude each other, and it is recognized that features of job analysis appear in the definition of competences, and action

learning sets may well use analytical techniques to guide their deliberations.

Furthermore, the culture of an increasing number of organizations varies from department to department according to the particular function, a situation described by Handy (1985) as a 'differentiated culture'; in this case, a variety of approaches is likely to be necessary. Each, however, has its own characteristics which affect the roles of administrator, trainer and learner as well as the learning process itself.

CHOOSING AN APPROPRIATE TRAINING STRATEGY

Having identified a need for training, and looked at the overall approach, the next task is to determine how best the learning objectives can be met. This can be a difficult decision because the range of possible strategy choices is considerable.

How then can an optimum training intervention strategy be determined? One solution lies in the application of a simple matrix which juxtaposes requirements and potential solutions. The two dimensions of the matrix are: the key *criteria* which must be satisfied if the proposed strategy is to be successful; and the *range* of possible training strategies. The use of this matrix (see Figure 9.1) helps to determine which strategy will best accommodate both the opportunities and the problems inherent in a particular situation. Attention is focused on a series of possible options at each stage when working through the process; the reasons for and against the potential choices are evaluated; and the optimum or 'best fit' solution emerges. It is important to stress that the use of the matrix does not

Possible training strategies

	Training within present job environment	Other planned in-company activity	Planned external activity	Internal courses	External courses
Training/ learning objectives					
Likelihood of transfer					
Organiza-tion reaction					
Organiza-tion poten-tial					
Trainee-related factors					

Criteria

Figure 9.1 A matrix of criteria and training strategies

provide automatic solutions! Its purpose is to raise a series of questions to enable careful and wide consideration of a range of possible options.

Which particular elements to include on each axis will be a matter for the user to decide, and the format of a matrix will therefore vary according to circumstances. In making this choice, account will be taken of such factors as the overall approach to training, as well as the level of sophistication of relevant staff.

The key-criteria dimensions of the chosen matrix (not in order of priority) are as follows:

- Training/learning objectives.
- Estimated likelihood of transfer of learning to the work situation.
- Probable organizational reaction.
- Organization potential for providing training, and resources available.
- Trainee-related factors.

The possible training strategies are grouped into the following main categories:

- Training within the present job environment.
- Other planned in-company activity.
- Planned external activity.
- Internal courses.
- External courses.

The main criteria

The need to achieve learning objectives is a key factor in the choice of training strategy. However, they have to be capable of being achieved and compatible with company training policy. Hence, at the same time as setting objectives, those responsible should think carefully about possible suitable strategies, and, if necessary, modify the training targets accordingly. For example, is the proposed training consistent with the company's policies? Is the strategy adequate in the sense that it can achieve the learning objectives within the required time horizon? By asking these kinds of questions in relation to each of the possible training strategies listed on the other axis of the matrix, the degree of compatibility with the objectives (revised, if necessary) can be considered and a short list compiled of the probable choice or choices.

The second criterion concerns the estimated transfer of the learning to the work situation. There is some force in the general argument that training which takes place away from the workplace suffers a built-in disadvantage when compared with on-the-job training. This is not to say that an off-the-job training strategy is always inferior, but that possible transfer of learning problems should be estimated. Bearing in mind the interim decision made in respect of the first criterion (compatibility of learning objectives), the user next considers in turn all the possible strategies listed in the matrix and, having rejected some as being less suitable, notes those that offer a high probability of good transfer.

Consideration must also be given to the general approach and likely organizational reaction if the strategy were to be implemented. This involves evaluating the strength of the support that the training may receive and the identification of possible organizational resistance. Off-the-job training which involves taking a large number of employees out of one department at the same time is unlikely to be supported by the manager who is not convinced of an overriding need for it. Again, an assessment should be made as to whether the proposed strategy has a reasonable chance of success.

Resources for training is a fourth criterion to be examined; a very important factor here is the extent to which intrinsic learning opportunities exist within the organization, providing wider scope for the use of more imaginative in-house training strategies. For example, compared with small businesses, large organizations, by their very nature, can provide a wider variety of learning opportunities. The availability of other resources, such as the time available, money, equipment and technical expertise, has to be checked and an evaluation made of their suitability in relation to the preferred strategies. Suitability here implies the capacity to contribute to the success of the training and that the contribution be cost effective.

A similar questioning procedure is followed in considering the final criterion on the matrix, 'trainee-related factors'. Trainee involvement in the selection of a training strategy can secure important motivational advantages in both the training and its subsequent application at the workplace. Factors to take into account at this stage include the learners' needs and personal agenda for training, the experience and current expertise of the trainees, their preferred learning styles, ages, and their history of training/learning experiences.

The possible strategies

The strategies listed in the matrix above are largely self-explanatory but of course they do not include all possible options. Each is briefly described for the sake of completeness.

'Training within the present job environment' is deliberately put at the top of the list to emphasize both the potential for learning of the present job environment (a reality which was poorly understood in the past) and, very importantly, that this form of training is typically extremely cost effective. It includes coaching, mentoring and deputizing for the boss.

The category 'other planned in-company activities' refers to training/learning opportunities available, either within the same department or elsewhere in the organization, and includes taking part in problem discussion groups, undertaking projects, and job rotation.

'Planned external activities' can include a wide range of initiatives such as secondments and visits to other organizations, representing the company on external bodies such as trade associations, taking part in working parties, or acting as a liaison officer. Such activities can often provide a valuable broadening experience and at the same time develop the capacity to exercise new kinds of responsibility.

'Internal courses' remain for many people synonymous with training. Such *109* courses can serve many different learning needs particularly where the nature of the learning is company-specific.

It is impossible to describe the very wide range of 'external courses' that is available. They include one-day conferences or workshops, residential programmes and, at the other extreme, qualification programmes which may last months or years. The use of new technology and distance learning enables cost effective study of 'external courses' at home or at work.

To summarize, the matrix can aid the selection of a 'best fit' training strategy. Trainers use their experience and judgement in weighing, at each stage in the process, the balance of opportunities afforded by each intervention against the costs (in many different forms) of its adoption.

CASE STUDY

The following short case history illustrates the way in which the choice of training approach affected the use of the matrix.

Two entrepreneurs (now owner-directors) started a highly successful company producing children's games. The company expanded rapidly, but the directors foresaw future management problems. The ten original employees, initially engaged as operators, had worked their way up as business expanded and were competent section managers, but had no other managerial experience and had received little formal education or training since leaving school. As they appeared to have potential, and their industry and application had contributed to the success of the business, it was decided to offer them training and development and to assess their suitability for promotion, rather than to recruit outsiders to levels above them.

The main concern was to widen their outlook and enable them to work together as a team towards corporate objectives. The directors investigated the possible learning strategies. There had been no formal training within the company before and no specialist training staff were employed. The matter had been discussed with the section managers who seemed enthusiastic, provided that the proposed training was really relevant to their jobs and did not involve long periods away from home. The directors considered the possible approaches. They discarded the analytical approach as the jobs were likely to be subject to constant change. They thought about a college-based course relating to management competences, but felt that at this initial stage perceived relevance to the job was paramount. There was an urgent problem of designing and planning the production, costing and marketing of a new game to be ready for sale the following Christmas. Hitherto, the directors would have dealt with this themselves, but they decided to form an action-learning group of the section managers to address the problem. A written report and demonstration would be made to the directors and further discussion would be initiated about the implementation and necessary follow up.

In this way, as well as introducing new developments into a specific area, each trainee gained an insight into the work and problems of other sections. During the course of the discussions other individual training needs cropped up, and the set considered more specific training strategies for themselves, obtaining help (both internal and external to the organization) when required. The programme resulted in useful developments within each section; it was achieved with minimum disruption to business; and because it was based on the actual job, learning transfer was not a problem. The section managers became highly motivated and gained in confidence; when the appropriate time came the partners had no difficulty in finding staff to promote. In this particular case, the ownership of the matrix in Figure 9.1, was passed to the set. Had a more trainer-centred approach been selected, a trainer or manager might have used it to assist the decision-making process. This case does not imply that other methods considered might not be useful in a different situation, but that they were not the most appropriate in the particular circumstances.

CONCLUSION

Training is expensive in terms of organizational resources and employees' time and effort. Selecting the most appropriate approach and training strategy merits extremely careful consideration and thoughtful planning. It is, however, important not to forget the long-term aspect, in that learning can create flexibility of mind and develop skills which will help in future learning. The need to focus on clear training/development objectives must never be overlooked, but just as a number of important scientific discoveries have been made during investigations of something totally different, and their significance not realized at the time, it is possible that on occasions, valuable self-developmental insights occur in an unplanned way and do not manifest themselves until much later. Thus, it would seem that whatever approaches and strategies are adopted, the concepts of continuity and self-development should never be totally ignored.

FURTHER READING

Annett, J. and J. Sparrow (1985), 'Transfer of learning and training. Basic issues: how to promote transfer', *Research and Development No.23*, Manpower Services Commission.

Beck, M. (1989); 'Learning organizations – how to create them', *Industrial and Commercial Training* **21**, (3), 21–8.

Boyatzis, R.E. (1982), *The Competent Manager: A model for effective performance*, Wiley.

Handy, C. (1985), *Understanding Organisations*, Penguin Books.

Hayes, C. *et al.* (1983), *Training for Skill Ownership*, Institute of Manpower Studies.

Humble, J.W. (1973), *Management by Objectives*, British Institute of Management.

Institute of Personnel Management (1990), *Continuous Development: People and work*, IPM.

Jackson, L. (1989), 'Turning airport managers into high-fliers', *Personnel Management*, October, 80–2.

Jacobs, R. (1989), 'Getting the measure of management competence', *Personnel Management*, June, 32–7.

Kenney, J.P.J. and M.A. Reid (1988), *Training Interventions*, IPM.

Klemp, G.O. and D.C. McLelland (1986), 'What characterises intelligent functioning among senior managers?' in R. Sternberg, and R. Wagner, (eds), *Practical Intelligence Competence in the Everyday World*, CUP.

Mintzberg, H. (1980), *The Nature of Managerial Work*, Prentice Hall.

National Health Service Training Authority (1985), report from review group chaired by Sir John Donne, *Better Management, Better Health*, March, NHSTA.

Mumford, A., G. Robinson *et al.* (1987), *Developing Directors: The learning processes*, Managing and People series, Manpower Services Commission.

Pedler, M. (1983), *Action Learning in Practice*, Gower.

Pedler, M., J. Burgoyne and T. Boydell (1986), *A Manager's Guide to Self Development*, 2nd edn, McGraw-Hill.

Reid M.A., H. Barrington and J. Kenney (1992), *Training Interventions*, 3rd edn, IPM.

Revans, R.W. (1983), *The ABC of Action Learning*, Chartwell Bratt.

Sloman, M. (1989), 'On-the-job training – a costly poor relation', *Personnel Management* , February, 38–41.

Steward, A. and V. Stewart (1981), *Tomorrow's Managers Today*, IPM.

Woodruffe, C. (1992), 'What is meant by a competency?' in *Designing and Achieving Competency*, (eds) Sparrow, P. and Boam, R., McGraw Hill.

10 The cultural mosaic

Phillip Wright

When this chapter on the cultural ramifications of training was first written (Wright, 1988), the task was straightforward. Peters and Waterman (1984) had awakened the business world to the concept of corporate culture, yet comparatively little was known about the complex and varied nature of micro cultures.

In the few intervening years, however, my work required one substantial rewrite (Wright, 1991) and now this second edition must include an abundance of new ideas that will help trainers to understand, change and work with cultural phenomena at many levels. Despite this rapidly evolving knowledge base, the fundamental underpinnings of what was known about organizational cultures have held firm. This chapter, then, will build upon previous work, integrating new concepts with knowledge that has continued through time, to be useful to trainers in a wide variety of settings.

The global economy and the painful adjustments that must be made to remain competitive, have raised the general profile of training, from a, sometimes suspect, peripheral activity where a high discount rate was applied to deferred benefits, to a mainstream function that has become part of many organizations' strategic direction (Garavan, 1991). Still, training can be a political activity requiring strong, high-level sponsorship within the firm.

Training and development professionals now must understand the strategic framework in which their businesses operate (Gainer, 1989). Strategy often relates to learning: learning to be competitive; learning to meet and to exceed customer expectations (Rayner, 1991). Indeed the entire organization can be seen as a learning organism, integrating the learning and personal development of all employees, while continuing to transform itself (Beck, 1989). It is within this context that the trainer must view culture, and work to ensure that training becomes part of the overall organizational fabric (McDonald and Gandz, 1991).

THE CULTURAL DIMENSION OF TRAINING

The study of corporate cultures has been taken far beyond what was previously *113* regarded as pseudo-science (Campbell, 1984) to become a topic of serious research enquiry (Isaac, Cahoon and Zerbe, 1992). Our original definitions, however, have remained the same. Campbell (1984), for example, defined corporate culture as 'the attitudes, values, beliefs and expectations of those who work in an organization', while Pascale (1984) indicated that culture was 'a set of shared values, norms and beliefs that get [sic] everybody heading in the same direction'. Similarly, Field and Davies (1984) referred to the 'behaviours, patterns and standards that bind it [the organization] together', and to Drake (1984) culture was 'a set of values and beliefs shared by people working in an organization'.

The common attributes, then, are values, beliefs and attitudes that somehow are shared. It must be remembered, however, that organizational characteristics can be functional or dysfunctional, and each organization will have a culture that bears strongly on its success, or failure. Organizations with outmoded management techniques, for example, have created dysfunctional cultures (Rhinesmith, 1992). These cultures contain the root causes of our recent industrial decline, in that the notion of corporate culture addresses the real human issues that often impinge on the success of an organization. It has been suggested, for example, that culture can anaesthetize leaders against problems that, from the outside, are painfully obvious (Wright, 1993). None of these ideas are new, yet we continue the struggle to transform cultures (Greco, 1992) and to fit training into this mosaic (Byrnes et al., 1990), that is, to create a training culture (Kramlinger, 1992).

THE MULTI-LEVEL CULTURE CONCEPT AS A VEHICLE FOR TRAINING

The training professional should look at corporate or organization culture (for the same phenomena are found in public sector organizations) as having three main pillars or facets – philosophy, activities and systems (see Figure 10.1). Indeed, trainers who are aware of the constantly unfolding cultural panorama in which they work and can respond to it at all levels, are in a position to make a valuable contribution to an organization's strategic and tactical objectives.

Philosophy

The development of a management philosophy is central to the creation of a functional corporate culture. Of primary importance is the attitude of top-level management (Anthony and Norton, 1991), as it is here that the necessary unifying philosophy and spirit originates. For example, the frequently used phrase referring to the 'family feeling' at Delta Airlines is attributed to a policy of open-door access to management, a feeling of caring and the president's attitude that one does not just join a company, one joins an 'objective'. This attitude leads to the conscious cultivation of internal guidance systems by impressing basic values and beliefs, thus reducing the need for external bureaucratic controls.

The process of developing internally motivated employees must begin with a strategic plan. It should incorporate senior management's desire to build the *114* necessary cultural infrastructure into the very foundation of the organization.

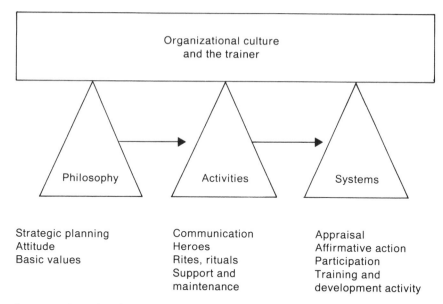

Source: adapted and presented with permission from the Canadian Institute of Management

Figure 10.1 The multi-level culture concept

Strategic planning does not end with a definition of purpose and general corporate direction, but continues on to develop the general philosophy of how individuals will be treated and managed throughout their working lives. Without constant visible support and encouragement, senior management will lose control of an organization's cultural direction, for organizations are constantly changing in response to a multitude of internal and external forces. This inevitable evolution can be either managed or left to chance; the choice is up to the senior management team.

The statement that 'people are our most important asset', for example, can be merely empty words in an annual report, or the guiding principle by which the organization is managed. It is becoming more and more obvious, however, that an emphasis on human resource is one of the key ingredients of success and profitability (Rollins and Fruge, 1992).

When an organization implements a specific umbrella strategy, training professionals should observe these strategic movements and seek to supplement them with a supporting strategic or proactive human resource development plan (Gainer, 1989). The design of an overall high-level strategy, then, is the first step in creating a viable organizational culture.

Next, the development of a corporate management philosophy could be an important determinant of a firm's success or failure. At this level, the trainer's main function is in the preparation of a cultural profile that will help to guide management in the cultural creation process, especially as it concerns the *115* development and training of the human resource. According to Dr Homer Hagedorn (1984), a consultant with the prestigious Arthur D. Little Company, a profile is 'the most candid statement possible of what a company stands for and what it can't stand'. In order to obtain the profile, he advocates a procedure based on a 'systematic' interviewing technique consisting of open-ended questions, so that a 'sample of experts' can be polled concerning their perceptions of the organization's characteristics. These people are asked both direct – 'What does the company do best?' – and 'evocative' questions – 'If you remember the founder of the company, what sort of person was he, and what did he expect of people?' With some practice, the answer can help to isolate 'internal patterns that are unique to a particular company' or organization. It has been found that by identifying the 'prudent warrior', that is, an experienced survivor, a list of 'critical symptoms' can be tabulated. Thus organizations can 'audit' their cultures just as they would audit other aspects of the business.

A specific example concerns an audit, performed within a public-sector organization, that stemmed from two isolated incidents. The first was a comment by a former associate who, when entering a virtually empty open-plan office, declared: 'Things sure have changed. When I was here you could walk in at 5 p.m. and still find all the employees sitting around talking. Look, it's only 4 o'clock and the place looks like an empty barn!' The second incident involved one of the original group of employees hired by the organization. Conversations with this individual determined that he found it an 'unpleasant place in which to work'. These two incidents suggested that the working environment had become less fulfilling. Through the development of a cultural profile, therefore, it was hoped to provide valuable insight into the contemporary culture. Only after the characteristics of the culture were understood could viable attempts be made to adjust it.

The audit process began by determining the factors that characterize an ideal workplace. The plan was to compare the present work situation with these data and then to determine where improvements could be made. It was found that the 'ideal' culture would have all of the following characteristics:

1. A unifying philosophy and spirit emanating from top management.
2. The conscious cultivation of internal guidance systems by inculcating basic values and beliefs.
3. Intensive initiation into the culture.
4. The provision of regular, positive feedback.
5. Intense communications.
6. Encouragement of internal competition.
7. Allowance for mistakes.
8. The use of 'heroes' or role models, rites and rituals.
9. Work would be given meaning through a general emphasis or orientation on caring and on people rather than the mechanistic side of management.
10. Sound human-resources management systems, such as:

   - adequate pay and benefits;
   - fair appraisal procedures;

- affirmative action programmes;
- promotion from within;
- a management style promoting participation, informality, visibility and accessibility; and
- insistence on high work standards.

While it was realized that no culture could be perfect in all these areas, a questionnaire containing open-ended questions was designed to test the respondents' perceptions concerning each of the characteristics listed above.

As a cluster sampling approach was used, the results were not valid in a strictly academic sense, but enough preliminary information was gathered to form a rough description of how the respondents viewed their working environment. For example, while it was the respondents' unanimous opinion that less than three years ago the work environment was 'friendly', 'trusting' and characterized by a family feeling, it was suggested that something had changed the ethos, or the central philosophy of the organization as set by the senior management team. With some exceptions, the respondents seemed to view senior personnel as aloof, uncaring and removed from the concerns of lower-level personnel. This pronounced 'we/they attitude' could inhibit the effective operation of the organization, since many employees were beginning to feel alienated.

It was interesting to note that not all aspects of the culture were viewed as dysfunctional. At the lowest level of abstraction, the systems area – work assignments, relationship with immediate supervisor, and so on (see Figure 10.1) – perceptions generally were positive. Pay and benefits were seen as adequate and sexual discrimination was not an issue. Similarly, at the worker level, there was intense social interaction during work hours, suggesting the existence of an underlying homogeneity and commonality of interest. The problem then appeared to be that the top was out of touch with the bottom of the organization.

A training programme

The trainer's role in this instance was to act as a consultant. In practical terms, attending to corporate culture means starting at the top and working down through the organization so that the general ethos or philosophy of the work group is changed. As this attitude toward the organization's major activities is, in large measure, set by senior management, the consultant in this case made the following recommendations:

1. Senior management must be made visible. The director and each of the vice-directors should spend at least one hour daily wandering about, chatting with employees in the lower echelons of the organization.
2. An intensive study must be made of the methods by which the various organizational levels communicate. Communication should be more intense and it must be more personal.
3. Although the process will take time, rites, rituals and rewards must be 'worked into the culture'.

The main training requirement that surfaced from this analysis or profile was to train senior management in the acquisition of a more open, people-oriented management style. Thus, the focus of training activity changed (for a time) from productivity and service issues at the bottom of the organization, to the top, where the existence of divergent cultural entities was not even suspected. In this case, the training activity would consist of developing a strategy (with the organization's director) for changing the primarily authoritarian management philosophy, and then administering a series of non-threatening formal and informal sessions to train senior management personnel in the art of organizational metamorphosis. This process would be supported by informal motivational sessions conducted privately by the director, culminating with the formal appraisal interview. It was suggested that this procedure would take from three to eight years, depending upon the size and complexity of the organization.

Cultural activities – their effect on the training function

At the second level of abstraction, the activities level (Figure 10.1), the trainer can focus on more traditional goals. For example, who would send a supervisor on a human-relations course and then return that same individual to an authoritarian work environment where 'theory X' is the dominant management style? Who would conduct a job description writing course in an organization where job descriptions are traditionally four years out of date and supervisors are not evaluated on their record-keeping abilities? Who would send junior managers to a communications course when the primary method of communication in their home organization is top-down with little room for feedback? Many senior and middle managers throughout North America and Europe will have to raise their hands in response to these questions.

Support and maintenance systems in training

What, then, should be done to integrate these activities into a cultural reality, to keep the training from becoming a cultural island, divorced from the mainland culture of the organization? (See Figure 10.2.) The answer goes beyond the traditional and necessary activity of training-needs assessment to a study of support and maintenance systems. For until these two vital elements are in place, training should not proceed.

A needs assessment in a health service organization by an outside consulting firm, for example, elicited the following concerns:

1. Budget planning.
2. Writing job descriptions.
3. Understanding job evaluation.
4. Line-staff relationships.
5. Orientation.
6. Performance management.

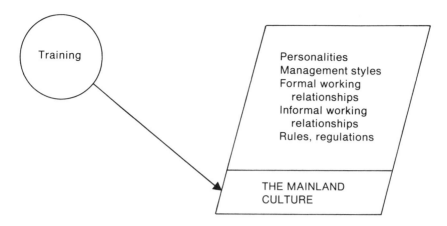

Source: reproduced with permission from the Institute of Training and Development

Figure 10.2   Training and the cultural island

The need	The support	The maintenance
1. Budget planning	Budget planning and control system	Regular budget planning meetings
2. Writing job descriptions	Standard format	Updating system
3. Understanding job evaluation	Job evaluation system	Job evaluation committee
4. Line-staff relationships		
5. The selection process	Policies and controls re authority to hire	
6. Orientation	Orientation programme developed	Check list for follow-up session
7. Performance management	**Policy re performance management problems**	Employee files
8. Stress management		
9. Conducting meetings	Policy re authority to call meetings	
10. Minute taking	Distribution system	File system
11. Labour relations	Policy and system re grievance processing	

Source: reproduced with permission from the Institute of Training and Development

Figure 10.3   Support and maintenance systems

7. Stress management.
8. Conducting meetings.
9. Minute taking.
10. Labour relations.

While it would not be difficult to design training modules for any of these topics, further investigation into the support and maintenance systems necessary to ensure training success (see Figure 10.3) indicated that some would best be omitted, and others required further support. The budget-planning process, for example, lacked a formal planning and central system that would require regularly scheduled meetings between the management and the supervisory groups. While this procedure was not difficult to institute, it was suggested that job evaluation (setting pay to a job description) be omitted, as the organization was in the throes of negotiating a labour agreement and a common job description format did not as yet exist. Nor could orientation be taught immediately. Management wanted further investigation into what new employees really needed to know. The result of this support and maintenance analysis was to delay the training programme by several weeks. But when training did commence, it was with the assurance that learning would be directly related to what the trainees needed to know and that knowledge gained during the formal course work could be applied in the work environment. The provision of support and maintenance systems, then, brought the training from the cultural island on to the mainland.

At this point it should be stressed that not all topics require support or maintenance. The request for more information concerning the Employment Standards Act could easily be met by obtaining copies of the Act and conducting a lecture/discussion while relating the salient points to current and possible organizational problems. A similar technique, fortified by the use of case studies, was found to be appropriate when presenting concepts such as motivation or informal groups. Even though the provision of support and maintenance systems is not a universal prerequisite for training, the process of analysing the state of one's own organization at the secondary or activities level may be as valuable as the training itself; for the installation of support and maintenance functions that integrate training into the dominant culture can result in a more effective operation.

Systems: the bottom line in training design

Cultural baggage

Much of the training in an organization takes place at the basic or systems level, for it is here that the 'how to' function often takes place. It must be remembered, however, that the trainer deals with people, and people come complete with cultural baggage. Leonard Nadler (1982), in his classic book *Designing Training Programs*, tells the story of the 'platform people'. In a certain bank in New York City, customers were using very few of the 35 services being offered to them.

Nadler was asked to design a training programme for employees who normally sat at desks away from the tellers' cages – the platform people. The idea was that these individuals would leave their desks, meet customers, and sell the bank's financial packages.

Unfortunately for the bank, this simple concept ran foul of cultural reality. It appears that a platform job was regarded as a promotion, a 'step up' in the world of banking. The desk itself was a symbol of long service and success and the platform people 'had no intention of getting out from behind their desks'. Accordingly, Nadler suggested that management either dismiss or transfer the platform people and replace them with others not imbued with dysfunctional cultural values. His advice was ignored:

> and a contract was given to somebody else to design the training program. Within six months the vice-president for marketing was fired and a different person was hired. Jointly, with this action, new people were recruited and selected for the new job category. Some of the platform people were retained for those activities which still needed to be done behind the desks. The new people hired knew that their main job performance was outside the bank, visiting customers, and selling bank services at the customers' place of business. (Nadler, 1982)

In other words, until the culture was changed (in this case destroyed) training would be ineffective in bringing about the massive changes required. As not every organization can adopt such expensive and draconian measures, it is wise to take cultural attributes into account when designing a training programme, rather than wait until evaluation produces negative results.

The trainer/trainee dichotomy

Another aspect of culture that can affect training delivery systems is the trainer/ trainee dichotomy. Too often, the trainer lives in a different cultural world from the trainees. Social class and community standing might be quite different, as well as age and educational achievement. With these differences come different value systems. For example, a book or a blueprint that is regarded with respect and valued as a 'good' thing in itself by a middle-class instructor, may be seen as a threatening object of suspicion and even punishment by working-class trainees. If books are not regarded as objects of value, time spent reading them or using them will not be valued. Therefore, trainees may be labelled as lazy or uninterested, when in fact, the wrong medium – one that has been rejected by the trainees' culture – is being used in the training process. Indeed, the mere sight of the traditional training room can trigger negative reaction and fear in some cultural groups.

Unless trainers understand the cultural ramifications of their work, disrespect for the students is inevitable. A 'we/they' attitude will inevitably create tensions. When trainers lose respect for their trainees, the entire teaching/learning interface is negatively affected.

Introducing new technology – the challenge to training

Culture too affects the introduction of new technology at a very basic or systems level, for cultural assumptions regulate employee receptivity to change. Is the workplace seen as a good place in which to work? Does management treat employees fairly? 'The real power of culture [may lie] in the area of assumptions – the way employees think about the organization' (Burdett, 1985). The trainer who works in a culture in which change is regarded as a constant rather than a threat, will not find the introduction of new concepts to be an onerous task. Conversely, if it is assumed that management has an uncaring, egocentric attitude toward 'rank and file' employees, cultural barriers will be thrown up to resist even the slightest change.

Trainers may unwittingly find themselves on the receiving end of activities that are designed to block impending change. If an organization is to flourish, however, a constant influx of incremental technical innovations must be accepted and utilized by both management and labour. This ability to introduce technological change can be a critical factor in the success or decline of individual business organizations, and even entire industries. Indeed, how technology is introduced is increasingly seen as the key to employees' accept-ance, which ultimately determines how much their productivity improves (Malbera, 1992).

Many years ago, as a junior systems analyst, I was responsible for training schedulers in the use of a computerized parts control system for a well-known small-appliance manufacturer. Several months after the system was on stream, it was found that considerable time still was being spent updating clandestine Kardex systems, kept hidden in desk drawers. While one might describe this incident as a reaction to fear of the unknown (computers, for example, were not widely used at that time) recent evidence suggests that present-day workers and management are no better equipped than their predecessors for the inevitable onslaught of new technology.

Most authors, however, while admitting that resistance to change is extremely commonplace, indicate that often there are good reasons for intransigence. Individuals do not always resist change, they sometimes welcome it. What people resist is change that threatens them or appears to threaten them, because it has been sprung too quickly or is too big for them to grasp. Other difficulties to overcome include feelings of inadequacy and fear of being unable to cope with the training involved (Kleinscheid, 1980; Wilkins, 1992).

Part of the answer to this fear of the unknown is in the use of a psychological technique that one might call 'success flagging', in which the instructor informs the students about the success of others who have gone before and/or suggests ways in which the trainees' jobs will be made easier, more profitable or whatever. In some cases, success flagging can be a simple statement: 'Not to worry, Jane, I've taken many people through this process. I know you'll do all right'. Sometimes, time taken to complete a tour of a facility in which the new technology is operational can solve the problem. Borrowing an employee who is familiar with the new technology – someone with the same cultural background and speech characteristics – from another employer or department can have beneficial results. The trainer must be innovative in designing methods to show employees that success is possible and that the new technology is used by other mere mortals like the present group of trainees.

Another significant reason for resisting technological change is that the difference between old and new is too big to grasp. Frequently, time and financial constraints necessitate an intensive immersion into the new ways. These short courses can be more threatening than the new technology itself. In many cases it might be wiser to take a more deliberate approach, both as to time and teaching technique.

The title of a Royal Navy training film seen over 30 years ago has long been relegated to the mists of memory, yet the scene in which the instructor enters the classroom with an eight-by-four foot, fully detailed, schematic diagram of a jet engine, remains vivid. Of course, the trainees (actors all, I'm sure) were horrified at the thought of absorbing that amount of new information. The next sequence showed the same instructor and the same classroom, but this time the diagram was covered by pieces of taped-on paper, so that only a small section of the schematic showed. Predictably, the material was received in a more positive fashion. Although this film illustrated an extreme case, the rate at which information can be acquired depends strongly upon culture. The trainer must take care to design learning experiences that match the rate at which the trainees feel they can absorb new data.

All efforts aimed at reassuring trainees will come to naught of course, if the instructors' actions are not compatible with the organization's overall cultural values. The process, then, has come full circle, in that while the trainers can create learning systems that are culturally sound, the ability to introduce new technology depends, in large measure, upon how successful they have been in helping to develop management philosophies and cultural activities that support the change process by creating a climate of trust between management and other employees.

Orientation and the psychological contract

A final aspect of systems-led culture that must be addressed, is the process of orientation. Much of what is done in industry is either superficial or of brief duration, when the employer should be taking the opportunity to socialize the new recruit into 'correct' cultural attitudes.

In this context, the salient issue is the infusion of core competencies. Core competencies have been described as the collective learning of the organization (Prahalad and Hamel, 1990). They are the key abilities, skills and even attitudes that give the organization competitive advantage (*Economist*, 1990; Jennings and Westfall, 1992).

The orientation system or programme must be redesigned to act as an entry portal into a new world – the trainer's corporation or public sector organization. Indeed, now we must cast our sights beyond the corporation/organization itself and include our customers and suppliers in the concept, as the new employee (at   *123* any level) will need to become committed to building long-term positive relationships with customers and other stakeholders (Rado, 1989). Even maintenance 'workers', for example, are now being oriented into the core competency/ customer focus concept, for only this external awareness allows firms to exceed customer expectations (Rayner, 1991; Hyden, 1991; Hanlin and Johns, 1991).

To focus (or refocus) orientation activities to provide smooth entry into sophisticated, participatory learning cultures, the training professional must be full business partners with senior management (Jennings, 1989), because as expectations change, so does the psychological contract! A psychological contract is a tacit understanding one reaches with a supervisor as to how the job should be done (see Figure 10.4), and the characteristics of the new employment system (Harriot and Pinder, 1992). This fundamental concept is particularly important in an era where trainees are likely to be transferred at frequent intervals, to be cross-trained, to be asked to work in teams and to take responsibility for their own quality control.

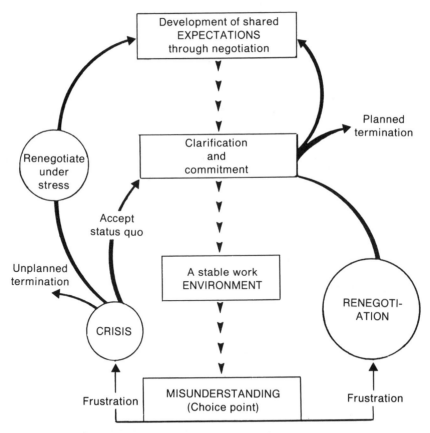

Source: reproduced with permission from the Canadian Institute of Management
Adapted from Sherwood and Glidewell as quoted in Kolb et al. (1979).

124   Figure 10.4   Management of the psychological contract

Even though individuals have control over their decision to join a company, the criteria they use in making this decision often affect their future level of participation or effort. While most individuals will make enquiries about items such as benefits and pay, few ask about the specific nature of the job or about future opportunity for personal development and growth – and even when they do ask, the response is likely to be perfunctory at best. Thus they join with scant knowledge of the considerable expectations about to be placed on them. Traditionally, Kolb's thought-provoking model (Figure 10.4) would depict a situation in which on-the-job reality did not match initial expectations, where the work does not fulfil needs for individual initiative, responsibility and challenge, resulting in frustration, poor or uneven performance, and, eventually, termination. Now, however, the same concepts can be used to describe situations in which core competencies are taught and absorbed into an employee's work consciousness.

Given the likelihood, then, that the new employee will, at least to some extent, bring false conceptions and expectations to the job, it is vital that supervisors be trained in the management of roles and/or work relationships. The result of misunderstanding is frustration, uncertainty, anxiety and/or resentment. Unfortunately, there is also a natural tendency for managers, who are often preoccupied with other matters, to ignore the early warning signs that signal a potential crisis situation.

Supervisors who take the time to acknowledge and to diffuse these misunderstandings are renegotiating the original psychological contract in search of a new stable working environment (see Figure 10.4). Those managers who choose to ignore, or are unaware that frustrations have developed, are choosing a different path, one that may lead to unplanned termination, or at best, a grudging acceptance of the new status quo within the organization. Forced acceptance of management's new norms can lead to the most insidious (and costly) type of termination – psychological termination in the form of apathy.

Apart from being aware that a psychological contract exists or does not exist, in practical terms, how can managers be trained to ensure its successful negotiation and inevitable renegotiation? The first step is to stress the importance of the key personnel documents – the job description (now often in flexible format), policy manuals and procedure specifications (now often team oriented) – as it is in these sources that many on-the-job expectations are outlined. The next step is to train managers to help the employee set challenging, but achievable goals that add value to the company/client relationship (Hyden, 1991). Finally, honest and, at first, frequent feedback should be stressed. It must be remembered that inexperienced employees need to be reassured more often than their more experienced counterparts. Those who have recently left school, for example, are accustomed to constant and immediate feedback – a grade or mark. They carry this expectation with them into the workforce. They are often shocked when their first manager seemingly is unconcerned with their day-to-day problems and anxieties (Cannon, 1990).

The psychological contract, then, also includes the new employee's expectations of the organization and how these expectations can be met. The key *125* variable in this process is expectation. It has long been known that if a teacher's expectations of students' classroom performance are low, performance will indeed be low; should instructor expectations be high, a higher level of learning will result. This concept applies as well to other social situations and to the work world, in that high expectations on the part of the company can produce increased individual contribution, and greater contributions will likewise raise expectations. Faced with this realization, the trainer's job is to make sure that managers have the social skills to prepare and to execute viable psychological contracts, not only at the entry levels, but at all stages in the career progression, be it transfer, promotion or the acceptance of a new position.

Managers ignore the concept of psychological contracts at their peril, for not only do employees make a decision to join a given organization, they also must make a decision to participate. It is in the level of this participation that most problems occur and where the trainer is most likely to become involved. But training activity directed at the poor performance may be addressing a symptom, when the real problem is a broken (and unmended) psychological contract.

PROFESSIONAL DEVELOPMENT: TREAT PROBLEMS, NOT SYMPTOMS

Kolb's model now must be left behind to discuss a widespread problem because in many organizations there may be some questions that should not be asked. The main 'players' may not be ready to accept the answer. What is accepted (and perhaps utilized) and what is ignored (or left unsaid) may vary with the personalities and the political/career agendas involved in, or affected by, the work environment (Punch, 1986). During a staff meeting in a large urban-based organization, for example, a vice-president lightheartedly remarked that 'stress management courses always seem to be popular around here'. Serious research into why stress management sessions were so well attended might have revealed a serious problem with overwork caused by personnel cutbacks, repetitive clerical tasks, job insecurity and constant demands for higher productivity.

Stress management training was not about to improve this situation in the long term, but management was unwilling to make the necessary organizational development interventions to improve the work culture. Indeed, the assumption that 'the most significant productivity improvements result from action directed at the people in the job' is one of the 'seven deadly sins' that block performance improvement. In fact, Norman Wright (1993) of the world-famous Kepner–Tregoe organization, suggests that over 80 per cent of performance improvement opportunities lie with the environment, rather than with people.

This concept has held true from its first introduction by T.F. Gilbert (1978) to the development of performance technology or performance engineering systems. These functions evolved from the realization that a training programme, no matter how well designed, often is not a very good answer to many job-related performance problems (Gordon, 1992).

A training director who runs a few extra sessions of stress management may be scoring political points, but is doing little to promote the long-term health of the organization. What can trainers do in work cultures steeped in political intrigue and/or management inertia? A partial answer lies in the development of 'significant input acceptance levels'. Although needs analysis, presentation and evaluation can be conducted using an authoritarian (isolationist) methodology, Geroy and Wright (1989), and more recent work by Wright, Nasierowski and Geroy (1993). strongly suggest that stakeholder-based activity can be used to provide both credibility and face validity. Under this rubric, a 'stakeholder group' is formed that reviews the training function at all stages and provides peer approval by limiting the curricula to that which is relevant and useful (Geroy, Wright and Caffrey, 1989).

Typically, the stakeholder group might meet three or four times during the life of a training project, but there could be much less contact, or the review process could be carried out individually at a distance. The key factor is that stakeholders participate in the design, presentation and outcome review stages, lending credibility (face validity) to the training process. Training methodology and curricula are therefore evolved according to organizational realities, as important participants are identified and actively involved in the total training experience. Quite simply, if those who are intended to use and/or to benefit from the training have continuous input into the process, they are more likely to use the results, thus distancing the research from the surrounding 'noise' of personality and political pressure.

A practical outcome from this approach is that training activity will tend to be part of a performance engineering process aimed at trainable problems. When managers have a personal stake in a training intervention, they invariably wish to be assured that the process is beneficial in cost/benefit terms.

Training that addresses symptoms, therefore, no matter how high-profile, will quickly be discouraged. The ultimate question becomes not whether the trainees learned the material, but whether or not their behaviour changed when they returned to the job (Gordon, 1992).

GUIDELINES FOR THE TRAINER

Trainers who are not fully conscious of the cultural milieu in which they work are doing only a partial job. It must be remembered that the training experience is itself a cultural phenomenon that must be inserted into an ever-changing, always different, and sometimes resistant work environment, in such a way as to become an intrinsic part of the organization's overall cultural mosaic.

From the trainer's viewpoint, the development profile appears to be a useful tool for influencing top management, for it is in the creation of a strategic corporate philosophy that the organization's cultural direction is determined. The answer, then, is to adopt a consultant's role, advising senior management in the art of cultural definition leading to core competency development.

After gaining an understanding of the culture in which they operate (and helping to model that culture), the next task is to ensure that all training activity *127* 'fits' the organization's cultural reality through careful application of support and maintenance systems and problem definition. Trainers have a very personal stake in this process, for failure to provide adequate support and maintenance will severely limit programme effectiveness.

Finally, trainers must know themselves. An understanding of one's own 'cultural baggage' is critical if one is to deal effectively with others from different backgrounds. Constant awareness of the trainee/trainee dichotomy is the first step in developing a climate of mutual respect.

FURTHER READING

Anthony, P. and L.A. Norton (1991), 'Link HR to Corporate Strategy', *Personnel Journal*, April.

Beck, M. (1989), 'Learning Organizations – How to Create Them', **21**, (3), May/June.

Beckham, J.D. (1991), 'Tools for Staying Ahead in the Nineties', *Healthcare Forum*, 34, (3), May/June.

Burdett, J. (1985), 'Building A Values Driven Culture', *The Human Resource*, Oct/Nov.

Byrnes, J., and W.C. Copocimo (1990), 'Develop a Powerful Learning Organization', *Transportation and Distribution*, **31**, (11), October.

Campbell, A. (1984), 'Knowing "Culture" of a Firm is Vital', *Globe and Mail*, 25 June.

Drake, M.A. (1984), 'Information and Corporate Cultures', *Special Libraries*, October.

Economist (1990), 'Competing with tomorrow', **315**, (7654), 12 May.

Field, L.M. and A. Davies (1984), 'Corporate Culture and Corporate Success', *The Canadian Manager*, June.

Gainer, L.J. (1989), 'Making the Competitive Connection: Strategic Management and Training', *Training and Development Journal*, 43, (9), September.

Garavan, T.N. (1991), 'Strategic Human Resource Development', *Journal of European Industrial Training*, **15**, (1).

Geroy, G.D., P.C. Wright and P. Caffrey (1989), 'Establishing a Multi-Craft Maintenance Operation: A Needs Assessment Approach', *Performance and Instruction*, **28**, (7), August.

Geroy, G.D. and P.C. Wright (1989), 'Evaluation Research: A Pragmatic Program-Focused, Research Strategy for Decision Makers', *Performance Improvement Quarterly*, **1**, (3).

Gilbert, T.F. (1978), *Human Competence*, New York: McGraw-Hill.

Good, T.W. (1989), *The HRD Practitioner*, New York: Nichols Publishing.

Gordon, J. (1992), 'Performance Technology: Blueprint for the Learning Organization?', *Training*, **29**, (5), May.

Greco, R.B. (1992), 'From the Classroom to the Corner Office', *Harvard Business Review*, **70**, (5).

Hagedorn, H.J. (1984), 'Everybody into the Pool', *Across the Board*, October.

Hanlin, J.R. and N.J. Johns (1991), 'Championship Training', *Training and Development*, **45**, (2), February.

Harriot, P. and R. Pinder (1992). 'HR Strategy in a Changing World', *Personnel Management*, August.

Hyden, H.E. (1991), 'Winning Organizations', *Executive Excellence*, **8**, (7), July.

Isaac, R., A. Cahoon, and W. Zerbe (1992), 'Values in Corporation – Who is in Charge ?' *International Journal of Value-Based Management*, **5**, (2).

Jennings, K. and L. Westfall (1992), 'Benchmarking for Strategic Action', *Journal of Business Strategy*, **13**, (3), May/June.

Jennings, M.P. (1989), 'Focus on the Future: Challenging Human Resources Issues', *Executive Speeches*, September.

Kleinscheid, W.A. (1980), 'Change and the People Factor: A Matter of Trust, Not Technique', *Administrative Management*, **41**, May.

Kolb, D.A. *et al.* (1979), *Organizational Psychology: An Experimental Approach*, 3rd edn, Englewood Cliffs, NJ: Prentice Hall.

Kramlinger, T. (1992), 'Training's Role in a Learning Organization', *Training*, **29**, (7), July.

Kravetz, D.J. (1988), *The Human Resources Revolution*, London: Jossey-Bass.

Malerba, F. (1992), 'Learning by Firms and Incremental Change', *Economic Journal*, **102**, (413), July.

McDonald, P. and J. Gandz (1991), 'Identification of Values Relevant to Business Research', *Human Resource Management*, **30**, (2).

McGill, M.E. J.W. Slocum, and D. Lei (1992), 'Management Practices in Learning Organizations', *Organizational Dynamics*, **21**, (1), Summer.

Mills, D.Q., and B. Friesen (1992), 'The Learning Organization', *European Management Journal*, **10**, (2), June.

Mumford, A. (ed.) (1986), *Handbook of Management Development*, Aldershot: Gower.

Nadler, L. (1982), *Designing Training Programs*, Addison-Wesley: Don Mills.

Pascale, R. (1984), 'Fitting New Employees into the Corporate Culture', *Fortune*, 28 May.

Peters, T. and R. Waterman (1984), *In Search of Excellence*, New York: Warner Books.

Prahalad, C.K. and G. Hamel (1990), 'The Core Competence of the Corporation', *Harvard Business Review*, **68**, (3), May/June.

Punch, M. (1986), *The Politics and Ethics of Fieldwork*, Qualitative Research Methods series, vol. 3, Beverly Hills: Sage Publications.

Rado, R. (1989), 'Connecting with the Customer', *Training and Development Journal*, **43**, (7), July.

Rayner, B. (1991), 'A Blueprint for Competition', *Electronic Business*, **17**, (6), March.

Rhinesmith, S.H. (1992), 'Global Mindsets for Global Managers', *Training and Development*, October.

Rollins, T. and M. Fruge (1992), 'Performance Dimensions', *Training*, January.

Schwind, H.F. (1985), 'The State of the Art in Cross-Cultural Management Training', *International HRD Annual*, **1**.

Ulrich, W.L. (1984), 'HRM and Culture: History, Ritual and Myth', *Human Resources Management*, summer.

Willis, N. (1989),: 'A Worker's Right to Train', *National Westminster Bank Quarterly Review*, February.

Wright, N.B. (1983), 'Seven assumptions that block performance improvement', *CTM: The Human Element*, October/November.

Wright, P. (1983), 'Strategic Planning and Human Resources Development: The Vital Link', *Training and Development Journal*, January.

Wright, P.C. (1988), 'The Trainer and Cultural Reality', in R.D. Bennett (ed.), *Improving Trainer Effectiveness*, London: Gower.

Wright, P.C. (1993), 'EDL Corporation', *International Journal of Case Studies and Research*, forthcoming.

Wright, P.C., W. Nasierowski, and G.D. Geroy (1993), 'Special Needs Groups Within Generic Needs Analysis', *Proceedings*, Eastern Academy of Management Conference, Providence, RI.

11 Practical approaches to culture and learning

Teresa Williams and Adrian Green

This chapter is about enabling learning by taking the implications of culture on the learning and development process into account. Cultural values are usually fundamental to our way of thinking, the learner's way of thinking, and to the way of doing things in an organization, yet culture is often one of the neglected factors in the learning process. It can be the vital link between the learners, the learning content and transfer of learning into the workplace.

Each of us faces different problems at different stages in helping with the learning process. At the present moment you may well be facing some of the following questions from a variety of sources.

Trainer How can I be more effective in the way I help people with the learning and development process?

Senior management How can we improve our return on investment in learning and development?

Learner How can I learn something I can use back at work? Will the learning event meet my needs?

Learners' managers Will the learning event make a difference to them when they return to work?

You may well find that achieving satisfaction in one question will create dissatisfaction in one or more of the other questions. The needs of each player sometimes appear to be mutually exclusive. This chapter demonstrates how to use culture as a tool to help with these differing demands on us as a trainer.

WORKING DEFINITION OF CULTURE

There are many definitions of culture but the working definition that we use for this chapter is: 'meanings, beliefs, understandings, values and assumptions subscribed to, by a group of people'.

The ideas in this chapter will demonstrate new ways of tackling common issues, such as those affecting learners in the following:

- Becoming 'sick' rather than attending a course.
- Being 'too busy' for training.
- Having to return to work to deal with a 'crisis'.
- Experiencing poor transfer of learning to work.
- Having low perception of relevance of material covered in sessions.
- Becoming withdrawn or obstructive with the group.
- Saying that 'it won't work in my department'.

Taking cultural implications into account is not a panacea for all learning and development problems and issues. You need to consider it as one of a number of important factors that you need to respond to if you are trying to maximize the effectiveness of time and other resources spent on the learning and development process.

By taking culture into account you will be better able to:

- Modify and design learning events to take account of each learner's needs.
- Reduce prejudice and stereotyping about learners.
- Run a learning event that does not force learners to compromise the culture they subscribe to. You may, however, decide to challenge their values and assumptions in a positive and constructive way.
- Gain a better return on the money and time invested in learning by working *with* culture, rather than ignoring it or inadvertently working against it.

WHY SHOULD TRAINERS CONSIDER CULTURE?

We suggest you consider the implications of culture on the learning and development process (see Figure 11.1) because a mismatch between the learner's culture at work and the culture of the trainers and/or other learners can lead to:

- Ineffective learning during a programme.
- Ineffective transfer of learning back to work.
- Longer-term loss of credibility, respect, and therefore effectiveness for those leading or facilitating the learning process.

With increasing cultural diversity becoming a feature of more organizations, the need to manage the implications of more than one culture during learning and
development is an issue relevant to an increasing number of trainers. An

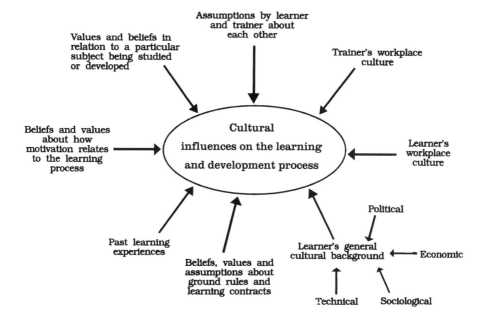

Figure 11.1   Cultural influences

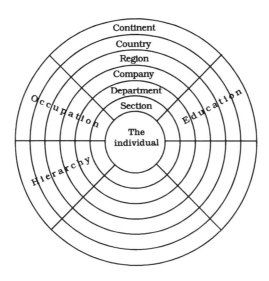

Figure 11.2   Cultural groupings

organization may experience differences in culture because its people are in different work groups or teams, departments, branches, regions, levels of the hierarchy, occupational groups, different countries, ethnic groups, or national groups. Figure 11.2 shows some of the many cultural groupings which learners can be part of.

There are many factors that are increasing (and will continue to increase) cultural diversity. These include the following:

- As industries and organizations change, fewer people are being employed in the same organization, or even the same field of work, for their entire working lives.
- Freer movement of labour across countries.
- Changing demographic trends, which force employers to extend their search to meet skill shortages.
- As organizations move to cheaper or more attractive locations, not all of their employees relocate with them. Organizations usually recruit some staff from the new locations and keep some staff from the old location –an inevitable mix of culture.
- Legislation has its effects too. Law relating to sex, race and movement of labour will all lead to increasing diversity of people employed.
- Technological changes such as improved transport. In many parts of the world this means that people are more prepared to commute, and thus have a wider choice of employment. Changing jobs becomes more feasible.

So when learners (either individually or as a group) and their trainers or learning facilitators come together, there is an increasing diversity in the cultures of those present. This means an increasing diversity in the beliefs, understandings, values and underlying assumptions which those people are bringing to the learning event.

We have found that you can increase the effectiveness of time spent on learning and development by taking culture into account. To do this you need to be able to:

- Identify how culture can influence the learning and development process.
- Recognize the main facets of your own culture and the learner's culture.
- Identify how cultural differences in a group of learners or between the trainer and learner can affect learning.
- Take these cultural differences into account when planning, developing, or delivering learning strategies and methodologies.

By recognizing learner culture you can help learners:

- Settle down more quickly within a group of learners.
- Learn from and help each other.

- Identify which ideas can be transferred effectively to their places of work.
- Identify alternative approaches which may be more suitable to the situations which they face.
- Adapt and modify suggestions, theories and models to take account of the culture in which they are working.
- Explain, discuss, and analyse issues that they regard as important because of the values and beliefs held by them or the people with whom they work.

You have one of a number of choices when there are significant cultural differences:

- You can ignore the differences.
- Either you or the learner can attempt to change.
- You may try to avoid the differences.
- You can manage the differences.

We are not implying that any of these options are right or wrong, merely that you need to be conscious of them and understand how culture relates to the effectiveness of the learning process.

RECOGNIZING CULTURE

As a trainer it is important to recognize the corporate culture and the learner's culture. What are the differences? How do they differ from the culture in which you like to operate?

If learners are experiencing uncertainty, threat, fear or change they are likely to cling to *their* culture, and to the ways of behaviour supported by that culture. If the training which you propose conforms to that culture then it is likely to be more readily received. If however, the training is encouraging people to break from that culture in some way, then the change process can be a much longer and more difficult one. It may result in only temporary change taking place because people may feel that the need to conform and be a full member of their old cultural grouping is more important than improving productivity or using more effective work methods.

A checklist

So, how can you recognize culture? Culture is present from a tangible and conscious level to an intangible and subconscious level. The following checklist is by no means exhaustive but it will give some pointers on what to look for.

Physical signs

- The way people dress – uniforms, rules about whether jackets can be   *135*

removed, sleeves rolled up, casual clothes or formal clothing such as suits to be worn, corporate styles and colours.
- Office layouts – open plan, private offices, more senior people seated where they can observe and control more easily, or in preferred places (for example, next to a window or a radiator), amount of space between desks, positioning of desks to ease discussion or minimize it, whether the quality of furnishings is related to seniority or job function.
- Noise level and music.
- Building design – purpose built, makeshift, functional, pleasing to the eye, taking human needs as well as business needs into account.

Way of life at work

- Work ethics.
- Management and leadership styles.
- How ideas are expressed and treated.
- Styles and methods of communication.
- How emotions are expressed and dealt with.
- Degree and type of rules, procedures, freedom.
- Methods of evaluating performance, reward, promotion.
- How external pressures and requirements are dealt with: for example, legislative requirements, customer demands, competitors.
- Pace of working life, hours worked, breaks and time off.
- Language, acronyms, jargon.

Published aspects

- Company logo.
- Corporate plan or general business plan.
- Mission and vision statements.
- Quality statements or customer charter.
- Advertising literature for products.
- Advertising literature for recruits.
- Training and development plans, statements, schemes, course specifications.
- Annual report and accounts.
- Minutes of meetings: for example, AGM, EGM, shareholders' meetings, board meetings, external liaison meetings.
- Appraisal and job evaluation procedures.

Underlying assumptions

Less tangible, and often unspoken aspects (unless an individual does not conform), are the underlying assumptions such as:

- What is regarded as good or acceptable practice.

- When it is acceptable not to follow the *modus operandi.*
- How much individualism is acceptable.
- To what extent people are expected to follow the rules even if the rules do not make sense on a particular occasion.

In the text which follows we have included three practical activities that will help you to understand more about culture.

ACTIVITY 1: PERCEPTIONS

Purpose

This first activity is designed to increase your awareness of how other people perceive the culture of an organization for which you have a training responsibility. It is specifically designed to:

- focus on the differences and similarities in perceptions at different levels of the hierarchy; and
- identify if there is any relationship between the length of time individuals have worked for the organization and their perception of the organization's culture.

Method

1. Familiarize yourself with the Recognizing Culture checklist. You may wish to photocopy the page and have it read as an aid to memory.
2. Choose at least four people to interview formally. For example:

   - someone who has recently joined the organization at a more junior level;
   - someone who has recently joined the organization at a more senior level;
   - someone long-serving and junior; and
   - someone long-serving and senior.

3. Spend ten to fifteen minutes asking these people how they perceive the culture of the organization. Use the checklist to help if they do not know how to start describing the culture.

It is preferable to wait to see which aspects they focus on, the words they use to describe those aspects, and which aspects they do *not* mention. Try *not* to lead them by giving your own perceptions. It is interesting that most people have a view on the organization's culture even though they are not conscious of exactly what they mean by culture.

Debrief

1. Look at the four (or more) different responses and check for similarities and differences.
2. How did the responses compare with your expectations? Are there any surprises?
3. What common perceived strengths or assets are there about this organization's culture?
4. What common perceived weaknesses or liabilities are there about this organization's culture?

Conclusion

An awareness of how the organization's culture is perceived is the first step towards being able to take that culture into account in a training context. The view that trainers have of an organization is often quite different from the ordinary workers view because trainers are:

- often more in touch with senior management;
- more likely to understand the corporate plan (where there is one);
- usually aware of issues in a more strategic way; and
- often a little more removed from the main work of the organization because they are part of a separate training or human resourcing department, or are external to the organization.

If the responses you received from your interviewees were in line with what you expected, ask yourself what it is that you do which helps you to keep so well in touch. Try to maintain that communication.

On the other hand, if the responses contained some surprises for you, then consider what action you can take to increase your awareness of: the organization's culture; how that culture is perceived in different areas; and how the culture is perceived at different levels and by people with different lengths of service.

ACTIVITY 2: ASSUMPTIONS WE MAKE

Purpose

This activity will enable you to start identifying the cultural assumptions and mind sets that you have about learners in general, or about a specific group of learners.

Method

Assumptions are what you believe but have not as yet checked. You can focus on the assumptions you make by either thinking about a learning event which is taking place soon, or about one which has only recently finished. Some assumptions which we have often heard trainers make are: 'they always learn better through participation'; or 'this one's nearing retirement and won't want to be bothered with all these changes'.

Write down ten assumptions which you tend to make about learners.

Debrief

1. Consider the implications of your assumptions.
2. How will you help a learner who does not fit the stereotype you expect?
3. What can you do to accommodate different learners?
4. What can you do to move from assumptions to evidence?

Conclusion

By identifying and working on your own assumptions you are in a better position to empathize with the learners you are in contact with. You are also better able to recognize and deal with the assumptions they are making about the learning process.

It is worthwhile checking with other trainers in your organization to see whether or not their assumptions are the same as or different to your own. If the same assumptions are being made by all the trainers are you missing an opportunity (that is, are you blind to certain possibilities)? Are different trainers trying to pull the organization in different ways because of different assumptions, and hence counteracting or negating each other's efforts?

ORGANIZATIONAL CULTURE

Breaking the rules

The material you provide for a learning event may support and strengthen the existing culture, or it may be designed to introduce new ways of doing things – ways that are different to those supported by the current culture. Your material may well be 'best practice', but how does it fit in with the prevailing culture?

Look carefully at what you are providing. If the material does support the existing culture, ask yourself the following questions:

1. Am I taking the easy way out, giving them what they want to hear about, rather than what is needed?
2. Am I reinforcing the existing culture when senior management are trying to take the organization in a different direction?
3. Does the material conform to existing culture because it makes me feel comfortable?
4. Am I reinforcing existing culture because it is the most appropriate one for the needs of the organization in the short to medium term?

If the material you provide does not conform to the existing culture ask yourself these questions:

1. Is the material different because my culture (or the culture of my section) is different from the culture of the main organization, or from the learner's cultures?
2. How much success can there be if the support for the ideas is not present because it is contrary to the prevailing culture?
3. Will flouting convention cause disapproval in other parts of the organization (for example, with learners' bosses, those who may influence your promotion, those who release budgets). Will the disapproval be beneficial to the organization – in the short term and in the long term?
4. Will nonconformity help to revive the organization? Will it inspire new ways of doing things and so help to change the culture to suit the organization's current needs?
5. Will breaking the rules – written or unwritten – help to win respect and credibility so that you can better facilitate the learning process?
6. Will breaking the rules be seen as inciting rebellion and upsetting the *status quo* which has been acceptable for the last few years?
7. Will providing material which is contrary to the existing culture be a waste of time when it comes to the transfer of learning back to work?

The need to look at organizational culture

Arthur Young (1986) says: 'As a trainer it is important for you to know the official company culture (stated values) and to compare it with reality.' There may well be one stated and dominant culture but you are also likely to find a number of sub-cultures in different departments, branches or levels of hierarchy. Let us look first at what organization culture is, how you can observe it, and then how that might influence the design and delivery of learning and development events.

Definition of organizational culture

Michael Armstrong (1989) defines corporate culture in this way: 'corporate culture is the pattern of shared attitudes, beliefs, assumptions and expectations which shape the way people act and interact in an organization and underpin the way things get done.' The third activity will help you to recognize your organization's published culture and to relate that to the type of learning events you are involved with.

ACTIVITY 3: YOUR ORGANIZATION'S PUBLISHED CULTURE

Purpose

140 Some insight into an organization's culture can be seen through the aspects which are deliberately made public, either orally or in writing. The purpose of this activity is to help you to gain a better picture of the published aspects of culture so that you can see if the actual culture is supportive or contradictory. You can also judge whether the training and development you are involved with supports or contradicts the published cultural image.

Examples of oral publishing are through an annual report to employees or shareholders, briefing groups, video recordings. Written examples include quality care statements, report and accounts, goal and policy statements, and advertising literature.

Method

1. Make some notes on your organization's culture under the following headings (it may be that you do not usually have access to certain information and you may have to be either assertive or creative in getting it):

   - Your organization's goal and policy statements.
   - Corporate philosophy as given in the annual report and accounts.
   - Customer care or quality statements.
   - Core values set by senior management.
   - Any other published statements about the organization's values and beliefs.

2. To get a full picture, talk to people at different levels, look through advertising literature for jobs or products, look through back copies of the in-house journal or briefing sheets, look at posters in reception on quality or corporate approach.

Debrief

1. From the information you have, summarize the culture in a short paragraph of three or four sentences.
2. From what you know about the culture already (for example, from the information gained in the previous activities) is the real culture and the published culture one and the same?
3. If there are differences, why do you think this is so?
4. If there are similarities, what has helped to achieve these?

Conclusions

Quite often senior management publish and operate a culture at senior levels that is not actively supported at lower levels. This is often due to poor communication from the top.

If you believe in the culture as published, or the culture which senior management promote, does the training and development you are involved with *141* help or hinder? Is it consistent with or contrary to the values and beliefs held by senior management?

TAKING CULTURE INTO ACCOUNT

There are many practical things which you can do to take culture into account throughout the whole life cycle of a learning event – through advertising material, joining instructions, ice-breakers, main activities, to methods of feedback and review. These are described in more detail in *Dealing with Difference* by Williams and Green (1994).

We recognize that people from different cultures have different ways of doing things – eating, language, beliefs, rituals, and family behaviour. But many of us are only just beginning to recognize and appreciate the different cultural frameworks influencing working life – the way we organize, manage, lead, motivate, or control. A culture which is geared up for avoiding uncertainty will manage situations very differently from one which is comfortable with uncertainty. Cultures see time in very different ways and short-term planning may be in terms of days for one culture and months for another in regard to the same project.

For trainers to work effectively across cultures is a challenging and sensitive task. Many trainers use Western (and particularly American) models for their design and delivery. A number of these models are based on being proactive, encouraging individual contribution, developing individuals; on 'humanistic' values concerned with integrating personal and organizational goals; on decision-making involving trust; and on equalizing power. However, bear in mind also that many organizational cultures are based on very different assumptions and rationales, and that those assumptions and rationales have validity in those cultures.

Trainers are in a special position to learn to listen to individuals from different cultures and to respond to them with sensitivity and awareness, to negotiate and manage the differences in a positive and beneficial way, and to accommodate differences in a way that will facilitate the learning process. With training and practice we can learn to recognize different cultural frameworks and the assumptions, values and beliefs on which they are based. By doing so we will be in a much better position to facilitate the learning process.

SUMMARY

When it comes to communicating effectively across cultures the following factors become clear:

- The same words mean different things to different people – and cultural context is one of the many factors influencing the outcome.
- We hear, see and feel things which were *not* communicated, and often not even intended.
- We do *not* hear, see or feel things which *were* communicated – we sift,

sort, miss, and misinterpret many of the communications around us and our culture is one factor influencing how this is done.

- We each perceive the same things in different ways.

If people have never had to consider a different culture, they tend to assume that their way of doing things is the right (or the *only* right) way. People who have worked in one section or one branch all their working life will naturally be entrenched in the values and beliefs of that section. Wider experience can help, but is not necessarily the answer if they carry those values with them and impose them regardless on their new companions.

Trainers often have wide cultural diversity on learning events, not in terms of country or nationality but in terms of functional, organizational or geographical culture. We need to recognize that those cultural frameworks are just as powerful and relevant to the learning process as if they were speaking a foreign language. Success in the future will lie in the trainer's ability to bridge and manage those cultural differences and to use them positively to facilitate the learning process.

The distortion caused by different cultural frameworks is an issue from which trainers cannot hide. It is one that can and has to be addressed if learners are to be helped to make progress.

THE WAY FORWARD

We said at the beginning of this chapter that there are many factors which influence an effective learning event. Culture, which is such a fundamental aspect, is often a neglected factor.

We identified a number of questions which you may well be facing at the moment. Let us now restate those questions.

Trainer　How can I be more effective in the way I help people with the learning and development process?

Senior management　How can we improve our return on investment on learning and development?

Learner　How can I learn something I can use back at work? Will the learning event meet my needs?

Learners' managers Will the learning event make a difference to them when they return to work?

You should by now be able to start addressing these issues by:

- Identifying and allowing for your own cultural biases.
- Being aware of the implications of taking others down the paths of your own values and beliefs.

- Recognizing the assumptions, values and beliefs held by each learner.
- Tailoring learning events, where appropriate, to take account of each learner's different assumptions, values and beliefs.
- Being aware that each organization consists of many cultures, some of which are extremely complex.
- Recognizing and taking these cultures into account so that learners can be helped more effectively with the transfer of learning back to work.

FURTHER READING

Armstrong, Michael (1989), *Personnel and the Bottom Line*, IPM.

Turner, Charles Hampden (1990), *Corporate Culture – From Vicious to Virtuous Circles*, Economist Books, Hutchinson.

Williams, Teresa and Adrian Green (1994), *Dealing with Difference: How trainers can take account of cultural diversity*, Gower.

Young, Arthur (1986), *The Manager's Handbook – The Practical Guide to Successful Management*, (ed.) Erica Hunningher, Marshall Editions.

There are also available two films – *The Eye of the Storm* and *A Class Divided* – based on experiments conducted by Jane Elliot. In these films she demonstrates the effects of discrimination and difference on the learning process. The films are copyright of Yale University, and are available from a number of suppliers, including Concord Video and Film Council, Ipswich, Suffolk, United Kingdom (tel: 0473 726012).

12 Organizational training needs

Stuart Dalziel

This chapter discusses the characteristics of training needs within an organization and suggests a practical framework for their identification.

Much learning at work takes place without people necessarily thinking of it as 'training'. Through interest, curiosity, ambition or criticism; or simply by having to cope with difficulties and changes, individuals become aware of 'learning gaps' or of opportunities for self-development. Often without official guidance or direction people grasp these opportunities or take action to fill the gaps. They watch others, try things out, reflect on their experience, seek (or are given) advice, or get hold of information. Whether pleasurably or otherwise, a good deal of the knowledge and many of the skills and attitudes that people acquire at work are learnt in this way.

Quite outside their work environment people can also become aware of ways in which their skills and knowledge can be improved. Through the media (articles, advertisements, TV series), and with the rapid advances in information technology and flexible learning facilities, such opportunities are dramatically increasing. They have focused more attention on what might be termed 'supply-led' learning needs, that is, needs which are not recognized or not accorded a high enough priority for action to be taken before opportunities occur. While they do not of themselves necessarily correspond with what the organization itself wants or thinks is important, they may sometimes be disconcertingly nearer the mark than some more formal and remote reviews, and their potential for the organization is too often overlooked.

This recognition of needs is largely informal. In contrast, when people use the word 'training' they generally visualize a more formal process, directed towards a practical, performance-related objective. They perceive 'training' as a deliberately planned and structured intervention into their informal day-to-day learning which requires *someone else* – a trainer, teacher or coach – to suggest, organize and control what they learn.

This view of training is too simplistic and is increasingly unfitted to current thinking. However, if the purpose of training is to ensure that employees have *145* the skills, knowledge and attitudes required for the organization to thrive and develop within its particular culture, then the identifying of what has to be learnt cannot be left purely to chance. A more systematic process is needed that will enable the organization to determine and keep under review its priorities for training and enable quick reactions to problems and opportunities. It should include both formal and informal activities, and should encourage and assist managers and others to play their own roles in providing a relevant learning environment.

It is of course important, when identifying needs, to take account of the national and organizational contexts within which organizations are working, and, in particular, current developments affecting training. These include:

1. The effects of legislation and national economic policies on the organization's markets and policies.
2. The pace of technological development and job change, which is increasing the requirement for learning needs to be quickly and continually reidentified.
3. More flexible policies for human resourcing.
4. The competitive impact of the European Community and the increasing recognition of Britain's comparative weaknesses in vocational education and training and in the possession of qualifications.
5. The establishment and use of detailed and nationally agreed competencies and National Vocational Qualifications in an increasing range of occupational, professional and management areas.
6. The increasing stress (sometimes in an uneasy relationship with the 'competency' developments) on continuous development. self-development and on people taking responsibility for their own learning.
7. The often rapidly changing pattern of government intervention in the control, encouragement, provision and funding of vocational education and training, and the various 'initiatives' launched by government departments.

WHAT IS A TRAINING NEED?

At its simplest a training need exists in an organization when there is a gap between the present skills and knowledge of its employees and the skills and knowledge they require or will require for an effective performance. One must not too easily assume, of course, that poor performance is being caused by a lack of competence on the part of the employee; the real problem may lie elsewhere. The following case exemplifies this point. Complaints about the attitude and manners of counter staff in a self-service cafeteria were reduced, not by increased social skills training, but by a redesign of the counter layout, an alteration of lunch-hour overlaps and a better organization of food to the counter. The fewer problems that did occur were then readily coped with by the counter staff, using the social skills they already possessed, and extra training was unnecessary.

The simple definition of a training need can only be a starting point. As an
146 organizational activity, a training intervention will require resources, support

and some structured activities. There may, for instance, be a cadre of instructors or on-the-job trainers, an 'open resource centre' which people are encouraged to use, external or internal courses, or a programme of planned experience. To be of practical value and enable training decisions to be made, a training need identification must recognize the resources implied and make a supporting case to those responsible for making decisions about resource allocations. The case has to demonstrate that the need described is directly related to operating policies, priorities, opportunities and problems and to budget constraints. (Indeed, a preliminary identification may be necessary in order to justify the expense and time of a more detailed exercise.) At a training officer course a newly appointed training officer was presenting to her managing director the results of a thorough analysis of the whole range of training needs at her factory. He congratulated her on the presentation of her project and then said: 'But tell me, what do you want me to start doing first next Monday morning?' She had no ready reply.

Nowadays a training need identification needs to do more than describe and justify (in terms of costs and benefits) what has to be learnt. It should also identify, and make some assessment of, wider factors, so that relevant and effective learning arrangements may be made. These have to do with the characteristics and circumstances of the learners and the opportunities and constraints present in their work environments. This aspect of needs identification has become inescapable now that, firstly, learning opportunities and resources can be made more flexibly available to people as to place, pace, sequence and mode, and, secondly, with the growing encouragement being given to self-development and taking one's own responsibility for learning. Thus the traditional boundaries of the process of identifying a training need as 'what has to be learned' have been extended to include 'how the learning can be achieved', that is, making a recommendation about what choices of training strategy are feasible.

TO WHOM MAY A TRAINING NEED APPLY?

In the last resort, training needs must apply to individuals, at whatever level in the organization, but the scope and grouping of application will vary considerably. As a consequence, the scale and characteristics of the related training will also vary, as will its importance and cost.

First, some training needs may cover everyone in the organization; for example, where the development and perhaps survival of a business depends on a much greater willingness on the part of its managers and workforce generally to accept change, or where the whole business is moving to a new site.

A second category, less wide in its scope, relates to specific groups of people within an organization. They may be in a particular unit, department, or section; at a certain level, such as supervision; within a particular occupation; or exercising a particular function such as designated safety officers. An example is when a new information system, linking all the retail outlets of a large chain store, leads to the requirement for training in the use of on-line computer terminals for certain grades of staff in all branches.

A third category relates to particular individuals. Examples of person-specific learning needs include: preparing an employee for a new job; activities in support of career or self-development; remedial training or coaching where work performance is not up to standard; and updating training, as, for instance, the requirement for the employee relations manager to keep up to date with court and tribunal decisions.

WHY DOES A TRAINING NEED OCCUR?

It can be argued that a training need occurs for one of three reasons only, or some combination of the three: the job or its setting changes; individuals change their jobs; or performance deficiencies exist in an existing job.

Job changes

While continuing to be employed by the same organization many managers and their staff, especially in recent years, have had to adapt to significant changes in their work or work environment, and on occasions be retrained for an entirely new kind of work. These changes have occurred as a result of new equipment, new methods, systems or procedures, computerization, reorganization and take-overs, changes in management styles, relocation, or legislation. That such changes occur is not new; what is new has been the frequency and pace with which they are now taking place. In this context, what employers are requiring, to a greater degree than ever before, is a workforce which is flexible and responsive to change.

Person changes

Individuals changing jobs, whether through choice or necessity, or preparing for future changes in their work within their present organization or elsewhere, are potentially in need of training. There will be a need for induction and initial training for young people commencing employment or for adults joining a new department or organization; 're-induction' and updating for women returning to work after a break; training as a preparation for transfer or promotion or as part of a longer-term career development programme.

Performance deficiencies

The emphasis placed on the need for training stimulated by technological and other changes should not eclipse the importance of identifying routine or maintenance needs. These are often more humdrum in character, not being associated with the adrenalin-rich environment of hi-tech investment or organization development, yet they are of great importance to all organizations. Indicators of learning needs that result from shortfalls in work performance include operator faults; customer complaints; the carelessness of familiarity and the 'forgetting' or 'becoming rusty' aspects of tasks, instructions and procedures

Why does the need occur?	To whom does the need apply?		
	To specific individuals	To specific groups of people	To the organization as a whole
Job changes, e.g. Technology/methods Systems Products/services Organizational Management style Legal requirements			
People changes, e.g. Young people starters Adult starters Transfers/promotions Career development Personal development			
Performance deficiences, e.g. Technical skills/know-how People skills/know-how Managerial skills/know-how			

Figure 12.1   Training needs matrix

that are carried out less frequently. This may often need what might be called 'reminder training', and is noticeable, for instance, in safety procedures.

The training needs matrix suggested in Figure 12.1 provides a summary of why training needs occur and for whom. It may be found useful in providing a 'synoptic map' of needs across an organization, in presenting these needs, and in justifying recommendations.

HOW DOES A TRAINING NEED BECOME RECOGNIZED?

There are many ways in which training needs can become recognized. First, they may be recognized by management in and through day-to-day events such as operating problems, staff shortages, faults or complaints, or the inability of staff to handle new systems. Some managers are adept at identifying that such problems may need a training solution, but only too often this occurs at a late stage in a planning cycle, or where there is a crisis. It is therefore important for training and personnel specialists to have their fingers on the pulse, to know what is going on, to be able to spot and/or clarify the real learning need, and to respond quickly and flexibly.

Sometimes individuals come to appreciate of their own accord that a deficiency exists in their knowledge, skill or attitude, and in a supportive environment – where to say 'I do not know' is not regarded as a sign of weakness *149*

– the need may be articulated by them. Because self-diagnosed needs are not found by someone coming in from outside, they are more likely to be owned by those concerned. Acceptance by individuals that they have a learning gap which cannot be filled by informal learning is an important first step in securing a positive attitude of mind towards taking part in training aimed at remedying the need. In the United Kingdom, with its absence of a tradition of continuous training and development, and where training is still not regarded as a normal feature of working life irrespective of age or status, this can be a difficult area in which to make progress.

As has already been stated, not all requirements for training will emerge in the above ways. Important needs will have to be identified through a number of different forms of more systematic investigation. These include carrying out training audits and setting up needs identification projects. Systematic methods such as interviews, questionnaires, job or task analysis, assessment centres, diary-keeping, and faults analysis are described in most books and booklets on planned training and form an essential part of the repertoire of training staff. Used without discrimination, some of these methods can be mechanistic and time-consuming and do not always reach the root of a problem. Skill and perception in the use of the tools of systematic analysis is therefore necessary.

Training needs may also be uncovered in a structured way by making sure that the consideration of training implications is built into an organization's policies, systems and procedures. These include the processes for deciding about and implementing objectives or introducing changes, and, of increasing importance, staff appraisal systems. The latter have a crucial role to play in ensuring that an individual owns his or her learning needs, and has a chance of contributing to their recognition.

Finally, another method of achieving both recognition and acceptance of learning gaps is to involve people in a review of current work practices where identifying training needs is a 'hidden agenda' item; this can be particularly effective when the individuals concerned are critical of the present arrangements and feel that their opinions will be taken seriously by management. This approach was successfully used with a group of sales managers who had a poor track record of recruiting and selecting their sales representatives, but did not see the fault as being theirs and blamed the company's system. The process of critically reviewing the current arrangements led to *their* requesting interviewing training and to the introduction of a more efficient system.

WHAT SHOULD A TRAINING-NEEDS STATEMENT AIM TO INCLUDE?

A statement of needs should aim firstly at achieving the commitment of resources, by demonstrating that such a commitment is warranted. Secondly it should enable informed decisions to be made about the kind of resources and where they should be focused. Thirdly, it should provide information which will enable a relevant and effective provision of learning resources to be planned. The following are some of the most important features that personnel and training specialists should consider, perhaps in general rather than detailed terms, in meeting these aims.

TO WHOM DOES THE NEED APPLY AND FOR WHAT GENERAL REASONS?

This has already been covered in Figure 12.1 and the accompanying text.

What needs to be achieved?

The overall objectives to be met should be clear. As well as performance requirements, objectives as to the training strategy proposed should be decided, particularly if this differs from any present strategy.

What is the justification?

Operational justification, priority and urgency should be considered. Priorities can rarely be neatly or clearly established. They may look different from different vantage points in the organization, or to managers with different interests, and there can be merit in opportunism!

What type of needs are they?

Are they, for instance, once for all, recurring, or continuous and changing? Do they require small amounts of training or more substantial, longer-term learning, or are complete areas of knowledge, skill or qualifications required?

What kinds of learning are required?

Does the learning needed, for instance, mainly consist of theory or knowledge; of adaptation and development of existing expertise; of practical know-how; of a need to be exposed to new ideas or sources of information; or of changing attitudes?

What about the people involved?

What is their present range of experience and knowledge; their likely motivation to learn and learning styles; their availability for training; the characteristics and circumstances of their working environment which might help or hinder learning?

What about the organization itself?

These are very important factors to be assessed (some may indeed need to be taken account of in *planning* a needs analysis rather than appearing specifically in the statement itself). Is the organization's culture hostile, neutral or supportive *151* to training? What opportunities and/or constraints are there as far as traditional forms of training are concerned? Who currently has access to training and of what kind? What facilities and opportunities do or could exist at the workplace or elsewhere? What is the strength of the organization's commitment to vocational education programmes or continuing development?

What kind of training provisions might be necessary?

What type of training provision might be the most effective or advisable both generally or in particular situations? What learning strategies are acceptable or might be made acceptable to the organization? For example, is there support for informal on-the-job learning, for updating, or for individual initiatives? What advice and help is available to initiate and sustain flexible individual learning? Is structured on-the-job training and coaching likely to be effective?

It could be said that the more the required learning is spasmodic, episodic and/or changing, the more discretion about timing and content should be placed in the hands of the individual or section. Thus if the learning is closely related to day-to-day problems and know-how, then it is more likely to be cost-effective and relevant if it is dealt with informally by training on-the-job trainers and providing flexible resources of learning material, information and advice which can be called upon when needed.

CONCLUSION

The traditional philosophy of training in the United Kingdom as an activity associated with preparation at the beginning of a working life – in the 'front-loaded' model of training – implies a once-and-for-all training need which could be met by a once-and-for-all episode. In a society with little, or only gradual, change in work patterns, processes and materials, such an approach to training may have been adequate. It is a totally inadequate approach in today's turbulent society.

A philosophy of continuing development is necessary to accommodate the reality that training needs are occurring on an unprecedented scale for the individual, the employing organization and society at large. To gain the maximum benefit which training (in its many forms) can bring at each of these levels, personnel and training officers must pay much greater attention to identifying learning gaps and how they can be filled.

FURTHER READING

Institute of Personnel Management (1984), *Continuous development: people at work*, IPM.

Kenney, J.P.J. and M.A. Reid (1986), *Training Interventions*, IPM.

Margolis, F.H. and C.R. Bell (1989), *Understanding training: perspectives and practices*, San Diego, Calif.: University Associates Inc.

Nadler, L. and Z. Nadler (1989), *Developing Human Resources*, 3rd edn, London: Jossey-Bass.

Turrel, M., *Training analysis: a guide to recognising training needs*, London: Macdonald & Evans.

Varlamm, C. and C. Pole (1988), *The training needs of trainers in industry and commerce: a feasibility study*, Sheffield: Training Agency.

13 Job training needs

Leslie Rae

This chapter continues the important theme of identifying training needs, with particular emphasis on the analysis of job requirements. It describes how to conduct analyses to produce effective job descriptions and job specifications which can be used to identify the training requirements related to a job, whether the job is itself a new introduction, or the job holders are inexperienced new employees or developing job holders who might not be performing to the competence level required.

At some stage, preferably in the earliest stages in the training cycle, a determined effort must be made by somebody – trainer, line manager, personnel expert or external consultant – to identify what the training needs of the job or jobs in question might involve. Too often an identification of this nature is taken for granted and a number of assumptions made. The common consequence of these assumptions is a training event which satisfies the trainers, is declared an enjoyable, excellently produced and run course by the learners and the training manager, but:

- satisfies none of the needs of the job because it scarcely relates to this; and
- fails to enable learning transfer to work because the learning does not lend itself to this.

A medical analogy would be that 'the operation was efficiently performed and was a huge success, but the patient died'.

A great deal of training is wasted as a result of this approach and there is a similar waste of resource and time for both the trainers and the learners. Someone at board or senior management level says: 'Wouldn't it be a good idea to have some training in .... So-and-so could tell them about x, so-and-so could tell them about y, and the trainers could cover a, b, and c.' This type of decision (and it is not fiction) is made without any real analysis of need or detailed requirements. Even
worse is when the training idea stems from the trainers themselves who hear of a

new technique or method and, wanting to try it out, put forward what appears to be a realistic proposal of 'Wouldn't it be valuable for the organization if we ran a course on. . .'.

There must be initially a very specific and reasoned decision to commence training, even though the trigger for this action is often simply a suspicion. Most training originates in this way, and fortunately there is nothing wrong with acting on a suspicion – many have been discovered to be founded on fact. But until a realistic analysis is made, the suspicion must remain at that level, as a pointer to something which may be needed. Usually a training need is identified by the failure of a person or group of people to fulfil effectively a task on which the product or service depends.

Let us trace the training needs identification of a job by using the example of a hotel receptionist. To determine what might be wrong in the performance of this job (the suspicion), it is essential to know exactly what the job involves and, as far as possible, what levels of competence must be attained.

JOB ANALYSIS

The first step in providing information about the needs of a job is to examine the basic employment document known as the job description. Every trainer or training-need assessor would like to think that every job and every job holder is the proud possessor of one of these, fully detailed and maintained in an up-to-date condition (many trainers would like to have one of their own!). Unfortunately, in spite of the value of such a document and the many exhortations over the years that one should always exist, it still remains a rarity, particularly to the really useful extent described.

JOB DESCRIPTIONS

A job description can be described as a statement about the whole job, showing, not only the duties, tasks and responsibilities of the job, but guidelines to attitudes and personal approaches where relevant. In so many cases the analysis produced is confined to the practical tasks alone, forgetting that few jobs consist of tasks only with no people or emotional involvement. The full extent of the description will be determined by the culture of the organization. It may also include hours of work, rates of payment and other aspects of the contract of employment, or it may simply be confined to a statement of the task facts.

If we use the hotel receptionist's job as an example, Figure 13.1 shows a typical job description. The 'duties' part of the job description is obviously the most important part of the document when a training-needs analysis is being considered and the analyst must ensure that it includes everything the job holder is required to do and should be able to do if the job is to be performed effectively. As far as possible the description should be couched in active terms and be simple and unambiguous, avoiding overlong descriptions of each task.

There might often be required in a description of the job, rather than the job holder's role in the job, an additional section which is concerned with the *155*

Job title:	Hotel receptionist.
Function:	To maintain the hotel's bookings, reservations and charge system, and be the hotel's principal customer-contact point.
Lines of communication	Upwards – to head receptionist. Downwards – to junior receptionists and hall staff.
Responsibilities	To – head receptionist. For – junior receptionists.
Hours of work	Shift system (detailed according to practice).
Principal duties	1. Dealing with room reservations made by telephone, letter, telex, fax and customer contact. 2. Allocating reservations and completing and maintaining records of these reservations. Records will be entered on the hotel computer. 3. Confirming reservations with customers by the appropriate means.
and so on.	

Figure 13.1   Example of a job description

occasional duties, or 'range statement'. This would describe the possible variations from the norm under certain circumstances; for example, the manual action to be taken in the case of computer failure; substitution for the head receptionist; additional secretarial duties, and so. But the principal part of the description, particularly for the analyst, will remain the essential part – what the job holder is normally expected to do to fulfil the requirements of the job.

JOB SPECIFICATIONS

The job description describes generally the job and the task requirements, and even at this stage there may be some evidence of the specific training requirements. The description itself is in effect the basic statement of training needs – a completely inexperienced person who might be engaged to do the job would have to be able (be trained) to perform according to the list. Consequently, any training function for a person of this nature in order to permit job performance would be to a large extent the list of job tasks described.

However, very few new employees, and certainly those for a responsible post as receptionist, would come to the job without some skills. The gap between the skills possessed by the person and those required by the job therefore define the training needs analysis of people of this nature for this job. It is thus necessary in the real situation, when employees with a range of skills, knowledge and attitude have to cope with the job, that the demands of the job are known in detail, much more so than in the job description.

The next step is to prepare a job specification. In order to produce this specification, the job must be analysed in detail in terms of *all* its skills, knowledge and attitude requirements. These details must also follow the rules of

156   definition which require complete objectivity (as far as that is possible), an

active description ('to understand' has very little relevance in a job – 'to understand *and* be able to perform' is an objective statement), and, where relevant, a time bounding.

In our analysis of the hotel receptionist job it is doubtful whether time bounding would be relevant over much of the job, except perhaps a requirement that the computer entries for a shift must be made before the end of an individual's shift or that a reservation made over the telephone must be completed before the telephone call is ended (or a timed call-back agreed). In some jobs, however, time bounding will become much more important and relevant.

Job title		Hotel receptionist.
Duties	1.	Reservations
	1.1	*Task:* determining room availability. *Knowledge:* number and types of rooms in hotel; number and types of rooms which are available during period required; availability of room chart and reservation sheets. *Skills:* ability to understand room charts and reservation sheets and be able to use the methods of making entries.
	1.2	*Task:* obtaining reservation requirements. *Knowledge:* types and lengths of reservation periods possible in the hotel. *Skills:* ability to ascertain with 100 per cent accuracy the date, length of stay, type of accommodation, number of beds, ages of children (if any), date of departure, special requirements (if any) – see checklist provided.
and so on.		

Figure 13.2   Example of job specification

A job specification details, as described above, the skills, knowledge and attitudes which are requires in the effective and efficient performance of the job. Part of the hotel receptionist job is making reservations. Consequently with the job specification there will be a section which is concerned with the detailed requirements for making reservations. Part of such a job specification is shown in Figure 13.2. In the case of the hotel receptionist there will also be many cases where attitude is of prime importance in the effective performance of the job. These requirements will obviously be inserted at the relevant points in the specification and notice must be taken of them by the analyst. The emphasis on training needs will vary considerably from job to job. Some jobs will have specifications which are highly detailed in the area of knowledge and skills, but minimally in those of attitudes and customer care and handling. In others, the skill elements will be low, but the ability to handle people in a variety of situations will be high. And, of course, many jobs will fall between these *157* extremes, requiring elements of all the requirements. The hotel receptionist is a good example of this latter type, in that there are considerable customer care and handling skills required, but these are balanced by extensive knowledge and system handling skills. Whatever the job, the more the detailed job specification details can be made available, the easier it will be for the training-needs analyst to identify where deficiencies lie.

Competences standards

Over recent years, a government initiative has started the development of a rather different form of job description from those described so far. The initiative requires a national approach to occupational-standards definition across all occupations. This task is currently being performed by what are known as Lead Bodies which are developing standards for occupations in industries and across industries. The principal purpose behind this move is to enable job holders to obtain credits by a variety of methods towards obtaining a national vocational qualification, although the standards will be available for general use in industry. In this latter context they will help in appraisal, recruitment, and certainly a full description of the occupation or job.

The standards descriptions are based on functional analysis which differs from many forms of task analysis in that it approaches the whole job function, rather than just the tasks involved. The emphasis is on skill and attitude (or personal competences) and although knowledge is recognized as forming part of the requirement for a person's competence, this is expressed as the outcome of knowledge rather than knowledge *per se*. This emphasis on outcomes in the form of activities rather than the process is reflected in the definition of competence which is: 'the ability to perform activities within an occupation to the standards expected'. The format of a competences standards description does not differ too greatly from the approaches already described, but there is the great advantage that the description is a nationally agreed one which is basically consistent.

Although there are variations from one Lead Body to the other, and some standards will be much more complex than others, a common format is based on key roles, units, elements, performance criteria, and range indicators.

Key roles

These are the general areas of responsibility within an occupation. In the Management Competences Standards description, a pattern seen in the standards of other occupations, although not every occupation includes key roles in its description, there are five key roles:

- Managing operations.
- Managing finance.
- Managing people.
- Managing information.

- Personal competences.

Units

Each key role contains a number of units. Let us take as an example the key role 'Managing finance', which contains the units:

- Monitor and control the use of resources.
- Secure effective resource allocation for activities and projects.

Elements

Similarly each unit will contain a number of elements. If we continue the finance key role example and concentrate our attention on the first unit we find:

- Control costs and enhance value.
- Monitor and control activities against budgets.

Performance criteria

The next aspect of the standards are the performance criteria. These can be described by looking at the element 'Control costs and enhance value' as an example. This element has eight performance criteria, for example:

- Expenditure is within agreed limits, does not compromise future spending requirements and conforms to the organization's policy and procedures.
- Requests for expenditure outside the manager's responsibility are promptly referred to appropriate people.
- Where appropriate, expenditure is phased in accordance with a planned time scale.

and so on to the total of eight criteria.

Range indicators

The final detail considered in the standards relates to the variations which can occur within an occupation. If all the possible variations were to be included, the standards statement would be too unwieldy. Instead, in any set of standards, the basic generic elements are shown, but all the possible variations are included as a final, separate item – the range indicators. Using the element example of 'Monitor and control activities against budgets', the relevant range indicators include the following:

- Monitoring relates to an accounting centre for which the manager has responsibility.

- Monitoring covers:
  - direct costs of: materials; staffing; and expenses;
  - relevant overhead charges;
  - any revenue earned by the accounting centre;
  - cash flow.
- Expenditure outside the manager's area of responsibility will be due to it:
  - being over stated budget limits;
  - subject to other organizational controls.

and so on.

When an occupation is analysed in this way, the description provided is another approach to identifying the characteristics of the job from which the job training needs can be identified. The obvious advantage of this programme is that eventually there will be a standards description for every occupation and these will be available for common use nationally. There will, of course, be some variations from job to job in the same industry or even company, but provision should be made in the standards for these variations by the range statements, the statements in a description which provide the alternatives and options possible. The provision of a complete set of national standards should encourage the greater use of job descriptions, which, once established, will require only minor updating and variation.

OBTAINING THE REQUIRED INFORMATION

It will be unusual if information to the extent described above is readily available to the analyst on demand; perhaps a minimal job description, but very rarely a complete job specification. The next stage in the analyst's task is consequently to produce a job specification which is sufficiently detailed to enable an effective analysis to be performed.

The next important question the analysts will be asking is, therefore, how is the construction of this specification to be approached. The methods of data collection are many and can range from complex and sophisticated question-naires backed by sampling or total interviewing and processed in compre-hensive computer programs, to the highly subjective interviewing techniques used by street interviewers to obtain the opinions of passers-by.

Questionnaires

Questionnaires can be very useful and time-saving in the initial stages, but considerable care has to be taken in their construction and their eventual interpretation. The biggest stumbling block is usually the differing interpret-ations placed on the questions by the completers.

Self-analysis

A simpler approach would be to request job holders to list all the things they do in the performance of their job. Unfortunately, this is demanding of the job holder the same skills required by a job analyst, and results of this type of approach are usually less than complete, rarely in the type of sequence required by the analyst, and couched in terms which, first, have to be interpreted and then have to be translated in to the objective language of analysis.

Observation

Observation of the job holder performing the job should eventually give the analyst with acute observational skills all the information required. But how long will this take? If the job is a relatively straightforward, mechanical-operation type of job, usually all that is required is a short observational period during which one or two cycles of operation are observed and recorded. Care has to be taken that occasional or range tasks are known and also observed. But with the more complex jobs, although observation will produce the required results, this observation might have to be undertaken over a considerable period of time. Certain tasks which occur may not be frequently repeated and, consequently, if they are to be observed, the observer will have to wait and perhaps waste considerable time in this waiting period. A natural response would be to suggest that while waiting, the observer might carry on with other work, perhaps the writing-up of the analysis to that stage. However, it may be that a lapse of observation may result in an occurrence of the awaited activity to be missed. The principal problem with observation might, therefore, be the long time utilization, a resource which may not be readily available.

Interviewing

Interviews are yet another approach to the analysis of the job. In such cases the analyst would conduct probing interviews with at least one job holder. The interview would help to guide the job holder through a detailed description of the job, with the analyst prompting at relevant stages with probe questions when the description became unclear, inconsistent, insufficient, and so on. The principal disadvantage to interviews of this nature is the requirement placed on the interviewer to have sufficient knowledge about the job already to know when the interviewee is being insufficiently helpful to the process.

Other methods

There are a number of other approaches to obtaining the information about the job in question. Such methods include:

- Co-counselling discussions between two of the job holders.
- Diaries which can be analysed for sequencing after completion.

161

- Brainstorming sessions of a group of job holders to ensure that the complete information set emerges.
- An interaction analysis such as 'behaviour analysis' (see pp. 165–6).

Co-counselling

Co-counselling in the context of methods of eliciting job specifications involves two of the job holders coming together and being encouraged to interview each other about their jobs – what they do, what their attitudes in and to the job are, how they see the good and bad aspects of the job. In an atmosphere of this nature, provided that the two people are reasonably compatible, a considerable number of views and amount of information can emerge. It does not matter too much that they may not have the skills of a trained analyst, but at least they are likely to talk about their common interest – the job – and because they are peers (perhaps friends) they are likely to talk easily. Usually in situations such as these so much emerges that perhaps the biggest problem is that of ensuring the recording of everything that emerges. Obviously a record must be made so that a subsequent job analysis can be produced from the mass of information. Various methods can be used for this recording, with the highest preference from the analyst's point of view being either a video or audio recording. If techniques of this nature are used, the analyst must ensure that the recording apparatus does not get in the way of a free discussion by inhibiting the co-counsellors. This will require, as a minimum, a statement by the analyst to the people concerned that whatever they say will be treated as confidential within the constraints of producing an analysis. An alternative would be for the analyst to be present during the discussion to record the relevant parts of the discussion. In such an event, the analyst must take care than under no circumstances would he or she make any contribution or intervention during the discussion – clarification, if necessary, could always be sought in a post-counselling discussion between the analyst and the two job holders.

Diaries

With this method, an individual or group of job holders are asked to maintain a 'diary', or its equivalent, at work over an agreed period of time. The entries in the diary will relate all the activities performed at work during the review period, although non-relevant activities can be omitted as this is not complete time or total-activity log. The diary can be in a traditional diary format or as activity sheets, specially prepared for the analysis. The latter can be as simple or as complex as necessary, provided that all the basic information needed is recorded.

A simple record might suffice with sequential entries of each activity performed – making a telephone call, receiving a telephone call, dealing with a personal customer reservation, making entries on the computer, and so on. In order to make it even simpler the sheets could be pre-prepared with headings for the main activities which are likely to be performed, so that all that is necessary for an entry would be a tick or cross. In this simpler type of diary there is every likelihood of entries being made fully and honestly.

The next useful step in the design of a diary format would be to add detail to the simple entries. For example, to 'making a telephone call' might be added 'to confirm a reservation with a customer', or to 'making entries on the computer' could be added 'summarizing the day's reservations'. However, in a more detailed format the dangers of omission or false inclusion increases 'because there should be an entry about that' (even though it may not have happened).

At the end of the agreed period of completion the entries can be examined and analysed to show the range of tasks involved and from which a job specification can be constructed. In effect, this is another form of self-analysis, replacing the simple, not always complete, personal self-analysis, and also the observation of the job in process by the analyst (or perhaps supporting these).

Brainstorming

Brainstorming is a well-known form of obtaining the largest possible number of contributions on a subject, usually a problem, from a group of people. This problem approach can be modified to simply obtain the maximum number of views about the job, if a group of job holders are brought together. The task they would be set would be to produce the maximum number of pieces of information about the job in which they are involved. Because of the larger number of contributions to the list of duties from a larger number of people than the individual in self-analysis or observation, or the two people in co-counselling, there is little likelihood of any aspect of the job, however small, being forgotten. The brainstorming approach is also valuable for revealing aspects which might otherwise not be mentioned, because the triggering action of a contribution by one person may result in the memory of another being jogged about something which was not being mentioned.

The free, fast-flowing contributions of ideas, thoughts, feelings, facts and views about the job will be listed as they emerge. After the brainstorming session, the analyst, possibly with the help of a job holder, can assess and analyse the list of contributions and produce a job specification.

All these methods can be examined in detail in published explanations. For the trainer's purpose the significant points are that there are many ways of approaching the situation and that some of the techniques will be the most effective for some types of job, whereas other jobs will require different treatments. This decision will obviously be the first one to be made by the analyst depending on the type of job to be analysed.

A POSSIBLE APPROACH

If the example of the hotel receptionist is continued, the practical application of some of the methods mentioned above can be examined. The analysis 'package' *163* recommended here combines several of the techniques, but is intended to suggest the minimum amount necessary for an effective analysis.

Stage one

The first requirement is a job description which, if available, should be checked for completeness and credibility – consistency, understanding and practicability. If such a description is not available, the organization and the job holder should be asked to provide one. It may be that this is not possible, in which case a job description can emerge as a summary of the job specification which will form the principal part of the analysis.

Stage two

Because the job is reasonably complex, but not overcomplex, and the job holders are likely to be articulate people, most of the job information can be obtained by interview between the analyst and the job holder. Preparation for the interview can be to request the job holder to attempt a self-analysis, having given some form of instruction in how to approach this. The self-analysis is likely to be incomplete, but should reduce the time necessary for the interview by providing at least what will almost certainly be the chief aspects of the job. The specification can be completed by filling in the gaps left in the self-analysis and building up the information provided.

A useful start to an interview of this nature is, having read the self-analysis before the interview, to ask the job holder to describe the job verbally. During this description, the analyst will be checking it against the self-analysis and identifying areas which need expansion and/or clarification. The probing can then begin until both the job holder and the analyst are satisfied that everything has been included. There can be no guarantee that the complete job specification will be obtained in this way; the job holder might omit aspects of information and the analyst may not realize the omissions or errors.

Stage three

The interview or interviews can then be followed up by a period of observation, the purpose of which is to satisfy the analyst that the information obtained at the interview(s) is accurate and complete. Concerns of the analyst at this stage usually include:

- that the job holder will not perform normally because of the presence of the observer; and
- that the job holder will be disturbed by the observer's presence.

Experience has shown that these concerns or fears are usually unfounded, or at least disappear soon after the start of the observation when the job holder
164 becomes immersed in the job and forgets the presence of the observer. Of

course, it is helpful if the observer can be unobtrusive and so permit this settling down to develop quickly, and persist. The observer must never interrupt the job holder performing the job even if something new occurs or the observer cannot understand why something is happening. A note can be taken to be discussed later with the job holder.

Observation will be at two levels. One will be the system observation, in which the processes, actions, procedures which should be followed are seen to be so (or not), the other, particularly in a people-type job such as that of the hotel receptionist, will be a behaviour analysis during which both the verbal and non-verbal behaviours of the job holder will be recorded.

Behaviour analysis

One of the most useful forms of observation where behaviour is involved is the 'behaviour analysis' model of interaction analysis. This simple but accurate technique was introduced and developed by Neil Rackham, Peter Honey, and Terry Morgan (1977) and uses a logging system of the verbal contributions made by people graded against a number of categories of behaviour. Initially the method was used to analyse the behaviour patterns of groups, but it has since been modified to analyse a number of different behavioural situations. Behaviour analysis can be used to observe the behaviours exhibited in negotiations, sales discussions and interviews of various natures.

If behaviour analysis (BA) is to be used in the observation of a hotel receptionist at work, the most appropriate categories need to be selected. They will fall generally in the area similar to those used to observe interviews in action, because the significant behaviours exhibited by the receptionist will occur when an interaction is taking place with a customer, either face to face or on the telephone. It may be necessary to use a preliminary observation period to determine the most appropriate behaviour categories.

When a receptionist is interacting with a new customer, let us say face to face, the principal behaviours will be as follows:

- seeking information;
- giving information;
- testing understanding;
- agreeing;
- using the customer's name; and
- suggesting lines of action.

To these can be added:

- any other positive behaviours (to ensure that all are included); and
- any 'negative' behaviours (interrupting, disagreeing without giving reasons, being unhelpful).

The 'seeking information' behaviour can be subdivided into the type of questions *165* asked, on the basis that some types of questions are more supportive, helpful and less time wasting than others – open, closed, leading, multiple, and so on. In most cases when behaviour analysis is used the categories included are normally constrained to eleven or twelve. The limitations in this case are not so stringent because the observer is logging the behaviours of only one person. Following the observation period, the BA sheet with its scored behaviours can be analysed and compared with a model of what is considered to be an appropriate behaviour pattern for occasions such as this.

But behaviour is not only verbal – some experts claim that some 70 per cent of our effective communication is by means of body language or non-verbal communication. Observing this type of behaviour is much more difficult, both in practice and in analysis. Ideally a non-verbal behaviour contribution should be identified at the same time that the verbal behaviour is being exhibited. In this way the congruence of the verbal and non-verbal behaviours can be confirmed. But this ideal approach may be too difficult for an observer to cope with, so perhaps the best that can be hoped for is a relatively simple non-verbal analysis sheet. The types of non-verbal behaviour categories to look out for will include:

- smiling at the customer;
- looking at the customer when the customer is talking; or when the receptionist is saying something to the customer;
- taking immediate notice of an approaching customer;
- speaking to the customer in a pleasant voice (a very subjective assessment!);
- visibly demonstrating listening; and so on.

Once more, after the observation period, it will be necessary to analyse the record against a constructed model of what has been agreed to be an appropriate behaviour pattern. It may be that more than one observational period might be necessary to ensure that all activities are observed, or so that different forms of observation might be used on the different occasions – system observation on one, behaviour observation on another.

Stage four

The final stage of analysis will be to examine:

- the job description;
- the interview records from which a provisional job specification would be constructed;
- the observation records; and
- the construction of a second provisional job specification.

At this point, before the production of a final job specification, the analyst and the job holder could usefully meet again to agree that the specification represented the full account of the job.

TRAINING NEEDS ANALYSIS

The job specification so produced can then be used in a variety of ways, depending on the type of training-needs analysis required. The full specification might be used to design a training event for new entrants to the occupation, or if the applicants present themselves with some skills, an identification of remaining skills, knowledge and attitude in which they should be trained to satisfy the requirements of the specification. Existing job holders can be assessed against specification, to ensure that they are working effectively or to identify areas of the job in which they could benefit from some, or further, training. Whatever the level of assessment, the basis will be the needs of the job, identified from the job specification, and the training needs identified from the gap between actual performance and the requirements of the job.

This may seem to be a lengthy process, and there is no doubt that feelings of this nature about the process have discouraged many from conducting analyses. However, it must be remembered that the full job analysis is undertaken once only, or perhaps infrequently updated. Training needs will only have to be identified when a new job is introduced, an existing job has been modified extensively, new inexperienced employees are recruited or transferred from other duties, or existing job holders require their skills to be developed, remedied or updated.

Updating of the job descriptions, specifications and resulting identified training requirements should be self-regulating, but experience has shown that a positive effort must be made and a planning programme introduced to ensure that at least the analysis is reviewed at regular intervals.

Job analysis will not only show all the aspects involved in the job, but it can be used to identify the priority areas in the job. These priority, or key result, areas are those which the job holders *must* be able to do to the satisfaction of the employer. If problems are demonstrated as a result of this, an immediate and urgent training need is identified. Or, in the case of new employees, these are the training areas which are 'musts' for the initial training event, 'musts' which training validation must eventually show to produce 100 per cent training effectiveness. The other aspects demonstrated in the analysis may then be considered for inclusion in the initial training events as 'should' items, left for later training, or allowed to develop in other ways.

A tried and effective approach to the identification of the training needs required by a job will pay considerable dividends throughout the whole training process. It will certainly avoid many of the problems which arise at different stages in this process, problems which have usually arisen because of lack of planning, foresight or the necessary information being available.

FURTHER READING

Annett, Duncan, Stammers and Gray (1971), *Task Analysis*, Training Information Paper 6, HMSO.
Bloom, B.S. (ed.) (1956), *Taxonomy of Educational Objectives*, Longman.

Boydell, T.H. (1976), *A Guide to the Identification of Training Needs*, BACIE.

Boydell, T.H. (1970), *A Guide to Job Analysis*, BACIE.

Davies, I.K. (1971), *The Management of Learning*, McGraw-Hill.

Pearn, M. and R. Kandola (1988), *Job Analysis: A Practical Guide for Managers*, IPM.

Rackhan, N. and J. Carlisle (1978). 'The Effective Negotiator Part 1: The Behaviour of Successful Negotiators', *Journal of European Industrial Training*, **2**, (6).

Rackhan, N. and T. Morgan (1977), *Behaviour Analysis in Training*, McGraw-Hill.

Rackhan, N. *et. al.* (1971), *Developing Interactive Skills*, Wellens.

Rae, L. (1991), *The Skills of Training*, 2nd edn, Gower.

Rae, L. (1991), *How To Measure Training Effectiveness*, 2nd edn, Gower.

Rae, L. (1992), *Guide to In-Company Training Methods*, Gower.

14 The trainer as manager

Peter Bowen

In this chapter we consider an approach to the management of corporate training based on the requirements of high-performance business organizations and of the people we can expect to find in such organizations. Implicit in the approach described here is the idea of 'balance' or 'contract' between organizations and their memberships. This is helpful in any review of the contribution of training to the performance of an organization.

Indeed, in any such review we need to make this contribution explicit. Too often what happens in the name of training is less than specific. This blurring of identity is unfortunate, and costly. It suggests an imprecision which undervalues training as an instrument of management control. It also suggests that a good deal of what is sometimes undertaken in the name of training is insufficiently targeted and inordinately expensive.

The effective management of a training function should begin with an explicit statement of purpose, and a clearly defined contribution to the organization in which it is located. It should continue with the design and delivery of a performance-related method of training which is geared, first, to the measurement of skill performance and, second, to the improvement of performance where weaknesses are acknowledged to exist. It should end with a recognition by the organization that the competences whose performances have been reviewed in training are valid. This enables the training sequence to begin again, but at a higher level of effectiveness than before.

Training functions are best considered in this way, as cycles of activity geared more or less purposefully to the organizations in which they exist. We can develop our understanding of what promotes effectiveness in the management of training by an examination of the following propositions:

1. Strategies for business should incorporate strategies for human resource development.
2. Human resource strategies are about the performance of skills.

3. The purpose of training is to develop the capability of people to perform skills to defined standards of competence.
4. Standards of competence can be improved, and it is a purpose of training to advance standards of performance.
5. Gearing planned improvements in the performance of human skills to planned improvements in the performance of the organization links the strategy for human resources to the strategic plan of the organization.

This is the primary cycle of training activity, and its successful accomplishment is the main criterion of effectiveness of the training function.

INTEGRATING HUMAN AND BUSINESS STRATEGIES

There are two aspects to this topic. The first is about how to create a human resource strategy within a wider corporate plan. The second is about the corporate infrastructure of training required to maintain the vitality of the training cycle. Let us consider each aspect in turn.

Building the human resource strategy

The first requirement of an effective training function is that its purposes derive from the objectives of the organization as a whole. Whether training is organized centrally or more diffusely, the risk is that training is permitted to go its own way. the result is usually disastrous for both the organization and its training function.

Conversely, successful organizations are identified increasingly by the existence of a human resources strategy. Typically, this will be a strategy in which the training and development programme occupies a central position. Successful organizations build in training to their operations as a way of life. Sometimes this conceals the energy which organizations need to invest in the strategic development of the human resource programme if the business is to advance effectively.

In principle, the importance of correctly positioning human resource strategies within wider business planning frameworks is acknowledged by corporate planners. In practice, the quality of 'fit' between planning for the business and planning for people is less than satisfactory. Individual human resource plans for pay, careers, roles, representation, development, security, benefits, and the rest are drawn up at different points in time. People plans are often formulated during periods of organizational growth, with insufficient flexibility for contraction and slack. Plans for people can erode more rapidly than marketing and financial plans. Above all, the assumptions which inform an organization's human resource planning may be far less explicit than those which govern the construction of its marketing and financial plans. For such reasons planning for people presents inherent but not insuperable difficulties for strategists and planners. Nevertheless, successful organizations can and do accomplish long-range planning for the development of people.

Most organizations have an obvious need to pace performance. Similarly, many will need to establish, review and revise performance futures within some kind of strategic business plan. A human resource strategy geared to business results will have identified and clustered those policies aimed at the improvement of people importance at its cutting edge.

Building a human resource strategy in this way takes us down two pathways. The first is that we must model the strategy in stages similar to those required in any corporate plan. The second is that we need to construct people policies with a rigour comparable to other corporate plans. Figure 14.1 sets out the main steps of strategic planning, including human resource planning.

1. Assess the future environment.
2. Set out the assumptions and guidelines.
3. Develop the broad objectives.
4. Define the specific targets.
5. Construct the plans and budgets.
6. Implement, with performance indicators and review.

Figure 14.1   The steps of strategic planning

This step sequence illustrates the outlines of a human resource planning cycle. We can place a time-scale on the sequence of, say, one year or more ahead of the present. Whatever the scale, a discipline of making explicit a preferred course of action is imposed, with a methodology of comparing and evaluating actual against planned performance of the preferred action.

In Figure 14.2 are set out some typical elements of a human resource strategy. Some are more concerned with the performance of people. Others are aimed at the improvement of security or at the protection of rights in employment.

1. Organization structure and management style.
2. Communication.
3. Productivity.
4. Remuneration and rewards.
5. Benefits and entitlements, including pensions.
6. Discipline.
7. Career planning.
8. Job evaluation.
9. Security of employment, including severance and redundancy arrangement.
10. Health, safety and welfare.
11. Representation.
12. Training and development.

Figure 14.2   Typical policy elements of the human resource strategy

This list is offered to illustrate the likely human resource policy interests of a large organization: there is no suggestion that organizations actually conform in detail. Within the total range, however, emphasis will be given in 'achieving' organizations to performance-related policies.

The integration of selective people policies for high performance has been approached by Walker (1979). Here a 'building block' method is suggested where relevant policies for staffing an organization are clustered around a core human resource strategy. Figure 14.3 illustrates this process in respect of manning and organization. Note how the cluster of policies depends upon the existence of a human resource strategy, the key building block in the set. But the use of policies in each case varies according to the task.

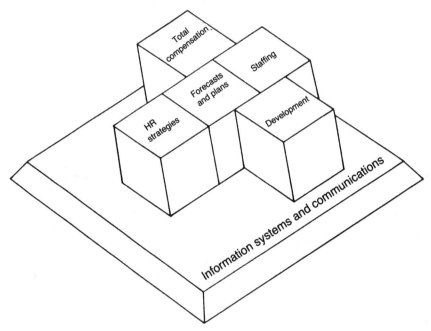

Based on work by James W. Walker (1979).

Figure 14.3   People policy building blocks

If, for example, a key objective of the human resource strategy is to secure and retain a higher calibre of manager in the organization, then the use of policy frameworks like those in Figure 14.3 will be relevant. The pursuit of other key objectives will involve different frameworks.

But in organizations whose business performance is required to progress measurably year on year, we repeat that the human resource strategy will need to be similarly performance-orientated. This means that the strategy must ensure the development of people in ways which enhance their capabilities. It must also be along lines which maintain a sense of equity and trust between organizations and their memberships. It is in this sense that the planned improvement of human performances must proceed, and why the notion of 'contract' between employers and employees is so important in this respect. The positioning of a *172* training and development policy in any cluster of performance-related policies is critical for this reason: training delivers benefits to both the organization and the membership. The human capability of the organization to achieve its business targets is increased by training, but so is the personal competence of each individual. This is the nature of the contract.

The construction of a performance-related training policy is discussed in more detail in a subsequent section. We turn now to the second aspect of integrating human and business strategies: creating a corporate infrastructure of training.

Creating a corporate training infrastructure

Clustering high-performance human resource policies, including the training policy, to align with the requirements of the business strategy of the organization is a first condition of effective management of the training function. The second is to create the means by which a training policy is implemented across the organization.

Training strategy, and the policy which delivers a strategy, is the property of the organization. Effective training requires the organization to communicate from the centre to the parts the objectives, authority, style and structure of a training policy and the plans and programmes which stem from it. Typically, the mandate to train comes from the directorate at the centre, but the licence to continue comes in reality from the line.

For these reasons an organization should review its training function at more than one level. Centrally, there is a need for a strategic review conducted at least annually. Here the directorate needs to confirm the value and vitality of its training investment, and especially in terms of its performance contribution to the business. This strategic review should be complemented by a more frequent scrutiny of training activities at the level of each separate division or individual business unit of the organization. Divisional reviews at something like six-monthly intervals are recommended.

At both levels, however, the chairmanship of these reviews should be conducted by the principals of organizations: managing directors for strategic review, divisional or business unit directors for divisional reviews. In this way the ownership of training is reinforced.

It is well worth the time and effort involved in getting this right. Effective training management depends upon a partnership between line management and trainers. Where training is conducted by training specialists for line management, the maintenance of confidence is vital. This requires the active influence of the line in determining and renewing its training plan. The most obvious sign of decay in such partnerships is when senior line management becomes indifferent to its own training.

However, such issues of ownership and involvement in training by the organization are eased considerably where the programming of training can be cycled into time-phases with distinct beginnings and ends. An important condition for effective training is where cycles exist: timeless training is a prescription for boredom and apathy. This involves the creation of a training year into which programmes can be inserted and removed, for which objectives *173* are set and plans prepared, and by which results can be evaluated. As far as possible, training and financial years should be identical. Above all, the development of a training strategy needs to occur within a predictable and measurable time framework.

The method of communicating training to audiences within large organizations is an important part of the corporate infrastructure. It should occur at predictable times within the training year, and provide a regular opportunity to update potential users on availability and content. The need for line managers to be familiar with the details of a training plan for their business unit is critical. The best way to do so is to issue a standardized guide to training year on year. Reinforcing the training message in a consistent format and at regular intervals ensures recognition and response.

At the core of the training infrastructure is the training plan. Here what is determined in advance in the training reviews described above can be keyed into the next cycle as a new training activity. In this way the content and quality of training advances from one cycle to the next. Effective training requires a planned response to need. Each large division of the organization should be encouraged to construct and agree its periodic training plan specifying the objectives, priorities, programmes and content of what is available during the current cycle, and what is likely to change in the next.

PERFORMANCE-RELATED TRAINING

Integrating the business strategy with a human resource strategy geared to the planned improvement of people performance is the first global requirement of an effective training function. Without this perspective, training is likely to remain out of focus. From such a standpoint, however, the pattern of a training strategy for high performance emerges much more clearly, and this we go on to describe.

The requirement for a strategy may well begin with quality issues of management, arising from developments or changes in the strategic business plan. For example, the organization misses new business opportunities because its existing management cadre is too narrowly specialized. Or its career planning indicates an insufficient supply of quality candidates for new positions created by expansion. Or because competition for the organization's business is increasing, and the skills of people are insufficient to match the pace.

These are not unfamiliar situations. The business changes, the human resourcing lags, an opportunity is missed. Always a cost is incurred. The aim of a performance-related training strategy must be to sharpen as well as to broaden the human capability of the organization to adapt to new situations. How can training make a direct contribution to the bottom-line performance of the organization?

Training functions are vulnerable to criticisms of performance blindness, failing to incorporate explicit targets, controls, or indicators of performance. *174* Performance-related training counters such criticisms. Designed at W.H. Smith by the author, and developed with his colleagues, this approach to the training of managers and staff emphasizes how:

1. Effective training depends upon identifying the key skills of jobs and exercising their performance to defined standards of competences.
2. Identifying skills, defining standards and exercising performances requires a distinctive training methodology. This methodology involves the profiling of skills to identify individual strengths and weaknesses, and a personal skill development plan where performance improvements are required.
3. Skill development can be undertaken by residential training, by directed self-study (open learning) or by both methods. It may address procedural deficiencies, practical skill requirements or knowledge-based weaknesses.
4. The purpose of performance-related training is to appraise relative skill performances and to produce the swiftest possible learning response. An effective learning response is accomplished when a performance improvement can be demonstrated in the skill under review. This is achieved by the administration of a final exercise.

Performance-related training became fully operational in W.H. Smith in 1986. During 1985 the methodology of profiling management skills performances was developed to:

- identify lists of core skills;
- ensure the authenticity of these lists;
- identify standards of competence in the performance of each skill, and similarly ensure the authenticity of these standards;
- devise benchmark tests and exercises to allow managers to demonstrate performance in relation to a standard in each skill under review, and to satisfy participants of the fairness of these exercises;
- administer a management skills profile to each participant; and
- devise a personal development schedule to improve skill underperformance to an acceptable standard of competence.

We can make two generalizations about this approach. The first is that a skills- or competence-based approach to training, one which is the primary characteristic of performance-based training, is the correct approach to the performance development of people in organizations. This is especially true of managers and the development of managerial cadre, and it is with managers that performance-related training should commence.

This emphasis upon skill and competence is vital in the growth of achievement and performance-oriented training strategies. And it is upon the measurable improvement in key skills that the approach advocated here depends. The argument for this is summarized as follows:

1. The source of identity in work is the practice of skilled activities.
2. The ownership of skills provides individuals with personal stimulus, targets, and standards.
3. People seek regular opportunities to improve skill performances, and to receive critical feedback on both stronger and weaker performances. Properly presented, such feedback provides a more powerful and a more enriching environment for individual learning and development than other, less demanding, approaches to training.
4. The most sensitive technique of feedback is that provided by a profile. Here, all the relevant skills for, say, a particular level of management in an organization can be profiled together, and a balanced picture of strengths and weaknesses derived.
5. The possession of such a personal profile of achievement against standards is a vital precondition of focused development where skill deficiencies can be identified clearly and where skill improvements can be driven by learning, and subsequently reprofiled. It is this facility to 'benchmark' performances in managerial skills which is the missing link in much conventional management education and training.

A second generalization about this skills-based approach to performance-improvement is that the quality of learning required to deliver measurable improvements in the practice of a skill must be consistently high. Effective training now requires the provision of training material for both managers and staff which is finely tuned to the improvement of specific skills. Let us look at how this can be done.

Effective training delivery

In organizations where focused skills training is critical to the performance of organizations and to the quality of the products or services offered, a delivery system which can distribute training swiftly and accurately to people is a vital requirement of modern management practice. The supply of information to assist staff in the conduct of tasks, even those which appear routine and simplistic, has increased enormously. Yet it is in the treatment of apparently simple task performances that well-directed training can be most effective. Raising the awareness of an individual to the personal opportunities for challenge and skill in such tasks is a massively important part of an effective training programme.

The requirement for high-performance organizations to advance the skill deliveries of their managements is no less important. Here the choices available may be more complex, and will include directed self-study as well as residential training. Again, it is the paramount importance of intensifying the volume and the specificity of learning material available to the manager which demarcates self-study, or open learning, as a key instrument of effective training delivery.

Let us examine training delivery systems for both large groups of employees in more immediate job-related training situations, and for managers with
responsibilities for the performance of departmental or business units.

Training for single skills performance

A training strategy seeking consistent performance improvements from employees will need to identify the primary skill requirement of each defined job. This can be more difficult than it looks. One problem is that jobs can be unwittingly deskilled by oversimplification of the task, or underskilled by setting performance requirements which lack lustre. There needs to be a clear identification of a core skill in each job, around which the main performance indicators can be expressed, and in terms of which the achievement of people can be set. Jobs which lack this characteristic are unlikely to command interest or provide more than minimal opportunity for human performance improvement.

A retailing example may be helpful here. A core retailing skill is selling a product to a customer. Even allowing for the scale of self-service purchasing by customers, the opportunity to sell products and the service of the business to the customer is manifest. Yet selling products and customer services, however important these activities rank in the priorities of organizations, are often assumed to be readily acquired by adults, requiring only superficial training and almost no reinforcement. Regrettably, these attitudes to selling remain commonplace. With such assumptions we can come to 'deskill' the very jobs on which the survival of the organization depends.

In reality, selling is a transactional skill of some complexity requiring a product knowledge, a selling technique, and an understanding of buying psychology. These elements can be organized into a framework of learning, and it is the command of such learning which enables the salesperson to grow in the skills of selling. We repeat, it is the primary purpose of effective training to communicate and transfer this sense of growth and achievement in the practice of a skill. Developing this sense in the salesperson as well as in the manager is the substance of all achieving cultures. Effective training is about the creation and maintenance of such cultures.

If people need to own skills and become multiskilled, achieving organizations are based upon terms of 'achieving' people. As individual and team access to self-paced learning systems intensifies, so also should be the awareness of skill and of high competence in its delivery.

How technologically sophisticated these systems are is much less important than their ability to sustain the learning requirement of the individual, and to produce a measurable improvement in the performance of a skill. Paper-based systems are as valid as computer-based systems in this respect, and much less expensive. Selecting an appropriate training delivery system becomes more rigorous as the options available range from low- to high-tech formats.

In larger organizations the opportunities to network skills training to workplaces become more cost-effective with the growth of communications infrastructures, and with the use of microcomputers in everyday business practice. Inevitably computer-based and video-linked training are becoming a key component of a flexible delivery strategy which might also include paper-based and face-to-face systems of training.

Indeed, effective training functions will possess a capability to select appro- *177* priate delivery systems for different performance needs with accuracy and confidence. The choice and cost of delivery will depend on the scale and urgency of the need. We can illustrate this by looking again at a core skill of retailing: selling.

To present to salespeople the challenge and skill of effective selling requires a sequence which will include the following elements:

- identifying the sales orientation of the salesperson;
- recognizing the purchasing styles of customers;
- exercising and developing the skills of recognition, interpretation, and evaluation of sales transactions; and
- selecting the right skills to manage the transaction competently.

Practising this sequence forms the basis of a skilled activity, one which can be consciously managed by the salesperson, and which can be worked and reworked with increasing confidence as performance improves. It follows that the power of the delivery system and its technology must be sufficient to assist learning and skill development accurately and to the standard required.

In high-performance organizations, a powerful delivery system will include the following elements:

- an appropriate technology: paper, computer-based training; paper-, computer-linked to video, videotext, videodisc, and so on;
- a student guide to the system; details of objectives, method, structure and routeing of the system;
- an appropriate structure: modules, segments, sections;
- an acceptable method of assessing performance;
- a process of providing critical feedback to the student; and
- a service of tutorial support.

Any plan for human achievement in organizations in the 1990s seems likely to incorporate a training strategy that includes delivery systems capable of streaming learning to people in workplaces for the primary purpose of skill development and improved performance. This capability to enrich work by paced skill development is the primary contribution of training to improved business performance.

Training for multiskills performance

When we turn to management training and its requirements for multiskills development, the real potential of performance-related training becomes evident. Here, the approach is to define management activities in terms of its key skills, using a methodology which allows for high specificity in skill definition. This methodology has been described already in the chapter. Here, we can say something about the follow-up training to profiling.

Identifying training needs in the way we have described already provides a powerful incentive for the student to correct an identified weakness as quickly as possible. Further, we can show that individual training needs in management are much narrower than is generally believed. Indeed, when one concentrates on a skills approach to management development, specific needs can be identified with precision. Finally, we can show that the skills themselves fall into two major categories. In the first are people-management, and interpersonal skills which can best be developed through interactive training on residential courses. In the second category are analytical, cognitive skills which are amenable to learning by self-study, or open learning.

The development of multiskills management performance depends on devising a suitable mix of interactive and analytical learning programmes.

At the end of each skill development programme, a final exercise should be offered to the student as the basis on which a measured improvement in skill performances can be determined.

CONCLUSION

In this chapter we have considered the following aspects of effective training management:

1. Linking human resource development strategies with business strategies.
2. Creating a performance-oriented human-resource development programme.
3. Designing and delivering a performance-related training programme.

Effective training management begins with an awareness by the organization that the performance development of its human resources is directly geared to the development of the business of the organization. Sustained business improvement cannot occur without sustained resourcing of people.

Effective training management requires, above all, the preparation and regular updating of an organization training plan. It is in this plan that the development priorities of managers and managed as human resources can be set out, reviewed, and renewed in an ongoing training cycle. In this way, the development of people is always phased to reflect the priorities of skilled development required to advance the business of the organization.

Effective training management requires this kind of recognition from those who direct the strategy of the organization. In achieving organizations, human resource planning is used to give the business a competitive advantage. Developing people to build, manage, and advance the performance of organizations is the real purpose of an effective training function.

CHECKLIST

The main steps to managing an effective training function are as follows:

1. Define a 'people' strategy, or a human-resources development strategy *179*

within the business strategy of the organization.
2. Define the role of training within the HRD strategy, i.e. create a training strategy.
3. Focus the training strategy on performance-related training, i.e. training geared to the measured improvement of core skills.
4. Create a focused learning response to individual skills profiling. This response to provide a mixed-media range of learning and exercising.
5. Create a company training infrastructure owned by the organization, and not by the trainers.

FURTHER READING

Armstrong, A. (1983), *How to be a Better Manager*, London: Kogan Page.

Bennett, R. (1981), *Managing Personnel and Performance – An Alternative Approach*, London: Business Books.

Bennett, R. (ed.) (1986), *'Get in There' – Managing the Business of Training*, five workbooks from Trainer Support Services, UK (see particularly Workbook 2 –'Business Needs and Plans', by Bennett and Laidlaw, and Workbook 4 – 'Managing for Success', by Jeremy Spoor).

Bowen, P. (1976), *Social Control in Industrial Organizations*, London: Routledge and Kegan Paul (ch.3, pp. 57–77 and ch.10, pp. 242–53 on 'balance' and 'contract' between organizations and their memberships).

Brodie, M. and R. Bennett (1979) (eds), *Perspectives on Managerial Effectiveness*, Thamesman Publications.

Camp, R.R. *et al.* (1986), *Toward a More Effective Training Strategy and Practice*, Englewood Cliffs, NJ: Prentice Hall.

Churchill, G.A. *et al.* (1985), 'The Determinants of Salesperson Performance: A Meta-Analysis', *Journal of Marketing Research*, **xxii**, May, 103–18.

Davis, H.L. and A.J. Silk (1972), 'Interaction and Influence Processes in Personal Selling', *Sloan Management Review*, **13**, (2), 59–76.

Futrell, C.M. (1980), *ABC's of Selling*, Irwin (ch.2, pp. 49–71).

Pepper, A.D. (1984), *Managing the Training and Development Function*, Aldershot: Gower.

Walker, J.W. (ed.) (1979), *The Challenge of Human Resource Planning: Selected Readings*, Human Resource Planning Society, 101–11.

Young, Arthur (1986), *The Manager's Handbook – The Practical Guide to Successful Management*, (ed.) Erica Hunningher, Marshall Editions.

15 Developing effective trainers

Roger Bennett

This chapter looks at ways in which trainers can develop themselves. It covers the non-formal, non-certified approaches to the training of trainers. There are two main thrusts in this chapter. First, different roles of the trainer are discussed, along with ways of developing effectiveness in each of them. Second, the question of competence is discussed and related to trainer effectiveness.

One key assumption is made: that trainers are responsible for their own development. While others will have an influence, ultimately only trainers can generate for themselves the necessary motivation to do something about their own development. The support of others is necessary, but not sufficient alone for this development to take place and work.

Finally, and as many recent reports have stressed, training is now becoming a vital 'centre stage' organization function in a changing and complex environment. Many of the traditional approaches to training are now less effective than they were. Cross-cultural business (for example, Europe, the trade agreement between the United States and Canada, and the opening up of Eastern European economies) presents many challenges. Continual development of trainers is crucial if other organizational members are to be equipped to meet these challenges.

ROLES FOR THE TRAINER

Although many classifications of trainer roles exist, the one used here is that presented by Bennett (1988). This contains five key roles, namely:

- the trainer;
- the provider;
- the consultant;
- the innovator; and
- the manager.

These are depicted in Figure 15.1. As will be seen, two of these roles (trainer and provider) are concerned mainly with maintaining levels of performance. Another two (consultant and innovator) are more concerned with training for change. The fifth – the manager – is concerned with integrating the activities and behaviours of the other roles but might also include aspects of these other roles. Thus, these roles are not distinct 'packages' of activities, behaviours and responsibilities. They each have a clear focus but do relate to each other, as already indicated in the descriptions given above. The manager role has a strong link with all others, by virtue of its very nature. Trainer and provider roles are more concerned with maintenance activities, while those of consultant and innovator are (often) involved with change and problem solving.

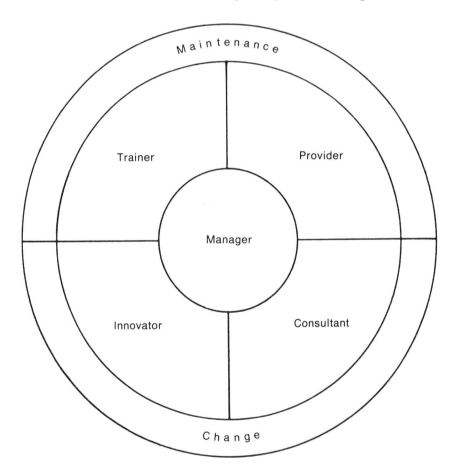

Figure 15.1   General trainer roles

The trainer   A training role that is primarily concerned with actual direct training. It is a role that involves the trainer in helping people to learn, providing *182* feedback about their learning and adapting course designs to meet trainees' needs. The trainer's role may involve classroom teaching and instruction, laboratory work, small group work, supervision of individual project work and all those activities that directly influence immediate learning experiences. In effect, the trainer is a learning specialist.

The provider A training role that is primarily concerned with the design, maintenance and delivery of training programmes. It will involve training-needs analysis; setting objectives; designing courses; choosing appropriate methods; testing out and evaluating courses or training activities; and helping trainers to deliver the training.

The consultant A training role that is primarily concerned with analysing business problems and assessing/recommending solutions, some of which may require training. It may involve some elements of the provider role but specifically concentrates on liaising with line managers; identifying their performance problems; advising on possible training solutions (where appropriate); working with providers and/or trainers to establish training programmes; advising training managers (where the roles are separated) on training goals and policies; and ensuring evaluation takes place and the results are used.

The innovator   A training role that is primarily concerned with helping organizations effectively to manage change and solve performance problems. It will involve working with managers at senior/middle levels, providing support and help to managers in coping with change; identifying where seminars and workshops can be a useful means of educating managers for change; facilitating change; identifying the real sources of power in the organization and linking with these to help bring about change; and advising the training function on how it can best help in the change process. (In 'organization development' terms, such a role might be called 'change agent', 'catalyst', or 'interventionist'.) The role frequently overlaps with that of the consultant.

The manager A training role that is primarily concerned with planning, organizing, controlling and developing the training and development activity or function. It will involve setting training goals, policies and plans; liaising with other departments and with senior managers about the contribution training can and should make to improving performance; ensuring that appropriate training activities are designed, developed, delivered and evaluated; acquiring and developing training staff; establishing effective lines of authority and communication within the training function; acquiring and effectively using non-staff resources; monitoring quality standards and controlling activities against a total training plan. Some provider roles may contain elements of the manager role in small organizations or in situations where providers have several training programmes to deliver.

Checking the role

Before any development can take place, it is important for trainers to be able to   *183*

Item	Do now	Should do
A Classroom teaching or instructing		
Small group work/seminars		
Role playing or other simulations		
Supervising individual project work		
Adapting course/training designs		
Researching your training/teaching subject		
Choosing and using specific learning methods		
TOTAL SCORE		
B Designing training courses/programmes		
Identifying training needs		
Setting course/programme objectives		
Choosing appropriate delivery methods		
Identifying contributors to training		
Pilot-testing courses/programmes		
Evaluating courses/programmes		
TOTAL SCORE		
C Helping analyse business/performance problems		
Recommending/assessing solutions		
Identifying where training can help		
Liaising with managers		
Advising managers on training issues		
Helping set up appropriate training		
Working to implement training solutions		
TOTAL SCORE		
D Identifying changing business priorities		
Helping managers cope with change		
Advising trainers on how to meet change		
Working with managers to solve problems		
Helping managers with training their staff		
Bringing in external experts to help		
Suggesting new ways of developing staff		
TOTAL SCORE		
E Setting training goals and priorities		
Establishing a training plan		
Acquiring training resources		
Developing training resources		
Liaising with other departments		
Monitoring training standards		
Controlling budgets and activities		
TOTAL SCORE		

Now add up the ratings under each column heading within each grouping of items (i.e., A, B, etc.) and put the result on the lines opposite 'Total score'. When you have a complete set of five 'Total score' under each column, do the following:

1. For the 'Do now' column, rank order your set of 'Total score' where rank order 1 would be the highest score.
2. For the 'Should do' column, repeat 1. above.
3. Write down on a piece of paper the group letters, with the appropriate rank number for each column against them. The roles indicated by each grouping are as follows:

    A   Trainer
    B   Provider
    C   Consultant
    D   Innovator
    E   Manager

Remember, these are not mutually exclusive categories. They do, however, give the main emphasis of each role. Which were your dominant roles in each column? Is there a significant change involved (i.e., are the score fairly close)? Answering these questions will determine what you may need to do.

Figure 15.2   Role identification checklist

identify their current main role(s) and those they might need to adopt in the near future. A checklist is presented in Figure 15.2 which can help in doing this. Listed in Figure 15.2 are a number of items that describe different facets of the roles training personnel operate. They are based on the general statement of roles presented earlier in the chapter. There are also two columns, headed 'Do now' and 'Should do'. For each item, give a rating out of 10 under each of these column headings. A rating of 10 would indicate that you do (or should do) a lot of that item; a rating of 0 that you do (or should do) none of that item. Ratings between these extremes can be used to indicate varying amounts. For example, against 'classroom teaching or instructing' you might have put ratings of 3 under the 'Do now' column and 8 under the 'Should do' column. This would indicate that you feel your role should contain more of this item in the near future. Remember, you are trying to assess how and to what extent your role needs to be extended, added to or changed. Write your score on the lines provided.

Developing the roles

Having identified the role(s) needed in the future, trainers are in a better position to develop themselves. This is, after all, the starting point. The next step is to isolate those items in the checklist under the 'Should do' column, and ask yourself seriously if these can be undertaken effectively. If the answer is 'no', a framework for a personal development plan can be drawn up. This should be discussed with colleagues, or a 'mentor', to establish whether any other elements should be added and precisely what development steps should be taken.

Because each development plan will be different, it is not possible here to describe ways in which each and every one can be executed. What can be done is to suggest some ways for developing each of the roles.

Developing the 'trainer' role

There are many opportunities for doing this. They include the well-tried and tested 'train the trainer' programmes offered by many centres in the United Kingdom and overseas, often leading to a qualification from a body such as the Institute of Training and Development in the United Kingdom. Institutes in other countries can give help and advice, and might provide formal qualifications. Some examples would be the Irish Institute for Training and Development, the New Zealand Association for Training and Development, the Singapore Training and Development Association and the American Society for Training and Development.

Many such courses are highly practical and give good foundation training. Enhancing the trainer role requires further work. Here are some ways in which this might be done:

- *Watching others in action* Going to conferences, workshops and training sessions conducted by people known for their effectiveness in direct instruction/teaching. Observe what is done, and how it is done. Take notes of these things and any actions that might be possible to put them into effect. Try them out and evaluate their success.
- *Working with others* This can apply across the whole spectrum of 'trainer' role elements. Ask what they do, how they do it and ask for an opportunity to do it and for feedback.
- *Confidential practice* Rehearsed in private, in front of a mirror, a tape recorder, microphone or a video camera can help on those finer points of personal presentation. Getting someone else involved to give feedback (still in confidence) is useful.
- *Reading* A useful but currently much maligned method of development. Reading current journals and new books can give insights into different training approaches, latest developments in the specialism and generally get people to think about what they are doing and how they are doing it.
- *Reflection* Sitting back and thinking about an event, how it went, what needs to be improved, and then taking action. Many 'trainers' talk about it but often don't do it!

There will be other things that can be done. Talk with experienced trainers and ask for their thoughts. Write them down here:

What   **How**

_____   _____

_____   _____

_____   _____

_____   _____

_____   _____

_____   _____

_____   _____

_____   _____

_____   _____

Reading hint: an extremely useful book that addresses many of the points the 'trainer' needs to look at is that by Pont (1990).

Developing the 'provider' role

To an extent, some of the approaches discussed in the previous section apply here also. In particular, 'train the trainer' programmes that focus on course design, delivery and management can be effective. However, some aspects of the role require the experience that, typically, some researchers have. This is especially true of pilot-testing and evaluation. Experienced providers will also have knowledge that can be passed on. Seek opportunities to watch them at work and to work with them. Form co-consulting duos or trios to exchange, explore and learn.

An approach that is extremely effective is to set up an action development group. Here is how it can be done:

- Identify five or six experienced providers from within and outside the company.
- Set up an informal meeting to explore mutual interests and development needs and agree to meet regularly.
- At each meeting, take one key element and explore it in depth. Search for examples, possible actions, sources of information, current practice.
- Go away and do something.
- At next meeting, review progress/outcomes.
- Give each member of the group the same opportunity.
- Repeat process until usefulness of group for all members has expired.

Other ways of developing the 'provider' role? Again, ask round, read the books and journals. List them here with actions:

187

What	How
_____	_____
_____	_____
_____	_____
_____	_____
_____	_____
_____	_____
_____	_____
_____	_____
_____	_____

Reading hint: again, Pont (1990) is useful; so is Buckley and Caple (1990), especially chapters 7, 8, 9, 10 and the two appendices.

Developing the 'consultant' role

To develop this role requires, as a basis, a good understanding of the previous two roles. Trainers as consultants must know the general field of training if they are to be credible. They must also be capable in the areas of analysis, problem solving and advising. There are external programmes that are geared to these and related aspects. An example is the programme on consulting and influencing skills for internal advisers offered by Oxford Management Consultants in the United Kingdom. For trainers moving into a consultant role, it is recommended that they attend such a programme. Again, some understanding of action-research methods will be an advantage.

Having gained this initial training, trainer-consultants will benefit from:

- Acquiring key social and political skills.
- Setting up action-development groups (as described in the previous section).
- Co-consulting with an experienced trainer-consultant.
- Talking with management consultants about latest trends and developments.
- Working/talking with action researchers.
- Establishing a network of key, senior managers in the organization with whom to talk regularly about business issues.
- Attending conferences and workshops specifically aimed at trainers as consultants.

188 Are there others? List them here:

What	How
_____	_____
_____	_____
_____	_____
_____	_____
_____	_____
_____	_____
_____	_____
_____	_____
_____	_____
_____	_____

Reading hint: an excellent book is available, specifically for the trainer as consultant, by Phillips and Shaw (1989). Among its many useful features is a self-development plan and a good reading list.

Developing the 'innovator' role

This is, perhaps, the most difficult role to develop. It overlaps with the consultant role but is much more ideas-based in relation to business strategy and change. It relates to the role of change agent but with a training and development emphasis. Good consultants can move into the innovator role but will have to think and act more strategically. They need to link training with the direction of the business. Thus, they need an understanding of business development, relevant environmental issues and they need to operate creatively, using the intervention approaches of the action researcher/change agent. In many senses, they need to develop some aspects of four of Margerison/McCann's (1990) eight team roles, namely:

1. reporter-adviser;
2. creator-innovator;
3. explorer-promoter; and
4. assessor-developer.

Being able to operate in such modes is a function of personality and preferences, as well as specific skills. It could almost be argued that innovators are born, not made. Certainly, not all trainers will be able to develop into this role. For those who can, experience at senior management level – as a consultant, management development advisor, non-executive director or whatever – will be most important. In addition, the regular use of the strategic training workshop is a very beneficial way of keeping in tune and developing key insights.

There are several forms such workshops can take, but the basic form is as follows:

- Set aside two or three days away from work.

189

together for the workshop key training staff and several senior managers.

Ask each person to come to the workshop with a list of their top five priorities for the business.

- Share these at the workshop, inviting comment and seeking agreement on key priorities.
- Work through the possible training implications, particularly those that have to do with substantial change.
- Work through options and actions, and agree next steps.
- Review process/achievements with the group within the next three to six months.

Some ways of keeping in touch and developing broader insights are:

- Meeting regularly with a network of colleagues from other organizations.
- Attending relevant large conferences and events of importance to the business.
- Taking on an 'academic guru' or adviser from an educational establishment or training consultancy.
- Study tours of overseas countries.
- Reading, reading and yet more reading!

Are there others?

What

_____

_____

_____

_____

_____

_____

_____

_____

_____

How

_____

_____

_____

_____

_____

_____

_____

_____

_____

Reading hint: difficult, this one. There is so much on change, but not too much which is specific to trainers. The Phillips and Shaw (1989) book is useful; as is Bentley (1990) which takes a strategic look at training. Jones (1988) also offers some valuable insights. Some cases are given in the Training, Enterprise and Education Directorate of the Employment Department report (1990) on the training and development of trainers.

Developing the 'manager' role

190 This is a complex role to develop, as it can combine elements of the four other

roles. Managers should at least have insights into these other roles and a real understanding of the contribution that each makes to the success of the organization. Managers must also be able to obtain and manage resources, manage their teams of trainers and provide a businesslike interface with the rest of the organization. In short, they must be *real* managers!

Here are some of the ways in which this role can be developed:

- Attending a programme on the management of the training function.
- Attending a general management programme.
- Working with effective line managers, to observe, note and act upon effective behaviours.
- Having a senior line manager as a mentor.
- Setting up a management development group with training managers from other organizations (similar to the action-development group discussed earlier).
- Having a spell in line management (probably for no more than two years) if this is practical to arrange.
- Spending time to talk with line managers about their problems (they might be similar!).
- Using an action-learning approach with other line managers.
- Combining self-development with any or all of the above.

Are there others?

What	How

Reading hint: a lot to choose from. Try Zenger (1985); Robinson (1985); Pepper (1984); and Pittam (1987), plus any of the general books on management.

THE QUESTION OF COMPETENCE

A good deal of effort, time and money is being spent (at least in the United Kingdom) on identifying the competences of trainers. There exist differing views as to whether this is feasible, or even necessary. However, the work has developed quickly, and the topic needs to be considered.

But what is 'competence'? There are in existence several definitions (as   *191* evidenced by Cowling, 1990) but the Concise Oxford Dictionary defines *competence* (and competency) as: 'sufficiency of means for living, easy circumstances, ability (to do, for a task), ...'. It further defines *competent* as: 'adequately qualified (to do, for a task) ..., effective, adequate ...'. The use of words such as 'sufficiency', 'ability', 'effective', 'adequate' in relation to the task, suggests more than just knowledge. This view is shared by Cowling (1990), and by Burgoyne (1989) who states that: 'it concerns doing and action, rather than the mere possession of knowledge. It is, however, a broader concept than skill and can usefully be thought of as encompassing knowledge, skill, understanding and will.'

For the purpose of this chapter, *competence* will be defined as: 'the general set of knowledge, skills and personal attributes necessary and sufficient to ensure tasks are carried out effectively, i.e., they lead to the desired results'. This leads to the question of whether universal competences can be established, or whether they are situation-specific. The Training and Development Lead Body in the United Kingdom would appear to believe the former and the Directorate seems to, not only for trainers but for managers and other professionals. Astute observers and writers such as Garrett (1990) believe in the latter (in the case of directors). The view taken here is that it is a bit of both. Certain skills, experiences, and so on, are required by most trainers: but not all will be able to put them to good use in the same circumstances. This is pointed up by Bennett and Leduchowicz (1983).

So, what are the competences required by trainers? The information emerging from UK-based studies would appear to suggest a rather large number, and in some detail. In the United States, the ASTD study (1983) identified some 31 competencies (note that the spelling differs – it does even among UK studies). It is this author's contention that such lists are too long, too unwieldy and will lead to paperwork systems that will render the usefulness of the concept close to zero. They will also continuously be out-of-date

Instead, the view is taken that focusing on role requirements is a more positive way of developing effectiveness. If, in addition, other factors that influence effectiveness are taken into account, genuine development of overall, situationally relevant competence will take place. The reader is urged to work through the checklist presented in Chapter 16.

Reading hint: the Training, Enterprise and Education Directorate of the Employment Department in the United Kingdom is publishing a number of reports on competence and the development of trainers. See for example Horton (1990); and Greenaway and Bill (1989). At the time of writing a draft Standards in Training and Development has been prepared by the United Kingdom's Training and Development Lead Body to provide a proposed Qualifications Framework. For the ASTD's US approach, see McCullough (1987). For a manageable set of competences related to the work of the 'facilitator', see Heron (1989, p.139).

FURTHER READING

192 Bennett, R.D. (1988), *Improving Trainer Effectiveness*, Gower.

Bennett, R.D. and T. Leduchowicz (1983), 'What makes for an effective trainer', *Journal of European Industrial Training Monograph*, **7**, (2).

Bentley, T. (1990), *The Business of Training – Achieving Success in Changing World Markets*, McGraw-Hill (UK).

Buckley, R. and J. Capel (1990), *The Theory and Practice of Training*, Kogan Page.

Burgoyne, J. (1989), 'Creating the managerial portfolio – building on competency approaches to management development', *Management Education and Development*, **20**, pt 1, 56–61.

Clark, R.E. (1992), 'New techniques for effective training management', *Journal of European Industrial Training*, **16**, (6), 3–6.

Cowling, A. (1990), 'The appraisal and development of managers', in A. Cowling and C. Mailer (eds), *Managing Human Resources*, 2nd edn, Edward Arnold.

Garratt, Bob (1990), *Creating a Learning Organisation*, Director Books.

Garrick, J. and R. McDonald (1992), 'Competence standards for industry trainers – alternative models', *Journal of European Industrial Training*, **16**, (7), 16–20.

Greenaway, R. and C. Bill (1989), *Competences of Development Trainers*, a report produced by and for the trainer development section of the Training, Enterprise and Education Directorate of the Employment Department.

Heron, J. (1989), *The Facilitators' Handbook*, Kogan Page/Nichols Publishing.

Horton, C. (1990), *The Training and Development of Trainers*, a report produced for and by the Training, Enterprise and Education Directorate of the Employment Department.

Jones, Alun (1988), 'The Skills of Change Making', in R. Bennett (ed.), *Improving Trainer Effectiveness*, Gower.

Margerison, C. and Dick McCann (1990), *Team management – Practical New Approaches*, Mercury Books.

McCollaugh, R.C. (1987), 'Professional Development', in R.L. Craig (ed.), *Training and Development Handbook*, 3rd edn, McGraw-Hill.

Pepper, A.D. (1984), *Managing the Training and Development Function*, Gower.

Phillips, K. and P. Shaw (1989), *A Consultancy Approach for Trainers*, Gower.

Pittam, J.L. (1987), 'Organisation and Management of the Training Function', in R.L. Craig, (ed.), *Training and Development Handbook*, 3rd edn, McGraw-Hill.

Pont, A.M. (1990), *Developing Effective Training Skills*, McGraw-Hill (UK).

Robinson, K.R. (1985), *Handbook of Training Management*, 2nd edn, Kogan Page.

Zenger, J. (1985), 'Training for organisational effectiveness', *Journal of European Industrial Training*, **9**, (7), 3–8.

16 The effective trainer checklist[1]

Roger Bennett

The research and workshops on trainer effectiveness carried out by staff of the then Thames Valley Regional Management Centre at Slough and Oxford, on behalf of the Manpower Services Commission, identified a number of key areas that influence trainer effectiveness. This checklist summarizes what were found to be the more important factors in each area. The purpose of the checklist is to provide some food for thought: it is not a definitive listing. All items must be considered in the light of the trainer's own situation. In using this checklist, you are invited to ask the following questions:

- How does this apply to me?
- Where do I stand in relation to each item?
- Where should I be?
- What things might I change to improve my effectiveness?
- Why should I change?
- How can I bring about the change?
- What help do I need to change?
- What other factors should I be considering?

There are no right or wrong answers. The process of asking and answering the questions will help clarify what you want or need to do to improve the contribution you can make to your organization.

TRAINER COMPETENCES

These can be numerous, but our research suggests the following at least must be considered:

---

[1]This checklist draws upon research sponsored by the Manpower Services Commission and on workshops, seminars and conferences conducted throughout the United Kingdom and overseas. Hundreds of trainers and managers contributed to the work on which it is based. Their contribution is warmly appreciated, as is the work of Tad Leduchowicz, of Slough College, who was Research Associate on the main project.

- Ability to motivate learners and to hold their interest.
- Capacity to communicate and present information, and ideas, in a meaningful way.
- Good knowledge of the subject matter or area in which people are being trained.
- Ability to relate the training to the practical world of the trainees, using appropriate examples.
- Clarity of thought and in use of analytical and logical skills.
- Capacity to stand back and work strategically.
- Being able to control the learning group.
- Exercising appropriate social and leadership skills.
- Being able to manage the training situation.

There will be others you would wish to add, based on your own experience.

Please do so:

_____

_____

_____

_____

TRAINER CHARACTERISTICS

The range of characteristics is clearly very diverse – as diverse as the people who make up the training profession. However, the research indicates the following to be important contributions to effectiveness:

- Being sensitive to the needs of the learners.
- Being prepared to listen to what learners have to say.
- Being approachable, responsive and sensitive, feeling the mood of the learners.
- Projecting enthusiasm, vitality, motivation, interest and dedication.
- Having confidence in and commitment to the approach adopted.
- Being patient and tolerant of the learners' problems and shortcomings.
- Being seen to be 'credible'.

Others you would wish to add:

_____

_____

_____

_____

TRAINER ROLE ORIENTATION

This refers to the way in which the trainer sees the role. Two key dimensions *195* were established from the research, and imply four basic orientations. Which orientation do you have?

- An orientation to the maintenance needs of the organization, that is, to ensuring the continuance of the existing activities, products or services.
- An orientation to bringing about change within the organization, that is, to ensure that training can respond to pressures for change from both outside and inside the organization to help it get geared up to meet new situations, objectives, and so on.
- An orientation to traditional methods of training, that is, methods and approaches adopting the educational or 'professional' model of training based largely on classroom-type techniques and curriculum design.
- An orientation to methods of intervention, that is, a 'change agent' approach to training that involves greater participation in bringing about changes in systems, procedures or technologies and in changing people's attitudes and approaches to work.

Do you have others?

_____

_____

_____

_____

TRAINER STYLE

There exist considerable variations in the way in which trainers go about their jobs. We found that a number of dimensions could be used to characterize trainer style. Where do you fit on each of these dimensions?

1. Use trainer-centred training approaches — Use learner-centred training approaches

2. Use persuasion to get people involved in training — Use own authority or the authority of others to get people involved in training

3. Work in a detached way — Pervasive in the organization

4. Adopt theory-centred approaches in training — Adopt problem- or need-centred approaches in training

5. Use interventionist strategies — Do not use interventionist strategies

6. Primary concern is for the need of the organization — Primary concern is for the needs of the individual

7. Respond to training needs as presented to you.

Diagnose the na
apparent training
before responding

_____

8. Structure training programmes highly

Adopt a more flexible approach to training programme structure

_____

9. Use standard/tried training approaches

Experiment with training approaches

_____

10. Tend to propose solution

Guide people through problem-solving

_____

11. Work strategically, plan ahead and set objectives

Respond to problems and needs as they arise

_____

12. Take steps to remain informed on subject matter and the organization

Do not take steps to remain informed on subject matter and the organization

_____

13. Choose specific areas for training initiatives

More concerned with teaching principles

_____

14. Obtain feedback to improve training

Not concerned with obtaining feedback

_____

15. Vary training approaches to suit learners

Tend to use the same training approach irrespective of type of learners

_____

Are there other dimensions you would add?

_____
_____
_____
_____

TRAINER ROLES

There is clearly no single, all-purpose trainer role. Trainers adopt a variety of roles, some being merged within an overall role. Which of the following roles do you perform?

- Training policy formulator
- Training need identifier and diagnostician

THE EFFECTIVE TRAINER CHECKLIST *(rotated)*

for training initiatives

ing objectives

riculum builder

nd developer

or and organizer

tor

ment agent, catalyst, facilitator

...ultant

- ...ent of learning transfer to the job
- Manager of training resources
- Trainer and developer of trainers
- Liaison officer
- Assessor of training quality
- Evaluator of training contribution

What others would you add?

_____

_____

_____

_____

ORGANIZATION CULTURE

Trainers operate in rather different cultures according to the nature of the organization in which they work. Many things characterize organization culture. The following represent a few of the key ones:

- The extent to which the organization is managed in an autocratic or democratic manner.
- The attitude of managers toward the training function.
- The level of involvement of line managers in the training activity.
- The degree of support for training, particularly at senior management level.
- The philosophy of the organization concerning education, training and staff development.
- The time span of senior management, that is, 'results today' or 'better performance in the future', or both.
- The nature and use of power in the organization (e.g. personal power versus positional power).
- The nature and use of sanctions.
- The form and nature of technology and the work to be performed.

198 Please add others of your own:

_____
_____
_____
_____

You will need to weigh up the kind of culture in which you operate and adopt a style appropriate to it – or seek to change it!

ORGANIZATIONAL NEEDS

It is difficult to be specific about these, since they are unique to the organization in question. However, you may wish to consider which of the following you are trying to satisfy:

- Ensuring adequate supply of properly trained personnel.
- Keeping present job performance levels up to scratch.
- Developing skills, abilities and attitudes for future job performance requirements.
- Building greater job deployment flexibility.
- Coping with fast-changing technologies.
- Moving into new markets.
- Meeting statutory training requirements.
- Coping with reduced staffing levels and redundancy.
- Preparing staff for retirement.

You can no doubt add specific needs that your organization is trying to meet:

_____
_____
_____
_____

PURPOSE OF TRAINING

These are really for you to define, in the light of the organizational needs that have to be met. But think about the following:

- Is training part of a general corporate strategy for improving organizational effectiveness?
- Is training carried out because it has a long history of existence in the organization: 'we do it because we've always done it'?
- Is training too concerned with satisfying external requirements (e.g. of government, of training organizations(?

Any others?

_____
_____

_____
_____

OVERALL EFFECTIVENESS

Finally, what do you feel are the outcomes of your work as a trainer? Are they:

- Evidence of changed behaviour/performance of trainees?
- Capacity of trainees to continue to apply learning to their work situations?
- Greater willingness of trainees to find better ways of doing things?
- Improvement in the cost effectiveness and efficiency of the organization?
- Improved productivity?
- Greater interest in training (e.g. as expressed in more post-training follow-up activities)?
- Measurable achievement of objectives?

Others:

_____
_____
_____
_____

SURVIVING AS A TRAINER

Trainers are increasingly under threat from economic pressures, the introduction of new technology and organization restructuring. To survive the threat and continue to make a positive contribution to the organization requires certain skills. These are listed below. What are you good/less good at? Which ones need developing? Who can help you develop them?

Technical   Skilled at:

- training methods and techniques;
- analysing organizational behaviour/structures;
- helping plan the business activities; and
- identifying environmental changes.

Personal   Skilled at:

- communicating ideas effectively;
- analysing training/business needs clearly and logically;
- generating enthusiasm for training; and
- building acceptance of your skills/role as a trainer.

Political   Skilled at:

- being visible to others within the organization;
- persuading others to support training;
- influencing events and decisions in the organization; and
- identifying and getting close to the real sources of power in the organization.

Innovating   Skilled at:

- scanning the external environment for new ideas/new approaches that might be helpful to your organization;
- generating new ideas for consideration by colleagues;
- experimenting with new ideas/approaches to demonstrate their usefulness in helping to meet business requirements; and
- helping the organization to learn from the uses of new approaches and develop more effective ways of surviving and meeting the business challenge.

You might have others – list them here:

_____

_____

_____

_____

Remember, the best means of survival is to make a direct contribution to the organization's business needs – to help it survive and grow. Check which activities you engage upon meet this requirement. For those that do not, can you afford to continue with them?

ATTITUDES TO TRAINING

Experience and research have shown that widely differing attitudes to training exist. The following represent some of those most frequently encountered. The first set are essentially negative (or pessimistic), while the second are positive (or optimistic) statements:

- Training is a costly luxury.
- Training is a waste of time.
- Training is a peripheral activity.
- Trainers are passive or reactive.
- Trainers are classroom-bound.
- Trainers are not adaptive to change.
- Trainers and training lack credibility with managers.
- Trainers do not put themselves about enough.

- Trainers and training do not contribute to organization success.
- Training is essential for excellent organization performance.
- Successful training is needs and change oriented.
- Trainers must and can get close to the heart of the business.
- Trainers can adopt alternative roles.
- Trainers need new skills to be successful in those roles.
- Successful trainers are politically aware but not necessarily politically active.
- Managers are more fully accepting their responsibilities for training.
- Credibility comes through positive action and visible success.
- Training and trainers make a direct contribution to organization success.
- Trainers are needed more than ever before.

There might be others you can think of. List them below:

_____
_____
_____
_____

Developing and showing positive attitudes to training and trainers is vital to the success of the training and development effort. Which attitudes do you hold? More importantly, which attitudes do your senior managers hold? If they are essentially negative, get working fast on changing them. Without a set of positive attitudes, a climate conducive to successful training cannot be established. What can you do:

1. To eliminate negative attitudes?
2. To build upon the positive attitudes?

Let us repeat that this checklist is not an exhaustive set of factors – it is a 'starter for ten' aimed at getting you to think about yourself as a trainer. We hope it will help you focus on items that could benefit from greater attention. But please bear in mind one important conclusion from the research – there must be the right kind of fit or congruence between each area. The role you adopt must fit the organization culture, or its needs – even if it really means being a bit of an irritant. Also bear in mind that successful 'irritants' have a power base somewhere in the organization!

17 Training the sales force

Ken Hill

It is not possible in one chapter to review all matters affecting the sales training function. Many of them warrant a chapter in their own right, and indeed some are covered in more detail elsewhere in this handbook. Accordingly, I shall confine myself to a strategic/tactical overview, and I shall attempt to be pragmatic rather than theoretical.

WHY TRAIN THE SALES FORCE?

At first sight, this may seem a strange question to pose. Yet we have all heard of new sales recruits who, on their first day, are told 'here are your samples, here are your customer records, get out there and sell'. In some cases, this situation may arise by design rather than mismanagement. Training is expensive, and the option to hire fully trained sales staff rather than train your own may seem tempting. Thus, employees of companies known to invest heavily in training are often targeted for recruitment by those who cannot or will not provide this investment. Indeed, this danger of poaching is often cited as a reason for restricting investment in training.

If your market is static, and the products/services of the industries competing in the market are very similar, there may be some merit in this argument. However, even in such markets, it is likely that the sales person will be a main differentiating factor in the buying decision, and as such, needs to be highly skilled – which implies highly trained. Even if recruited in a highly trained state, natural skills erosion needs to be met by some form of remedial training. Also, very few markets nowadays are static – customer needs change, new products/ services are launched, and competition is fierce. All these factors point to a need for training.

An additional factor needs consideration. Consumers in most markets are becoming increasingly knowledgeable about the products and services they buy and their rights as consumers. In some cases (e.g. the financial sector) there is a legal obligation to have competent sales staff capable of giving customers *203* best advice. Even if no legal obligation applies, there is certainly a moral one. Only by subscribing to this view will selling be perceived as a 'profession'.

On balance, therefore, the case for some investment in training seems self-evident. The question is rather, how much? This is a much more difficult issue. A number of variables will affect the decision, some of which are as follows:

1. What is the current gap between actual attitudes/knowledge/skills and the desired level?
2. What is the risk/cost of accepting this gap (prosecution/sales lost to competitors, and so on)?
3. How able are the line managers at delivering training (obviating the need for training specialists)?
4. How complex are the products/services/customer applications and how rapidly are they changing?
5. What is the quantity and quality of competition in the marketplace?
6. What is the company's financial ability to invest in training?

Individual companies must decide for themselves how to balance these factors. National norms are very hard to come by, but seem to vary in the range of 1–5 per cent of turnover. Traditionally, UK industry, with few notable exceptions, has tended to under-invest. It is interesting to note that high investors are often market leaders (e.g. Marks and Spencer, Prudential, IBM, Hewlett Packard).

TRAINING NEEDS ANALYSIS

Having taken the decision to invest in training, what should be trained? The answer may seem obvious, and indicated by an area of poor business perform-ance (e.g. low sales of a particular product), but two factors need to be considered. First, is the problem a training problem? All too often there is a tendency to 'throw some training at it' and hope that the problem will go away, and trainers refer to being 'asked to sprinkle the magic dust'. Clearly, this is not always the answer. A sales person who does not sell much product 'A', because it pays far less commission than product 'B' may respond more positively to a change in the commission rates than to extra training on product 'A'. This whole subject is covered elsewhere in this handbook. Secondly, there are usually far more training requirements than there are resources to satisfy them. Conse-quently, one just has to do the best one can within the financial limitations. Both these factors can be addressed by ensuring that a systematic 'training needs analysis' is carried out. As this subject is also covered in detail elsewhere, I shall concentrate here only on specifics concerning the training of the sales force.

Training needs analysis has to be considered at two levels: 'corporate' and 'individual'.

At a corporate level, the starting point of the trainee is defined initially by the new-entrant recruitment profile. This should describe in detail the attitudes, knowledge and skills the new entrant starts off with. This process may well 204 include formal ability and personality tests. A company which is unable to train from the beginning will have a more demanding new entrant profile. Similar standards should be defined to describe the 'entry level' when an employee is promoted. It is then possible to define a standard minimum competence, in terms of product knowledge and application (selling) skills. The difference between entry level and minimum competence represents the training gap, for which a programme can be designed. This programme, because the benchmarks are defined across the board, becomes a standard programme applicable to all.

At a second level, the training-needs analysis has to be considered for each individual. Information allowing entry level to be assessed can be qualitative and quantitative. Quantitative data will relate to primary sales performance (sales volume, mix, profitability, and so on) and should also encapsulate secondary performance factors (calls per day, existing business vs. new business calls, contact to order ratios, and so on). Most disciplined sales operators will support the view that one must *manage* sales activity and can only *measure* the sales result. This implies some form of activity/results reporting system which should track 'actual' against 'plan' for the previous period, and 'plan' for the coming period.

This quantitative data will indicate individual training needs. For example, a sales person who makes high numbers of telephone calls to get appointments, but obtains only low numbers of confirmed appointments, may need training in where to look for prospects and/or how to make such calls. A sales person who generates high numbers of proposals, but low numbers of orders, may need training in analysing customer needs (and thus making the right proposals), presenting proposals, or closing. These ratios, of quantitative activity to result, provide valuable clues. To pinpoint what is actually happening, the sales manager needs to conduct field sales accompaniments to collect qualitative data.

The process of field sales accompaniment – accompanying the sales person on actual customer calls – should form an important part of the workload of a first-line sales manager. It will not only identify individual training needs, but is also one of the most powerful media for addressing such needs; one-to-one coaching on the job. A brief reprise of the principles involved is appropriate.

Field sales training

Perhaps the first principle is the clear understanding that it is the line manager's accountability to train and develop his or her staff. Any training specialists must be positioned as a 'staff' (i.e. not 'line') function. Nowhere is this more critical than in sales training, as there are very few instances where good, regular, frequent field sales coaching can be bettered.

In my opinion, the first-line sales manager should spend at least one full day per month with each of his/her sales people, observing a typical working day, and coaching to improve skills. The purpose of this day should be field sales training, not customer public relations, or helping the sales person close a difficult case, or whatever. The latter should be regarded as over and above the training day. One day per month should be seen as a minimum; one day a week *205* would be worthwhile. A new entrant, or someone experiencing particular difficulties, should receive more. Spans of control need to be taken into account in arriving at a sensible balance.

Making such accompaniments regular and frequent is one way of overcoming apprehension on the part of the subordinate that 'the boss is checking on me'. It is essential that the process is seen as supportive and positive, not as a threat. Thus, the sales manager should give suitable warning (1–2 weeks), not just arrive unexpectedly, and should take the trouble to position the exercise.

Before each call, the sales manager should review the pre-call preparation with the sales person and agree a call objective and strategy. The latter should include the roles both parties will play, and some 'signalling' system for 'passing the control' between the parties, if this is appropriate.

Normally, the manager's role would be that of 'observer', and this needs to be explained to the customer in the introductions. Play down the manager role or the customer may not interact normally with the sales person, defeating the object of the visit. To facilitate observation rather than intervention the manager should position him/herself slightly back from the sales person, but be able to observe both customer and sales person. The observer role should be maintained, even to the point of allowing the sale to be lost. Only by being allowed to make mistakes can the sales person learn from them. Premature intervention results in the sales person taking the line 'I was going to do that but you beat me to it', and the manager will never know whether or not this is true. This is one of the hardest things for sales managers to come to grips with, but there are very few situations which the sales person cannot retrieve after the call, and after the learning point has been made.

Agreement should be reached on the standard being met by the sales person, and documented. The debrief should include the setting and recording of the objective for the next call on this customer. Figure 17.1 shows a typical document for recording the skills standard after each call. This is very much a stylized version – it should be designed to reflect the company's specific sales process, and highlight those parts of the process thought to be particularly critical.

A grade – A, B, C or D – should be *agreed* for the items under review. This raises three issues. First, only four grades, disallowing any indecision and obviating meaningless shades between say, 7 and 8 out of 10. Secondly, the assessment role is, by skilful positive questioning, to get the subordinate to recognize for him/herself areas which could be improved, suggest a suitable improvement plan, and, by implication, agree a grading of the current standard. This process is a most important skill of a field sales manager, which could fully justify its own chapter. Chapter 28 on 'Mentoring and coaching' covers the generics. Thirdly, grade the form for the terms under review. It is not necessary to complete *every* box on the form. With an inexperienced trainee, the manager should concentrate on the first steps first. With an experienced person, concentrate on those areas where scope for improvement has been agreed. The standards set should be absolutes for the sales team, not relatives for the individual. In other words, an improvement from D (below standard) would only gain a C (acceptable) if it was up to standard, not just to reflect an improvement by that individual.

Sales process	Observer									Sales Person	
	Call									General comment	Strengths
	1	2	3	4	5	6	7	8			
Preparation											
General Call objective Sales materials											
Approach Establish rapport Gain interest Sell interview											Areas for development
Needs analysis Information Problems Needs											
Presentation Relevant Benefits Sales aids											
Close Objections Buying signals Closing											
Departure drill											Signed Date

Figure 17.1   A stylized field sales accompaniment form

By using this process, the manager not only builds up a hopefully improving trend for each individual, but also develops a strengths and weaknesses matrix for the team. On-the-job coaching will, as mentioned earlier, go a long way to addressing individual training needs. The wider picture will also indicate what training needs are common and may be usefully addressed by more formal off-the-job courses.

STRUCTURING THE SALES TRAINING FUNCTION

Whether your training operation is run by you alone or a multistaffed department, certain training functions need to be addressed. My own operation has functional specialists in each of the areas described below. Smaller operations may need individual staff to be able to perform a variety of tasks.

Research, development and design

The R & D function must be constantly in touch with line managers and operatives to ensure there is an up-to-date appreciation of the real training needs. This should preferably be proactive rather than reactive, implying early communication of company developments which may give rise to a training need (e.g. new markets, new products, and so on).

The research function should also keep up to date with the latest methods of meeting the training needs defined above. This is particularly important where the size of the sales team to be trained is large (Prudential Home Service Division is 12,000 strong). In the latter circumstances, traditional face-to-face training in small groups is often not practical, or cost effective. Hence the full range of alternatives must be explored. These range from distance learning books, audio cassettes, prerecorded video, computer-based distance learning, interactive video, through to satellite broadcasting. The last is in its infancy in the United Kingdom and can only be justified for high volume applications, particularly where immediacy is important. However, there is no doubting its effectiveness, given these circumstances.

Increasingly, ways should be sought to impart *knowledge* by some form of self-managed learning, leaving expensive face-to-face time with a skilled trainer for developing *application skills.*

Once needs are accurately identified, and an appropriate delivery medium is decided, the training can be designed and documented. I strongly recommend the use of a standard format for documenting training plans. Even if only one trainer will do all the delivery, and that trainer is also the training designer, the benefits to be gained in consistently delivering to a standard are significant. When numbers of different trainers will design and follow up the training, any less disciplined approach would be inviting failure.

OFF-THE-JOB DELIVERY

208 Though on-the-job field sales training, by way of one-to-one coaching, is probably the most powerful way of improving sales performance, there is still a place for formal training courses. For one thing, not all sales managers have the skills to delivery on-the-job coaching to the standard required. There are also benefits to be gained from a more formal training environment, removed from job and line management pressures.

Assuming we are addressing skills development, in the context discussed earlier, the groups should be kept small. A ratio of 1 trainer to 12 trainees should be a maximum, with 6–8 being an ideal number if a high proportion of role playing is to be employed (which it should).

Role plays

It is on this specific – sales role playing – that I wish to concentrate. Sales people are often reluctant to role play for a number of reasons which I am sure the reader either knows, or can imagine. The following advice may therefore be useful.

Realism Write up a detailed customer brief. This should, if possible, be based on a true-to-life situation, although some poetic licence can be granted to drive home particular training points. It is often fruitful to ask the trainees to provide these by completing pro formas on selected customers, prior to attending the course. The pro formas need to cover the customer profile, the buyer profile, what approaches will provoke a positive, neutral, or negative buyer response, and so on.

Relieve the pressure Ideally, only the 'customer' and 'sales person' should be present for the role play. The observers should observe on a TV monitor in another room, the picture being relayed (and recorded for later analysis) by closed-circuit TV camera. A lower-cost alternative is to split the group into threes – 'customer', 'salesperson' and 'observer'. By rotating the roles amongst the whole group collusion can be obviated.

Role briefing Position the role plays as a significant responsibility for all participants, but with no one individual being on the spot. The sales role may call for a pause if things get out of hand. The customer must be briefed to avoid the extremes (from ready capitulation to bloody-mindedness) and play it realistic-ally, and the observer must use a structured observation form to give meaningful feedback. The trainer should make it clear that *all* roles are being assessed, not just the sales role. Usually, a realistic customer is critical. this can be facilitated by the briefing notes described earlier, particularly if the 'customer' is playing one of his/her own real customers.

The debrief Always follow the sequence: 'sales person', 'customer', 'observer', 'trainer'. The sales person is often very aware of areas for further improvement. The customer can provide valuable input on how it felt being sold to. The observer should demonstrate an understanding of what was happening, against *209* the sales process being trained. The trainer should bring the key points out of each player and keep the learning experience positive.

ON-THE-JOB FOLLOW-UP

Field accompaniments by the sales manager have already been covered. However, the role of the trainer in field sales accompaniment is slightly different. The emphasis is on *field validation* of the formal training given in the training room. In my own operation we use a behavioural observation document which tracks 19 discrete defined sales behaviours. The field sales trainers record every behaviour observed in the sales call, categorized under the 19 behaviour types, further categorized according to the stage in the sales process being executed by the sales person. Test tapes, where the number and category of behaviours is known, are used to check trainer accuracy, using a statistical technique (which is yet another chapter).

Using this approach, it is possible statistically to correlate behaviours trained on the course against behaviours used in the call (i.e. is the training working?). By coding the call outcome, it is also possible statistically to correlate behaviours used in the call with sales success (i.e. are we training the right behaviours?).

This approach is totally objective, which is significant. Neither the trainee, the line manager, the training deliverer nor the training designer can dispute the findings. The trainee either did, or did not, ask 87 information questions (one of the 19 behaviours referred to) – it is not a matter of opinion or value judgement. This cannot be said of the more simplistic approach suggested earlier for the line manager, where a grade of A, B, C or D against a stage of the sales process is clearly a value judgement. This may not be a problem with a sales manager relating to a direct report. It does become significant with a field training specialist giving feedback to the parties referred to above.

Thus, the role of the field sales training specialist is firstly on-the-job validation. The feedback from this process may result in a review of training delivery, or design, or both. Only after validation should coaching take place.

THE TRAINER

The above functions hint at the 'person profile' of the sales trainer. Again, the generics are covered elsewhere so I confine my comments to sales trainers.

There is a wonderful Yorkshire expression which states: 'them's can, do – them's can't, teach'. No doubt most trainers have had this charge levelled at them at one stage or another. However, I believe it is a particularly strongly held view of sales trainees. As a consultant, I have trained many job roles in many industries, in many countries. I have trained Parts Managers from motor dealerships in techniques of computerized stock control. No one asked me when I last ran a Parts Department. But when training sales people, if they do not actually say it, you can almost hear them thinking 'when did you last sell anything?'. And if you have no sales experience, you have a significant credibility problem.

The problem is not insurmountable, and it is true that the best sales people do not necessarily make the best sales trainers. However, for most purposes, I recommend that the 'person profile' for sales trainers should include a period with a successful track record in selling. Training, and particularly sales training, should not be seen as the refuge for those who could not make it in the 'front line'.

In many companies a spell in the training function is almost a prerequisite for career advancement. This is a philosophy we follow in Prudential, to ensure that sales training always keeps its feet on the ground – even if we expect the R & D function to spend at least some of the time with its head, figuratively speaking, 'in the clouds'.

VALIDATING SALES TRAINING

This subject has been touched on in discussing the role of the field sales trainer. In very broad terms, the sales trainer should constantly ask this question: 'Is what I'm doing going to help our sales people sell extra product, at higher profit margins?' By constantly asking this apparently simple question, proper focus for sales training should result. By proving the answer to the question is affirmative, the ultimate validation is also achieved. However, it is worth being less simplistic, and viewing training validation as a four-stage process. Again, I will bias my comments around the sales training situation.

Reaction

Numerous designs of delegate-reaction forms are handed out at the end of training courses. I do not intend to enter into the argument for or against specific designs. In respect of sales training validation, I believe two factors in particular should be measured. First, was the training *perceived* to be *relevant* to the trainee's job? Sales people are usually commission earning, and understandably resist being taken away from the workplace (and hence ability to earn) for any reason, including training. It is thus *vital* that they perceive that the training will directly help them sell more on returning to the workplace. Secondly, was the training enjoyable? If the sales trainer can deliver training which is perceived to be relevant in an enjoyable, motivational manner, then the further stages of validation are likely to follow.

Knowledge

What does the trainee know as a result of the training? It may be useful to pre- and post-test, to establish a measure of learning. Certainly, a final standard should be established. As mentioned in the early part of this chapter, some industries are regulated by law – the Financial Services Act being relevant in the case of Prudential. Accordingly, Prudential sales people are 'licensed' (by LAUTRO – the Life Assurance and Unit Trust Regulatory Organisation in general, and by the company in terms of specifics). Each product carries a licence seal, without which the sales person is not permitted to sell it. The seal is granted on *211* acquiring product knowledge via distance learning booklets and/or CBT, which is tested, in this case by multiple choice test papers.

Behaviour

Knowing 'how to' is one thing: being 'able to' is another. Hence the importance of behavioural validation; can the sales person apply the knowledge in such a way as to identify and solve customer problems and achieve a sale? Behavioural results of training should be validated off the job by using structured observation forms to evaluate role plays. It should be validated on the job by field sales accompaniments. Both processes have already been covered. If the trainee is proved to be able to do the right things in a sales situation (simulated or real) then the final stage of validation should follow.

Results

We have come full circle. Remember the opening question. 'Is what I'm doing going to help our sales people sell extra product, at higher profit margins?' If investment in sales training is to be justified, this is the ultimate test. A word of caution, though. The further down the validation process, the more tenuous the link between trainer input and the outcome. A good or poor reaction is almost entirely under the control of the trainer. At the result end of the equation, many factors other than training have an influence. For example:

- Is the product design right, and is it correctly packaged, priced, advertised, etc?
- What is the competition doing?
- Is the sales force correctly motivated and directed?

A good sales training programme can impact significantly on the sales result. Indeed, good sales performance almost always results from good sales training. However, the investment/return equation is not easy to determine. I do not advocate that it should not be undertaken, only that the assessment should be tough but realistic.

CONCLUSION

This has been a brief argument in favour of training the sales force, and has visited some of the key areas for consideration. As a starting point, sales managers need to play their part, and the role of field sales training by the line manager should not be underestimated. Done well, this can also be a finishing point. This is not to demean the role of the sales training specialist. This chapter started with the question 'why train the sales force?'. I hope the value of sales training has been established. Perhaps a quote from my General Manager would provide an appropriate finishing point: 'If I had to choose between marketing and sales training against a limited discretionary budget, I would invest in sales training.'

FURTHER READING

Forsyth, P. (ed.) (1984), *Managing Sales and Marketing Training*, Gower.
Lidstone, J. (1986). *Training Salesmen on the Job*, 2nd edn, Gower.
Lidstone, J. (1991), *Manual of Sales Negotiation*, Gower.

18 Performance appraisal

Andrew Stewart

A great deal has been written about performance appraisal. A great deal more has been said. It is odd that, despite all this attention, so few organizations say that they are satisfied with their particular way of conducting appraisals of employee performance. It is all the more strange since the task is, in principle, very straightforward. Two people, one the manager and one the managed, sit down together perhaps once during the year, in order to find answers to the following four questions:

- What did we set out to achieve during the year?
- Have we achieved it?
- What are we going to do next?
- How will we know if we have done it?

Anything more elaborate than the above could be said to be complicating a simple matter more than it merits, and to the confusion of all concerned. This chapter presents some of the approaches that have been adopted to try to obtain satisfactory answers to those four questions.

First, some of the more usual varieties of appraisal system will be described, together with a discussion of the performance criteria associated with them. Some comments will be offered about system design, and this will be followed by an account of some of the ways in which organizations try to train their managers to use their systems. Ways in which systems can be monitored and controlled will be presented, and then two further issues will be explored which often cause difficulty: assessing potential, and problem performers. Some future trends will also be discussed. Finally, there will be a simple checklist to help managers to ensure that all necessary steps towards a successful performance appraisal interview have been carried out.

VARIETIES OF SYSTEM

214 People do not learn unless they are given feedback on the results of their actions. For learning to take place, feedback must be both regular and frequent, should register both successes and failures, and should follow soon after the relevant actions. In the daily rush of getting things done, much of this can be forgotten or not put into effect. Performance appraisal schemes give people the chance to learn how they are doing, to correct their mistakes and to acquire new skills. Since manager and appraisee are together reviewing past performance and planning to meet the needs of the future, it should follow that some of the necessary conditions for the successful management of change are also being met. A performance appraisal scheme can also offer the opportunity to consider and agree longer-range targets for achievement, thus making positive growth more likely for the organization, and avoiding the trap of doing nothing more than daily firefighting. Finally, since employees are expensive, it makes sense to try to encourage their best efforts. A performance appraisal interview can be one of the most motivating events in an employee's year. Badly handled, it can be a disaster.

There are usually four parties to an appraisal: the appraisee, the appraiser, the central planning and personnel departments, and external bodies such as training organizations, trade unions and bodies set up in the interests of equal opportunity legislation. The interests of the first two parties should dominate. If the main focus is either planning or defence, then the chief objective of the exercise may be lost.

Appraisal systems may be used for three main purposes: remedial, mainten-ance and development. A system should have a mix of all three. Systems become out of balance if any one purpose predominates. If the remedial purpose is foremost, then the appraisal interview may become a disciplinary interview, and the form a charge sheet. If maintenance is the main objective, then the process can become a short, skimped, unthoughtful ritual. If there is too much emphasis on development, then the focus falls on the next job rather than the one presently in hand, and the interview may be construed as a promise of future progress.

Above all, the appraisal interview is a time for listening. The appraisee probably has a good idea of how his or her performance appears to him or her, and this is unlikely to be badly at variance with his or her manager's view. Indeed, there is some evidence that an appraisee is likely to be harder on him/herself than his or her manager intends to be.

Many variations in appraisal systems have been tried in order to support the basic purpose of looking backwards in order to look forward. The chief ones appear to be:

1. Eligibility: all staff, or managers and salaried staff only.
2. Appraiser: immediate line manager, technical specialist, personnel specialist, 'grandfather' or 'grandmother' (manager's manager).
3. Employee access: employee sees all the form, some of the form, or none of the form.
4. Self-appraisal or preparation-for-counselling form used, or not used.
5. Past performance only, or past and present performance measured.
6. Measurement against: performance targets or objectives, rating scales of   *215*

performance, rating scales of personality, or no measurement criteria specified.

7. Rating scales: present or absent, together with variation in the number of divisions on the scale.
8. Opportunity to set targets for future performance, or not.
9. Discussion of training and development needs: for present job, for next job, or for longer term.
10. Potential rated: on a one-dimensional scale, a multidimensional scale, or no formal rating of potential.
11. Discussion of salary: forbidden, mandatory, or optional.
12. Frequency and regularity of appraisal interviews.
13. Disputes: resolved by appeal to grandfather, or personnel, or no procedure.
14. Who may see the appraisal forms, and for what purpose.
15. Use of forms for central planning purposes.
16. Use of forms for day-to-day management and coaching purposes.

Each of these variations is held to be helpful by different practitioners, depending on the circumstances in which they are working. It is not possible to offer a single best method, merely a selection from which a choice may be made. The area which seems to cause the most anxiety, however, is the link with salary.

If salary is seen as compensation for work done, then perhaps the link with performance is more tenuous. If salary is used as an incentive, to reward outstanding work and to encourage rising standards, then some form of link seems inevitable. If salary review and performance appraisal occur at the same time, there may be a tendency to drift the rating unjustifiably upwards in order to be able to offer a satisfactory increase. One way to prevent this is to have both performance and salary rated on the same scale and in the same way, but to have the events occur six months apart. In this way all concerned understand the system, but managers have the freedom to vary the salary rating if the employee's performance has either improved or worsened since the performance review.

PERFORMANCE CRITERIA

In order to be satisfactory, both to those directly involved and to the law, the criteria for a performance appraisal system should be genuinely related to success or failure in the job, and should be as far as possible amenable to objective, not subjective, judgement. In addition, it is helpful if they are easy for the manager to administer, appear fair and relevant to the employee, and strike a fair balance between sensitivity to the needs of the present job and applicability to the company as a whole.

Most appraisal systems offer some guidance to appraising managers on the way they should measure performance. There are two principal kinds of measure: personality measures and performance measures.

Personality measures have largely fallen into disuse. They are difficult to apply reliably, depend too much on the quality of personal relationships rather than employee performance, and if the employee is judged deficient on a personality measure there may be little incentive or ability to change. Their use is now generally discouraged.

Performance measures have replaced personality measures in most cases. They have two main forms. There are rating scales which are generally printed on the form and held to apply to all employees. There are objectives, which are an individual performance measure, agreed between manager and employee. Rating scales allow the measurement of change in one employee over time. They also allow comparisons between employees. They are, therefore, necessary if the appraisal records are to be used for any kind of central manpower audit, leading to the planning of salaries, careers or succession. They have the disadvantage that not all scales may be equally applicable to all employees, and that managers may not share similar standards in the use of the scales. Objectives give greater freedom to both manager and the employee in deciding how performance will be measured. They may also have a greater motivational effect by demanding that standards be discussed and understood by manager and employee, whereas rating scales can be imposed without the opportunity for understanding. The disadvantage of objectives is that no common yardstick may exist between different appraisers and appraisees. It may be possible and desirable to have both rating scales and objectives in one system.

Personality measures might include such items as drive, loyalty or integrity. Performance measures might include accuracy, clarity, analytical ability. Objectives might include 'sell x widgets by y date to z customers'. Clearly these measures are offered in increasing order of precision. Some systems have aimed at the maximum precision at the expense of measuring what is important but not easily quantifiable. Under these circumstances, a qualitative measure, the meaning of which is clear to both parties to the interview, is probably preferable to a quantitative measure which assesses with great accuracy something which is not important.

The derivation of performance criteria demands research. A specification for the universally effective employee does not seem likely to be a realistic target. Each organization should evolve its own performance measures, and should monitor them continuously to ensure their relevance. The needs of organizations and individuals change. If the performance criteria do not change as well, preferably a little ahead of the need, then the appraisal system will serve no useful purpose, and may even do damage by insisting on performance measures which no longer relate to the work in hand. A variety of methods for establishing performance criteria will be found in the chapters on diagnosing needs.

SYSTEM DESIGN

Each of the four main parties to an appraisal has different but overlapping purposes, all of which have implications for system design.

The appraisee will wish to make a contribution to the appraisal process, which *217* implies a face-to-face interview. If acceptance of the appraiser's evaluation is to be indicated, or at least evidence that the appraisee has seen the comments is required, then the appraisee may need to sign the form at the end of the interview. If there is to be an opportunity for long-term guidance, then the system will need to provide for planning or objective setting for the future, together with discussion of ambitions, training needs, and abilities not yet evidenced in the work currently being done. If appraisal is to be used for self-development, then goals will need to be agreed during the interview, some variety of preparation for counselling form might be helpful, written objectives should be retained by both manager and appraisee, and there should be further mini-appraisals during the year.

The appraiser will want the employee to work to agreed goals, which implies the setting and recording of objectives and personal goals. These goals may need co-ordinating with those of other employees, which will require control over the timing of appraisals from the top of the organization downwards, with the minimum time lag possible between appraisals at top and bottom, and fairly close co-ordination and control of appraisals from the centre. Coaching the employee will require the setting of specific performance targets, as much as possible suggested by the employee, including both targets and measures, and both parties will need to keep records and use them for frequent and regular reviews. To encourage the appraiser to listen to the employee, a preparation for counselling form should be strongly encouraged, and the appraiser may wish to record the employee's comments separately, possibly for later integration. In order to make the early detection of problems more likely, general, open-ended questions should be used concerning aspirations, unused skills, constraints on performance and other self-rating techniques. The preparation-for-counselling form can be a vital aid here, as can the need for the grandfather to sign off the appraisal form before the interview takes place. In this way it is also possible to achieve some measure of equity between employees. The management information system can also be used to detect broken trends or unusual patterns if rating scales are being used. If the training of subordinates is to be controlled, then there needs to be a record of both training needs and the extent to which they are being met. If money is being used as compensation, then a salary increase may be communicated at the appraisal interview, since pay and performance are not directly linked. If money is being used as an incentive, then it is suggested that the salary review should be a separate but related exercise.

Central planning and control may have a wide range of purposes, but some of the most common are mentioned here. A manpower skills audit will require that there are some common performance criteria across all employees, and that there be central collation of measures on these criteria. For manpower planning purposes the form may need to record not only the employee's performance as measured on required characteristics, but also information about age, job history, mobility, family circumstances. Succession planning also requires that some form of assessment of employee potential takes place, as objectively as possible, and that information about employee aspirations, judged suitability, and current performance is co-ordinated. Salary planning may require that the manager gives an overall performance rating across all characteristics, and central collation will be necessary, either with or without intervention to produce conformity to agreed norms. A record of training needs will be needed if overall decisions about training priorities are to be taken on an informed basis. Equity between employees can be monitored by defining and communicating the scope of the scheme to all concerned, by grandfather signing off appraisal ratings, by central monitoring of both quality and promptness of appraisals, and by a formal system for handling unsatisfactory performers. Problem and grievance detection and handling becomes easier if the employee signs off the completed form, if the employee is invited to comment on the form, if grandfather or central personnel have the power to intervene in critical situations, and if there is a formally defined and agreed procedure for improving the performance of those judged to be unsatisfactory, followed by a declared system for asking them to leave the organization. Finally, downward transmission of organization objectives can be achieved by centrally co-ordinated cascading of appraisals, so that no manager is put into the position of having to agree objectives with a subordinate in the absence of their own agreed objectives.

Outside parties can also have interests which impinge on the appraisal system. Industry training bodies may lay down requirements for schemes, compliance with which offers levy exemption. Local, industry or national codes of good practice can usually be adhered to by ensuring that the performance criteria are relevant to the job, that no group of employees is given special treatment, and that appropriate guidance is offered on the use of appraisals with poor performers. Pay restraint has been a feature of many political programmes in the recent past. In this case, the system needs to ensure that both immediate parties to the appraisal understand clearly the restrictions on the manager's discretion, and increased use needs to be made of the remaining motivational characteristics of appraisal. Finally, privacy or right of access legislation may require that forms be designed so that the employee can see the whole form, adequate safeguards are in place against misleading interpretation – such as employee sign off and comment space – a formal grievance procedure is in place, and there is a clear policy about who has access to appraisal data and for what purposes, together with location and duration of storage of records. This is now a particularly sensitive area where any part of the records is stored in a computer.

Rather than approaching this set of problems in terms of the various purposes of the parties involved, it is very common to spend much time and effort designing the paperwork. Given the strong arguments sometimes put forward for a blank piece of paper being the ideal appraisal form, some of this enthusiasm may be misplaced. Assuming, however, that the purposes have been thoroughly investigated, certain specifics then need clarification. If individual objectives are to form the core of the process, then a common form is simply a blank piece of paper divided down the middle, with objectives on the left-hand side and standards of performance on the right. It is important to offer some guidance so that managers do not try to set too many objectives, try to set objectives to cover *219* the whole job, or only set as objectives those things than can be measured quantitatively.

If narrative summaries are to be used, then the form will contain a list of key words, such as accuracy, speed, cash control, or timing, and the manager will be asked to write a two-line summary of the employee's performance on each of these characteristics. This method has the advantage that it does apply common yardsticks across large groups of people, but does not demand undue precision. Differences may occur in the way in which individual managers interpret and judge these characteristics, however.

Rating scales require that the appraisee is rated on each characteristic, using a scale with a number of divisions. While useful, rating scales carry some issues which need resolution. There is no point in offering more than five divisions on the scale. Scales with seven, nine, or even thirteen points have been seen. Managers tend to use them as if they were slightly vague five-point scales. There is often dispute about whether there should be an odd or even number of points on the scale. It is possible to avoid this discussion entirely in the following way. Label the points on the scale, avoiding the use of the word average, so that the first four are concerned with above-the-line performance and only the fifth records below-the-line work. For example:

- Exceeds in all respects.
- Exceeds in most respects.
- Exceeds in some respects.
- Meets basic requirements.
- Fails to meet basic requirements.

In this way, ratings are being made against the requirements of the job and not against colleagues, and the scale can be described either as a five-point scale, or as a four-point scale with an extra box for the unsatisfactory performer. It can also be helpful to offer a separate 'not applicable' box. Any overall rating should follow the separate rating scales, preferably at a distance. It might also be useful to consider a separate column to record immediate past performance. This emphasizes the fact that the appraisal is supposed to be a review of the entire previous year, and allows any recent changes in performance to be noted without unduly affecting the rest of the year's evaluation.

Perhaps the most important consideration in system design is to ensure that the system responds to the developing needs of all those using it, and to avoid the situation in which an entrenched system dictates inappropriate behaviour by those upon whom it is inflicted.

TRAINING

Appraisal training falls into three parts. They need to be kept distinct and to be carried out in the sequence shown, otherwise confusion and ineffective implementation are almost certain. The first stage involves obtaining managers' commitment. The second stage trains them in the formal systems and procedures. The third stage trains them in the necessary interview and inter-personal skills.

Commitment

Commitment is best obtained by holding a series of meetings at which all those who will be affected by the system have an opportunity to hear what is being proposed to discuss it. It may be helpful to lobby one or two key managers in advance; there should be a clear statement about the purposes of the appraisal system, there should be a readiness to negotiate about system design, but it is better to avoid being side-tracked into form design. This should follow as simply as possible from the agreement of purposes. It may also help to de-emphasize the judgemental role of the appraiser and to stress the benefits that employees will gain from being appraised – in other words, help them discover what they will be able to do as a result of appraisal which would otherwise have been difficult or unlikely. If no such benefits are apparent, the value of the system as proposed must be questioned.

Systems and procedures

Training the systems and procedures should only occur after commitment has been obtained, otherwise much time will be consumed trying to answer the question 'why' when the training is designed to answer the question 'what'. This stage of the training should include the history of the appraisal system and the organizational problems it is supposed to solve, what actually happens in the interview, how the form is filled in, when, and by whom, who receives the form, what happens to the information, and whose responsibility is to see that actions recommended on the form are actually carried out. Special emphasis should be given to ensuring that managers understand the grievance and poor-performer procedures. Practice in handling and completing forms should be offered, together with the opportunity to criticize and spot mistakes in forms already completed. This stage of the training would respond well to some form of programmed instruction, either in text form or on a computer.

Interview and interpersonal skills

Training in skills depends on successful completion of the previous two stages, otherwise disruption is highly likely. Three training techniques may be worth considering.

Role play

Role play is used automatically by many trainers. It can have many drawbacks, including the passivity of most of the audience and the fact that participants can always opt out by stating, correctly, that it is not real life. Poorly chosen role plays can compound these difficulties. Role play can be useful, however, particularly *221* where attitude change is important. Trainees can be asked to play the part of someone whose attitude they need to understand, such as someone passed over for promotion. They can also be useful in unfreezing people by trying on a completely new appraisal personality.

Real-life counselling

Real-life counselling involves one participant counselling another about a genuine work or personal problem, while the remaining participants observe. This certainly lacks the artificiality of role plays, but can get a little sharp. For this reason, perhaps, it is generally a better vehicle for learning counselling skills than the normal role play.

Live appraisal

Live appraisal of real tasks involves the following sequence:

1. A participant performs an appraisable activity while the remainder of the small group observe.
2. All prepare to appraise the volunteer, who prepares to be appraised.
3. One person then appraises while the rest observe.
4. All prepare to appraise the appraisal, while the appraiser prepares to be appraised.
5. One person then appraises the appraisal, while the rest observe.

This module can be repeated as often as necessary, and concludes with a general review. The exact nature of the kick-off task is relatively unimportant, so long as there is enough to appraise. Subsequent appraisals quickly become surprisingly real, and the whole approach can be highly successful at making apparent issues of objectives, standards and measurement. Rich feedback is essential, and should be as accurate as possible, backed perhaps by video recording the entire episode. Objective matters should predominate, such as the balance of talking at various points of the interview, the amount of time devoted to extremes of performance versus the amount of time used to talk about the regular performance, the use of open and closed questions, and the amount of positive versus negative feedback offered.

An interesting variant is to offer training in being appraised. This has worked particularly well where managers have been reluctant to appraise or to be trained. The prospect of their subordinates being better equipped than they are has sometimes led to both appraiser and appraisee being better equipped to fulfil their roles.

Issues arising

222   The most common issues arising in the skills-training stage include:

1. Knowing one's own biases.
2. Being prepared to discuss both good and poor performance in a straightforward manner.
3. Using open, closed or reflective questions.
4. Handling conflict.
5. Listening and summarizing skills.

Common pitfalls

The most common pitfalls encountered in appraisal, which therefore require to be looked at in training, include:

1. The halo effect.
2. Avoiding extremes of rating.
3. Talking too much.
4. Failing to support opinions with evidence.
5. Inadequate briefing of the appraisee.
6. Pre-judging performance.
7. Not allowing adequate time for the interview.
8. Not choosing the right environment.
9. Basing assessments on feelings rather than facts.
10. Over-stating weaknesses or strengths.
11. Failing to take account of special circumstances.
12. Basing judgements on too short a time span.
13. Making false assumptions.

Understandably, looking at that list, skills training can be a fairly intense experience which has benefits well beyond the immediate task of the appraisal interview.

MONITORING AND CONTROL

All appraisal systems need constant monitoring, and from time to time they need alteration of some kind. In the early implementation of a system the designer should look out for two main kinds of misunderstanding.

Misunderstanding of terms may occur, particularly such common ones as objective, job description, man specification, training needs, development needs, counselling, personality, performance and behaviour. These may well be familiar to trainers and management developers, but many line managers have no real idea of what is meant by them, or may have developed some eccentric definitions.

Misunderstanding the system will be shown by forms going to the wrong place or being filled in late, inadequate coverage of certain employees or groups, peculiar use of rating scales, or partial completion of the forms.

Later on, as part of a more general research programme, some other types of monitoring may seem possible and appropriate. Appraisal action may be *223* checked by following up the actions recommended on the appraisal forms to see if anything has actually happened as a result. The types of objectives set can also be reviewed as part of this process. Appraisal predictions, particularly of potential, can be checked to see if they are actually proved to be correct in practice. Employee attitudes can be checked, either with a purpose designed survey or as part of a larger attitude survey. Examples of some items that have proved significant indicators of effective interviews in the past include:

- I had a clear idea of his/her career path.
- He/she and I had the same idea about the direction of his/her career.
- My manager agreed with my rating.
- My rating came as no surprise to him/her.
- She/he accepted my rating of her/him.
- My manager agreed with my rating of her/him.
- She/he fitted in with the rest of the work group.
- We wanted the same outcome from the interview.
- I could visualize him/her as my manager some day.

Whether the interview was conducted in the office or outside, and whether the manager had selected the employee for the job initially or not, were not significantly related to the effectiveness of the interview.

As any survey of employee options will increase their expectations, there should be a policy about feedback of results, a method of feeding back locally useful results fast, and a commitment by top management to action should the results indicate a need for change.

IDENTIFYING POTENTIAL

Performance appraisal is designed to look backwards in order to look forwards. The best predictions of potential, using performance appraisal as the basis, are made when the next job is not greatly different from the previous one. The greater the proportion of new demands, the less likely that track record alone will suffice. Performance appraisal seems to be essential but insufficient as a predictor of future performance.

Objections to the use of performance appraisal records for the prediction of potential include the following. Single-scale measures of potential, such as most systems still use, are too simple to permit a full statement of what the employee may be able to do. Although supported with words, it is the number that goes into the manpower planning system. In addition, a statement of the kind 'ready for next move in x months/years', if seen by the employee, can be construed as a promise. Managers' confidence in their ability to make ratings of potential is usually very low, and they are very rarely trained in using the potential assessment part of the form. Thus, they receive the least support at precisely the point where they feel they most need it. Managers find it difficult to assess the potential for positions much above their own or in parts of the organization with
224 which they are not familiar. Promotion solely on the basis of past performance

almost inevitably leads to promotion to the person's level of incompetence. Discontinuities in the system will occur, where past performance is a particularly poor indicator of success in the next job, for example, the first move from a non-management to a management position.

Poor performers who are in the wrong job are difficult for the system to detect. For them, appraising potential on the basis of past performance is doubly unfair. Finally, in the absence of experience, the appraisee has no basis for judging whether the post under consideration would appeal to them. The more people know about the job for which they are being considered, the more likely it is that they will succeed in it.

There are many alternatives and additions available to performance appraisal as a means of identifying potential. These include assessment centres, psychological tests, assignments, secondments, peer and self-assessment and action-learning programmes. Ideally, ratings of potential should involve the use of more than one criterion or trait, more than one assessor, and more than one technique. In this way a more reliable judgement may be reached.

If the performance appraisal system is to play a useful part in the prediction of potential, then it should ensure that appraisal is on the basis of performance, not personality. The performance criteria should be related to success in the job for which potential is being assessed. Appraising managers should be trained to use this part of the form and to extract appropriate information during the interview and at other times. Promises of specific jobs should neither be made nor implied. Preparation for counselling forms should be used. Ratings of potential should be checked as a matter of course rather than as part of the grievance procedure. There should not be sudden and significant discontinuities in the requirements for jobs in adjacent grades. Finally, there should be a buyer's market for important staff.

Unsupported by other techniques, performance appraisal can be seriously misleading as a predictor of potential. The information which it yields is a vital component of any decision reached by whatever other methods may be used.

PROBLEM PERFORMERS

People perform unsatisfactorily for a wide variety of reasons. The first task is to discover which particular combination of reasons applies in the specific case. The problem may lie in a number of factors:

- Intelligence – too little, too much, specific defects of judgement or memory.
- Emotional stability – over-excitable, anxious, depressed, jealous, sexual problems, neurosis, psychosis, alcoholism, drug addiction.
- Motivation to work – low motivation, low work standards, lack of organization, frustration, conflict.
- Family situation – domestic crises, separation from family, social isolation from peer group, money worries.

- Physical characteristics – illness, handicap, strength, age, endurance, build.
- Work groups – fragmented, over-cohesive, inappropriate leadership, wrong mix of personalities.
- The organization – inappropriate standards, poor communication, too little investment and management support, span of control too large, responsibility without authority.
- External influences – employment legislation, consumer pressure, safety legislation, changing social values, economic forces, changes in location.

The appraisal system can be used as part of the process for dismissing people who do not perform satisfactorily. Alternatively, and preferably, it can be used to manage those people so that their performance improves. This can be achieved in a number of ways:

- Counselling – self-appraisal, preparation for counselling, some form of job climate questionnaire, vocational guidance, mid-career guidance, medical help, financial counselling.
- Training and development – as a reward and encouragement, not punishment, set up with precise, measurable objectives, careful monitoring and close follow-up.
- Changing the job – physical layout, timing, induction, responsibility without authority, no feedback on performance, late or distorted feedback on performance, too many figurehead duties, little or no control over the job content, insufficient warning of changes, shared management of subordinates.
- Termination – which does not have to be rushed or graceless, can take proper account of financial arrangements, time off to look for a new job, vocational guidance, interview training and exit interview.

Note particularly that there is an option to change jobs within the organization. Several appraisal schemes specifically exclude this possibility. The options there are either to improve performance in present post to an acceptable standard, or to dismiss. This runs the serious risk of sending away someone who could do a perfectly satisfactory job if they were in the right place. While the logic of not wanting managers to shuffle poor performers around the system instead of addressing uncomfortable issues cannot be denied, it seems potentially wasteful to make a rigid rule that prohibits trying an employee in a different role.

There are particular groups who perform badly simply because they are unhappy or bewildered in some way. These people might include new graduates who are experiencing a mismatch of abilities and assigned task with inadequate induction. Older employees might be feeling that they have reached their ceiling or be experiencing difficulty with the slower learning patterns that can come with older age groups. People without clear career paths would appreciate information and options. People with a sad history in the organization need help to discover whether the problem is real and not merely a reputation which is following them around without justification. The performance appraisal system should be able to generate information, objectives and controls to assist with most of these situations, making the unhappy necessity to dismiss for poor performance rarer, but more sure-footed when it does occur.

FUTURE TRENDS

The only certain thing about today's business environment is that it is changing rapidly and somewhat unpredictably. It follows that no performance appraisal system should expect to be the same in five years' time as it is now. There is therefore a need for continuous monitoring and control of the relevance of the system to the organization's shifting requirements.

Some of the primary influences on the change as it affects performance appraisal include increasing public scrutiny of performance criteria, coupled with open record systems. It does after all, seem perverse to deny access to information about someone when that someone is the person who might benefit most from knowing it – quite apart from the ethical issue about whether there is any right to deny access to information about an individual to that individual. Self-appraisal is a growing component of many systems, and is a logical outgrowth of the open record. The increase of on-the-job training and self-development, wherein people take responsibility for their own learning, increases the inevitability of self-appraisal, and matrix management makes the older, hierarchical approach to performance appraisal almost unworkable.

Pressure towards professional and technical career paths to parallel the more traditional managerial career progression also puts pressure on performance-appraisal systems. Managers have to be better informed about the technology they are managing, or have to hand over some of the responsibility for appraising performance to those who do not manage but do perform a technical/professional function.

Special efforts need to be made to counsel those who are experiencing mid-career change, possibly coupled with personal life crisis. The phenomenon of middle managers who feel that their worth is in question, reinforced maybe by redundancy, is more common. Many more people are now questioning whether they are pursuing the right path, and would welcome informed advice about alternatives. There are pressures to bureaucratize. While it is true that some of these pressures can legitimately be traced to the door of government at various levels, more come directly from within the organization. The first reaction to difficult trading conditions is often to tighten controls and to administer more effectively what is already there, rather than go all out to discover new ways to do things or new things to do. Under these circumstances, negative feedback and talk of where people are failing, becomes the norm, and the appraisal system becomes the vehicle for stifling initiative and motivation rather than a stimulus to new directions and originality.

There is a feeling that smaller business units may be helpful. Some organizations have become too large to manage, and breaking up the monolith into *227* more viable pieces needs to be accompanied by local control and adaptation of the appraisal scheme. It might be necessary for the large unit to put things on to a computer, but a manual system may be perfectly adequate for the smaller organization. The move to smaller units offers an encouraging chance to simplify over elaborate systems.

Finally, there is a greater inclination to treat people as valuable investments, not merely as units in a card index or computer file. The return to an organization on investment in good recruitment, selection, induction, appraisal and assessment of potential practices is now more rarely questioned. Performance appraisal systems are being seen as less concerned with discipline, control and record-keeping, and more oriented towards development, self-development and growth. This seems to me to be a useful trend.

APPENDIX: PERFORMANCE REVIEW SEQUENCE

The following is offered as a rough guide to the sequence of events which a manager might wish to initiate in order to be fairly sure that nothing of importance in the performance appraisal process has been overlooked:

1. Agree a time and date for the review well in advance.
2. Arrange for the location to be private and free from interruptions.
3. Set aside at least an hour and a half, and possibly two and a half hours.
4. Bring all relevant results and information concerning the appraisee's performance in his or her area of responsibility.
5. Ask the appraisee to review his or her performance in the work situation point by point.
6. Ask the appraisee about any problems which might affect performance.
7. Ask the appraisee about the implications of any problems or events, and their effect on the individual, the team and the work.
8. Ask the appraisee what needs to be done by either of them to help improve performance.
9. The appraisee should ask about anything which he or she feels is affecting his or her performance.
10. Agree the key result areas.
11. The appraisee should set/agree standards of performance for the next review period.
12. The manager should set/agree standards of performance for the next review period.
13. Agree future action.
14. Close with a firm date for the next interim review.

FURTHER READING

Boyatzis, R.E. (1982), *The Competent Manager*, Wiley.
Fletcher, C. (1993), *Appraisal – routes to improved performance*, IPM.

Fletcher, C. and R. Williams (1985), *Performance Appraisal and Career Management*, Hutchinson.

Handy, C.A. (1985), *Understanding Organisations*, 3rd edn, Penguin.

Stewart, V. and A. Stewart (1977), *Practical Performance Appraisal*, Gower.

Stewart, V. and A. Stewart (1982), *Managing the Poor Performer*, Gower.

19 Using evaluation techniques
Bernard Wynne and David Clutterbuck

Evaluation of training has always been difficult, and it is perhaps worth considering why. Generally, trainers have not liked the idea of other people auditing what they do. They have not been very happy with the evaluation techniques that have been applied. It is also true to say in their defence that many of the traditional techniques have been more concerned with form-filling and report-writing than with delivering the goods. While regretting the demise of the training organizations – because of the danger of losing focus and emphasis on training – many were grateful to see them go because of the bureaucratic systems they required of trainers.

Looked at from another perspective, the lack of effective evaluation can be seen as responsible for keeping training in a subordinate, non-strategic role within many organizations. Most aspects of a business come under the scrutiny of the board from time to time. Boards have been interested in looking at costs in relation to benefits delivered by marketing, finance, research and operations divisions. They have largely been unable to do so in relation to training. The result has been a lack of management information, which may have contributed to a lack of belief in the ability of the training function to input at a strategic level into business as a whole.

All managers and trainers should be asking: 'What are the benefits of training?' They should be seeking to put into place systems of measurement which will assist in the assessment of the benefits. Without systems of measurement, evaluation cannot be carried out.

This chapter will aim to introduce to managers and trainers a range of techniques which they can use to assess the effectiveness of the training they are delivering. Before looking at techniques, however, it is important to see evaluation as an integral part of the training cycle (see Figure 19.1). Evaluation may appear to be the final phase of the training cycle, but consideration should be given to it at each stage. It is also important to build it in as a phase on its own in order to evaluate the total process.

The starting point for any attempt to evaluate the effectiveness of training has

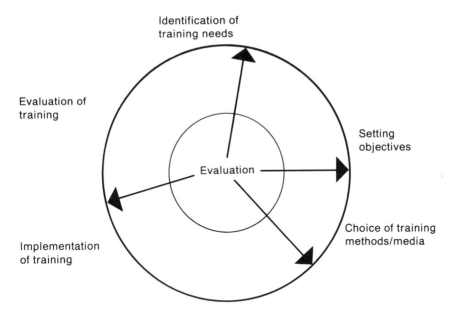

Figure 19.1   The training cycle

to be the relationship between training and the strategic objectives of the company. The trainer clearly needs to be aware of the strategic objectives and relate these to the most effective training response. In the most progressive organizations, the human resources view will be considered during the setting of strategic objectives and will not be seen to be bringing up the rear. Many organizations, however, still make strategic decisions which have a massive impact on the training requirements and manpower resources of an organization without paying any attention to such requirements. Therefore, not only should training relate to the strategic needs of the business; it should aim to be party to setting the strategic objectives.

Assuming that a set of clear and effective strategic objectives exists, the trainer needs to ask a series of questions, as follows:

- If we are to achieve these strategic objectives, what are the implications for the skills, attitudes and knowledge of all the people at various levels throughout the company?
- What is the current position and does that indicate any gaps in skills, knowledge and attitude?
- Can I design an effective training response to bridge this gap?
- How will I know when I have achieved success?

The last question above is the most important. Also, before decisions are made, the trainer will need to carry out an identification of training needs. Without a *231* clear identification of need and an assessment of the current level of skill, measurement will be difficult.

Before beginning any specific training intervention, the trainer should set clear and measurable objectives. Here the trainer needs to define:

- the skills it is proposed to teach;
- how and why they are needed;
- the method to be used;
- how the trainee will demonstrate that the skills have been learned; and
- how the trainer will assess that the learning has been applied.

Objectives are always more effective when set in behavioural terms – terms which describe the expected behaviour at the output of training. For example, which of the following objectives would most effectively assist the application and measurement (evaluation) of the training?

1. *Course objective*   To train managers to conduct interviews.

or

2. *Course objectives*   On completion of training managers will:

- understand the purpose of an appraisal interview;
- have developed effective listening and giving feedback skills;
- have practised these skills in simulated role plays; and
- have received feedback on their performance.

It is clear that in the second case the trainer is much more likely to be able to measure his or her effectiveness than in the first, where the objective is set for the trainer and related to the input. In the second example the objectives are related to the trainee and concerned with outputs. The problem with measuring inputs is that all you can really hope to do is to measure the content of the training and not whether people have achieved the learning required – and more importantly whether they have applied it.

Once objectives have been set, the trainer can turn to methods of implementation, a subject which is considered in other parts of this handbook. However the choice of media and method of implementation also has an impact on evaluation, and must be evaluated as part of the training cycle as well as form part of a final evaluation of the whole process. The choice of method and media can have significant effects on the measurement and assessment of the outcome.

Having identified needs, set objectives and chosen the media we can now concentrate on post-training evaluation.

WHAT IS EVALUATION?

232   It is useful to look at evaluation in three related but distinct phases.

Immediate

This relates to changes in knowledge, skill or behaviour immediately after a training experience. In other words it attempts to assess whether or not training has been effective in communicating the message. Have people learned the skills you were setting out to teach? Do they understand what is now required of them? Have they been equipped with the necessary behaviours to be able to implement the learning?

Intermediate

This refers to evidence that knowledge, skill and behaviour which has been learned is being put into use on the job. In other words, can the trainee, manager and colleagues identify changes in behaviour, skill and attitude as a result of the trainee's attendance?

Long term

This refers to the long-term effectiveness of the individual, the unit and perhaps even the organization. This ultimate evaluation is difficult and only possible if the training in the first instance has been related to the real corporate, strategic and business needs of the organization. What the trainer is attempting to evaluate is: 'does the individual now make a real contribution to the business needs of the organization, or has training just been a comfortable and hopefully enjoyable experience which has brought about little change?'

Evaluation is about determining the value of the training delivered. It should seek to assess:

- The effectiveness of the training.
- The effectiveness of the learning process – in other words, whether the trainees have learned what we set out to teach them.
- Whether the learning has been applied.
- Whether the applied learning has brought about the changes required in relation to attitudes, skill or behaviour.

If trainers can begin to think about evaluation within the context of the three phases outlined above, it should be possible to design and apply a range of evaluation techniques appropriate to each phase. Of course, many techniques will be appropriate to all phases, but some will apply primarily to one or the other.

As well as thinking of the three phases during which evaluation can be carried out, the trainer also needs to think of using appropriate methods of evaluation in relation to the particular training being delivered. Assessing the effectiveness of training in relation to attitude and interpersonal skills may require the application of different assessment techniques from those required in assessing the effectiveness of learning a motor skill. It is often assumed that it is relatively easy *233* to assess knowledge gain. However, what is often overlooked is retention levels. Ask any students two months after an important exam to remember the learning at the level they achieved just prior to the examination; you will find that retention level is directly related to the method and purpose of learning and the activity participated in immediately afterwards, and much of the learning may well have been lost. Therefore, while it may well be possible to assess and measure knowledge gain effectively, it is more important for the trainers to assess retention and application levels.

THE APPLICATION OF EVALUATION TECHNIQUES

We now set out 15 possible methods of assessment:

1. Post-course assessments.
2. Pre- and post-course tests.
3. Management briefing.
4. Management debriefing.
5. Questionnaires.
6. Appraisals.
7. Promotability.
8. Assessment/development centres.
9. Repertory grids.
10. Surveys.
11. Trainer interviews.
12. Trainer-observed behaviour.
13. Participant observation.
14. Records of performance.
15. Action plan follow-up.

These methods are repeated in Figure 19.2, in which you will see possible applications in the matrix, concerned with immediate, short-term and ultimate evaluation, and also that each method is linked to the assessment of knowledge, skills and attitudes. There follows a brief description of how each of these techniques can be developed and applied within an organization.

Post-course assessments

Post-course assessments are often called 'happiness sheets' because trainers usually ask for them to be completed immediately after the end of a training experience, before the post-course euphoria dissipates. They are probably the most frequently used method of evaluating a training programme. If the training has been effective and has been delivered in an effective and acceptable manner, the trainees will probably respond positively, not so much because of the effectiveness of the learning process, but because of their enjoyment of it. But that should not detract from the use of post-course assessments. They provide us, nevertheless, with a useful means of assessing how trainees received the

Evaluation techniques	Trainer requirements					
	Rapid immediate feedback	Considered but early feedback	Medium-term considered feedback	Long-term results	Assessment of skill changes	Assessment of attitude/behaviour change
1. Post-course assessments	✓					
2. Pre- and post-course tests		✓	✓			
3. Management briefing		✓	✓			
4. Management debriefing		✓				
5. Questionnaires				✓		
6. Appraisals				✓	✓	✓
7. Promotability				✓	✓	✓
8. Assessment/development centres				✓	✓	✓
9. Repertory grids				✓	✓	✓
10. Surveys			✓			
11. Trainer interviews		✓				
12. Trainer-observed behaviour	✓				✓	✓
13. Participant observation	✓					
14. Records of performance				✓		
15. Action plan follow-up	✓	✓				

Figure 19.2 Selection of the most appropriate evaluation techniques.

235

training. Clearly, trainers should not place too much emphasis on individual comments taken from a post-course assessment. However, complete analysis of a set of assessment forms can provide useful insights into those parts of the programme which the trainees believe to have been the most effective. Given that most training is concerned with adult learning, the views and opinions of the trainees should not be discarded lightly, particularly if a consistent view is expressed by a range of people.

The method can be especially useful in assisting the trainer to evaluate and assess the effectiveness of particular instructors or presenters, especially if evidence about similar sessions or courses being presented by other people is available. It may well be that one of the most useful benefits of a post-course assessment is in assisting the trainer to assess the skill of the instructor.

Pre- and post-course tests

An ideal way of measuring learning is to measure before, or at the start of a programme, and then to measure the same set of knowledge when it is over. It is often helpful in deciding what needs to be built on, particularly when teaching a specific skill.

Management briefing

Here the trainer moves out of the area within his or her own responsibility and becomes much more reliant on the trainee's line manager. Ideally, of course, training should always be the responsibility of the line manager, but experience teaches us that many are reluctant to accept this as part of their responsibility and are only too willing to pass it off to the trainer. Management briefing can be a useful way of involving line managers, as well as assisting the trainer in the evaluation process. The commonest way of conducting a management briefing is for the trainer to provide the manager with a detailed set of objectives and an outline of the content of a particular programme. The manager then discusses this with the trainee, and together they work out some personal and specific objectives which may be related to the trainee's knowledge, skill or attitude. The trainee who attends a programme having been fully briefed by the manager and who is fully committed to achieving personal objectives will be well prepared for the learning process.

Management debriefing

This method of evaluation also requires the complete commitment of line managers. They should review the learning process with the trainee after the programme. It is important, however, to understand that it is not only the learning process which should be reviewed but the application of that learning within the job the trainee is expected to do. A fundamental problem, identified by the vast majority of people who attend training programmes, is that there is little or no

opportunity for them to apply the learning gained when they return to an inevitably busy work situation. Management debriefing can overcome this problem, not only by reviewing the learning, but also by assisting the trainee to understand how to apply it in the work situation.

Questionnaires

A systematic approach to evaluation often involves the Training Department in following up, at various intervals, people who have attended specific programmes. If the objective is to assess retention and application, the questionnaire should be designed primarily to assess the level of skill or knowledge which the trainee has retained during the period following the training – after three, six or twelve months, whichever period the trainer deems to be appropriate. Trainees should be encouraged to answer honestly and openly without reference to notes or handouts.

A second but no less important use of questionnaires is to identify how and how well the learning has been applied. What benefits have trainees gained and what opportunities do they now have for increasing their learning? Considerable benefit can also, of course, be obtained from negative responses. The trainer would want to know what learning has *not* been applied and why. Is it, for example, because the learning has not been relevant or is it because the timing was not opportune? On the basis of such responses, the trainer can assess whether or not the training being delivered is relevant and applicable to the particular circumstances which need to be evaluated.

Appraisals

An essential part of any appraisal system should be to assess the effectiveness of training delivered during the previous period, and also to assess training needs in relation to future objectives. The application of training effectiveness for the previous period can be assessed by a few simple questions. This applies whether training has been carried out on formal programmes, by the process of self-development or by learning on the job. Because the appraisal is usually conducted by the immediate supervisor of the trainee, it should be possible for the two people working together to assess the applicability of the training needs of the trainee.

Once again using this method provides very effective feedback, both in terms of evaluation and in terms of the value of the training which has been delivered. Only when it is known that the training is not being used is the trainer in a position to ask 'am I delivering the right type of training?'.

Promotability

The value of this method depends partly on who is responsible for promotion procedures within an organization. If they are the one-off responsibility of departmental line managers, for example, it may be less valuable. Decisions may be dismissed as particular idiosyncrasies of the manager. If, on the other *237* hand, promotion procedures are well considered and involve some objective form of assessment, the training experience of individuals who are promoted is likely to have some relevance to an evaluation of training procedures. Trainers should track and monitor the career progress of trainees, relating their promotability back to course performance. If people who attend programmes are not coming through in terms of promotion, some serious questions must be asked about the value of the training being given. If, on the other hand, those with training experiences are seen to be promoted on a regular basis, the trainer will soon find a queue of people wanting the same standards of training. This method also assists the trainer in assessing whether the training is genuinely associated with, and related to, business needs. In a company with well-considered promotion procedures, only those people who are capable of meeting business needs are likely to be promoted.

Assessment/development centres

Many companies now run centres designed to assess employees' potential (assessment centres), or to provide people with an opportunity to assess their own development needs along with skilled assessors (development centres). Either type of centre provides a trainer with a lot of useful information which will be of relevance to the processes of evaluation. In assessment centres, the potential identified will frequently relate back to previous training experience and will assist the trainer in evaluating how effective previous training delivered to an individual or group has been.

Development centres provide the trainer with a rare opportunity to check that the identified training needs of individuals are being met. It is not often that trainers can offer proof that they are responding to the direct and individually identified needs of a group of trainees. Evidence which emerges from development centre work, however, provides an ideal basis on which to build evaluation programmes designed to test the effectiveness of training delivered against a checklist of specifically identified needs (assuming, of course, that other techniques of evaluation are applied to the training given).

Repertory grids

Grid analysis helps trainers assess performance on two dimensions simultaneously. Frequently the trainer will be concerned to assess performance both in relation to the skill level and the motivational level. Many people who have the necessary degree of skill to do a job effectively lack the motivation, and vice versa. Grid analysis assists the trainer to evaluate both factors and to plot them on a grid. Working with line managers, this type of approach enables the trainer to assess real training requirements and also to follow up the delivery of the training once it has been completed. Trainers wishing to explore this area in more detail should refer to Jackson (1989) or Rae (1986).

Surveys

Many organizations now carry out a whole range of surveys and market research into customer attitudes. Even surveys into employee attitudes and communications audits are now all common management experiences. Such information provides a useful base on which to assess current performance and to build future performance. Along the same lines, surveys have been conducted in relation to the assessment of organizations' training needs – and they apply with equal force to the evaluation of training delivery. A full-scale or even a shorter, more qualitative survey can be carried out effectively in most organizations. Sometimes the information the trainer is seeking may be of a more confidential nature. Then, it may be necessary either to employ the services of an external consultant or to allow people to respond anonymously.

Questionnaires can also be used to assess how people believe they have benefited from training experiences in the past and to identify what they believe would be the most valuable training experience for them in the future. This method of survey is often most effective if followed up by shorter qualitative interviews based on the initial findings.

Trainer interviews

Trainers sometimes find it useful to interview former trainees to assess in detail the effectiveness of the training they have received. Interviews are most effective if they follow a structured pattern, with each interviewee being asked the same questions. This allows for more effective analysis of response, and also helps keep the interview on track.

Interviewing is time consuming and therefore demands commitment of a significant resource. Before starting a set of interviews, it is important that the trainer is sure this kind of research will yield real benefit which cannot be obtained in an easier, less resource-demanding way.

The great benefit of interview-based evaluation, however, is that the trainer can gain a great deal of information through a mixture of closed and open questions designed to probe in detail the trainee's responses. Such an approach can cover knowledge, skill and attitude assessment, both in the initial and latter phases of evaluation. If this approach is linked with a more quantitative approach, as outlined earlier, it can provide trainers with a good feel for the effectiveness of the programmes they have been responsible for delivering.

Trainer-observed behaviour

This type of evaluation is most valuable in relation to action-based learning, including role plays and simulations. The trainer can observe how behaviour has changed as a result of learning and feedback, and can reinforce this with additional feedback to the trainee after a particular exercise or experience. It should be noted, however, that feedback is an essential part of this type of *239* evaluation, and that trainers cannot expect sound behaviours they observe to be repeated unless they provide some kind of positive reinforcement.

Participant observation

As with trainer observation, trainees learn a great deal from colleagues observing and giving opinions, particularly about behaviours identified for the purposes of a training experience. Once again the essential part of this is feedback. As an evaluation technique, observation is most effective where the trainer or participant is concerned with immediate evaluation of the learning, and has less application to the long-term benefits of training.

Records of performance

Where records of performance are kept, either through detailed appraisal systems or through the use of effective personnel reports, it is possible to use them to identify training needs and, at a later stage, to evaluate training delivered. Working closely with the line manager, the trainer needs to identify through performance records how effective an individual employee has been in relation to the training received. As with all methods of evaluation, those performance records which provide a real measure will be most effective. If, across a whole department, for example, trainers can identify those people who have been most successful, they should be able to obtain clear indication as to the effectiveness of training delivered – assuming people have attended similar training experiences. It should also be possible for the trainer in this situation to identify those people with low performance levels who perhaps have not received the same training experiences as the others. Again, this can provide evidence of training need, as well as a measure of the effectiveness of training within that department.

Action plan follow-up

After most training experiences, trainers usually ask participants to complete an action plan. Far too often, unfortunately, action plans are left to gather dust on a shelf or are hidden away in a drawer of the participant's desk and only unearthed many months later when the time has come to put them in the bin. However, such plans can be used most effectively as a means of evaluating the effectiveness of the training delivered. It requires a joint effort by the line manager and the trainer, who can follow up by interviews, a survey or just a brief letter to all participants to assess whether or not the action plans so 'enthusiastic-ally' made on the final morning of the course have now been implemented – and if not, why not. What, in other words, have been the barriers to implementation? If this method of follow-up is to be effective, trainers must develop close relationships with line managers and must be seen to have a genuine desire to assist and evaluate rather than forcibly to impose their own solutions which, in any event, are unlikely to be as effective as if they had been undertaken willingly.

There are two other techniques of evaluation not included in our matrix but which managers and trainers may like to consider using:

- Control groups.
- Self-assessment.

Control groups

The trainer chooses a group of people who represent, as nearly as possible, an ideal match with the group to be trained. The control group should be similar in terms of age, experience and in every other way possible. They should receive no training, and no indication that they are being used as a control group. Nor should the trainee group be informed that there is a control group in existence. This requirement may appear over-secretive and even unacceptable, but it will be very difficult otherwise to prevent competition between the groups, leading to the results of the evaluation being contaminated.

This technique can be used to assess the short-term effectiveness of the training given and the ultimate long-term impact of this training on the business. It should only be employed when clear objectives have been set for its use and the trainer is very clear about what it is that is being measured.

In practical terms many trainers feel that control groups, while providing a good basis for evaluation, are unrealistic in industrial and commercial enterprises. It is clearly difficult to ensure that the control group remains separate. In a modern, fast-moving organization, some will feel that not to provide training for one group yet expect them to do the same job is a risk they cannot afford to take.

Self-assessment

A technique which has possibly received too little attention in the past, but increasingly, as we recognize that learning must be centred around the needs of the trainee, has much to commend it. Self-assessment can be carried out in a variety of ways, but is, perhaps, most effective when it involves the trainees in reflecting on the learning received and its application to their own needs. Trainees should be encouraged to build a portfolio of learning experiences in the form of a training log or diary. In it they should record their training experiences, and more importantly their learning experiences. In our view, learning experiences occur every day, while a training experience is more specific. The really important thing, however, is to encourage trainees to reflect on what they have learned and how they will use it. An interesting discussion about reflection as a key learning tool can be seen in Honey (1990).

The trainer's role is to work with trainees in helping them to reflect productively. At the same time the trainer can assess the long-term development of the individual and the role formal training has played in this development. As more organizations seek to gain accreditation, leading to some form of certification of in-company training, through the credit accumulation and transfer *241* scheme (CATS), the role of self-assessment and training logs will assume greater importance.

CONCLUSION

The real purpose of evaluating training is to ensure that it improves the overall effectiveness of the organization. In too many organizations, and for far too long, training has been making its way quite separately from the needs of the organization. In looking to the future, training will be effective, and be seen to be effective, only if it responds to real business needs. Recent reports and the increasing emphasis we now see placed on training, both in the national press and in the management journals, indicate that, for the future, what will be required is a much more professional approach to training.

Training is increasingly being recognized as having a significant strategic role to play in organizations. It is important that trainers grasp the opportunities presented by this change in our environment and ensure that they are equipped to demonstrate the benefits which can accrue from effective training. There are two specific things that trainers can do to ensure that they demonstrate this. One is to keep fully in touch with the business themselves; this means having a close working relationship with key line managers in order to understand and be responsive to the needs of the business. The second is to ensure that they design and implement appropriate evaluation procedures for all the training they deliver. Methods of evaluation which relate back clearly to the real business needs of the organization are likely to be by far the most persuasive.

FURTHER READING

Bramley, P. (1986), *Evaluation of Training*, BACIE.

Honey, P. (1990), 'Confessions of a learner who is inclined to lapse', *Training and Development*, **8**, (6).

Jackson, T. (1989), *Evaluation: relating training to business performance*, Kogan Page.

Kenny, J. and M. Reid (1986), *Training interventions*, IPM.

Newby, A.C. (1992), *Training Evaluation Handbook*, Gower.

Pepper, A.D. (1986), *Managing the training and development function*, Gower.

Rae, L. (1986), *How to Measure Training Effectiveness*, Gower.

20 Training records

Keith Marshall and Lind

The need for training records varies according to the user's role in the training system. These needs will be discussed from a variety of viewpoints in the first section of this chapter. The chapter will then describe a case study of the training records used currently by the Engineering Training Authority (EnTra) and how these will need to evolve as training systems change as a result of the introduction of National Vocational Qualifications in the United Kingdom.

TRAINING RECORDS AND THEIR USERS

Training records can be thought of either as records purely used for training purposes or, more widely, as the records used by the people involved in the learning and training function. This second wider consideration is the one used in this chapter.

This first section will look at training records from a number of different points of view. It is intended to be a description of the different ways that records can be used rather than a detailed description of a system. Rather more detail is given in the second half of the chapter when dealing specifically with EnTra's training records.

The trainee

The first point of view considered is that of the trainee. Traditionally records of an individual's performance on a particular education or training course are confined to the assessor and the awarding body (e.g. examiners and BTEC). The only information that the trainee or candidate gets is a grade, which may either relate to a performance criterion or a norm group of other candidates. Even on a course run by the trainee's company, any records of performance may only be held by the trainers or perhaps the personnel department. Increasingly, the responsibility for owning the learning process is moving to the trainee or learner. For this to work effectively, the learner must have detailed feedback on   *243*

therefore a copy of any performance records must be kept. ...e trainees or learners to keep track of their current and past ...nd to take an active part in plans for future development. One ...chieving this is profiling, where the learner keeps records of all ...ts including the outcomes of both formative and summative assess- ...other, less comprehensive approach is the National Record of Achieve- ...NRA) which has been introduced by the Employment Department and the ...onal Council for Vocational Qualifications. This National Record is a docu- ...nt case designed to contain all the records of achievement in vocational qualifications throughout the working life. One example of trainee ownership of records is seen in EnTra's logbook system which will be described in more detail later in the chapter. Here the results of continuous and final assessment are recorded alongside the trainee's own notes of the work that has been carried out.

In addition to having copies of records of performance for development planning, the trainee may at some stage wish to show them to a future employer, whether within the organization or in a new one. This leads on to the next group of people who need training records, personnel staff.

Personnel staff

Selection

Obviously records of an applicant's performance are desirable when recruiting someone into a team or organization. The new system of National Vocational Qualifications (NVQs), with all the units of competence contained on a national database, will enable prospective employers to have a very clear idea of the competence of their applicants in the workplace as well as in a training or academic environment.

Manpower planning

Clear and readily accessible records of the workforce's areas of competence are evidently very important for the effective use of manpower resources. Keeping records of the competences that an individual has on joining the company, and acquires during training – both on and off the job – will give a detailed picture of where in the organization the skill and expertise in a particular field lie. Additionally these records, when cross-referenced with such information as age profiles and management objectives will enable succession planning and rational development of staff to take place. In the current climate of demographic change in the United Kingdom, it will become increasingly important to tap internal resources effectively, and so be able to identify individuals who could be developed to fill vacancies internally.

The records needed to support this come from several sources. An application form can be used to collect information on the competences that people bring with them to the team. The formal acquisition of units of competence and NVQs must also be recorded for planning purposes. In addition, it is likely that there will be a need to supplement this with information gathered from individuals about their own aspirations, and from the line management, about day-to-day performance and their opinions of potential for development. A common way of collecting this information is through an appraisal system.

Remuneration

Many engineering companies have their rates of pay linked to the completion of craft or technician training. Training records are therefore needed to trigger the necessary increase in pay at the appropriate time. There may be a case in future for some increase in pay to coincide with the attainment of units of competence or NVQs.

Outplacement

If a change in company fortunes or objectives makes it necessary to lay off staff, then contractual restrictions and industrial relations issues must be supplemented by a consideration of the competences of the staff for whom redundancy is being considered. Those staff with competences most fitted to the new situation should be retained in preference to those less well prepared. For those who are to go, records of their competences can be used to counsel them about future prospects outside the organization and what further development they might need.

These issues overlap with those of selection when trainees on special schemes – such as TEC-funded programmes – are coming to the end of work placements. Records of performance can enable the decision, whether or not to retain these people, to be made on a rational and objective basis.

The instructor

The instructor will often be responsible (perhaps in partnership with the learner) for compiling many of the training records. The instructor can either be working solely on instruction or this role may be combined with other responsibilities (e.g. assessment and/or production or supervisory work). For the instructional role itself, however, the instructor will make considerable use of training records.

The first aspect will be to monitor the performance of the trainees for whom the instructor is responsible. A considerable amount of information will be carried in the instructor's memory about the performance of individual trainees. However, if this information is recorded, then it is more easily shared with other people interested in the trainee's development. Trends in performance will be more readily identified, as will exceptionally good or poor performance. This information can be fed back into the individual's training plan and used to guide training.

The training plan itself also forms part of the portfolio of records. It can be used *245* to form the objectives of the training and can comprise a set of milestones against which progress can be measured. Increasingly, training plans are being drawn up for each individual, tailored to suit particular training needs. Examples of this system can be found in the Action Plans of the NRA.

As a complement to using training records to reflect on the trainee's performance, they can be used to reflect on the instructor's performance, too. This can either be done formally with training management or informally by the instructor alone or with peers. Different content or techniques can be tested and evaluated; the instructor's own performance can be evaluated and the development plan proposed.

Training management

Evaluation

If training records can be used for local evaluation by instructors, then equally they can be used by training management when looking at overall costs and benefits. The costs are usually straightforward to identify and quantify, providing the records have been efficiently kept! The benefits can often be more difficult to measure, as many variables can affect improvement in an individual's performance and so many more can affect improvements in productivity overall. Careful phrasing of the all important questions on benefits can often elicit the required information from line managers. This can either be done during discussions with the trainee and line management or in a larger exercise using questionnaire techniques. Either way, records of the training objectives, trainees' performance and the costs of delivery are essential to the evaluation process.

Objectives and planning

Both the corporate objectives and the lower-level management objectives need to inform the planning of the training provision in any organization. Without this information the training function cannot demonstrate its contribution to the organization meeting those objectives. Accordingly, records of these objectives must be readily available to training management, whatever its status in the organization.

Similarly, records of the developmental objectives of individuals or groups within the organization must also contribute to the planning process. As mentioned earlier, this is often done using an appraisal system where individual objectives are recorded. This overlaps with the section on manpower planning earlier in the chapter.

The assessor

This separate role will be new to many people. The person carrying out

assessment of work competence will probably not be new, in that assessment will often be carried out in the workplace or training centre by the same people who are involved now and have the role of: instructor, supervisor, facilitator of learning, coach or line manager. None of these categories is new, nor are they necessarily separate people: in many organizations they will be combined in the same person. Assessment of the competent performance of the worker or trainee is a key function, and similar questions are asked in all of the above roles; for example:

- Are the correct processes being used?
- Is the quality what it should be?
- Is the speed of work what is required?
- Is the person competent to do the job?

Emphasis is rapidly moving towards the answers to these questions where certification for vocational qualifications is concerned. This is discussed in more detail later in the chapter in the section looking at changes for National Vocational Qualifications. It is sufficient to say here that assessors will need to keep records of evidence of competent performance as the systems focusing on competence are introduced.

The people considered as using records so far have mostly been inside the organization that is managing or providing training. The people, or rather organizations, which follow are mainly from outside this organization.

Awarding bodies

A range of organizations is included here, and the following list gives some examples:

1. Institutions offering professional qualifications, for example in:

   - accountancy;
   - engineering;
   - psychology;
   - medicine; or
   - personnel.

2. Industry bodies responsible for developing national standards for competent performance as part of National Vocational Qualifications, for example:

   - Engineering Training Authority.
   - CAPITB for the clothing industry.

3. Vocational examining bodies, for example:

   - SCOTVEC (Scottish Vocational Education Council).
   - BTEC (Business and Technical Educational Council).

247

- CGLI (City & Guilds of London Institute).
- RSA (Royal Society of Arts).

As the measuring of results increasingly focuses on workplace competence, those awarding bodies listed above which do not already require records of performance at work will do so more and more.

Funding bodies

Organizations which make contributions to the costs of training naturally require evidence that the training has taken place and often want some evidence of its quality. This is the same whether the money comes from central sources (e.g. the Department of Employment, the European Social Fund, Industry Training Organizations) or from local provision, notably the Training Enterprise Councils (TECs). Each funding body (and awarding body) has its own requirements in terms of records of training, but clearly none of these can operate without such records in some form.

Licensing bodies

Some occupations have licensing bodies which insist on evidence of competence before a licence to operate can be granted; for example, where the competence of the individual doing the work is vital for public safety, such as drivers or pressure-vessel welders. It is likely that, as National Vocational Qualifications gain widespread recognition, these will become part of this system. This will add to the necessity of keeping accurate records of assessment.

Customers

The last category of those making use of training and assessment records, albeit indirectly, is customers. The customer can be someone who takes note of the certificates hanging on the pharmacist's wall, or a large industrial concern demanding compliance with the British Standard 5750 on quality control which contains sections on the training of staff (BSI, 1990). Both are taking an interest, and may be deciding to place their custom, on the basis of training records.

Records are often neglected because they are not seen to be contributing to the learning, training and achievement of the people at the working front. They are often considered to be a hindering bureaucracy rather than another tool in the training kit; however, training records are a fundamental part of the training administration system. Indeed, used effectively, they can be shown to contribute a great deal more. How often is it said that the training administrator runs the place? Often this is said flippantly, but with an effective system of records, used efficiently, the smooth running of the training function is ensured and the overall effectiveness of the training provided is greatly enhanced.

ENTRA RECORDS

EnTra records are principally concerned with recording the achievements of the people who have received training in the engineering industry, or training in engineering skills in other industries. Certification is given to those people who follow EnTra-approved programmes of training, and the vast majority of such training is currently in craft or technician areas of work.

Craftsmen and women have a wide range of skills, allowing them to interpret engineering drawings and instructions so as to convert ideas and designs into the finished product. They must be able to plan the order in which the work is to be done, set up the job and then do it. They work in such jobs as fitting and maintenance, tool making, welding, fabrication and sheet metal work (ECIS, 1989).

Technicians have the detailed knowledge and practical expertise upon which engineering decisions are made. They can be found in engineering departments, often working as part of a team in which they would be expected to solve problems as well as come up with new ideas. They often work in supervisory or management positions.

Currently, work is being undertaken to enable EnTra to recognize and certificate those skills held by operators. Operators have at least one manufacturing skill and play a vital role in the manufacture of a tremendous range of different components and products. They work in such jobs as assembly, paint-spraying, packing and store keeping.

There are two main aspects to EnTra records: logbooks and certification, each of which is now to be described.

Logbooks

Logbooks are the mainstay of record keeping for both craft and technician training. They are used by the trainee for keeping a record of all the tasks that are carried out during both off- and on-the-job training. They can also be used during the further education components of training, too. The following sentence is offered as a definition: 'The logbook is a commentary on the relationship of training to achievement' (EITB, 1985).

An example of a typical exercise from a craft logbook is shown in Figure 20.1 (EITB, 1987).

The role of the logbook begins at the training planning stage. It enables the work carried out by the trainee to be related to the plan of training included in the EnTra system. In craft training each part of training has associated skill and training specifications. The skill specification indicates the range of skills which are required to be developed and, where appropriate, the standards to be reached at the end of training. The training specification gives details of how the training is to be carried out (EITB, 1985). The trainee is given copies of these and is required to record on the training specification the reference numbers from the logbook of three jobs which included the particular item in the training specification. Figure 20.2 shows an extract from a training specification. *249*

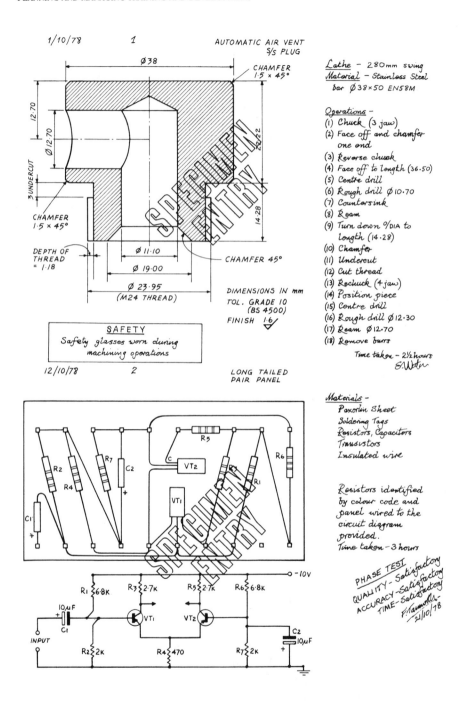

Figure 20.1   Typical logbook entry taken from EnTra's Training Logbook

Oxyacetylene welding

1. Practice in safely and correctly operating oxy-fuel gas welding equipment, including:

    1. selection of correct size nozzle and/or injector head

    2. gas pressure regulation

    3. flame ignition and regulation

    4. selection of filler rod (type and size)

    5. normal maintenance and routine care

2. Practice in tack welding, appropriate to the thickness of material being welded, to the standard required for welds in BS 4872

OR

Tungsten-arc gas shielded welding

1. Practice in safely and correctly operating tungsten-arc gas shielded welding equipment, including:

    1. selection of appropriate electrodes

    2. setting electrical conditions

    3. setting gas mixture and flow rates

    4. selection of filler rod

    5. initiating the arc and terminating deposition

    6. normal maintenance and routine care

2. Practice in tack welding, appropriate to the thickness of material being welded, to the standard required for welds in BS 4872

OR

Metal-arc gas shielded welding

1. Practice in safely and correctly operating metal-arc gas shielded welding equipment, including:

    1. selection of electrode wire

    2. setting electrical conditions

    3. setting wire feed

    4. setting gas mixture and flow rates

    5. initiating the arc and terminating deposition

    6. normal maintenance and routine care

2. Practice in tack welding, appropriate to the thickness of material being welded, to the standard required for welds in BS 4872

Issue No 2 (February 1986)

EITB/8/88

Printed by EITB Reprographics

Figure 20.2   Extract from an EnTra Training Specification showing the training and skill specification for welding and fabrication

251

The next role of the logbook is in assessment where it is used both by the trainee and the assessor or instructor. Trainees are advised to write up their logbooks weekly or at least fortnightly. Often their instructor or supervisor will allow some time for this during the working day, but much of the work may need to be done in the trainee's own time. When each job has been satisfactorily completed and written up in the logbook, the entry is then checked and initialled by the instructor or supervisor. If the job concerned is part of the assessment procedure, for example, a test piece that has been set, then this is indicated by the supervisor in the logbook and the assessment result is included. The logbook should provide a basis for regular discussion between the supervisor and the trainee, and provide a focus for both summative and formative assessment.

The logbook complements the assessment of test pieces as an important part of the assessment system itself. In addition to being initialled by the supervisor each trainee's logbooks are examined by a licensed EnTra verifier and certain items are discussed with the trainee during a validation interview. Validation (or verification as it is sometimes called) is the process when a licensed EnTra verifier checks that the assessment in the training centre or workplace has been carried out to the correct standards, and that all of the areas in the previously agreed training plan have been covered. When looking at logbooks during validation, an EnTra verifier is looking for the following things:

1. All training records are complete and up-to-date.
2. Correct skill specifications are being used.
3. All mandatory items in the specifications have been covered.
4. Logbooks contain all the relevant information, and the entries are cross-referenced with the specifications and practical work.
5. All practical work and written work meets specification criteria.
6. All necessary tests/projects/assessments have been completed to an acceptable standard.
7. The instructor/tutor has signed off performance at all stages.

However, it is usually only possible to look at samples of the trainee's work at any given time. [EnTra internal document]. Validation usually takes place at the end of training but may also take place at other appropriate times such as the end of a Youth Training (YT) scheme or the end of first year off-the-job training.

A special logbook has been published to be used by YT trainees during their work placements (EITB, 1982). This has a broader range of tasks for the trainee to carry out concerning the working environment, as well as tasks carried out during training. Examples of the tasks are:

- Preparation: what is work really like?
- Work diary.
- Tasks: keeping within the rules; equipment and tools, company costs, the organization.
- Follow-up: the good will of your employer; selling yourself – interviews.

Extracts from a BBC publication on work are also included in the YT logbook.

There is not a specifically published logbook for technician trainees, although they may use the same logbooks as craft trainees early in their training. Generally, loose-leaf files are used but the entries are assessed and cross-referenced in the same way as the other logbooks. As the ability to produce an accurate record develops, the trainee is encouraged to make increasing use of various forms of graphical communication including drawings, tables, graphs and flow charts, as well as written information (EITB, 1983).

The last important function of a logbook is to help the trainee develop the essential skills of communication, and so it is not merely a record but also an active part of the training.

To summarize, the chief functions of logbooks are:

1. To provide a record of training received.
2. To provide trainees with a source of reference which may be useful later.
3. To identify in a logical manner, through the discipline of writing, the knowledge and application of techniques which trainees need to understand and use.
4. To provide a means of assessing the trainee's progress and achievement.
5. To develop ability in written communication, by providing an opportunity to practise the skills learned in school, in training and in further education.

Registration and certification

With the EnTra craft system, it is necessary for all trainees who will require certification to be registered with EnTra at the commencement of their training (or employment, if their employer has changed during training), and must register again when they want to begin a new phase of training (e.g. a new segment or the objective training section of the technician programme). Computerized records are kept by EnTra on all registered trainees and each time a trainee completes a section of training (e.g. basic engineering training, segments, objective training and so forth) the record is amended. The purposes of these procedures are:

1. To provide a system of control in respect of methods and standards specified by EnTra.
2. To ensure that the trainee receives the appropriate certificate in confirmation that the training has been to the standards specified by EnTra.
3. To ensure that all such trainees are duly recorded on the national training files maintained by EnTra.

At the end of training, and at some other convenient points, the trainee is issued with a certificate which is often awarded jointly with another awarding body (CGLI, BTEC, or SCOTVEC) which has covered the further education component of the training.

The records of completion of sections of training have been kept since the *253*

Engineering Industry Training Board was set up more than twenty years ago, and will continue to be kept and updated as necessary for the foreseeable future.

CHANGES FOR NATIONAL VOCATIONAL QUALIFICATIONS

The introduction of National Vocational Qualifications (NVQs) has led to a change in emphasis for EnTra's training records. Previously EnTra focused on the quality of the training process and made the assumption that, if the training is valid and of good quality, then the trainee will become competent to do the job. The emphasis is now changing towards collecting evidence of competent performance in the workplace and not prescribing how that competence is developed. The records that EnTra will be concerned with in future will contain information about the evidence of competent performance and how that evidence has been collected. As far as EnTra certification is concerned, individuals will be considered competent when they have demonstrated that they can consistently meet performance criteria which are being laid down (after thorough consultations with industry) in published EnTra Units of Competence. An example of a draft unit of competence is shown in Figure 20.3.

Most of the evidence of competent performance will be collected during continuous workplace assessment. Records will need to be kept of the method of assessment; for example: observation, questioning, examination of work pieces, and so on. The outcomes of assessment will also need to be recorded: was the trainee or candidate judged to be competent or not yet competent?

It is important that there is not a bureaucratic overload on the person carrying out the assessment or gathering evidence of competent performance. If it is possible to glean evidence of competence from existing records, for example, quality control or production records, then these, or extracts from them, will become part of the evidence submitted for assessment, and hence, training records. In addition, the logbook is likely to maintain its status as a key part of the record system. Both formative and summative assessment can continue to be recorded, although in future the activities recorded are more likely to have taken place in the workplace rather than in the training centre.

The person carrying out the assessment will need to establish that the methods used were both reliable and valid. Assessment is reliable in that the assessment could be carried out on another occasion or by another assessor and, given that the candidate's competence is unchanged, the outcome would be the same. It is valid in that the method used is measuring as much of the competence to do the job as possible, and not skills in passing exams or high levels of verbal communication that would not otherwise be needed to do the job. Policies are currently being developed to enable reliability and validity to be demonstrated.

The records required for certification will also change. When sufficient evidence of competence has been collected to cover an entire unit, a Certificate of Validated Achievement (CVA) can be issued by EnTra on application. This will list the units achieved, will be laminated with plastic, and will be suitable for framing or including in a National Record of Achievement (NRA). The final

component in the new certification system is the National Vocational Quali-

ELEMENTS OF COMPETENCE   LNW 001

1. Prepare Oxy-acetylene Equipment for Use

Performance Criteria

		1	2
1.1	All equipment is checked for damage before assembly. · · · · · · · · · · · · · · · · · · ·	☐	☐
1.2	Cylinder/gas supply is cracked open before connection of regulators. · · · · · · ·	☐	☐
1.3	All equipment is correctly assembled and tested to ensure that joints are gas tight. ·	☐	☐
1.4	Where appropriate flash back arrestors and hose check valves are installed. · ·	☐	☐
1.5	Appropriate nozzle size and gas pressures are selected for material and type of joint. ·	☐	☐
1.6	Filler rods are free from contamination and of appropriate size for thickness of material. ·	☐	☐
1.7	Blowpipe is adjusted to produce a neutral flame. ·	☐	☐

2. Apply Safe Working Practices

Performance Criteria

2.1	Gas bottles and hoses are positioned to avoid damage and hazards. · · · · · · · · ·	☐	☐
2.2	Appropriate welder protective clothing is worn to include eye protection with correct shade of filter. ·	☐	☐
2.3	A suitable means of fume ventilation is used. ·	☐	☐
2.4	The working area is maintained clean, tidy and free from hazards and fire risks. ·	☐	☐

3. Weld Single Fillet Lap and Close Outside Corner Joints in Carbon Steel in the Flat Position

Performance Criteria

3.1	The joints are welded using a single run, (to include welds at least 150mm long and materials up to 3mm thick). ·	☐	☐
3.2	Where appropriate a suitable sized filler wire is used. · · · · · · · · · · · · · · · · · · ·	☐	☐
3.3	All welds are regular in width with even and regular ripple formation, uniform in appearance and free from excessive undulations. · · · · · · · · · · · · · · · · · · ·	☐	☐
3.4	Undercut and overlap are minimal and stop/starts are smooth with no pronounced "Hump" or "Notching". ·	☐	☐
3.5	Penetration on corner joints is present, but not excessive and is continuous for at least seventy five per-cent of the joint length. · · · · · · · · · · · · · · · · · · ·	☐	☐
3.6	Weld finishes are built up. ·	☐	☐

4. CLOSE DOWN OXY-ACETYLENE WELDING EQUIPMENT

Performance Criteria

4.1	Blowpipe valves are turned off in correct sequence. ·	☐	☐
4.2	Cylinder/supply valves are closed, pressure regulators relieved and hoses purged. ·	☐	☐
4.3	Blowpipe and hoses are stowed safely. ·	☐	☐

UNIT OF COMPETENCE COMPLETED

Assessor's signature	Date	Place of assessment

Figure 20.3 Extract from an EnTra Unit of Competence showing the elements of competence and performance criteria for a foundation unit in basic oxyacetylene welding *255*

fication (NVQ). These qualifications come under the auspices of the National Council for Vocational Qualifications (NCVQ) and have its seal of approval. Particular combinations of units of competence are approved by the NCVQ to make up an NVQ at a particular level. When the candidate has acquired the combination of units required for an NVQ, then a certificate can be issued to that effect.

EnTra's system of records clearly does not meet all the needs outlined in the first section of the chapter: it was never designed to. However, it does give insight into how some of those needs can be met. Each organization must develop systems and records which best meet the needs of those using them. It must be remembered that training records used effectively enhance the learning, training and development objectives of both individuals, teams and organizations. They should not be regarded merely as an imposition to keep the administrators happy.

FURTHER READING

BSI (1990), *Quality Systems Part 4. Guide to the use of BS 5750*, BSI Standards.
ECIS (1989), *Engineering Option*, Engineering Careers Information Service.
EITB (1982), *Work experience guide and log book YT17*, EITB Publications.
EITB (1983), *The training of technicians in engineering, TR21*, EITB Publications.
EITB (1985), *Training in engineering craft skills, TR23*, EITB Publications.
EITB (1987), *Training logbook, MSO2*, 2nd edn, EITB Publications.

Part Three
WAYS AND MEANS

21 Learning *how* we learn

John Giles

In the past 20 years more has been discovered about how our brains function and how people really learn than in all of our previous history. That information led Dee Dickinson, President of the international educational network, New Horizons for Learning, to declare: 'We know enough now to make a difference. A big difference. What's needed is to put that knowledge into action' (Dickinson, 1991).

The period from the late 1970s has produced a valuable growth of research findings about our physical and mental make-up, which, if sensibly applied, can help us cope with the accelerating accumulation of knowledge and change which threatens to overwhelm some people.

Links of shared understanding between the physical and the social sciences were seen as the most promising routes towards meeting the gathering momentum of change in society. Physiology joined with psychology to provide opportunities for discovering and meeting the varied ways in which individuals prefer to learn.

It was recognized that people learned through their senses in a much broader, more diverse combination than that provided by the traditional Western method of 'sit still and listen to me'. It was realized that to optimize learning the whole brain, together with the emotions, needed to be involved. Supporting that need, Dr Jean Houston of the Foundation for Mind Research in New York reported:

> Much in European-derived education and the understanding of intelligence tends to reward those students who respond well to verbal, linear styles of education. And yet we humans are as different as snowflakes one from another. Our brains are as different from each other as our fingerprints, with enormous variations in styles and talents of perception and learning. Some people are naturally kinesthetic thinkers, others think in images, others in sounds. Children can learn almost anything and pass standard tests if they are dancing, tasting, touching, hearing, seeing and feeling information. They can delight in doing so because they are using much more of the mind–brain–body system than conventional teaching generally permits. (Houston 1990)

THE TRIUNE BRAIN

From the physical sciences we can draw valuable understanding of our mental *259*

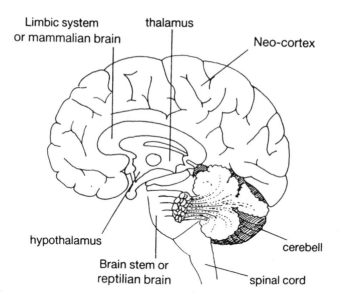

Figure 21.1 The Triune Brain

resources. In 1973 Dr Paul MacLean coined the term 'The Triune Brain' to emphasize the three vertical divisions of that most important human resource (see Figure 21.1).

1. The reptilian brain (or brain stem), which emerges directly from the spinal column and controls the very basic instinctive responses.
2. The limbic system or mammalian brain, which controls emotions and pleasure centres.
3. The neo-cortex, which controls the intellectual processes.

These three parts of the brain illustrate its evolution from pure instinctual responses, via the acquisition of controlled emotional response and the beginning of memory, to the incredible complexity of the new brain or neo-cortex. It is of considerable significance that the limbic system tends to be the channel through which impulses are transferred from instinctual, involuntary behaviour to 'rational' thought. Personality is said to be determined by the interaction of the limbic system and the neo-cortex and that most learning occurs between the 'old' and 'new' brains via the limbic system.

Writing in *Scientific American* in 1987, Mishkin and Appenzeller, building on the work of Paul MacLean at the National Institute of Mental Health, showed that four specific elements in the limbic system have a crucial role in learning. These are the amygdala (an almond-shaped structure), the hippocampus (shaped like a sea-horse), the thalamus and the hypothalamus (see Figure 21.2). These four areas are interconnected and act as a sort of central switchboard for the brain.

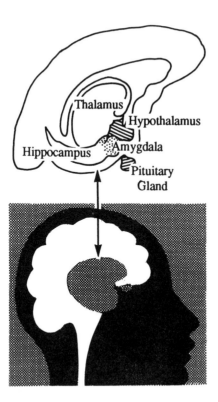

Figure 21.2   The limbic system

Here are controlled our emotions, our immune system, our hormonal system and some key elements of our long-term memory.

This leads to the positive conclusion that learning is enhanced when information is conveyed in ways that engage positive emotions, and explains the common observation that information with emotional impact is well remembered. On the negative side, learning is inhibited when people feel under threat or stress. The limbic system may actually filter out the information so that it never reaches the neo-cortex. Further, as researcher J. Levy has shown, when a person faces a stressful or threatening situation the brain downshifts from the intellectual thinking part to the lower, more instinctive levels.

People's state of mind determines how well they learn. Learning is facilitated by a low-stress environment, a state of relaxed alertness and a sense of confidence in one's capacity.

THE THINKING BRAINS

In addition to the vertical divisions of our brain, there is a horizontal division of the neo-cortex into left and right halves with each having specialist functions.   *261*

This was first shown by Roger Sperry and Robert Ornstein of the California Institute of Technology in their Nobel Prize winning submission.

Although the two halves of the neo-cortex are connected by a rich bundle of nerves so that they do not normally function independently, they do perform somewhat specialist tasks. Sperry and Ornstein showed that the two halves of the neo-cortex tend to function as follows:

1. The *left* brain emphasizes:

   - language;
   - mathematical formulae;
   - logic;
   - numbers;
   - sequence;
   - linearity;
   - analysis;
   - words of a song.

2. The *right* brain emphasizes:

   - forms and patterns;
   - spatial manipulation;
   - rhythm;
   - musical appreciation;
   - images/pictures;
   - imagination dimensions;
   - tune of a song.

Sperry and Ornstein also attributed to the right brain the ability to deal with certain kinds of conceptual thought – intangible 'ideas' such as beauty, love, loyalty. It is now known that the right half of the neo-cortex which tends to be more intuitive and responsive to imaginative thinking works many times faster than the left brain. (One estimate by Hainer is 1,600 times faster!) The right brain responds to the challenge of making sense from rich complex data.

Recent research also shows that when people are exposed to material with a positive emotional content, opiate-type chemicals are produced in the brain. They make one feel good and naturally make one want more. This, in turn, stimulates a further reaction and the chemicals noradrenalin and acetylcholine are produced. They appear to make the passage of thoughts along the electrical pathways of the brain smoother and more efficient. Within the average adult brain there are some ten to fifteen billion nerve cells, each one capable of making thousands of contacts; the possible permutations of connections thus runs into the trillions.

Dr Marian Diamond, Professor of Anatomy at the University of California, Berkeley, has ascertained that the anatomy of the brain can be changed by the environment. Her studies show conclusively that positive, nurturing, stimulating environments that encourage interaction and response are the prime conditions for developing the more complex neural networks that appear to be the 'hardware' of intelligence. Her work also indicates the ongoing influence of the environment, experience, learning and emotions on neural equipment development throughout life. According to Diamond, the number of connections between brain cells and the size of the cells increases when one is exposed to continuous, sensory-rich, learning environments.

'*NO LIMITS TO LEARNING*'

Between 1979 and 1980 the Club of Rome's report *No Limits to Learning*, co-authored by Dr James Botkin, was published in more than twelve languages (Botkin *et al.*, 1979). It undertook a study of innovative learning and, as a primary feature of it, 'anticipation' – preparing people to use techniques such as forecasting, simulations, scenarios and models. Anticipatory learning was to encourage the consideration of trends, to make plans, to evaluate future consequences and possible side-effects of present decisions and to recognize the wider implications of actions.

Re-examining the position a decade later, Dr Botkin found schools world-wide hopelessly out-of-date. Despite a widespread recognition of inadequacy, the response had been 'more' for the future of what had not worked in the recent past. More hours, more homework, more science and mathematics had been the guiding principles, rather than new teamwork, focus on values or holistic learning.

> No country in the world has been able to figure out how to divest itself of a system built for another age and to start afresh in redesigning formal education. Meanwhile, problems of drugs, dropouts and deprivation go universally unchallenged as a growing fact of classroom life in all western countries. (Dickinson, 1991)

To his surprise Dr Botkin found that: '... the place where there is promising action in reforming education and modernizing learning is the international business community.' He was referring to the forward-looking work of some multinational bodies including: the Scandinavian Leadership Initiative in Northern Europe; the Alliance for Learning in North America; the Consortium Senior Managers Development Programme operating in Geneva, Boston, Tokyo and Budapest; together with his own International Corporate Learning Association which he launched with Eric Vogt in Cambridge, Massachusetts and Santa Fe, New Mexico.

In the United States the White House has a Task Force on Innovative Learning of which Dee Dickinson is a member; she also currently chairs the Educational Advisory Board of their National Learning Foundation, having been Vice-President of the International Association for Accelerative Learning. Her report, *Positive Trends in Learning: Meeting the Needs of a Rapidly Changing World*, was commissioned and published by the IBM Corporation in 1991.

People from many parts of the world are contributing to innovative or accelerative learning, as it is more often called. Organizations concerned with *263* the sharing of ideas, methods and systems have expanded. In America there is the Society for Accelerative Learning and Teaching (SALT) and in Europe the Society of Effective, Affective Learning (SEAL).

Our knowledge of how the brain is constructed and how it uses its capacities has been brought up-to-date by many of the individual contributions to these organizations. Thus a useful marriage of the physical and social sciences gives rise to the prospect of important developments in our ability to learn how we learn.

A SIX-STAGE MODEL OF LEARNING

Based in the United Kingdom, but operating on an international basis, is Accelerated Learning Systems, led by Colin Rose, which produces programmes for organizations and individuals that incorporate a distillation of much of the recent discoveries made by both the physical and social sciences.

Rose has developed a six-stage model of learning that is not intended to be definitive but which does act as a simple, easily understood framework for both the facilitator (trainer/teacher) and the learner. The six stages are as follows:

1. State.
2. Intake.
3. Explore.
4. Store.
5. Act.
6. Review.

We will examine each of these stages separately.

1. State – developing a resourceful state of mind

Most Britons have a negative experience of some aspects, or indeed, of the whole of formal learning activity. A study has shown that 82 per cent of children entering the school system at ages 5 or 6 have a positive self-image of their ability to learn. That positive self-rating drops to an average of 18 per cent by the time they are 16 years old. This suggests that four out of five students and adults start a new learning experience with a feeling of some insecurity: that is, they find it somewhat threatening and/or stressful.

An important element of the learner's state of mind is motivation. Dr Csikszentmihalyi, Professor of Human Development and Education at the University of Chicago, says: 'It seems increasingly clear that the chief impediments to learning are not cognitive in nature. It is not that students cannot learn, it is that they do not wish to' (Csikszentmihalyi, 1988). He claims that if facilitators invested a fraction of the energy on stimulating the students' enjoyment of learning that they now spend in trying to transmit information, we could achieve much better results. The motivation to learn can be enhanced not only by a realistic assessment of the extrinsic rewards attendant on the learning, but also by making learners aware of how much fun learning can be. He continues:

> This strategy is something facilitators can do something about; it should be easy to implement, it does not require expensive technology and it is proven to be a more efficient way to empower learners with the tools of knowledge. Finally, it is preferable because it adds immensely to the enjoyment learners take in the use of their new abilities and hence it improves the quality of their lives.

Dr Diamond's researches suggest that positive, nurturing, stimulating environments that encourage interaction and response are prime conditions for developing neural networks that appear to be the 'hardware' of intelligence. Learning helps the brain to grow!

Colin Rose believes that the low or hesitant expectations of the learners need to be met by a sensitive, supportive, low stress, confidence-building approach right from the first contact between the provider and recipient. Motivation will be improved if the learner is brought to visualize the successful outcome of the learning, the value of the new skills or knowledge, and to believe in that outcome. 'Learning is a function of two things – will and skill. Or, to put it another way, a positive state of mind and appropriate strategies.'

In a group learning situation the reception environment should be warm and welcoming, with informal arrangement of furniture, supportive wall decorations and relaxing background music. The facilitator's attitude to the learners needs to be warm and approachable and to the subject enthusiastic.

An early opportunity should be taken to do four things:

1. develop rapport between participants;
2. find out what is on their minds, in order to clear the decks for learning;
3. define the roles of facilitator and learner; and
4. establish whatever administrative rules are needed to conduct the learning.

A 'big picture' or overview needs next to be presented. This is 'the picture on the box of the jigsaw puzzle – enabling learners to see how it all fits together, where they are heading and how they will do it'. These things, done sensitively, should establish a stress-free atmosphere in which the learner is in a state of relaxed alertness, has identified 'What's in it for me' and recognizes 'If it's to be – it's up to me'.

2. Intake – via the three primary senses

All new information enters our brain through one of the five senses, but few of us use our sense of smell or taste in learning. Surveys indicate that 25 per cent of people are mainly auditory learners; 35 per cent are mainly visual learners and 40 per cent are mainly physical (kinesthetic) learners. No one is exclusively one type of learner but, as Dr Jean Houston has pointed out, each of us has a unique combination that we like to use.

The work that highlighted the significance of our varied forms of sensory perception was, perhaps, best developed by Richard Bandler and John Grinder (1979) whose book *Frogs into Princes* is a classic in the field. But it was Robert Dilt's *Neuro-Linguistic Programming* that gave us the initials by which it is now popularly known – NLP (see Chapter 33).

Our sensory preferences are sometimes indicated by our language. Auditory learners may typically say: 'That sounds right', 'Suddenly it clicked', or 'That rings a bell'. Visualizers might say: 'I see now', 'I get the picture', or 'That looks right to me'. Kinesthetic (physical) learners sometimes use: 'That feels right', 'I have a firm grip on the matter', or 'It's a smooth answer to a tough problem'.

To allow facilitators and/or individuals to identify their preferred learning style Colin Rose uses an adaptation of the well-researched *Learning Style Analysis* by Harry Reinart and issued by the Edmonds School District, Lynnwood, Washington, USA. This enables respondents to identify whether they prefer to learn by visual, verbal/visual, auditory, kinesthetic (physical), or multisensory routes. Having identified their individual preferred learning style, Rose goes on to show how that style can be brought to bear effectively in any learning situation. As he points out, learning how to learn is a skill for life!

Arthur Costa, Professor of Education at California State University, has shown that, as we grow up, many people learn naturally by doing, then thinking, then talking, then theorizing. The problem, he points out, is that this natural human sequence is too often reversed in our formal learning situations. The abstract theory comes first, then, perhaps, a discussion and, only maybe, some physical activation.

'Why,' said the Dodo, 'the best way to explain it is to do it' (Lewis Carroll).

It has been claimed that, on average, we remember 20 per cent of what we read, 30 per cent of what we hear, 40 per cent of what we see, 50 per cent of what we say, 60 per cent of what we do, but 90 per cent of what we see, hear, say and do! As remembering is an important part of learning, it pays if we can learn in ways that combine seeing, hearing, saying and doing, as Dr Jean Houston shows. Houston adds that learners delight in so doing because it uses so much more of the mind–brain–body system in a smoothly co-ordinated way (Houston, 1990).

In Colin Rose's system facilitators are reminded:

- of the Sperry/Ornstein need to engage the whole brain;
- to give the 'big picture' first, because most people are more 'global' thinkers:
- that an emotional content makes the brain function better and helps to secure the transfer of information to long-term memory; and
- to ensure that the presentation appeals equally to audio/video/kinesthetic learners.

3. Explore – thinking about it

Clearly this stage spreads across the learning activity, but here it is focused on the new material.

'Intelligence is not a static structure, but an open, dynamic system that can continue to develop throughout life!' So claims Dr Reuven Feuerstein after studying in Geneva and at the Sorbonne and working in both east and west Europe before taking the Chair of Education at Barr Ilan University, Israel. Using his theory of Structural Cognitive Modifiability, Dr Feuerstein spent some years training French workers, managers and executives in the skills of intelligence.

Feuerstein's claim may have yet to be widely accepted by the psychological and educational establishments, but he is in good company with professors at both Yale and Harvard universities. At Yale the IBM Professor of Psychology and Education is Robert J. Sternberg who has a Triarchic Theory of Intelligence. The types are 'componential' (primarily composed of linguistic and logical–mathematical abilities), 'contextual' (the source of creative insight) and 'experiential' (the 'street smarts' of intelligence). He states that while the 'componential' is the one that most tests are designed to assess, the other two, which are of enormous value to society, are neither reinforced nor given much opportunity to develop in many learning arenas.

He is developing the Sternberg Triarchic Test (STAT) which will be suitable for administration to nine levels from kindergarten age to adults. It will offer separate scores for analytical ability, synthetic ability (coping with novelty), automatization and practical – intellectual skills. Crossed with those fields will be scores for three content areas (verbal, quantitative and figural) yielding twelve separate sub-tests per level. STAT differs from conventional tests in a number of ways, including:

- Measuring skills for coping with novelty.
- Measuring practical abilities as well as academic intellectual skills.
- It places more emphasis on ability to learn than on what has been learned.

Along the road at Harvard, Professor Howard Gardner at the Graduate School of Education seems to endorse Feuerstein's claim and widen Sternberg's range. Gardner believes that we have seven identifiable intelligences – but that we mainly train and teach to just two. The two intelligences that we favour and train/teach to in Western society are:

1. *Linguistic*   Skill with words, as exemplified by writers, negotiators.
2. *Logical/mathematical*   Skill in analysis and logic, as exemplified by scientists, economists.

These are accepted as vitally important, but there are five more intelligences according to Gardner:

3. *Visual/Spatial*   The ability to visualize, as exemplified by architects, artists, navigators, photographers.
4. *Musical*   The ability to create and identify complex patterns of sound, as exemplified by musicians.

5. *Kinesthetic* The ability to use physical intelligence, as exemplified by athletes, builders, dancers, surgeons.
6. *Interpersonal* The ability to communicate effectively with others and to show empathy, as exemplified by gifted facilitators and therapists.
7. *Intrapersonal* The ability to create one's own goals and plans, to be reflective.

Use of the seven intelligences can usefully be illustrated by elements of learning to drive a car:

- Linguistic – reading up on written advice.
- Logical/Mathematical – working out braking distances.
- Kinesthetic – practising the skill, steering, brake, gears.
- Visual/Spatial – manoeuvring into a parking space.
- Musical – making a jingle of key facts in the Highway Code.
- Interpersonal – asking advice from the instructor.
- Intrapersonal – encouraging oneself to cope with road hazards.

In Colin Rose's system he builds on the two 'normally used' intelligences by using the other five in a variety of ways. Spatial intelligence is involved by creating highly visual memory maps, charts, graphs and posters with lesson content. Kinesthetic intelligence is used in role play, drama, visualization and in active games. Musical intelligence is added when facts are memorized in raps or songs and when classical music is used as a background to a spoken summary of what has been learned. Interpersonal intelligence is involved through the inclusion of paired learning and through group games and competitions. Intrapersonal intelligence is catered for by including time to reflect, to review and to plan how to transfer what has been learned to one's life or one's job.

4. Store – filing for easy recall

As Paul MacLean has shown, the limbic system of the brain controls our emotions and some key elements of our long-term memory. But what we receive passes first to our short-term memory. It has been estimated that 70 per cent of what one learns one day is forgotten by the following day – unless there is a deliberate attempt to consolidate the material in the long-term memory.

One of the most dramatic and effective ways of achieving the transfer was developed by the doyen of practitioners in accelerative learning, Dr Georgi Lozanov, a medical doctor and a leading research psychologist in the Bulgarian University of Sofia. The United Nations Education, Scientific and Cultural Organization (UNESCO) welcomed Lozanov's technique as an important advance in education. They did so after a disbelieving group of their people learned to recognize 1,200 new words of a foreign language in a single day! The Lozanov method involves six main principles:

1. Remove the negative mental blocks that cramp natural learning ability.

2. Relax – because relaxation creates the ideal condition of stress-free alertness, when information is rapidly and effortlessly absorbed.
3. Create a mental map of the information to be learned.
4. Hear the 'active concert'. This is a dramatic reading of the main elements of the text to the accompaniment of classical music. The musical choice is mainly that composed between 1700 and 1750 by the Baroque composers including Bach, Corelli, Haydn and Vivaldi. The brain is known to store information in a rhythmical way, so the use of rhythm as an external aid is seen as logical.
5. A series of games, puzzles and playlets designed to review the material learned, presented in a 'fun' environment. It is stress free and character-ized by high expectations of success. Mistakes, if they occur, are taken as an indication that the learner is deliberately stretching for the new material and are seen as a sign of ambition and lack of fear.
6. The 'receptive concert' – to develop familiarity with the material being studied. Learners relax in their chairs, close their eyes and just concen-trate on the music; this creates an ideal mental state for an effortless absorption of the material.

Peter Kline, an experienced trainer using the Lozanov method, claims that 'The whole of the lesson brings about a coordination of the left and right brain in a synthesis that creates a quantum leap in learning speeds and retention. You can't separate the intellectual from the emotional. An emotional content to learning makes it easier to remember because people remember more in a higher state of arousal.' The music works by activating the right brain and in this way the left and right brains are directly and independently stimulated to speed the information into the memory in a positive and enjoyable environment.

Dr Thomas Budzynski of the University of Colorado Medical Center and the Biofeedback Center, Denver, appears to confirm Kline's point. Writing in *Psychology Today* he states:

Apparently the right hemisphere processes verbal matter better if it is coded in rhythm or emotion. When someone speaks in a monotone, only the verbal hemisphere is activated. If the speaker adds intonation, the nonverbal side starts to pay attention. The right hemisphere's language is not the logical content of what is said, but the emotions conveyed by how it is said. Lecturers, preachers and politicians who are famous for their oratory know intuitively what to do with their voices to generate emotion and thereby persuade their audiences.

The medium is the message?

Colin Rose first applied the system he had developed to languages – French, German, Italian and Spanish. He gained students in various parts of the world and they seemed to bear out the 'accelerated' pace of learning. In Australia, test schools in the New South Wales school system successfully 'taught two years' French in three months'. In the United Kingdom, the Savoy Hotel group measured the system as ten times faster than conventional methods. Many other British and   *269* foreign organizations use accelerated learning languages for their staffs.

Recognizing the four distinct aspects of memorizing – review, registration, retention and recall – Rose uses a wide variety of techniques including: memory mapping, flash cards, diagrams, flow charts, rhymes, raps and mnemonics. He appeals to aural, visual and kinesthetic preferences and the seven intelligences. He also uses 'active' and 'review' concerts in his programmes for facilitators and individual learners.

5. Act – show you know

Learners need to act – to provide a spoken, written or physical demonstration that the new information has been learned, or that behaviour has changed. The act of discussion with peers is not only a proven study strategy, it is also a proven way of ensuring action. In Rose's 'Accelerate Your Learning' programme it is called the 'Study Buddy System'.

A now famous experiment by Dr Kurt Lewin of the US Department of Agriculture underlines the usefulness of discussion. He set out to persuade American housewives to consider eating some of the less popular cuts of meat like liver, kidneys and heart. The experiment took place in Iowa between two groups of housewives. Group One were given a lecture on the value of a type of meat; they were also given leaflets explaining the high nutritional value and were given recipes. Group Two were given the same lecture, information and recipes, but were also given time to discuss the information together. The proportion of each group that acted on the information – that is, actually served the cuts of meat – was 3 per cent in Group One but 32 per cent in Group Two. In other words the presentation, plus discussion, was over ten times more effective than a lecture alone. (Quoted in *Readings in Social Psychology*, ed. G. Swanson.)

The rationale is that discussion ensures that arguments are marshalled more logically and the decision to act comes from the individual instead of being imposed from an outside source. Robert Sternberg has demonstrated that students who talk problems out loud – even to themselves – arrive at a higher number of quality solutions. Discussion also encourages a higher level of commitment.

At this stage Rose looks for a high level of participation in a stress-free, fun-based environment. In his 'Training and Development Programme' he provides more than 70 activations – games puzzles, competitions, exercises. The inter-action is always encouraging, supportive and rewarding. In this way errors are seen as useful guidance and feedback on the need for a change in approach – not as a threat or a negative.

6. Review – short and longer term

This stage in Colin Rose's programmes reflects the Lozanov method and the 'review concert'. In group learning situations the facilitator will have a summary of the key points that have been learned during the session and will read it to music while learners relax quietly in their seats. Alternatively, the key points can be projected on to a screen while the learners watch and listen.

The 'review concert' is so different from other forms of conclusion that it is important to remember why it is effective:

- Learning occurs optimally when learners are relaxed.
- Using music as part of the delivery engages the emotional centre of the brain where an important element of long-term memory is located.
- Learning is helped when the whole brain is working on the task. Music stimulates the right side of the brain.

We have all absorbed the words of many songs with little, if any, conscious effort – the 'review concert' sets out to reproduce a similar state of relaxed absorption.

Following the 'review concert' an opportunity is given to identify 'What went well' and 'What could have gone better'. This gives learners an opportunity to participate in determining the quality of their class experience, and also a sense of involvement, even control. It gives the facilitator valuable feedback on making the group as effective as possible. It also reinforces the concept of self-review that so much needs to be developed in self-directed learners.

Consolidation of learning is a further part of Colin Rose's system and lies in 'The Personal Progress Plan'. This invites the learner to record what has been learned and to what use it will be put; but it also asks that the material be reviewed on a predetermined frequency. In a study reported in *Practical Aspects of Memory*, Mangold Linton kept a diary over a four-year period. She was able to show that those events in the diary which she never reviewed were 65 per cent forgotten. Even a single review cut down forgetting significantly, whereas four reviews over the four-year period reduced the probability of forgetting down to about 12 per cent. Just four reviews could produce an 88 per cent probability of recall!

CONCLUSION

A recent survey reports, as others over the years have done, that 10 per cent of our young people compare well in performance with any of our international competitors. But, the survey adds, further down the percentage scale our young people fail significantly to match up to their opposite numbers in our competitors' populations. This could portend a significant economic handicap in the relatively near future. Have we concentrated so exclusively on academic excellence that we have overlooked the needs and failed to recognize the abilities of most of our people?

Hear Sir John Cassels, Director of the National Commission on Education, writing of 'A' levels, which he calls 'the "gold standard", this highly prized qualification at 18'. 'They are', he says, 'a bind.' They 'cast a wide blight on all other avenues of study, not because of any defects they may have but purely for reasons of history and supposed prestige. They make everything else second-rate.'

If, as our earlier study shows, less than 20 per cent of young people aged 16   *271* retain a positive self-image of their ability to learn, the size of our educational and occupational training problems becomes enormous. It requires a rapid re-evaluation of the ways people may be helped to learn and a massive re-allocation of resources, so as to equip educators to both appreciate and effectively apply what we now know from research.

Perhaps Dr Botkin in his 1990 report to the Club of Rome is right: 'The place where there is promising action in reforming education and modernizing learning is the international business community.' However, there is evidence that we may be in danger of concentrating as much on the top 10 per cent of employees as educators appear to have done on pupils.

It is most prestigious to be seen to be training 'managers, executives and administrators'; most of our effort and much of our writing is directed at developing those albeit important occupational groups. At our peril, though, do we overlook the largest proportion of our workforce. Those who, currently, have poor experiences of formal learning, to the point where their confidence is low, their attitude pessimistic and their feelings coloured by threat and/or stress when facing new formal learning situations.

Occupational learning facilitators must overcome these basic hurdles before they can start to produce efficiently the lively, challenging, outward looking, flexible, capable, occupied personnel who will be essential to retain their organization's and the nation's place in the global economy.

Colin Rose's contribution to that end are his unique 'learning how to learn' programmes for facilitators and individuals. They are already enabling some multinational and some relatively local organizations, here and overseas, to meet the development needs of their people through accelerated learning methods that owe much to the application of the most recent validated research on how humans learn.

FURTHER READING

Bandler, Richard and John Grinder (1979), *Frogs into Princes*. Moab, Ut.; Real People Press.

Botkin, James, Mahdi Elmandjra, and Malitza Mircea (1979), *No Limits to Learning*, New York: Pergamon Press.

Costa, Arthur (ed.) (1985), *Developing Minds*, Alexandria, Va.: ASCD.

Costa, Arthur and L.F. Lowery (1989), *Techniques for Teaching Thinking*, Pacific Grove, Calif.: ASCD.

Csikszentmihalyi, Mihaly and Isabella (1988), *Optimal Experience*, Cambridge Mass.: Harvard University Press.

Diamond, Marian Cleeves (1988), *Enriching Heredity*, New York: Macmillan.

Dickinson, Dee (ed.) (1991), *Creating the Future*, Aston Clinton: Accelerated Learning Systems.

Dilts, Robert (1990), *Changing Belief Systems with NLP*, California: Meta Publications.

Entwistle, N.J. (1990), *The Handbook of Educational Ideas and Practices*, London: Routledge.

Feuerstein, Reuven, Yaacov Rand, and John Rynders (1988), *Don't Accept Me As I Am*, New York: Plenum Press.

Gardner, Howard (1982), *Art, Mind and Brain*, New York: Basic Books.

Gardner, Howard (1983), *Frames of Mind*, New York: Basic Books.

Gardner, Howard (1989), *To Open Minds*, New York: Basic Books.

Houston, Jean (1990), *Mind Games*, New York: Marlboro.

Lozanov, Georgi (1978), *Suggestology and Outlines of Suggestopedy*, New York: Gordon & Breach.

Machado, Luis Alberto (1980), *The Right to be Intelligent*, New York: Permagon Press.

MacLean, Paul D. (1990), *The Triune Brain in Evolution*, New York: Plenum.

Ornstein, Robert (1977), *The Education of the Intuitive Mode: The Psychology of Consciousness*. London: Harcourt Brace.

Rose, Colin (1985), *Accelerated Learning*, Aston Clinton: Accelerated Learning Systems; New York: Dell.

Sternberg, Robert (1988), *The Triarchic Mind: A New Theory of Intelligence*, New York: Viking Press.

Sternberg, Robert (ed.) (1990), *Wisdom: Its Nature, Origins and Development*, New York: Cambridge University Press.

22 Preferred learning styles

Peter Honey

I always remember reading a piece written over twenty-five years ago by Chris Argyris where he predicted, amongst other things, a move

> *from* management development programmes that teach managers how they ought to think and behave
> *to* programmes with the objective of helping managers to learn from experience.

He argued that it was necessary because 'no one can develop anyone else except himself. The door to development is locked from the inside.' He went on to say 'Emphasizing the *processes* of how to learn, how to diagnose administrative situations, how to learn from experience – these are timeless wisdoms.' His conclusion was that we needed less emphasis on developing *learned* managers and more on developing *learning* managers.

When I first read Argyris's words I agreed with them wholeheartedly, but I did not fully understand how to put them into practice. What exactly were the processes of learning from experience? How could management development be designed to give managers practice in these 'timeless wisdoms'? Was it just a question of exposing managers to different experiences and hoping they would learn from their successes and mistakes? Or did the mechanics of learning need to be understood and designed into management development as a deliberate strategy?

I confess I did not know the answers to any of these questions. Then I came across Kolb and Fry's Learning Style Inventory together with their description of the stages involved in the business of learning from experience. This was the spur for many years of work in conjunction with Alan Mumford which has resulted in our publication *The Manual of Learning Styles* together with its sister booklet *Using Your Learning Styles* (Honey and Mumford, 1982 and 1983). In these publications we describe the full range of uses of learning styles information in the design of programmes, boss/subordinate relationships and selection of structured learning activities.

In this chapter I intend to concentrate on the use of learning styles by individuals for themselves. I shall:

1. examine the process of learning from experience and the short cuts that managers characteristically take to truncate the process;
2. describe four different learning style preferences and show how they affect the sort of activities managers learn from;
3. show how it is possible to develop an underdeveloped learning style and thus become an all-round learner from experience.

THE PROCESS OF LEARNING FROM EXPERIENCE

Alan Mumford and I have developed a simplified version of Kolb's model (Kolb, 1984) which looks like Figure 22.1.

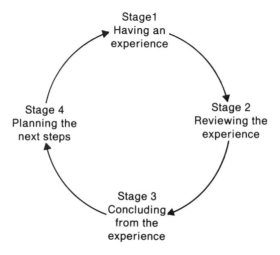

Figure 22.1   The process of learning from experience

It is rare to find managers who consciously discipline themselves to do all four stages as shown in Figure 22.1. Depending on their learning style preferences (this will be discussed later) managers are likely to take a number of liberties with this process. Some of the better known ones are as follows:

1. Indulging at stage 1, that is, rushing around, having lots of experiences and keeping frantically busy, but never bothering to review, conclude or plan. Such managers equate having lots of experiences with learning, and conveniently assume that if they have experienced something they have automatically learned from it.
2. Limiting stage 1 by repeating familiar experiences over and over again, and never going out on a limb and trying something new or different.
3. Avoiding stage 1 by being a 'voyeur' and learning from other people's *275*

experiences rather then their own. This reduces the risks of making mistakes or making fools of themselves.

4. Avoiding stage 2 by having a stock of conclusions, and forcing experiences to fit the conclusions rather than the other way round. This is closely akin to the well-known process of jumping to conclusions. The attraction is that it avoids the uncertainty of reviewing an experience and the hard work of reaching conclusions.

5. Limiting stages 2 and 3 by collecting ready-made ploys and techniques of the 'how to do it' variety. This avoids the hard work of discovering and creating practical ways of doing things via reviewing and concluding experiences.

Of course, all these short cuts are entirely understandable and all have their attractions, but they, and others like them, all tend to erode the amount that can be learned from experience.

DIFFERENT LEARNING STYLE PREFERENCES

Kolb and Fry's Learning Style Inventory suggested that people develop preferences for different learning styles in just the same way that they develop any other sort of style – management, leadership, negotiating, and so on. Naturally, I did the inventory to discover my own learning style and started to include it on training courses I ran as a way of predicting who would respond in what sort of way and so anticipating learning difficulties. Unfortunately, whilst I bought the theory, I found some problems with the inventory itself (the predictions were not as accurate as I wished and the face-validity was poor). Accordingly, together with Alan Mumford, I started to develop a questionnaire that would do a better job.

After three years of intensive experimentation the result was an 80-item questionnaire that takes ten minutes or so to complete, and identifies whether someone is predominantly:

- *Activist*   What's new? I'm game for anything.
- *Reflector*   I'd like time to think about this.
- *Theorist*   How does this relate to that?
- *Pragmatist*   How can I apply this in practice?

The learning styles tie in with the four stages of learning from experience as follows:

- A preference for the *activist* style equips you for stage 1.
- A preference for the *reflector* style equips you for stage 2.
- A preference for the *theorist* style equips you for stage 3.
- A preference for the *pragmatist* style equips you for stage 4.

276   All-round learners, or integrated learners as they are sometimes referred to, are clearly best equipped to manage all four stages. However, most people develop learning style preferences that assist with some of these stages and hinder others.

These style preferences very significantly affect the sort of activities that people learn best from. For example, we have found that activists learn best from activities where:

1. There are new experiences/problems/opportunities from which to learn.
2. They can engross themselves in short 'here and now' activities, such as business games, competitive tasks, role-playing exercises.
3. They have a lot of the limelight/high visibility.
4. They are thrown in at the deep end with a task they think is difficult.

Reflectors, on the other hand, learn best from activities where:

1. They are encouraged to watch/think/chew over activities.
2. They are allowed to think before acting, to assimilate before commenting.
3. They have the opportunity to review what has happened, what they have learned.
4. They can reach a decision in their own time without pressure and tight deadlines.

Theorists learn best form activities where:

1. They have time to explore methodically the associations and interrelationships between ideas, events and situations.
2. They are in structured situations with clear purposes.
3. They have the chance to question and probe the basic methodology, assumptions or logic behind something.
4. They are intellectually stretched.

Pragmatists learn best from activities where:

1. There is an obvious link between the subject matter and a problem or opportunity on the job.
2. They are shown techniques for doing things with obvious practical advantages currently applicable to their own job.
3. They have the chance to try out and practise techniques with coaching/ feedback from a credible expert.
4. They can concentrate on practical issues.

The dovetailing between learning styles and learning activities has led us to postulate some key questions that people can use to assess the appropriateness of different learning opportunities.

Key questions for activists

- Shall I learn something new, that is, something that I did not know/could not do before?
- Will there be a wide variety of different activities? (I do not want to sit and listen for more than an hour at a stretch!)
- Will it be OK to have a go/let my hair down/make mistakes/have fun?
- Shall I encounter some tough problems and challenges?
- Will there be other like-minded people to mix with?

Key questions for reflectors

- Shall I be given adequate time to consider, assimilate and prepare?
- Will there be opportunities/facilities to assemble relevant information?
- Will there be opportunities to listen to other people's points of view – preferably a wide cross-section of people with a variety of views?
- Shall I be under pressure to be slapdash or to extemporize?

Key questions for theorists

- Will there be lots of opportunities to question?
- Do the objectives and programme of events indicate a clear structure and purpose?
- Shall I encounter complex ideas and concepts that are likely to stretch me?
- Are the approaches to be used and concepts to be explored 'respectable', that is, sound and valid?
- Shall I be with people of similar calibre to myself?

Key questions for pragmatists

- Will there be ample opportunities to practise and experiment?
- Will there be lots of practical tips and techniques?
- Shall we be addressing real problems and will it result in action plans to tackle some of my current problems?
- Shall we be exposed to experts who know how to/can do it themselves?

BECOMING AN ALL-ROUND LEARNER FROM EXPERIENCE

A knowledge of learning styles can either be used to help dovetail learning activities to suit learning styles or be used as a starting point for self-development. The latter option is the one I want to explore now.

The advantages of having a broader range of learning skills are that you become a more effective learner from life's events and, if you are a trainer as I am, you are more likely to be able to help a greater range of trainees by being a more effective trainer. I want to illustrate how I personally have made use of a knowledge of my own learning style preferences to become a more effective trainer. I do this not in any boastful way, but as a means of trying to encourage readers to develop their own learning skills and thus become better at helping other people to learn.

THE PROBLEM

I have been an active trainer since 1965, but it is only recently that the implications of my own learning styles really dawned on me. My own preferences are for the activist and pragmatist styles. This means that my strengths and weaknesses tend to be as follows:

As an activist, my strengths are that I am:

- flexible and relatively open minded;
- happy to have a go;
- happy to be exposed to new situations; and
- optimistic about anything new, and therefore unlikely to resist change.

As a pragmatist, my strengths are that I am:

- keen to test things out in practice;
- practical and realistic;
- businesslike and down to earth; and
- keen on specific techniques.

That's the good news! On the other hand my preference for the activist and pragmatist styles means that I have some important weaknesses.

As an activist, my weaknesses are that I am:

- likely to take the immediately obvious action without considering alternatives;
- likely to take unnecessary risks;
- likely to do too much myself and hog the limelight; and
- likely to get bored with implementation and consolidation.

As a pragmatist, my weaknesses are that I am:

- likely to reject anything without an obvious application;
- not very interested in theory or basic principles;
- likely to seize on the first expedient solution to a problem; and
- impatient with disorganized people who 'waffle'.

Clearly, these strengths and weaknesses affect my performance as a trainer. For example, I am likely to design training courses that are *279* packed with lots of activities and to sell people short on theory and basic principles. I am likely to warm to trainees who display activist tendencies and to have difficulties with trainees who hold back and are more cautious and less assertive. Also, paradoxically, the more I try to jolly along trainees who have reflector/theorist preferences, the more likely they are to take fright and withdraw still further.

THE CHOICES

Once I knew my own learning style preferences (the Learning Styles Questionnaire together with its score key comes as a package with *The Manual of Learning Styles*) and realized their implications for me as a trainer, I had two choices. Either I could specialize and only train fellow activists and pragmatists, or I could set out to develop my underdeveloped reflector and theorist styles so that I was better equipped to help a broader range of trainees.

The idea of specializing has some practical difficulties and, having seriously toyed with the idea, I dropped it in favour of self-development. The practical difficulties are not by any means insurmountable – indeed, on an in-company basis, where there may be a team of trainers with various styles, there is much to be said for more thoroughly matching trainer and trainee styles. It would require a system where trainee's learning styles are identified *before* they attend a training programme so that they could be catered for either by allocating them to courses designed to suit their styles or to trainers with compatible styles.

THE SOLUTION

I decided to set about consciously strengthening my reflector and theorist styles so that, through an extended repertoire, I would be in a better position to adopt styles suitable for all types of trainees. More specifically, I set myself the goal of strengthening my reflector style by becoming:

- more thoughtful, thorough and methodical;
- better at listening to others and assimilating information; and
- more careful not to jump to conclusions.

In order to strengthen my theorist style I set about becoming:

- more rational, objective and disciplines;
- better at logical (vertical) thinking; and
- better at asking probing questions.

MY SELF-DEVELOPMENT PROGRAMME

Here are some of the things I did in order to strengthen my reflector and theorist styles.

1. Each month I sat in the public gallery at the Town Hall, observing our local district councillors during their meetings (for an activist this is ideal because you are not allowed to speak – only to observe). I kept a careful record of what was said, and later did an analysis of the arguments used, and the processes that led up to a decision.
2. It so happened that a general election was called soon after I had embarked on my self-development plan. I bought myself copies of the manifestoes for the three main parties and did a painstaking analysis of the policies each was advocating. Having done this, I designed a self-scoring questionnaire to help people decide which policies they agreed/did not agree with.
3. I put myself on a rational emotive therapy (RET) course. RET is a rigorous form of therapy that surfaces and challenges your irrational beliefs, and as such is an excellent vehicle for developing the theorist style in particular.
4. I read articles in the 'quality' newspapers and did a thorough analysis of the arguments they were using, and tried to identify and write down the fundamental assumptions they were based on. I compiled a list of probing questions that I wished to put to the authors.
5. I forced myself to compile lists for and against a particular piece of action. I tried this on domestic decisions, not just work ones, and it nearly drove my wife mad! Never mind, it helped me to think of alternative courses of action rather than revelling in instant (activist) on-the-spot decisions.
6. I deliberately increased my serious reading. To give myself an incentive, I volunteered to write reviews of books. This is an excellent way of forcing yourself to read the book in question carefully enough and analyse its good and bad points.
7. I took a list of criteria to be used as the basis for designing an assessment programme for middle managers and broke each down into a number of specific behavioural indicators. Previously, the criteria had been global and vague (leadership, flexibility, decision-making, and so on). I spent a concentrated day pinpointing six key behaviours for each criterion.
8. Finally, and perhaps most helpful of all, three times a week I make an entry in my learning log. The procedure I have devised is as follows:

   - Start by thinking back over an experience and selecting a part of it (a 15-minute period or so) that was significant or important for you.
   - Write a detailed account of what happened during that period. Do not at this stage put any effort into deciding what you learned – just concentrate on describing what actually happened.
   - Then, list the conclusions you have reached as a result of the experience. These are, in effect, your learning points. Do not limit the number and do not worry about the practicality or quality of the points.
   - Finally, decide which learning points you want to implement in the future and work out an action plan which covers what you are going to do and when you are going to do it. Spell out your action plan as *281*

precisely as possible, so that you are clear what you have to do and that it is realistic.

I have been so impressed with the worthwhileness of keeping a log like this that I have introduced it as a twice-a-day feature on most of the training programmes I run. Activists need some cajoling: reflectors, theorists and pragmatists take to it more easily.

IDEAS FOR STRENGTHENING THE ACTIVIST AND PRAGMATIST STYLES

Of course, none of my personal examples will help those who want to develop their activist and/or pragmatist styles. Here then, taken from *The Manual of Learning Styles*, are some 'thought starters' for people in that position.

Self-development activities to develop the activist style

1. At least once a week, do something new, that is, something that you have never done before. Hitch a lift to work, visit a part of your organization that you have neglected, go jogging at lunch time, wear something outrageous to work one day, read an unfamiliar newspaper with views that are diametrically opposed to yours, change the layout of furniture in your office, and so on.
2. Practise initiating conversations (especially 'small talk') with strangers. Select people at random from your internal telephone directory and go and talk to them. At large gatherings, conferences or parties, force yourself to initiate and sustain conversations with everyone present. In your spare time go door-to-door canvassing for a cause of your choice.
3. Deliberately fragment your day by chopping and changing activities each half-hour. Make the switch as diverse as possible. For example, if you have had half an hour of cerebral activity, switch to doing something utterly routine and mechanical. If you have been sitting down, stand up. If you have been talking, keep quiet, and so on.
4. Force yourself into the limelight. Volunteer whenever possible to chair meetings or give presentations. When you attend a meeting, set yourself the challenge of making a substantial contribution within ten minutes of the start of the meeting. Get on a soapbox and make a speech at your local Speakers' Corner.
5. Practise thinking aloud and on your feet. Set yourself a problem and bounce ideas off a colleague (see if between you, you can generate 50 ideas in ten minutes). Get some colleagues/friends to join in a game where you give each other topics and have to give an impromptu speech lasting at least five minutes.

Self-development activities to develop the pragmatist style

1. Collect techniques, that is, practical ways of doing things. The techniques

can be about anything potentially useful to you. They might be analytical techniques, such as critical path analysis or cost benefit analysis. They might be interpersonal techniques such as transactional analysis, or assertiveness or presentation techniques. They might be time-saving techniques or statistical techniques, or techniques to improve your memory, or techniques to cope with stress and reduce your blood pressure!

2. In meetings and discussion of any kind (progress meetings, problem-solving meetings, planning meetings, appraisal discussions, negotiations, sales calls, and so forth), concentrate on producing action plans. Make it a rule never to emerge from a meeting or discussion without a list of actions, either for yourself or for others or both. The action plans should be specific and include a deadline (e.g. 'I will produce a two-page paper listing alternative bonus schemes by 1 September').

3. Make opportunities to experiment with some of your new-found techniques. Try them out in practice. If your experiment involves other people, tell them openly that you are conducting an experiment and explain the technique which is about to be tested. (This reduces embarrassment if, in the event, the technique is a flop!) Choose the time and place for your experiments. Avoid situations where a lot is at stake and where the risks of failure are unacceptably high. Experiment in routine settings with people whose aid or support you can enlist.

4. Study techniques that other people use and then model yourself on them. Pick up techniques from your boss, your boss's boss, your colleagues, your subordinates, visiting salesmen, interviewers on the television, politicians, actors and actresses, your next door neighbour. When you discover something they do well – emulate them.

5. Subject yourself to scrutiny from 'experts', so that they can watch your technique and coach you in how to improve it. Invite someone who is skilled in running meetings to sit in and watch you chairing, get an accomplished presenter to give you feedback on your presentation techniques. The idea is to solicit help from people who have a proven track record – it is the equivalent of having a coaching session with a golfing professional.

6. Tackle a 'do-it-yourself' project – it does not matter if you are not good with your hands. Pragmatists are practical and, if only for practice purposes, DIY activities help to develop a practical outlook. Renovate a piece of furniture, build a garden shed or even an extension to your house. At work, calculate your own statistics once in a while instead of relying on the printout, be your own organization and methods man, go and visit the shopfloor in search of practical problems to solve. Learn to type, learn a foreign language.

CONCLUSION

If management development is designed to provide managers with learning opportunities, then the process of learning from experience is an essential *283* ingredient, perhaps the *most* essential. In my view any respectable management development programme should offer explicit help with learning how to learn by doing some or all of the following things:

1. Helping managers to know the stages in the process of learning from experience and how their learning style preferences help and hinder them with parts of this process.
2. Helping managers to work out how to develop an underdeveloped learning style, so that they can aim to become better 'all-round' learners.
3. Providing managers with a safe haven, where they can practise developing an underdeveloped style and help learning from experience to be a deliberate, conscious process.
4. Helping managers to identify learning opportunities in their current jobs and plan how to utilize them.

FURTHER READING

Argyris, C. 'Human relations: a look into the future', *Management Record*, **2**, (3), (1985).

Honey, P. and A. Mumford (1982), *Manual of Learning Styles*, Honey.

Honey, P. and A. Mumford (1983), *Using Your Learning Styles*, Honey.

Kolb, D. (1984), *Experiential Learning*, Prentice Hall.

23 Individual and group learning

Carol Law

People can, of course, learn by themselves as well as learning through interaction with others. However, group learning can offer the members mutual support, since it soon becomes clear that no one person's difficulties are peculiar to that person and this is reassuring at a personal level. Group members can help each other solve their difficulties and give each other feedback, as well as receiving it from a group facilitator. Groups also offer increased opportunities within which learning can take place. They offer the opportunity for individuals to increase their self-awareness through interaction with other group members. There are those who consider learning as a social event, and more effective learning takes place through interaction with others.

Trainers need to be aware that there are many ways of learning and that their new role in today's changing world, where the skills learnt today may not be those needed tomorrow, is that of a learning facilitator. The key component is to help people develop as individual autonomous learners, so that they can transfer their knowledge and skills from one situation to another, that is, to become versatile and confident of coping with change. Autonomous learners are those who have developed learning skills; that is, they have developed ways of organizing and co-ordinating learning activities so that any change in behaviour or disposition is retained. Economically and socially, there appears to be an urgent need to help people become autonomous learners. Autonomous learners are those individuals who take responsibility for their own learning, whether that learning takes place by individual study or within a group. Practitioners who take on a facilitative role set about integrating, within a training programme, *how* something is learnt so that it goes hand in hand with *what* is learnt. This can be done whether working with individuals or working with groups. What is needed is a framework that relates *what* is learnt to *how* best to learn it, and also a knowledge of the training approaches and methods that can aid effective learning both for the individual studying alone and for groups of learners.

LEARNING THEORIES AND TAXONOMIES

What goes on while learning takes place apparently goes on in the learner's head, but mental events are not very accessible and sometimes not accessible at all. Thus, most researchers into learning have made the focus of their researches the observable behaviour of the individual. Gagné (1977) defined learning as 'a change in disposition or capacity which persists over a period of time and which is not simply ascribable to the process of growth'. Over time a highly complex body of theory about the nature of learning has been built up. Generalized learning theory attempts to fit all learning together within one framework such as Thorndike (1932), Skinner (1938) and Hull (1952) in terms of stimulus and response, or Kohler (1925) and Tolman (1932) in terms of cognitive theories. All these outline ways in which learning takes place, and are helpful in indicating how practitioners can make learning more effective by altering the way in which the material to be learnt is presented. They do not discuss how people can improve their own learning.

Taxonomies of learning also attempt to deal comprehensively with all learning activity and are therefore, by necessity, very sophisticated and depend for their interpretation on well-developed powers of analysis. Examples of such taxonomies are Bloom (1956), Gagné (1965) and De Cecco (1974).

Fully elaborated taxonomies are not particularly useful for trainers in their day-to-day activities. In 1976 the Industrial Training Research Unit (ITRU) produced a much simpler classification of five categories of learning called CRAMP from its initial letters, as follows:

1. **Comprehension**
2. **Reflex action**
3. **Appropriate attitude**
4. **Memorizing**
5. **Procedural learning**

CRAMP is a practical instrument designed to help trainers choose between different types of training methods for different types of learning task. In other words it relates *what* is to be learnt to *how* best to learn it.

Comprehension Comprehension in a task refers to understanding how, why or when things happen; for example, knowing how to price articles in a shop.

Reflex action Reflex actions in a job are skilled physical movements and fine perceptual capacities developed over a period of time; for example, operating a till quickly and efficiently.

Appropriate attitudes These are expressed in relationships with other people and in behaviour appropriate to the job or task; for example, showing courtesy to customers even if the sales assistant feels they are being unreasonable.

286

Memorizing Remembering information required to carry out a specific job efficiently; for example, product prices, stock location, job numbers.

Procedural learning Procedures organize activities or tasks into a set or preferred sequence of action. Job aids, checklists, and so on, can be used by the employee without decreasing performance levels. Learning procedures usually involves one or more of the other types of learning, especially a willingness to follow the routine (appropriate attitudes).

In 1981 ITRU published the results of a project undertaken for The Further Education Unit (FEU) entitled *How do I learn?* The project was commissioned by FEU to introduce young people and their tutors to the proposition that there are many ways of learning, and to develop a programme to help develop learning skills. During the project an even simpler way of classifying learning material into facts, concepts and activities learned by memorizing, understanding and doing (MUD) was developed.

Learning by memorizing This enables individuals to recall material in the same form as it was originally learned.

Learning by understanding Understanding is an active mental process involving thoughts which link or group ideas together in a new way that make sense to the individual.

Learning by doing This involves learning a procedure and then practising until the individual becomes skilful.

Subsequent projects undertaken by Sylvia Downs and Patricia Perry of the Occupational Research Unit, Department of Applied Psychology, UWIST, have shown that the MUD classification is workable and straightforward enough to be used not only by tutors of young people but also training practitioners in industry (Downs and Perry, 1984 and 1987). There does not appear to be any reason to justify a more complex taxonomy for practitional purposes.

The research commissioned by FEU and the later research by Downs and Perry provide evidence that the development of learning skills by individuals leads to considerable improvement in the rate of learning. However, for individuals to develop these skills they must be prepared to take responsibility for their own learning and develop autonomy.

LEARNING AND AUTONOMY

The work on learning skills is directly linked with research by those who are concerned with developing autonomy and individual responsibility for learning. M.S. Knowles has been a proponent of learning autonomy. He describes efforts to instil the idea of learners becoming self-directing and the difficulties of dealing with people's concepts of learning. He said, 'The minute they walk through a *287* door labelled education or training they put on their dunce hat of dependency, sit back, fold their arms and say OK, teach me!' (Knowles, 1980). He has through his own work with adult learners put forward his own theory on adult learning, since he states: 'My strongest impression was that these (learning) theories had all been based on research on animals (mostly rodents, at that) and children, and I had trouble seeing their relevance. In fact it dawned on me that educational psychologists had not been studying learning at all but reactions to teaching' (Knowles, 1984a).

Knowles has put forward a new approach to learning – the 'androgogical model' – as opposed to the model of traditional learning – the 'pedagogical model'. The pedagogical model is the one most people have had experience with. In fact, for most people it is their only way of thinking about education/ training, since it has dominated all education – even adult education – since schools began being organized in the seventh century. Within the pedagogical model the learner is a totally dependent personality, for the teacher has full responsibility for making all the decisions about what should be learned, how and when it is learned and whether it has been learned. In the androgogical model the learner is self-directing. In fact, the psychological definition of an adult is 'One who has arrived at a self-concept of being responsible for one's own life'. Adults have a deep psychological need to be perceived by others, and treated by others, as capable of taking responsibility for themselves. Conflict arises because of the pressure exerted by teachers to make adults dependent, and their deep psychological need to be self-directing. Children, too, desire to be self-directing. *The Observer* newspaper ran 'A school that I'd like' competition, and from thousands of entries there stood out above everything else the children's desire to teach themselves, rather than to be the passive targets of teaching.

Knowles regards the pedagogical and androgogical models as parallel rather than antithetical. There are now two sets of assumptions about learners. In some situations, such as when learners of whatever age are confronting a totally strange territory of content or are confronting a machine they have never seen before, they may be truly dependent on their teacher before they can take much initiative for their own learning; in such situations the pedagogical assumptions of dependency would be realistic and pedagogical strategies would be appropriate. In many more instances, however, with adult learners, the androgogical assumption would be realistic, particularly if the learners have some orientation towards self-directed learning.

LEARNING SKILLS

Learning skills have been described as ways of organizing and co-ordinating learning activities so that any change in behaviour or disposition is retained. In the early stages of the research by Downs and Perry (1984), a number of aspects of learning were placed under the umbrella of skills of learning. However, as the research progressed it was considered that there is one group of learning skills *288* which is internalized and the elements of which are most likely to be present in most people to some extent. The difference in performance of skills of learning might be differences in capacity, but it is also likely that these elements are individually active or latent.

Internalized learning skills

A list was compiled of those internalized learning skills that were identified during the research programme.

- Questioning self and formulating questions.
- Imaging.
- Clarifying, ordering, grouping, summarizing, relating, comparing, contrasting, associating, structuring.
- Reviewing, monitoring, checking.
- Predicting.
- Evaluating, assessing.
- Formulating hypotheses.
- Deciding.
- Selecting.

Observable activities

The second group comprised a form of halfway house which was called observable activities. They could be confused with internalized learning skills because they are the overt expression of a combination of some of these skills and quite often lead to another stage in the learning process. It was argued that they incorporate the skills of learning and are not themselves such skills but are the observable activities arising from them. They are:

- Recording.
- Following written instruction.
- Expressing ideas.
- Writing, documentation.
- Problem solving.
- Using equipment.
- Note taking.
- Manual dexterity and co-ordination.
- Identifying and correcting errors.
- Questioning.

Products

A third group was identified and called simply products, and included such items as:

- A report.

- A project.
- A presentation.
- A plan.
- A procedure.
- A performance.
- An analysis.
- Output.

A fourth group was also identified and called motivational impetus and included such descriptions as 'identifying one's own personal needs' and 'taking advantage of learning opportunities'.

Downs and Perry point out that the lists are not exhaustive and will continue to be refined. They stress the importance of concentrating on the internalized learning skills. It is naturally very tempting to shift to the observable activities, just because they can be seen, but this involves the danger of deviating from the cause to the effect.

The research programme convinced the researchers that developing the skills of learning is crucially important to the individual and the community. Trainees involved in the research programme who had been educated in traditional ways appeared to see each item of product learning as discrete and more often than not of no interest. The ability to transfer and translate was therefore minimal. It is essential to change from *product* teaching to developing *processes*, which involves helping to develop the skills of learning.

LEARNING BLOCKAGES

Lack of learning skills obviously prevents people from learning efficiently and effectively, but there are undoubtedly other barriers or blockages that prevent people from using those learning skills they have, let alone develop them more fully. What are the common blockages? For example, the learners may:

- be afraid to look stupid;
- be afraid of failing;
- not know what is worth learning;
- feel too old to learn;
- feel they cannot remember things;
- lack self-confidence; or
- remember they never did well at school.

The causes of these blockages often lie within the learners themselves. For instance, it may be that:

- they lack learning skills;
- they have never learnt to learn;
- they had bad learning experiences, for example, they were: not allowed to ask questions; swamped by too much information; not encouraged to understand; expected to achieve results too quickly;

- they think that learning equals memorizing; or
- they perceive that the quality of their own learning is outside their control.

Practitioners need to help learners overcome their learning blockages as they prevent effective learning taking place, whether the individual is learning on their own or in a group. Practitioners who help their learners learn to learn, as well as helping them learn specific knowledge and skills, will help their learners overcome many learning blockages.

MOTIVATION TO LEARN

People not only need to learn, but must also want to learn. Much has been written about motivation (for example, Herzberg, 1966; Maslow, 1970). While it is acknowledged that people will respond to extrinsic motivators – a better job, a salary increase, paper qualifications and the like – the more potent motivators are *intrinsic* – self-esteem, recognition, better quality of life, greater self-confidence and the like. The androgogical model put forward by Knowles predicts that intrinsic motivators are more important for adults. Children and young people too are naturally more motivated by intrinsic rewards than by external pressures; it is schools that have conditioned them to be otherwise.

LEARNING CONTRACTS

A learning situation must be structured in order that effective learning can take place. It has traditionally been the role of the practitioner to identify the learning objective of any training session. This has been done by undertaking a skills/job analysis and the writing of learning objectives that specify not only what people will do but how well they will do it – to what standard (e.g. quantity, quality, time, cost, and so on).

The process of establishing learning objectives has so far only involved the practitioner. Most people want to have some say in their learning objectives and the methods by which they will learn, and this freedom increases their motivation to learn as fast and as well as they are capable of doing. For this to happen, a learning contract must be negotiated with the learner. Learning contracts are an effective way to help learners structure their learning. Some people have difficulty with the term 'contract' because of its legalistic flavour and substitute 'learning plan' or 'learning agreement'. But learning contract is the term most often found in the literature. There are four stages to negotiating a learning contract:

1. The learner translates a diagnosed learning need into a learning objective that describes the terminal behaviour to be achieved (which is appropriate for most basic skills training) or the direction of improvement in ability (which is appropriate for more complex learnings).

291

2. The learner next identifies with the practitioner's help the most effective resources and strategies for accomplishing each objective.
3. The learner then specifies what evidence will be collected for indicating the extent to which each objective was accomplished.
4. Finally, the learner specifies how this evidence will be judged or validated.

Negotiation of a learning contract is the key activity in preventing problems that a learner may have in studying and should be undertaken before any training programme begins. It is the first opportunity to start forming a relationship of mutual trust and respect between practitioner and learner.

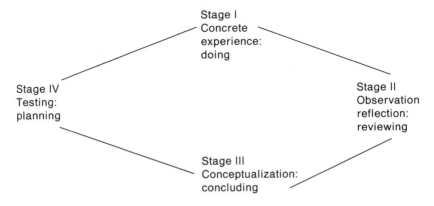

Figure 23.1   A model of Kolb's learning theory

LEARNING STYLES

Kolb (1971) put forward his own theory of learning that was based on the assumption that learning involves both thinking and doing. He developed this idea into the model shown in Figure 23.1. Honey and Mumford (1982) took Kolb's model and agreed that all four stages were essential, but that people would prefer to learn in any one of the four stages. They describe the four types as shown in Figure 23.2.

Figure 23.2   The four learning styles

Most people are a mixture of styles, with a preference for one or two. Such information is useful for practitioners in designing training programmes because a range of training methods should be included in the programme that allows trying out new ideas, reflecting on ideas, observing ideas in action, and so forth.

People have a more general preference. There are those who are happy to learn by themselves and for whom such approaches as 'Open learning' and 'Computer-based training' work well, while other people, most likely the majority, prefer to learn through interaction with others.

TRAINING APPROACHES

In negotiating the learning contract the practitioner must help the learners choose the most appropriate approach to meeting their learning objectives. Practitioners need a knowledge of the training approaches and methods than can aid effective learning in order that they can advise learners on how best to meet their needs. They must gather a great deal of information from their learner while negotiating the learning contract (e.g. attitudes to learning, previous experience, learning preferences, anxieties, and so on). Such information will help them advise the learner on what is the most appropriate training approach. There are other factors besides the needs of the learner that may constrain the choice of a training approach, for example: the time and resources available if the learning is to take place within an organization; the expectations the organization has about training; and the numbers of people who need to learn. Nine training approaches will be described and they are divided into three categories: trainer-centred; group-centred; and individual.

Trainer-centred approaches

Presentation

This is the giving of information, facts or procedure by a straight talk or demonstration, with little participation from learners except for taking notes and possibly asking occasional questions. Aids such as slides, overhead projector (OHP), handouts, samples, and so on, may be used. This approach is used when the type of learning to take place is understanding. It is a cheap and flexible approach and is often the expected approach of people, particularly those with a background in higher education. The approach does not involve the learner at all, and much of the information received is soon forgotten.

Presentation/discussion

This is a structured presentation by the trainer, followed by a discussion. The limits are clearly defined and the trainer plans and guides it so that all important topics are covered. It is an approach used when the type of learning required is understanding. It is, again, a cheap and flexible method, but if the trainer's presentation is too expository there will be little learner participation. However, the approach can be group-centred if the trainer has taken on board the androgogical model and therefore is learner-centred when giving the presentation. The presentation can be very much group-centred if it is given by *293* a member of the group and the trainer permits a free-ranging discussion to follow.

Group-centred approaches

Group discussion

This is when a group, controlled by the group members and not the trainer, debate a topic or perform a task. This is an approach used when understanding and sometimes memorizing are the types of learning required. It is a participative approach, and often, trainers need to be trained specifically in its use. Learners often need to learn additional skills to participate effectively in groups (e.g. helping others to participate, sensitivity to group processes, discussion, leadership). Future expectations about training may be radically altered by this approach.

Project work

Imsie (1968) identified four types of project group:

1. Projects based on the learners' past experience in their own firms.
2. Projects requiring original work.
3. Projects in which learners go to a new firm to tackle a specified problem.
4. Project reports based on discussions with other learners.

Project work is undertaken when the type of learning requires is understanding. Traditionally, it has been used with managers and potential management trainees, though it can be used equally successfully with more junior employees (e.g. supervisors, workers when using quality circles).

Team training

This approach is designed to help learners recognize the role and contribution of the individual to the team. From an understanding of their own actions/ contribution, an appreciation of the differing but effective approaches of other team members is gained. The approach is used when the type of learning required is understanding.

Individual approaches

Discovery learning

Unlike traditional expository training, the trainer's verbal instruction or demonstration is not the source of the learners' understanding. A sequence of graded problems designed to suit the learners' knowledge and ability enables them to develop for themselves an understanding of the subject. All the information required for solving the problem is in the situation and the trainer does not give extensive help. Discovery learning actively involves the learners and gives them autonomy; however, it may be costly in terms of time. It is an approach that can be used with groups as well as with individuals.

Open learning

This is self-directed learning which may be linked with an institution (e.g. Open University) or involve personal learning projects with limited tutorial support. Through open learning, learners may become autonomous, that is, they can learn at their own pace, at a place of their own choosing and in their own time, but they do need to be highly motivated. Well-managed support systems can lessen feelings of isolation that learners may have. Open learning may well be a cost-effective format, and can be used for all three types of learning.

One-to-one discussion

A one-to-one discussion is used to convey information, ideas and opinions, usually by the discussion of a concept or a procedure between the trainer and the learner. It may be based on a written essay or other piece of work and is an approach often used in higher education, where learners may become the target of a one-way lecture. The type of learning that it aims to bring about is understanding.

Computer-based training

The use of computers to train individuals with or without the aid of a trainer. Computer-based training encompasses both computer-assisted instruction and computer-assisted learning. In computer-assisted instruction, the computer is seen as a medium for instruction like a textbook or video. The main problem is how to present instructional materials most effectively. In computer-assisted learning the computer is seen as a tool like a calculator, and the main problem is how to help leaners use their computer to enhance their learning. With computer-based training (CBT) learners have control of their learning, as CBT can be self-paced. It provides learner-satisfaction due to the personal involvement, individual feedback and the capacity to assess one's own progress. Some CBT programmes enable learners to develop their own learning strategies.

TRAINING METHODS

In theory, all training approaches can be used with all training methods. However, some training methods are more appropriate to one type of learning than another and should be selected by considering what types of learning are involved in the task to be learned.

Below are listed 27 training methods and three procedural ways of learning. *295*

Also listed are the types of learning for which each method is relevant. A full description of each training method can be found in the CRAMP booklet (ITRU, 1980).

	Method	**Type of learning**
1.	Basic concepts, basic skills – identifying what the learner *needs* to know in the early stages of training, not what is *nice* to know. More detail can be added during the final stages of training.	Memorizing Understanding Doing
2.	Lecture video.	Understanding
3.	Demonstration	Understanding Doing
4.	Case studies	Understanding
5.	Interactional analysis – designed to develop specific job-related interpersonal skills, e.g. interviewing by observing behaviour and giving feedback.	Understanding
6.	Role play – presenting a real or imagined situation to the learners who deal with it as a real situation.	Understanding
7.	T group – aims to improve social skills by group members examining their behaviour as it happens.	Understanding
8.	Encounter group – similar to T group, but more structured.	Understanding
9.	Coverdale – develops individuals by working in group, but more structured.	Understanding
10.	Adventure training – use of outdoor activities to develop the individual within the group in leadership and the effective management of people.	Understanding
11.	Team skills.	Understanding
12.	Synetics – enhancing the creativity of a team by turning competitive energy into co-operative energy.	Understanding
13.	Individual projects.	Understanding
14.	In-tray exercises – an in-tray representative of the job is presented to the learner. It contains documents, letters, reports, notes of meetings, and so forth, most of which require action to be taken.	Understanding
15.	Textbooks, manuals, handouts.	Memorizing Understanding
16.	Mnemonics and jingles.	Memorizing

17.	Rules and deductive method – dividing or structuring material to ease the learner's memory load.	Memorizing
18.	Progressive part method – used for teaching a task which consists mainly of skilled movements. The sequence of micro-motions is easy to get right but the task involves a heavy memory load. Breaking the task into parts does not destroy it.	Memorizing Understanding Doing
19.	Cumulative-part method – used for teaching a task or material involving a lot of difficult memorizing. It is particularly suitable when breaking the task into parts destroys or distorts it.	Memorizing Understanding Doing
20.	Drill and practice – the traditional way of teaching knowledge and skills.	Memorizing Understanding Doing
21.	Self- and CBT-testing.	Memorizing Understanding Doing
22.	Database inquiry – learning how to use a computer to look up information, solve problems and make decisions.	Understanding
23.	Simulation, games.	Understanding Doing
24.	Simulators.	Understanding
25.	Discrimination method – learners to distinguish between closely similar items.	Memorizing Doing
26.	Cueing and fading – helping learning to discriminate on a small number of points by adding something, e.g. colour-coded keys on a keyboard.	Memorizing Doing
27.	Magnification method, i.e. used for teaching skilled physical tasks which involve fine perceptual judgements rather than skilled bodily movements.	Memorizing Doing
28.	Embedded training, i.e. instructions for use are provided within the computer-based system.	Doing
29.	Job aids, checklists, simple instructions.	Doing
30.	Complex instructions in audio programme and algorithm form.	Doing

THE ROLE OF THE TRAINER

Over the past years the Industrial Training Research Unit (ITRU) has been doing research into the differences in training style. It was observed that two trainers might be following the same training plan, using the same visual aids – and yet *297* have very different success rates. The difference between them lay in the detail of *how* they put across information and dealt with errors. This difference was called their training style (ITRU, 1984).

Observation of effective and less effective trainers enabled the identification of characteristics of style that are important to helping people learn. These included: developing a rapport with learners; having a flexible approach to accommodate the individual needs of learners; and trying to adapt to the different type of learning which jobs involve. In short, effective instruction has a learner-centred approach to training.

The research also noted that the influence an effective training style has upon learners is wide-ranging. Not only does it bring about better job understanding, but it also develops self-reliance and confidence in learners. This confidence instilled in the learners manifests itself in their ability to deal with a variety of new learning situations successfully. In other words, not only do effective trainers help learners to learn specific job skills, but they also help them to develop their learning skills and to become autonomous learners.

The following techniques have been identified during various research projects as those used by effective trainers in helping learners learn and in encouraging independence in learners (ITRU, 1986).

Helping memory

1. New information is presented in a logical sequence and in a series of manageable chunks so that learners do not have to take in too much at any one time. This will also prevent errors arising. Learners can revise in manageable chunks for tests or exams. This would be a more sensible way to revise than the commonly adopted procedure of reading through a topic from start to finish. Fewer errors will creep into their recall.

2. The amount of information presented to learners is limited at the beginning of training to what they need to do the job, not what is thought nice to know. At a later stage of training, learners will be able to handle more information, but they can be helped to identify what are the key parts they need to remember and what is detail. Example: 'That is the important thing to remember; the rest is detail.' Learners can begin the process of sifting through information to identify the important points which must be remembered.

3. New information can be linked with what the learners may already know themselves, or have covered in a previous session, so that the context of the material is set and, thus, the trainees remember more easily. Examples: 'How is the sewing machine different from the one you used to use at school?'; 'Remember we learnt something about this when we dealt with ...'. Learners can begin to make up associations to help them remember information more easily.

4. Trainers can ask specific questions at regular intervals to check that new information has been absorbed by the learners, but more general questions, such as 'did you get all that?', do not give any positive feedback

that the trainees have remembered anything. Examples: 'You'll forget a lot of that detail if you don't revise it from time to time, so let's go over it now' (followed by specific check questions to which the trainee must give a detailed answer, not just 'yes' or 'no'); 'We covered how to do this the other day but we'll go through it again now, just to make sure it sticks in your mind'; 'So tell me why you do . . .'; 'And what would happen if . . .'. Learners can check what they have remembered by testing themselves and each other at regular intervals.

Helping understanding

1. Trainers can ask questions of their learners. They can be asked for explanations of facts and procedures, and so on. By doing this the learners will be mentally involved in the learning process and get feedback on whether they have understood the information put across. Example: 'Why do you think we do it this way?' Learners can begin to develop the habit of thinking things through for themselves, and have confidence to ask questions if they feel they have not been given all the information they require. The art of asking the right questions is probably the single most important skill they can acquire.
2. Trainers can ask questions to help learners understand why their mistakes occurred and how to prevent them happening in the future. Example: 'Why do you think it happened?'; 'That's the sort of mistake which will crop up again and again – you need to work out carefully how to stop it. Have you any ideas?' Learners can begin to work out for themselves why things went wrong and transfer their knowledge to a variety of different circumstances. They can begin to interpret errors, not as signs of failure, but as opportunities for learning how to proceed more effectively in the future. This will help them not only become independent employees but also independent learners.
3. Trainers can again ask questions to develop their learners' judgement of their own work and progress. Examples: 'Do you think this piece of work is up to standard?'; 'Why?' Learners can begin to assess their own progress and identify their own learning needs. Self-assessment is an important life competence because it contributes to personal growth and independence.

Helping doing

1. Trainers can state the objectives of each training session at the beginning so that learners are reminded of what is to be achieved. Example: 'Today I'm going to show you how to make a Victoria Sponge'; 'We're going to concentrate on three-point turns today'. Learners can begin to realize the importance of setting realistic objectives for themselves when they set about learning something on their own.
2. Trainers can identify the key point that learners must be aware of before they give a demonstration. There is a need to demonstrate slowly so that *299*

the learners have time to observe such things as body movements, how the tools and materials are held, and so on. Trainers should also do their demonstration with as little excess talking as possible so that the learners can concentrate on what is going on and ask questions when they need to. Learners can begin to understand how to get the most out of watching a demonstration. They need to become proficient at getting the information they need; they need to find out the purpose of the activity, the procedures involved and to make sure that they get 'hands on' experience of any equipment being used in the course of the demonstration.

3. Trainers can let their learners practise the job or parts of the job as soon as possible, provided, of course, that there is no danger to the learner or anyone else and that expensive materials will not be wasted. Involving the learner physically in the learning process will give feedbacks on how much the learner has taken in. Learners can begin to practise various manual skills as soon as it is practical to do so, and begin to realize that in learning manual skills they must practise as often as possible.

4. Trainers can identify those mistakes which may hinder the learning of manual skills, and should take action to rectify them immediately. Once having gone through a sequence of movement wrongly, it is very difficult for learners to unlearn. This must be prevented from happening. Example: 'Hold on! Before you begin to saw, you're holding the saw wrongly'. Learners can concentrate on getting it right first time when practising, rather than trying to hurry and consequently making mistakes. Trainers can begin to build up a strategy for dealing with errors. First, by not allowing those errors to happen which would have serious consequences in terms of safety, loss of time or expensive materials. Secondly, by identifying those errors that must be corrected immediately because they will delay learning. Thirdly, by identifying those errors which the learners make that can be turned into learning opportunities; that is, by getting learners to work out for themselves the cause of the errors, the consequences of the errors and how to prevent them happening in the future.

In conclusion, people can learn either by themselves or in groups. There are several advantages to learning with others (e.g. increased learning opportunities, mutual support, and so on). Many consider learning a social event, and much more effective learning takes place through interaction with others. Individual study demands that the learner is highly motivated.

There is an urgent need to help people become autonomous learners and develop learning skills. To help people take responsibility for their own learning and develop their learning skills, practitioners must have a learner-centred approach; that is, they must respond to the individual studying alone or learning in a group. To do this they must relate what is learned to how best to learn it, and they must have a knowledge of training approaches and methods that can aid effective learning, both for individuals studying alone and for groups of learners.

FURTHER READING

Abercrombie, M.L.H. and P.M. Terry (1974), *Aims and Techniques of Group Teaching*, Society for Research into Higher Education.

Adams, J.A. (1979), 'On the evaluation of training devices', *Human Factors*, **21**, 711–20.

Ayres, R. (1977), *A Trainer's Guide to Group Instruction*, London: BACIE.

BACIE (1970), *Case Studies*, London: BACIE.

Barber, J.W. (1968), 'Discussion leading and group training trends', Ch. 17 in J.W. Barber (ed.), *Industrial Training Handbook*, London: Illiffe.

Belbin, E. (1964), *Training the Adult Worker: Problems of Progress in Industry*, no. 15, London: HMSO.

Belbin, R.M. (1969), *The Discovery Method in Training*, London: TIPS/HMSO.

Belbin, R.M. (1981), *Management Teams: Why they Succeed or Fail*, London: Heinemann.

Belbin, E. and R.M. Belbin (1972), *Problems in Adult Retraining*, London: Heinemann.

Belbin, E., S. Downs, and P. Perry (1981), *How Do I Learn?*, London: Further Education curriculum, Review and Development Unit, PR9.

Bloom, B.S. *et al.* (1956), *Taxonomy of Educational Objectives: Handbook 1: Cognitive Domain*, New York: David McKay.

Coverdale Training for Development (1967), London: Training Partnership.

DeCecco, J.P. (1974), *The Psychology of Learning and Instruction*, 2nd edn, New Jersey: Prentice Hall.

Downs, S. and P. Perry (1984), *Developing Skilled Learners Learning to Learn in YTS*, Research and Development Series BN022, Sheffield: Manpower Services Commission.

Downs, S. and P. Perry (1986), 'Can trainers learn to take a back seat?' *Personnel Management*, March, 42–5.

Downs, S. and P. Perry (1987), *Developing Skilled Learners. Helping Adults Become Better Learners*, Research and Development Series No. 40, Sheffield: Manpower Services Commission.

Fleck, V. and C. Law (1986), *CRAMP: A Guide to Training Decisions*, Cambridge: Industrial Training Research Unit.

Gagné, Robert M. (1965), *The Conditions of Learning*, 1st edn, New York: Holt, Rinehard and Winston.

Gagné, Robert M. (1977), *The Conditions of Learning*, 3rd edn, New York: Holt, Rinehard and Winstone.

Garett, R. (1971), 'Project Based Education and Development', *Management Education and Development*, **2**, (1), 40–9.

Gibb, G.I. (1974), *Handbook of Games and Simulation Exercises*, London: E. & F.N. Spon.

Gibbs, G. (1981), *Teaching Students to Learn: A Student-Centred Approach*, Milton Keynes: Open University Press.

Herzberg, F. (1966), *Work and the Nature of Man*, Cleveland: Word Publishing.

Honey, P. and A. Mumford (1982), *The Manual of Learning Styles*, Maidenhead.

Hull, C.L. (1952), *A Behaviour System*, Yale University Press.

Imsie, J. (1968), 'The Project Method', Ch. 14 in J.W. Barber (ed.), *Industrial Training Handbook*, London: Illiffe.

Kearsley, G. (1983), *Computer-based Training*, Reading, Mass.: Addison-Wesley.

Kield, J.R. (1973), *How Adults Learn*, Chicago: Follet.

Knowles, M.S. (1980), 'How do you get people to be self-directed learners?' *Training and Development Journal*, May, 96–9.

Knowles, M.S. (1984a), *Androgogy in Action*, San Francisco: Jossey Bass.

Knowles, M.S. (1984b), *The Adult Learner: A Neglected Species*, 3rd edn, Houston: Gulf.

Kohler, W. (1925), *The Mentality of Apes*, New York: Harcourt, Brace and World.

Kolb, D.A. (1971), *Organisational Psychology: An Experienced Approach*, London: Prentice Hall.

Law, C. (1986), *Helping People Learn*, Cambridge: Industrial Training Research Unit.

Maslow, A. (1962), *Towards a Psychology of Being*, New York: Van Nostrand.

Maxwell Towers, H. (1969), *Role Playing for Supervisors*, Oxford: Pergamon.

Newsham, D.B. and J.M. Fisher (1984), *What's in a Style*, Cambridge: Industrial Training Research Unit.

Powell, L.S. (1970), *Lecturing to Large Groups*, London: BACIE.

Prince, G.M. (1982), in Olson, S.A. (ed.), *Group Planning and Problem Solving Methods in Engineering*, Chichester: Wiley.

Rackham, N., P. Honey and M.J. Colber (1971), *Developing Interactive Skills*, Guilsborough: Wellens.

Reynolds, J.I. (1980), *Case Method in Management Development: Guide for Effective Use*, Geneva: ILO.

Rogers, C.R. (1973), *Encounter Groups*, Harmondsworth: Penguin.

Shank, J.H. (1982), *Working in Teams: A Practical Manual for Improving Work Groups*, New York: AMACOM.

Shulman, L.S. and G.R. Keisler (eds) (1966), *Learning by Discovery: A Critical Appraisal*, Chicago: Rand McNally.

Skinner, B.L. (1938), *The Behaviour of Organisation*, New York: Appleton–Century–Crofts.

Smith, R.M. (1982), *Learning How to Learn: Applied Theory for Adults*, Chicago: Follet.

Stammers, R. and J. Patrick (1975), *The Psychology of Training. Essential Psychology*, London: Methuen.

Taurney, D.A. (1979), *Learning through computers*, London: Macmillan.

Thorndike, E.L. (1932), *The Fundamentals of Learning*, New York: Teachers College.

Tolman, E.C. (1932), *Purposive Behaviour in Animals and Men*, University of California Press.

Toye, M. (1968), 'A rethink on basic skills', *Industrial Training International* **4**, 112–19.

Whitaker, F.P.G. (ed.), (1965), *T-Group Training*, Oxford: Blackwell.

Wood, A.E. (1979), 'Experiences with small group tutorials', *Studies in Higher Education*, **4**, (2), 203–9.

Zoll, A.A. (1969), *Dynamic Management Education*, Reading, Mass.: Addison-Wesley.

24 Flexible learning

Hilary Temple

Once we know something of how people learn best, it is necessary to be able to put these principles into daily practice if training is to be effective. Learners need opportunities to think, experiment, test, and reflect on their experience. They all learn at different speeds and in different ways. Adults rarely benefit from sitting in groups being told things, if only because it reminds them of school. Rigidity of any kind is inappropriate for the organic process of growth which is implied by learning (though this is not to say that there should not be rigour of control of quality and standards). So it is sensible to assume that a flexible approach to training is needed if learners are to get the best out of their learning experience. Flexible learning is one of the most exciting developments in training in recent years. Its effects are even more far-reaching than those of computer-based training, even though they are less dramatic at first sight.

WHAT IS FLEXIBLE LEARNING?

What do we mean by flexible learning – also known as open learning? Open learning in particular has often been defined in ways which contrast it with conventional (that is, face-to-face) training. A useful discussion of the various terms associated with flexible approaches to learning appears in *The A–Z of Open Learning* (Jeffries, 1990). 'Flexible' and 'open' are, unfortunately, words in vogue which can mean practically anything we want them to mean; and in the education/training context they can be associated with particular brandnames or administrative structures like the Open University. Flexible learning is about flexing up learning in one or more respects, so that its users find it easier, more accessible, quicker, better related to their needs, or more effective. In terms of managing a training system, flexible learning means getting better value for money. So what flexible and open mean in this context is certainly not learning which is lacking in substance or ill-defined. If anything, the outcomes of training accomplished by flexible learning are more clearly defined than those of conventional courses.

FLEXIBLE LEARNING AS STRATEGIC CHANGE

The learner at the centre

It is easier to describe what flexible learning does than what it is, because it is essentially an approach rather than a method or system. At its core, it seeks to make training systems *learner-centred*. This is not as simple as it sounds. Courses, handbooks and textbooks tend to tell learners what the experts think it is good for them to know. Most trainers have a sense of having given a good performance at the end of a rewarding training session where the learners have taken it all in and hung on every word. In the conventional situation the trainer is at the centre, as the controller of information, inspiration, feedback and pace. Putting the learner at the centre is about more than fulfilling individual training needs. It is a little like discovering that the sun does not revolve around the earth. As Galileo's detractors found, it is difficult to acknowledge that you are not the centre of the universe. But the days when trainees were passive recipients, with the trainer the only active person in the room, are gone for ever.

The implications of learner-centredness

Own pace – and perhaps own place

Because we are human beings instead of planets, relationships are changed as a result of this change of perception. If learners are to learn at their own pace, making a group proceed in lock-step (so that some are kept waiting or given fill-in tasks to do while others struggle to keep up) becomes irrelevant. When learners learn at times and in places of their own choosing it is impossible for trainers to check from minute to minute that they are doing what they said they would do – not that this is always possible even in the classroom! All the learners' customary indications of agreement, understanding, non-comprehension and learning difficulty have to be made in different ways if learners are not physically in sight of the trainer all the time that they are learning.

Work-related learning

A flexible training programme will quite often be based on real-life work situations, so that learners will use resources other than the trainer to facilitate their learning: line-managers, colleagues, workmates, even their own family and neighbours. And because flexible learning tends to start from where learners are, the traditional course structure of theory followed by practice will frequently be reversed, so that learners are encouraged to generalize from their own observation and experience.

Changed course structures

Flexibility does not reside simply in the way in which people are encouraged to *305* learn, but in what they learn. If starting and finishing times are flexed up, assessment has to be flexible as well: otherwise there would be an absurd situation where a flexible learner had to wait, perhaps for many weeks, to take an examination for a national qualification. The self-paced nature of much of the learning means that testing assumes a new importance: for the learner, in order to consolidate what has been learned before moving to the next step; and for the trainer, to keep track of where learners are in the programme. The logical first stage in making a training programme flexible is, thus, to break it into modules, which may or may not need to be studied in a particular order.

Learner approaches to choice

Once modules of training are offered in a flexible way there is a choice for the customers (individual or corporate) of training, who no longer have to buy the whole menu but can choose appropriate items from it. This produces more far-reaching consequences than mere mixing-and-matching, or tailoring of training to specific needs, attractive though these are. After a flexible-learning approach is well established in a company it is not unusual for learners to decide for themselves, in consultation with line management and the training department, what they should study next. And where flexible-training facilities are made available to the workforce in their own time, it is quite common for people to choose general educational modules at least as much as strictly work-related ones, thus helping to bridge the education/training divide. Taking responsibility for one's own learning can be a powerful motivator in improving general performance, and is often an aspect of the introduction of broad-based quality initiatives.

Flexible learning does not equal distance learning

Open and flexible learning are equated in many people's minds with distance learning and correspondence courses. Partly, this is because in the past flexible-learning packages have been supplied to learners with obvious access problems, such as lighthouse-keepers and oil-rig workers! The advantage of a flexible-learning package is that it can indeed be studied anywhere suitable, even if this is many miles from the training department or from a tutor. Equally, and more usually, the package can be studied in the workplace. Nor need the loneliness associated with the long-distance learner ever set in: a typical flexible learner in a company scheme will do most of the following:

- attend an initial group briefing on the programme;
- discuss a timetable and work-method with the trainer, subject tutor or workplace mentor;
- arrange a date for completion of the first stage of the work, such as an assignment;
- take away a pack for individual study;

- discuss problems or interesting points with fellow-learners, in scheduled or unscheduled sessions;
- meet a tutor for individual (and possibly group) discussion;
- meet regularly with a mentor whose responsibility it is to provide personal support to the learner, often separately from technical expertise;
- negotiate revisions to the learning schedule as appropriate;
- have information about how to access help in between timetabled tutorials, such as a hotline to a local college.
- develop an action plan to be carried out after the end of the open-learning programme.

The point is that the meetings and group activities should have a purpose and that they should be arranged in accordance with learners' needs, not with the administrative convenience of the training provider.

The pervasiveness of flexible learning

All this flexibility is much less tidy than the face-to-face course. For example:

- Learners will start and finish according to individually negotiated schedules.
- More time in the workplace will be allocated to learning.
- A wider variety of people will be responsible for helping learners.
- Learners (and/or their managers) may have more choice over what is learned.

Learning is thus diffused very much more broadly within the organization. New communication patterns may be established by learners seeking help where the relevant expertise resides rather than according to hierarchy. The pervading sense of staff development is similar to that seen in quality improvement initiatives. In fact, the two sit well together, since one of the ways of ensuring total quality management is to ensure better learning. The 'Investors in People' standard specifically includes the requirement to review staff development on a regular basis and provide for job-related development needs. But any apparent untidiness is worrying to those who visualize training in terms of what they themselves have experienced. They are only reassured when it is made clear that the management and administration of the flexible learning programme is purpose-designed and even more meticulous than that of conventional courses. *Open Learning in Industry* (Paine *et al.*, 1987) is a package which is particularly helpful for planning a flexible training system and introducing it into the organization.

Changes of role

Non-training staff

We have already seen that many more people will be in contact with learners as *307* a result of introducing flexible learning. This implies a change of role for a number of them. Staff not labelled as 'trainers' may find that learners are using them as a resource for their open learning, perhaps as a result of workplace activities signalled by an open-learning programme. Line managers and other colleagues likely to be involved will need to be briefed to make time available and to give effective help. Being flexible, the material should be highly work-related and it is not always possible or desirable for the trainer responsible for the programme to be involved in the context-specific detail, which is better discussed with staff of the learner's own work-team. It is the resulting analysis which the learner can take back to a tutor or trainer for discussion of the implications for that stage of the learning. The new approach generated by flexible learning often causes a number of ripples in the organization. Good planning and communication ensures that these are positive. 'How can I join in this?' is a common response among non-participants hearing of an open learning programme.

The trainer

The role of the trainer plainly also changes as a result of the structural change brought about by flexible learning. For a start, the basis of the content of the flexible-training programme is often an open-learning package. This saves the trainer a great deal of time which would normally be spent in the training room presenting the material and checking understanding. This time is, instead, transferred to the management of the programme: briefing and induction of those involved in the programme, the individual tutoring (or arrangement of individual tutoring) of learners; organizing of any group and practical work, possibly to encourage peer-group support of learners; organizing assessment; and the monitoring, evaluation and presentation of results to senior management.

Management of the programme may involve anything – choosing learning packages, guiding learners in their choice of programme, setting up a full-blown learning centre, arguing the case for resources, organizing the awards ceremony at the end, and so on. Some trainers become involved in the development of learning packages, especially with the advent of affordable wordprocessing and desk-top publishing systems. Self-evidently, flexible training is not something which a trainer undertakes in order to gain spare time in the week. Nevertheless, many find it more satisfying than acting as what David Tinsley has called 'a two-legged tape-recorder'. Depending on the job which the trainer was originally doing this can be something of a transformation from an operative to a managerial role.

Trainers need to allow themselves adequate training to benefit from the change; such opportunities are most frequently taken by those who intend to develop their own flexible learning packages, probably because the need to acquire a new technique is so apparent. But the change of technique from running group sessions to individual tutorials, to counselling and guiding learners and possibly to dealing with learners at a distance, is just as great as is the management and marketing of what has become, in effect, a new internal consultancy.

The external training provider

The training provider who is at one remove from the organization buying the training is less exposed than the in-company trainer when it comes to setting up more flexible learning programmes. The upfront investment of resources is likely to be the main difficulty at the outset. Flexible learning is a positive benefit to the marketing of the organization's services, since purchasers of training find the potential for individually tailored programmes offered by flexible training very attractive. At first sight it may seem unpleasantly likely that any fly-by-night individual (especially one with a couple of personal computers and some basic software) can set up a flexible learning centre in a front room and operate as a training provider, without the overheads of established providers. Any such operators would soon find that the infrastructure needed to support open learners cannot be produced at short notice: the 'fling the package at them and run' approach to flexible learning being the shortest way to consumer dissatisfaction and business failure that is known to the training world.

The learner

Changes to the person experiencing training are, of course, usually built in to training programmes. It is expected that trainees completing a programme will know more, have acquired new skills, or have changed attitudes about something essential to the organization's good functioning. Flexible learning, however, produces profounder changes. Conventional courses tend to reinforce the dependency of the learner upon the expert. Well-designed flexible programmes should, rather than transferring that dependency to the learning package, encourage learners to stand on their own feet, to learn to manage their own learning and, perhaps as importantly as anything, to see themselves as learning individuals.

Despite the amount of learning we do as adults in the ordinary course of our lives, too many people regard learning as something they finished when they left school – and were probably bad at – or as something academic and remote from the real world. Courses are still too often regarded as a way of keeping the ambitious quiet, or as a good 'day out' for the unscrupulous, while the real work gets done by others. Flexible learning opens up learning not only to its participants but to those around them, by making the whole process more transparent. Trainees completing a flexible programme more frequently comment on the extent to which the experience has 'made my brain come alive' than do their conventional counterparts.

The organization

The possibility of some quite fundamental change in the organization as the result of flexible learning has already been hinted at. Where expertise is sought for its own sake, and not because of any status attaching to the person who owns it, any organization becomes necessarily less hierarchical, if only for the *309* purposes of those transactions associated with flexible learning. But even where flexible learning is introduced on only a limited experimental basis, it is evident that many more diagonal and lateral communications occur than is the case in a normally hierarchical organization. And even larger changes naturally result where flexible learning is not only given the backing of senior management, but is experienced from the top down. This also avoids any difficulties resulting from managers being insecure about their subordinates benefiting from training opportunities of a kind which they themselves have missed.

WHAT DOES THE ORGANIZATION NEED TO DO?

Typically, flexible learning is initiated in an organization because a trainer or a manager has seen some form of flexible learning at work in another similar organization, or has heard about it at a conference or other presentation. There are also regular events at which flexible-learning materials are demonstrated (notably, in the United Kingdom, at the Education & Training conference in Birmingham in July each year and at the Human Resource Development conference in London in the spring). This tends to lead straight into a 'what shall we do with it?' approach, which, though natural, is not wholly satisfactory.

Ideally, an organization going into flexible learning needs first to answer the question 'why?'. The answers may be self-evident, especially to trainers; but they need to be spelt out to the whole of the organization if the venture is to be anything more than marginal. Some of the reasons most often adduced by users are:

- A backlog of training which cannot otherwise be cleared.
- A large population requiring training for a particular purpose (e.g. the introduction of a new computer system).
- A large population requiring updating or reskilling (e.g. the multiskilling of mechanical engineers).
- People with very different starting points needing to go on the same course (again this often happens with new technologies).
- A small number of people in a minority subject for whom a conventional course is not an economic proposition.
- Inability to spare key staff for conventional training.
- Large overhead costs of sending staff on residential courses (often happens in management courses).
- Desire to broaden the range of people undertaking training.
- Desire to get learners to share responsibility for their training.
- Special needs requiring sensitive handling (e.g. literacy problems).

The wide-ranging nature of the items on this list can surprise those who imagine that flexible learning is only for the highly academic or white-collar worker, or that it offers some kind of second-best, second-chance training.

Only if the organization is clear why it is undertaking flexible training will such
310 an innovation become anything more than an interesting experiment. Ex-

perience in all kinds of establishments suggests that a large amount of work, planning and enthusiasm can be wasted simply because the flexible learning enthusiasts got carried away by the intrinsic worth and interest of their programme, instead of visualizing it as a far-reaching structural change requiring carefully orchestrated managerial backing.

Once the fundamental reasons for introducing flexible learning are established, the questions 'who', 'what', 'how', 'when' and 'where' can then be answered, probably in that order. As with any strategic change in an organization, objectives must be carefully established and communicated, preferably as a result of extensive consultation. Trainers do not often find themselves in a strategic role and it is important not to underestimate the scale and significance of this planning. Marketing a new idea within one's own organization is far more difficult than ordinary marketing to those outside, but this is the process that will have to be undertaken, first to senior management and then to the workforce.

What will be involved?

Trainers will need to do any or all of the following:

- Plan the system.
- Evaluate existing flexible learning packages commercially available.
- Adapt/create materials where none exist, or commission them.
- Support learners.
- Support their line managers or mentors.
- Monitor learner progress and the detail of the programme's administration.
- Ensure that learners' achievement is acknowledged by the organization.
- Evaluate the results and report to senior management, making recommendations on future developments and on the resourcing levels needed.

This sounds like a great deal of work, but there is no need to go it alone. There are always organizations which have previously travelled a similar route, and if these are felt to be too idiosyncratic there are many professional flexible-learning organizations listed in the *Open Learning Directory* (Pergamon Press) which can advise on setting up a system as well as buying in packages. Local colleges of further education may also be helpful in this respect. Taking advice from experienced sources saves the labour of identifying and evaluating individual learning packages, of which there are now many thousands, as well as ensuring that a vital planning element is not omitted.

What makes a good learning package?

Although it is perfectly possible to have flexible learning without a learning package in sight, many programmes do in practice depend on input made by such a package, in the form of text, video, audio, computer program, practical kit, *311* or any permutation of these. The medium (or, often, mix of media) does not matter, so long as it is appropriate for the objectives to be achieved. In the real world, however, choice is often influenced by financial and, possibly, political considerations. Everyone has experienced periods in their organization's history when it seems easier to obtain a large amount of money for some attractive technology than smaller sums for more mundane kit. But, subject to such constraints, the flexible-learning system should be user- not technology-driven.

There is no particular mystique about gauging the quality of flexible-learning packages, since the normal criteria for assessing the likely quality of the learner's experience apply. Indeed, the highly visible nature of the content and presentation ensures that better judgements can be made in advance about such packages than about, for instance, residential courses. But there is an important extra dimension to the flexible learning package: usually learners will be working individually through it. This has a number of implications for the design and style of presentation of the material, which must, at least partly, replace the normal trainer input. Given that a package is technically correct in its subject matter, it is also necessary to check that it meets the following criteria:

- Objectives, outcomes or competences to be achieved through use of the package are clear and relevant.
- Introduction gives learner a clear idea of what is expected, including any necessary pre-test or hints on studying.
- Sequencing of the material is clear and logical.
- Learners are required to be active in a variety of ways, and to relate the material to their own experience (not just read text and tick boxes, or press keys to move from screen to screen in a computer-based program).
- Learners can easily gauge progress (through self-assessment questions, activities, final assessment).
- Assessment measures all the objectives or competence specified at the beginning of the package.
- There is a variety of assessment activities (not just multi-choice or straight recall).
- Feedback to all forms of assessment is positive and helpful.
- Pace and tone are appropriate to the target group (with material being appropriately divided into units than can be absorbed at a sitting, difficult concepts being 'unpacked', clear and unpatronizing explanations).
- Illustrations and examples are free of race and gender stereotypes.
- Reading level is appropriate.
- Style is lively without being over-friendly.
- The layout contributes to understanding of the material, with clear headings, good typeface, helpful signposting and diagrams, good use of white space to avoid overcrowding, and of colour if appropriate.
- There is enough space in the workbook for learners to write responses.
- Any multi-media material is well integrated (so that, for instance, there

are activities associated with a video rather than its providing light relief – or prestige!)

- Guidance for trainers/tutors is adequate.
- The package looks as if it will provide a worthwhile learning experience, even to someone working in far-from-ideal conditions.

Again, this seems like a lot of work, but, as before, it is not necessary for each trainer to perform such evaluation from the very beginning except to gain understanding of the approach. Open-learning organizations of all kinds will offer a quality-controlled service, and the *Open Learning Directory* cited above lists packages which meet the criteria of the open learning industry's Code of Practice (Employment Department) as well as organizations offering flexible-learning services. Specialist guidance on quality in open learning for TECs and LECs is being developed to enable their staffs to advise clients, especially small firms. Nor is activity on quality confined to the United Kingdom: the European Community has set up a working group under the SATURN programme to produce guidelines on the provision of open-learning goods and services that can become a standard across the member states.

Successful implementation of flexible training

Organizations which have had the most successful results with flexible learning, measured in terms both of cost-effectiveness and of user satisfaction, have almost always ensured that the following factors are present in their system:

- Genuine and observable interest has been shown in the initiative by senior management.
- Resistance has been previously identified and as far as possible dealt with.
- Adequate briefing is given to all staff.
- Objectives are carefully planned and monitored.
- Learners are given clear guidance on: the purpose of the training; self-management of learning (including: allocation of time; regular, short study sessions; systematically completing exercises; relating what they learn to their own situation; sharing ideas and experience with other learners; and consulting managers, colleagues, trainers, tutors, and so on); their own progress; and the overall schedule of the training (including any negotiable features). 'Flexible' does not mean saying to learners 'finish any time you like', as this can lead to demotivation and drop-out.
- The system is tested with a small pilot group to gauge its strengths and weaknesses.
- Results of the scheme are disseminated and learners visibly rewarded (for instance with company certificates of achievement where a programme does not carry a National Vocational Qualification).

313

THE NEED FOR FLEXIBLE LEARNING

The logic of introducing flexible learning in the present industrial context is inescapable. It is appropriate at the level of the individual because it puts into practice what we know about successful learning. It is a commonplace that, in the United Kingdom and many other European countries, the decline in the number of young people means that more mature entrants to the labour market will be much sought after, requiring different recruitment, retention and training strategies. What is less apparent is that the background of such young people as there are (and numbers will start to rise again towards the end of the century) is going to be very different from that of previous generations of school-leavers. Curriculum and other changes are producing youngsters who have been encouraged to learn independently, to negotiate and set work objectives, and to undertake work experience. Both these and their adult counterparts will be demotivated by old-fashioned classroom-style methods of training, and are likely to be much more aware of themselves as consumers of training, with all that this implies.

Flexible learning is also well advertised as meeting employer needs. Reskilling, upskilling and updating as an ongoing process for all in employment (as well as those seeking to return to employment) is becoming the norm in the context of technological advance and the demise of unskilled jobs. Our increasingly information-based society will need to have training available as a resource in exactly the same way as it has telecommunications systems – available at will, with the right messages going to exactly the right recipient. And the new UK competence-based vocational qualifications system makes a flexible training approach virtually essential. It is designed to restructure the 'qualifications jungle' by providing a single framework within which qualifications are expressed as what a person can do and at which of five (clearly defined) levels. Apart from the unfortunate mismatch between these levels and those of the European Community, which results almost entirely from the appalling neglect of training in the United Kingdom, this has great potential for strengthening the vocational qualifications structure. Employers can be sure that a National Vocational Qualification is based on what the industry requires, and employees will be able to build up credits towards a vocational qualification by undertaking short modules of training rather than a pass-or-fail programme. Since flexible training is modular in nature, it exactly meets these new needs. Publishers of flexible-learning materials will now have to express the objectives or outcomes of their material in the same language as the vocational qualifications competences, so that customers can be sure of buying the correct product. A stimulus to this market may result from the marketing of a set of databases for each occupational area, developed under the Employment Department's Matching Programme. Available on computer disc, each matches the occupational standards for the sector (examples are 'Retail' and 'Training and development') against published flexible learning materials. A simple coding system indicates how closely the material enables users to develop competence in each element.

In this last decade of the twentieth century we have far too many people in the workforce who believe that training is something that they should have done to them – if indeed it is necessary in the first place – by an expert. Yet the world we live in, with its demographic and technical change, the impact of a single European market, the modularization of qualifications and the move towards total-quality management, demands that all individuals should assume greater responsibility for their own learning. Under present conditions, people are unlikely to take this responsibility without some structure to help them, so organizations need to make training a resource to be accessed by anyone at any time. Training has to become a commonplace, daily occurrence for most adults.

Since the possible consequences of neglecting this need are too unpleasant to contemplate, this chapter has attempted to focus upon the positive and the achievable. It is simplistic to say that flexible learning is the only successful means by which we can meet the training needs of the working population into the twenty-first century, since flexible learning is not a single entity. It encompasses all the delivery methods known to training, from private study to group discussion, and from the new technologies of computer-based training and interactive video to the low technologies of text and face-to-face conversation. It also incorporates some of what we know about achieving 'best value' out of learning, even beginning, in a minority of cases, to accommodate different preferred learning styles.

These two factors on their own are powerful enough to make flexible learning a good option for most users. The case becomes overwhelming, however, when contextual factors such as the new vocational qualifications and the increasing pace of change, particularly in technology, are taken into consideration. Once we have faced up to the change of approach which flexible training demands, we shall wonder how we ever managed without it.

FURTHER READING

Developing Good Practice in Open Learning, series commissioned by the Training, Enterprise and Education Directorate of the Employment Department and produced by a team of practitioner organizations (Capel Manor, ITUR, National Extension College, OPTIS, SCOTTSU.) Modules on different aspects of flexible learning and at various prices are:

- *A taste of open learning*
- *Opening learning – understanding your learners*
- *Open learning – supporting your learners*
- *Open learning – assessment*
- *The case for open learning*
- *Open learning – selecting your staff*
- *Implementing open learning in organisations*
- *Open learning – selecting and adapting materials*
- *Implementing open learning in colleges*

Jeffries, Clive *et al.* (1990), *The A–Z of Open Learning*, Cambridge: National Extension College. As well as clarifying the extensive jargon used in flexible/open learning it highlights key issues in the development of systems and materials.

Paine, Nigel (1988), *Open Learning in Transition*, Cambridge: National Extension College. A book of readings for those interested in the history, politics and diversity of flexible/open learning.

Paine, Nigel *et al.* (1987), *Open Learning in Industry: a Guide for Practitioners*, Baldock: Flex Training. Multi-media package (5 books, video, audio, pocket guides) in open-learning format with practical help on the benefits, strategy for introducing flexible learning into the organization, selecting/adapting/developing a flexible learning package, providing support for learners and managing the system. Not cheap, but cheaper than the consultancy it offers.

Rowntree, Derek (1990), *Teaching through Self-instruction*, Kogan Page. An invaluable handbook to assist with developing flexible-learning packages, very down-to-earth despite its academic-sounding title.

Training, Enterprise and Education Directorate of the Employment Department (1988), *Ensuring Quality in Open Learning: A Handbook for Action*, Sheffield: Employment Department. Guidance on good practice for producers, deliverers and users of flexible learning. New sections on quality in technology-based training produced in 1990.

Open Learning Directory, published annually, Oxford: Pergamon Open Learning/Employment Department Group. Contains details of suppliers of flexible training materials, producers and the packages themselves. All organizations with entries in the directory agree to abide by the code of practice in the Employment Department's *Ensuring Quality in Open Learning: A Handbook for Action* (see above).

25 Self-managed learning

Ian Cunningham

The term 'self-managed learning' (SML) was coined in order to distinguish this approach from close relatives. My colleagues and I were particularly interested in bringing together the advantages of various learning methods whilst avoiding some of their disadvantages. In this chapter I shall give a practical example of a self-managed learning (SML) course, before commenting on some of the methods and theories drawn upon.

SML has been introduced in a wide variety of settings over the last fifteen years. It has mainly been used with managers, but programmes in, for example, Cable and Wireless have shown the value of the approach for secretaries, technical staff and others. I have always been keen to include assessment of people's learning in SML programmes and in some cases this has led to qualifications being gained by course participants. In Shell, for example, we negotiated with BTEC for managers to gain the Certification in Management Studies as a result of carrying out a self-managed learning programme. In other organizations, assessment of learning has had a purely internal focus. In British Airways successful 'graduates' from an SML programme for younger managers were given accelerated promotions. In the BBC, a one-year programme for newly recruited personnel staff provided the basis for them gaining managerial posts. In contrast, Allied Lyons (see Hurley and Cunningham 1993), the NHS and the London Borough of Lewisham have used the approach for senior managers.

A CONCRETE EXAMPLE

Let me now illustrate what this approach means in practice. In contrast to the organizational examples mentioned above, I shall focus on the part-time Post Graduate Diploma in Management (by SML) which was offered by North East London Polytechnic – now the University of East London (see Cunningham, 1981). I shall indicate incidents an observer would actually see or hear, and follow each of these with an explanation of why they would observe such episodes. This should provide a better insight into the course than a purely abstract discussion.

Observed

New course members arrive on a Friday evening in October for the opening of the Diploma course at a residential weekend. They join with existing (second-year) course members and do some fairly standard 'getting to know each other' exercises, in addition to finding out more about the course. So far, this looks very similar to many other management courses. However, as the weekend goes on, differences become apparent. The residential weekend has been organized by a planning group consisting of second-year course members plus two staff. This group steers the weekend, but staff, whilst actively involved in particular sessions, are not controlling what happens.

On Saturday a session is devoted to helping first-year course members form into 'sets'; the sets are groups of five or six course members, together with a staff member and a second-year course member (who together act as co-set advisors). The session is disorganized, and sometimes chaotic, as people try to find a sensible basis with which to group themselves. Eventually they do, and the sets settle down to their first meeting, one of many they will have over the next two years.

Also on Saturday, all first- and second-year course members and staff gather together for a *community meeting*, in which they discuss and decide upon course issues. This meeting is chaired by a course member, and whilst staff join in on discussions they have only a minority voice in the proceedings. The community meeting decides:

- who shall be on the planning group for the next residential weekend; and
- which workshops and other events shall take place before the next residential weekend, which is in the next term.

Explanation

1. SML is not necessarily an individual activity. Managing one's own learning includes *involving oneself in the learning of others*.
2. SML events are sometimes quite tightly structured. The difference between SML and other modes is *where the structure* comes from. In most college or university run courses, tutors lay down the structure: in SML the structure comes from collective agreement involving course members and

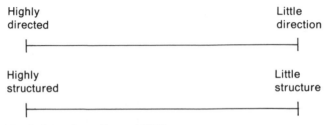

Source: the idea is taken from Heron (1977)

Figure 25.1   The self-managed learning structure

staff. This issue of structuring is important. Just because course members control their own learning it does not make the course unstructured. 'Structure' and 'direction' (or control) are two relatively separate variables, and courses can be more or less structured and more or less directed by staff. This can be shown as in Figure 25.1

A course can, for instance, be highly directed with little structure. This fits certain T-group or interpersonal skills programmes where staff dictate a low structure format. Most so-called taught courses have high direction and high structure: staff impose both content and timetabling (structuring). Certain self-development groups come into the low structure/low direction category: the trainer adopts a low profile on content and structure.

The SML mode is unusual in providing a great deal of structure within a framework which has little staff direction over course content. In Figure 25.1 I am suggesting that a total lack of structure is not possible – an unstructured course is a logical nonsense since to have a course is to provide a structure of some kind, even if it is only to arrange a time when people meet together.

3. The community meeting is a key event since it demonstrates the notion of a self-managing community operating to make collective decisions about the course. All course members are able to be involved directly in decisions about what goes on, though the community meeting delegates specific tasks to groups (such as the residential planning group).

4. Sets are important in providing *support groups* besides meeting other needs. Each set is assisted in its operations by the presence of the co-set advisors. Second-year course members who want to develop their skills in this area have found it valuable to apprentice themselves to a staff member in order to work with a first-year set. The set also gets the benefit of the presence of someone who has been through the first year.

Observed

After the first residential weekend, John, a manager in a construction company, is at home in the evening working on what he should put into his programme of study. He has to write a learning contract which he then has to present to his set for approval. Some aspects of this contract seem much easier to write than others; he has had no problem in covering his past experience, and he has made a reasonable effort at describing his strengths and weaknesses (helped by diagnostic material provided by the college). However, working out learning goals is proving less easy. He knows that he wants to advance within his own company, but specifying a balance of objectives is not simple. So he decides to take a rough draft of what he has written to his next set meeting in order to receive feedback and comments from the other members.

Explanation

Paul Tillich called the fatal pedagogical error: 'To throw answers like stones at *319* the heads of those who have not yet asked the questions' (in Brown, 1971). Managing involves asking questions and formulating problems *before* looking for answers and solutions. Thus for managers to manage their own learning, they need first to formulate the questions: the problems.

I define a 'problem' as existing when we cannot go from where we are to where we would like to be simply by action. If I want to know something about company procedures, and these are written in a company manual, I can simply go and look it up; that is no problem. However, if I currently feel unassertive and lacking in confidence – and I want to be assertive and self-confident – I may well have a problem. It is probably not at all clear how I can move from my current to my desired state.

In the Diploma course managers are advised that they may find it helpful to address themselves to five questions:

1. *Where have I been?*   What are my past experiences?
2. *Where am I now?*   What strengths and weaknesses do I have? What is the current situation that I am in?
3. *Where do I want to get to?*   What goals/targets/objectives do I want to set for myself?
4. *How will I get there?*   What programme of study should I design to achieve my goals?
5. *How will I know if I have arrived?*   What criteria can I apply to assess my learning?

Most people find this sequence helpful in assisting them to formulate and choose their problems. I say 'choose' because any problem is a choice. If one decides to accept the situation and does not wish to change, then there are no problems. It

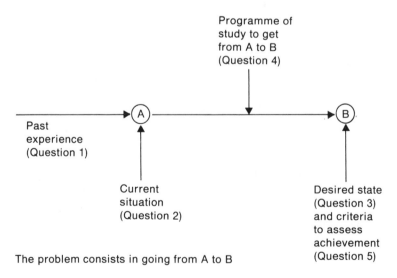

Figure 25.2   The five-question self-managed learning sequence.

is only when a person *chooses* to change that problems become identifiable. The situation can be shown diagrammatically as in Figure 25.2. This indicates the link with the five questions outlined above.

In Figure 25.2 the person has the problem of going from A to B. The position is chosen on the basis of the person's values and beliefs; it is not an externally defined objective reality. My stance, then, is to reject what I often hear from trainers and lecturers. 'That manager says he wants to learn *X*, but that is not the real problem. What he really needs is *Y*.' The arrogance of such statements is in part based on a notion that 'real problems' exist out there in the world, detached from people, which I regard as an unacceptable standpoint. I may disagree with the goals a manager has set, but that is just my view against his or hers. As a trainer I believe that I have the right to challenge and question a learner, and in the process they may change their formulation of the problem. However, in SML courses the staff do not have the right to impose goals on learners, no matter how subtly they may wish to do it.

I have argued here for the principle of learners setting their own goals; however, there are also practical reasons why this is important. The research evidence on managerial learning is quite conclusive in supporting the notion that learning is enhanced if managers consciously *set their own goals*. Kolb and Boyatzis (1984) quote a number of studies which demonstrate remarkable improvements in learning and performance when managers were given the chance to set their own goals, and such changes tend to be independent of how difficult the goals are that people set for themselves.

Observed

John has returned from the set meeting where his draft learning contract has been discussed. His proposals have been analysed in detail, and many of his ideas have been exposed, under questioning, as being ill-thought out. He had been annoyed at the time, for he felt he had put a positive effort into his draft contract. However, now that he can re-read his proposals he realizes that they were not as good as he had thought. Just saying that he wanted to 'learn about management finance' and to 'improve interpersonal skills' clearly was not specific enough. He decided to talk to his boss, since he had put 'improve interpersonal skills' into his draft contract partly on the basis of feedback at his last appraisal interview. He now recognizes that he needs to be clearer about what his boss actually meant by this.

Explanation

1. Sets are often at their most supportive when they confront individuals about what they *are or are not doing*. Woolly non-judgemental feedback ('I like what you've done') is as inappropriate as destructive judgemental assessment ('You'll never make a good manager'). Supportive confronting involves supporting the person as a person and valuing their worth as a human being, whilst at the same time commenting, positively and negatively, on *321*

what they do. This can be expressed simply as: support *being* (that is, the person); confront *doing* (that is, what they do).

2. Part of helping people to manage their own learning is assisting them to specify the precise problems which they wish to tackle. In order to get *good answers*, one needs first *good questions*.

3. It is valuable if managers can build into their learning contracts evidence they gain from colleagues, bosses, subordinates and others at work. However, our experience is that much of this evidence is too vague. We have encouraged managers to seek out *good feedback*, so that they can have a better basis on which to decide what to learn. Sometimes set members (staff or course members) have gone to a person's place of work to assist in this information gathering, especially if the boss or work colleagues are built into the contract as sources of learning.

Observed

Jane has had her contract agreed by her set at the end of the first term, and she now finds she has to start to put her plans into operation. She decides that her wish to learn about basic elements of marketing can best be met by attending a module on this topic, which is already provided on the Diploma in Management Studies course. The module is one evening a week for one term. Her employers have given her study leave for one day a week, so she comes into the college to use the library in the morning, prior to going to her set meeting in the afternoon. She feels she has a problem in running meetings, and looks for books in the library on this topic. However, in the catalogue she comes across an entry of a video tape on the subject. She signs out the tape and views it in one of the soundproof booths provided by the library.

Later in the term she decides to pluck up courage and tackle her antipathy towards statistics. She arranges a meeting with a tutor, who shows her how to use material on the PCs on open access in the computer room. Now she realizes how valuable it has been for her to be able to discuss her concerns about statistics in the set, as her colleagues were not only able to reassure her, but also helped her to clarify the kind of questions she needed to put to the tutor. The tutor occasionally gets overenthusiastic about pushing her into the broader aspects of the subject, but because she is clear about what she wants, she is able to steer him back to her own needs.

Explanation

1. A person managing his or her own learning can choose a *variety of ways to learn* what he or she wants to learn.

2. *Back-up learning resources* are important, though many are ill-designed for easy access. Libraries are often organized to suit librarians, and it can be a problem getting the flexibility and responsiveness needed for SML work. The use of learning resources in SML programmes is unlike their use in so-

called open and distance learning; much of the latter is not very 'open' at all, being predefined packages which give little or no choice to managers – they are like Tillich's stones being thrown at the heads of managers who have not formulated the questions (and are not going to be allowed to). It is a Henry Ford approach to learning ('You can have any course you like, so long as it's this one').

3. Tutors may also not be ideally responsive. However, part of the skill of managing one's own learning is to *manage experts*; the experts do have things to offer, and it is short-sighted of managers to ignore this. Managers are, though, rightly suspicious of experts who wish to push their own field of interest too much. To quote Greenberg's First Law of Experts: 'You don't ask a barber if you need a haircut' (Peers and Bennett, 1981). However, if you decide for yourself that you need a haircut, a barber can be useful.

Observed

Jim, a senior manager in local government, meets his tutor from college. They sit down in Jim's office and go through a time diary Jim has kept for the last two weeks. As they analyse his activities, Jim realizes how much time he has been devoting to unproductive work. He appreciates now why his staff have complained about the amount of time he is out of the office or otherwise not available to them. With his tutor he discusses ways in which he could reorganize his time to fit more closely with his priorities.

After they have been through the time diary, they discuss how Jim processes paper (since this is another problem he has decided to tackle). Jim calls in his secretary, so that the three of them can consider how to change the filing system.

Explanation

1. SML can be about learning both high-level abstract theory and 'nitty-gritty' practical skills.
2. Learning can take place at work, in college (or anywhere).
3. Course members choose one staff member (not the set adviser) to act as a 'specialist tutor' to assist them with specific learning that needs expert help. Ideally, the specialist tutor works with the learner over the two years, although in practice people often switch tutors as their interests or requirements change. This special relationship does not preclude the course member from using other tutors on an occasional basis.

Observed

It is a sunny July Saturday afternoon and this is the third residential weekend of the year. Course members can be observed around the building and outside it. Eight people are struggling with a computer-based business game: some are *323* from the public sector, and they are finding the commercial aspects of the game difficult to handle. Ten people are in a seminar on industrial relations negotiations run by one of the tutors. Tom, Jenny and Tim are busy in the computer room, each working on his or her own specific work problems. Tim has been testing out some proposals his employers are about to implement, and he finds a serious flaw in their calculations. He subsequently reports this to his organization, and they save a seven-figure sum by revising their figures along the lines that Tim suggests.

Arthur sits under a tree in the grounds reading a book on operations research, and every so often he glances at a group of nine people on the lawn who are painting and drawing. They are in a session on integrating left-brain and right-brain working. Later on, he observes them all lying down listening to a guided fantasy, and he wonders whether he should not have joined that group rather than choosing to work on his own.

Meanwhile, in a darkened room in the main building, a group of seven is watching a video of Tom Peters, oblivious of the sunshine outside. Along the corridor Tony, Mike and Sue are using video equipment to practise their counselling skills. Janet, who is on the course, but is also a management tutor in a college, is assisting them, as she runs counselling training courses in her own college.

Down by the lake, well away from the main building, Simon and Carol sit on a bench. Simon is very upset: his father died a few days ago; he does not feel like going into any of the planned activities, and Carol, who is in his set, has agreed to sit with him for the afternoon. Simon is confused because his dominant feeling is one of anger, not sadness, at his father's death. Carol knows that Simon's relationship with his father has been fraught, as it has come up in the set discussions, and she tries to help Simon make sense of his feelings. Eventually, they wander slowly back from the lake.

It is now late afternoon and a discussion group is about to start on the lawn, led by one of the tutors. Tim and Jenny leave their computers to join it, along with Simon and Carol. Mike and Sue emerge from their video session to take part, and Arthur decides to take a break from his book to join them.

Inside the building, a session on theorizing is being held, and people do various exercises to assist them in being more effective at developing theory from their experiences. In one exercise, course members form into small sub-groups. One person (the problem owner) talks about a problem whilst the others write on cards the concepts used by the person as he or she talks. Together they arrange the cards in a 'concept map' in order to help the problem owner to *model the problem*. The problem owner is then assisted in elucidating the hypotheses with which he or she is working, so that concepts, models and hypotheses can be linked together as theory.

Explanation

1. Residential weekends provide a range of options to cover what course members request. Sometimes people spend time outside formally organized sessions: this is part of *managing one's own learning*.

2. The activities exemplify the *holistic orientation* of the programme; most people are pleasantly surprised at how valuable it is to attend to their learning needs as whole persons: they find they change intellectually, emotionally, physically, socially and sometimes spiritually. All of this is relevant to management.

3. Course members *learn from each other*. The course provides a network that allows people to meet others with matching interests and concerns: it also facilitates mutual support in times of personal difficulty. This networking often continues after the formal ending of the course. There are facilities for ex-course members to meet up and be in contact with each other. One set which went through the programme in 1980–82 has continued to meet of its own volition up to the present day.

4. The style of the residential course is in keeping with a both/and orientation: people work hard and they have fun; they are active and passive; they engage in rational and non-rational activity; they plan rigorously and they respond to serendipitous whims.

5. I like to feel that the SML approach is genuinely scientific in the sense that Bateson (1973) has supported; that is, that one counterposes theory and existing knowledge with experience, and tests each against the other. I agree with Sirag (1979) that 'the future of physics rests in the hands of those who have an equal toleration for mathematical rigour and free-wheeling fantasy' (p. 18). A similar statement could be made about management.

Observed

The two-year course is coming to its end for Mike's set, and they are dealing with assessment, in order to decide who receives the Diploma and who does not. Mike has already presented various essays and reports to the set, and these have been discussed. He is now at the set meeting at which they are looking at the totality of his work. First, he shows a video tape where he is counselling someone, and after that he gives his reasons why he thinks this has satisfied the criteria in his contract on this subject. Other course members and the staff member (set adviser) question him on this, and eventually they agree he has met the required standard. Mike then distributes copies of assessments carried out by his boss and his subordinates on aspects of his performance at work. In discussion it seems that there is doubt on some aspects of these, particularly as to whether Mike has met all his previously contracted criteria. The set agrees that they cannot make a decision on this information, and the task of going to Mike's company to talk to his boss and his subordinates is delegated to two set members. After this discussion, Mike's specialist tutor joins the set, and he reports on Mike's work in the areas of finance and economics. The set quizzes him on his report, and eventually agrees with Mike and the tutor that the required criteria have been met. The set then considers Mike's other (written) work, which they have already seen. They agree that if the two set members seeing Mike's boss and subordinates get the required information, they can proceed at the next set meeting to decide on a pass.

Explanation

It is central to SML that the learner manages the assessment process in conjunction with *relevant others*. In the context of this college course 'relevant others' means at the very least other set members and the specialist tutor. In Mike's case above, the person's boss and subordinates were also involved. At no time are judgements imposed externally on the learner: the assessment process matches the initial contracting process in being a *collaborative negotiation*. I have discussed elsewhere other aspects of assessment (see Cunningham, 1983).

WHERE DOES SML COME FROM?

The roots of SML lie in a particular view of learning and in a range of methods and approaches to learning, some of which are now briefly described.

Learning approaches

Independent study

From work in the North East London Polytechnic, I wanted to use the idea that individuals can *plan and carry out their own learning programmes* (Cunningham, 1981).

Action learning

The value of individual managers *assisting each other* in their learning (through the use of sets) was clearly demonstrated in various action learning programmes in which I was involved (e.g. GEC's Developing Senior Managers' Programme; see Casey and Pearce, 1977).

Autonomy labs

Harrison's (1974) work in creating courses where managers were free to do what they liked (almost), impressed me. Restricting the trainer role to providing *rich resources and to assisting others in their learning* (through counselling and coaching) seemed a healthy stance.

Humanistic education

Rogers (1969) has been an influence on many management developers in the United Kingdom, and his passionate advocacy of a *'person-centred'* approach provided important philosophical underpinnings for SML.

Holistic education

326 It seems self-evident to me that managers are not disembodied brains (see also

Mant, 1977): they exist in physical bodies, they feel (even if they pretend they do not), they value and believe in particular ideals (even though it is not always apparent). Schutz (1979) is one of many writers who have promoted a *holistic perspective* on learning. His holistic studies MA at Antioch University in San Francisco was one of a number of American programmes I was able to experience at first hand when working in the United States in the late 1970s.

Self-development

Self-development methods and ideas flourished in the late 1970s. The idea of managers managing their own development through starting with their *own needs* has proved very effective. However, 'self-development' has tended to become a catch-all term to include almost anything that is not traditional learning. Some of the proponents of self-development also started to see the need to consider the *context* within which the person was learning (usually their organization). Hence the idea of developing 'learning organizations' came more to the fore.

Work-based management development

These are the methods one can use to assist managerial learning *without managers leaving their place of work*. Coaching, the use of work assignments, job rotation, and apprenticeship are examples of such unglamorous (but often highly valuable) methods. My experience of consulting in various organizations indicated that these approaches could be the most cost-effective learning modes for much managerial learning (see Mumford, 1980 for further discussion of this topic).

OTHER INFLUENCES ON SELF-MANAGED LEARNING

As well as influences from learning approaches, SML has benefited from:

1. Developments in *psychotherapy*, which have provided ideas on how people change (for example, neuro-linguistic programming: see Chapter 33 below; and Bandler and Grinder, 1979).
2. Research on the *nature of management* (for example, Stewart, 1982), which indicates that managing is not a neat subject discipline that can be taught in compartmentalized, standardized chunks.
3. Research on *brain functioning*, which shows up the different contributions that the left and right hemispheres of the brain contribute to our ways of thinking (see Mintzberg, 1984).
4. Ideas from philosophy about the *nature of knowledge and of reality* (Bateson, 1973 and Watzlawick, 1978 were specific influences); the notion that 'reality' cannot sensibly be conceptualized as a concrete entity outside ourselves is a central tenet of SML. Managers create their own reality, and teachers and trainers have to respond to that.

327

5. *Eastern philosophy*, particularly Taoism, has provided a subtle and powerful antidote to narrow Westernized modes of thought; this is especially so in relation to the idea that one can work in a *both/and* rather than an *either/or* mode: I shall comment specifically on this in the next section.

BOTH/AND OR EITHER/OR?

In organizing SML to benefit from the different strands outlined above, it was guided by the notion that we could work in a 'both/and' rather than 'either/or' mode: we did not need to choose between apparent opposites, since many things that are supposed to be opposites are not. Let me pick out one writer (amongst many) who has categorized management education programmes on an either/or basis, and indicate how his reasoning is unhelpful.

Handy (1975) identified what he claimed were the polar opposites in management education – instrumentalism and existentialism – and argued that management teachers had to choose between these two schools. He described the *instrumental* school as believing that education was *subject-oriented*: that one teaches things to people; that the success of a course is judged on the basis of the person's contribution to society or to an organization; that reasoning and learning are deductive (practice follows theory); that entry to courses is on the basis of organizational sponsorships only. The *existential* position he described as concentrating on the individual (and his or her freedom), not on the group. The view of reasoning and learning held by this school, he said, was *inductivist* (theory emerges from experience). He stated that teachers in this camp disliked assessment and talked instead of allowing feedback. They also preferred to take people onto a course on the basis of personal choice rather than organizational sponsorship.

He further argued that it was not possible to 'ride two horses at once' (Handy, 1975, p.61) and that all management teachers had to choose one or the other position. The evidence I have gathered from my own research (Cunningham, 1984) indicates that effective management teachers or trainers do not conform to Handy's assumptions. The people in my research talked very much in terms of working with *both poles at the same time*. Everyone was, for instance, in some way interested in the development of the person and in the person's contribution to society, their organization or their area of work. The notion that a management teacher *has* to choose to help *either* the person *or* society (and cannot do both) is nonsensical. For one thing, the notion that 'organizations' and 'society' are objects which can exist separately from persons is difficult to sustain; secondly (and conversely), it pre-supposes that managers can manage *outside a social context*.

To refer back to the case of the course I described earlier:

1. We recruited individuals as self-sponsored *and* as organizationally sponsored.
2. We took assessment seriously, and pass-or-fail decisions were faced not as a necessary nuisance, but as an important judgemental process to be set *alongside* the less judgemental feedback mode.

3. We valued people who were independent *and* interdependent. The course could work only if people *both* considered themselves and worked on their own problems *and* considered others and worked with them on their problems.
4. The course demanded that a person be involved in a *learning community*, as well as pursuing *individual* and *small group* work.
5. Course members used subject-based knowledge and they used their personally created knowledge. Theory and practice were continually counterposed in ways which transcended simplistic deductive–inductive modes.

I have indicated here the notion of a holistic integration of poles, but I recognize that there are 'management teachers' who operate according to one or other of Handy's opposites. I have come across messy, self-centred existentialist programmes which have degenerated into chaotic disasters. The history of much of the 1960s and 1970s radical and humanistic education movement showed that many programmes collapsed because of this unbalanced mode of operation (see Swidler, 1979; Rogers, 1983; Leonard, 1979; Deal, 1975).

Equally, degenerate instrumental programmes have tended to survive because of a combination of authoritarian control mechanisms – that is, the exclusiveness and secretiveness of staff – and the investment by course members in pretending that their course is satisfactory (otherwise it would undermine their qualification, and if they have learned the hidden curriculum of instrumentalism they would not want to put their careers at risk).

What I have expressed above is my own interpretation, based on my experience of a number of institutions. However, in my research, people time and again expressed their rejection of narrow instrumentalism. They criticized the lack of involvement of such programmes with the lives of course members, the wastefulness of fixed curricula, and the lack of effectiveness of standardized taught courses.

CONCLUSION

SML approaches have been tried and tested in a wide variety of contexts over many years and with thousands of managers. Evaluation studies have shown the depth and breadth of learning for individuals from this approach. More importantly, people who have been through SML programmes comment on the way they learned to learn for themselves for the rest of their lives. They say, in evaluation studies carried out in a variety of organizations, how much they value becoming self-managing learners. Ultimately it is the *process* of SML which appears to provide the richest and most profound pay-off for learners and for their organizations.

FURTHER READING

Bandler, R. and J. Grinder (1979), *Frogs into Princes*, Moab, Ut.: Real People Press.

Bateson, G. (1973), *Steps to an Ecology of Mind*, London: Paladin.

Brown, G.L. (1971), *Human Teaching for Human Learning*, New York: Viking.

Casey, D. and D. Pearce (1977), *More than Management Development: Action Learning at G.E.C.*, Aldershot: Gower.

Cunningham, I. (1981) 'Self Managed Learning and Independent Study', in T. Boydell and M. Pedler, (eds), *Management Self Development: Concepts and Practices*, Aldershot: Gower.

Cunningham, I. (1983), 'Assessment and Experiential Learning' in R. Boot and M. Reynolds (eds), *Learning and Experience in Formal Education*, Manchester monograph, University of Manchester.

Cunningham, I. (1984), 'Teaching Styles in Learner Centred Management Development Programmes', PhD thesis, University of Lancaster.

Deal, T.E. (1975), 'An Organizational Explanation of the Failure of Alternative Secondary Schools', *Educational Researcher*, **4**, (4), 10–16.

Handy, C.B. (1975), 'The Contrasting Philosophies of Management Education', *Management Education and Development*, **6**, (2), August, 56–62.

Harrison, R. (1974), 'Developing Autonomy, Initiative and Risk-Taking through Laboratory Design', in J.D. Adams (ed.), *New Technologies in O.D.*, La Jolla: University Associates.

Hurley, B. and I. Cunningham (1993), 'Imbibing a New Way of Learning', in *Personnel Management*, March, 42–5.

Herson, J. (1977), *Dimensions of Facilitator Style*, British Postgraduate Medical Federation.

Kolb, D.A. and R.E. Boyatzis (1984) 'Goal Setting and Self-Directed Behaviour Change', in D.A. Kolb, I.M. Rubin and J.M. McIntyre (eds), *Organizational Psychology: Readings on Human Behaviour in Organizations*, Englewood Cliffs, NJ: Prentice-Hall.

Leonard, G. (1979). 'Frontiers in Education: Past and Present', *AHP Newsletter*, May, 5–6.

Mant, A. (1977), *The Rise and Fall of the British Manager*, London: McGraw-Hill.

Mintzberg, H. (1984), 'Planning on the left side and managing on the right', in D.A. Kolb, I.M. Rubin and J.M. McIntyre (eds), *Organizational Psychology: Readings on Human Behaviour in Organizations*, Englewood Cliffs, NJ: Prentice-Hall.

Mumford, A. (1980), *Making Experience Pay*, London: McGraw-Hill.

Peers, J. and G. Bennett (1981), *1001 Logical Laws*, London: Hamlyn.

Rogers, C.R. (1969), *Freedom to Learn*, Columbus, Oh.: Merrill.

Rogers, C.R. (1983), *Freedom to Learn for the Eighties*, Columbus, Oh.: Merrill.

Schutz, W. (1979), *Profound Simplicity*, London: Turnstone.

Sirag, S.P. (1979) 'Physics Education', *AHP Newsletter*, May, 17–18.

Stewart, R. (1982), *Choices for the Manager*, London: McGraw-Hill.

Swidler, A. (1979), *Organisation without Authority*, Cambridge, Mass.: Harvard University Press.

Watzlawick, P. (1978), *The Language of Change*, London: Basic Books.

26 Computer-based training

Peter Wynn

Increasing competition, a global marketplace, the shift in the working population – all these developments mean that patterns of training are set to change. This chapter offers an insight into maximizing the use of training resources by the application of modern technology. With the right planning this additional facility can be utilized as successfully by smaller companies as by the large organizations. It should be studied by all trainers who are seeking to be proactive, and also by senior management who are responsible for budget setting and results. A glossary of technical terms has been included at the end of this chapter.

WHAT IS COMPUTER-BASED TRAINING?

Computer-based training (CBT) is an effective and flexible method of training and can be used by all levels of staff. It is effective because:

- It engages learners in activity.
- It enables learners to study at their own pace.
- It provides opportunities for learners to check their understanding.
- It supports self-development.

Its strengths

- It is readily available at many company locations and can be fitted in with their work commitments.
- It enables time and resources to be used effectively.
- It can be a cost-effective way of meeting the needs of the business.
- It can be used on a stand alone basis, or it can be used to complement other forms of training.

Its constraints

- This form of training requires a greater commitment by the manager and the individual.
- Since individuals work on their own, they may feel a degree of isolation.
- Some people may be anxious about using computers for training purposes.

HOW DOES CBT WORK?

As with other effective training, computer-based training must involve the manager and the individual learner. Together they identify the individual's training and development needs and set clear and specific objectives. This ensures that the outcome of the training is measurable and the added value provided by the training can be seen in enhanced achievement by both the manager and the individual concerned. The individual should then complete the training programme by using the computer, the disk containing the training material and associated workbook to achieve the knowledge and understanding of the specific topic. As will be seen later, interactive video can also be used in conjunction with the computer.

An action plan should be prepared and jointly discussed, and the manager should offer help and assistance. In this way the transition from the learning situation to enhanced job performance will be greatly facilitated. A follow-up discussion should take place after a suitably elapsed time, to review the situation and to discuss future training activities.

WHAT ARE THE ADVANTAGES OF CBT?

- People can work through the material at their own speed.
- The programmes are designed to check understanding of the subject matter.
- Many programmes allow for studying only those sections that are relevant to the training needs, by means of a menu facility (all the content items are listed and a selection is made).
- The time devoted to the training is highly flexible and can be agreed by the manager and the individual.
- Training is usually carried out on an individual basis, but people with similar training requirements can pair up. The exchange of views expressed can result in mutual sharing of ideas and issues.
- People are away from their workplace for a minimum amount of time.
- It promotes consistency in training throughout an organization.

HOW DO I GET STARTED IN USING CBT?

Provided that there is access to an IBM-compatible PC, then this can be done very inexpensively. First of all, undertake a needs analysis to ascertain the training need and formulate objectives. Next, contact one of the many suppliers of generic material and ask for a preview disk on the subject matter you require. Most suppliers will send you a demo disk which contains a selected amount of material from their published course, and this will give you a flavour of the quality of the material and the amount of interactivity required by the learner. Beware the supplier who only provides electronic page turning courseware!

Having contacted several suppliers and tested their products, you can then make your choice and purchase the full course. Prices start well under £100, so you will not break your budget by trying one. With the disk and the use of an IBM-PC compatible computer, you can run through the material for yourself. It would also be useful to select a few volunteers to do the same for preview purposes. Make sure that you question them on their views of CBT as a training method when they have completed their previewing. You have now sampled CBT and obtained a collective viewpoint.

THE NEXT STEP

Repeat the above exercise with further analysis into training needs, and obtain new CBT programmes until you have a number of disks that have addressed a variety of training needs.

You will now have a decision to make – either to do a presentation to managers in the organization about CBT, or to prepare some in-company material. The reason for the latter is that most managers will be more supportive of training endeavours if they can see its direct relevance to their own organization and current business problems. It is unlikely for a generic product to be able to address all of their specific requirements, so a tailor-made programme would help sell CBT to the organization.

THE FEASIBILITY OF SETTING UP AN IN-COMPANY CBT/IV FACILITY

The costs of such a study are small, but the investment of time at this stage could enhance any agreed future implementation – or prevent a disaster from happening. An example of a disaster situation is where expensive facilities are organized and set up at remote locations, but, because of poor communication and control, are then infrequently used. It is also important to arrange for visits to companies where successful implementation has taken place, and to find out at first hand what specific hurdles had to be overcome.

The following items will serve as a starting point for most investigative studies.

1. The attitudes of the people involved – from the points of view of both potential customers and those who hold the purse strings as far as any budget allocation is concerned. Company policy on training and information technology; who will be providing the hardware for running the courses? Is the hardware already in place, and can time be made *333*

available for people to use it? If not, will the CBT budget have to allow for hardware provision?

2. The medium- to long-term view in terms of investment pay back – particular note should be given to market competition and the changes taking place in the market sector of the company concerned.

3. Immediate problems which will require a solution; for example, staffing issues (internal or external recruitment); financial resources available for the start-up phase; the cost of promotional material; and the time/cost factor of briefing managers about the new venture.

4. A forecast of likely future budget requirements. A start will usually be made with CBT, but at some stage the company may require the additional facilities which only interactive video can offer, which has considerable cost implications.

5. A list of the benefits and a demonstration of how cost savings/performance improvement could be made to certain current training activities. (An example is reducing the length of a course, by having certain of the knowledge aspects handled by CBT as pre-course study).

6. To do this activity effectively means breaking down the costs of conventional training activities and matching them against the projected cost of CBT.

7. Conducting a training needs analysis.

8. Setting course and performance objectives.

9. Calculation of course development costs: for example, producing course materials including handouts, tutor notes and transparencies; (cost in person hours, materials, and so on). All associated overheads, including accommodation costs.

10. Training costs: for example, tutor costs in delivering training (person hours); cost of training accommodation (in-house or hotel); trainees' salaries and overhead costs attributable to being away from the job; travelling and subsistence allowances for tutors and trainees.

11. Administration costs associated with organizing and running the particular course: for example, arranging nominations, preparing and issuing joining instructions, booking venues, and so on.

12. Costs associated with CBT and IV use: for example, provision of local accommodation (it is unrealistic to expect people to study effectively at their own desk, even if it is equipped with a PC); equipping local accommodation with the required hardware and software. It is a good idea to enlist the help of your DP department for this, and to ask them about the relevant benefits of buying, renting or leasing the hardware.

When the feasibility study has been completed, arrangements should be made for a formal presentation to the decision-making group concerned. By arranging a face-to-face meeting, the opportunity is gained to sell the idea and to resolve any lack of understanding or disagreement in constructive discussion.

TOWARDS EFFECTIVE CBT

The overall effectiveness of the produced material will depend on how it is presented to the trainee. The following items are the key to a positive result.

Screen design

Training research has shown that when training material is well designed and presented, then users are much more motivated to use it – and to pass on their favourable views to their colleagues. The use of colour is most important as it enables users to focus attention and provides continuity through the material. Screen messages can be placed at specific points on the screen to offer comments on the trainee's progress, and help screens should also be made available if requested. It can also be used to draw attention to errors and reinforce correct responses when dealing with user input. Check the use of colour combinations carefully and do not use too many on one screen; an easy mistake in designing initial programmes. Font size and type-style are also important and it is useful to experiment with different examples in the early stages of production and reflect these back to prospective users for their views and comments.

CGA graphics

Colour Graphics Adaptor (CGA) mode which gives medium screen resolution (640 x 200 pixels), and a basic colour choice of three foreground colours and one background colour.

EGA graphics

Enhanced Graphics Adaptor (EGA) which offers a screen resolution of 640 x 350 pixels and up to sixteen colours on the screen at any one time from a palette of sixty-four.

VGA graphics

Visual Graphics Adaptor (VGA) which gives a definition of 640 x 480 pixels and the choice of 256 colours on screen at any one time from a total of 262,144.

With the aid of a mouse input device, very sophisticated diagrams, cartoons and pictures can be reproduced on screen, thus adding to the user's interest. Animation also contains many facilities for highlighting key learning points. Graphics can also be used for simulating main frame screens on PCs, and all design charts of both an industrial and commercial nature can be reproduced using a CAD/CAM system.

335

Interactivity

This is a key feature of all CBT material. It enables the users to check on their understanding, and to progress through the material by routes depending on their success. The interaction can take several forms; for example, quizzes, business games, questioning techniques and matching. An important design feature is the anticipation of possible wrong answers and the development of appropriate feedback and encouragement. An incorrect response may well require branching the user to a separate path in order to reinforce a particular learning point and to offer more required responses. Good design makes this transparent to users; they think that their requirements are being met as individual users.

Support documentation

It is useful for the learners to have printed details of their training by way of bullet-point summaries. Where a printer is attached to the PC, screen details which are identified by the user as being particularly useful for future use can be printed off.

HOW DOES A COMPANY MAKE ITS OWN PROGRAMMES?

This can be achieved by the use of external consultants (expensive), recruiting a CBT specialist, nominating and training one of your current team, or by doing it yourself. Whichever method you use, it is vital to ensure that your first in-house production is a success.

If in-house staff are to embark on this project, then please ensure that some specialized training is undertaken first. This has to be said, because many sellers of CBT authoring systems will say that their product is so user-friendly that no other training is required. Not so! The skill of achieving good results with CBT is to do a proper analysis, talk to the subject matter experts and prepare a paper-based flowchart before you even touch an authoring system.

Authoring systems have been designed for trainers to use; they remove the need for being a computer expert but do require a time input to become proficient. Selection of the appropriate authoring system is outside the scope of this chapter. Please remember one important thing: always be looking forward; do not get locked into suppliers who are not investing in their product for future enhancements.

Screen design is an important aspect of CBT and it needs particular attention. There is general tendency to clutter screens with too much information. It is far better to reveal the information in stages, so that it can be more easily digested. Print size and font type require consideration as do the colours used for the final production. Graphics will depend on the PC being used; the quality may be CGA, EGA or VGA. The computer manual supplied with the machine will contain all the relevant information.

You will also need to check on the memory availability of your computer, to ensure that the authoring system will work on it and that there is a sufficient amount left for designing and storing the new programmes that are developed.

Distribution of your programmes will require decisions as to whether they are run from the hard disk, or the disks which will need to be supplied. Depending on the type of programmes being designed, there may be a need for a printer to be attached to the computer when it is being used by trainees.

Finally in this section, a word about mainframe CBT. This is possible, but you will have to budget for extra costs, and there is always a problem of response time back from the mainframe when the trainee has entered an answer.

COMPUTER-MANAGED LEARNING

This further aspect of CBT is an important one, as it generates user records and collates records of their performance. This data can then be analysed by the trainers and designers with the objective of making the training material even better. Many authoring systems have this facility built in, but test out what you require the systems to provide you with before purchase.

RECORD KEEPING

The question of keeping records on any computer system must be thought through realistically. An analytical and ordered approach will determine what output is required; this will then quantify what data is required to produce the desired outcome. Another important aspect is to consider carefully the implications arising from the Data Protection Act when keeping records on a computer system.

The requirements that arise from the above analysis will probably include some of the following headings:

- Name of trainee.
- Personnel number/student number.
- Course title and number.
- Start date.
- Details of all input responses.
- Test assignment results.
- Paths through the course arising from test results.
- Time taken to complete modules.
- Completion date.
- Comments of users keyed in at the completion of the training.

The above items are going to demand disk storage space and analysis arrangements. The size of the organization concerned and the amount of CBT usage will determine the resource required both in person and computer terms. The benefits of such a facility must, therefore, be weighed up carefully at the analysis stage of the CML project.

INTERACTIVE AUDIO

This is a facility which can be used by inserting a voice card into one of the expansion slots of the PC and loading the appropriate software. The price of the voice card will determine the voice output quality; it can be quite impressive and individual voices can be recognized. The sound output is routed to a small external loudspeaker. The use of such a device adds a further dimension to CBT and the voice output can reduce screen presented information. Feedback to user's input can also be directed back via this speaker system.

On the more advanced systems, the voice card can also be set to receive voice commands from the user which reduces dependence on the keyboard. A test run is done at the beginning of the programme, whereby the user speaks into the microphone and the computer builds up a voice pattern for use during the course.

INTERACTIVE VIDEO

A system which offers the full facility of using video sequences during the programme. The video is stored on a laser disk and this is enclosed in a laser player during use. The computer has another two cards inserted into its expansion slots, and these control the video and digital signals before presenting them on the screen with accompanying audio.

The computer and its internal program entirely control the use of the laser disk. It can be used to show full video and associated audio, still frame (no sound), and audio only (no picture), the computer itself delivering the text and graphics on to the screen. The user runs the programme using just the keyboard; all the equipment is electronically linked together when it is switched on.

Once again, generic laser disk training material is available from suppliers on a variety of subjects. Company-specific programmes can also be commissioned, but the cost here will run into thousands of pounds. However, this can still prove to be cost effective where there are a large number of employees, and the costs are looked at on a per capita basis and the life of the finished programme.

Future activities in this area are being concentrated on the compact disc. This has the ability to store large amounts of information and can be coupled to the computer in the same way as the laser disc mentioned above.

DIGITAL VIDEO INTERACTIVE

DVI is the first available technology on the commercial market to enable designers to produce full screen, full motion video from a compact disc. These compact disks can also store audio tracks, text information, graphics and photographic stills. This brings the full scope of 'Multimedia' to users of the latest PCs, which have a compact disc drive fitted as an optional extra; or, by linking an existing CD–ROM player to the computer system.

Modern PCs now have the capability of handling the large amounts of digital
338 data that make up full motion video and delivering it to high-definition monitors.

The key to the system is the special DVI plug-in cards which are located in the expansion slots of the computer system unit, plus the associated software.

'Multimedia' now offers the designer the ability to mix CBT, interactive video, and audio and publish multi-language versions of the programme using the same compact disc.

TOWARDS THE FUTURE – SATELLITE TRANSMISSION

Technology moves on apace, and it is appropriate to conclude on this latest area of development. This form of transmission will provide live broadcasting to company audiences at specific times, and local automatic recording facilities, so that staff unable to be present at the live transmission can view the material subsequently. It will also enable organizations to transmit data during the night at cheap rates, ready for staff to use next day. By this method CBT material can be transmitted to selected offices and used immediately. Print-based material can also be transmitted and printed out locally on high quality laser printers.

Effective and timely training should be the watchwords of any successful trainer. Are you exploiting technology to the full for your organization?

GLOSSARY OF TERMS ASSOCIATED WITH CBT AND IV

Authoring systems
A computer software package that contains programs for compiling CBT courses. They can be used by trainers in most cases, and provide useful tools for producing quality results.

Bar code
A series of parallel black lines used on products to transmit data via a scanner to a computer. This device can also now be used to produce and send signals to interact with a laser-disk player via a light pen.

BASIC
One of the most common programming languages for personal computers. It stands for Beginners All-purpose Symbolic Instruction Code.

Board
A flat card of plastic containing microchips and circuits which plugs into an expansion slot in the PC to provide extra facilities, such as the control and graphics card used with interactive video.

Boot
The process of starting up a computer at the beginning of the working day. A re-boot is where the data in the working memory is removed and the screen is cleared.

Branching
An instructional design facility which allows for users to be routed to different   *339*

parts of the course, depending on their input response to questions or statements.

Brief

The document used in the tendering process when involving external production houses. It contains the background to the project and an idea of the desired outcome.

CAD/CAM

Computer Aided Design/Computer Aided Manufacturing. Sophisticated software packages that enable complex design and drawing to be done using non-keyboard input devices.

CBT

Computer Based Training. It represents the delivery of training material by use of a computer and can also include the use of interactive audio and interactive video.

CCTV

Closed circuit television.

CD

Compact Disc – used in music recording to produce high-quality sound output. Can also be used to store computer data and a combination of still and moving pictures. CD–I Compact Disc–Interactive; CD–ROM Compact Disc–Read Only Memory; CD–ROM–XA – eXtended Architecture: all items that are developing now and should be carefully studied.

CPU

Central Processing Unit – the control, memory, and logic unit of a computer.

CGA

Colour Graphics Adapter – offers medium screen resolution and limited colours on the screen.

Check disk

A glass or plastic prototype videodisk which is prepared for the customer who can then test before final production.

Compression facilities

Devices which can reduce the space required on a disk. Usually used for storing pictures or complex graphics.

Computer graphics

Diagrams or art work used in delivering courseware, which has been generated using a computer.

Cursor

A short flashing line, or icon, on the screen which denotes where the next input item will be displayed.

Delivery system

The hardware and software required to present courseware to a user.

Disk drive
The part of the computer which spins the disk and reads information to and from the computer disk.

Diskette
The disk which contains the data and which is used in the disk drive mentioned above.

Dot matrix
A type of computer printer which produces characters by a series of dots. The number of dots per inch determines the quality of the finished document.

Download
The transfer of data from one computer (usually a mainframe), to a PC via a network. This facility can be used during the night to transfer CBT courseware. It is then available for the user at the start of business the following day.

EGA
Enhanced Graphics Adapter. Offers a higher degree of resolution than CGA and greater availability of foreground and background colours.

End user
The person who actually uses the CBT or IV material. This usually takes place in the working environment, although modern portable computers mean that the training can be done almost anywhere.

Entry test
Can be used to ascertain the knowledge level of a particular individual on a specific subject, to determine the route through a CBT or IV course.

Evaluation
The process of monitoring the performance of an individual after training has taken place.

Feedback
A vital part of CBT and IV delivery, where the user is offered congratulations, help, and re-try facilities when responding to questions, quizzes and business games.

Field testing
This is where a representative group of potential users are asked to complete the course and offer comments on the design, accuracy and user-friendliness of the course material.

Generic material
CBT and IV courses which are produced and marketed by specialist companies.

Genlock
An electronic system which locks differing input signals such as video and computer graphics, to produce a screen display.

Hard copy
The transfer of computer data to paper, 35 mm slides and overhead transparencies.

Hardware system
The component parts of the CBT or IV such as the systems unit, keyboard, monitor and laser player.

IBM compatible
Personal computers based on the industry standards determined by IBM.

Interactive audio
CBT systems which have the added advantage of having a voice card or compact disk linked into the delivery process alongside text and graphics on the screen.

Interactive video
The combination of video pictures and sound coupled to text and graphics on screen. This powerful medium has the ability of fully engaging users and portraying real life situations. The laser player is controlled by the computer via the keyboard or mouse device.

LD
Laser Disk. Describes the 12" videodisk which is used in a laser player to offer full motion video and accompanying audio.

Menu
A screen list of available options, any one of which can be selected by the user to activate the programme.

Mouse
A small input device which when moved across a working surface controls the movement of the cursor or arrow device. Clicking the mouse buttons selects or confirms the information required.

NTSC
The American television standard, which uses a 525 line system.

Off-line edit
The initial stages of video editing, where all of the shoot material is put through the editor to produce an initial master.

Overlay
The electronic process which enables the designer to overlay text and graphics on a video picture.

PAL
The European Television standard which uses the 625 line system.

Peripheral
An item of hardware which is linked by a cable to a computer; keyboards, printers and laser players are three examples.

Ports
The input and output sockets of a computer, which connect the peripherals.

Project manager
The title given to the individual who heads up a team involved in the making of CBT and IV courses.

Resolution
The picture quality as it appears on screen. This is determined by the number of pixels (points of light) that occupy a screen area.

Script
The documentation used in the production of a videodisk programme. It contains all the details relating to the scene shooting, treatment of each shot, audio information, including voice-over, and the inclusion of music and captions.

Software
This relates to the computer programs and associated instructions which are contained on the disk, together with the video and audio contained on the laserdisk.

Stand-alone
The term given to PCs and their associated peripherals which are not connected to the mainframe or local area network.

Storyboard
A series of sketches which help to visualize the shots for the video production work.

Synchronization
The electronic process which locks the video and computer inputs together, and then presents a combined picture and audio output on the monitor.

Touchscreen
A monitor that has been fitted with a special screen device which is able to accept the touch of a finger as another type of input device.

VGA graphics
Visual Graphics Adaptor. This new graphics standard was developed for the IBM PS/2 computers for their model 50s and above. It offers a high screen resolution and up to 256 colours on screen at any one time.

Videodisk
This contains all the video, sound, still frame and voice-over data. The benefits of using a laser disk as compared with videotape are its fast access speed and continuously good reproduction.

Voice-over
A commentary which accompanies still frames, computer-generated graphics or text based screens. Remember to keep volatile data on the computer disk, which can be easily altered as compared with having to produce a new videodisk.

FURTHER READING

Barker, Philip (ed.) (1989), *Multi-media Computer Assisted Learning*, Kogan Page.

Dean and Whitlock (1988), *A Handbook of Computer Based Training*, 2nd edn, Kogan Page.

Hartley, James (1987), *Designing Instructional Text*, Kogan Page.

Haynes, George (1989), *Opening Minds: The Evolution of Videodisks and Interactive Learning*, Videodisk Monitor.

Luther, Arch (1989), *Digital Video in the PC Environment*, McGraw-Hill.

Megarry, Jacquetta (1989), *Compact Discs and Computers: Converging Technologies*, Kogan Page.

Picciotto, Robertson and Colley (1989), *Interactivity: Designing and Using Interactive Video*, Kogan Page.

Tucker, Richard (ed.) (1989), *Interactive Media: The Human Issues*, Kogan Page.

27 On-line education and development

Vivien Hodgson and David McConnell

As information technology (IT) becomes ever more ubiquitous in both organizational and domestic life, it is increasingly important for educationalists and trainers to use IT to its optimum potential. In this chapter, we discuss as yet little-used technology in the educational and training world. Computer-mediated communications systems (CMCS) offers enormous possibilities for enhancing educational provision by the potential they give to offer on-line education.

COMPUTER-MEDIATED COMMUNICATIONS SYSTEMS

The term computer-mediated communications[1] systems is currently used to cover any form of communication that occurs over a network of computers. CMCS involves the use of computers to send and receive textual communications. The text is often held in a mainframe computer, where it can be retrieved at any time by those wishing to read it. Electronic mail provides a example of this 'store and retrieve' principle; E-mail is perhaps most suitable for person-to-person communications. Where interactive group communication is important, computer conferencing allows groups of people to communicate in a way that they can all share the text of the group messages. A record of the proceedings of the group communications is kept permanently on the mainframe and can be read linearly (equivalent to following a discussion from start to end), or can be searched in a variety of ways depending on what information a user is looking for (equivalent to using it as a database).

Communications via CMCS usually occur asynchronously, although occasionally users do co-ordinate times when they are 'on line' together. But the asynchronous nature of these systems is often cited as a positive benefit to busy workers and learners who prefer the flexibility of communicating whenever it

[1] Other terms currently used include: computer-supported co-operative work (CSCW) (Greif, 1989); groupware; computer-supported co-operative learning.

Direct PSTN Link:

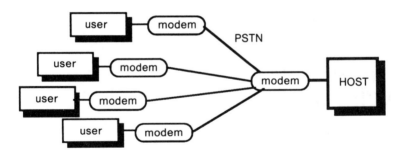

PDN Link:

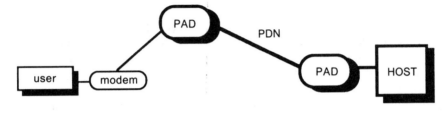

Leased Circuit:

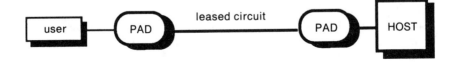

Local Area Network:

346 Figure 27.1   Four possible routes to the host computer

suits them. Electronic meetings – the social presence, process and outcomes – differ from face-to-face meetings (McConnell, 1990) and possibly require new ways of thinking about the meaning of group work when it is mediated via computers.

WHAT IS NEEDED?

The basic set up requires a host computer where the CMCS software is held, and computer terminals or personal computers capable of connecting with the host to allow users to interact with the CMCS software. If there are large numbers of users and if access is needed by several users at the same time, then the host computer will usually be a mainframe computer.

Users can access the CMCS software by a variety of methods, using a variety of equipment. Four basic scenarios are suggested in Figure 27.1.

Direct PSTN link

Accessing the host using the public switched telephone network (PSTN) requires each user to have a personal computer with wordprocessing software, communications software, a modem (modulator–demodulator – a piece of equipment that changes the digital signals from your computer to analogue signals which can be transmitted down the telephone line), and a new '600' series telephone point (most telephone points are now of this type; the telephone need not be dedicated for teleconferencing; it can be used for ordinary 'voice' calls as well).

The user simply directs the communications software to connect their computer with the host via the modem and the public telephone lines. The cost of connecting in this way is the same as the ordinary cost of the telephone connection to the location where the host is held (this of course varies depending on the time of the day and the location of the host). The quality of the connection varies enormously with the quality of the PSTN, and data is often corrupted due to 'noise' on the line. Transmission of data can be rather slow via this method, although rates from 2,400 bits per second up to 19,200 bits per second are possible.

PDN link

The public data network (PDN) provides a better quality connection to the host than PSTN often does. In the United Kingdom, both British Telecom (BT) and Mercury provide a data network service. The BT service is called Packet Switch Stream (PSS), the latest version of which is PSS Dialplus. The Mercury service is called Mercury Packet Data Service. Users take out a subscription to the PDN, which costs approximately £60.00 for Dialplus and £20.00 for Mercury plus quarterly charges. In addition, there are usage charges of about £1.10 to £1.80 per hour depending on the time of day and day of week.

Using this method, access is gained by dialling the local PDN node via any *347* ordinary telephone line and connecting to their PAD (packet assembler disassembler – a device for sending and receiving 'packets' of data; PDNs use packet switching to send 'packets' or parts of a message rather than the complete message; the packets are reassembled at the other end into the complete message). The user then has access to the completely digital data network to connect to the host. These services provide error correction and various other supports which make data transmission quality very high. Speed of transmission is also higher using PDN – ranging from 2,400 bits per second using standard modems to 48,000 bits per second with higher quality modems.

Leased circuit

Where volume of use from one location is high (e.g. many users in the same buildings accessing a distant host) and quality and speed of data transmission are important, it may be preferable to lease a digital line. Leased circuits provide permanent connections to the host, and users may access the host from a terminal connected to the line, or via a personal computer connected to it. No modems or telephone points are required. The costs of a leased line vary, depending on the distance between the two points being connected and on the data transmission speeds required. For example, a leased line to connect two locations 9 kilometres apart costs about £3,000.00 per year for a 9,600 bits per second link, and £4,300.00 for a 64,000 bits per second link. There are no limits on the usage of the line, and no additional usage costs. However, there would be the cost of buying and installing the in-house cabling and PAD, which might cost around £5,000.00. This configuration would allow at least 16 simultaneous users to access the host. A leased line is clearly not feasible for single users, but may be beneficial where there are many users in close proximity. The higher band width of a leased line enables large volumes of data to be transmitted.

Private local area network

Many organizations have private local area networks (LANs) which function in a similar way to a leased line. LANs are usually installed within a building (several LANs in different buildings may be connected together) and would connect the users to a host computer also situated within the same building.

It is, of course, possible to combine any of these data networks with any of the others (e.g. PSTN and PDN can be linked together, and a public leased line can be combined with private LANs, and so on).

HOW IT WORKS

Computer-mediated communications systems include electronic mail, computer conferencing, bulletin boards and on-line databases. For clarity and convenience, we shall limit our discussion to the use of computer conferencing (cc) since that is the most appropriate medium for training, education and development work with groups of people. We currently use cc in a variety of higher education programmes, but will focus here on our use within a computer-mediated MA in Management Learning at Lancaster University.

Members of a computer conference are able to carry out the following basic operations:

- Read the text of the conference.
- Add their own items (i.e. freestanding textual communications) to the conference.
- Add responses to other people's conference items (or indeed to their own items).
- Send private messages to any number of individual conference members.

Thus members of a computer conference can have both one-to-one communication via the conference system and one-to-group communication. They are able to link into the conference at any time and on any day of the week. Whenever they do link into the conference they are told what new activity has taken place in the conference since they were last on line. That is, they are informed of:

1. How many new items have been added to the conference.
2. The number of new responses that have been added to items.
3. How many new personal messages they have received.

Conference items and responses are a way of organizing, ordering and structuring inputs into a computer conferencing system.

Levels of organization

Conferences

A conference is the most general level of order or organization. Any group of CMCS users may set up as many conferences as they require. On our computer-mediated MA programme there are three main types of conferences: general, tutor group, and specific.

Everyone on the programme contributes to and participates in the general conference as a way of keeping the whole group in touch with each other. Substantive management-learning issues are discussed collectively, and we can inform each other of developments in other conferences or activities occurring elsewhere. This conference also acts as a noticeboard for the programme as a whole.

Each member is also joined to a tutorial group conference. These have smaller numbers of participants and are primarily concerned with discussions around the assessed work on the course and personal development issues.

The specific conferences are meeting places: to discuss such things as the design of residential workshops; to share information about books and papers *349* that participants have read; and to place resources (bibliographies, research papers, and so on) to share with others.

Items

The next level of organization is an item within a conference. Items are basically sub-topics of the general conference theme or purpose. Any member of a conference can add an item, and there can be as many items as are required by participants.

Responses

The final level of order is that of a response. For each item added by a conference member, others can add responses to that item, so that a form of dialogue or discussion emerges around the item topic. Responses are added either until the discussion concludes, or until a decision is made that the discussion has moved sufficiently far from the original topic focus that it would be more profitable to start a new item, in order to acknowledge the change of focus and start a fresh dialogue around the new emerging ideas.

Thus, the metaphor of the conference being the meeting place to discuss a general theme, the items being the sub-themes or sub-topics, and the responses being the group dialogue, provide a way of helping us to understand the nature (process and product) of an electronic meeting. In our use of cc, we apply a useful title to each conference which helps us orient ourselves to the purposes of that conference each time we join it. In these ways we try to provide a 'living' electronic learning environment which has meaning for our participants, and which embodies an aura of belonging and support.

An example of the text of a computer conference is provided in Figure 27.2. The example is taken from one of our own MA conferences. The discussion is about grading and assessment on the MA programme. Names have been changed to ensure anonymity.

COMPUTER SKILLS REQUIRED

There are three levels of computing operations ideally required for computer conferencing: wordprocessing skill; telecommunications skill; conferencing skill.

Wordprocessing skill

To use CMCS most effectively it is best to prepare the text of items, responses and personal messages before going into a conference. This is perhaps less important if you are working from a terminal with a permanent link to the host; you can then use the on-line conferencing editor to prepare text, although the text editors on most conferencing systems are so primitive that the experience can often be excruciating! For those linking into the host by PSTN or PDN it is
350 usually preferable to prepare the text in advance, using ordinary wordprocess-

Item 9   26–JUN–90   9:45   Geraldine Crosbie
Assessment on MAML programmes

This is my account of a discussion held during CSML's work week. It is about assessment on MAML programmes. I thought you might be interested – here goes

During our work week at Borwick, a session about assessment within MAMLs was led by Robin Snell. He was discussing whether there should be a move from a system of marks to one of a simple pass/fail. Within CSML there were different views about this and as a result he agreed to do some research into the issue for asession at work week.

Robin conducted a questionnaire survey of pastMAML participants and about a third replied. Of these, just over a half were in favour of a moveto the pass/fail option.Many of the opponents of the marking system emphasised the pain and anxiety experienced, the absurdity of haggling over 1 or 2 marks and the contradiction between the student-centred/humanist leanings of the programme.

Pro-markers emphasised the need for the feedback that marks gave and also the motivation. Some felt that the whole issue of marks was relatively trivial when compared with some of the other controversial issues such as tutor role and power in general, admission to the programme, the awarding of a degree.

(item cut here for brevity)

   4 Discussion responses
9:1) Charles Rayburn   27–JUN–90   14:26
   Hi Geraldine
   Very interesting.
   I'm a pass/fail with comments, person myself.
   Love
      Chris!
– – – – –

9:2) Ian Fleming   30–JUN–90   14:48
   Hi geraldine thanks for putting this on. It certainly appears to polarise the debate on assessment. I know from my own experience that I found grading particularly difficult but I also realise that I would be unlikely to fail my own work no matter how bad it was but I would be prepared to mark or grade myself accurately e.g see gradings in K.g.B conference. So as you can see most people come down firmly on one side or the other although I could see occasions where I would edge my bets. What a fence sitter I could become on this issue.
   What do others think.?
   See you soon
– – – – –

9:3) Daniel McBride   02–JUL–90   23:00
   Very interesting. I agree with Ian's point that you'd be unlikely to submit a piece of work which you saw as a fail, but having to give it a mark does, however uncomfortably, focus you to evaluate it more finely. I've found the very process of grappling with how you will mark yourself quite self revealing. Maybe I'll get bored with it by the end of the course!
– – – – –

9:4) Zoe Cunnigham   03–JUL–90   16:29
   This must be short cos I am getting cramp from one and a half hours typing! well it wasn't all typing! Anyway at the level of taking part broadly in the debate I thouhgt Geraldine's summary was v. good. I guess I am a pro currently for the very reasons that Ian and Daniel suggest. Also I thingk it gives a better indicator of movement and progress as one travels through the programme! Zoe.

Figure 27.2 Edited transcript of a computer conference item.   *351*

ing software, save it on the personal computer and 'upload' it to the host when connected.

Telecommunications skill

Communications software is used to link the personal computer to the host computer through one of the methods described above. Although simple enough in theory, this part of the process is often the most bewildering, confusing and frustrating aspect of teleconferencing. It is an application of computers that is little understood, and where so much can go wrong that even so-called computer experts fail to offer corrective guidance when called in to give advice.

The procedure involves the users setting the PC communications software to match those required by the host, instructing the PC to dial into the PSTN or PDN and connect to the host. After logging into the host (by providing a user identity and unique password), the PC keyboard is used to instruct the host computer to run the conferencing software.

Everything that the users do now originates from their own keyboards; all instructions to the host are sent from the PC down the line (which may be a few miles long or several hundred or thousand miles long). The users typically join the conferences of interest to them and download (i.e. receive on their own PCs) conference text and personal messages; they upload similar text into conferences and send personal messages to other users; they often also type in text whilst in a conference, and move in and out of the conference system and their own PC text-processing systems.

Conferencing skill

When joined to a computer conferencing system, a user needs at the most basic level to be able to:

- read new items and responses as required;
- read items and responses that they have previously read;
- add new items;
- add new responses; and
- send personal messages.

There are many other operations that the more sophisticated user of any particular conference system is able to do which enhance the potential of the medium. Some of the more obvious ones are:

- list all the conferences on the system;
- list all the items (briefly or in detail) in a conference;
- check which conferences they are a member of and the number of new items and responses that have been added since their last visit;
- check which members of a conference have visited the conference recently;

- search a conference for key words or phrases; and
- set up a new conference, customize its users and 'design' the nature of the meeting that will take place in the conference.

THE ROLE OF THE CONFERENCE ORGANIZER

As with most educational and training situations, the person organizing and running a computer conference (the trainer, tutor, facilitator or whatever term you prefer) is crucial to the success of the venture. Their role is to set up the conference (which is usually a fairly straightforward set of procedures) and help prepare the participants for the event. Once the conference is under way, the organizers (or moderators, as they are often called) have a similar role to the professional trainers or facilitators. They have to have skill in working with people, in creating a positive and supportive group culture on line, and in allowing participants to use the medium in ways that they think appropriate. CMCS will only be successful if the process emphasizes *group* learning.

The moderator has to ensure that there is a real meeting of minds on line – not just unassociated pieces of text. The role of the moderator of an online conference is as complex as that of any teacher or trainer in a face-to-face situation. Issues of educational philosophy, relationships with learners, power and control, the nature of knowledge and learning, and so on, are as important and problematic in CMCS as they are in face-to-face meetings. Some authors have written about the role of moderators (e.g. see Kerr, 1986; Feenberg, 1986).

SOME CHARACTERISTICS OF ON-LINE EDUCATION AND TRAINING

On-line education and training is clearly different from face-to-face meetings. Some of the more significant differences that we have identified are as follows:

- People from geographically distant sites are able to 'meet' without physically travelling to one location.
- There are savings in time and travel (and therefore financial savings, although there will be initial capital set-up costs, and recurring costs).
- Meetings are continuous – a meeting on line can take place over a defined time span (e.g. a week or a month) or can continue indefinitely (for months or years).
- Interactions (responses to contributions, and so on) are not instantaneous or immediate.
- People can contribute to the meeting whenever they feel they want to (i.e. without waiting their turn or interrupting others).
- Contributions can be made at any time of the day or night, seven days a week.
- A user can contribute from any geographic position (e.g. people who have to travel in their work can link in from almost any location).
- Communication usually (but not necessarily) happens in a slower, more sporadic fashion.

- There is a permanent record of the meeting and of everyone's contribution to it (this can be manipulated like a data base).
- Participants can access electronic resources and data bases other than those used for the particular programme.
- Social presence, process and product of cc meetings often differ from face-to-face meetings.
- The opportunity to work collaboratively in groups is enhanced – cc can support co-operative learning and group processes in ways that may be difficult to achieve in face-to-face meetings.

As yet, CMCS is a relatively new medium in education and training and very little research has been carried out into its relevance and effectiveness. There is a growing body of opinion, however, which is substantiated by initial research into the medium, that one of the important aspects of CMCS as an educational medium is the opportunity it offers for the democratization of educational exchanges. This is believed to be associated with not having to interrupt others or talk over people in order to say what you want to say within a conference. All users have the same access to the dialogue. In addition, visual cues which can be used to denote status and power are eliminated. Thus, CMCS potentially offers the possibility for what Roger Boshier recently identified as Habermas's 'ideal discourse', which Boshier (1990) claims should be 'free from coercion or distorting self-deception, is open to other perspectives and points of view, is accepting of others as equal participants'.

SOME USES OF CMCS

It is possible to discuss at least four possible uses of computer conferencing within education and training. Computer conferencing may be used as a *complete replacement* for face-to-face meetings, as an *adjunct* to them, as a *multi-media approach* to teaching and learning, and as a *fully integrated approach*.

Complete replacement

Computer conferencing may be used to replace conventional face-to-face meetings, either by offering these meetings electronically at a distance for geographically isolated learners, or by offering them as a viable alternative to in-house courses.

Computer conferencing is being used in North America in the direct provision of on-line courses. The Connected Education programme at the New School for Social Research in Manhattan offers entire courses via this technology. The conventional college environment is mirrored in these electronic courses: the classes are conducted by computer conferences where the main interactive teaching and learning occurs. There are also conferences to create the 'electronic campus' – a 'café' for students and staff; a 'student lounge'; a 'tutor lounge'; an electronic library and newsletter. Connected Education attracts students from the Western USA, Tokyo, Singapore and United Kingdom as well as from the New York area itself (Kaye, 1985).

Computer conferencing is also being used in the provision of continuing education courses for industry and commerce, and for teacher in-service education work. It is also used in undergraduate degree courses at the New Jersey Institute of Technology where over 60 staff use the system for tutoring both internal and external students. Subjects taught by CMCS include anthropology, management practices, maths, computer science and introductory sociology (Hiltz, 1986).

Adjunct method

The technology of electronic communication is also suitable as an adjunct to face-to-face meetings. Electronic seminars and tutorials can add a useful and interesting focus to on-campus and in-house courses. Material covered in lectures can be added to and complemented in a computer conference. Students can question the lecturer or trainer about the course, request additional information, or, indeed, add their own information to the conference for the benefit of the class as a whole. Face-to-face sessions can also be extended into asynchronous meetings for continued discussion of points raised or items which were unable to be discussed face-to-face. Alternatively, education and training offered solely via computer conferencing can be conducted throughout the year, with learners and tutors participating in them as and when they like. This has the benefit of allowing participants time to consider substantive topics over longer than usual periods of time (see McConnell, 1990).

Multi-media approach

The multi-media approach is perhaps exemplified by resource-based learning which emphasizes a variety of different media and approaches to teaching and learning. An example of this approach is an Open University course in information technology. In addition to all the usual packaged learning materials provided as part of the course (course text units; audio-cassettes; broadcast television; a course reader; supplementary readings; course guides, and so on), students are also given access to computer conferences for such activities as course information and updating, course tutoring and self-help groups. Here, computer conferencing is only one of several alternative ways of learning on the course. The variety of media available can begin to meet the varying learning needs of the students (Mason and Kaye, 1989).

Fully integrated approach

New designs for educational and training programmes which fully integrate CMCS are now feasible. At Lancaster University, we are experimenting with the design of a part-time MA in management learning which involves two distinct but highly complementary learning environments. Over a two-year period, *355* participants attend five residential workshops where they examine relevant research and theory. In between these workshops they join the 'electronic learning environment' where they continue discussing issues raised in the workshop, plan their assignments and assess them, work in action learning sets, and so on (see Figures 27.3 and 27.4). The electronic meetings are an important and integral part of the whole programme, not just an added extra. We are currently doing research into this new programme design which should help us understand the nature and effectiveness of on-line education.

- Personal computer prices are continuing to fall, and PCs are increasingly being used at home and work and are becoming an integral part of many people's professional lives.

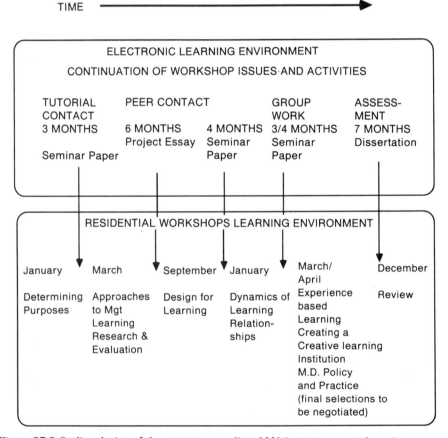

Figure 27.3 Outline design of the computer-mediated MA in management learning

CONCLUSIONS

Several factors may now lead to a wider use of CMCS within education and
training:

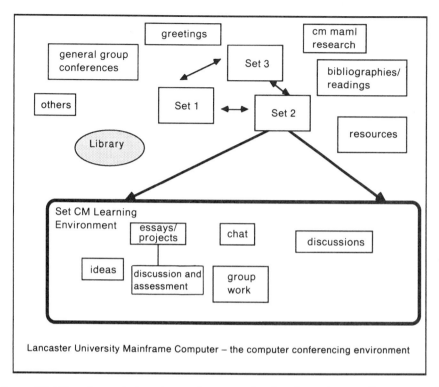

Figure 27.4 The electronic learning environment showing the various conferences used to support the MA programme participants

- Text processing and communications software is becoming more sophisticated and easier to use.
- Networks for on-line education and training are widely available – users can access CMC systems via ordinary telephone lines, via data lines or through private local area networks.

The introduction of CMCS into in-house and distance learning courses and activities offers an alternative to conventional face-to-face work. The exploration of the possible benefits to teaching and learning offered by the new information technologies is challenging and necessary, especially when the technology, as with computer conferencing, offers the hope of bringing people together who might otherwise never have the opportunity to meet and discuss educational and training issues.

FURTHER READING

Boshier, R. (1990), 'Socio-psychological factors in electronic networking', *International Journal of Lifelong Education*, **9**, (1).

Feenberg, A. (1986), 'Network design: an operating manual for computer conferencing', *IEEE Transactions on Professional Communications*, PC **29** (1), March.

Greif, E. (ed.) (1989), *Computer Supported Cooperative Work: A Book of Readings*, San Mateo, Calif.: Morgan Kaufman.

Hardy, V. (1992), 'Introducing Computer-Mediated Communications into Participative Management Education: the impact of the tutor's role', *Education and Training Technology International*, **29**, (4), 325–31.

Hiltz, S.R. (1984), *Online Communities*, Norwood, NJ: Ablex.

Hiltz, S.R. (1986), 'The virtual classroom: using computer mediated communication for university teaching', *Journal of Communication*, **36**, (2), 95–104.

Hiltz, S.R. and M. Turoff (1978), *The Network Nation : Human Communication via Computer*, Reading, Mass.: Addison-Wesley.

Hodgson, V. and D. McConnell (1992), 'IT-based Open Learning: a case study in Management Learning', *Journal of Computer Assisted Learning*, **8**, (3), 136–50.

Johansen, R. (1988), *Groupware: Computer Support for Business Teams*, London: The Free Press (Macmillan).

Kaye, Tony (1985), *Computer Mediated Communication Systems for Distance Education: Report of a Study Visit to North America*, Project Report CCET/2, Milton Keynes: Open University, Institute of Educational Technology.

Kaye, A.R. (1992), 'Collaborative Learning Through Computer Conferencing: the Najaden Papers', NATO AS1 Series F: *Computer and Systems Sciences*, Special Programme AET, Vol. 90, Heidelberg: Springer-Verlag.

Kerr, E.B. (1986), 'Electronic leadership: a guide to moderating online conferences', *IEEE Transactions on Professional Communications*, PC **29**, (1), March, 12–18.

McConnell, D. (1990), 'Case study: the educational use of computer conferencing', *Education and Training Technology International*, **17**, (2), 190–208.

McConnell, D. (1991), 'Computer, Electronic Networking and Education: Some American Experiences', *ETTI*, **28**, (3), 171–87.

McConnell, D. and V. Hodgson (1990), 'Computer mediated communications systems – electronic networking and education', *Management Learning and Development*, **21** (1), 51–8.

Mason, R. and T. Kaye (1989), *Mindweave: Communication, Computers and Distance Education*, Oxford: Pergamon Press.

Meeks, B.N. (1985), 'An overview of conferencing systems', *BYTE*, December, 169–85.

28 Mentoring and coaching

Ed Moorby

People develop and grow by their own individual efforts and/or with help from somebody else. On your own, you may read a book, study a computer-based training programme or discover things for yourself. With others, you may join a class and be helped by a teacher, join an action-learning set and be helped by your comrades-in-adversity, or learn together with an individual master, for example, a craftsman or a martial arts 'sensei'.

A highly significant proportion of the skills we acquire are learned by imitating or copying others or by trial and error. Both these processes can be improved enormously by exchange with somebody who has experience and can pass it on to speed up imitation or to cut down on mistakes. This field of accelerating or improving the application of skill and knowledge is often the domain of the mentor or coach. It is often asserted that over 90 per cent of what we learn as adults is acquired in the process of working; the 'university of life' has its tutors and professors. This chapter, therefore, seeks to identify just what coaching and mentoring are, why they are important, what are the benefits and obstacles to be expected, what are the skills and how does one go about being a successful coach, what is your performance like as a coach, and where does coaching fit into the training and development scene.

WHAT ARE MENTORING AND COACHING?

The role of training and development is one which is most closely interrelated with the supervisory and managerial role, and needs clear identification within it. First, both terms address the development of on-the-job skills, either in the sense of specific skills, such as coaching a subordinate to make a better presentation, or in the sense of holding a career discussion with a young graduate engineer to clarify the satisfactions to be gained from either an engineering role or a supervisory role. The term 'counselling' is often used to describe either of the processes, and it is correct in the sense that counsel or advice is given. Coaching in the sporting context is used to describe not only the 359 acquisition of basic skills, but also the process of squeezing out that extra application necessary to become a champion. An interpretation of each process is as follows.

Mentoring

The term 'mentor' has a dictionary definition of 'experienced and trusted adviser'. It has had a long history, being founded in Greek mythology in Homer's *Odyssey*. Mentor was appointed as adviser of the young Telemachus by his father Odysseus. The term reappeared in management literature in the 1970s, arguably more strongly in the United States than the United Kingdom, where it was popularized by Clutterbuck's book in 1985.

In practical terms, mentoring involves an individual entering into a relationship with somebody to act as adviser, counsellor or even role model. It often involves a senior manager keeping an interest in the development of a protégé throughout a significant aspect of his/her career. Mentors may be asked to adopt a high-flyer on a management course, or provide advice or assistance to a young professional, such as a prospective chartered engineer or accountant. The role may occasionally be informal, where a senior manager takes an active interest in the career development of a younger employee. It may be time-consuming or undertaken only occasionally. Various American surveys have indicated a wide use of mentoring, and that it is seen as highly significant in determining success for senior executives. It could, of course, also be regarded as the 'old boy network'.

Coaching

A somewhat more ambiguous word. The verb is described as to tutor or to train (pupil for examination, crew for race), to give hints to, to prime with facts. Coaching as a development activity was again written about significantly in the United States rather earlier than elsewhere. Walter Mahler in the *American Society for Training and Development Handbook* (1967) was one of the first to write about the process, followed in the United Kingdom by the author (Moorby, 1973) and Edwin Singer (1974) in *Effective Management Coaching*. Coaching essentially involves some specific and hopefully planned activity designed to improve the skilled performance of another. It is about helping someone to 'grow'. A survey of coaching practice carried out in 1973 showed that the main purpose of coaching was to get people to do things differently and more cost effectively. Coaching as described here could involve:

- Boss coaching subordinate.
- Teacher coaching student.
- Subordinate coaching boss.
- Coach coaching individual athlete.
- Coach coaching team.
- Set adviser coaching action-learning set.

- Peer coaching peer.

In other words, coaching can be one-to-one or one-to-many and hierarchically upwards, downwards or sideways in organizational level.

Counselling

This term is included as it is often used, interchangeably with coaching or mentoring. The dictionary tells us that counselling is to advise (person to do), to give advice to (person) professionally on social problems, to recommend. In practice, counselling is often regarded as more concerned with personal or non-task advice, i.e. more in the social context. However, the term 'counselling' is used in place of the term 'appraisal' and is often used in the context of career counselling, i.e. advice on what career direction an individual should take. It is probably closer to mentoring in this sense. A useful split might be the degree of concentration on short-term performance associated with coaching, the emphasis on the personal/social context often associated with counselling.

In order to avoid what would be overprecise distinctions between the activities of mentoring, coaching, counselling, sponsoring or managing, those activities aimed at improving performance through work will be referred to as mentoring or coaching in this chapter. The conventional emphasis on mentoring being more career or strategically oriented is recognized, though coaching takes place within most mentoring relationships and much coaching has a strategic aim (e.g. to win the Wimbledon Ladies' Singles Final for the tenth time, or to improve my delegation to a particular individual).

WHY UNDERTAKE MENTORING OR COACHING?

The advocate of coaching usually recognizes that work is central to growth, and that by adopting a proactive approach great productivity gains can be achieved. The approach is very much in line with the behavioural or theory Y style of management as opposed to the autocratic or theory X style, and fits closely with ideas of agreeing objectives and reviewing performance. In periods of high rates of change, coaching and mentoring can be crucial means for changing the organization's values and culture. Thinking such as inverting the organization structure and having senior staff in support of or serving those who serve the customer imply clear mentoring and coaching roles, and the provision of role models by senior management in organizations such as Scandinavian Airlines Systems (SAS).

The following are some of the reasons why individuals undertake mentoring or coaching activities.

Management process

It is an integral part of the manager's or supervisor's job. In agreeing objectives *361* and ensuring their achievement, it is necessary to provide continuous support and guidance through coaching.

Achievement

To get the best out of staff, the competent coach agrees challenging tasks that help them to grow in competence. Continuous review and practice help to ensure that they stay at the peak of their ability.

Standards

Coaching is probably the best way of achieving excellent performance. By giving examples of the standards that individuals are expected to achieve, exemplary service standards can be achieved.

Time

By showing others how to achieve tasks, such as monitoring the group's performance, more time is available to represent the function outside in the community.

Practice

To improve the level of customer service, staff have had to learn new skills. Some have practised greeting customers and registering them, just as a tennis player learns to improve the backhand. That is how they all became champions.

Reputation

If a bank branch is known to be successful, it reflects well on the manager, particularly if performance was average before he/she arrived. By really getting the staff to work as a team through coaching, the manager's reputation will grow.

Removing difficulties

One of the factors which stopped some pilots from becoming captains was that their landings were too hard. Coaching in how to achieve good landings every time quickly removed operating difficulties in an airline.

Growth

The graduate trainees often know which particular manager will provide the opportunities for them to do meaningful work and to grow in competence. They want the chance to show what they can do, rather than to sit around and just watch.

Succession

One divisional general manager really entered into acting as a mentor for one of the managers on the young manager programme. She said it kept her in touch with what the younger executives were thinking and it helped her to assess what level of ability was available for succession.

Coaching the boss

The secretary was really pleased that the boss wanted to learn wordprocessing. After eight hours' coaching it was noticeable that far fewer words were being used in dictation and typing instructions for alterations were so much clearer.

Master craftsman

It was felt that the only way to ensure that new entrants to the engineering profession would be properly developed was to appoint mentors. Their task was to provide advice and guidance in the early years rather like the master craftsman of old.

Theory into practice

The material being taught on the four-week general management programme was being seen as too theoretical. It was felt by a number of senior managers that a good deal of effort and money was being wasted. Senior managers agreed to act as mentors, attended project presentations, acted on appropriate recommendations and met 3–4 times a year with two participants each. The whole atmosphere and implementation changed. Mentoring linked the academic world of management education with the real world of uncertainty and change.

It can be seen that the reasons for undertaking mentoring and coaching are many and varied. The reasons may be to help the individual being coached or to promote the interests of the coach. Ideally, the reason should provide mutual benefit to the participants while bringing improved performance to the organization.

A number of professional institutions lay great emphasis on the development of talent. The Institute of Personnel Management's Code of Professional Conduct states that members are expected to adhere to ten principles of behaviour. Number 6 – development of others – states that 'Personnel practitioners will seek to achieve the fullest possible development of the capabilities of individual employees to meet present and future requirements of the organization, and to encourage others to develop themselves'.

OBSTACLES TO SUCCESSFUL MENTORING/COACHING

Descriptions of many approaches to improving management skills or techniques *363* make it seem so straightforward and obvious that one must ask why everybody does not use them. However, there are real obstacles to be overcome by those managers who want to coach or act as a mentor. Before considering the considerable benefits which can be achieved, it would be sensible to consider these obstacles.

Lack of time

This is perhaps the most common cry. To give some indication of the spread of allocation of time in practice, a study of 62 subordinates carried out by the author identified the estimates of how much time each received by way of coaching in an average week (see Figure 28.1).

Estimate of time per week	Number receiving time
Up to 1/2 hour	10
1/2 hour–1 hour	21
1–2 hours	7
2–3 hours	10
3–4 hours	3
More than 4 hours	11

Figure 28.1 Estimates of coaching time received

To put these figures into perspective, to give four subordinates four hours' coaching each in a week would consume 40 per cent of the time available to the boss, and make coaching the most significant use of time in the week, exceeding the average time spent at meetings by a factor of 4. It would also only allow each subordinate 45 minutes per day with the boss. However, the research and subsequent seminars involving several hundred managers indicated that somewhere in the order of 1 in 5 to 1 in 10 managers did allocate significant time to coaching and, on their own evaluation, made a good job of it.

A useful way of focusing attention on coaching is to ask the question of both boss and subordinate, 'how much time do you spend on coaching in a week?', probably having discussed what is coaching first, and then to probe whether the individuals think that the time is sufficient and whether what is provided is adequate to sustain good performance.

Lack of skill

This leads quite naturally to the next big obstacle – lack of skill. Coaching and mentoring require a number of sophisticated skills coupled with specific motivational/personal characteristics. These can be developed, as described later in the chapter, and a few people – perhaps 1 in 10, seem to acquire them naturally. In summary, some of the skills or competencies are:

- Effective listening.
- Interactive skills.

- Discussion skills.
- Process skills (e.g. timing of interventions).
- Conflict and problem-solving.
- Identification of objectives and targets.
- Measurement of performance.
- Learning process skills.
- Giving constructive feedback.
- Learner-centred approach.

Lack of will

Any approach to coaching or mentoring contains some important assumptions about the psychological disposition of the 'players'. People vary markedly in their motivational drives, and the successful coach or mentor will need at least four distinct drives or themes, which, if absent, will make it highly unlikely that the individual will succeed as a coach/mentor. An approach developed by Selection Research Inc. (SRI) has identified the following as four out of 11 themes necessary to be a successful manager and they describe well the motivations one would expect to find in a good coach.

Developer

This manager takes satisfaction out of each increment of growth of associates. At the highest level, this manager enjoys training and developing people who become future leaders for their company.

Delegator

This theme is indicated when a manager assigns responsibility to people in terms of what each person is ready for. The optimum outcome of good delegation is that the person feels he or she owns the assignments. Managers high in this theme get associates involved and stretch the right people.

Growth orientation

A manager who is high in this theme would be continuously orientated towards recruiting and attracting talented people, focusing upon the strengths of people and maximizing business opportunities by moving from strength.

Individualized perception

Managers who have this quality think individually about each of their employees. They know that each employee is different, rather than treating them all basically the same.

365

Without a positive commitment in these four areas, it would be difficult, though not impossible, to build substantive coaching skills.

Another aspect of lack of will is the psychological make-up of the prospective mentor or coach. Some – it could be argued many – individuals have pathological needs to control others, or are fundamentally insecure and have a corresponding high need to impose control on their environment and the future. They do not delegate, positively punish mistakes, plan to obsessive degrees and need to give their personal approval to the most mundane detail of tasks under their control. They live their life through others and must control the totality. This is clearly a significant obstacle to any individual learner-centred or trans-formational approach.

THE SKILLS OF MENTORING AND COACHING AND HOW TO DEVELOP THEM

Coaching requires line management commitment. It is an approach to managing which can flourish or wither depending on the culture around it. Most of the skills are not unique but need to be developed and applied sensitively. In many ways, it needs to be an opportunistic activity or one which permeates the management style of those involved. Since it can have a significant multiplier effect on other training and development investments, it merits inclusion in a company's strategic planning and review process. It must, of course, be consistent with the business strategy if it is to succeed. The following skills are required.

Ability to identify development needs and opportunities

This involves spotting development needs and matching them to opportunities which are often part of the job and may be fleeting. However, many tasks lend themselves to practice. A salesman introducing himself is a classic example of how a less-experienced person can be coached, with actual performance being rehearsed before a call and reviewed at a kerbside conference after the sales meeting.

Listening and giving constructive feedback

These interpersonal skills are often underdeveloped and sometimes require significant modification to current behaviour. Patience and the ability to give feedback, free of personal criticism and aimed at the event and not the person, are the ideal. *The One Minute Manager* by Blanchard and Johnson (1982) gives excellent guidance on what the authors refer to as one-minute praisings and one-minute reprimands. Coaching does require a commitment to positive improvement while recognizing shortcomings. Listening skills are essential to give the coach sound information on which to give feedback.

Process skills

366 The competence to set up the coaching meeting or experience, knowing how to use timing in discussions, experience and skill in building confidence and gaining commitment, and the ability to manage or initiate the overall process, are all process skills.

Problem-solving skills

Things will sometimes go wrong. The ability to think through situations and identify courses of action is necessary, coupled with the ability to act as a mirror and reflect possibilities, so that people being coached or receiving mentoring can identify and own courses of action.

Learning process skills

An area where the natural coaches will often be gifted. They will know how far to push, when to push and when to leave people alone, what size learning steps to use, how to give reinforcement and how to deal with learning obstacles. Just watch a skilled parent moving a child on from learning words to learning phrases, or a swimming coach getting learners to swim out of their depth. These skills can all be learned, but reasonable fluency to start with would considerably improve the chances of achieving excellence.

Adopting a learner-centred approach

Perhaps the most difficult aspect of coaching, certainly for the author, is that of helping the coaching along. The balance between not getting too involved, but also not entirely opting out of the situation, can be very demanding. It is natural to want to sort things out when presentations are going wrong, sales are at risk or that report just lacks bite. For many years it was my job to charge the battery in my wife's car. Of course, when it was flat, I was usually a hundred miles away. By showing her how and then charging the battery together, she quickly learned how to do the job. Result – more independence for the learner, more time and less hassle for the coach.

Not getting involved (i.e. doing nothing) is one of the most crucial skills in coaching or mentoring. By supporting but not doing, the coach or mentor facilitates the basic aim of the whole process – to enable acquisition of skill by somebody else.

Reviewing the process

Coaching and mentoring for many people will be enhanced by a regular systematic review process. For the less reflective learners, be it coach or person to be coached, this may not come naturally. However, a formal and privileged opportunity to review progress, discuss what might be done differently and explore how the mentor/coach feels about progress, will add to effectiveness. The follow-up meeting to review action, so beloved of course designers, really *367* does need to take place away or at least aside from the everyday hurly-burly if the process is to be fully exploited.

Technical or professional competence

While there are those who may take the opposite view, experience in the field in which the person is being mentored or coached is invaluable and arguably essential. In theory, non-directive questioning and total learner-centredness should enable a skilled coach to work in any environment. In practice, competence in managing or banking, tennis or judo, are closely entwined with the coaching process which involves undertaking real tasks in the actual environment and not case studies in the classroom.

Clearly, many of the skills involved are those required of a competent manager. Some occur naturally, some are taught. All can be developed and improved.

IMPROVING MENTORING AND COACHING SKILLS

There are a number of steps that can be taken to improve an individual's competence. This section will describe as follows those which can readily be undertaken at work, and will then outline the content for a course designed to improve coaching/mentoring skills:

1. First, individuals can sharpen their awareness and commitment to planning or seizing learning opportunities. Awareness of the issue, coupled with basic skill practice, can make a positive contribution to improvement.
2. Finding the time and creating an atmosphere that encourages develop-ment are also key factors. Often, the urgent drives out the important. Time spent with younger staff, in particular on career direction and the acqui-sition of basic skills, can have significant overall payoff in creating standards.
3. Talking to other managers about either coaching or mentoring can add to an individual's breadth of options, opportunities and feedback.
4. Learning from a good practitioner, or a bad one if the right lessons are taken, can be very powerful. Working as number two to an experienced politician or a top-class chef can improve skills tremendously. In top restaurants, young chefs pay to work with a master. Similarly, the managements of some organizations acquire the reputation of providing top-class experience. Ford Motor's Finance and Personnel departments, Procter & Gamble's Marketing, Marks & Spencer's Retailing, and many other organizations, have at various times had this sort of reputation. One needs to pick the right time to work for them, of course.
5. Experimenting, listening and generating discussion and awareness are also important components. The learning organization concept captures this view of a high commitment to individual growth and the recognition and practice of the manager's coaching and mentoring role.

6. Attending a course can build skill, either by specifically concentrating on coaching, or by addressing the skills involved in communication, interactive skills, the learning process and learning styles. Awareness of career routes and the organization's particular schemes for management trainees, graduate trainees and high-flyers and the skills of counselling are also useful modules for those with formal mentoring responsibilities. There are few courses aimed specifically at mentors. In general, there is some evidence to suggest that about one in three managers receive training in coaching, though this applies in a sample which probably has a significant commitment to training. Mentoring was less widespread and fewer managers received training in how to undertake the role.

An example of a framework for a training course on coaching which provides the basis for a half-day to two-day programme, together with a follow-up meeting, is shown in Figure 28.2. The duration of the seminar depends on the amount of practice involved, in particular for interpersonal skills and understanding the learning process. The framework has been used for half-day to two-day seminars, and Session 2 can be readily combined with the development aspects of conventional appraisal training.

PROGRAMME FRAMEWORK

Seminar
Session 1.   What is coaching and why coach?
Session 2.   The skills of coaching
Session 3.   Using learning to improve performance
Session 4.   Practical exercise
On-the-job activity   Preparation and implementation of action
                                    plans
Review   Individual action plans and coaching pro-
                                    cess

Figure 28.2   Programme framework

A brief description of the aims and conduct of each component outlined in Figure 28.2 now follows.

Session 1

This aims to relate the practice of coaching to the everyday management experience of individuals. It may be in the context of appraisal, total quality, organization culture change or in its own right. It seeks to establish the relationship between learning, improving performance and work. A significant proportion of the first session will be spent on clarification of what is meant by the concept and in exploring and modifying attitudes. It is important that the group establish for themselves what they will get out of the approach. Typically, one or two individuals will already be positively committed to the concept. Their experience should make a helpful contribution.   *369*

Session 2

The aims here will either be to discuss what the skills are at a cognitive level or to develop a level of competence in some or all of the skills through practice. The skills have been described elsewhere in this chapter. Practice or skill building was achieved by using triads working on actual coaching situations which the participants planned to implement. A degree of role-playing may be necessary if interpersonal skills are to be practised. Equally, participants can act as coaches for the setting-up, objective setting and planning aspects of the role.

Session 3

This session aims to create an understanding of the learning process and of learning styles. It requires a somewhat more structured input and needs to link participants' experience of learning – often gained many years earlier at school – with their present experience at work.

Session 4

This session concentrates on the skills and is designed to give practice on live coaching situations. The use of video-recording and a thorough review of the interpersonal skills aspects can significantly enhance the process.

On-the-job activity

Individuals are strongly encouraged to practise coaching over a 4–6 week period and a date was agreed for a review meeting lasting 3–6 hours.

Review

The aim of this session was to review the principles of coaching and individuals' actual successes and failures in action. Perhaps the most memorable issue in the sessions was the number of people who were surprised by the positive responses they found.

THE BENEFITS OF COACHING AND MENTORING

So what do managers hope to get out of the energy and time they are encouraged to spend on the development of others? Some of the benefits identified by the managers when discussing the use of coaching are:

1. Better communication and understanding achieved with staff.
2. Loyalty and the willingness to do that little bit extra when things get tough.
3. More time available for the manager who knows that subordinates are contributing with minimum supervision.
4. Fewer mistakes with customers.

5. More productive teams.
6. More ideas put forward by staff and greater sense of ownership for plans.
7. Succession cover improved and manager's own promotion ensured as result of the mentoring provided.
8. Staff more self-reliant and able to deal professionally with unexpected events.
9. Lead times shorter on projects as a result of improved discussion of and estimates for jobs.
10. Better presentations being delivered and more contracts being won.
11. Strategic direction of employee development changed to include open learning.

Other important benefits are the linking of formal off-the-job training with application back on the job, and the growth of the coach through learning from the process. Mentoring can provide improvement in the placement, development and retention of high-flyers and graduate trainees, and an improvement in the quality of the information and data base on high-potential staff which can then be used to achieve better promotion decisions.

KEY QUESTIONS ON MENTORING AND COACHING

The following questions are suggested for you to reflect on and to identify your own situation. The first group are about the individual coach/mentor and how the process is being carried out. The second are more strategic in nature and concern the organization and its response to coaching and mentoring.

The individual as coach/mentor

1. How much time have you spent on coaching in the last four weeks? Is this a typical period and are you satisfied with the amount?
2. Do you think through in advance how you will approach a coaching task or a mentoring review meeting?
3. Write down what development through coaching you plan for each of your subordinates or associates over the next week, month, year.
4. Is your performance as a coach compared to six months ago:

   - worse?
   - about the same?
   - better?
   - much better?

5. Write down examples of how the performance of your subordinates/associates has improved through coaching over the last year.
6. What benefits to you and the organization can you identify from coaching and/or mentoring?
7. Identify two individuals whose careers have thrived as a result of your interest, influence and advice through mentoring over the last 1–2 years.   *371*

8. What are your plans to improve your success as a coach/mentor over the next twelve months?

Strategic questions for the chief executive/HRD director

1. Do the culture and mission of your organization suggest that the principles and concepts described would contribute to your business performance?
2. Are openness and self-direction what you want and what you need in your business?
3. Do you make sufficient provision to provide the skills described?
4. Do you have a strategy for using open learning, computer-based training, action learning, self-development or resource centres, and if so is it understood and supported?
5. Who are the key players you need to influence if you want coaching and mentoring to work across your organization?
6. Will you be able to deliver the quality and service levels you require at the point of sale without some form of coaching programme?
7. Who will provide the skills necessary in this area and how much are you prepared and able to spend?
8. *Do you have the skills in your organization that it will need to survive?*

FURTHER READING

Moorby, E.T. (1973), 'The manager as coach', *Personnel Management*, **5**, (11), November, 30–3.

Singer, Edwin J. (1974), *Effective Management Coaching*, London: IPM.

Clutterbuck, David (1985), *Everyone needs a Mentor*, London: IPM.

Blanchard, K. and S. Johnson (1982), *The One Minute Manager*, London: Fontana/Collins.

29 Using training aids

Chris Bell

WHAT TRAINING AIDS ARE AVAILABLE?

There is a vast range of aids available to help the trainer deliver successful training. They can be classified into a number of broad categories:

Printed materials   All texts, handouts and the like.

Non-projected materials   A variety of visual display materials, for example realia, models, photographic prints, posters, flipcharts and markerboards.

Still projected material   Overhead projector transparencies (viewfoils), slides and microfilm.

Video materials   Video tape, video disc, broadcast television and film.

Audio materials   Audiotape, record, compact disc and broadcast radio.

Computer-based materials   These may involve the application of a computer alone or a computer used in conjunction with other materials (for example, compact disc, video disc, audiotape) thus enabling multi-media training aids to be constructed.

There is, of course, overlap between the above categories. For example tape-slide presentations employ still slides with an audio commentary; the production of slides, viewfoils and printed material can be greatly facilitated by use of computer technology. The features, strengths and weaknesses and techniques for use of many of the aids noted are described below, or in subsequent chapters. Those with the greatest versatility and most applications are described in detail, others in less detail.

WHY USE TRAINING AIDS?

Training is about helping people learn: assimilating new knowledge or modifying existing knowledge. Well-chosen training aids, or instructional materials, can enhance the effectiveness of the training/learning process. For example, training aids can:

- add variety to the learning process, thereby helping maintain involvement and motivation;
- benefit those learners whose learning style responds better to one type of approach than another;
- provide certain stimuli not available without their use;
- encourage interaction; and
- act as a valuable 'lesson plan' to the trainer, facilitating planning and preparation before the training session.

These advantages can only be realized in practice if the aids are chosen and used paying due regard to:

- the objectives of training;
- the characteristics of the learners;
- the characteristics of the various aids available; and
- how the aids will be integrated with other facets of training.

To help ensure optimum use of training aids, it is often useful for the users to ask some basic questions of themselves:

- What am I trying to achieve?
- Why am I trying to achieve this?
- Who will use the aids?
- What are the characteristics of the users?
- What is the essential content of the aids?
- How will concepts be developed?
- How will the aids be used?

Remember also that when developing aids, they should, ideally, be tried out before actual use and evaluated during and after use.

SELECTING APPROPRIATE TRAINING AIDS

Although a fully rational means of selecting training aids has yet to be developed, there are important considerations to contemplate when selecting the most appropriate aids for any given training need.

Research indicates that most aids can perform most instructional functions, but that some are better than others for achieving certain objectives. The starting point for planning any training must be to establish what objectives are to be achieved and whether these are best achieved by mass instruction, group or individual learning. Only then can the trainer start to consider the most appropriate aids.

The fundamental criterion for judging the appropriate use of training aids is their relevance. Training aids must be relevant to the purpose for which they were created and to the learner's level of understanding. Detailed paper handouts at the start of a training session to which the trainer never refers are a typical misuse of a potentially valuable aid.

Different aids lend themselves to different types of training/learning systems (mass, group or individual instruction). Almost all training aids can be employed as vehicles for mass instruction in one form or another. Many can be employed in group or individual instruction, although their use is likely to be different.

Some authors (for example, see Ellington, 1985) present algorithms to facilitate the selection of appropriate aids for each learning system. Others adopt an approach based on theories of learning and communication and the psychological attributes of the training aids. The latter approach helps understanding of the selection of appropriate aids and will be discussed briefly. For a fuller explanation see Cheek (1977) where many references are also given.

When considering the choice of aids to satisfy a particular learning objective, the physical attributes of the aids (e.g. markerboard, television) are of less consequence than their psychological, or functional, attributes: the ways in which learners interact with the aid. The main functional attributes of the learner's senses, through which all communication must occur, include:

- Persistent – fleeting.
- Diffused – focused.
- Concrete – abstract.

Each of these dimensions should be seen as a continuum, the functional attributes of any aid being able to be located somewhere on each continuum (Cheek, 1977). These continua can be considered to form a three-dimensional space, as shown in Figure 29.1.

Persistent – fleeting

Aids with predominantly persistent characteristics are generally visual, either written, still projected, photographic or regalia, and are good at allowing learners to study detail, seek relationships, synthesize information, and so on. 'Fleeting' aids tend to be sound stimuli, excellent for attracting, stimulating and alerting the learner. Visual aids used in a transient way (e.g. the overhead projector with an image turned on and off quickly) can also be 'fleeting'. Learners with different characteristics tend to respond to fleeting stimuli with different effect. Activists (or extroverts) react well, learning more effectively when they are frequently stimulated with changes in pace and style. Reflectors (or introverts) react less well.

The degree of 'fleeting stimulation' most appropriate also varies with the *375*

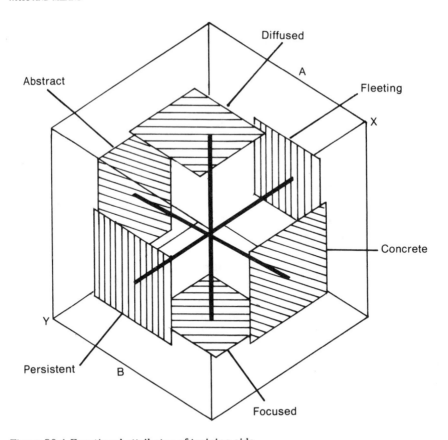

Figure 29.1 Functional attributes of training aids

cognitive level of the learning. Higher levels (conceptual tasks, synthesis, evaluation, problem-solving) generally require greater stimulation, whereas lower levels (simple learning, rote learning) generally require less.

Diffused – focused

Aids with predominantly 'diffused' characteristics are good at attracting attention and helping learners recall existing knowledge. Sound is probably the best example. 'Focused' aids are generally visual, are optimum for tasks involving analysis, comparison, and for studying similarities, differences, relationships, shapes, and size.

Concrete – abstract

Location of training aids on the 'concrete – abstract' dimension is relatively obvious. For example, words, symbols and numbers tend to be abstract, whereas real objects, photographs, video, role play, and so forth, tend to be concrete. This 376 dimension is closely related to the degree of feeling and involvement experienced by the learner. In general, concrete aids have more effect on the feelings, on the emotions, than do abstract ones.

The intersections of each of the six planes in Figure 29.1 indicate aids with a particular set of characteristics. For example the intersection between the 'diffused' and 'fleeting' planes (marked A) is indicative of aids which are good at attracting attention: for example, verbal messages, the transient image. Opposite to this, the interaction between 'persistent' and 'focused' (marked B) is indicative of aids useful for helping learners concentrate on detail.

The recorded sound of an engine, perhaps with a fault, or birdsong, is an example of use of an aid with diffused, fleeting and concrete characteristics good at attracting attention (located at point X in Figure 29.1). Text, which is focused, persistent and abstract (located at Y) is good for tasks which require the learner to focus upon detail or undertake higher-level cognitive tasks.

Consideration of training aid characteristics, and their desired purpose, will help the trainer locate the most suitable aid for any given situation.

OVERHEAD PROJECTION

The overhead projector (OHP) is one of the most versatile training aids available for mass instruction and can also be useful for use in small groups. Its use is, therefore, described in detail. The OHP is well proven, simple, versatile and relatively cheap. It allows you to project any prepared or impromptu image onto a screen. The image is usually drawn on an acetate 'viewfoil' placed on the platen of the OHP, but can also be a model or real object. Images can be pre-prepared or drawn in 'real time'.

Strengths

- Simple to use, versatile, relatively cheap; clean and quiet.
- Can be used in much the same way as a markerboard, but with the advantages of greater clarity and the ability for the user to maintain eye-contact with the learners (if certain points are taken into account).
- Can show pre-prepared materials; this allows the use of high-quality images, enables the trainer to build up banks of notes, diagrams, and so on and helps give confidence to both trainer and learners.
- Can be used to reveal, or build up information.
- Information is generally better understood and retained if it is seen as well as heard.
- Can make presentations more lively, immediate and effective if used well.
- Can be used without blackout, thus allowing learners to make their own notes.

Weaknesses

- Can too easily be used in ways which hinder, rather than aid, learning (see below).

377

- Needs an electricity supply and suitable screen.
- Can become monotonous if used too extensively.

Some uses for the overhead projector

- To show the structure and objectives of the whole training session so that the learners know where they are going.
- To list important points and to draw attention to key words, phrases, and so forth, to provide a focus for what is being discussed.
- To collect and display points and opinions from the learners; the trainer can write on acetate, or if using, for example, buzz groups or pyramiding, the learners can record feedback on slips of acetate which can be immediately displayed; the sheets can also be photocopied for later distribution.
- To display diagrams, charts and graphs.
- To display real objects (for example, small items, models, experiments, e.g. magnetic fields).
- To focus the attention of learners.

Tips for successful use

The full benefit of the OHP will only be realized if adequate attention is given to:

- How its use will be integrated within the training session.
- The design and preparation of viewfoils.
- The way the OHP is set up in the training room.
- The ways in which the OHP is actually used.

The first of these considerations is discussed earlier, the remaining three are elaborated below.

Design and preparation of viewfoils

When designing viewfoils, aim to:

- Keep them simple; do not have too much information on the screen at any one time; for text, 8–10 lines are adequate.
- Limit each foil to one main idea.
- Make certain that the area of the viewfoil written on is not larger than the area of the OHP to be used; many blank acetate sheets are larger than the effective size of the OHP platen.
- Keep them bold; fine line pens can get spidery, normal text-size typeface is useless.
- Avoid clutter; underlining, lots of arrows, inappropriate use of colour, and so on, all help confuse.
- Use colour where it helps clarity; this does not mean every line in a

different colour, but used with reason, colour can highlight important points, make diagrams and graphs more meaningful and help in the use of overlays (see below);

- Consider layout; use white space, symbols, illustrations, and so on, to achieve maximum clarity and impact.

Text and diagrams must be sufficiently large for the intended use. The screen size, distance between screen and most distant viewer, and room lighting should all be taken into account when designing viewfoils. Assuming that the screen size and location have been carefully chosen, then aim for letters no smaller than 5 mm (¼ in.) high, preferably larger. Go to the back of the room you are using and check whether or not information can be clearly seen.

Viewfoils can be prepared in a variety of ways. Felt pens (either spirit or water soluble) are useful for hand-drawn work, both text and diagrams. Keep text sufficiently large and use bold colours (not yellow or orange for text, but these colours are ideal for shading areas). A ruled grid placed under the acetate sheet is very useful. Keep the lettering style simple, preferably lower-cased, not joined-up.

Adhesive film such as Letraset or Kroy lettering and symbols, in either black or translucent colours, can be used directly on to acetate. Coloured translucent adhesive sheets are available for covering large areas of a viewfoil in colour. Black letters on paper can form the original from which copies on to acetate can be made by one of the techniques noted below. The advantage of using such techniques is a clearer, more professional result, but at the expense of speed of preparation. Computer-based systems have largely replaced these as viable techniques in the training field for the majority of applications.

Computer-based systems (wordprocessors, desk-top publishing and graphics programs in particular) can be used to produce excellent viewfoils. Remember to take into account the design considerations noted above, in particular the size of text and the use of adequate white space. Many printers, in particular lasers, can print directly on to acetate in either black or full colour. Alternatively, print can be on to paper, with one of the techniques noted below being used to produce viewfoils.

A photocopier or thermal copier can be used to transfer information from paper to special acetate. Many photocopiers allow enlargement and reduction. Enlargement is particularly useful! Thermal copiers allow the use of colour: coloured lettering on a clear background, black lettering on a coloured background or clear (or gold) lettering on a dark coloured background.

Photographic techniques can be used to produce very high-quality viewfoils, but the process itself is best left to professionals.

Setting up the overhead projector

Despite near universal use, many trainers fail to get the best from OHPs either because they are set up incorrectly or else are used poorly. A few basic rules will help ensure correct setting up as follows:

- Ensure that the screen can be seen from all parts of the room. If you have the choice, use the largest screen commensurate with the size of the room; it is often better to put the screen in one corner of the room rather than centrally.
- Try to avoid 'keystoning', which occurs when the OHP is incorrectly aligned either horizontally or vertically with respect to the screen (see Figure 29.2).

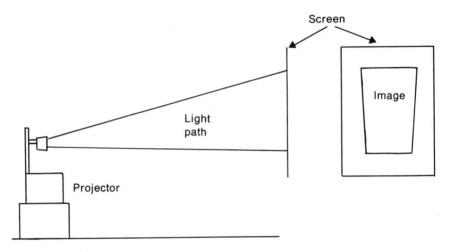

Figure 29.2 'Keystoning' effect on the overhead projector screen

- Adjust the distance between the OHP and screen so that the image fills the screen.
- Try to avoid placing the OHP in such a position that it obstructs the view of any learners.
- Make certain that the lenses and platen are clean.
- Remove coloured 'fringing' by using the appropriate adjustment on the OHP (sometimes inside – remember to disconnect from the electricity supply before removing the cover).
- Make certain that the image is in focus.

The overhead projector in use

As with most training aids, there is no one best way to use the OHP; techniques should be related to what the trainer intends to achieve. Some obvious aspects to take care with include:

- Not standing in such a position that either the light from the projector or the learner's view of the screen is obstructed.
- Only having the projector switched on when it is being used; some users like to turn off when changing transparencies, turning back on again attracts attention;

- Not just reading what is on a viewfoil; visuals should work for the user, adding something to what is said.

There are a range of techniques which will enhance the use of the OHP:

- Progressive revealing of prepared viewfoils is a basic technique and one which can aid learning. All or part of the viewfoil is initially covered, being progressively revealed as the presentation proceeds. Learners are focused on the point in question, and are not 'cluttered' by unnecessary information. Covering can be by a sheet of paper placed over the foil or by masks of thin card taped to the foil, or frame, which are folded out of the way to reveal what is underneath. Masks are particularly useful when using diagrams, flowcharts and so on.

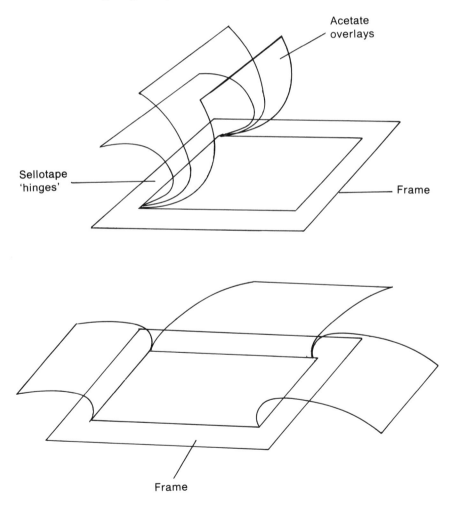

Figure 29.3   Overhead projector overlays

- Overlays, using several sheets of prepared acetate, each with part of the complete information, differ from progressive revealing in that the whole screen is seen all the time, with new information being added as the presentation proceeds. One advantage of this technique is the easier use of different colours on each overlay, if, for example, a thermal copier has been used. Each sheet of acetate is best fixed to a card frame with tape, thus ensuring accurate registration (see Figure 29.3).
- Animation, using models, moiré fringes (producing apparent movement when two grids of fine lines are moved over each other) or polarized acetate, can be used to good advantage in certain circumstances, for example to show the movement of water along a pipe.
- Real objects, for example, small opaque objects, can easily be magnified by placing them on the OHP platen.
- Experiments, for example, the use of iron filings to show magnetic fields, can be conducted on the platen.

Handouts can be used to good effect to support the OHP, particularly when using pre-prepared diagrams. The handout can be a mirror of the viewfoil, or can have certain information missing which the learners complete. The latter has the advantage of encouraging greater interactivity.

PAPER-BASED MATERIAL

Paper-based materials (handouts, textbooks, charts, maps, diagrams, and so on) are almost universal in their use in training within mass, group and individual instruction. Unfortunately, surprisingly little thought is sometimes given to their design, preparation and use. In this section, emphasis is on the use of handouts or small booklets. More ambitious projects (textbooks, individual instructional materials and so forth) are beyond the scope of the section; several of the sources noted in the bibliography will provide ideas.

Strengths

- Simple to use, versatile, relatively cheap, clean and quiet.
- Provides learners with information they can take away.
- Can show pre-prepared materials; this allows the use of high-quality images and enables the trainer to build up banks of notes, diagrams, and so on.
- Can be used in a wide variety of ways to support mass, group and individual instruction.
- Can be used to encourage interaction.
- Can allow large amounts of information to be disseminated relatively quickly (this can also be a severe disadvantage!).
- Can be used to support the majority of other training aids.

Weaknesses

- Can too easily be used in ways which hinder, rather than aid, learning.
- Easy to present too much information.
- Can become monotonous if used extensively.

Tips for successful use

The full benefit of paper-based materials will only be realized if adequate attention is given to:

- How their use will be integrated within the training session.
- The layout and preparation of materials.
- The ways in which the materials are actually used.

The design of printed material is a complex subject; several of the references at the end of this chapter give fuller details than space here permits.

Layout

The reader needs to be able to read and scan quickly, locate easily the required information, and be motivated to use the materials. Blocks of dense text are unlikely to achieve any of these needs! In addition to what is written and the style in which it is written, headings, the appropriate use of white space, illustrations, the choice of typestyle (i.e. typeface and size) and line length all have a marked effect on the usability of paper-based materials.

Computer-based production facilities (wordprocessing and desk-top publishing in particular) greatly facilitate the development of attractive, easy-to-use material. They have also facilitated the production of less well-designed materials, using multiple typefaces, many columns and near random layout!

After deciding upon the page size, often A4 or A5 (half the area of A4), plan a 'reference grid' which indicates the outer margins of the text, space around each level of heading and margins for notes, and for headers and footers if these are used.

The optimum line length of text depends upon the type size and face and interline space. Too many or too few words on a line and the text becomes more difficult to read. For a clear type of size 12 points (a common size in self-produced materials) with adequate interline spacing, a line length of 15 cm (6 ins.) is reasonable. This equates to A4 paper with margins of about 3 cm (1¼ in.) at each side.

PARAGRAPHS IN ALL UPPER CASE ARE MORE DIFFICULT TO READ THAN TEXT IN THE NORMAL MIXTURE OF UPPER AND LOWER CASE LETTERS. *Likewise, blocks of italic text are often considered more difficult to read than upright text.* Both UPPER CASE and *italic* can be used to emphasize words or headings, although **bold text** and larger-size type can be used to good effect.

The comprehension of text and retrieval of information can be greatly *383* facilitated by the appropriate use of white space: the space around the text, between columns, between paragraphs and around headings and illustrations. White space should be used to:

- Separate units of thought (e.g. paragraphs or points in a list); an extra line space between paragraphs is to be preferred to indenting only.
- Separate headings from the text; use adequate space around the heading and slightly greater space above headings than below.
- Separate illustrations from the text.
- Separate 'notes in the margin' from the main body of text if this type of layout is used.

Using printed materials

Printed materials can serve a number of valuable purposes, for example:

- as a complete learning medium (e.g. in some individualized training systems; the textbook);
- to support other training aids (e.g. OHP, audio, tape-slide, the trainer's verbal messages);
- as a note-taking guide;
- to encourage interaction;
- to provide prescribed reading.

How the printed material is used is crucial. Distributing a handout which is subsequently not used or referred to is less than useless! As with all training aids, the use of printed material must be carefully planned and integrated into the training session. The notes following provide ideas on the use of some types of handout.

Some types of handout

Handouts and the like can take many forms, from straightforward blocks of text to mind-maps, information maps and interactive handouts.

Mind-maps

Mind-maps, or spray diagrams, are an alternative to linear notes. They can be useful for both presenting information and for note-taking by learners, having the advantage that connections and links between parts of the information can be easily shown. To produce successful mind-maps takes practice; their particular style also tends to be 'personal' to the writer, what is optimum for one may be less so for another.

Information mapping

384 Information mapping is a way of structuring the presentation of information to

Handouts: use of illustrations	
Possible roles	Affective: enhance interest and motivation
	Attentional: attract and direct attention
	Didactic: showing, providing information
	Retentional: aiding long term recall
Advantages	Useful for conveying concrete images (e.g. a diagram of a valve may be worth many words of description)
	Appropriate when explaining visual or spatial concepts
	Useful to convey ideas that have to be presented simultaneously (aids multiple discrimination)
	Can provide holistic information well
	Tends to increase learner motivation and retention of learning (if used appropriately)
Disadvantages	Can be distracting
	Often time-consuming to produce
	Words often better to present sequential information
	Conventions may not be known by readers
Positioning	Positioning is very important to facilitate learning
	Should be placed immediately after textual reference if possible
	Captions should be close to illustration
Reference	Jonassen, D. (1982), *The technology of text*, vol 1, Educational Technology Publications.

Figure 29.4   Information mapping

make it more easily comprehended by the reader. Each 'map' presents one idea or concept, is laid out in a particular way and is cross-referenced to other maps or sources of information. Figure 29.4, presenting information about the use of illustrations in written material, gives an example of information mapping.

Interactive handouts

Many handouts tend to be purely presentational. However, those that encourage some action on the part of the reader are likely to encourage more effective learning. Two examples of interactive handouts are given in Figures 29.5 and 29.6.

FLIPCHARTS

Flipcharts, large sheets of paper hung from a support bar or easel so that they can be flipped backward and forwards, can be used in a similar way to markerboards and overhead projectors. They can be used to display pre-prepared sheets or can be written on in 'real time'.

Using handouts

Think of a short training session of about 10–15 minutes in which you are planning to use handouts. Briefly note the following:

Aims of the session:

Mode of instruction (mass, group or individual)

Main instructional method used

Purpose of using handouts

Most appropriate type of handout

Figure 29.5   Interactive handout: example (i)

Strengths

- Simple to use, versatile, cheap and quiet.
- Sheets can be torn off and displayed around the room.
- Can be used to reveal and build up information in much the same way as an OHP.
- Can easily be completed by learners (e.g. working in groups) for later display.
- Some people find it easier to write on paper than on OHP acetate.

Interactive handouts

The aims of interactive handouts are to:

- encourage learners to become involved in their learning;
- help the reader learn; and
- help the reader retain information.

Evidence suggests that once the brain has become activated, it is more likely to retrieve not only the information presented, but also the thought patterns which led to it. To make a successful transfer from short- to long-term memory, requires reiteration by the learner (out loud, on paper, in buzz groups, and so on) within about 30 minutes. By writing in their own words, the learner is more likely to

```
┌─────────────────────────────────────────────────────────────────┐
│                                                                   │
│                                                                   │
│                                                                   │
│                                                                   │
│                                                                   │
└─────────────────────────────────────────────────────────────────┘
```

The designer can indicate the appropriate length of notes by

```
┌─────────────────────────────────────────────────────────────────┐
│                                                                   │
│                                                                   │
│                                                                   │
│                                                                   │
└─────────────────────────────────────────────────────────────────┘
```

and so on.

Figure 29.6   Interactive handout: example (ii)

Weaknesses

- The size severely limits the amount of information which can be put on one sheet.
- Can encourage writing/diagrams too small to be clearly seen.
- The presenter probably needs to turn away from the learners when writing.
- Some people find it more difficult to write on flipcharts than on OHP acetate.

Some uses for flipcharts

- To show the structure and objectives of the training session so that the learners know where they are going.
- To list main points and to draw attention to key words, phrases, and so on, to provide a focus for what is being discussed.

387

- To collect and display points and opinions from the learners (if using, for example buzz groups or pyramiding, the learners can record feedback on flipchart paper which can be immediately displayed).
- To display diagrams, charts and graphs.

Tips for successful use

The full benefits of flipcharts will only be realized if adequate attention is given to:

- how their use will be integrated within the training session; and
- the design and layout of each sheet.

The first of these considerations is discussed earlier. However, when designing and laying out sheets, aim to:

- Keep them simple, do not have too much information on any one sheet.
- Limit each sheet to one main idea.
- Keep writing and diagrams bold and sufficiently large to be seen from the back of the room (walk to the back and check).
- Use colour where it helps clarity; this does not mean every line in a different colour, but, used with thought, colour can highlight important points and make diagrams and graphs more meaningful.
- Consider layout, use white space, symbols, and illustrations.

MARKERBOARDS

The use of markerboards (whiteboards or chalkboards) is ubiquitous, particularly in mass instruction and often in group instruction. Whiteboards have the advantage of being cleaner and generally clearer than chalkboards. In addition, many whiteboards are metallic, allowing objects to be affixed with magnets.

The majority of the applications of markerboards can be fulfilled as successfully, and possibly more conveniently, by the overhead projector. Much of the information previously given about the OHP also applies to markerboards, therefore this section is less detailed.

Strengths

- Simple to use, versatile, cheap, clean (whiteboards) and quiet.
- Information is generally better understood and retained if it is seen as well as heard.
- Can be used without blackout.

Weaknesses

388

- Can too easily be used in ways which hinder, rather than aid, learning.

- Can easily become monotonous if used too extensively.
- The user probably needs to turn away from the learners when writing.
- Some people find it difficult to write legibly on markerboards.

Some uses for markerboards

- To show the structure and objectives of the whole training session so that the learners know where they are going.
- To list main points and to draw attention to key words, phrases, and so on, to provide a focus for what is being discussed.
- To collect and display points and opinions from the learners.
- To focus the attention of learners.

Tips for successful use

The full benefit of a markerboard will only be realized if adequate attention is given to:

- How its use will be integrated within the training sessions.
- The ways in which the board is actually used.

Despite a long tradition of use, many trainers do not make the most appropriate or effective use of markerboards. It is all too easy to transfer notes from paper to the board in order that the learners can blindly copy! If the board is used to display key words, phrases, equations, and mathematical workings, and so forth, either originated by the trainer or by the learners, then it is likely to be a more effective aid to learning.

When using a markerboard:

- Make certain the board is clean to start with; whiteboards must only be used with the correct 'dry-marker' types of pen; if not, they may be very difficult to clean.
- Make sure that the writing can be clearly seen; if in doubt, check from the back of the room.
- Try to avoid talking and writing simultaneously; it is better to face the learners when talking.
- Do not obstruct the learners' view of the board more than necessary.
- Use colours to give appropriate emphasis; however, there must be a rationale for the use of colour.
- Use the space on the board logically; if it is large, try mentally (or with lines) dividing the board into different areas.

Electronic markerboards

'Electronic markerboards' are generally small (A0 or A1 size) whiteboards which can be written on with pens just as on a normal board. However, the image *389* can quickly be transferred to paper so as to produce a permanent black and white record of what is written. Electronic markerboards are particularly useful in small group instruction where learners can be given instant copies of the boards' content; for example, when brainstorming or collecting feedback from buzz groups. Their main disadvantage is cost.

AUDIO

The importance of talking, both as a training aid and as a communication skill which learners need to develop is increasingly becoming recognized. Audio recordings can be used in mass, group and individual instruction. Tape (both cassette and reel-to-reel), compact disc and vinyl records are all capable of good quality reproduction.

Strengths

- Simple to use, relatively cheap.
- In certain circumstances (for example, music) audio is the only appropriate medium to convey the required information.
- Can stimulate interest.

Weaknesses

- Obviously only applicable to presenting audio information.
- Requires appropriate equipment and an electricity supply.

Some uses for audio

- To bring real sounds into the training room; music is obvious, but also the sound of mechanical processes and the like may, under certain circumstances, be invaluable.
- To replay off-air broadcasts (taking due account of copyright laws).
- To act as a vehicle for managing or guiding learning; for example, guiding learners working alone or in groups through specific tasks, in much the same way as a trainer would.
- To record interviews, discussions or role play to allow later analysis.
- To play speech and record learner responses for later analysis, particularly in language learning.
- To record the trainer in his or her normal work, useful as an aid to evaluation.

Tips for successful use

Although the use of audio playback is widespread in everyday life, in a training
situation its full potential will only be realized if adequate attention is given to:

- How its use will be integrated within the training.
- The quality and audibility of the medium.

If playing back commercially pre-recorded audio in a mass-instruction situation, then quality and audibility is largely a function of the replay equipment. This must be sufficiently powerful, taking account of the size of the room and its audio characteristics (for example, soft furnishings, curtains and carpet tend to absorb sound). The use of headphones for individual or small group work is likely to have fewer potential problems.

When recording:

- Make sure that the material being recorded is of as high a quality as possible; get people to speak clearly and, unless impromptu, plan, prepare and rehearse before recording.
- Use the highest possible quality of recording equipment available; good quality external microphones are superior to those built in to cassette recorders; use the appropriate microphones (for example, omni-directional for group work, bi-directional for interviews or gun for distant sounds).
- Try to optimize the recording environment; make sure it is free from extraneous noise and is neither too reverberant nor too dead.
- Get to know how to use the equipment well in advance of using it; it is best to seek advice from a knowledgeable person.

PHOTOGRAPHIC SLIDES

Photographic slides can be an excellent way of providing visual illustrations to support mass, group or individual instruction. Slides are commercially available or can be produced specially by photographing actual scenes, systems or material carried on other media (be aware of copyright laws!).

Strengths

- Once prepared, simple to use.
- High quality; full colour slides are easy and relatively cheap to produce and can have a high impact.
- Can show complex diagrams and the like with relative ease (take care not to display too much detail).
- Can be used for mass instruction via a projector and group, or individual-ized instruction via a viewer or back-projection unit.

Weaknesses

- If using a projector (for example in mass-instruction) blackout is neces-sary, thus making it difficult for learners to take notes.

391

- Possibly less flexible than the overhead projector, in that sequencing cannot easily be changed on the majority of projectors.
- Unless using equipment utilizing two or more projectors, the pauses between slides and abrupt changes of visual images can be annoying; fades and build-up of information cannot effectively be achieved.

Some uses for photographic slides

- To provide illustrations where clarity and high quality are important; for example, in photographs.
- Where visual impact is important.
- In 'professional' presentations, quality slides generally impress.

Tips for successful use

The full benefit of slides will only be realized if adequate attention is given to:

- How their use will be integrated within the training.
- Their sequencing.
- Their design, preparation and quality.
- How they are actually used.

If slides are assembled for use in a carousel projector (or back-projector for small group viewing), their sequence will be fixed unless a sophisticated random-access projector is available. Therefore, even greater attention needs to be paid to sequencing and integration.

Design and preparation of slides

When designing slides, aim to:

- Keep them simple, try to convey only one idea on each slide.
- Avoid clutter; avoid the temptation to photograph existing overcomplex diagrams; it may be necessary to redraw these.
- Consider layout carefully, when photographing real objects, scenes, and so on, consider what message the slide is intended to convey.
- Keep the aspect ratio to about 3:2 (for example, a 'frame' of about 15 cm x 10 cm ($6'' \times 4''$) is ideal for text to be photographed).

There are a variety of techniques of slide preparation. The majority involve photography of the object or illustration on to 35 mm film, either colour or black and white.

Actual photographic techniques are outside the scope of this chapter; several of the texts noted in the bibliography carry further details. It is often more appropriate to seek professional help. However, one technique worth noting is the use of computer-generated text or graphics to form the basis of slides. There is some excellent hardware and software available to facilitate the preparation of slides.

SYNCHRONIZED AUDIO AND SLIDES

Synchronized audio and slide (or tape–slide) presentations involve the use of a slide projector which is linked to a specially coded audio tape, the tape both presenting audio information and controlling the automatic changing of slides. Alternatively, a computer can be used to control sophisticated multi-projector audio-visual presentations. Tape–slide presentations can be useful in all types of learning systems, a projector being used for mass instruction and groups, and a back-projector with an integrated audio-tape for small groups and individual instruction. Much of the information presented under Photographic Slides and Audio is also applicable to tape–slide.

Strengths

- Relatively straightforward to use.
- High-quality full-colour slides can have a greater impact than video.
- Can be used unattended at displays, exhibitions, and so forth.

Weaknesses

- Time consuming if being self-prepared.
- If using a projector (e.g. in mass instruction) blackout is necessary, thus making it difficult for learners to take notes.
- Less easy to set up than a video and TV.
- Requires suitable equipment, including a synchronization unit to link the projector and audio tape.

Planning and designing linked audio and slides

When planning to use multi-media presentations, it is even more important to ensure that the planning and design considerations noted at the start of this chapter are taken into account. Once the objectives, characteristics of the intended learners, content, and so on, have been decided, then the basic steps in producing a simple tape–slide presentation are:

- Produce a story-board for the presentation, both slides and audio.
- Obtain the appropriate slides; if slides are to be taken, then always allow time to take more than you plan to use, and to retake those that are not satisfactory.
- Assemble the slides into the required sequence.
- Script the audio, including the length of time each slide/associated audio will last, pauses, and so on.
- Record the audio, including pauses, using the highest-quality equipment *393*

available; it is helpful to view the slides as you are recording.

- Add synchronizing pulses to the tape at the appropriate places where slide-change is required.

For fuller details, refer to one of the texts listed under Further Reading.

VIDEO

Video is a powerful training aid increasing in popularity in all types of instruction. The production of video material is beyond the scope of this chapter; some of the texts noted in the bibliography give further details. However, the services of a knowledgeable person, or attendance on a course, is recommended to anyone planning to produce video materials for the first time. Here, only the use of pre-prepared video is considered.

Strengths

- Versatile (within the obvious limits of the medium).
- Excellent for displaying movement.
- A wide variety of commercially available materials (if recording off air, consider copyright).
- Used appropriately, can provide an excellent stimulus to learning.

Weaknesses

- Watching uninterrupted video generally becomes a passive activity with little learning taking place.
- Equipment can be expensive, particularly video projectors for use in mass instruction.
- Video projectors require blackout.

Some uses for video

- To bring a wide range of concrete examples to the learners; particularly useful to stimulate interest, provide an overview, present material for discussion, and so on.
- Can be used to display almost any visual images (for example, computer-generated graphics in place of the overhead projector).
- To record, and later play back for analysis and discussion, a wide range of training activities; for example, role play, simulations, micro-teaching.
- As a magnification medium to display small objects, processes, and so on, to a large group; for example, microscope work, chemical reactions, machinery.
- Combined with a computer, interactive video opens a wide range of interactive training possibilities.

Tips for successful use

The full benefit of video will only be realized if adequate attention is given to:

- how its use will be integrated within the training session; and
- the ways in which the video is actually used.

Passively sitting in front of a monitor is unlikely to promote optimum learning, although it is relatively easy for the trainer to organize! Properly integrated into training, video offers a wide range of applications: consider carefully the information given at the start of this chapter.

An obvious factor, often overlooked, is the need for the video image to be clearly seen by the learners. For small groups, one large monitor may be adequate, possibly sited to one side of the room. For larger groups, either several linked monitors or a video projector will be required.

If used in mass or group instruction, do not be afraid to stop the video frequently to emphasize points, promote discussion and allow learners to make notes. Video used in conjunction with interactive handouts (see earlier in this chapter), for example, provides a powerful learning medium. When used in individual instruction, either make sure that the material has been developed for this mode of learning, or else produce paper-based material to accompany the video.

FURTHER READING

Anderson, R.J. (1976), *Selection and developing media for instruction*, Van Nostrand Reinhold.

Ashcroft, K., G. Gibbs, D. Jaques and C. Rust (1990), *Using Audio-visual Aids Creatively*, Standing Conference for Educational Development.

Cheek, V.P. (1977), 'Some factors in the selection of media', *Programmed Learning and Educational Technology*, **14**, (3), 223–30.

Ellington, H. (1985), *Producing Teaching Materials*, Kogan Page.

Hartley, J. (1985), *Designing Instructional Text*, Kogan Page/Nichols Publishing.

Kemp, J.E. (1980), *Planning and Producing Audio-visual Materials*, Harper and Row.

Murphy, S. (1990), *The Manager's Guide to Audio-visual Production*, Kogan Page.

Newble, D. and R. Cannon (1989), *A Handbook for Teachers in Universities and Colleges*, Kogan Page.

Romiszowski, A.J. (1986), *Developing Auto-instructional Materials*, Kogan Page.

Part Four
TRAINING FOR SKILLS

30 Communication skills training

Dave Francis

Ronald Reagan was not a noted intellectual, but as President of the United States he had to take decisions of great complexity. Experts on foreign affairs, defence, law and economics lined up for his attention. Each expert wanted the President to make a decision on highly involved and contentious matters. How was this done?

Fascinating techniques were developed. President Reagan learned well from television, and videos were made to brief him for the fireside summit with Mikhail Gorbachev in 1985. Teams of illustrators and cartoonists worked at the White House to bring complex issues down to earth.

Robert Stockman, once Reagan's director of the Office of Management and Budgets, reports that he devised a multiple-choice budget quiz to help the President understand the issues involved in making budget cuts. The quiz gave the President fifty choices, and his task was to review each item, decide whether to cut deeply, lightly or not at all. Apparently, the President was entranced with the quiz and spent hours, pencil in hand, deliberating on the options. Stockman was delighted; he had found a way of communicating some of the most difficult choices to a president who was uncomfortable with intellectual pursuits.

All of those who presented information to him had to be skilled individual communicators, otherwise the President was likely to become bored and go for a game of golf.

The skills of the communicator make a real difference to the intelligence of individuals, governments and organizations. This does not only apply to management. Every day, in any sizeable organization, there are millions of communication transactions. You can imagine what is happening by visualizing electrical activity in the brain. It is impossible to analyse each act of information exchange but it is crucial that this buzz of communication enables intelligent decisions to be made.

Effective communication skills are especially important in today's organizations. Routine jobs are becoming increasingly mechanized, automated or computerized. More people are dealing with non-routine situations, unexpected *399* problems and strategic decision-making. Such tasks require a high order of personal communication skills. The pressure is on. People must work together skilfully to solve complex problems.

What are personal communication skills? The following extract from a description of a candidate for a management job gives some vital clues:

> Elvis Woodman is widely recognized as an effective manager. He took initiatives to learn about good interpersonal relationships by attending training workshops. He has thought deeply about how his personality affects others. He is sensitive without being soft. He is attentive to what others say and do. He is an excellent listener who quickly gains rapport with people. As a leader he is capable of giving support or direction as appropriate. In meetings he uses a logical approach to solving problems and seizing opportunities. When difficulties occur, he acknowledges the emotional aspects but delves into the facts so as to make a positive decision. In groups, he is capable of steering other people constructively and dealing with destructive people. Those who work with him develop new insights and skills. He encourages others to make the most of their potential. He stimulates new ideas and is open to positive criticism.

This is a description of a skilled communicator. By studying the details on Elvis Woodman we can analyse twelve primary ingredients of effective personal communication skills, most of which are also relevant to other white-collar workers, as follows:

1. Accurate perception of how one's personality affects others (self-insight).
2. Prepared to stand firm (assertion).
3. Good listening skills (active listening).
4. Supportive and directive leadership as necessary (leadership).
5. Methodical approach to problem-solving and decision-making (systematic approach).
6. Acknowledges the importance of feeling and emotion (counselling).
7. Capable of steering meetings well (chairmanship).
8. Able to deal with unco-operative people (interpersonal problem-solving).
9. Developing the competence of others (trainer competence).
10. Prepared to consider and implement new ideas (creativity).
11. Able to communicate effectively through the written word (writing skills).
12. Able to communicate effectively through the spoken word (oral communication competence).

These twelve communication skills are valuable to all managers. Where they are lacking, the quality of decision-making in the organization suffers. In order to clarify how this happens, we will examine briefly each of the twelve skills.

Self-insight

Self-insight is gained as we reflect on ourselves, experience new situations and receive feedback from others. We become clearer about our own values and *400* potential, understanding our unique character so that we can be more true to our nature. Such insight is hard to quantify or convey to others. The quest for self-understanding is always a personal search.

Self-insight is valuable to managers because:

- An inaccurate self-concept irritates, upsets or distresses other people.
- People with high self-insight seem to be able to handle stress and pressure.
- Self-insight improves objectivity.

A practical way of deepening self-insight is by gathering feedback from others. The term 'feedback' describes the process whereby a person gains information about the impression he or she makes on others. Training programmes have been devised to help develop sensitivity to others. Small groups, which develop a close and supportive climate, enable participants to be truthful about themselves and how they perceive others. An extraordinary exchange of insights takes place which can have a profound effect on all involved.

Assertion

It is common observation that some people are much better at getting their own way than others. The ability to be firm, clear and personally powerful is termed 'assertiveness'.

Assertiveness is valuable to managers because:

- Energy is released and the person feels stronger.
- Other people take more notice of an assertive manager.
- Good ideas get the hearing they deserve.
- Dominant people are less likely to get away with bullying behaviour.
- Relationships with others improve – difficulties are resolved rather than festering underneath the surface.

Managers can increase their assertiveness in a practical way by attending specialized seminars which help them to examine their personal backgrounds and identify attitudes which inhibit the expression of natural assertion. Such seminars teach special assertion skills such as delivering clear messages, avoiding 'flak', repeating your point, giving emphasis, and so on. Assertion seminars are especially useful for minority or disadvantaged groups like black or women managers.

Active listening

It is difficult to listen to others. Other people's inputs may be regarded as an unwelcome interruption of your line of thought. Some people even say: 'I don't have time to listen!' Unless you are truly concerned to hear others' viewpoints, the motivation to listen is inadequate. You need to develop 'relaxed concentration' that signals to others 'I am ready to hear you'. There are special *401* techniques to assist the active listener, like reflecting, summarizing, clarifying and probing.

Active listening is valuable to managers because:

- More data are available.
- More good ideas are voiced.
- Problems are aired rather than supressed.
- Relationships with others are improved.
- People feel more committed to their work.

A practical way of improving listening skills is to practise and get feedback on your own capability. Active listening is a set of skills that, like riding a bicycle, can be learned and improved. Effective listeners are made, not born.

Leadership skills

Effective leadership is a crucial set of communication skills. Fortunes have been lost through the use of inappropriate leadership styles. Organizations apparently suffering death throes have been 'reborn' under excellent leadership. Truly outstanding leaders become folk heroes and are revered in our hearts and minds. Effective leaders have two outstanding qualities: the capacity to devise and communicate a 'compelling vision' (see Chapter 35) and the communication skills needed to support and direct those who follow them.

'Supportive behaviour' means that you must get to know subordinates, concern yourself with what they think and feel, and encourage them to give their best. 'Directive behaviour' means telling subordinates what to do and instructing them in the right way to do it. Each follower requires a blend of support and direction depending on his or her willingness and ability to perform particular tasks. As people become more able, so they require less supportive behaviour from their leader.

Leadership skills are valuable to managers because:

- Most managers are measured on their ability to perform in this role.
- Unsatisfactory behaviour is reduced.
- Overall standards improve.
- People give more of their natural ability, so they have greater job satisfaction.
- The organization benefits through improved exploitation of talents.

Managers can improve their leadership skills in practical ways with specialized training courses, imitation, on-the-job counselling and coaching. They can benefit from obtaining feedback on their existing style, often collected by questionnaires completed by subordinates. These data, when discussed, reveal strengths and weaknesses. In addition, there are many training exercises which stimulate leadership situations, ranging from intellectually demanding business *402* games to hazardous wilderness projects.

Systematic approach

For many years army officers studied decision-making and realized that there were disciplines which, if rigorously followed, resulted in fewer blunders and a greater chance of victory. A structured approach enables decision-makers to make wiser choices between considered options.

Non-military organizations have the same needs. They have been forced to cope with an increasing rate of change and have come to realize the great benefit of a structured approach to problem-solving and decision-making. As one manager put it: 'We found that there was a technology for finding answers to difficult questions, rather than depending on a hunch or toss of a coin.'

Systematic approaches to problem-solving and decision-making emphasize rational, logical, rigorous and methodical attitudes and skills. They draw from the best traditions of scientific research, but need to incorporate intuitive and creative processes.

A systematic approach is valuable to managers because:

- Problems are solved effectively.
- Decisions are more intelligent.
- Managers are less likely to be overwhelmed and suffer stress.
- Leadership ability is improved.
- Meetings are more effective.
- Time is saved as people devote less effort to unrewarding pursuits.

There are practical ways to improve your capacity to use a systematic approach by trial and error learning, first-hand experiences, reading, watching experts at work and participating in specialized training courses. When managers discover the value of a systematic discipline it is a small jump for them to realize the tremendous benefits in the day-to-day management job.

Counselling

At first sight it may seem strange to include counselling in a list of communication skills for managers. It is often believed that management is a rough and tough occupation and has no place for the 'soft' skills of a counsellor. This is not the case. Human behaviour is influenced by feelings and emotions. Managers should be practitioners in the art of building constructive relationships. This requires the counsellor's sensitivities and skills.

Counselling helps people to understand themselves better, to resolve personal problems and to take a truthful but positive approach to life. It requires that feelings and emotions be respected, even if they appear illogical. Managers will not wish to delve into the complex topic of therapeutic counselling, but they can improve their ability to cope with feelings such as anger, frustration, stress, depression, anxiety, pride, enthusiasm and fear.

Counselling is valuable to managers because:

- The manager relates to others more effectively.
- People with personal or work problems can be helped.
- Potentially serious problems are detected earlier.
- Emotional factors are taken into account when planning change, so action plans have a greater chance of success.

You can improve your counselling skills by guided practice and review. A framework of concepts is a useful starting point but skills are only developed by practice. Supportive but critical feedback is essential. In particular, closed circuit television assists managers to develop a skilful but authentic style.

Chairmanship

Some managers detest meetings and believe that they are the epitome of all that is bad in organizational life. Yet meetings are constantly held, often at huge expense, for no one can think of a better mechanism for exchange of information, co-ordination, decision-making or planning. Despite their drawbacks, meetings are the most ubiquitous integrating mechanism and are with us to stay.

Few individuals have the skills and wisdom to behave impeccably in meetings, so discipline and control are needed. This role is played by a chairman who acts as the 'process manager' and exploits human resources towards objectives. Chairmanship requires many of the skills described in this chapter, especially a high order of self-insight. You must clarify objectives, adopt a systematic approach, encourage or control members and build bridges between factions.

Chairmanship is valuable to managers because:

- Ineffective meetings waste time and resources.
- Effective meetings are better able to make decisions and solve problems.
- Effective chairmen tend to have more progressive careers.
- Participants respect competent chairmanship.
- Action plans are more likely to result.

You can improve your chairmanship skills by observing an 'expert' at work, coaching in real situations, and attending specialized training seminars which provide a combination of theory, skill training and practice. Sound intellectual competence is a necessary qualification for the role. Equally important, the chairman should have a measured personality which is capable of integrating different personalities.

Interpersonal problem-solving

It is comparatively easy to relate to others who behave nicely. Friendly,
supportive, rational and interested people provoke few interpersonal problems.

But a person who is unfriendly, unsupportive, irrational or uninterested may be rightly described as a 'pain in the tail'.

Six important questions will help you to solve a difficult relationship:

1. How is your own approach contributing to the problem?
2. What precise differences in behaviour do you want to see?
3. How does the 'difficult' person or group see the issues?
4. What kinds of power are you attempting to use and why is it not being effective?
5. Do you have a conscious strategy for influencing which escalates from feedback and counselling to firm disciplinary action?
6. What are you going to do if your strategy fails?

Interpersonal problem-solving is valuable to managers because:

- Low-performing people are confronted and performance may improve.
- The manager feels stronger and more potent.
- High performance is encouraged because people see that interpersonal problems are being positively tackled.

A practical way to develop your interpersonal problem-solving skills is through 'learning by experience', under the guidance of a mentor. Techniques can be taught but the most useful insights come through experiment, feedback and counselling.

Trainer competence

One of the key tasks of a manager is to become increasingly redundant by developing others. This approach strikes fear into the hearts of the insecure but it is the only progressive way to manage. Training and developing are essential tools for improving the quality of performance. Some managers think of training as a low-priority assignment which distracts them from their primary task of getting things done. This is an unproductive stance; in fact, training is one of the most powerful managerial tools available.

Training techniques include instructing, experimenting, counselling, coaching, getting feedback, distance learning, team building, reviewing, appraisal and project assignment. These techniques can often be used informally, as there is no need for special facilities or equipment. Managers can develop their areas into 'learning environments' and thereby gain greater resourcefulness and improved motivation.

Trainer competence is valuable to managers because:

- Managers have an acceptable technique for controlling behaviour.
- Morale is raised as people become more competent.
- Inadequate performance is reduced.
- Standards of output are improved in quality, quantity and reliability. *405*

You can develop your training competence by reading, coaching and attending specialized training courses. Managers benefit from acquiring some of the skills of a good teacher, especially a sound awareness of the stages of human development and what factors help or hinder adult learning.

Creativity

Industrial and technological change has a great impact on managers today. The only constructive response to external threat is to counter attack with innovation and a rigorous questioning of the status quo. Managers must become bolder and more creative.

Communicating for creativity requires different attitudes and skills from those required to maintain an existing situation. You have to generate ideas, collect information, undertake research, evaluate risks and make choices. The creative individual works with others to look beyond the conventional and grapple with uncertainty and confusion. Decisions have to be taken with inadequate information so gifted people become skilled at making hunches. Insight seems to come from the darker recesses of the mind as the subconscious self contributes powerful but subtle information.

Generating ideas is only part of the creative process; new concepts and methods must be communicated to others. Creativity is not always easy to handle. Divergent and radical ideas are seductive. Innovation can be undertaken without sound preparation as excitement takes over from common sense. Successful creativity requires that new approaches work in the real world. Managers must learn how to manage dialogue between imagination and realism if they are to play a truly creative but practical role.

Creativity is valuable to managers because:

- Creative managers are more likely to cope effectively with problems and opportunities.
- Both the quality and quantity of decision-making improve as managers and teams become more creative.
- Individual managers get more challenge and satisfaction from their jobs.
- The customers of the organization obtain better products or services.
- Competitive advantage is more likely to be sustained.

Practical ways to develop your creativity are by self-study, practising creative techniques, team building and project work. The basis of creative achievement is freedom in oneself; so the individual has to examine personal blockages to creativity. Assignments can help by forcing the individual into situations where creativity is demanded. Creative individuals need to learn how to contribute their ideas to others constructively.

Writing skills

406 Most managers spend a lot of their time reading, writing and analysing statistics.

Their task is to manage what is too complex for a computer to handle. They also have to look ahead and decide what could and should be done. Improvements to buildings, production technologies, changes in markets, and revised personnel policies are just a few of the topics to be considered. Such matters are complex and arguable. A written analysis is essential to sharpen debate and give a balanced presentation of facts.

The skills of writing include word choice, sentence construction, paragraphing, logical argument, report structuring and graphical presentation. Behind such skills lie expertise in logical thinking, appropriate use of concepts, story telling and practical orientation. Discussion papers, reports and proposals are only part of the manager's written output. Visual aids for presentations, letters, memoranda, and regular reports are also required.

Writing skills are required throughout the hierarchy. A technician must be capable of writing well-considered reports and a sales clerk able to write lucid and balanced letters. These written documents present the image of the company to the outside world. The capacity to write well is especially important at senior levels. The complexity of managing a large organization requires substantial intellectual competence which can only be communicated through the written word.

Writing skills are valuable to managers because:

- Important ideas are more likely to be considered.
- Complex situations can be better explored.
- More thought is devoted to considering written submission.
- Writing something down is a valuable discipline.
- People are judged on the quality of their written work.

You can develop your writing skills by accepting critique from acknowledged experts or by attending short training workshops which teach the elements of preparing written work. Managers can also learn by imitation: examine highly regarded written documents and see how they have been constructed.

Oral communication skills

The presentation of the spoken word used to be considered a great skill. Greek and Roman leaders were taught the art of oratory. They became highly competent in conveying important ideas and swaying emotions in speeches and conversation.

Today few of us have been trained as orators, yet the skills remain valid. As Shakespeare's Mark Antony said: 'Friends, Romans, countrymen, lend me your ears.' Managers too are assessed on their capacity to be coherent, confident and persuasive when they present their views and ideas in speech.

Oral communication skills include accurate choice of words, logical flow, full explanation, avoidance of digression or redundant information, objectivity and capacity to hold interest. The good speaker uses every word to add impact. Care   *407* is taken to balance seriousness with humour. Visual presentation adds to the weight of the spoken word.

Oral communication skills are valuable for managers because:

- Important concerns get expressed and discussed.
- The manager is more persuasive, so more able to win support.
- Agreement between colleagues is more likely to occur.
- Misunderstandings are less frequent.
- The quality of debate is high, which improves decision-making.

You can improve your oral communication skills by obtaining feedback on your personal style. Closed-circuit television is a particularly valuable medium. Skills are acquired by practice and review under the guidance of a competent mentor or tutor.

CONCLUSION

These twelve communication skills can be isolated for analysis but, in reality, they complement each other. Those senior politicians entering Ronald Reagan's oval office knew that they had to be orators, counsellors, trainers and cartoonists. Their personal communication skills could materially affect the wellbeing of millions. Perhaps the lives of us all.

FURTHER READING

Adair, John (1988), *The Effective Communicator*, London: Kogan Page.
Francis, Dave (1989), *Organizational Communication*, Aldershot: Gower.
Scott, Bill (1986), *The Skills of Communicating*, Aldershot: Gower.
Stanton, Nicki (1986), *The Business of Communicating*, London: Pan.
Stuart, Cristina (1989), *Effective Speaking*, Aldershot: Gower.

31 Interpersonal skills training

Annette Bradley and Keri Phillips

Interpersonal skills training (IST) can be defined as helping people to learn more about themselves and their impact on others. Traditionally in management development this has meant training in such areas as team-building, coaching, interviewing, counselling, leadership, assertiveness and group problem-solving. While this definition and the associated activities are valid, they offer only a partial understanding of the challenges IST now faces in making a worthwhile contribution to the creation of a healthy world. This chapter describes some of these challenges.

THE CONTEXT

The central goal of IST is clarity about self. This is based on the assumption that the most important relationship one has is with oneself. Seeing oneself clearly is vital for seeing others clearly. People who have this clarity will be able to:

- Recognize the distinction between their own feelings and those of others (e.g. in a counselling session they will not absorb the despair of their client).
- Distinguish between their old feelings and current ones (e.g. as they begin to get angry about a piece of equipment not working, they recognize this is an old childhood pattern which is a cover for the fear of being seen as inadequate).
- Know what they want, as opposed to living a life based solely upon the actual or presumed expectations of others.
- Be open to the possibilities of change, and, equally, do not seek change simply for its own sake.

These capabilities, while essentially personal, can only be discovered and acted upon when in relationship with others. This indicates a core dilemma which many people struggle with for most of their lives: how to be fully oneself   *409* and yet be in relationship with others; how to be close without being engulfed; how to be separate without being abandoned. This confusion has been deepened in recent years by some of the strongly contradictory, yet often equally balanced, forces which flow within and between organizations. Many organizations are currently engaged in efforts to come to terms with these polarities. They are particularly potent because they echo many individuals' personal dilemmas, and also because society as a whole is engaged in active decisions about just these issues as the millennium approaches.

Freedom vs control

On the one hand, there has been a drive to 'empower' and liberate individuals; that is, giving them the opportunity to make mistakes and learn from them, and to take full responsibility for a defined area of work, with considerable scope to grow beyond it. At the same time, many organizations have sought to exercise much tighter control, often through financial incentives and penalties, over the work and ideology of their members. These organizations have often been prompted by a fear that if people are allowed to develop, they will start to pull in different directions. In times of significant social, political and economic change, as organizations seek to hold on to stability and familiarity by increasing control over members, this can become critical.

Economic growth vs planetary survival

Until recently, limitless economic growth was generally accepted as a positive goal for individuals, organizations and societies. Some have seen the simple accumulation of wealth as positive, while others have seen it as a means to provide better living standards in the form of improved health care, housing, and so forth. However, environmentalists have warned of limits to growth, and it has now been widely acknowledged that the unbridled economic growth of recent years has inflicted serious damage on the planet. Through the sheer volume and toxicity of waste, the destruction of natural habitats and the drive to get more for less, many non-renewable resources have been squandered. Many organizations are now beginning to give consideration to their impact on the environment as part of their strategic planning.

Competition vs collaboration

Organizations are often filled with military metaphors portraying other organizations, other groups within the company, and even other individuals, as the enemy to be 'beaten'. An alternative perspective stresses the importance of collaboration and the sharing of knowledge in order to be successful.

Leadership vs teamwork

410 Members of an organization are expected to work together as a team, sharing information and ideas, assisting others in their development and making co-operative decisions about projects and their implementation. There is often also an expectation that they will lead, inspire and push, not be afraid of making tough decisions and, if necessary, drive through the opposition.

Survival vs growth

At times, especially when external conditions are unfavourable, there is a strong emphasis on survival; that is, dealing only with short-term operational necessities, slimming down, cost-cutting and discarding anything or anyone not making a direct and immediate contribution to profitability. At other times, or in other parts of an organization, there may be an emphasis on the longer-term viability of that organization through new initiatives.

The impact of these polarities on the development of an organization and the individuals within it can be profound. They are difficult to address, and may perhaps never be confronted with sufficient openness to allow the declaration of widely differing assumptions. Also, an organization may give its members conflicting messages about what is valued, or change the message so frequently that people become confused about how to be successful within it.

These questions can have an impact on people within an organization on a much deeper level, often beyond conscious awareness. IST has an important role in helping people to recognize, accept, and, where appropriate, transform their responses to these fundamental issues. However, IST has itself been both enriched and impoverished by its own struggle for identity.

In recent years, there has been a growing expectation that IST would produce tangible and quantifiable benefits to organizations, and a reluctance to pay for people simply to learn more about themselves. More emphasis has been placed on the acquisition of specific behavioural skills, such as being assertive, managing conflict, and interviewing techniques. In some ways this rigorous attention to outcomes has been a valuable discipline. At its worst, however, it has fed the 'three-minute culture', and led to a considerable pressure on IST trainers to produce instant results. Some trainers have, for various reasons, colluded with this, and have produced programmes whose participants may well be able to 'talk the talk' but often cannot 'walk the walk'. That is, the new skill has not been well integrated. In interaction, the person may leave others with a sense of incongruity and discomfort. Trainers may themselves have been trained in this way, and therefore not have achieved the depth of self-awareness which many of the newer approaches to development require. They may produce a well-honed performance, but use the jargon of IST to avoid, rather than facilitate, an authentic relationship (e.g. 'I appreciate your honesty in telling me I drive you crazy. Is there anything else you would like to share with me?').

The other polarity in IST's struggle for identity has been whether, or how, to incorporate the spiritual aspect of personal development, which has been expressed as 'love in the workplace' (Harrison, 1987), meditation, ecology, the promotion of right-brain capacities and the insights of oriental religions.

At its best, it is a way of integrating the inner and outer aspects of identity and *411* purpose; in other words, a way of legitimizing and encouraging managers to reflect on what is really important to them, to become familiar with an ethical and moral force which goes beyond each individual. This has provided an impetus for raising fundamental questions about the appropriateness of organizational goals (e.g. the value of expansion as an end in itself) and about how people within organizations should treat each other, and their customers. Along with this, there has been the much greater attention paid to the role of organizations within the community. Sometimes this has led unfortunately to distortions of the truth in an attempt to convey an attractive corporate image; sometimes it has been in the pursuit of aims which are of benefit both to the organization and the community (e.g. in building links with schools and providing them with computers, an organization may be able subsequently to attract recruits at a time of skill shortage).

At its worst, consideration of the spiritual can become detached from reality, and trainers can lose sight of the operational necessities of the organizations they are employed to support. A credibility gap can then develop between the producers and the facilitators; each could learn from the other, but it becomes difficult to discover the common ground. Thus, the opportunity for those interested in influencing the spiritual orientation of the organization is lost.

So, this is the new context for IST. It is a context where interpersonal skills trainers need to create and recreate their role, while helping managers do the same. In the rest of this chapter we consider some of the features of organizations which are providing particular challenges for IST.

THE GROWING RATE AND EXTENT OF CHANGE

One of the important requirements to manage change effectively is the capacity to step back from the immediate pressures and to taken an objective, bird's-eye view. Even in times of relative stability this can be quite difficult:

- People are usually recruited to fit into a culture, and often, as a result, reinforce it.
- After recruitment there are usually a number of initiation ceremonies which reinforce the fit, such as acquiring the jargon, learning how to get listened to, or discovering who are the people with real influence.
- Within organizational groups, there is often a drive to recreate old family patterns. This may be fostered by the leaders' attempts to establish a 'family feeling', and may encourage people to continue in old, stereotyped modes of behaviour (Ketz de Vries and Miller, 1985).
- There may be a growing commitment to the company, both financially (e.g. low interest loans) and emotionally (e.g. social and professional networks), which make the expression of disagreement less likely.
- By definition, the more embedded one becomes in a culture, the more difficult it is to step outside it (for example, the company sets up a complicated series of working parties in order to discover why it is so slow in decision-making). Any act to change a culture can easily

reinforce it. External consultants can be chosen apparently to promote change, but actually the deeper, often unaware, choice is to employ somebody who will help the organization stay stuck. Organizations frequently have their favourite consultants; this fit could be the result of the consultant using highly elaborate intellectual models which mean that the highly rational organization does not consider any of its emotional blocks; similarly, the collusion might be between a consultant who works well at an emotional level but does not support the organization moving forward into action; or a consultant who likes to do everything in a hurry is chosen by a 'fire, fire, aim' organization, and neither party takes necessary reflective time.

- An organization can be seen to have a darker or 'shadow' side containing its disowned aspects, so that it may be seen by itself and others as caring and socially responsible, whilst in reality, it is also ruthless and cut-throat. As members of the organization will generally possess some of these disowned qualities, any exploration by the organization of its shadow will also involve a personal confrontation. Thus, the individuals and the organization will collude to keep the shadow hidden.

In turbulent times, therefore, objectivity can be even more difficult to achieve. People may retreat to a highly defended position where their capacity for healthy and productive change is reduced. They can then become locked into old patterns of behaviour and ways of experiencing themselves and others. One useful way of illustrating this is Stephen Karpman's (1968) 'drama triangle' (see Figure 31.1). He identified three roles which people may adopt:

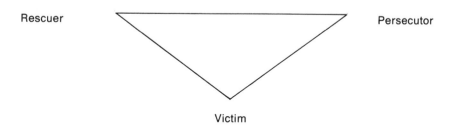

Figure 31.1   The drama triangle

Rescuer   'My role is to help all these poor and inadequate waifs and strays, and to protect them from themselves and the cruel world.'

Persecutor   'My role is to make these useless inadequates do their jobs properly.'

Victim   'My role is to get pushed around by Persecutors and looked after by Rescuers. I just can't help myself.'

None of these roles is authentic, and when people are in them they are responding in old ways to old situations on an unconscious level rather than dealing with reality in the present.

Once on this triangle, each acts out a drama – outside awareness – which reinforces their chosen way of seeing themselves and the other players. In this defended position, they will not be receptive to new information, and will filter and distort it to fit the drama which is being acted out. Thus when someone adopts a position on the drama triangle, they will expend considerable energy in making circumstances fit their perception. Any confrontation of their perception may arouse powerful feelings of fear and anger.

IST has a vital role to play in exposing the underlying messages and challenging these dynamics. For example, at a surface level (content) a group of managers might discuss their market share while at a deeper level (process), they may be experiencing many powerful feelings about the other managers and themselves. This process level will be the most important determinant of the outcome, and yet will generally be paid least attention. An understanding of the complexity and intensity of individuals' emotional responses to organizational life is crucial to the development of a healthy organization.

The transition curve (Spencer and Adams, 1990) is a very useful model describing some of these quite intense personal reactions to change (see Figure 31.2).

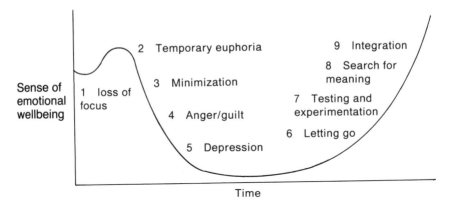

Figure 31.2   The transition curve

1. *Losing focus*: shock and disorientation (e.g. 'Do they really mean to reorganize everything?'; 'How on earth will I cope without my partner?').
2. *Temporary euphoria*: delusion that everything is going to be all right ('I'll cope very well'; 'This relocation is a golden opportunity; everything will be wonderful now').
3. *Minimization* ('There are a few little problems, but nothing to worry about').
4. *Anger/guilt*: perhaps blaming those who initiated the change ('What on earth made them think I was suitable for this promotion?'), or blaming self ('How could I have been so stupid as to leave?').

5. *Depression*: ('I'll never get out of this mess').
6. *Letting go*: learning to cope with the new reality and relinquishing the anger, guilt and illusions which were part of the previous phases.
7. *Testing and experimentation*: taking on the new role and circumstances with full force; looking to the possibilities in the new job, new relationship, new location, and so on.
8. *Searching for meaning*: looking back on the whole episode and its significance ('What does it tell me about myself and what I value?').
9. *Integration*: the change has been completely absorbed by the person and is almost taken for granted.

Organization change strategies have often ignored these powerful reactions to change, the individual processes of holding on and letting go. People need to be able to let go of the past before they fully take on the future. However, those responsible for promoting change will sometimes urge and expect everybody to embrace the 'new dawn' (i.e. move immediately to integration upon announcement of the change) without a recognition that it is quite normal for people to have many strong feelings in the face of change and that these need to be fully acknowledged and worked with. For example, even where a change is generally welcomed, people may still need to grieve the loss of old relationships and locations. A few hours in which people are encouraged to talk about their sense of loss can help them move more willingly towards the new. Regrettably, grieving can be too readily interpreted as holding on to the past, whereas frequently it is simply honouring it.

With this model in mind, interpersonal skills trainers need to be aware of the transitions in their life and where they are in them. It is perhaps more likely that internal trainers will get stuck at the same point on the transition curve as those they are trying to help (e.g. minimize the problem of dealing with a client who does not fully acknowledge the extent of the problem he or she is facing).

THE DRIVE FOR EXCELLENCE

Increased competition has caused many organizations to see excellence as a way of maintaining their competitive edge. This has meant paying close attention to quality, customer satisfaction and the establishment of values and goals which will help people give of their best. To make excellence the norm, however, requires a commitment of the heart. Continued top performance clearly cannot come simply from going through the motions. A consequence is that some organizational leaders have wanted to create (sometimes mistakenly impose) a vision of the future which will energize and encourage all employees to be wholehearted in their commitment to the company. The model in Figure 31.3, adapted from the work of Robert Fritz (1984) will be used to illustrate how IST has a role to play in this.

A powerful 'future vision' is made up of the best hopes that people have for themselves and their organization; it represents an ideal in terms of the type of business it is engaged in, the quality of relationship with customers and its *415*

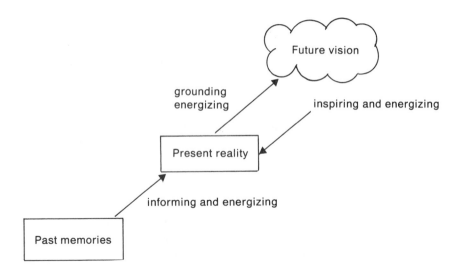

Figure 31.3 Focusing change

contribution to the community at large. The power of the vision comes from being shared at the level of the heart. Quite often, however, individual visions do not include the company; if this is so, it will need to be uncovered and addressed, otherwise the vision will simply be a mouthed and empty catechism. If those in charge of organizations want wholehearted commitment, then they need to accept that they are more likely to encounter some quite profound resistances because they are approaching the core of the employee. One aspect might simply be the amount of time people are willing to give to work. Will there be any heart left to give at home? Another aspect might be concerned with the values associated with the 'future vision'. It can be a matter of opening Pandora's box. If people are encouraged to talk about what they really want and what they really believe in, then it may not include their current employer. This is not necessarily a bad thing, since it opens the possibility of the organization changing to accommodate people's values, or of people leaving now rather than half-heartedly going along with the changes. IST has a contribution to make in helping people to express what they want, and, indeed, to listen to what others want.

This is also true when working with 'present reality'. The quality of the 'future vision' is dependent upon truthfulness in assessing 'present reality'. As clear a definition as possible of current resources, both human and material, will provide the best base for launching into the future. If information is hoarded or distorted to produce a better picture of current circumstances, then the 'future vision' will be fatally flawed.

Sometimes, also, 'past memories' will need to be explored; the encouragement to identify and learn from the successes and failures of the past, the revisiting of traditions to consider which need to be retained and which relinquished.

This exploration of past memories, present reality and future vision can require courage by all parties. Chris Argyris has written about skilled incompetence, in which certain aspects of organizational life are regarded as undiscussible (e.g. the shadow side) and people become skilled not only in not discussing it, but also in not discussing the undiscussibility. It was with a child-like naivety that the little boy said, 'but the emperor has no clothes'; a manager or trainer is likely to have lost that early innocence and will require determination and courage to tell the truth as he or she sees it.

Interpersonal skills trainers will need to work with individuals and groups in the context of past, present and future, sometimes taking quite a narrow focus, such as helping two managers to give and receive some feedback; at other times, it might be a much larger undertaking, building bridges between many groups.

THE GROWING EMPHASIS ON SELF-DEVELOPMENT

Self-development means individuals and groups taking the initiative to organize and use the resources necessary to support their professional and personal learning. It reflects a trend towards flatter structures, local responsibility, and responsiveness to the needs of both internal and external customers. Where an organization is engaged in self-development some of the more obvious signs could be: mentoring, action-learning sets, a learning resource centre and support groups. However, although less obvious, just as – perhaps even more – important would be high-quality coaching and counselling, an encouragement to work in other parts of the business and general support for trying something different. In other words, the technology is less important than the values which underpin it. For example, a mentoring scheme would be a shallow exercise if the mentors failed to be as fully open to the possibilities of learning as their protégés.

Two assumptions underlie self-development:

1. If staff have developed the capacity and confidence to pursue their own learning, then they will anticipate and meet problems quickly; they will be more creative in building and sustaining an organization that is not only financially profitable, but also an enjoyable place to be.
2. If staff can also learn how to work with others, not only to achieve tasks but also to support each other's development, then previously hidden reservoirs of energy and enthusiasm can be tapped.

A number of factors have caused this impetus towards self-development.

- The growing recognition that standard training courses, especially if they are isolated events, have a number of limitations: that is, actual or perceived unreality; problems of the transfer of learning; the cost of time away from the workplace to attend the course; and the fact that not enough can be provided to meet rapidly changing skill needs. One could argue that training courses reflect the old organizational hier- *417* archy, with the trainer, albeit with a variety of styles, exercising control and managing events. This can be the case even where the course is run in a highly participative way. If the trainer chooses to give power to the group, then this is simply an indication of how much power he or she has.

- The need for organizational flexibility and resilience in responding to dramatic change. This carries with it the notion of proactivity and self-motivated individuals and teams learning from and supporting each other as they go about their business. This is sometimes known as the 'learning organization'.
- The creation and refinement of technology that supports individual self-paced but monitored learning (e.g. interactive video, computer-based training).
- The fact that fewer companies offer life-time employment. Increasingly it is the case that all employees have to be responsible for their own career.
- The growing importance of qualifications based on work experience. This requires the person to be responsible for gathering sufficient evidence to merit accreditation.
- The growing prevalence of the notion that quality requires individuals actively to seek out opportunities for continuous improvement in their products and services.

At its best an organization using self-development is a place of great creativity and commitment. To reach this ideal, self-responsibility is crucial. This is where IST can make a contribution.

Self-responsibility means being willing to take full responsibility for one's feelings and actions, recognizing that each person's life (assuming minimum conditions of physical and emotional wellbeing) is a matter of choice; blaming others or living in a world of what might have been is fruitless. Full acceptance of self-responsibility is a rare and hard-won achievement, and yet a large measure is required for management self-development to be effective. The mechanisms for avoiding self-responsibility can sometimes be quite intricate and are likely to have been the subject of many basic IST courses; for example: generalizing, not answering questions directly, being vague, putting self down, using passive language ('It just seems to happen to me'). Growth in the sense of maturation, requires separation, and underlying the challenge of self-development is the challenge of really growing up and being truly oneself. Organizations are quite often ambivalent about this, because it necessarily brings with it some loss of control. In the not too distant past, hierarchical organizations, such as large financial institutions, functioned on dependency: people generally doing what they were told. Many now recognize that hierarchies are unhelpful for dealing with rapidly changing market conditions; however, whilst wanting to change to some extent there is also a desire to maintain the status quo. So a mixed message is given, 'We do want you to change and be proactive, but not too much'; or even more disabling. 'We do not know what the limits are but we'll punish you when you exceed them'.

This ambiguity can be reinforced by the manager's own fears and vulnerability in working in a flatter organization. There are fewer places to hide; role cannot be relied upon; and the direct personal contact becomes vital. Self-development means moving beyond technique and seeing oneself as an important instrument for change. This necessarily has consequences for those responsible for supporting and developing the self-developers. They will need to be alert to 'educational opportunities', matching them to the self-developer whilst providing a challenge. In broad terms this will mean the self-developer either being exposed to new tasks or new ways of doing the same task; specifically the possibilities are endless, including managing meetings, trouble-shooting, carrying out an interview, writing a report, secondment to a totally different industry, making a presentation to the board, and so. However, learning requires more than the self-developer simply doing something different. Much of the writing about learning organizations emphasizes the importance of being an aware learner, so the self-developer will need to be specifically helped to learn from those experiences; highly refined listening and questioning skills are crucial for this, in order to uncover what is important technically and emotionally, and in planning future action.

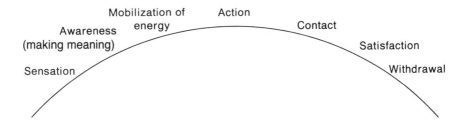

Figure 31.4   The energy wave

We offer a model drawn from *Gestalt* psychology (Zinker, 1977, Clarkson, 1989) to illustrate this (see Figure 31.4). It is based on the assumption that in 'normal' and 'healthy' functioning, energy is generated and focused towards meeting a succession of physical and emotional needs; as each need is satisfied, then another emerges to take its place. Eating can provide a simple example.

- I am watching television.
- I become aware of pangs in my stomach (Sensation).
- I recognize this as hunger, rather than, for example, indigestion (Awareness–making meaning).
- I go into the kitchen (Mobilization of energy).
- I make a sandwich (Action).
- I start chewing on the sandwich (Contact).
- My hunger pangs abate (Satisfaction).
- I go out of the kitchen (Withdrawal) not sure what to do next.

This can also apply to emotional needs:

- I notice I have a pain in my neck (Sensation).
- I recognize that it is because I am angry with a colleague who did not, as promised, support me in a meeting (Awareness).
- I leave my office and go to see him (Mobilization of energy).
- I express my anger (Action).
- I fully experience my feelings and the situation (Contact).
- I leave my colleague's office having done and said what I wanted (Satisfaction).
- I have now left that situation and may decide to go back to my office (Withdrawal).

This is not based on the principle of hedonism (I must always satisfy my feelings so as to maximize pleasure), but rather acknowledging the validity of feelings and deciding what appropriate action to take. For example, some people might decide to ignore the hunger pangs because they are on a diet; or, might decide not to express anger because they realize the colleagues involved are under stress at the moment.

However, there can at any stage be blocks; these prevent the identification and meeting of the need (see Figure 31.5).

- *Denial* I may be quite abrupt with one of my staff but not realize it.
- *Minimization* I may recognize that I am 'a bit' annoyed, but not accept that I am actually furious with my colleague.

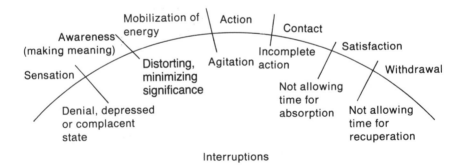

Figure 31.5   Blocks on the energy wave

- *Agitation* Rather than go and see my colleague I divert my energy into other activities – phone calls, filing, smoking.
- *Incomplete action* I go and see my colleague, but minimize my complaint.
- *Not allowing time for absorption* Not acknowledging to myself that I followed through with a difficult task.

- *Not allowing time for recuperation* I immediately rush into another task, rather than giving myself time to identify what is now important.

Learning means being able to move through all the stages of the 'energy wave'; where there are blocks the learning will not take place, or be incomplete. Self-developers may well need help in moving through each stage. Below are some examples of how this might be done.

Block	Possible interventions
Denial	Generate data: facts on costs, quality, turnover, absenteeism; customer satisfaction surveys; questionnaires. Hold 'sensing' meetings. Hold briefings and feedback; confront mismatches between what people say and how they say it. Move people around; break up groups; point out mismatches between 'fantasy' and reality. Bring in outsiders (e.g. a customer); 'devil's advocate'. Encourage self- and peer assessment against core management competences.
Minimization	Encourage people to collect own data. Check and probe feelings and wants. Hold grieving/dumping sessions. Express own fears/doubts/hopes. Press people on the conclusions they draw from the data. Encourage the identification and expression of work and/or personal priorities.
Agitation	Focus people on outcomes. Run a visioning workshop. use planning frameworks. Give reassurance to encourage clarity of thought and feeling. Set tight targets. Use problem-solving structures (e.g. brainstorming, synectics, force-field analysis, wall charting).
Incomplete action	Check and re-check on people's satisfaction. Offer own observations. Gather 'objective' data. Refer back to original plan/objectives. Revisit what people may already know about how they block themselves at the earlier stages.
Lack of celebration	Encourage the expression of appreciations, even if there is incomplete success. Set up a mechanism for the giving of both positive and negative feedback. Initiate celebration rituals, while respecting individual preferences for how to celebrate. Review learning from what went well/badly. Identify considerations for next time.

Lack of recuperation   Build in time to reflect. Reconsider priorities. Watch out for people becoming workaholics; encourage people to take time for themselves outside work and to develop other interests. Counselling.

The intervention has to be where the block is. It is no use encouraging people to plan how to solve a problem if they are denying its existence. Once again this points to the necessity of self-knowledge for those engaged in interpersonal skills training, including the development of developers. For example, somebody who finds it hard to celebrate is more likely to be blind to this need in others.

Supporting the self-developer assumes a generosity of spirit and willingness by trainers and personnel to create the conditions where staff development takes place, rather than directly undertaking the development work themselves. In other words, they move away from being developers to being the developers of developers. As a consequence the range of possible roles extends to include some, or all, of the following: coach, counsellor, mentor, set adviser for action-learning groups, mediator, meetings co-ordinator, writer of 'how to' guides, devil's advocate, resource link (to people and places, both inside and outside the company), course designer, and facilitator of group facilitators. A common strand in all these roles is acknowledging the need to let go, that is, to relinquish control. Such acknowledgement can be hard for those trainers and personnel specialists who have, in the past, prided themselves on being problem-solvers and the providers of right answers. The change in role described above does not mean giving up this capacity completely, but it does mean using it more sparingly, in order to allow others to be truly self-responsible (although even this carries with it an edge of arrogance).

CONCLUSION

In the last ten years the domain of IST has increased dramatically, helping managers on significant inward and outward journeys which ultimately converge. The inward journey has been a very personal one about one's relationship with oneself: feelings, values and life priorities. The outward journey has been a recognition that no person, no organization, no community and no country can exist in isolation. This continued attention to both the outer and the inner aspects will be important for the health of the world; it means continuing to be open both to oneself and to pressing moral, economic, political and spiritual questions, despite the strong temptation to pretend they do not exist. This does not mean that an answer, let alone *the* answer will immediately appear, but it requires the capacity and willingness to hold the chaos and confusion until a window of clarity appears.

FURTHER READING

422   Argyris, C., 'Skilled incompetence', *Harvard Business Review*, **64**. (5).

Clark, Neil *et al.* (1984), *Unfinished Business: The Theory and Practice of Personal Process Work in Training*, Gower.

Clarkson, Petruska (1989), *Gestalt Counselling in Action*, Sage.

Fritz, Robert (1984), *The Path of Least Resistance*, Salem: Stillpoint Publishing.

Harrison, Roger (1987), *Organization Culture and Quality of Service: A Strategy for Releasing Love in the Workplace*, AMED.

Karpman, S. (1968), 'Fairy tales and script drama analysis', *Transactional Analysis Bulletin*, **7**, (26).

Ketz de Vries, Manfred and Danny Miller (1985), *The Neurotic Organization*, London: Jossey-Bass.

Phillips, Keri and Tony Fraser (1984), *The Management of Interpersonal Skills Training*, Gower.

Phillips, Keri and Annette Bradley (1993), *A Practical Guide to Self-Development in Organizations*, KPA.

Spencer, Sabina and John Adams (1990), *Life Changes: Growing Through Personal Transitions*, Impact Publishers.

Zinker, Joseph (1977), *Creative Process in Gestalt Therapy*, Vintage.

32 Business language training

Michael Woodhall and Ian MacKay

This chapter deals with the strategic and tactical issues associated with language training in business organizations. It considers questions relating to the place of language competence in the achievement of corporate objectives, the formulation of a corporate language strategy, the conduct of a language audit to identify language training needs and the fulfilment of these needs through different types of learning programmes.

INTRODUCTION

'When abroad, the British show a blithe disregard for any language other than their own: they believe that they will be perfectly well understood providing they speak slowly and rather loudly – in English!' This statement is less true today than it has been in the past, although it still contains more than a grain of truth. We are well known for our reluctance to learn and speak foreign languages. Such a stance must be eradicated if we are to gain real advantage from our membership of the European Community in the future. It is not merely good business sense to do so: it is a matter of necessity, even survival.

So how can you, the executive responsible for training and development in your organization, ensure that the organization you represent not only survives, but actually thrives in world markets by communicating effectively in the relevant languages? To ensure that appropriate staff can achieve business results in the language of the customer, whatever it may be, is no easy task, although, as some organizations have demonstrated, it can be achieved with effort provided a systematic approach is adopted. Such an approach is illustrated in Figure 32.1.

CORPORATE OBJECTIVES

The first stage in developing relevant language skills is to conduct an analysis which examines your organization's corporate objectives as they are now and as

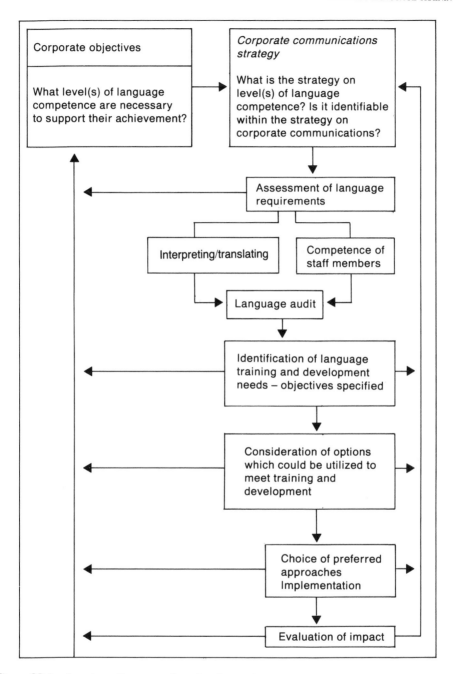

Figure 32.1   A systematic approach to developing language skills

they may become. The object of the analysis is to assess the extent to which these objectives require varying levels of language competence to support their achievement.

The analysis itself should incorporate questions similar to those illustrated in Figure 32.2

1.	What are your organization's corporate objectives for the current financial year?
2.	To what extent have these objectives changed from the previous financial year?
3.	To what extent may they change in the next financial year?
4.	Just how far is the achievement of current corporate objectives dependent on:

- information derived from foreign sources (patents, specifications, techniques/scientific developments and the like)?
- information translated into foreign languages (sales brochures, instruction manuals, operating manuals and similar literature)?
- effective communications with foreign nationals (through telephone contact, business letters, meetings and visits)?
- joint contracts with foreign companies?

5.	What is the contribution now by linguistically competent staff at all levels in your organization to current corporate objectives?
6.	Just how much may the situation change in the foreseeable future? Could your organization's dependence on such competence grow more significant in the future? By how much in broad terms? Critically?

Figure 32.2   Corporate objectives and language support

LANGUAGE LEARNING STRATEGY

Having considered your organization's corporate objectives and the broad role played by language ability in their achievement, your next task is to decide what your organization's strategy should be towards language learning.

Example: corporate strategy

In the mid-1980s GKN Technology acquired a German company. Training Officer Richard Thurlow realized well in advance that a whole range of GKN people would need to be able to talk to their opposite numbers frequently and in depth. He realized too that not all these Germans would be able to speak English, nor would a lot of them – understandably – want to.

Thurlow made time to look at a number of language training providers and delivery methods. He invited language training providers to meet and discuss with the key staff the company had identified. In this way the language training provider got to know at first hand the strengths and needs, hopes and fears of the learners. The format which learner (GKN technology) and provider (Michael Woodhall) agreed on and refined was one week per month over four months, each week being Wednesday to Wednesday, excluding weekends, each day being from 8.00 am till 1.00 pm.

The provider selected was a Language Centre based firmly in a business school. This was an important factor in the decision. The business learner is, in general, not a linguist – by background, training, or inclination. The business learner benefits from the business trainer.

Strategic issues

Strategic issues which must be considered include the following:

- Should language competence at different levels displayed by individual employees attract additional payments beyond basic salary?
- Alternatively, should language competence be incorporated within your organization's job evaluation system?
- Should language competence be sought actively throughout the recruitment selection process?
- Should staff exchanges with partner companies, agents or subsidiaries be positively encouraged, and planned for, to extend the language competence of those involved as part of the organization's strategy on career development?
- Should the appointment of foreign nationals to full-time positions within the organization be actively encouraged?
- Should the organization's approach to language learning be viewed within the context of a wider communications strategy?
- Should an evaluation of the need for any development in language competence be conducted at every performance review (appraisal)?
- Should the responsibility for encouraging language competence be written into the terms of reference (job description) for every manager at every level?
- Should language training take place within a wider cross-cultural perspective?

Decisions on these and related policy issues will provide a framework for the design of your organization's language learning strategy to meet corporate needs. Your responses to the preceding questions will provide the basis for more detailed analysis in each of the following principal areas of language activity, the first two of which may be the responsibility of specialist staff: interpreting at meetings involving the organization; translation of documentation; and the language proficiency of staff generally in conducting the organization's business. Each is considered in turn in the next section.

FORMAL USE OF LANGUAGE SERVICES

Interpreting

An assessment of the present contribution of interpreting to the fulfilment of corporate objectives should be carried out to establish both its efficiency (is it carried out accurately?) and its effectiveness (is its use directed at critical issues?). Questions which may be posed in this context are illustrated in Figure 32.3.

---

1. Why are interpreting services required?

   - For face-to-face business meetings with foreign nationals?
   - For telephone conversations with foreign customers, agents, and so on?
   - For other purposes? If so, what?

2. What language(s) are involved, principally?
3. How is the requirement met currently?

   - By specialist internal staff?
   - By other staff with some language knowledge?
   - By full-time specialist interpreters from outside the organization?

4. Is the requirement primarily for simultaneous or consecutive interpreting?
5. Is the requirement met effectively? How do you know?

   - For instance, if interpreting is carried out at business meetings by the organization's own staff, do they possess any necessary technical/commercial knowledge of the topics under consideration to facilitate quick/accurate interpretation?

6. In specific terms, to what extent is the achievement of your organization's corporate objectives dependent on interpreting services? Just how far may such dependence change in the future? In what direction? To what extent may it be changing, even now?

Figure 32.3   The impact of interpreting on the achievement of corporate objectives

Translation

Larger organizations are increasingly establishing specialist translation departments employing 'into-mother tongue' translators to meet their foreign languages documentation requirements. Whilst your organization may not have reached this stage of development yet, it is necessary to establish just how far translation activities contribute to the achievement of corporate objectives currently. There are three main responses to translation needs other than by establishing a separate department: on an *ad hoc* basis by the organization's staff, by external contracts, or by using translation companies, as illustrated in Figure 32.4.

Following a review of the questions posed in Figure 32.4, you may care to consider what poor translation of product names may have had on your organization's corporate reputation in the past. Two examples dramatize the point:

1. Some time ago, a certain people's car was to be marketed in Germany as a competitor for the Mercedes 600. Its name, 'Silver Mist', was hastily changed to 'Silver Shadow' when the meaning of *mist* in German – manure – was realized.
2. A Japanese car manufacturer marketed its new sports car in France as the MR2. Said quickly in French, the slip soon became apparent!

Your responses to the questions, about the contribution of interpreting and translation to the achievement of corporate objectives currently, may have

Ad hoc by the organization's staff

1. Are translations carried out effectively? How do you know? Are translations edited/checked:

   - By technical/commercial specialists where necessary?
   - By appropriate foreign nationals for translation from English into other languages?

2. What is the cost of this *ad hoc* translation to your organization currently?

   - Financially?
   - In terms of possible conflicts of interests?
   - In terms of corporate image if, for example, instruction booklets are written in unintentionally humorous, or nonsensical, language?

Ad hoc by external contacts

3. How have these contacts been developed?

4. Is their use effective when compared with the alternatives available?

   - How do you know?
   - When was the last time the situation was reviewed?
   - Should it be reviewed again? How soon?

5. Are these contacts effective?

   - Is their language skill/knowledge acceptable?
   - Is any required technical/commercial knowledge up to date?
   - Are translations edited and, for into-foreign-language work, checked by mother tongue-foreign specialists?

6. What was the cost to your organization of using external contacts for translation purposes in the last financial year? The year before that? What is the trend? Are you getting value for money?

Use of translation companies

7. How were the companies chosen? What criteria were used? Are those criteria still valid?

   - Are the companies members of the Institute of Translation and Interpreting?

8. How much did use of translation companies cost your organization in the last financial year? The year before that? Again, what is the trend? Is it acceptable?

Figure 32.4 The impact of translation of documentation on corporate objectives.

signalled the need for changes to present practices in this respect within your organization. It may be that you have identified language training needs which should be fulfilled to help the integration of these elements of language requirements into corporate activities. If this is the case, you are advised to seek specialist help from language consultants before taking any action.

The next task is to review the extent of language proficiency amongst staff in your organization.

Staff language proficiency

An assessment of such capability amongst staff currently may be achieved by conducting a languages audit. If such an audit has been carried out in the past it *429*

Private and confidential

Name	Section/Dept/Division

Language (please specify)

	Used at work	Skill
	Never at all/A little/A lot	A little/A lot/Fully competent

Focus

Listening/speaking
Conversations with customers face to face.
Conversations with visitors.
In-house business meetings.
Conversations on the telephone.
Giving verbal instructions.
Making statements in public on behalf
of the organization.

Writing
Routine correspondence.
Non-routine correspondence.
Company telex, notes, etc.
Articles for publication in journals.
Public Relations releases.
Report writing/
Specialist material (contracts, patents, and so forth).

Reading
Routine correspondence.
Non-routine correspondence.
Instructions.
Telex, notes, and so on.
Journal articles.
Public Relations releases.
Reports.
Specialist material (contracts, patents, and so on).
Please indicate the name(s) and level(s) of any language courses you have undertaken in past years

Language	Level

Figure 32.5   Language audit questionnaire: an example

would be worth questioning its current validity and whether it should be updated again now. If an audit has never been carried out, then its completion should be regarded as a priority.

The object of language audit is to establish, in detail, the qualitative and quantitative extent of language skills (both written and spoken) present with the organization. Some companies have been agreeably surprised by the extent and depth of language competence amongst staff when first conducting such an audit.

A simple self-completion form can be used to conduct a preliminary stage of such an audit, an example of which is shown in Figure 32.5. Following return of the completed forms to a central point the information generated can be checked and claims for proficiency can be investigated further in the audit's second stage, which should be conducted with the help of language consultants.

The language consultant will undertake with you a four-part approach to the full language audit. First, you will be asked to complete a questionnaire to identify your 'shopping list' of language needs, which may include entertaining visitors, using the telephone, reading memoranda and reports, attending conferences and making presentations. The results form the basis for the second stage of the audit, a discussion with the consultant to agree a broad plan of action.

The individuals nominated then undertake one of two tests:

1. *Diagnostic* For those with some language ability.
2. *Aptitude assessment* To establish likely success at language learning.

The Dorset Business School Language Centre utilizes both tests as an integral part of its assessment of language needs in particular organizations. The diagnostic test comprises a 30-item questionnaire to establish the precise level of an individual's foreign language capability. The language aptitude test is used to predict the likely degree of success of foreign language learning in individual cases. It consists of a 5-part multiple-choice test, two parts of which focus on listening to the language being spoken, while the remaining three parts focus on reading skills. On completion, individual results are given as a percentile figure accompanied by a written report. Experience shows that the test, which can be taken as either 75-minute or 30-minute variants, is predictive of future success. The results certainly contribute to informed decision-making on suitability for language training from both the individual's point of view and that of the organization.

Both tests, diagnostic and aptitude assessment, provide a factual base for the third stage of the audit: a corporate language training needs diagnosis, which identifies any gaps which exist between current language competence at particular occupational levels and for individual staff, to perform their jobs effectively both now and in the foreseeable future. These gaps (the needs) at both group and individual levels must be closed off if the organization is to meet present and future corporate objectives. The needs will be translated into proposals for training objectives, with required end-states specified as appropriate and with relevant and realistic time-frames clearly indicated. The proposals themselves constitute the fourth and final part of the audit.   *431*

It is worth remembering, as you consider any proposals, that extending language competence is not amenable to the 'quick-fix' solution. It takes time to develop such skills: you cannot, for example, graft language ability into your technical staff in a few weeks, where none existed before. Learning a language is a much longer-term commitment, as some organizations have found to their cost. 'Distress' purchasing of language packages with an expectation of near-instant results is just not realistic.

In addition, any proposal must be viewed not only against the likely perceptions of staff towards language learning, but also against the various approaches which may be taken to such learning. These issues are considered now.

LANGUAGE LEARNING: SOME MISPERCEPTIONS

People expect and accept change in many professional areas, but tend to assume that language learning now will be exactly like it was for them at school. They will conveniently forget that at school they did not have computers, cassette recorders, audio-active language learning machines – in short, the whole range of educational hardware which is an integral part of language learning now. They may also be unrealistic in their expectations of how quickly they will progress up the learning curve of language proficiency. Just because of the familiarity with difficult computer programs, for example, previously the exclusive preserve of the program designer, they may exhibit an unrealistic expectation of acquiring a language with the same degree of ease. Someone else, they assume, will have done the basic work for them and that all they have to do is press a button.

Whichever methods are proposed in support of the language learning objectives, these potential misperceptions will need to be borne in mind. Nevertheless, some people are beginning to realize that language competence can help particularly in fulfilling career aspirations. Such realizations can provide a very real motivation to succeed, whatever learning methods are used. The main methods open to you are considered now.

THE LEARNING OPTIONS

What are the choices open to you in planning to help the sales staff to market your organization's products effectively in foreign markets? Or to collaborate with others in joint development projects? There are five basic options.

Self-study

There is currently a wide selection of high-quality self-study material. The main advantage of this material is the personal control over the material exercised by the learner. For example, staff who frequently make lengthy car journeys, or who travel regularly by train or plane, can utilize what would otherwise be 'dead time' rather more effectively with such self-study aids. On the other hand, the main complaint of learners is that they lack the self-discipline to follow this approach to learning: they are incapable of managing their personal time effectively. Indeed, managing such time more effectively may be a parallel training need!

Open learning

Open learning for the business person taking a foreign language is a very powerful resource indeed. Open learning talks the language of the business person – setting objectives, constructing a critical path, reviewing progress, arranging 'milestone' meetings.

The learner is able to make a personal contract based on: targeting tangible outcomes, forming a sensible appreciation of the personal and technical resources available; and harnessing these resources to provide a realistic framework. In short, the learner is able to do many of the things that the traditional training and classroom setting proscribes.

In the field of business language learning, open learning is a popular method with the personnel and training function – with employees learning in their own time, a single investment in re-usable equipment, learners taking responsibility for their own learning, and so on. It is a fact that over approximately a three-year period a move toward a carefully constructed open learning system – using specially prepared materials, incorporating an individual 'pathway to progress', and involving regular monitoring – can halve the training budget for languages while increasing the effectiveness of the learning for those who follow through their own programmes.

However, an investment has to be made by the company in order to identify and provide the right kind of resources and to put its chosen open-learning project into the hands of a committed training organization. And as well as investment in terms of materials and methods, there is also a vital investment necessary in terms of internal marketing. This latter investment is required because open learning is not always popular with the learner. Typically the idea of a move towards open learning for languages generates the same kind of emotional response as does a projected move towards open-plan offices. With open-plan offices the perceived fear is of lack of privacy and increased exposure; with open learning the fear is of losing contact with a human trainer and of being isolated.

One company that has identified open learning as the answer to its business language-learning needs is the Damart Group in France. The personnel director, the motivator behind the change, was seeking control over the objectives, personal involvement from the learners, and a dramatic reduction in his training budget. He achieved all three requirements with a specially constructed open learning system.

Individual tuition

Tutors can be employed to give individual tuition either on the organization's 433 premises, or at learners' own homes. The primary advantage here is that your organization, as a client, can agree programmes of meetings to fit with the operational constraints of both learner and tutor. A complaint is that contingencies arise, causing postponement or even cancellation of the sessions. It is certainly true that once the rhythm of such sessions has been lost, there is frequently a feeling that progress too has been lost.

Commercial providers

Many of the commercial providers see the answer to semi-formal individual tuition as being the prepaid, pre-designed, one-to-one programme which takes place either with your organization or on their language training premises. The learning is entirely geared to participants' needs and, because the programme has been paid for in advance, there is an additional pressure on participants to keep to the programme.

Group courses

Such courses fall into three main categories. First are the classes run by local educational colleges. Typically these are evening classes with 10–15 participants, catering for a wide range of objectives and very often starting from scratch. Second, are the group or groups from one particular organization where nominated staff meet together at a pre-arranged time to learn the language. Finally, there is the inter-organization course where participants from a variety of employers come together in groups in which the language competence level is compatible, to learn together.

Do not be too ready to accept that one-to-one tuition must be the best route, the most effective way of learning a foreign language. Certainly, this approach has the advantage of flexibility, intensity and clear focus. However, small group courses, where the participants come together from a variety of backgrounds, have an extra dimension which is of enormous value to the business learner. First, the learner is not alone. Business people do tend to be very aware of their own mistakes. They are always seeing a glass as being half-empty rather than half-full; that is, they notice what they cannot do, rather than what they can do. Learning in a group situation enables learners to be realistic about their achievements and the pace of learning. It enables them to seek help from fellow-learners rather than from the tutor who, by definition, is always better at the foreign language than they are. Tutor dependence is, therefore, reduced and a more natural communications framework is developed. The construction engineer who has to build a large animal-rearing station in French-speaking Africa is forced to practise French by explaining the problems and constraints to the textile sales representative trying to penetrate the French market, and vice versa.

MAKING THE CHOICE

As with any form of learning, there are both advantages and disadvantages to each of these methods. Your choice will depend, at least in part, on the operational constraints (including budget considerations) within your organization. Nevertheless, there are a number of questions you should pose before you make a final choice. You have already identified the individual training needs of potential participants, including the skills nominated as priority items (for example: small group negotiations, entertaining visitors, instructing trainees) and the level at which such skills are to be used, called here the target level. Armed with this information, and the knowledge that it will take around 120 hours of study for a 35- to 45-year old business person to attain minimum oral competence in a foreign language from absolute beginner status, you can now choose the option, or combination of options, which most effectively meets your needs. In any event, it is worth re-emphasizing that, whatever your choice, language training is a longer-term commitment. Whatever training is initiated for particular staff (occupational groups, vertical slices through the organization, or horizontal 'rafts' of employees), progress beyond genuine minimum proficiency (the ability to make a clear presentation of self, employer, employer's products, requests) will not be forthcoming quickly. As an example, the language training scheme at Peugeot Talbot indicates a probable 500–600 hours of contact to achieve a high level competence, such contact being spread over several years.

Example: implementation

Time & Data Systems International, a small dynamic hi-tech company from Poole, Dorset, supplies markets throughout the world with sophisticated security systems. The commercial strength of the West German market made it a prime target. Because the product is best sold via distributors and because distributors want a rapid response to the demands of their customers, coupled with technical support from TDSI, the British sales engineers have to have German. The chairman of TDSI is a man of wide international experience who has lived and worked actively in a number of foreign language cultures. There was no need to tell him that a 'four-week intensive' was not what he was seeking for his technically highly qualified but linguistically unable staff.

A small-group, company course based on short learning bursts was the delivery system chosen. The trainers came from a management development/ languages background with the knowledge of the specialist learning skills of letting the learner(s) identify and use their own language models based on their own learning skills.

Not for them the rigid division of first-person singular, followed by second person singular, followed by . . .! Why study the past tense, when your business is in the future?

EVALUATING LANGUAGE TRAINING

Language training at any level is not cheap. It therefore makes sound business *435* sense to check the worth of any language training programme you initiate. The bottom line must be cost-effectiveness in achieving agreed objectives.

Elsewhere in these pages you will find advice on methods of evaluating training which will help you to assess the degree of 'fit' between the training objectives, the training design, its implementation and the method(s) chosen to evaluate the results of such training. Evaluation of the elements which constitute a training programme is just as important for language training as it is for any other area of business activity.

Example: evaluation

'What level will I be at when I've finished?' 'Will it be like "O" level?' are typical questions from the learners. 'How will we know your programme has been successful?' is a typical question from the personnel and training function. All three questions miss the point, however,

The ultimate 'level' or 'success' will be rubber-stamped not by the trainer or by personnel, but by the marketplace. Measuring measurables are useful milestones. Orders from overseas are the bench marks of success.

Stephen Moseley, Sales director from Dell Quay Marine, Poole in Dorset, is one person who has achieved this success. Dell Quay Marine makes dories. In the late 1980s this company realized that it needed to balance a flat home market. West Germany was identified as an existing market which needed revamping. The method chosen was to appoint more distributors to give a wider regional spread. The BOTB, working through the commercial attachés at the British Consulates, helped Dell Quay to identify potential distributors.

How to get Stephen Moseley's rusty 'O' level in German to the right level for a presentation to a range of potential distributors? In reality, the Language Centre Moseley approached turned this question round and asked 'how can your existing language, suitably de-rusted, enable you to present and elicit the information crucial to you?' A five-day 'presentation skills in German' programme was the answer. Stephen Moseley cut this short after three days. Why? Because he felt himself that he had the right language and structures available. The marketplace confirmed this. By the early 1990s orders were still coming in from the German market as a direct result of the late 1980s activity.

CONCLUSION

If your organization is to prosper in the global marketplace of the future, language competence, and a sensitive awareness of the customer's culture and ways of doing business, must be reflected in a broad spectrum of your staff and not merely by one or two people. To achieve such competence requires a genuine clarity of purpose, an acceptance that language learning cannot be achieved overnight, and a clear corporate language policy which itself reflects the aims and objectives of the organization.

What more should you do now to help your organization respond positively to
436 its own language needs?

FURTHER READING

Bannock Report, The (1987), *Into Active Exporting*, occasional paper, April, BTOB.

Blackburn, P.N. (1989) 'The Threlford Lecture: Language, Education and Industry – towards 1992', *The Linguist*, **28**, (3), 74–80.

DESKPICKUP (1987), LX Centre Briefing, no. 1, October.

Embleton, D. and S. Hagen (1992), *Languages in International Business*, Hodder & Stoughton.

Fox, J. *et al.* (1992), *Perspectives in Modern Language Learning*, a report by the University of East Anglia for the Learning Methods Branch of the Department of Employment.

Hagen, S. (ed.) (1988) *Languages in British Business*, Newcastle upon Tyne Polytechnic Products Ltd in association with the Centre for Information on Language Teaching and Research (CILT).

Hogg, E. (ed.) (1990), 'Language Training', Factsheet No. 25, *Personnel Management*, January 1990.

Language International, the journal of the language professionals: Praetorius.

Liston, D. and N. Reeves (1985), *Business Studies, Languages and Overseas Trade – A Study of Education and Training*, MacDonald & Evans Ltd and the Institute of Export.

Scullard, S. (1989), *The Provision of Foreign Language Training to Industry*, Further Education Unit (FEU).

Skapinker, M. (1987), 'British Executives: Too often lost for words', *Financial Times*, 16 October.

Van Mesdag, M. (1988), 'Use your customer's language', *The Linguist*, **27** (4), autumn, 150–1.

Wickland, N. (1989), 'Executive/Linguist or Linguist/Executive?' *The Linguist*, **28**, (6), 210–13.

Woodhall, M. (1986), 'A business-like approach to language training', *Training and Development*, September.

Woodhall, M. (1990), 'Profile of the business learner', in *Corporate Language Policy*, proceedings of 15th Annual Conference of the International Association of Languages for Business, Praetorius.

33 Neuro-linguistic programming

Roy Johnson

I have always believed in what might be termed the techniques of 'mild' management. By this I mean that small interventions, carefully thought out, can have an effect far out of proportion to the amount of effort involved in the actual intervention. (Harvey-Jones, 1988)

Neuro-linguistic programming (NLP) is an aid to 'mild' management. Its skills and principles provide managers with subtle but powerful means of communication, influence and change.

NLP has its roots in studies of renowned humanistic psychotherapists in the mid-1970s. From these studies emerged specific models of communication and personal change that enabled others to achieve similar results to those studied. The skills and processes encapsulated by the models applied to one-to-one communication, and the processes of change helped people to achieve the results they wanted by developing new ways of thinking and hence new behaviours. Since then, practitioners have taken NLP into education, arts and business throughout the world. NLP is of value in self-management and one-to-one communication, and also, through the recent work of Robert Dilts and John Grinder, in the leadership and management of groups and organizations. The following quote from Richard Asquith's article in the *Telegraph Weekend Magazine* describes the beginnings of NLP:

NLP began in the early 1970s, in the USA, when John Grinder, a professor of linguistics, and Richard Bandler, a mathematician, conducted a study of three celebrated communicators, all of whom worked as therapists. All three regularly achieved excellence in their work; the aim of the study was to determine the precise behavioural details of what this excellence involved.

One of their earliest discoveries was that the three therapists instinctively mimicked their clients' physical behaviour, and this 'body-matching' seemed to encourage clients to relax and talk freely. They also found that the therapists were responding to the clients' physical behaviour so that, for example, a slight increase in muscle tension might be interpreted as part of an answer to a question, altering the meaning of the spoken answer and shaping the therapist's response to it. But the real breakthrough came when they began to organise their data. Using linguistic analysis and mathematical notation, they described the patterns of behaviour on which the therapists' excellence seemed to depend in a complex 'model' or set of hypothetical rules. This model was then learned by other therapists – who found that, as a result, they began to achieve the same superb results as the three therapists in the original study. In other words, Grinder and Bandler seemed to have found a way of analysing excellence and transmitting it to other people.

This chapter sets out to provide a practical guide to the use of NLP under the following headings:

- self-management;
- the micro-skills of communication; and
- change skills.

For those who wish to explore the subject further, the books referred to in the text make interesting reading. At the end of the chapter I have listed training organizations that will help to turn the reader's know-how into usable skills.

THE PRINCIPLES OF NLP

NLP is, however, more than a set of skills. Its underlying principles provide an ethical framework.

The map is not the territory (Korzybski)

Whenever two people are involved, at least two versions of events will emerge. Any manager who has investigated a problem will know this. Ask your friendly local police officer and he or she will tell you how witnesses vary in their account of events. This is unavoidable. We perceive information through a series of filters. First, there are our neurological filters – the limits of our five senses. For example, close one of your eyes and hold one hand over it. As you look with your one eye you should see a two-dimensional world. What you probably see is a three-dimensional world that is only available to us because of binocular vision. Your brain makes the adjustment outside your consciousness (see Bateson, 1985).
  The culture into which we were born and the parents to whom we were born create powerful filters. Language itself is a filter. Is it 17 or 70 words Eskimos have to describe snow? In either case, Eskimos' discriminating sense of snow is enabled by their language. Finally, the culture within which we operate as a manager acts as a filter. White shirt and blue pin-stripe suits are outward signs of professionalism in some places; in others they are signs of a stuffy and uncreative establishment. Managers who imagine that theirs is the only true version of events are deluding themselves fundamentally. Yet it is this false view that is the root of many breakdowns in communication.

Communication is a systemic process

You reach agreement at the end of a meeting. You summarize in the time- *439* honoured way and you check that the people involved understand, agree and commit to specific actions. Does it happen as you expect? Only rarely, I suspect.

Sometimes communication is taught as if it were subject to Newton's laws of action and reaction. In a game of marbles, if you know the force with which you nip a marble, the coefficient of friction of the marble and the school playground's surface, the angle with which it hits the next marble, and so on, you can predict that the marble struck will end up in the gully. On the other hand, if I kick my dog, the law of action and reaction will not be useful in predicting where my dog will end up – probably her teeth will be somewhere in the vicinity of my ankle, if I am lucky.

People's response to a chairperson's expert closure to a meeting depends not only on the expert closure but also on other elements in the system. The relationship between them, influences in the wider system of the department and company, and their thoughts and feelings at the time of receiving the message, all influence their subsequent actions. This was put succinctly by Gregory Bateson (1972): 'The behaviour of the governor (leader) is determined ... by the behaviour of the other parts of the system, and indirectly by its own behaviour at a previous time.' Thus, each element in a system has influence; no one element has unilateral control.

According to Richard Bandler and John Grinder (1979): 'With just one *choice of action* you are a robot, with two choices you have a dilemma and with three choices you have the beginnings of freedom.' NLP is about offering more choice of thought and action. It is not about taking choice away. Even if people's actions seem negative, they are left with this choice. If they can find from within their own resources actions with more positive outcomes, then they are likely to take those choices.

There is a *positive intent* behind people's behaviour. If a colleague is doing something that annoys you, then look for the positive intent behind the behaviour. If you can find their positive intent and offer alternative ways of your colleague achieving it, then they may stop annoying you. That, of course, is after you have thought about how what you are doing in the system of communication is encouraging your colleague's behaviour in the first place.

Within this framework, NLP can be used for 'mild' management – the little things that mean a lot.

SELF-MANAGEMENT SKILLS

It is trite to say that change starts with yourself. You are, however, the person most in your own control. Creating change within yourself has an impact on the whole system. The specific skills we shall talk about are:

- *Outcome thinking* Using mental rehearsal to pre-condition successful behaviour.
- *Anchoring* Using positive experiences in your life as resources for today's challenges.

Outcome thinking

John Sculley states, in *Odyssey: Pepsi to Apple*, 'It wasn't the quality of their planning that got many big companies into trouble; it was the quality of their perspective' (Scully and Byrne, 1987). Management by objectives is less successful than it might be because written objectives remain an abstraction until they are translated into an imagined experience. It is this imagined experience that is called 'outcome thinking'.

The mnemonic PRINCE, represents the outcome thinking process.

Positive

Those of you with children will know that if you ask one of them to carry a cup of tea across the room and say, 'don't spill it', then the next thing you are likely to see is the cup wobbling on the saucer in the child's hand. Why? Because in order to think of not spilling it you have to think of spilling it. So often we express things we would like to change in the negative. We want to stop smoking, to lose weight, to stop leaving the desk cluttered, to stop dissent in the team, to arrest a decline in sales. It is not until you can say what you want instead, that you have a positive outcome that you can rehearse and achieve. After many failed attempts to stop smoking, I succeeded when I was able to imagine the fresh smell of curtains and clothes in our house, the positive comments of my children, a pleasant taste in my mouth on waking, and so on. In the same way, outcomes stated in the positive might be to achieve a specific weight, to have harmonious relationship in the team or to achieve a specific level of sales.

Rehearsal

Until people imagine the outcome, how can they know whether it is achievable, whether it feels right for them, and whether it is achievable within their present personal and external resources? The act of mental rehearsal preconditions successful behaviour. Ask Jack Nicklaus: 'First, I "see" the ball where I want it to finish, nice and white and sitting up high on the bright green grass. Then the scene quickly changes, and I "see" the ball going there: its path, trajectory, and shape, even its behaviour on landing. Then there's a sort of fade-out, and the next scene shows me making the sort of swing that will turn the previous images into reality.' Notice that he is not restricting himself to mental pictures, he is also feeling the swing.

The more you can engage the senses of sight, hearing, feeling (touch and emotion), taste and smell as you imagine achieving your outcome, the more likely it is that your mental rehearsal will be successful. Create the picture of what you want as if you are watching yourself on a screen. When the outcome seems satisfactory step into the picture and experience the feelings. If it does not feel right, then step out of the picture and change it until you can step into it and feel committed to its achievement. Continue this stepping in and out of the picture until you are satisfied with your creation. If you find visualization difficult, *441* then feel or hear what the outcome will be like. When you have the feelings you want, then see what it's like when you have those feelings.

In Bandler and Grinder's (1979) book *Frogs into Princes* they describe an outstanding project manager who looks, in his mind's eye, at the whole project, and only starts that project when the whole of it has been 'seen' through.

Initiated and maintained by you

So often we set objectives that are outside our control and blame ourselves when they are not achieved. It is important to know where the line is between our own and others' responsibility. If the objective involves others, than a shared vision will be important.

Next steps

In describing his transition from Pepsi to Apple, John Sculley shows an intuitive grasp of NLP principles and skills. He talks about back-to-the-future planning: 'Our planning is quite different and simple. We've separated preparation of our business plan (a moving twenty-four month outlook) from the process of long-term planning about Apple's future direction in the 1990s. For the latter we project ourselves out into the future and work back into the future in small increments of time.'

Say your outcome is achieved in two years' time, step into that future and imagine what it will be like. You are here in the future, now look back and find out how you got there. This brings planning to life allowing you to look back from a 'known' future. (Again, if you find it difficult to perform these visual gymnastics, feel what it is like in the future and then get in touch with the concrete steps you took to get 'here'.)

Conserves positive by-products

When you (and others) want to make a change but are frustrated in your attempts then it may be because there are hidden benefits in the present situation. One of my bosses ran a regular weekly management meeting. It was a bore. He dealt with issues that involved only one person at a time while the rest sat in silence. When, at last, we prevailed on the boss to hold monthly meetings and *ad hoc* meetings with people concerned, we found that communication between managers in the department deteriorated. Part of our boss's resistance to change was the unexpressed feeling that his weekly meetings had an unstated purpose. It was up to us who were proposing the change to tease out the hidden by-products and ensure that they were taken into account in the change.

Ecological

Consider the larger system – your department, your company, your family, society in general. Is your outcome worthwhile at each of these levels? If not, reconsider it and cycle back to the beginning of the mnemonic.

442

Anchoring

'Courage is not fearlessness. Courage is the willingness to move forward with your fear', as Phil Laut has stated.

Once you have defined the outcome, you need to mobilize resources to achieve it. The most important of these resources is yourself. It is a question of mobilizing the resources when and where you want them. Managers need to be in a resourceful state when they make an important presentation or meet with their boss to sell an idea, or face a supplier or colleague in a tricky negotiation, or need to switch mental state in order to deal sensitively with someone's personal issue. Here the concept of stimulus and response is useful. The smell of fresh-cut grass may take you back to a vivid childhood memory. The prospect of meetings with particular colleagues may either enliven you or enervate you. Your responses come automatically. They have been programmed in, as with Pavlov's dogs.

Stimulus and response can be used consciously to set up responses that you want for particular challenges. First, you think of a response that you want. It might be confidence for a presentation, or clarity and enthusiasm for selling an idea, or flexibility and focus for a negotiation, or relaxed attention and openness for counselling. The response is one that is appropriate to you and to the situation. Next you need to associate with the response a particular stimulus – the NLP term is 'anchor'. It must be an anchor you can reproduce exactly each time it is used. It can be a mental picture, a touch, a sound, or, indeed, a taste or smell. It might be any of the following:

- a favourite view in your mind's eye that gives you a pleasurable feeling of relaxation and wellbeing;
- breathing out as if blowing out a candle;
- a characteristic gesture, such as clasping hands, twiddling with a wedding ring; or
- saying the words to yourself, such as, 'relax, relax'.

The steps are as follows:

1. Imagine yourself in a setting in which you want a particular response. In that setting ask yourself what personal resources, such as confidence, you need to achieve your desired outcome.
2. Take each of the resources you want in turn. Recall a time when you had the resource that you want. The closer it is to the situation you are planning for, the better, but this is not crucial. You can take the resource from a non-work situation – an interest, a hobby, a social situation or a special event. Recall the time as if you were there. Remember what you saw, what you heard and what you felt.
3. When you reach the peak of the experience anchor it. Make a character-istic gesture, or blow air from your lungs, or say a particular word to yourself and see a particular picture in your mind's eye. Anchoring the resourceful *443*

state with touch, sound and vision makes it easier to reproduce the state when you want it.

4. Then take your attention on to something else. Look up and around at the room or get up and move.
5. Now move on to the next personal resource that would be useful to handle your challenge. (The first resource might have been confidence, the second might be alertness for instance.) Repeat the above steps, using the same anchor.
6. Before you make the presentation, walk into the negotiation or settle down to discuss a personal issue, use the anchor you have set up as a stimulus for the resourceful response you want.

This process will enable you to make best use of the knowledge and skill that you have (see Bandler and Grinder, 1979; and Bandler, 1985).

Just as you can use your mind to change the way you feel and behave, so you can use your body to change the way you think. When you feel under pressure of time at your desk, or from an irate customer or a critical colleague, you may sense a deterioration in your posture. Your head may drop, your shoulders droop and your chest slightly cave in. You look down and you feel down. Changing your posture can help to change your mental state. Being mentally stuck can be synonymous with being physically stuck. Move. Sit up, breathe deeply and move to a balanced position. Under fire from difficult questions, take a few steps, breathe deeply and assume a balanced posture before answering the question. Remember, NLP is about 'mild' management. It is not 'chest out, chin in, shoulders back', but movement to a softer, more relaxed posture.

THE MICRO-SKILLS OF COMMUNICATION

John Harvey-Jones (1988) likens 'mild' management to 'making a small movement near the centre of the see-saw which makes a much more obvious impact at the end'. NLP skills of communication are simple skills that potentially make a large difference and enable you to have:

- the *awareness* to know whether you are progressing towards your outcome; and if not,
- the *flexibility* to change your behaviour as required.

Awareness

John Grinder states: 'I take verbal reports to be rumours until they are confirmed by non-verbal behaviour.'

Non-verbal behaviour

How do people communicate with each other? Of course they use words, but
444 research shows clearly that the bulk of the information is transmitted non-

verbally: through the behaviours that accompany the words. Estimates suggest that non-verbal behaviour provides between 75 per cent and 95 per cent of the meaning. Gestures, postures, facial expressions, voice tone, tempo and volume – parts of our behaviour that are non-verbal that are often outside of our awareness – are what people unconsciously pay attention to in order to derive meaning from our words. It is as if the words provide the 'headline content' and the behaviours provide the 'context' within which to make sense of them. Apparently, Shakespearean actors need at least 17 different ways of saying 'no', varying from 'No' (means: 'yes, but I have to say "no" for the benefit of others') to 'No' (means: 'No, absolutely not!').

As professional communicators, it is the responsibility of managers to communicate effectively. This means paying attention to people's words and, as important, their behaviour (more important, if you believe the research). Awareness of non-verbal behaviour is not mind reading. You will get clues to people's thinking in their behaviour and this is a moment for you to ask questions to find out what is going on or to ask yourself a question and to watch the person's subsequent behaviour for the answer (see Figure 33.1). So, for professional communicators: 'The meaning of the communication is the response they get.'

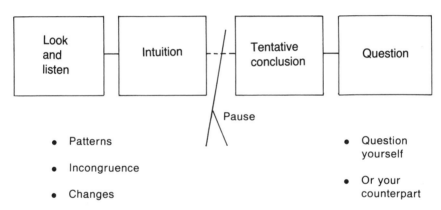

Figure 33.1   Awareness of non-verbal behaviour

Representational systems

A special contribution of NLP has been a model of the way in which we think. We experience the world through our senses – sight, hearing, feeling (touch and emotion), taste and smell: so, for example, when on a beach on holiday you experience the sight of the blue sky and the golden sand, the sounds of children playing, the rough feel of the sand under your feet and the sense of relaxed wellbeing, the salty taste remaining after your last swim and the fresh scent of ozone in the air. At a later time when recalling the holiday, some people will have a strong memory of the sights, others of the sounds and yet others will have a strongest sense of the feelings. Words interpret and describe these inner experiences. For example:

445

- A person who prefers to think in pictures might use a visual language style: 'I remember vividly the beautiful, blue sky and the golden sand.'
- A person with a preference for sounds might say: 'I recall the shrieks and high-pitched laughter of the children.'
- And a person with a preference for thinking in terms of feelings might say: 'I felt so relaxed, the sun was warm on my back as I lay on that lovely, soft sandy beach.'

The words people use are a description of their internal experience. And the words they use give a clue to this internal experience. (The way in which they represent experience, hence 'representational systems').

Try this exercise as a test of your preferred representational system:

1. Write out a couple of sentences of a passage you would like to say or write with greater impact.
2. Now write the passage again, using words that express the visual sense (exclude words that express auditory (sound) and feeling sense).
3. Then write the passage again using words that express feelings.
4. Finally, write the passage again using words that express the auditory sense.

The sense you found easiest to express in words is a rough indication of your preferred representational system. The one you found most difficult is the sense of which you are likely to be least conscious. Our research shows that the preferred representational system of the majority of business people in the United Kingdom is visual, backed up by the feeling sense. Least preferred is the auditory sense. All representations are available to all of us but we have a preference for certain of them.

In order to gain understanding, it helps to identify and to communicate in the other person's preferred representation. With a group, use a variety of representational system, both in your words and in the experiences you provide.

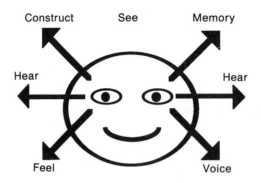

Figure 33.2 Accessing cues

Eye movement is another clue to the way in which people are thinking. Figure 33.2 illustrates this. To think visually, people tend to look up; to their left to recall and to their right to construct or create a picture. When they think in terms of feelings they look down and to their right. In talking to themselves they look down and to their left. When thinking of sounds (remembering a tune, for instance, or making up a tune) they look level and to their left or right. This is true of most people who are naturally right-handed. People who are naturally left-handed tend to look to the right to recall and to the left to construct. This, of course, is a generalization. And like all generalizations, it is a lie. (As is that sentence.) Each person has to be treated as being unique, so that you find out for the individual what way he or she looks to access information.

What does this mean for the practising manager? First, when people are moving their eyes when you are in discussion with them, it is a sign that they are thinking and it is time to be quiet to allow them to do so. Secondly, looking people in the eye continuously may prevent them from thinking well, so look away occasionally. You will need to, anyway, to think yourself. Thirdly, it gives you an indication of how they are thinking. So, if a person is expressing a lack of understanding and looking up to the right, then it tells you to show the person by demonstration, with pictures, video and diagrams. If they look down and to the right, then explain by using feeling words. Help them to come to grips with the subject until they are comfortable with it. Provide time for hands-on experience.

The importance of this subject stretches beyond communication to the thinking that guides our behaviour. Thinking can be thought of as a manipulation of our internal senses. The strategies we use in this manipulation make the difference between effective and less effective performance.

Flexibility

Rapport

Have you ever been in a situation in which your helpful suggestions are met by an implacable resistance? It is like stirring syrup with a whisk. Perhaps in a problem-solving interview with a colleague you suggest rational solutions to a problem and are met with the deadly, 'Yes, but ...'. There is apparent agreement, but you know that the 'Yes, but ...' makes it likely that your colleague will ignore your ideas. In selling an idea, a product or service you fall at the first hurdle if your prospective buyer will not give you a fair hearing. He or she may be polite, but you know you are on to a loser from the start. These responses are a consequence of a lack of rapport. Rapport is the lubricant of good communication. (Or, to save mixing metaphors, it is the warmth that makes the syrup flow.)

But what is rapport? If you look at people in places like bars or airport lobbies you can probably tell which groups are friends and which are not. If you observe the patterns of behaviour of the different groupings you may notice a consistent difference between the groups who are 'friends' and the groups who are 'not friends'. Typically, the 'friends' – those groups in good rapport – will be engaged in something resembling a dance of mutual responsiveness. The movements of *447* one person will be 'echoed' or 'mirrored' by another or others in the group. For example, one person leans forward; the person they are talking to may also lean forward or shift posture slightly in that direction. This naturally occurring process is termed 'matching' and is exhibited intuitively by all good communicators as a means of gaining rapport at an unconscious level.

There are many ways in which you can gain and maintain rapport. Some are listed below. All you need is willingness to change the way you habitually do things.

Whole body matching   Take on the general posture of your counterpart, move as he or she moves. Relax: follow your partner gently. There is no need to follow all of his or her shifts of posture at exactly the time he or she does. Just follow easily and naturally.

Half-body matching   When you do have a desk between you and your partner, then use half-body matching. This is typical of sales situations and offices where you do not have control of seating arrangements. When you control seating arrangements, perhaps get out from behind your desk when working with people. This is particularly important in helping situations like counselling, coaching and joint problem-solving when rapport is vital to achieve a successful outcome.

Head/shoulders matching   Match the angle between your partner's head and shoulders. It gives you a new angle to look at the world and an insight into the view of your partner.

Facial expressions matching   Match frowns, lifting eyebrows, smiles, narrowing eyes and so on.

Gestures matching   If your partner uses his or her hand to talk, then use yours. It will intrude if you wave your hands around as he/she talks. (Cross-over matching as described below is used.) But when you talk, then use similar gestures.

Voice-quality matching   Our voice quality is usually out of conscious awareness. Each of us seems to think that his or her own speech rate is natural. I can remember being unable to influence a marketing director, not for the want of trying. He was, and still is, an energetic and decisive man. He talks fast and fires off ideas. I could not get a word in edgeways. That is, I could not until I increased the tempo of my speech and started to respond quickly to his ideas and to throw in my own. For the first time I was able to get a word in edgeways. He listened and I felt satisfied that our meeting had been of value to both of us. Matching voice quality comes into its own on the phone. Do not mimic people's accent – that they will notice – just alter your tempo and volume to match the person at the other end of the line.

448 *Breathing matching*   A profound and subtle way of gaining rapport at an

unconscious level is to match breathing. It really does put you in touch with another person. (And it is said to be a great way of making contact with the opposite sex at parties.) The rate, depth and pace at which people breathe is an indicator of their inner state and a change in breathing pattern is a sign of a change in the state of a person's mind. It is not so easy to spot if your partner is wearing loose clothing or if someone's breathing is shallow. You can usually detect it, however, if you watch a fold of clothing, or the tops of your partner's shoulders, or simply de-focus on your partner's torso. If you look in a relaxed way until you match it, you will be able to keep track with your peripheral vision. Indeed, movement is detected with peripheral vision, so it helps to use the facilities deliberately. Not only that, staring at chests all day may earn you a dubious reputation.

Cross-over matching Sometimes it is unpleasant or potentially embarrassing to match. If you are faced with your boss racing up and down in his office, then it may not go down well for you to pace up and down with him – even if there is space. Or you may be working with someone who is depressed or very agitated. Matching breathing with them may be quite uncomfortable. And obviously, it would not be very healthy to match breathing with an asthmatic person. The answer here is to cross-over match. Choose a particular behaviour and match it with a different aspect of your behaviour. For instance, tap your foot in time with your boss's paces across the office floor. In a counselling situation, match the rise and fall of your voice to the rate of the counsellee's breathing. A story – perhaps apocryphal – serves both as illustration and warning. Richard Bandler interviewed a counsellor who was reputed to be particularly good at putting her clients quickly at ease. Without being aware of it she matched Bandler's behaviour closely. Bandler gradually shifted forward on his chair. Bandler stopped at the edge of the seat, the counsellor fell off.

Matching and leading

Rapport, then, is a mutual responsiveness in behaviour. But how do you know when you have rapport? Assuming that matching is both a way of gaining rapport and its outcome, then the way to test for rapport is to change your behaviour such that you mismatch your partner. If your partner follows your lead, then you have established rapport – there is a bridge between you; if your partner ignores your lead, then you simple re-match and try a lead at some later time. Wait at least 60 seconds after you lead for your partner to follow. When that happens, the groundwork has been laid for open communication. As the relationship develops, it will not be clear who is leading and who is following. It will be a dance whose outcome is mutual understanding.

Leading, therefore, is not only a test for rapport, it is also an aid to communication. Matching and leading is also an elegant way of helping people to consider new choices. With non-verbal rapport you have the tools to create the conditions for open, two-way communication, provided you have the flexibility to use them.

Matching language styles

As well as matching non-verbal behaviour you can match the language people use. There are four steps to using language styles to gain rapport:

1. Ask neutral questions so that the words you use do not refer to any particular sense. For instance: 'How did you decide on your present policy?'
2. Listen to the language styles used in reply. A visual manager: 'I looked around a lot of other companies in the group and saw their managers a few times. It took a few months but in the end I saw enough to make my decision.' An auditory manager: 'I sounded out colleagues of mine in similar positions in other companies and spoke to experienced business consultants. At the end of two months I'd heard enough to make a decision.' A kinesthetic manager: 'I got a feel for the impact of policies offered from friends in other companies. In the end I was comfortable about my decision.'
3. Use words from the same sense in reply. For instance: 'I see. What specifically are you looking for in the policy?', or 'Sounds clear. What sort of things do you like to hear about policy before you decide?' or 'What fits. What do you need to know before you can feel confident that a policy will work?'
4. If appropriate, lead the manager from one sense into another. For instance, if you want a manager who uses kinesthetic words to picture the future, you might say: 'I understand how you feel about the problem. If you were satisfied that we had resolved the problem, how would that look to you?'

Matching and leading is a universal concept that applies to groups as well as to individuals, to values as much as to behaviour.

Self-projection

'It's not what you do, it's the way that you do it. That's what gets results.' The 'way that you do it' is associated with your non-verbal behaviour. Before making a presentation, use a resource anchor to create the sort of internal state that will allow you to put your subject over as best you can. Then make sure you choreograph the presentation. How will you stand, how will you use posture and gesture to support your words, how will you use facial expression to create an atmosphere? How will you vary your voice tone, tempo and volume to create interest? Make your presentation to friends and get them to give you feedback on your voice quality and body language. Their feedback will be subjective; but it will allow your friends to tell you 'what your best friends wouldn't tell you'. Knowing your subject is vital but, in my experience, more proposals have been lost through poor presentation than have through lack of knowledge of the subject.

Precision questions

'When *I* use a word', Humpty Dumpty said in a rather scornful tone, 'it means exactly what I choose it to mean – neither more nor less.' (Lewis Carroll, *Alice Through the Looking Glass*)

Managers get their information from people, so questioning is a critically important skill. Take this statement for example: 'There's no way we are going to make progress. Top management must come up with an agreed strategy. We can't wait much longer!' What questions would you ask? Most people ask questions to fill in the gaps in their own understanding. This approach makes the assumption that the understanding they have is accurate and the understanding they gain after questioning is sufficient. NLP's unique contribution is that the questions asked are based purely on the language patterns used by the speaker. Their purpose is to uncover the deep structure of people's thinking revealed by the surface structure of their words (see Figure 33.3).

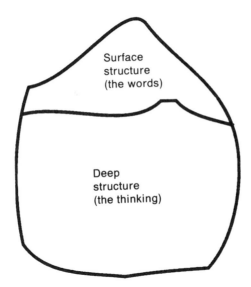

Figure 33.3   Thinking and surface structure of words

The questions offer the possibility of a shared understanding of a person's thinking and movement beyond limits within a person's thinking. The questions listed here are drawn from the meta model, NLP's first contribution to therapy. this shortened version is known as the precision model.

Gathering information

Nouns and verbs (e.g. productivity, communication, intimidates, harasses, and so on)

ask: 'who/what/which/how . . . specifically?'

Comparators (e.g. more, less, better, worse)

> ask: '... then what?' (for basis);
> or: 'what is the right amount?' (for outcome)

Expanding limits

Universals (e.g. every, each, all, etc., or none, never)

> ask: 'is there any exception?'
> or: interrogative emphasis on universal.

Necessities (e.g. must, need)

> ask: 'What makes ... necessary?' (for reason);
> or: 'What would happen if ... not?' (did not happen).

Limitations (e.g. can't, impossible, etc.)

> ask: 'What prevents ... ?' (for reason);
> or: 'What if ... ?' (did happen).

Changing meaning

Mind reading (e.g. 'they think, people know, he feels')

> ask: 'How do you know they think ... ?' (for specifics);
> or: 'What experience do you have that ... ?'

Cause/effect (e.g. they make me (us))

> ask: 'How, specifically, do they make you do that?'

To illustrate the idea, let us apply the model to a few of the words in this passage, 'There's no way we are going to make progress. Top management must come up with an agreed strategy. We can't wait much longer!', as follows:

• no way	No way?
• (Universal)	Has there ever been a time in which we have progressed without knowing the business strategy?
• we ((Pro)noun)	Who is we?
• make (Verb)	How do we want to make progress?
• must (Necessity)	What will happen if we do not have a strategy?
• can't (Limitation)	What stops us waiting longer?
	What would happen if we did wait longer?
• longer (Comparator)	How much longer can we wait?

452   The first question to ask yourself is, 'Do I need to know this information or do I

need to not-know?' There is no benefit in gathering more detail than we can hope to use or understand. The questions are direct and sometimes un-grammatical. To avoid them sounding like the 'third degree' it is important to:

- gain rapport before asking questions;
- use polite voice tones and emphasis; and
- soften the questions with such phrases as 'I'm curious as to which ... specifically? or 'I wonder how specifically you're thinking about ... ?'

The questions can be asked with finesse by matching the speaker's preferred representational system. For example, the manager says, 'I'd need to look at some detailed performance information before deciding'; we know that the information gap is in the visual channel, so we could ask: 'I'm curious as to which performance information specifically you'd like to see?'

Change skills: first and second order change

Watzlawick *et al.* (1974) stated: 'it follows that there are two different forms of change: one that occurs within a given system which itself remains unchanged (first order change), and one whose occurrence changes the system itself (second order change).'

An organization that introduces a new information system to improve its efficiency is undergoing first order change (it may involve the systems depart-ment in second order change), whereas an organization which shifts its market focus, decentralizes its operation into profit centres and delegates decision-making power to operating units is undergoing second order change. In a sense, first order change is change within the established rules, whereas second order change operates by changing the rules themselves. It is important to distinguish first and second order change. To enable second order change thinking 'outside the box' is needed. Such thinking will avoid resistance.

Reframing

Richard Bach, in *Illusions*, wrote: 'What the caterpillar calls the end of the world, the master calls a butterfly.'

Reframing is a way of looking at something in a new way which often leads to new feelings and new choices of action. It enables people to step out of an old framework into a new one. Techniques like reframing are like the Eastern martial arts, where an opponent's force is utilized rather than opposed – the 'mild' management of John Harvey-Jones.

Sometimes our thinking becomes fixed because we view a situation within a particular frame or class. A glass tumbler can be seen to be a member of a class of glass objects, or a class of drinking vessels, or fish bowls, or pastry cutters, and so on. Once we label an object as a member of a particular class, it is extremely difficult to see it as belonging also to another class. In effect, this class membership becomes reality. Reframing enables us to see alternative class *453* memberships. Once seen, we cannot easily go back to the trap of a former fixed view of reality.

If I pour water into the glass to occupy 50 per cent of its volume, some people would believe that the glass is half-empty, whilst others would equally strongly believe that the glass is half-full. These represent profoundly different attitudes. You can reframe then by changing either the context or meaning of a particular statement, behaviour or event.

Changing the context (in what other context might it be of value or acceptable?)

For instance, a senior airline stewardess who was particularly good at handling difficult passengers often used reframing. Soon after the smoking of cigars had been banned on passenger airliners she had to deal with an Arab passenger who smoked a cigar and refused to stop. Several of the stewards and steward-esses on board had tried and failed to persuade the passenger to stop and the smoke was beginning to annoy other passengers. Her approach was to explain to him that they were flying into Saudi Arabia and that she was going to go into the country to stay overnight. She told him that whilst she was in there she would obey the laws and religious customs of that country and although she enjoyed a drink she would abstain from drinking alcohol until she left the country again. In this way, she was able to persuade the passenger to stop smoking.

Changing the meaning (what else might it mean?)

A consultant who complained that his client was not paying him for the extra time that he had put in provides an example. The conversation with him went something like this: 'So, you have been working for X Ltd for the past year and have a contract with them for 100 days' work which they have paid you for, and yet the work they are asking you to do requires at least 20 more days to enable you to get it done properly and you have put in these 20 days? You believe that your core manager is aware that you are putting in extra time and you are aggrieved that he has not offered to pay for your extra time without being prompted. It is as if he doesn't value your services, and yet *your* behaviour is telling him that you value your services as being worthless. You put in the extra time that is needed and you neither remind your client that you have done this – nor invoice him. In effect you are saying to him that these services of yours are worth nothing.' The consultant strongly believed that his services were of value and that the project would have failed without his extra time. Having been offered this alternative frame to view his behaviour, he spoke to his core manager and put in an invoice.

Metaphors

Gregory Bateson writes: 'There's a story which I have used before and shall use again: a man wanted to know about mind, not in nature, but in his private large computer. He said, "Do you compute that you will ever think like a human being?" The machine then set to work to analyse its own computational habits. Finally, the machine printed its answer on a piece of paper, as such machines do. The man ran to get the answer and found, neatly typed, the words: "That reminds me of a story". A story is a little knot or complex of that species of connectedness which we call relevance. Surely the computer was right.'

Like reframing, the use of metaphors offers people ways of seeing new points of view that might not be possible by more direct efforts, such as explaining, requesting, suggesting, advising or instructing. Metaphors seem to work by appealing to the unconscious mind. They help people to shift their limiting beliefs about themselves and make desired changes of behaviour. Suggestions that a person might resist consciously if offered directly are considered and, if in line with a person's desired outcomes, are acted upon through an unconscious route.

A metaphor is defined as a figure of speech that uses a 'description that is not literally applicable' (New Oxford Dictionary). In helping people to find new choices in difficult or problematical situations the story or metaphor needs to have three parts:

- the present situation – a beginning;
- the resources the person would find useful in moving from the present situation – a middle; and
- the desired outcome – an end.

The kind of stories that are most useful are those that have a specific and clear message which is to the point of the discussion at hand and to the outcome. The further removed they are from the immediate content of the discussion, the more successful they are likely to be, since they are not likely to elicit resistance. If they are distant from the subject but related to the person's interest, then they are likely to be very effective. Here is an example.

The most important division of a large international company had been unable to persuade its salespeople of the benefits of team selling. Customers were beginning to centralize the buying decision and to involve not only the buyer but also senior managers affected by the purchasing decision, such as systems managers, financial managers and operational managers. To get the message across the company's sales director used a metaphor which was successful in creating a small change in behaviour that overcame the inertia and lead eventually to a change to team selling. He said: 'When you go walking in the foothills, even in bad weather, you can safely go on a trek by yourself providing you wrap up warmly, wear a good pair of boots, take emergency supplies and let somebody know when you are due back, so that they can take the appropriate action if you are overdue. Were you to carry on like this to climb a mountain you would soon find, to your cost, that your own resources are insufficient to get you safely to the top and back. You need equipment and clothing to cope with every eventuality. You need a base camp with whom you are in regular contact so that you are aware of changing conditions of weather, on the mountain. You need to work in a group, securely roped together, with anchor points on the mountain. *455*

Each person in the team has a different specialization and strength and can be called upon to contribute in different ways. There will be a leader, there will be people who cook, there will be people who man the base-camp as well as the two or three climbers who, in the end, scale the peak. Ladies and gentlemen, in our marketplace we are scaling mountains.'

Use metaphors to aid change, to open up new choices for people and to show different points of view to people who may be finding it difficult to see any other viewpoint than their own.

CONCLUSION

The 'mild' management skills of NLP enable people to:

- Use their imagination to create compelling outcomes.
- Mobilize their strengths in achieving those outcomes by using the anchoring technique, for instance.
- Be aware of people's responses so that they know if they are moving towards their outcomes.
- Adapt so that they can gain rapport with a variety of people, share outcomes and create the changes they want.

If what you are doing is not working, do something different!

FURTHER READING[1]

Bandler, Richard (1985), *Using Your Brain – For A Change** Utah: Real People Press.

Bandler, Richard and John Grinder (1979), *Frogs into Princes**, Utah: Real People Press.

Bandler, Richard and John Grinder (1982), *Reframing*, Utah: Real People Press.

Bandler, Richard and John Grinder (1976), *The Structure of Magic*, pts 1 and 2, California: Science and Behaviour Books.

Bateson, Gregory (1985), *Mind and Nature*, London: Fontana.

Bateson, Gregory (1972), *Steps To An Ecology of Mind*, Ballantine Books.

DeLozier, Judith and John Grinder (1987), *Turtles All The Way Down*, California: Grinder DeLozier & Associates.

Dilts, Robert (1990), *Changing Belief Systems with NLP*, California: Meta Publications.

Harvey-Jones, John (1988), *Making It Happen*, London: Fontana.

Laborde, Genie (1983), *Influencing With Integrity*, California: Syntony.

Pile, Stephen (1989), *Visionary Leadership*, an Action Research Project presented to Pepperdine University, California.

Robbins, Anthony (1986), *Unlimited Power**, New York: Fawcett Columbine.

[1]Books marked * in this list will be of particular interest to readers new to NLP.

Sculley, John and John A. Byrne (1987), *Odyssey: Pepsi to Apple*, London: Collins.
Seymour, John and Joseph O'Connor (1990), *Introducing Neuro-Linguistic Programming**, Crimble.
Watzlawick, Weakland and Fisch (1974), *Change*, New York: Norton.

Training organizations

The following organizations provide practitioner and personal development training:

International Teaching Seminars, 1 Mulgrave Road, London NW10 1BS

PACE Personal Development, 86 South Hill Park, London NW3 2SN

Sensory Systems, 28 Bellwood Street, Shorelands, Glasgow G41 3ES

The NLP Training Programme, 22 Upper Tooting Park, London SW17 7SR

The following organization focuses primarily on business training:

PACE, 54 Queens Street, Henley-on-Thames, Oxfordshire RG9 1AP

Part Five

MANAGEMENT TRAINING AND DEVELOPMENT

34 Effectiveness in management development

Alan Mumford

This chapter presents the view that effective management development (MD) is based first on awareness of effective managerial behaviour. Secondly, it proposes that awareness of effective learning processes must also be a prime constituent. Thirdly, it suggests that development is most likely to arise from real work rather than from abstract knowledge or even simulations of real work.

In the mid-1980s I was still defining management development as 'an attempt to improve managerial effectiveness through a planned and deliberate learning process'. I later came to the view that a great deal of management development is not 'planned and deliberate', and probably never can be. In two books (1988, 1989) I have developed and illustrated the idea that management development must be considered to include *informal* and *accidental* processes, as well as those defined as planned and deliberate. Of course, most personnel directors and management development advisers reading this *Handbook* have operated to a planned and deliberate definition, and advised formal planned and deliberate processes which they have understood to be, uniquely, 'management development'. While in this chapter I shall be giving much more emphasis to formal processes of management development, the additional material I have given on effective learning processes particularly brings out the point that a great deal of the development of managers is brought about by activities which have not been influenced at all by planned and deliberate interventions in the traditional sense.

The question of our definition of management development and of the areas in which we as advisers choose to intervene, is of course vital in considering issues of effectiveness: however effective our intervention may be on formal processes, if (as has largely been the case) we do not intervene in those informal accidental day-by-day activities through which managers learn, their effectiveness is both reduced and partial. Reduced because we may succumb to the temptation of dealing only with those managerial issues which we can *under-* 461 *stand* and *influence*; partial because we are acting only on a small and often *highly untypical* part of the manager's life – a big decision about a job move, or the occasion of attendance on a course. So part of the case made in this chapter revolves around the idea that we must embrace a wider vision of what we understand 'management development' to be, in order to expand our contribution to the manager's learning and development capacity. That wider vision is expressed in the following definition of management development: an attempt to improve managerial effectiveness through a learning process.

THE THREEFOLD NATURE OF EFFECTIVENESS IN MANAGEMENT DEVELOPMENT

Effectiveness in management development is best achieved when we bring together three different aspects of effectiveness:

1. A contingent definition of effective *managerial behaviour.*
2. A developmental process which emphasizes *activities* in which managers are required to be effective, rather than emphasizing the *knowledge* necessary for action.
3. The identification of learning processes which are effective for the *individual or group*, rather than economical and convenient for tutors or trainers.

It should be noted that in 'the effectiveness triangle' shown in Figure 34.1, the triangle is *equilateral*: this means that all three aspects are equally important. Moreover, the particular presentation offered in Figure 34.1, which could be interpreted as showing two contributors to 'effective managerial behaviour', is not the only way of representing the triangle. In some situations, the triangle could be moved round so that effectiveness was seen as depending on a triangle resting on a single point – effective learning processes. As presented in Figure 34.1, the triangle gives emphasis to the desired end conclusion – effective managerial behaviour.

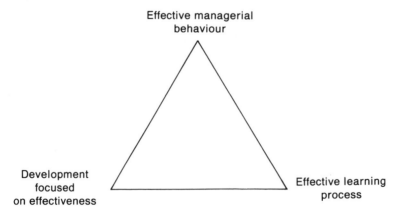

462   Figure 34.1   Effectiveness triangle in management development

EFFECTIVE MANAGERIAL BEHAVIOUR

It is, of course, absolutely fundamental to recognize that the prime purpose of management development is effective managerial behaviour; it is not just knowledge, or attitudes, although these clearly can often be significant contributors to effective behaviour. As anyone with experience of management knows, there are managers who have been extremely knowledgeable but who have not been effective, and managers with appropriate attitudes who also have not been effective. An 'effective manager' is one who does the right things in the right way – and it is the emphasis on 'doing' which is the key requirement of a manager, as distinct from a researcher, writer or academic. Unless we also recognize the necessary features of what effective managers *do* and what proportions of emphasis are appropriate in different situations, then the purposes of management development will be as badly aligned as they will be if we give too much emphasis to issues of knowledge and attitude.

For many years the formal process of MD followed what might be called the 'classical view' of the nature of management. A familiar version of this could be summarized under five heads:

1. Forecast/plan.
2. Organize.
3. Motivate.
4. Coordinate.
5. Control.

These terms, and the concepts and misunderstandings underpinning them, still survive in some formal courses. Rosemary Stewart (1976), Henry Mintzberg (1980) and John Kotter (1982) have provided research which shows that the basis of these concepts is unscientific. All three authors have also argued strongly that these inappropriate statements have led to structures for developing managers which have been unrealistic, and therefore unhelpful. Since each has then proceeded to his or her own statement of key managerial activities, it might be argued that their demolition of one list of managerial tasks and its replacement by another is simply due to differing perceptions and personal preferences when describing those managerial activities.

In fact, for management development purposes an even more significant common theme is that any generalized statement about managerial activities, including their own, is likely to be at least partially (and possibly substantially) incorrect for any particular manager or group of managers. They found substantial variations in required managerial behaviour in different organizations; the managerial activities in which any individual had to be effective were seen to depend on the specific kind of function and job, or the manager's interpretation of that job or role, and others' interpretation of the manager's role and responsibilities within that job. The main features of their analyses are conveniently spelled out in Mumford (1988).

It still seems to be the case that these discoveries have not had the impact on *463* management development processes that they ought to have done; the more intellectual courses probably include such analyses as important and thought-provoking contributions to the debate about what managers do. The consequences of their discoveries do not, however, seem generally to have been used to develop the course itself. Take as an example the importance given by Kotter and Mintzberg to the way in which *networks*, and their *effective use*, can contribute to effective managerial performance. Many courses will include sessions about interpersonal relationships; how many include sessions on the effective use of networks? Even more important, as we shall see in the next section, how many include practical work on the effective use of networks?

While the generation of more appropriate generalizations, and their incorporation into appropriate management training, seems not to have been fully carried through, some improvement does seem to have been made in producing more organization-specific training. It is still unfortunately true that in many (probably most) organizations, needs analysis is relatively superficial and leads to the facile adoption of training courses whose content differs remarkably little from one organization to another. There have been two problems in adopting a more rigorously analytical approach. Even where the professional management development adviser knows what he ought to do, there can be considerable obstacles in terms of actually engaging line managers in the analytical process. The definition, and interpretation, of what is meant by 'effective behaviour' takes time and energy, which managers on the whole would rather give to some other activity. This is most obviously true for a demanding process such as the repertory grid; although well used by some organizations, it has not been adopted as an appropriate approach by most of them.

The alternative approach receiving most attention in recent years has been that of management competences. Originating with the work of Boyatzis (1982) and being more widely aimed through the revived national management development debate in the United Kingdom in the late 1980s, this is an approach found helpful by a large number of organizations. It has the advantage of not requiring managers to start totally from scratch, as with the repertory grid; it is possible to start with the list produced by Boyatzis, or (in the UK) the material produced by the Management Charter Initiative. A debate about the appropriateness – or, as many would see it the inappropriateness – of a national list of competences may produce two not wholly intentional consequences. The first is to make organizations think specifically about what managers in those organizations need *to be able to do*, and the extent to which a nationally agreed list is appropriate. The second is to focus attention on the actual *content* of the competences, which has sometimes appeared to be a rather strange conglomerate of skills, attitudes and end results.

Although there has been this shift in at least some organizations towards what managers need to be able to do, the shift has in many not gone far enough, if it has even started. It is slightly surprising to see surviving into the 1990s one cause more understandable in the 1960s and 1970s – an overemphasis on developing managers for the future instead of working on issues of *current requirements*. While organizations have certainly helped to sustain this emphasis, the argument applies with even greater strength to many training and educational institutions offering taught experiences outside the organization. The identification of the nature of effectiveness in management has scarcely influenced the design of their programmes – as distinct from making a contribution to parts of the syllabus. The traditional business schools, all of whom now offer in-house programmes, have not on the whole shifted themselves substantially towards issues of effectiveness. They have stayed in the areas which they understand – those of knowledge, particularly *conceptual or theoretical knowledge*. With few exceptions, their in-company programmes have largely mirrored such 'open' programmes where there has been an inevitability about the generalized views of management processes on offer. Although there has been some shift to the design of specific material for particular companies, it has been relatively cosmetic, and again one looks in vain in many programmes for sessions designed to help managers to define and improve their own *effectiveness criteria* rather than sessions designed to convey only generalized management knowledge.

If we look, as we should, on the traditional business schools as the intellectual leaders in defining effective managerial behaviour, we see them largely still locked in the confusion between efficiency and effectiveness described by Peter Drucker in 1974: 'Efficiency is concerned with doing things right. Effectiveness is doing the right things.'

DEVELOPMENT PROCESSES EMPHASIZING EFFECTIVENESS

Just as too much management development has been based on an inappropriate view of what managers need to be able to do in their specific organizations (an intellectual failure), so there has also been a complementary failure of a different kind. Management development processes have too often been detached from the reality of the *perception and understanding of managers themselves*. With rare exceptions managers are not concerned about the knowledge possessed by a boss, colleagues or subordinates; their characteristic judgement on a manager's effetiveness is whether or not he or she can get things done. The fact that they are not aware of, and tend to be impatient about, the knowledge and skills required to enable a manager to get things done is not, of course, in itself an argument for not providing these things. It is a practical and psychological argument from two sides of the same coin – for starting from the reality of *where managers are*, rather than imposing on them our views about what they need.

Since effectiveness is defined clearly by managers in terms of the results actually secured, and not by the knowledge someone possesses, it would seem sensible to concentrate in our processes on helping managers to learn from *actions undertaken*, rather than providing them with conceptual statements of what managers have done (or might have done). Instead of giving emphasis to the provision of knowledge and asking managers to interpret and use that knowledge in subsequent action, it would be both more appropriate and more likely to be successful if we gave attention to issues of *action*, and only secondary attention to issues of the required *knowledge*: knowledge and the capacity to *465* analyse and produce solutions to problems are necessary but insufficient contributors to effective action. Primary attention to managerial skills may similarly be misplaced, although not inappropriate: the first stage of attention should be on a *desired managerial result* rather than the skills required for managerial activities.

In the United Kingdom, of course, the original definition of the benefits to be derived from working through real past experiences was provided by Reg Revans (1982) and then by John Morris.[1] My own research follows their pioneering statements by putting forward views about the kind of development experiences it is possible to identify, and to use effectively (Mumford, 1988; 1989).

It may be inevitable that good ideas are sometimes misunderstood and later watered down. The original work of Revans and Morris has frequently been misinterpreted simply as being about the use of a defined project by an individual, or the creation of a group of managers discussing their own projects; so, increasingly, management training and education courses have included projects as part of the syllabus, and in such cases projects have been yet another interesting variant within a set menu. Virtuous though this may be in programmes otherwise suffering from a surfeit of conceptual and analytical exercises, it is not an adequate representation of what is meant by using real-life experience.

Similarly, the view that managers ought to work on some kind of direct problem-solving, presented as a simulation of effectiveness issues in management, is a misunderstanding of what is desirable and possible. Whatever the arguments for introducing bridge-building with lego bricks, or outdoor experiences requiring managers to bridge chasms and climb cliffs, they are stronger as arguments directed to providing variety in learning activity than they are to using real work issues for development.

Courses which give primary attention to managerial skills such as interviewing, negotiation or interpersonal relationships, or to skills involved in dealing with information technology, can be significant contributors to the improvement of managerial performance. This will, again, be more likely to be true if such courses are built on a proper analysis by the organization – and preferably by the managers themselves – of what they have to do, rather than on someone else's judgement that all managers need to be good at some given list of skills.

Four cases are now given, illustrating the kind of shift of emphasis in which I have been involved, and where I find other organizations working with what I believe to be an inappropriate idea of what can be achieved.

Case 1

The final stages of a two-week programme were geared to the participants reviewing the corporate strategy of the group for which they worked. The intention of the sessions, which included a presentation to the chief executive, was that participants should be more familiar with the reasons for the corporate strategy, instead of just criticizing it from their own level in the business. In later programmes we made a significant change, since it seemed to us less relevant that participants should know the corporate strategy than that they should be encouraged to *take action on strategic issues affecting their own business*. They were instead asked to make proposals on a significant business problem currently affecting most of them: one example was the nature of, and possible reactions to, competition from Japanese manufacturers. While they could not do anything about corporate strategy – except perhaps understand it better – they could do something in their own companies about the Japanese 'threat'.

Case 2

A company which had revised its sales objectives and organization structure had some concern that the managers involved might not have the skills necessary to achieve the changed objectives. As a result of analysis with them it became clear that although probably a number of them were lacking in some skills, the larger problem was that, although apparently committed to the revised objectives, they had not fully set up the action necessary to *implement* them. The prime effectiveness was not therefore the skills of sales management, but the identification of specific actions to implement the broad objectives agreed.

Case 3

A company which had changed the composition and structure of its marketing function found that a number of those involved would be unable to produce what was required because they were not fully equipped with marketing skills. In the course of discussion with them the emphasis was shifted from the *acquisition* to the *implementation* of skills. An in-house marketing programme was devised which, in addition to giving managers the necessary tools, took them through to the identification of specific marketing projects which needed to be undertaken. The programme was designed to meet general marketing skill requirements in the organization, the specific requirements of the projects which had to be undertaken, and the completion of real work to meet the needs of the business.

Case 4

MBA progammes normally provide participants with a better understanding of the various functional areas of management such as marketing, finance and production. The expectation is that managers who have acquired this knowledge may be able to manage these functions better, or may through a better understanding have an improved relationship with other departments. IMC's MBA programme starts at the other end of the process, by requiring our associates to analyse the nature of *relationships between their own function and others in the business*, and to make proposals for improvement. While we believe that it may be important for most managers to 'understand finance better', we see it as at least as important that they should be helped to take specific actions relevant to their own needs in dealing with other functions.

Some of the central principles of action learning have been misunderstood and *467* misapplied (see Mumford, 1991). Another problem has been that the simplistic generalization that 'all managers should learn through doing a project' has too often been expressed entirely in terms of *doing* the project, and very little in terms of *learning from it*: learning processes concerned with effectiveness must always deal with the reality of the manager's job, and always involve him or her in action on it. A manager will, however, not learn enough simply by taking action, and it is clear from most of the literature on action learning that this is not sufficiently understood, and certainly is given too low a priority. The emphasis has been on projects and action to the exclusion of any serious discussion of the learning process while people are *undertaking the project.*

One other opportunity for development processes related to concern for effectiveness is now beginning to emerge. Managers have always expressed themselves in the cliché that: 'I have learned from experience'; it is often clear in fact that their learning has been partial, inefficient and ineffective – though that may not be always clear to them. One of the reasons is that learning from experience at work is very rarely designed, and even more rarely discussed; while formal management development processes will, for example, highlight the relevance of a particular job move from one function to another, from one country to another, or from one product to another, very little will have been done to make sure that effective learning occurs *within those experiences.*

We encounter now the essential paradox of management development which is that managers claim to learn from experience; they talk about the jobs they have done, the projects they have completed, the bosses they have worked for and even about the courses they have attended (see Mumford, 1988). Yet management development – because, as I argued at the beginning of this chapter, it has seen itself as being concerned with formal processes – has paid very little attention to this. Management development has been defined purely in terms of formal off-the-job training and education, and formal processes for moving people around. Not only have these schemes offered a prescription which does not meet the managers' realities; as already described, the processes themselves have given no help to managers in reinterpreting, and making better use of, their on-the-job development opportunities.

Clearly if we actually want to focus our development on effectiveness, rather than purely on discrete knowledge or skill, the on-the-job experiences present the prime vehicle. What we need is both a conceptual understanding that management development must embrace those accidental informal opportunities, previously ignored by most management development advisers, and practical processes for integrating real work experiences and formal schemes of development. A great deal of that integration will be accomplished by managers and their bosses with no intervention from the management development educator or trainer, except perhaps through some introductory sessions on a course or the use of some reading material or workbook.

Our understanding of the opportunities here, first illustrated on a large scale by Revans and Morris, is now being enhanced by more recent work. In the United States the work of McCall and his colleagues (1988) describes and 468 analyses the kind of experiences to which managers are exposed. My own work

Type 1: 'Informal managerial' – accidental processes

Characteristics
- occur within managerial activities
- explicit intention is task performance
- no clear development objectives
- unstructured in development terms
- not planned in advance
- owned by managers

Development consequences
- **learning is real, direct, unconscious, insufficient**

Type 2: 'Integrated managerial' – opportunistic processes

Characteristics
- occur within managerial activities
- explicit intention both task performance and development
- clear development objectives
- structured for development by boss and subordinate
- planned beforehand or reviewed subsequently as learning experiences
- owned by managers

Development consequences
- **learning is real, direct, conscious, more substantial**

Type 3: 'Formal management development' – planned processes

Characteristics
- often away from normal managerial activities
- explicit intention is development
- clear development objectives
- structured for development by developers
- planned beforehand and reviewed subsequently as learning experiences
- owned more by developers than managers

Development consequences
- **learning may be real** (through a job) or **detached** (through a course)
- is more likely to be **conscious, relatively infrequent**

Figure 34.2   Types of management development

with my colleague Peter Honey (1989) builds on my original 1988 research work in spelling out how managers can actually engage successfully in learning terms with the opportunities open to them. The use of learning experiences at work is by far the greatest area for attention for productivity in management development: it meets the criteria suggested by centring on what managers actually have to do, and on issues of their personal effectiveness; and it removes the problems of simulation and of transfer of learning. Increased recognition of such opportunities – whether at the design level by management developers, or by individual managers for themselves – will nevertheless not necessarily lead to effective learning. It is one of the most potent criticisms of formal management development schemes that in proposing to provide additional development opportunities – whether through courses or job assignments – we have largely assumed that *learning will necessarily follow.*

The argument of this section has been that formal management development processes can (and should) be focused on and operated through effectiveness issues, but that management development must also embrace the ways in which managers *learn to be effective* – learning by experience, largely outside normal schemes. The model I have developed to describe this view of Management Development is given in Figure 34.2.

> One of the determining factors about the success of improved development on the job – Type 2 in my model – will be the effectiveness of managers in developing not only themselves but their subordinates and indeed their colleagues. In formal management development schemes the role of a coach or mentor has increasingly been identified. Important though such formal approaches can be, we really need a much more extensive understanding and use of less-structured opportunities for one manager to help another. (Mumford, 1993)

EFFECTIVE LEARNING PROCESSES

If we manage to work successfully on the issues of managerial effectiveness in the ways described, we create the potential for a virtuous learning circle (see Figure 34.3).

It is clear that for many managers involvement in formal management development processes off-the-job has created a vicious learning sequence (see Figure 34.4). Modern motivational theory tells us that behaviour which is not rewarded is not willingly engaged upon again. Some managers have had training or educational experiences they regard as useful or interesting or stimulating, and they are willing to return to similar experiences subsequently; others are relatively unwilling to attend in the first place and/or experience nothing like stimulation or utility during the course. All too often this can be traced back to the failure of courses to deal with the issues of what managers really do, and to deal with them in the ways most related to their normal managerial work processes.

If trainers and educators have grappled successfully with the issues of *evaluation*, then corrective steps could have been taken to improve results; *470* either the programme could have dealt with effectiveness issues in the ways I

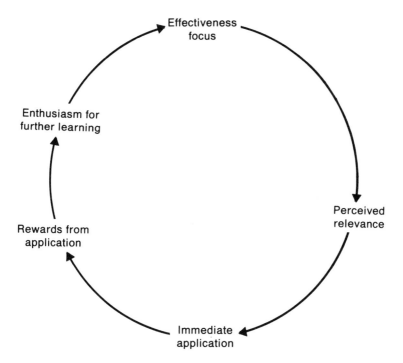

Figure 34.3   The virtuous learning circle

Figure 34.4   The vicious learning sequence

471

have recommended, or if they did not they would at least have dealt with broader issues of knowledge or skill in a more effective way. The absence of evaluation is particularly ironic in that, for those programmes which do emphasize the acquisition of knowledge or skill, evaluation is not only necessary but achievable (see Easterby-Smith, 1986); emphasis given to effectiveness issues makes the evaluation more difficult to separate for evaluation purposes. It is probably also less necessary; if you design a process actually to engage people in action you *reduce* the requirement to *test the extent to which they have applied that which they have learned*: I use the verb 'reduce', not remove.

The whole shift of emphasis to action-based learning helps us to remove one of the traditional problems of management education and training. It is a logical oddity that having created a situation of unreality (i.e., a structured off-the-job learning experience), and then having done in many cases very little about directing attention to those issues of real personal concern to managers, tutors and trainers have then complained and written learned articles about the problems of transfer of learning. If we create unreality and do not deal with issues of effectiveness, we ought not to be surprised that managers have problems in transferring what they are supposed to have learned back into their real job situation. Nor should we be surprised that the boss and colleagues to whom they return from the off-the-job experience gives no welcome to the kind of learning which the managers bring with them.

Concentration on those issues which are relevant to the manager and his or her colleagues in the real-life situation certainly reduces the transfer problem, both because of the perceived reality of what the manager is engaged in, and because there need literally be no 'transfer' in the sense that he or she can be involved in projects and real-time problems *drawn from his or her own work* that do not then have to be 'translated'. Where learning activities are not primarily and directly based on the manager's own work, we should tackle the transfer problem on our programmes instead of leaving it to the manager to resolve on his or her own on return to work; this means less time on teaching, and more time on how the manager will *implement* what he or she has learned.

Emphasis on effectiveness and reality will nonetheless not, as some writers seem to assume, in itself completely overcome the need for careful choice of effective learning processes. Management development has been far too subject to 'flavour of the month' approaches, each of them claiming to be uniquely appropriate to developing managers. Over the years we have been told that T-groups, grid training, coaching, self-development, action learning and now outdoor training were, successively, the answer to our management development problems. In my view, the adoption of any single technique as the predominant answer to our management development problems is lazy and incompetent; nor is the answer a further proliferation of management development processes. In his most helpful book, Huczynski (1983) identifies around 300 management development techniques. While in no way wishing to inhibit future creativity, it is my view that productivity in management development will derive from the appropriate methods already relatively well known and tried, rather than the identification of new processes.

I take this view because the application of management development methods is at the moment so clearly both inefficient and ineffective; we have failed to fit our processes to the *needs of the learner*. Just as we have not satisfactorily dealt with the reality of how a manager *manages*, so we have not dealt with the reality of how a manager *learns*. Just as we have swept aside the common perception of managers that they learn through on-the-job processes (a matter of common experience apparently too simple for researchers to cope with), so we have ignored the reality that different managers actually *learn differently from the same process*.

It is an extraordinary fact that educators, trainers and developers know very well that if Brown and Jones both have the same need to improve an aspect of their managerial performance, and both are taken through the same learning experience, Brown will learn and Jones will not. It seems that most tutors having stumbled across this truth painfully, when an individual reacts badly to a learning process, then pick themselves up and hurry on as if nothing had happened. In designing courses the best that may occur subsequently is that the designers offer a catholic menu of activities, hoping everybody will get something out of the course. Thus the supposedly well-designed course will include role plays, films, case studies, lectures, an afternoon in the resource centre: if you are bored by one, there is always tomorrow.

It is an extraordinary commentary on management education in both the United Kingdom and the United States that only in the years since 1980 has there been attention at any level of significance to differences in the ways in which people learn. The field was for a long time dominated by fundamentally sterile debates about the virtues of case studies, of business games, or of experiential exercises. I emphasize again the absence of action on the part of the traditional business schools because of their perceived dominance in the rest of the management development world. I cannot think of any significant university-level contribution in this field apart from the original innovative work by Kolb, and the work done by the Department of Management Learning at Lancaster who have made a considerable contribution in the literature on issues of the general design of different kinds of learning event, and the significance of the interaction between the tutor and the learner. Although much of their written work is understandably directed at the tutor I believe they would share with me the view that one of the problems is that the tutor has been given too great a prominence in the learning process: their efforts, quite rightly, are geared to helping the tutor be more effective by assessing the learning situation in which he or she is involved.

No doubt because I started from a different kind of environment my own concern has been as much with the learner as the tutor. Peter Honey and I have developed Kolb's original concept of the learning cycle, and have advised the designers of learning experiences how they need to pay attention to *all stages* of the cycle, designing total programmes, sessions within programmes, or particular kinds of on-the-job learning experience. We also took Kolb's original concepts of individual learning preferences, developed our own method of determining these, and then provided direct guidance to the learner on how to make use of this information (Honey and Mumford, 1986; 1992).

473

Honey and I have also argued that knowledge of the *learning preferences* of managers actually arriving on a learning experience can be used to provide a more appropriate experience. We think it is irresponsible simply to throw a ragbag of activities at a group on the assumption that their learning styles will be different. Our general proposition is, of course, that the experience should actually be designed as a *learning*, not as a *teaching*, experience. This undoubtedly increases the difficulties for the designers and operators of learning events, and perhaps it is the prospect of such difficulties that has deterred training and education institutions from actually thinking seriously about the learning process. Nor would understanding by designers and providers of development experiences, while helpful, go sufficiently far. It is surely another prospective leap forward in management development that we should share with managers our improved understanding of learning and cause them to recognize and improve their own learning processes: that is to say, that we should incorporate our improved understanding not merely in the design of a more effective event, but that we should treat learning as an *overt part of the programme*. Instead of being an implied and unstudied part of most management development activities, learning should be placed in the forefront as an explicit activity; nor should it be confined to an interesting session at the beginning of a programme, with perhaps some review of personal development growth at the end of it. We must provide time and resource to help managers consider their learning processes *during the programme itself.*

I have carefully used the word 'programme' rather than 'course', because I see this as being applicable just as much in the situation in which an advisor is counselling someone's development on the job as it would be where a tutor is running an off-the-job experience. The reason for this extended attention to the learning process is not merely a matter of logic – of the extraordinary fact that many programmes which claim to help managers to learn never actually address that issue – but also that it is essential as one of the ways in which we will manage to draw together on-the-job and off-the-job development experiences. If in our off-the-job experiences we give sufficient time and attention to engaging a manager in understanding his or her own learning, we can also help him or her to see how to apply this knowledge so that he or she *continues to learn* from similar or equivalent learning experiences when he or she is back on the job. Just as dealing with issues of effectiveness will help reduce substantially the problems of transfer of learning, so by giving substantial attention to the learning process itself we can reduce the notorious problems of managers seeing experiences as a series of one-off events, with no connection with each other in learning terms.

The phrase 'continuous learning' is now becoming popular; it will be no more than a promotional phrase if we do not provide the *learning processes* necessary to secure it. It seems clear that some of the people writing about continuous learning are really talking only about a series of training events, and not in fact about continuous learning at all; for learning to be *continuous*, rather than simply a series of events, we need to equip people to learn effectively *outside and around those events*: we need to do so for the obvious reason that for most managers most learning will occur – or not occur – *on the job*. Continuous learning and 'learning how to learn' will become empty clichés unless real effort is put into enabling individuals to understand what is involved, and to develop the necessary skills. In addition to our work on learning styles, Honey and I have increasingly concerned ourselves with further practical exercises to facilitate an individual's understanding of his or her own learning (Honey and Mumford, 1989; 1990).

In the same way that definitions of managerial effectiveness are most sensibly couched in specific organization terms, effective learning processes are defined most appropriately by the *learner*, not by the tutor. In my experience, it is salutary for advisers and trainers to be exposed to an analysis of their own preferred approach to learning and then to see how far what they offer – and how they offer it – is dominated by their *own preferences*, not by the individuals they are supposedly trying to help.

SUCCESSFUL MANAGEMENT DEVELOPMENT

I have used three different aspects of 'effectiveness' in this chapter. If we understood these issues better, and carried out our work on the development of managers more appropriately in relation to them, we would be much more likely to produce effective management development. Most specifically, we would increase the chance that we would be offering processes which managers themselves recognized as being effective and were therefore prepared to engage in for themselves and offer to others. I think we need to recognize that the continued unpopularity of management development (the formal process) is due at least as much to our failures as designers and implementers of formal processes as it is to unwillingness of managers to spend time and devote energy to formal management development.

Of course, there is more to successful management development than the three main themes I have mentioned here. Margerison (1991) offers a substantial review of causes of success and failure in management development; I agree with many of his items, but have expressed my own views as well (Mumford, 1988).

It seems to me that too many management development schemes are dominated by issues about the 'system' and too little influenced by the needs, requirements and potential for growth of individuals. We will not have effective management development as long as we encourage systems which are in fact geared to processing people seen as a *concept*, rather than as *individuals* who can be assisted to develop. I shudder when I hear a personnel director or management development adviser say 'All our managers have been through . . .': it has become all too obvious that some management development schemes measure results by the number of people who have 'been through', rather than by *achieved results in development*.

I have already argued that we need a more substantial contribution from the organizations who ought to be leading management development. Definition of what effective managers do, and the identification of learning strategies and *475* techniques – two out of my three areas of effectiveness – ought to receive much more attention. On the first, the marvellous work of Stewart, Mintzberg and Kotter surely cannot be the last word. On the second we need a substantial research effort from the business schools; perhaps the subject is too difficult for them to tackle, because it raises too many questions about the purposes of management education. I have argued for a focus on effectiveness, and the practice of most business schools certainly does not take them in that direction. (If they had a coherent philosophy, perhaps that, too, would inhibit them from pursuing the areas I have indicated.)

Although I have particularly strong views about the associated issues of learning and effectiveness, I am not alone in my criticisms. Over the last twenty years we have seen the views of Livingston (1971), who told us that formal management education 'tends to distort managerial growth because it over-develops an individual's analytical ability, but leaves his ability to take action and to get things done under-developed'; this kind of criticism was repeated by Peters and Waterman (1982) and Behrman and Levin (1984).

There has been no equivalent research and analysis of the output of UK business schools. This is not to say that we have lacked comment – from business schools vocal about their excellent contribution; from individuals such as Gordon Wills critical of that same contribution; and from the potential customers who have voted with their feet to be absent. An optimistic view would be that the debate largely engendered by the Management Charter Initiative may encourage a concentration on issues of effectiveness. A pessimistic view would be that the traditional business schools will unconsciously follow the advice offered by Peters and Waterman, and that they will therefore stick to their knitting – offering programmes geared to a view of management education as essentially concerned with the identification and application of theory and concepts, with all too little emphasis on *application.*

NOTE

[1]See John Morris (Chapter 38 in this volume).

FURTHER READING

Behrman, J.N. and R.L. Levin (1984), 'Are Business Schools Doing Their Job'. *Harvard Business Review*, January.

Boyatzis, R. (1982), *The Competent Manager*, New York: John Wiley.

Drucker, P. (1974), *Management Tasks, Responsibilities, Practices*, New York: Harper & Row.

Easterby-Smith, M. (1986), *Evaluation of Management Education, Training and Development*, Aldershot: Gower.

Honey, P. and A. Mumford (1992), *The Manual of Learning Styles*, 3rd edn, London: Honey.

Honey, P. and A. Mumford (1986), *Using Your Learning Styles*, London: Honey.

Honey, P. and A. Mumford (1989), *The Manual of Learning Opportunities*, London: Honey.

Honey, P. and A. Mumford (1990), *The Opportunist Learner*, London: Honey.

Huczynski, A. (1983), *Encyclopaedia of Management Development Methods*, Aldershot: Gower.

Kolb, D. (1984), *Experiential Learning* (Englewood Cliffs, NJ: Prentice Hall.

Kotter, J.P. (1982), *The General Manager*, New York: Free Press.

Livingston, J.S. (1971) 'The Myth of the Well-Educated Manager', *Harvard Business Review*, January.

Margerison, C. (1991), *Making Management Development Work*, Maidenhead: McGraw-Hill.

McCall, M., M. Lombardo, and A. Morrison (1988), *The Lessons of Experience*, Lexington, Mass.: Lexington Books.

Mintzberg, H. (1980), *The Nature of Managerial Work*, Englewood Cliffs, NJ: Prentice Hall.

Mumford, A. (1988), *Developing Top Managers*, Aldershot: Gower.

Mumford, A. (1989), *Management Development: Strategies for Action*, London: IPM.

Mumford, A. (1993), 2nd Edn., 'Learning in Action', *Personnel Management*, July.

Peters, T.J. and R.H. Waterman (1982), *In Search of Excellence*, New York: Harper & Row.

Revans, R. (1980), *Action Learning*, London: Blond.

Stewart, R. (1976), *Contrasts in Management*, London: McGraw-Hill.

35 Team-building[1]

Bill Critchley and David Casey

TEAM-BUILDING – AT WHAT PRICE AND AT WHOSE COST?

It all started during one of those midnight conversations between consultants in a residential workshop. We were running a team-building session with a top management group and something very odd began to appear. Our disturbing (but also exciting) discovery was that for most of their time this group of people had absolutely no need to work as a team; indeed, the attempt to do so was causing more puzzlement and scepticism than motivation and commitment. In our midnight reflections we were honest enough to confess to each other that this was not the first time our team-building efforts had cast doubts on the very validity of teamwork itself, within our client groups.

We admitted that we had both been working from some implicit assumptions that good teamwork is a characteristic of healthy, effectively functioning organizations. Now we started to question those assumptions. First, we flushed out what our assumptions actually were. In essence it came down to something like the following.

We had been assuming that the top group in any organization (be it the board of directors or the local authority management committee or whatever the top group is called) should be a team and ought to work as a team. Teamwork at the top is crucial to organizational success, we assumed.

We further assumed that a properly functioning team is one in which:

- people care for each other;
- people are open and truthful;
- there is a high level of trust;
- decisions are made by consensus;
- there is strong team commitment;
- conflict is faced up to and worked through;

 [1]First published in *Management Education and Development*, **15**, (2), 1984.

- people really listen to ideas and to feelings;
- feelings are expressed freely; and
- process issues (task and feelings) are dealt with.

Finally, it had always seemed logical to us, that a team-building catalyst could always help any team to function better – and so help any organization perform better as an organization. Better functioning would lead the organization to achieve its purposes more effectively.

The harsh reality we now came up against was at odds with this cosy view of teams, teamwork and team-building. In truth, the director of education has little need to work in harness with his fellow chief officers in a county council. He or she might need the support of the chief executive and the chair of the elected members' education committee, but the other chief officers in that local authority have neither the expertise nor the interest, nor indeed the time, to contribute to what is essentially very specialized work.

Even in industry, whilst it is clear that the marketing and production directors of a company must work closely together to ensure that the production schedule is synchronized with sales forecasts and the finance director needs to be involved – to look at the cash flow implications of varying stock levels – they do not need to involve the *whole* team. And they certainly do not need to develop high levels of trust and openness to work through those kinds of business issues.

On the other hand, most people would agree that *strategic* decisions, concerned with the future direction of the whole enterprise, should involve all those at the top. Strategy should demand an input from every member of the top group, and for strategic discussion and strategic decision-making, teamwork at the top is essential. But how much time do most top management groups actually spend discussing strategy? Our experiences, in a wide variety of organizations, suggest that 10 per cent is a high figure for most organizations – often 5 per cent would be nearer the mark. This means that 90–95 per cent of decisions in organizations are essentially operational: that is, decisions made within departments based usually on a fair amount of information and expertise. In those conditions, high levels of trust and openness may be nice, but are not necessary; consensus is strictly not an issue and in any case would take up far too much time. There is therefore no need for high levels of interpersonal skills.

Why then, is so much time and money invested in team-building, we asked ourselves. At this stage in our discussion we began to face a rather disturbing possibility. Perhaps the spread of team-building has more to do with team-builders and *their* needs and values, rather than a careful analysis of what is appropriate and necessary for the organization. To test out this alarming hypothesis we each wrote down an honest and frank list of reasons why we ourselves engaged in team-building. We recommend this as an enlightening activity for other team-builders – perhaps, like us, they will arrive at this kind of conclusion; team-builders work as catalysts to help management groups function better as open teams for a variety of reasons, including the following:

- They like it – enjoy the risks.

- Because they are good at it.
- It is flattering to be asked.
- They receive rewarding personal feedback.
- Professional kudos – not many people do team-building with top teams.
- There is money in it.
- It accords with their values: for instance democracy is preferred to autocracy.
- They gain power. Process interventions are powerful in business settings where the client is on home ground and can confuse the consultant in business discussions.

All those reasons are concerned with the needs, skills and values of the *team-builder* rather than the management group being 'helped'. This could explain why many team-building exercises leave the so-called management team excited and stimulated by the experience, only to find they are spending an unnecessary amount of time together discussing other people's departmental issues. Later on, because they cannot see the benefit of working together on such issues, they abandon 'teamwork' altogether. Such a management group has been accidentally led to disillusionment with the whole idea of teamwork and the value of team-building.

We began to see, as our discussions went on through the small hours, that there is a very *large* proportion of most managers' work where teamwork is not needed (and to attempt to inculcate teamwork is dysfunctional). There is, at the same time a very *small* proportion of their work where teamwork is absolutely vital (and to ignore team-working skills is to invite disaster). This latter work, which demands a team approach, is typified by strategic work but not limited to strategic work. It is any work characterized by a high level of choice and by the condition of maximum uncertainty.

Most people find choice and uncertainty uncomfortable. Many senior managers attempt to deny the choice element by the employment of complex models and techniques. We do not think most people's management experience teaches them to make choices about the future, for instance; it puts the main emphasis on establishing as many facts as possible and reviewing options in the light of past experience. That is why models like, for example, the Boston portfolio model and the General Electric matrix are so popular. They provide comforting analytic frameworks for looking at strategic options, but they are appealing really to our operational mentality. The hope often is that they will somehow come up with a solution to the strategic question. But, of course, they cannot make choices for people and they do not throw any light on the future.

The top team of an organization, if it is to achieve quality and commitment in its decisions about future directions, will need to pool the full extent of each individual's wisdom and experience. That means something quite different from reacting to a problem in terms of their own functional knowledge and experience. It means *exposing fully* their uncertainties, taking unaccustomed risks by airing their own subjective view of the world and struggling to build *480* some common perceptions and possibilities. This is where that much abused word 'sharing' really comes into its own. In this context it is not merely a value-laden exhortation, it is vital to the future of the organization. Ideas and opinions are all we have to inform our view of the future, but if we are to take a risk with a fragile idea or opinion, unsubstantiated by facts, we will only take it if the climate is right. Conversely, if we take the risk and the sheer vagueness and vulnerability of the idea attracts forth a volley of ridicule and abuse, then it will die quickly and be lost forever.

Most functional executives, brought up in the turbulence of politics and interfunctional warfare, find the transition from functional to strategic mode very difficult to make. They do not always see the difference, and if they do, they are reluctant to leave their mountain top, the summit of knowledge, experience and hence power, for the equality and shared uncertainty of strategic decision-making. And yet this is one area where real teamwork is not only necesssary but vital.

We had by now got ourselves thoroughly confused. We seemed to be forcing team-building on groups which had no need to be a team and missing the one area where teamwork is essential – because choice and uncertainty are at a maximum and for this very reason managers were shying away from the work – work which can only be done by a team. We resorted to diagrams to help clear our minds, and these new diagrams form the basis of the next section of this chapter.

THEORETICAL CONSIDERATIONS CONCERNING MANAGEMENT GROUPS

We found these kinds of discussion taking us farther and farther away from team-building and closer and closer to an understanding of why management groups work, or do not work, in the ways they do. In the end, we developed two basic diagrams, showing the relationships between the following variables which operate in management groups:

1. The degree of uncertainty in the management task.
2. The need for sharing in the group.
3. Modes of working.
4. Different kinds of internal group process.
5. Different levels of interpersonal skills.
6. The role of the leader.

We would now like to present these two framework diagrams as diagnostic tools, which a dozen or so management groups have found very useful in coming to terms with how they work and why. These simple diagrams are helping groups to see what kind of groups they are, and when and if they want to be a team, rather than jumping to the conclusion that all groups need team-building.

Throughout the discussion, we will be talking about the management group – that is, the leader plus those immediately responsible to him or her, perhaps five *481*

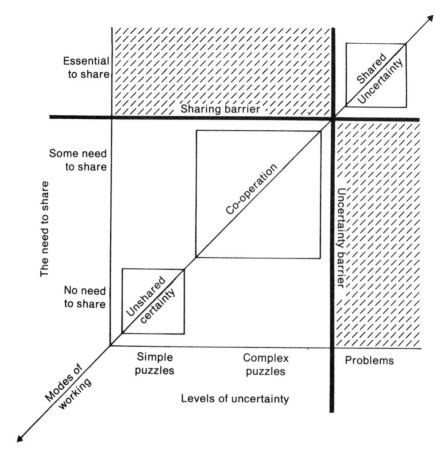

Figure 35.1   The more uncertainty in its task, the more any group has to share

to ten people in all, at the top of their organization or their part of the organization.

The level of uncertainty and the need to share

The first diagram (Figure 35.1) shows the relationship between the level of uncertainty inherent in any group task and the need for members of that group to share with each other. Expressed simply: 'the more uncertainty – the more need to share'. Everyday examples of this truism are: children holding hands for comfort in the dark or NASA research scientists brainstorming for fresh ideas on the frontiers of man's knowledge. Any uncertainty – emotional, physical or intellectual – can best be coped with by sharing.

However, the converse is also true – where there is less uncertainty, there is less need to share. The same children will feel no need to hold hands round the breakfast table where all is secure; the NASA scientists during the final launch will each get on with their own well-rehearsed part of the launch programme in relative isolation from each other. Only if something goes wrong (uncertainty floods back) will they need to share, quickly and fully. It took us a long time to realize the full significance of that in terms of the need to share in a management group.

We are dealing here only with the top group of the organization where task is the dominant imperative. There are other situations in which other objectives demand sharing; for instance, if one is dealing with the whole fabric of a complete organization and attempting a global shift in attitudes, then culture-building may become the dominant imperative and sharing at all levels in that organization may become necessary. But that is a different situation – we are looking here at the top management group where task must be the dominant imperative.

In Figure 35.1 we have used Revans' powerful distinction between problems (no answer is known to exist) and puzzles (the answer exists somewhere – just find it) to describe different levels of uncertainty. To illustrate the difference between a problem and a puzzle: deciding about capital punishment is a problem for society; tracking down a murderer is a puzzle for the police.

Work groups dealing with genuine problems (of which strategy is only one example) would be well advised to share as much as possible with each other. They should share feelings to gain support, as well as ideas to penetrate the unknown. Figure 35.1 shows two shaded areas. These shaded areas must be avoided. The shaded area on the right indicates the futility of tackling real problems unless people are prepared to share. The shaded area at the top indicates that there is no point in sharing to solve mere puzzles.

Two 'barriers' appear on our model; they indicate that a positive effort must be made if a breakthrough to a new level of working is to be accomplished. For instance, the uncertainty barrier represents a step into the unknown – a deliberate attempt to work in areas of ambiguity, uncertainty and ambivalence. To avoid the shaded areas and arrive in the top right-hand corner, the group breaks through *both* barriers at the *same* time. This is the *only* way to solve genuine problems. Most management groups stay behind both barriers in Figure 35.1 and handle work which is in the nature of a puzzle – and to achieve this they co-operate, rather than share with each other. As long as they continue to limit their work to solving puzzles, they are quite right to stay within the sharing and uncertainty barriers of Figure 35.1.

Modes of working

As teambuilders, we now see that we must spend time identifying which modes of working any management group operates. The three modes of working come out in Figure 35.1 as the diagonal and we would like to describe each mode, by working up the diagonal of Figure 35.1 from left to right.

Mode of unshared certainty   The proper mode for simple puzzles of a technical nature in everyday work, where every member of the group is relatively competent within his or her field and speaks from the authority of his or her   *483* specialism. Ideal when the work issues are independent of each other – as they often are. A healthy attitude is: 'I will pull my weight and see that my part is done well.' Attitudes can become unhealthy if they move towards 'my interests must come first'.

Mode of co-operation The appropriate mode for complex puzzles which impinge on the work of several members of the management group. In this mode (very common in local authorities), group members recognize the need for give-and-take, co-operation, negotiation and passing of information on a need-to-know basis. The attitude is: 'I'll co-operate for the good of the whole and because other members of this group have their rights and problems too.' Sharing is restricted to what is necessary, and each group members still works from the security (certainty) of his own professional base, recognizing the professional bases of his colleagues.

Mode of shared uncertainty A rare mode – partly because it is appropriate only for genuine problems (such as strategy) where nobody knows what to do, uncertainty is rife and full of sharing between members is the only way out; and partly because, even when it is the appropriate mode, many management groups never reach these professional heights. The attitude of members has to be: 'The good of the whole outweighs any one member's interest – including mine. I carry an equal responsibility with my colleagues for the whole, and for this particular work I am not able to rely on my specialism, because my functional expertise is, for this problem we all face, irrelevant.'

Clearly, the top mode of 'shared uncertainty' is extremely demanding, and it is not surprising that many management groups try hard to avoid it. We know several boards of directors, and even more local authority management 'teams', who have devised a brilliant trick to avoid handling genuine problems requiring genuine sharing in the top mode. Quite simply – they turn all strategic problems into operational puzzles! How? There are very many variations of this trick available; for example:

- appoint a working party;
- ask a consultant to recommend;
- recruit a corporate planner;
- set up a think-tank; and so on.

To make sure the trick works, the terms of reference are: 'your recommendation must be short and must ask us to decide between option A or option B.' Choosing between A and B is an operational puzzle they can solve and it leaves them with the comfortable illusion that they have actually been engaging in strategic problem resolution work, whereas the truth is they have avoided uncertainty, avoided sharing their fears and ideas, avoided their real work, by converting frightening problems into management puzzles. And who can blame them!

We do not feel we have the right to censure top groups for not working in the top mode of shared uncertainty. We do feel we have the obligation to analyse quite rigorously how top groups actually work, before we plunge in with our team-building help.

In Figure 35.1, the size of the box for each mode indicates very roughly how frequently each mode might be needed by most management groups. Sadly, we see many management groups working in modes which are inappropriate to the work being done. It is not just that many top groups fail to push through to the top mode; many management groups get stuck in the bottom box quite a lot of the time, when they should be working in the middle mode. On the other hand, other groups go through a pantomime of sitting round a table trying to work in the middle mode, but, in truth, feeling bored and uninterested because the middle mode is inappropriate and each member of the group could carry on separately with his own work, without pretending to share it with his colleagues, who do not need to know anyway. In other words, their appropriate mode is unshared certainty and attempts at sharing are boring or frustrating façades.

Our diagram shows an arrow on both ends of the diagonal, to illustrate that all three modes of working are necessary at different times, and effective work groups can and should slide up and down the diagonal. We do not see any management group working in one mode all the time – the really effective group is able to move from mode to mode as the task requires. Although it may think of itself as a management 'team', a top group will be truly functioning as a team only when it is operating in the top mode.

We use the word team here, in the sense used in the first part of this chapter, which we believe is the sense used by most team-builders in team-building work. Because we now believe that working in the top mode of shared uncertainty is called for infrequently – by the nature of the work – and is actually practised even less frequently, we now doubt the value of team-building work with most management groups, when there is so much more urgent work to be done with these groups.

We found in Figure 35.1 that when we plot the level of uncertainty in the work, against the need to share, we discover three modes of working, on the diagonal of Figure 35.1. These three modes of working are: unshared certainty; co-operation; and shared uncertainty. We now want to go on to answer the question 'How does a management group work in each of these modes? What *processes* are needed, what *skills* are required, and how does the *leader* function?'

The format of Figure 35.2 is the same as Figure 35.1, only the variables are different. The vertical axis of Figure 35.2 is the diagonal lifted from Figure 35.1 (modes) and two new variables are introduced – processes on the horizontal axis and interpersonal skills become the new diagonal.

Processes

To start with the horizontal axis – processes. We distinguish three levels of process in any group. At the most perfunctory there are *polite social processes*, very important to sustain the social lubrication of a healthy group but not focused *485* on the work itself. The work is accomplished largely via *task processes* – the way work is organized, distributed, ideas generated and shared, decisions made, and so forth. The third level of process concerns people's feelings (*feelings processes*) and how these are handled by themselves and by others.

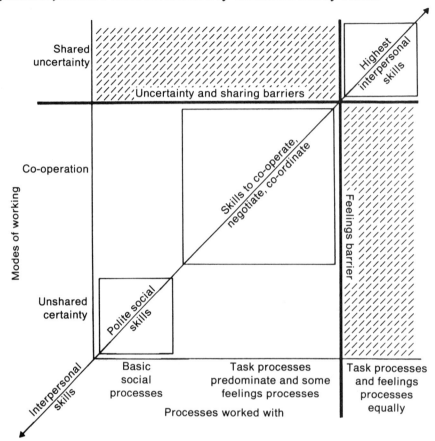

Figure 35.2   Different modes of working require different methods

Reference to Figure 35.2 will make it clear that as the mode of working becomes more difficult, ascending the vertical axis, from unshared certainty towards shared uncertainty, so the processes needed to accomplish this more difficult work also become more difficult, as the group moves along the horizontal axis from simple basic social processes, through task processes, towards the much more difficult processes of working with people's deeper feelings.

Many groups never reach the top mode of shared uncertainty, where people's feelings are actually *part of the work* and all is uncertainty, excitement and trust.

The shaded areas are to be avoided (as in Figure 35.1). The right-hand shaded area indicates that it is absurd to indulge in work with people's feelings if the group is working only in the two lower modes of unshared certainty and co-486   operation – to engage in soul-searching to accomplish this kind of work is ridiculous and brings team-building into disrepute. The top shaded area indicates similarly that there is no need to share deeply when only the two lower levels of processes (basic social processes and task processes) are operating.

However, a management group faced with the need to tackle uncertainty can either avoid the whole thing, by staying safely behind the barriers (which is what most management groups appear to do), or it can have the courage to break through both barriers simultaneously, arriving (breathlessly) in the top right-hand corner, where the mode of working is shared uncertainty and the necessary processes are task and feelings processes together. Those few management groups which accomplish this become *teams*.

Interpersonal skills

The final variable is the diagonal of Figure 35.2, 'interpersonal skills', and clearly there is an ascending order of skill from the lowest (but not least important) level of polite social skills to the highest possible level of interpersonal skills required in the rarified atmosphere of highest uncertainty and real teamwork. But, for the middle mode, a solid raft of straightforward interpersonal skills is needed by all managers – empathy, co-operation, communication, listening, negotiating, and many more. We have come to believe that here is the greatest area of need.

The leader's role

The group leader and group leadership have not been mentioned so far, in an attempt to keep things simple. The whole question of leadership is fundamental to the operation of all management groups and we would like to make some observations now.

Leader's role in the mode of unshared certainty

The leader is hardly needed at all in the unshared certainty mode and, indeed, the social lubrication process of a group working in this mode may well be carried out much better by an informal leader – there is nothing so embarrassing as the formal group leader bravely trying to lead the group through its celebration lunch in the local inn!

Some local authority chief executives (so called) suffer an even worse fate – they cannot find a role at all, because the members of their management team (so called) steadfastly refuse to move out of the bottom mode of working, tacitly deciding *not* to work together and denying the chief executive any play in the organization at all! This is not uncommon.

Leader's role in the mode of co-operation

The leader's role in the central (co-operation) mode, is well established in management convention. For example, a clear role at meetings has been universally recognized to enable the leader to manage the task processes in 487 particular. This role is of course the chairperson. Co-ordination of the task is at its core, and most group leaders find this role relatively clear.

Leader's role in the mode of shared uncertainty

No such role has yet been universally recognized to deal with the processes in the highest mode, of shared uncertainty. In Britain, we have the added difficulty of our cultural resistance to working with feelings (in action-learning language, 'No sets please, we're British'). In this sophisticated mode of working, the word 'catalyst' seems more appropriate than the word chairperson and often a team-builder is invited to carry out this role. But where does this leave the group leader? All management group leaders have learned to be the chairperson, very few have yet learned to be the catalyst. And in any case, to be the catalyst and the leader at the same time, is to attempt the north face of the Eiger of interpersonal skills. It can be done, but not in carpet slippers. If, on the other hand, the role of catalyst is performed by an outsider, the leadership dynamic becomes *immensely* complex and adds a significant overlay of difficulty when working in a mode which we have already shown to be extremely difficult in the first place. No wonder team-building often fails.

CONCLUSIONS

Many teambuilders are unaware of the shaded 'no go' areas and dreamily assume that any progress towards open attitudes, free expression of feelings and genuine sharing in any management group, is beneficial. This is not so – to be of benefit there needs to be a very delicate and deliberate balance between what work the group has decided to pursue (what level of uncertainty) and the degree of sharing and expression of feelings the group is prepared for, to accomplish that work. Only if the balance is right will the management group be able to aim accurately at the top right-hand corner of Figures 35.1 and 35.2 and succeed in breaking through all the barriers at the same time to experience real team-work. Attempts to push through only one barrier (trying to handle uncertainty without sharing; sharing for the sake of sharing; being open for the sake of being open) will fail, and in failing will probably make things worse for that management group.

Strategic planners are often guilty of pushing management groups towards handling uncertainty without the concomitant abilities to share and work with feelings. Team-builders are often guilty of the converse sin – pushing management groups to be open and share their feelings, when the group has no intention whatever of getting into work where the level of uncertainty is high. Neither will succeed. It is no coincidence that both strategic planning and team-building can fall quickly into disrepute; it may be too late to save strategic planning from the management scrapheap – it is not too late to save team-building.

FURTHER READING

Adair, John (1986), *Effective Teambuilding*, Aldershot: Gower.

Belbin, R.M. (1981), *Management Teams: Why They Succeed or Faii*, London: Heinemann.

Hastings, C., P. Bixby, and R. Chaudhry-Lawton (1986), *The Superteam Solution*, Aldershot: Gower.

Woodcock, Mike (1989), *Team Development Manual*, 2nd edn, Aldershot: Gower.

36 Developing women managers

Judi Marshall

When I first reviewed literature on women managers in the late 1970s, I was surprised to find so many articles asking whether women and men are *really* different. Most of the authors were trying to prove that they are not, so that women could be endorsed as suitable management material, because men were taken without question as an ideal norm. In the main the authors were able to find data to serve their purposes, for example on leadership behaviour. But this is only part of the story. It is more appropriate to see men and women as broad social groups, each highly diverse, which are both the same and different, sharing fundamental aspects of human existence but also potentially approaching issues from different bases and social positions.

Certainly research shows that women and men can *behave* similarly as leaders, but it also reveals contrasts in their perspectives and in how others respond to their behaviour. Women often bring different values to the workplace from those of most male colleagues (Marshall, 1984); for example, valuing co-operation in working relationships, and seeking to lead balanced lives. Many women favour exercising power *with* others rather than *over* them (Loden, 1985). Moreover, women are often inhibited in using position power because other people reject or undermine their authority, stereotype them in devalued 'female' roles, act dependently towards them, and so on.

It is now becoming more common to accept that women managers may sometimes be different from men, and for women to be seen as equal rather than inferior in any comparisons that are made. However, differences now identified should not be treated as fixed, essential qualities of either gender, lest they create new constraining stereotypes. Articulating them is part of an evolving and shifting learning process, providing us with a broader map of possible human characteristics, activities and ways of being, within which we can accept more diversity from *all* individuals.

Despite much current social change we are still greatly influenced by a deeply ingrained history of sex role stereotypes that constrain men and women, and contribute to stress for both. I therefore argue below that we now need to explore women's distinctive needs, rather than acclaim their undoubted similarities to men, as a necessary phase in movement towards true equal opportunities. In the remainder of the chapter I shall discuss the training and development initiatives currently arising from such an analysis.

POTENTIAL DIFFERENCES BETWEEN WOMEN AND MEN

There are two interlinked bases for my assertion that women and men are sometimes intrinsically different. The first involves theories of archetypal patterns, in terms of which women as a group broadly represent a different range of potential human characteristics from those of men. The second involves recognizing that because of inequalities in social power, men's qualities have traditionally been valued more than women's, and so have shaped organizational life. These frameworks help identify women's development needs and show why these are currently so important.

Male and female values

Various theoretical frameworks distinguish between male and female values as two potentially complementary viewpoints on the world, reflecting an archetypal polarity (Marshall, 1984). This is especially clearly expressed in the Chinese concepts of *yang* and *yin*, and has close parallels in Jungian psychology. Drawing on these sources, the male pole is characterized by self-assertion, separation, control, focused perception, classifications, rationality, thrusting out, and contractual arrangements. The female pole is characterized by interdependence, merging, acceptance, awareness of patterns, wholes and contexts, emotional tone, personalistic perception and containing.

Male and female values are qualities to which both sexes have access, rather than the exclusive properties of men and women respectively. But through physical make-up, social role and social learning, women are more likely to be grounded in the female archetype and men in the male archetype. As managers, then, many women draw, to varying degrees and in individualistic ways, on a distinct base of values which distinguishes them from men. Individual development involves balancing the capabilities of one's grounding with appropriate aspects of the other perspective. This offers a more flexible array of abilities than does either set of values alone. But this is to some extent an ideal picture.

Social power

In its recent history, Western society has emphasized male values, and these have shaped its organizations, cultural norms, language, and so on. Female forms are relatively devalued and underdeveloped. This is such a pervasive aspect of our culture that, until recently, it has been unusual to identify ways in which women differ from men without the assumption being made that women are somehow at fault. All too easily, men become the unquestioned norm against *491* which women's behaviour is judged, and any deviations are seen as unusual and therefore to be penalized.

In this chapter, differences are not viewed as faults of either sex. Rather they are aspects of our cultural and gender heritage that can be used either productively and creatively or inappropriately and degeneratively. It cannot be assumed, for example, that what men do in organizations is necessarily right. Their management styles and career patterns reflect a selective range of possible options. There are disadvantages of which men themselves are aware. Established ways of working contribute to job stress and coronary heart disease; hierarchical forms of organization restrict development opportunities for all but a small group of successful people. (It is worth questioning whether we know what men's development needs really are.) It is possible, however, to overidealize female values in contrast, and this too should be avoided. For example, openness to other people's views can be degenerative when it results in becoming overwhelmed, invaded and dependent.

The social dominance of male values has inhibited the development of complementary, female alternatives. This is shown culturally by an emphasis on individualism, competition, rationality and control, and limited attention to interdependence, collaboration, intuition and acceptance. Along with other commentators (for example, Capra, 1982), I see the re-emergence and elaboration of female values as a significant aspect of a current re-vision in Western society, with potential benefits for men and women alike. But unless these values are taken seriously and allowed considerable space for experimentation, they will continue to be constrained by the current pattern of culture. Women's separate development is, then, an essential element in any social evaluation.

Women's development needs

Many women now want to enter employment and benefit from the financial rewards, achievements and personal growth it offers. They are joining a world still largely dominated by male values, and in doing so, they have conflicting needs. They want both to prove their rights to membership and also to have the freedom to be congruent with their own self-images. Until recently, equal opportunity initiatives concentrated on gaining acceptance for women by emphasizing their capability to work similarly to, and as well as, men. Women's competence in these terms now seems well-proven, although they are still poorly represented in top management positions (taking only approximately 2 per cent of them in the United States, Canada and most European countries), suggesting that their acceptance has limits. So far, though, most women have felt under pressure to conform to prevailing organizational norms to prove their legitimacy. Yet the foundations of many women's identity as managers are different, as are their experiences of organizational cultures. Many women now want to express more of their own perspectives in the workplace and in shaping their careers. Some also want to question fundamental organizational assumptions and to incorporate more female values and more diversity into organiz-

492

ational life. But women – and men – who are too challenging of established norms are likely to be resisted and may be expelled.

Therefore women engage in any development activity with an implicit, but highly charged, choice. They can either adapt to male norms of management where these still prevail, or develop their own notions based on a wider, combined, heritage of values. Many writers now criticize the former option, suggesting that it entails collusion with limited cultural norms which have traditionally constrained women's social and organizational participation, and so reinforces them. Gordon (1991) calls women who have succeeded through such strategies, 'prisoners of men's dreams'. More women are becoming aware of this central dilemma and are seeking ways to understand and live with its challenges.

I shall now explore some of the specific implications for women managers arising from this tension of values. I am concentrating on pressures women managers experience in employment; these are balanced by many satisfactions and opportunities for achievement which women value. Also there is no common picture, as women's situations vary greatly; I therefore chart a range of potential needs.

Many women managers are operating from values, assumptions, and perspectives that reflect their female grounding but are not widely represented or accepted in organizational life. This creates conflicts and pressures, and many describe themselves as working in 'hostile environments'. In their everyday work and career prospects, women are continually affected by inequalities in social power, although usually these are in the background rather than foreground of their experience. These inequalities become apparent when women are placed in one-down positions because of their gender, find that others reject their use of authority power because it contravenes stereotypes of femininity, or that they are passed over for promotion despite appropriate qualifications and experience. It is common, for example, for female managers to be mistaken for the assistants of male colleagues, for their opinions to go unheard in meetings, or to be denied development opportunities such as assignments abroad because it is assumed they will not cope. Maintaining their own self-image and confidence, and managing relationships with others, thus require great insight and skill.

As female stereotypes have not corresponded to traditional images of good management, women have been encouraged to play down their femaleness and copy male management styles in order to succeed. Many have done this to great effect, and have developed capabilities which would otherwise have remained dormant. But this often leads to conflict between their work and their personal self-images. Some managers are currently acutely aware of the strains of working in male-dominated environments, and of what they have given up in order to succeed organizationally (Marshall, in press). They are looking for more female-compatible ways of working, and organizational cultures more influenced by female values. Their reservations are particularly reflected in dilemmas about management style. The influence-based, person-oriented management style which many favour (Marshall, 1984), is in sharp contrast to the aggressive, independent, achievement-oriented model most see around them. It can make *493* them personally vulnerable, prove ineffective in competitive environments and limit their chances of promotion. Women managers I interviewed in the retailing and book publishing industries (Marshall, 1984) wanted to blend aspects of several approaches into a more robust approach.

Recent research shows that some, possibly many, women are developing alternative management styles, high in attention to both task and people. In doing so they are both refuting earlier stereotypes of them as only skilled in managing relationships, and are showing their competence in terms of a new ideal – that of transformational leadership (Rosener, 1990). The latter approach is depicted as interactive, motivating subordinates to meet personal and corporate goals simultaneously, achieving high-quality performance and inspirational in times of change. These findings, however, should not be interpreted as guarantees that women are now wholly accepted as managers. Ideals keep changing – some commentators would suggest they often do so just as women have proved themselves able to match previously stated criteria. Women therefore need to be aware of the standards against which they are being judged – and of their own views on these standards.

Some women managers are looking for flexible ways to fit employment into their lives, and find the standard, life-long career pattern constraining. They typically consider a wide range of factors, including intrinsic job challenge, their health, relationships and their sense of personal identity, in any decisions they make about work. Female values thus shape their engagement with employment (Marshall, 1989). They are simultaneously ambitious in their own distinctive ways. But being employed is one highly significant role amongst several, which they seek to balance, if not at one specific time, at least during their life course.

Research suggests that women can bring a different range of viewpoints to management. Gilligan (1982), for example, distinguishes between two moral codes, one used more consistently by men and the other by women. The male moral system views the world in terms of rights and principles, which can be defended and used as the basis for decision-making. The female system perceives life as a network of social relationships, with the individual at its centre. Right and wrong become relative and pragmatic, dependent on the situation. Gilligan concludes that women 'speak in a different voice', a view that is widely held amongst linguistic analysts, too (Spender, 1980). Other authors identify intuition, which involves subjective and contextual awareness, as an approach to understanding that has much to offer in organizations. Nevertheless, women managers' perspectives tend to go unheard if they differ from established frameworks, and this may eventually undermine women's own faith in them. Many have therefore learnt to translate between languages, to express their views in more commonly accepted terms. This is both a strain and a potential skill, as they see the world simultaneously from more than one viewpoint. Overcoming silence and finding voices for their experiences are currently highly important priorities for women managers (Belenky, Clinchy, Goldberger and Tarule, 1986).

494   Until recently, women have had few female role models to look to in their

search for alternative approaches to management. The women who had reached middle and senior level jobs had mainly copied male styles. Stereotypes of hard, lonely, older women managers are still common, and the expectation that they might become like this deters some women from aspiring to top positions. Those women who have survived without copying dominant styles have mainly remained invisible, their learning and accommodations kept private. This dearth of role models is partly because female values remain in the background of organizational life and do not impact its public face. It is also because women have tended not to identify or mix with each other at work. To gain acceptance, particularly at senior levels, they have identified with their male colleagues rather than with other women.

This situation is changing, there is now more networking and sense of alliance between some women. But there are also signs of tensions that need to be addressed, as the increasing numbers of women in management make differences amongst them more apparent. For example, individuals have adopted particular styles to cope with the nature of employment as they see it. Some have become outwardly tough, others have presented themselves as professional before all else, others have accentuated their femininity, and so on. These differences in style can set them apart, and may lead some to feel undermined or upstaged.

Tensions are also surfacing between some older and some younger women managers at the moment. The latter are criticizing the former for having adapted to male-dominated cultures, and claim that this is certainly no longer necessary as equal opportunities are now firmly established. Older managers can feel both misunderstood – thinking that they previously had little choice given prevailing cultural norms – and cynical – doubting whether their younger colleagues really appreciate the dynamics of power they may encounter as they move up the organization.

For the various reasons outlined above, women need opportunities to share their perspectives, experiences and ways of coping, as a process of peer support or mentoring. They also need to discuss their differences, rather than acting these out in covert contests.

The analysis of needs above reveals seven main development priorities for women, as follows:

1. Developing an awareness of how organizational cultures are created and maintained, and how power is deployed to shape values and behaviour – especially those which are gender-related.
2. Creating their own management styles, drawing on a full range of potential options.
3. Developing strategies and management skills for being effective in current organizational cultures.
4. Developing strategies and skills for influencing and changing cultures.
5. Developing confidence in their internal voices, and skills to articulate their viewpoints.

495

6. Exploring how they manage power, both when they might be undermined by others and when they have potentially 'superior' power.
7. Reviewing what they want from employment as a continuing life process, and devising strategies for achieving quality in the portfolio of life roles they choose.

Shared development needs

This chapter concentrates on differences, and so has little to say about the many development needs which women share with men. These are particularly in the realm of specific skills or general management raining such as Master in Business Administration (MBA) programmes. Women need to gain access to a wide array of training, in which they are underrepresented relative to men, and to see promotion opportunities ahead of them to make their experience meaningful. However, as social values have been so firmly male-dominated until recently, no training can currently be assumed to be gender-neutral. Any course should explore whether its roots incorporate gender-biased assumptions; for example, by devaluing management skills previously stereotyped as female, or by treating as complete 'knowledge' frameworks derived only from studies of men in male-dominated organizations. This inquiry is best done both in course development and as an active process with participants.

In the remainder of this chapter I explore the current training and development provision for women managers. In taking this perspective I do not assume that women are deficient in some way, need to be socialized into 'normal' organizational behaviour, and should necessarily adapt. This was an implicit assumption of much early development for them (taking for granted the superiority of male over female values), which lingers on covertly in some activities. Rather I think that to achieve true equal opportunities, organizations need to grow and change as they incorporate more women. Any training and development for women managers is therefore best undertaken as part of a committed, long-term organizational change initiative.

MANAGEMENT DEVELOPMENT PROVISION

There is now a wide range of courses and other development opportunities directed at women managers. Company support for this provision fluctuates significantly with other social and economic factors. The last ten years have seen at least two important renewals of interest in women's development in the United Kingdom. The first was in response to expected skills shortages as a result of demographic trends. Some organizations introduced training for women returners and enhanced child-care provision. Interest waned, however, when recession caused rising unemployment. The potential boost for women's fortunes largely failed to materialize.

In 1991 the launch of Opportunity 2000, a Business in the Community initiative to
496 increase the quality and quantity of women's participation in the workforce, drew

renewed attention to women's development. By the end of Opportunity 2000's first year, 150 companies were involved, representing approximately 20 per cent of employees in the United Kingdom (Hammond, 1992). These companies have set their own individual agendas for change, some more robust than others. The more committed have introduced substantial training programmes for women – and some gender awareness training for men – as part of wider cultural change initiatives.

The activities discussed below are not solely relevant to women, but do directly address their concerns. In some areas, such as assertion, men are now showing an interest in training initiated for women; in others, women's training shares a label with men's but typically takes a different form in practice. It is important to recognize that the unequal patterning of social power which has helped shape women's development needs can also hamper appropriate attention to them. For this reason training structures are as significant as specific course topics. These aspects are dealt with separately.

Training structures

Networking

As they become more involved in the world of work and reflective about their places in it, many women are looking for people of 'their own kind' to mix with. They also often feel cut off from established channels of communication and information sharing. These various motives have led to a growth in women's networks and associations, some official (like the European Women's Management Development Network), others informal; some with a specified constituency such as women in publishing or computing, and other looser groupings of people who feel they can benefit from dialogue. Broadly based networks offer members reference points outside their immediate work contexts and news on current developments. Informal networks within a company or locality serve other, more supportive, functions as well.

As these activities grow, women are exposed to possible role models as well as friends and contacts. Coaching by mentors higher up their organizations has been a significant factor in many women managers' success; networking offers more lateral coaching relationships. Some organizations are deliberately creating opportunities on induction programmes for new female recruits to meet established women managers, making such relationships more possible. Advice to trainers and members on creating and fostering networks is also now available.

Women-only training and groups

Although we are experiencing their re-emergence in society, female values remain fragile and their development tentative. They need protection if they are not to be swamped or overriden by their robust male counterparts. Similarly in their development, women need the comparative safety of working in women- *497* only groups. Here participants can, to a certain extent, suspend dominant cultural stereotypes, and explore and compare experiences which either men do not share or which affect them differently. Even patterns of conversation make this more difficult to do in mixed company. Men and their opinions tend to dominate and either leave women out or assign them to supportive roles. This pattern occurs even in mixed sex discussions of *women's* issues. Men often speak for women with a clarity that is difficult to counter, or women may be reluctant to contradict if their own ideas are more diffusely formed or grounded in socially muted values. In women-only groups participants can concentrate on understanding and supporting each other, and finding clear expressions of their own needs, rather than on competing for attention. They are also more able to take risks.

Early initiatives in assertion and management training, and the recent impetus from Opportunity 2000, have done much to establish women-only courses as viable and valuable activities. Their number is increasing, despite debate and some criticism. Amongst other things, this reflects a growing identification amongst women, and in this way, too, provides new models of possible working practice. There is also more attention and respect for women's diversity, reflected, for example, in the emergence of some training specifically for black women managers.

Women-only organizations and networks are also flourishing. These vary widely in their ways of working and the issues they address. Some act as support groups, in which members talk through attitudes, motivations, problems and choices, gaining new perspectives and sharing ways of coping. Some are organized on a company or occupational basis and have a clear objective of professional development, running seminars on management skills, inviting guest speakers and so on. Some represent women's viewpoints to their organization or industry.

Women-only activities also bring their challenges. Sometimes conflict within a group is suppressed, partly as a relief from more combative relationships outside, and harmony becomes more important than allowing a diversity of views. Managing conflict and dealing with envy, competition and betrayal are now emerging as important issues for women to work on generally. Many of them reject competitive, rivalry-based models for handling differences, and are looking for alternatives which combine mutual recognition and self-assertion.

Many men find women-only activities bewildering and threatening, and it is therefore no easy path to introduce them into organizations. (There are also, now, increasing numbers of men who understand, respect and support such initiatives.) Once a women's group is set up it is not unusual for individual men to make powerful bids to join or to find out what is being discussed. Sometimes women are subtly deterred from being members by male managers' comments. For example, some women have been asked in appraisal interviews whether they *really* need to belong to a particular industry's women's network, their managers implying that doing so demonstrates weakness or aggression on their part. Also women can be hesitant about joining women-only activities: some are unwilling to attract attention; others think that separate development may harden stereotypes which might otherwise be shifting. Any women's group which intends to report back to and influence the rest of the organization must consider how this can be achieved without creating conflict inappropriately or breaching the safety of the group. These 'safe spaces' need, then, careful management and attention.

Flexibility

A keynote of women's development needs as outlined above is exploration. Predetermined course formats are not usually sufficiently flexible to meet this requirement. Sometimes, therefore, open time is scheduled on courses during which participants can work individually or in small groups on topics of their choice, using trainers as facilitators. The diversity that women bring to training is also accommodated by attention to contracting at the start of and during a course. Participants may be asked, for example, to write down three things they want from the programme, three things which will stop them achieving these objectives and three things they have to offer. These are then displayed publicly. Contracts help participants clarify their expectations, and give trainers an opportunity to state clearly those which the course can and cannot meet. Contracts can be reviewed part-way through the event to monitor progress. They help increase the course relevance and tailoring, and demonstrate participants' responsibility for their own learning.

Different approaches to development opportunities

Women's development activities so far have given priority to issues that men, whose choices about employment have seemed less problematic, might view as 'background'. This contributes to differences between men and women in how they approach development opportunities. From my own experience, and discussions with other trainers, it seems that women tend to bring their whole selves, their full range of life roles, to any activities, and are open to being changed by them. Men more typically present themselves as organizational people, looking for relevance within a particular area of expertise, and doubt whether radical change in adult life is possible. One consequence is that women may need help to integrate employment-based learning into the other life areas it affects. Assertion training, for example, may improve their management skills but create temporary havoc in relationships at home. Trainers will need to be alert to, and prepared to work on, these wider repercussions.

Dispersed training

A crucial need identified above was for women to increase their competence in potentially inhospitable organizational cultures. Once-and-for-all training is seldom the best way to achieve this, despite its practical and financial advantages. Instead, some courses meet at regular intervals for several weeks or months, with opportunities for members to test out their new skills in between. *499*

This format has been especially successful for some assertion and self-development training.

Self-development groups

Opportunities for maximum flexibility are offered by self-development groups for women. A group meets at regular intervals, with a trainer acting as facilitator. Participants manage their own process, identify their individual and collective needs, and plan and run a programme of activities to address these. The emphasis is on holistic development, addressing employment in the context of other life areas, and recognizing the interdependence of thinking, feeling and doing. Such groups can be highly successful, supporting their members in significant work and personal learning. Managing the group's development and decision-making themselves gives participants valuable experience, and opportunities to experiment with varied styles and strategies.

Training topics

Assertiveness

The single most significant and impactful training topic for women so far has been assertiveness; this directly addresses their traditionally inferior social position, and offers ways to reclaim personal and organizational power. Assertion training helps women develop their personal self-confidence and their interpersonal skills, including their abilities to express and honour their own perspectives, even when these do not conform to established organizational norms and ways of thinking. Participants tend to favour styles which reflect their female grounding and reject behaviours they find too aggressive or competitive.

The basic principles of assertion training are: respect for self and others; equality; responsibility for one's own needs; maintaining appropriate boundaries between oneself and others; and choice – including when and whether to be assertive. Typical exercises involve practising assertive techniques such as dealing with anger, accepting or giving criticism, and saying 'no'; role plays of problem situations; explorations of non-verbal behaviour and its implicit messages; and distinguishing between assertive, passive and aggressive behaviour. Dickson (1982) provides a valuable primer.

Some organizations recognize the benefits of assertion training and offer it widely. Many courses, however, go on outside companies as part of women's development for themselves, but with obvious job implications. Assertiveness is a valuable first rung of management training for women. Its basic principles are being incorporated in other types of programme.

Management courses for women

Many companies, higher education establishments and training organizations *500* now run management training courses for women, some targeted at those in senior positions. Opportunity 2000 has provided a significant boost to activities.

Courses cover an established range of skills such as leadership, time management, negotiating, stress management and decision-making, but take on a distinctive flavour because their participants are women. In sessions on stress, for example, the pressure of working in competitive, male-dominated environments and conflicts between life roles usually figure as concerns. As identity issues are central to many participants' approaches to work, activities to explore personal values and reinforce self-confidence are typically included.

Three topics are particularly gaining prominence in management development for women. The first is power. Women managers encounter power in many overt and covert ways. Assertion training largely addresses their potential powerlessness. They need also to explore how they handle their own various sources of power, especially that of organizational status, which is relatively unfamiliar to them and may prove initially uncomfortable for their colleagues. Many have co-operative ideals, wanting to exercise power with others rather than over them, and must develop strategies for doing this effectively, especially in organizations which are still largely hierarchic.

More women are also becoming interested in how power can be used to shape values and norms of behaviour, to define reality for people. Through such processes cultural habits become established, or may be changed. In their experiences of male-dominated organizational cultures, women managers are experiencing this form of power in action, and appreciate how resilient it is to influence. Learning about definitional power therefore has several purposes: developing their abilities to notice when such power is used against their potential interests; strengthening skills for countering such moves; and giving them access to strategies for establishing and defending their own viewpoints within the culture. However, many women reject the dominant view that organizational politics, through which such agendas are achieved, are necessary or desirable. They want to find more open ways of negotiating between differences.

Secondly, and on a related theme, increasing attention is being paid to organizational cultures, how they work and how they can be changed. Many women see culture change as the essential next step to achieving equal opportunities in practice; some are now in positions from which they can influence norms and values.

The third topic which now appears widely on training course agendas is 'self-presentation'; its prominence is intriguing and gives appropriately mixed messages about women's acceptability as managers. Similar titles cover diverse offerings. Some seem to advocate adjusting to dominant cultural norms: by dressing for success, learning to make a confident first impression, maintaining a professional, unemotional, image, asserting authority, and so on. Such advice could reinforce any uncertainties women have about being accepted or taken seriously as managers, and persuade them to adopt masks to gain legitimacy. Other courses, with which I have more sympathy, encourage self-expression by seeking congruity between outer and inner self-images and exploring possibilities of style. They advocate play, enjoyment and choice.

As women engage in development they often question established values and assumptions, and arrive at new formulations. Alternative perceptions of leadership, effectiveness, power, and so on – ones more compatible with female values – are thus emerging. More important than potential new guide-lines, however, are the freedoms individual women are being offered, and are taking, to explore for themselves and achieve their own uniquely appropriate blend of female and male values from which to operate.

Life-planning and career building

An early training concern amongst women was life-planning, and this is still an important priority. The basic format of reviewing one's past history, assessing strengths and weaknesses, identifying unfulfilled ambitions and so forming plans for future development is already well established. Women bring several distinctive concerns to these activities, and their own patterns of life phases. The early thirties are emerging as a critical time for many, as they review their career progress and wonder whether to have children.

Balancing careers with a home life is a continuing focus of attention, as is how to manage potentially conflicting needs in dual-career families. Whether to interrupt their career at some point is a particularly difficult decision for women. Some companies are now offering 'returner schemes' to allow extended leave for parenting, with opportunities for keeping in touch through occasional training or work experience. Although such measures are helpful, the dilemmas and practical difficulties remain. Also research in other contexts suggest that women who interrupt their careers are likely to be significantly disadvantaged in terms of pay and promotion opportunities in later working life. Improving child-care facilities, including after-school care, is an alternative approach which offers greater potential career continuity, but may encourage over-busy lives as being the norm for women and men.

These choices are related to how ambitious, in conventional terms, women want to be. Many are now setting out with the intention of pursuing careers continuously and with commitment and see no need to limit their expectations. Many also want to combine involvement in a sequence of satisfying and challenging jobs with leading a balanced life and achieving congruity between their work roles and inner senses of meaning (Marshall, 1984 and in press). Women, and their partners where appropriate, are seeking strategies and life-styles to achieve these complex aims. They are using life-planning to explore possible options, often putting their whole lives in the balance at a particular choice point.

In their planning, women have a choice between two core strategies, reflecting male- and female-based options, or they can combine the two. Much career literature gives highly directive advice, telling women to be exceptionally clear about their objectives and persistent in pursuing them. This is an idealized male model of development. Some women reject its potential rigidity and point to their own success through more opportunistic progress. They have
502 let their lives evolve following their own intuitions, and have found external

challenges as necessary. This – more female – strategy provides an alternative model for women and men as employment possibilities become more flexible (Handy, 1990).

Sexuality

An area which is now receiving some training attention is sexuality at work. Courses on sexual harassment are becoming available, aimed at advisers to victims and/or victims themselves. As women and men work together more often as equals, individuals are more exposed to dilemmas about sexual attraction. Some women are concerned about the management of sexuality in intimate working relationships, and are looking for opportunities to explore their feelings and strategies. This may well become an additional topic in assertion or management effectiveness courses. Addressing such issues also means examining dominant social assumptions that sexuality is mainly heterosexual, and paying attention to the experiences of lesbian managers.

Women and men as colleagues

The initiatives covered so far have concentrated on building bridges between women and the organizations in which they work. Workshops which take 'men and women as colleagues' as their theme offer more direct opportunities to influence organizational cultures. Typically, participants work in both single- and mixed-sex groups, reporting back in full session. Attitudes to work, sex role stereotypes, management styles, and so on, are both discussed and put to the test in role plays and problem-solving activities. Training objectives are enhanced understanding of the similarities and differences between women and men, individual learning about one's own attitudes and behaviours, and awareness of how organizational structures and cultures carry and enforce norms and values about gender. When training is company-based rather than open-access, it is hoped that further development will happen on participants' return to work.

Such workshops require considerable skills from the trainers involved. Sex differences in power, language, values and emotional expression all figure prominently in the discussions themselves and need careful handling if underlying assumptions about gender are to be adequately revealed and explored. The dialogue such arenas offer is a vital next step to developing women's and men's relationships at work and so must be fostered, despite its challenges. Use of this kind of format for gender-related training is therefore likely to increase in the future.

CONCLUSION

In this chapter I have charted women's current development needs and training provision. I have also outlined some of the issues, particularly of potentially conflicting values, which require attention in any initiative. This is an area of continuing change. Development for women still requires justification in many *503* organizations; and often this has to be argued within dominant value frameworks that may well not appreciate women's potential talents or believe they have a legitimate right to be in management. Recent developments, such as Opportunity 2000, have created renewed interest in achieving fuller realization of equal opportunities and have given more public prominence to women's development. Furthermore, an increasing number of women now see employment as a principal activity in their lives and are taking action both to maximize their individual prospects and to influence their working environments.

But there are also contrary voices. Some men resent attention being paid to women's needs; they are especially unconvinced that women require increased access, particularly as employment opportunities generally contract. Some women are hesitant about identifying themselves as having separate concerns, lest they be seen as troublesome. We need more open expression of such views and issues so that we can manage them overtly and productively, rather than negotiating round them covertly. This means being willing to engage in culture change together. If we do not establish more open dialogue we risk perpetuating current power differences and cultural patterns in any development activities we undertake, so continuing to devalue and limit women's perspectives. To guard against this we need both separate development for women, to strengthen their voices, and joint development through dialogue between women and men.

FURTHER READING

Belenky, M.F., B.M. Clinchy, N.R. Goldberger and J.M. Tarule (1986), *Women's Ways of Knowing: The Development of Self, Voice and Mind*, New York: Basic Books.

Capra, C. (1982), *The Turning Point: Science, Society and the Rising Culture*, Aldershot: Wildwood House.

Dickson, A. (1982), *A Woman in Your Own Right*, London: Quartet Books.

Gilligan, C. (1982), *In a Different Voice: Psychological Theory and Women's Development*, Cambridge, Mass.: Harvard University Press.

Gordon, S. (1991), *Prisoners of Men's Dreams: Striking Out for a New Feminine Future*, Boston, Mass.: Little, Brown.

Hammond, V. (1992), 'Opportunity 2000: A culture change approach to equal opportunities', *Women in Management Review*, **7**, (7), 3–10.

Handy, C. (1990), *The Age of Unreason*, London: Arrow Books.

Loden, M. (1985), *Feminine Leadership, or How to Succeed in Business Without Being One of the Boys*, London: Times Books.

Marshall, J. (1984), *Women Managers: Travellers in a Male World*, Chichester: Wiley.

Marshall, J. (1989), 'Re-visioning career concepts', in M.B. Arthur, D.T. Hall and B.S. Lawrence (eds), *Handbook of Career Theory*, Cambridge: Cambridge University Press, 275–91.

504   Marshall, J. (in press), 'Why women leave senior management jobs: my research

approach and some initial findings', in M. Tanton (ed.), *Women in Management: The Second Wave*, London: Routledge Press.

Rosener, J.B. (1990), 'Ways women lead', *Harvard Business Review*, Nov.–Dec., 119–25.

Spender, D. (1980), *Man Made Language*, London: Routledge and Kegan Paul.

37 Management development and organization development

Graham Robinson

INTRODUCTION

I wrote the original version of this chapter in 1986. At that time Great Britain was emerging from the most significant recession since the 1930s and showing signs of the recovery and attendant optimism which preceded the disastrous boom of 1989. In writing a piece on the relationship between organization and management development, I was concerned about what I considered to be a dangerous fragmentation between increasingly specialized disciplines, each of which purported to be serving managers endeavouring to cope with an exponentially accelerating rate of change. I was writing in the heady, post-Peters and Waterman days when everything was *excellent* and every management text contained at least one superlative in its title.

For the next edition of the handbook I revised the chapter to take account of the significant changes which seemed to be heralded by the impact of the Management Charter Initiative and the concept of national standards for management qualification. In my introduction to the chapter, I bemoaned the fact that, in the midst of all this change, organization development appeared to have come to occupy more and more of a back seat.

Now, in 1993, I am writing from a perspective which has changed dramatically once again. Depending on who your favourite economic guru or political pundit happens to be, we are presently crawling out, or are still in the middle, of an even deeper and longer recession than that of the 1980s. Manufacturing in the United Kingdom in general, and in the south-east of England (the garden of 'Yuppiedom') in particular, has been particularly hard hit. Mobile young managers find themselves landed with the yoke of negative equity, and the name of the managerial game, and that of its advisers, has moved on yet again. Organizations have 'rationalized', 'downsized' and 'rightsized'. Tom Peters' exhortation to managers to create fewer, flatter, structures and bash bureaucracy has largely become a regular feature of organizational life. Not, I suspect, as a response of true believers espousing his cause, but as part of a generalized and increasingly desperate bid for survival (with a bit of encouragement from political dogma). ICI is in the midst of splitting itself into two or more separate businesses following the predatory bid from Hanson. IBM and General Motors have recorded the largest corporate losses in the history of capitalism, while Microsoft, founded, managed and largely owned by Bill Gates, still under 40 and dismissed as 'nerdy' by a senior executive in a competitor company, has recorded a higher turnover than the once seemingly indomitable IBM.

In this world turned upside down, organization development as a distinct discipline appears to have faded even further from view. At the same time, some of the underlying assumptions and values of management development (derived to a great extent from experiences gained in supporting the big corporate guns) have been opened up to some serious questioning, as the organizations in which they were developed vie with one another to see which can operate with the leanest corporate office of them all.

If all this were not sufficient, the focus of attention has begun to fall increasingly upon smaller and medium-sized enterprises (SMEs), encouraging the question: 'What have organization and management development ever done for them?' While such businesses have always represented a large slice of most Western economies, it is really only the conspicuous failure of so many big organizations that has drawn their smaller fellows into the sights of management and organization development practitioners. As the Russian proverb puts it, 'When the devil is hungry, he will eat flies'.

All of this sugested to me that I should scrap the original chapter and start all over again, reflecting the new realities (at least as they appear in 1993!). However, the distinctions described in the original chapter, between organization and management development, still have an important influence upon the mindsets of many of us who provide advice and guidance to managers on how they might improve their own or their organization's performance. As mindsets lead to actions that are guided by assumptions lurking somewhere below the conscious level, it is as well to have them articulated and made explicit, particularly if economic circumstances may have served to drive them even deeper below the level of surface awareness. I have, therefore, decided to leave the core of the chapter largely unchanged, even at the risk of some of it now seeming a little quaint.

If you don't know where you have come from it may be a little more difficult to see where you are going.

THE BACKGROUND

In his *Encyclopaedia of Organisational Change Methods*, Huczynski (1987) suggests that organization development (OD):

> ... is now generally regarded as being concerned with helping the members of an organization to improve its total ability to manage and develop itself, so it is able to

507

respond to the environmental pressures it faces. Development implies that the organization needs to learn how to adapt and change its culture so that it can continue to survive and achieve its core purpose. ... if an organization's members are to develop and learn how to adapt and change, they need to acquire skills additional to, or other than, those they already possess.

If this is the case, and I believe Huczynski to be right, I would argue that the connections between effective management, effective management develop-ment and effective organization development must be seamless. The variations between the particular contributions to organizational learning, achievement of purpose and, ultimately, to survival made by the different disciplines are largely ones of accountability, emphasis and preference. A significant and, hopefully, beneficial outcome of the recession for the practice of management may have been to hammer a nail into the coffin of the self-indulgent interdisciplinary rivalries beween those disciplines which must now co-operate in making a concrete (that is, measurable) contribution to organizational performance or leave the stage to those who can.

First, however, it is necessary to be clear about terms. I quoted from Huczynski's 1987 description of organization development above, by way of a first definition of the subject. In 1990 I used the following quotation from Ralph Kilmann's (1989) book, *Managing Beyond The Quick Fix*, to place organization development in its current context:

> The field of organization development, as it first emerged in the 1950s was envisaged as offering methods for systemwide change that would significantly improve the function of entire organizations. For the most part, however, this majestic vision has been lost and forgotten. ... Today, however, as many organiz-ations are coming to realise that 'future shock' is upon them, the need for fundamental, systemwide change is being voiced more and more frequently. Now entire organizations must be transformed into market driven, innovative, and adaptive systems if they are to survive and prosper in the highly competitive, global environment of the next decades. Given this situation, there is an urgent need to rejuvenate the theory and practice of organization development – to supply programmes for systemwide change.

Many of the new approaches to achieving of organizational transformation – such as performance management, total quality management, and the Investor in People initiative – *do* borrow heavily and appropriately from 'the theory and practice of organization development' but, having been tempered by economic turmoil, with somewhat less of the latter's idealism and naiveté. At the same time there has been a recognition of the requirement for managers to be able to develop and learn with less of the prescriptive arrogance that characterized many of the traditional, centralized, specialist-owned programmes of manage-ment development.

Much of the distinction between organization development and management development was made possible by their mutual separation from the guts of politics of organizational and managerial performance. The debates over the
distinctiveness of either reduced the effectiveness of both, leading in turn to an

increased separation from the client managers for whose benefit they were both supposed to exist.

But now the situation is changing, largely as a consequence of force majeure as opposed to a conscious recognition of the requirement to change. Perhaps this does not matter, so long as we developers have learned along the way and, more importantly, our management clients have derived a benefit from that learning.

Let us now examine the aims and intentions of management and organization development more closely. Management development has been described as: 'an attempt to increase managerial effectiveness through planned and deliberate learning processes'. The customers for such processes, client managers, have tended to have fairly clear views about management development within their organizations, and they have usually had few problems in making a distinction between their perceptions of management development on the one hand and management training on the other. While the latter has been perceived as a process necessary to the acquisition of skills (such as budgetary development and control), management development tends to be viewed as a broadening, educational process by means of which the individual is initiated, shaped or fitted to the attitudes, values, rites and rituals of successively higher levels within the organization. As such, management development may or may not encompass formal training, and it may be self-managed. Many organizations have attached especially high value to processes of management self-development, even to the extent of welcoming back the prodigal manager who, having resigned 'to gain experience in another environment', now returns to the fold with renewed vigour. Others stress the value of a broad base of experience, but tend to reward 'loyalty and long service', which automatically places severe constraints on the perceived benefits and wisdom of pursuing opportunities for such broadening.

To an extent, then, client managers would relate management training to a process by means of which the individual acquires the skills associated with a specific management job or level. They would tend to regard management development as having much more to do with career development and progression. This difference in perception tends to be thrown into much sharper relief in organizations where responsibility for management training is assigned to the training function, while management development is assigned as a personnel responsibility. This distinction is further reinforced where there is, real or perceived, competition between the two functions over which is accountable for what and as to where the senior status lies.

As industry struggles to recover from the impact of two very deep recessions in little over a decade, this separation of functions has tended to be reduced as part of the slimming down process. The single, leaner function which has succeeded separated training and personnel functions in a great many organizations, under the title of 'human resource management' (HRD), and has narrowed the gap somewhat. But, as with management development and organization development, the separate mindsets associated with skills training on the one hand and with personal growth and development on the other, still linger on. *509*

Whatever the situation in a specific organization, there would appear to be a general consensus among client managers that both management training and development are a 'good thing' and that their organization probably has not done, or is not doing, enough in these areas.

The views of client managers towards organization development are quite different. For a start it tends to be less immediately meaningful to managers outside the human resources, personnel and training functions themselves. In response to an illustration or example of a piece of organization development work, client managers will tend to respond with a reference to the name of a particular consultant or academic who 'once did some work with the company along those lines', rather than indicate any familiarity with, or expectations of, organization development *per se*. As a consequence, organization development tends to be known in terms of what particular practitioners do, rather than as a process or discipline with which managers are naturally familiar.

I have long been intrigued by human resource specialists' use of the acronym OD in discussions relating to the organization development processes and practice. Unlike other management specialisms developed over the past thirty years, the acronym does not appear to have passed into common usage among client managers themselves. Thus, while it would be quite unremarkable to hear an experienced line manager make reference to HRD (human resource development), O&M (organization and methods), OR (operations research) or to IT (information technology), the letters of OD roll rarely off the tongues of the same individuals. Similarly, personnel and training people infrequently, if ever, make reference to MD or MT to refer to the areas of activity mentioned earlier in this chapter. However, the use of the label 'OD' may provide a clue to one of the significant areas of difference between management development and organiz-ation development, and this difference relates to management's sense of identification with and ownership of the two processes.

In the 1960s, operational research was perceived as having a particularly significant contribution to make to the resolution of highly complex management problems in conditions of high uncertainty and risk. It had already made dramatic contributions in the military field during the Second World War, when interdisciplinary teams of scientists had applied the scientific method to the analysis, modelling and resolution of previously intractable problems. At about the same time in the 1960s a number of reports were circulating in the United States which were highly critical of current business school practice. Such practice was, at that time, highly dependent upon 'crude, non-rigorous, highly specific descriptions of a particular business. There was little if any general-ization across many businesses to formulate a set of general principles that could apply to many situations' (Mitroff and Kilmann, 1984). The successful application of scientific method to the resolution of complex management problems offered by the OR people contrasted strongly with the perceived inadequacies of the business schools. The latter, argued Mitroff and Kilmann, over-reacted, con-sciously trying to emulate the academic departments that had spawned the successful scientists and technologists. They hired newly accredited PhDs from prestigious universities who had been trained in the so-called pure (that is,

510

untainted by practical application) sciences and academically respectable disciplines, such as computer science, economics, industrial engineering, mathematics, political science, psychology, sociology, and so on. As a result, the academic respectability of the business schools went up enormously.

The expectations that organizations had of the scientists in the OR teams, both in the university departments and in their client organizations in the private and public sectors, were extremely high and many successes were achieved (for example, the development of critical path analysis and programme evaluation review technique (PERT)). Not unnaturally, therefore, the suggestion was made that the success of the natural sciences should be capable of being emulated by the behavioural scientists. Initially, this emulation took the form of the development of 'human factors' groups within the OR teams (in the United Kingdom within the British Iron and Steel Research Association (BISRA), and the National Coal Board, for example) and direct consultation from the universities and research institutes, such as Birkbeck College and the Tavistock Institute. In the United States, specialist behavioural science teams sprang up at the interface between business and academic institutions to examine the specific contribution that behavioural science would make to the development of these organizations – and thus, organization development (OD) was born.

There was a fundamental difference in the antecedents of management development and organization development. Management development was always a process 'owned' by the organization itself. It may not have been done particularly well, but the manager within the organization could identify with it as a process that had specific meaning for him, within the context of the norms and values of the organization by which he was employed. Organization development, on the other hand, was more specialized, more specific and, in aspiration at least, more scientific. It tended to be the domain of the business school and the research institutes rather than incorporated into the organization itself. Although not writing specifically about organization development, Mitroff and Kilmann (1984) provide a possible insight as to why the values and concepts of organization development have rarely been incorporated into the organizations that it was meant to be serving:

A PhD straight out of graduate school who had never in his or her life even been near a real business organization, could teach, write, and do research on business and management. While they thus achieved greater prestige in their own network, they increasingly lost touch with the business community and the world at large. Intentionally or unintentionally, they shut out from the halls of academia the very reality they were supposedly in the business of studying'.

The Mitroff and Kilmann argument may tend towards the extreme and, as noted above, they are not referring to organization development as such but to the relationship between the business schools and business in general. It does, however, provide a backdrop for the image of the organization development practitioner as an 'outsider'. The practitioners themselves have tended to prefer this role, as facilitator and change agent, as consultant and catalyst, as opposed to *511* that of integrated participant in the hurly-burly of the organizations which they have aspired to develop.

With the dramatic economic changes which commenced in the 1980s, the increase in uncertainty at all organizational levels, and the reduction in confidence in the ability of Cartesian logic to come up with the right answers to the complex problems of organizational and business life, there began a process of challenge to the contributions offered by all the specialisms which had developed so rapidly and with such promise in the 1960s. Line managers tended to become much more suspicious of operations research, other than in those areas of complexity where it has an established track record (vehicle scheduling, stock control and reordering, life-cycle forecasting, and so on). It tends to be perceived as 'esoteric, back room stuff', highly mathematical and largely beyond the comprehension of the managers whom it is there to serve. O&M too has lost much of the gloss that it had in the 1960s, not least because its emphasis on rationalism leads to a natural (though not always fair) association with rationalization, which in turn means 'putting the squeeze on my department'. Organization development has suffered in its turn from its identification with outsiders to the organization. Its emphasis on humanist values has had a rough ride in organizations forced by economic necessity to experience the massive employee shake-outs of the late 1970s, 1980s and now again in the early 1990s. At the same time there is a much greater awareness of the limitations to the skills that managers have at their disposal to enable them to tackle the challenges that the new circumstances present. Therefore, of the four specialisms mentioned (operational research, organization and methods, organization development and management development), managers might naturally be expected to identify more closely with the latter than with the others. As a manager, it is *I* who am looking for help in raising my capability to deliver against frightening levels of demand and expectation. It is *I* who need that support in order to maximize my chances of survival. It is *my* head on the block. I am apt in these circumstances to ask, very forcibly, the question, 'What's in it for me?', when offered support from any specialist practitioner purporting to be able to assist in the solution of my most pressing problems. By and large, the acceptable answer is more likely to come from the management developer than from the other specialists with fewer personally perceived concerns.

ORGANIZATIONAL DEVELOPMENT FRAMEWORKS

Before pursuing the theme of similarities and differences between organization development and management development further, it would be helpful to be clear about the particular frameworks within which organization development has endeavoured to operate. The word 'frameworks' is used, rather than 'definition' or 'frame of reference' because the field has become too imprecise, in the view of this writer, for any one of the many attempts at definition to be entirely adequate. Bennis (1969) described organization development as 'a response to change, a complex educational strategy intended to change the

beliefs, attitudes, values and structure of organizations so that they can better adapt to new technologies, markets, and challenges, and the dizzying rate of change itself'. Such a description places organization development at the apex of the organizational pyramid. It is strategic, it is concerned with values and it is concerned with structure. If organization development interventions are to be effective in terms of Bennis's description, then they must be made with the full participation and commitment of top management. Beckhard (1969) wrote:

> In an organization-development effort, the top management of the system has a personal investment in the programme and its outcomes. They actively participate in the management of the effort. This does not mean that they must participate in the same activities as the others, but it does mean that they must have both knowledge and commitment to the goals of the programme and must actively support the methods used to achieve the goals.

Perhaps less elegantly but with a shrewd eye for the realities of organizational life, Reddin (1977) wrote: 'When change agents tell me that they plan to attempt a change from the bottom up, I remind them of the military dictum that the penalty for mutiny is death.'

But is this insistence on top management involvement realistic? In the current climate such involvement is usually the result of massive and usually externally induced change, such as merger, take-over or bottom line crisis. There are a great many examples where such involvement has been the springboard for the initiation of successful organization-development-type interventions. But in the majority of organizations, the demands of running the operation in a difficult, but not necessarily catastrophic, environment may make the demand for such involvement unrealistic. Highly motivated teams operating just below but with the blessing of such top managers may provide a more realistic driving force for organizational transformation and development (Katzenback and Smith, 1993). Bennis himself goes on to suggest that his description of organization development may be to provide 'an abstract and perhaps, useless, definition'. In order to clarify his position, therefore, he goes on to provide four examples of organization development in practice:

1. Team development.
2. Intergroup conflict resolution.
3. Confrontation meetings.
4. Feedback.

Each of these examples is concerned with 'process' issues having an impact on the effectiveness achieved by particular work groups, either internally or at the interface between groups. Each is also concerned with the intervention of a third party 'change agent' or facilitator. Margerison (1978), writing ten years after Bennis, picks upon this latter point to suggest a simpler framework for organization development than that of the earlier writers: 'The term "organization development" ... means the skills and methods used by people to facilitate organizational improvement.'

While Margerison's description may reflect what organization development *513* has often become (and may provide an explanation as to why client managers have a hard time in recognizing the term 'organization development' at all), it has lost two key elements of the Bennis and Beckhard requirements. The first of these is strategy and the second is top level commitment. While the earlier writers' aspirations may have been too high (reflecting Mitroff and Kilmann's concern about business schools' distance from organizational realities), Margerison's description opens the door to the cynical comment that organization development is what organization developers do when it is successful. When it is not, it is what the client manager did and, therefore, is not organization development.

A really useful framework would probably lie somewhere between the two and would include a reference to the areas of knowledge, the particular skills and methods the organization developer would characteristically employ. Margulies and Raia (1972) went a long way towards meeting this requirement when they stated that 'organization development borrows from a number of disciplines, including Anthropology, Sociology, Psychology and Economics. It generally involves the use of concepts and data from the behavioural sciences to attempt to facilitate the process of planned change.' The toolbag is specified with the references to the disciplines upon which organization development practitioners draw, and the stress upon planned change goes some way to meet Bennis's emphasis upon organization development as a strategic activity (though it would not be argued here that a strategy and a plan are one and the same thing). Margulies and Raia went on to write that:

> Organization development is essentially a systems approach to the total set of functional and interpersonal role relationships in organizations. An organization can be viewed as a system of coordinated human activities, a complex whole consisting of a number of interacting and interrelated elements or subsystems. A change in any one part will have an impact on one or more of the other parts ... organization development itself can be viewed as a system of three related elements – values, process and technology.

They then provided examples of what these three elements might comprise, which are summarized here.

Values

1. Providing opportunities for people to function as human beings rather than as resources in the productive process.
2. Providing opportunities for each organization member, as well as for the organization itself, to develop to his full potential.
3. Seeking to increase the effectiveness of the organization in terms of all its goals.
4. Attempting to create an environment in which it is possible to find exciting and challenging work.
5. Providing opportunities for people in organizations to influence the way in which they relate to work, the organization, and the environment.

6. Treating each human being as a person with a complex set of needs, all of which are important in his or her work and in his or her life.

Process

1. Data gathering.
2. Organization diagnosis.
3. Action intervention.

Technology

1. New ways of organizational learning.
2. New ways of coping.
3. New ways of problem-solving.

The set of values provided by Margulies and Raia are essentially humanist in orientation. This provides another clue to the externalization of organization development from the organizations within which it is practised. The values as listed are desirable to most people, but the experience of recent life in large organizations has not done much to suggest that these values are shared within the organizations themselves. More difficult still, because organizational members can identify with them at an individual level, they are easily espoused by the organization in formalized expressions of its values: 'Our greatest asset is our people and their unswerving commitment to company goals.' But, to paraphrase Argyris (1974 and 1976), the values in use are demonstrably different. 'Despite the best endeavours of senior management the economic pressures have meant that we have had to release 500 valued members of the workforce.' Thus, the experience of organizational members during the 1980s and early 1990s has tended to be at odds with the stated values of organizational functionalist or pragmatic values concerned with being clear about terms and conditions of staff (or, increasingly, subcontractors), equipment, finance and time. These values place emphasis upon effective and efficient delivery as opposed to the more general values of human potential and satisfaction.

This is not to disagree with those who argue that it is possible to have *both* sets of values represented (and, hopefully, shared) within the same organization, but to suggest that the emphasis placed by organization development practitioners upon humanist values puts them in a frame of reference that is essentially external to that of their client organizations. In the 1970s, as the pressures of impending recession increasingly made themselves felt, the discussion was frequently to be heard as to whether the organization developer should remain professional and independent of the politics and in-fighting within organizations (in which individual and corporate survival were becoming dominant themes), or whether they should regard themselves as part of the process and be there in the thick of it. In the 1980s and beyond, it can no longer be a matter for debate – the value position of the practitioner will have to be made clear.

Galbraith (1977) does not start from the same, humanist, standpoint that *515* characterizes the writers referred to so far. He is, however, very much in tune with the systems orientation espoused by Margulies and Raia and places great emphasis upon the importance of strategy, in common with Bennis. But perhaps the most significant difference in style in Galbraith's work from those alluded to previously is the sense that he is writing for the manager who *owns* the problem rather than for the organization development practitioner who can *analyse* and *understand* the problem. Indeed, he refers to organization design as the key issue and not to organization development:

> Organization design is conceived to be a decision process to bring about a coherence between the goals or purposes for which the organization exists, the patterns of division of labour and interunit coordination and the people who do the work. The notion of strategic choice suggests that there are choices of goals and purposes, choices of different organizing modes, choices of processes for integrating individuals into the organization, and finally, a choice as to whether goals, organizations, individual or some combination of them should be changed in order to adapt to changes in the environment. Organization design is concerned with maintaining the coherence of these choices over time. (Galbraith, 1977)

These choices are fundamental and confront the manager with increasing frequency.

Writing some time later, Galbraith (1983) developed his systems orientation further to indicate that organizations 'consist of structure, processes that cut the structural lines like budgeting, planning teams, and so on, reward systems like promotions and compensation, and finally, people practices like selection and development'. This approach is considerably more in harmony with the prevailing, functionalist orientation that is characteristic of the 1990s management style, than is the humanist approach characteristic of Bennis, Margulies, Raia and others. His emphasis upon the notion of choice and, in particular, strategic choice, would also find favour with Mitroff and Kilmann who berate the business schools and their academic antecedents for their post-1960s emphasis upon training students to tackle exercises rather than to solve problems:

> It is vital as a culture that we come to appreciate that there is a vast difference between structured-bounded exercises and unstructured-unbounded problems .... In a phrase we have bred a nation of certainty-junkies. We have trained the members of our culture to expect a daily dosage of highly structured-bounded exercises. The difficulty is that the problems of organizations and society have become highly unstructured and unbounded'. (Mitroff and Kilmann, 1984)

Their reference to 'certainty-junkies' will strike a chord in the hearts of management trainers who are asked so frequently to 'dispense with the theoretical stuff and give us some techniques to fix these problems once and for all'. All too often the expectation seems to be that provided one has the analytical ability to take a problem apart and break it down into its constituent parts, it will be possible to examine it logically and resolve it with precision. Unfortunately, the resolution of organizational and managerial problems tends to be less about elegance and simplicity and a great deal more about subtlety, ambiguity and

choices.

LOOKING FOR A SILVER LINING

In the 1930s the sale of comics, escapist 'penny dreadfuls', sky-rocketed. The same period saw the rise of Hollywood and the Busby Berkley musicals. Both had as much to do with the harsh realities of an economically depressed industrial society as the 'Fame' musicals have to do with youth unemployment in the 1980s and the 'Terminator' movies have for the 1990s. These situations do require a catharsis, a discharge from the unremitting gloom of the dole queue and company insolvency. It is not surprising then, that the studies of excellence and success from the McKinsey Group (Peters and Waterman, 1982; Deal and Kennedy, 1982) and others (Goldsmith and Clutterbuck, 1982; Kanter, 1984 and 1989) proved so successful. The intention is not to suggest that these works are to management in the 1980s a precise equivalent of the penny dreadfuls and Hollywood to the unemployed of the 1930s. There are, however, certain parallels. Peters and Waterman do leave the reader with a warm feeling for the anecdotes of successful organizations awash with style, shared values and champions. They do not, unfortunately, leave the same reader with any prescription for action if that reader happens to be the manager of an organization which is manifestly unsuccessful or in a declining industry (a serious omission which Peters (1987, 1992) sought to rectify in his later books, *Thriving on Chaos* and *Liberation Management*.

Nevertheless, the McKinsey 'Seven-S' model offered by Peters and Waterman in 1982 has some close affinity with the systems model offered by Galbraith:

- strategy;
- structure;
- systems;
- staff;
- skills;
- shared values; and
- style.

The elements of the McKinsey model are very similar to Galbraith's (for 'people' in Galbraith, read 'staff' and 'skills' in Peters and Waterman, for 'systems' read 'processes', for part of 'shared values' read 'rewards', and add 'style'). Both emphasize the importance of strategy as a cornerstone in fostering corporate success.

But Peters and Waterman make no reference to organization development as such, though they do refer to one or two practitioners by name (including Bennis). Writing for an audience of managers, the concepts, values (even the name) of organization development, do not enter the pages of the best-selling book on management practice in the last decade. Once more, this would appear in keeping with the view of organization development as an externalized process as opposed to an accepted area of effective management practice to be internalized within the organization.

The key to opening the door of management practice to the processes of *517* organization development lies in the strategic focus emphasized by Bennis, reinforced by Galbraith, and central to the McKinsey 'Seven-S' model. Unless the organization development process (and, indeed, the management development process) is closely related to, and in keeping with, the organization's driving strategy, it cannot be effective. This may well mean that the practitioner may have to forgo the lucrative assignment where the strategy espoused (or used) by the client organization is inconsistent with those humanist values referred to by Margulies and Raia. He will certainly have an obligation to make them explicit, change his values, or play Iago to his client's Othello.

Strategy as the integrating theme

As long ago as the early 1980s Professor Phillipe de Woot (1984) sounded a loud cautionary note about the enthusiasm among European managers for the findings of the McKinsey Group and, by implication, for Goldsmith and Clutterbuck in the United Kingdom as well. He pointed out that the assumption underlying their approach is that most companies are overmanaged in what they refer to as the 'hard Ss' (strategy, structure and systems). They have developed these to an extent where the individual manager is reduced to being an administrator of a decision system rather than being required to be a decision-taker, and certainly not a risk-taker, himself. The experiences of the turbulent economy since de Woot's work was undertaken have only served to reinforce his point. But has the move to leaner, meaner and more efficient management structures made all that much difference?

The writers on corporate excellence concentrated much of their attention on reviving interest in the so-called 'Soft Ss' (staff, skills, shared values and style), which, one might think, should be regarded as a shot in the arm for the humanist values of organization development. But, argued de Woot, this only makes sense if the underlying assumptions of overmanagement and overcontrol were correct. In the European context he found little evidence to suggest that they were.

The results of a six-year research programme headed by de Woot suggested that very few European organizations practised the basics of strategic management which are a prerequisite for corporate success regardless of whether the management emphasis is hard, soft, or balanced. An organization committed to these basics would demonstrate that commitment through elements such as clarity over corporate goals, systematic management development at all levels, and a range of sophisticated decision-support processes and systems. In the absence of these, he argued, to jump upon the 'excellence' bandwagon may be meaningless or downright dangerous for an organization lacking in professionalism and 'tightness' (clear operating procedures, control systems, levels of authority, and so on). Such 'tightness' needs to exist not only at the centre but throughout all of its operating units. No large company can be truly innovative and entrepreneurial (let alone intrapreneurial) if it has not developed a highly professional base for its total operation. De Woot warned against interpreting this professionalism too narrowly, stating that 'tightness' based only on financial controls is totally inadequate since it gives the headquarters no ability to provide strategic direction and to communicate fruitfully with its off-shoots.

Such was the state of apparent strategic backwardness in Europe in the early 1980s that de Woot found:

1. That a number of top managers did not believe in defining clear objectives, and making them explicit throughout the company. 'I am not the Pope', he quoted one as saying. Such companies, he reported, 'suffer from "Shakespearean" intrigue and instability';
2. that top management frequently failed to set a strong lead; and
3. that employees 'are often slaves to external social values, rather than to the organization's culture'.

Once more the critical finger is being pointed at the negative consequences of adherence to values that are external to the organization itself, whether these external values are those of society at large, or those of the academic community, as claimed by Mitroff and Kilmann, or those humanist values claimed to be at the heart of organization development by Margulies and Raia.

In the absence of a clearly expressed strategic framework and an associated and consistent organizational value system to which their contribution can relate, organization and management developers alike are likely to share a common experience of floundering around in a sea of apparently random, at best feudal, managerial behaviour. In such an environment, development, whether organizational, managerial, group, or individual employee based, is likely to be characterized by a series of fits and starts and sudden changes of direction resulting from the importation of new techniques having all the characteristics of short-term popularity.

If de Woot was correct, and experience would suggest that at least he was on the right track, it is clear that the thrust of both management development and organizational development in Europe should be towards the specification, clarification and communication of organizational strategies and values. In order to be effective in this role, the developers have to earn the right to contribute. They have not always been particularly successful in so doing, not simply, as Mitroff and Kilmann argue, because they have used inappropriate models imported from inappropriate cultural and value sets, but because they have not had the corporate power to be heard. Perhaps the two things go together.

Have things changed as organizations have slimmed down in order to survive? The harsh reality is that a great many who *did not* change *have not* survived, and not just in Europe. Many of the problems currently being encountered by the 'excellent' companies of the 1980s are precisely those summarized by de Woot early in that same decade. Tom Peters now argues very strongly for much fuzzier or softer structures, dedicated to the achievement of clearly articulated strategic intentions that are known by and which have the commitment of organizational members at every level in the organization. In such an environment the boundaries and distinction between sales, production and R&D become increasingly irrelevant. How much more must this be true of supporting disciplines such as management development and organization development? *519*

ON THE HORNS OF A DILEMMA

To summarize, for organization-development interventions to be effective they must be consistent with and contribute to the strategies and values of the organizations within which the intervention is made. However, it has been suggested that most European organizations pay scant attention to managing strategically, preferring to adopt a more reactive, 'seat of the pants' style. This unsystematic approach creates a vacuum which is filled by the importation of values and quasi-strategies from outside the organization, for example, from government statements, from business schools, from external change agents or from internal specialist functions, such as personnel or training. But because these are imported values and do not form part of a 'tight' whole, they are fragmented and essentially ephemeral. Beckhard's response to this situation, presumably, would be to argue that this is precisely why organizational development interventions should only be made with the involvement of top management. Unfortunately, experience suggests that the internal specialists rarely carry the corporate power to make effective interventions at that, top management, level. Therefore, when the need for such an intervention is recognized it is more often than not assigned to an external adviser who owns another set of values ... and so the process is perpetuated. The resolution of the problem must lie within the organization itself, and a resolution is essential to corporate survival, for the non-European competition does not appear to share this problem to anything like the same degree. 'If we do not create a managerial revolution,' warned de Woot, 'we will wake up one bright morning and discover that ... we have become underdeveloped and colonized. By then it will be too late.'

It is interesting to note that similar concerns are expressed among management developers. For example, Critchley and Casey (1984) argue against the conventional approach to team management development. A view which would suggest that before a management group can seriously address such issues as strategy formulation or the determination of key tasks, it is first necessary for them to build a degree of openness and trust. They argue that, on the contrary:

> High levels of openness and trust are only rarely needed, and management groups get most of their work done very well without them, preferring for safety and comfort to remain relatively closed, and, covertly at least, distrustful. To ask such groups to make a major cultural shift, to take such big risks with each other as to be fully open and trusting, requires some mightily cogent justification ... if their purpose is to be of real value to their clients ... they [should] start by encouraging their clients to clarify the role and purpose of the management group in question, to identify the nature of the tasks which they need to address as a group – complex puzzles or real problems, and then to consider the appropriate modes of working, and the skills and processes that go with them. When we have reached this stage, most of us have the skills and technologies to provide what is needed. What is often left out is the diagnostic work which gets us to that stage. (Critchley and Casey, 1984)

CONCLUSION: RESOLVING THE DILEMMA

If management development is effective it *will* result in positive organization development, with effectiveness being measured in terms of enhanced organizational capability. It has been asserted in the earlier part of this chapter that management development is more generally recognized by in-company management as a 'good thing' than is organization development. This is because highly stretched managers can usually identify a potential personal benefit to themselves from an effective management development process. This benefit may not necessarily be obtained directly; 'my boss should go on this programme' is a statement not unfamiliar to the management trainer.

It was also asserted that expectations of management development programmes, with some notable exceptions, tend not to be very high. However, the very fact that management development as a potentially 'good thing' is a commonly shared value in a great many organizations gives the management developer a significant boost. It is eminently sensible for the management developer to ask the question of senior management: 'Management development for what?' Indeed if the question is not being asked, then the organization ought to be seriously questioning the value of having management developers in any case. The answers to the question should lead, step-by-step, to a clarification of the role and purpose of the management group. This is the investment in the diagnostic process argued for strongly by Margulies and Raia, and so frequently neglected in practice, as observed by Critchley and Casey.

Presented with the results of the diagnosis, the next step needs to be placed firmly in the hands of the management group itself, and that is a questioning of the group's contribution to the achievement of overall organizational strategy, aims and objectives. If the answer is not apparent, then either the group has misjudged its role and purpose, or the strategy, aims and objectives are unclear. Whatever the reason for the situation in a specific instance, the group, which owns the problem, should push and push hard for its resolution. In this the members of the group must be supported and encouraged by the management developer. He cannot afford to sit on a professional fence for, if he does, he will have earned the comparatively low expectations that are so often expressed about his chosen field. If, on the other hand, he does get involved in the uncomfortable process of questioning and reappraisal that will result, he will have made a significant contribution to a genuine process of organizational development. Such a process will not of necessity incorporate the humanist values espoused by writers such as Margulies and Raia; it may even bring about the management revolution felt by de Woot to be so vital for European economic survival. Some practitioners who go down this road will do doubt wish that they had heeded Reddin's warning that 'the penalty for mutiny is death'. But whatever the outcome for the management developer, going through the process should make a significant contribution to the two things that all the writers referred to in this chapter seem to be agreed upon: that genuine organization development is contingent upon the espousal of clearly formulated and communicated strategies on the one hand, and internally developed shared values on the other. *521*

The pain of the recessions of the 1980s and 1990s has been shared by managers, management developers and organization developers alike. This trial by ordeal has probably – for those who have survived at least – served to break down the barriers and to develop a community of shared values which should have been there in any case. But the most powerful of necessary lessons will often only be learned as a response to a substantial crisis.

It is currently fashionable to describe those organizations which *do* adapt, change and, perhaps, even flourish in times of economic adversity as 'learning organizations'. There is a risk, of course, that the embattled manager may dismiss the term as just another example of specialist, 'consultant-speak' (like management development or organization development). On the other hand, the term might just be indicative of a much needed shift in emphasis, as a consequence of which managers, management developers and organization developers *all* begin to recognize and appreciate the value of their various, different contributions, and to demonstrate an enthusiasm and willingness to learn – really learn – from one another to the benefit of themselves and of their organizations.

FURTHER READING

Argyris, C. and D.A. Schon (1974), *Theory in Practice: Increasing Professional Effectiveness*, San Francisco: Jossey-Bass.

Argyris, C. (1976), *Increasing Leadership Effectiveness*, New York: Wiley.

Beckhard, R. (1969), *Organization Development: Strategies and Models*, Reading, Mass.: Addison Wesley.

Bennis, W. (1969), *Organization Development: Its Nature, Origins and Prospects*, Reading, Mass.: Addison Wesley.

Critchley, B. and D. Casey (1984), 'Team-building', *Management Education and Development*, **15**, (2).

Deal, T.E. and A.A. Kennedy (1982), *Corporate Cultures: Rites and Rituals of Corporate Life*, Reading, Mass.: Addison Wesley.

de Woot, P. (1984), 'Le Management Stratégie des groupes industriels', *Economics*, Paris, quoted by Christopher Lorenz, *Financial Times*, 26 November.

Galbraith, J.R. (1977), *Organization design*, Reading, Mass.: Addison Wesley.

Galbraith, J.R. (1983), 'Strategy and Organization Planning', *Human Resource Management*, **22**, (1/2), spring/summer.

Goldsmith, W. and D. Clutterbuck (1984), *The Winning Streak*, London: Weidenfield & Nicholson.

Huczynski, A. (1987), *Encyclopedia of Organizational Change Methods*, Aldershot: Gower.

Kanter, R.M. (1984), *Change Masters*, London: George Allen & Unwin.

Kanter, R.M. (1989), *When Giants Learn to Dance*, London: Simon & Schuster.

Katzenbach, J. and D. Smith (1993), *The Wisdom of Teams: Creating the High Performance Organization*, Harvard Business School Press.

Kilmann, R. (1989), *Managing Beyond the Quick Fix*, London: Jossey-Bass.

Margerison, C. (1978), *Influencing Organizational Change*, London: IPM.

Margulies, N. and A.P. Raia (1972), *Organization Development: Values, Process and Technology*, New York: McGraw-Hill.

Mitroff, I. and R. Kilmann (1984), *Corporate Tragedies*, New York: Praeger.

Peters, T. (1987), *Thriving on Chaos*, New York: Alfred Knopf.

Peters, T. (1992), *Liberation Management*, London: Macmillan.

Peters, T. and R. Waterman (1982), *In Search of Excellence*, New York: Harper & Row.

Reddin, W.J. (1977), 'Confessions of an Organizational Change Agent', *Group and Organization Studies*, International Authors, BV, March.

38 Action learning: the long haul

John Morris

Action learning has been around for quite a long time. The undisputed father of the approach, Professor Reg Revans (of whom more later) claims that he wrote his first article on the subject in 1938. But, as he would be the first to recognize, it has been around in spirit for much longer. Learning by doing, and from doing, has a long history. And yet the notion of action learning is far from self-explanatory. This chapter attempts to present both a summary account of action learning – its achievements and disappointments – and an argument that throws light on fundamental difficulties encountered by this approach. The argument can be briefly stated. It is that action learning positively demands the long haul, together with the courage and endurance to take it. It seeks the opportunity of becoming part of a way of life, rather than a short-lived current fashion.

This challenge is hard to meet, both in line management and in the centres dedicated to education and training. Most of us in training and development have settled for the short-term expedient. We have probably done this reluctantly, and in the hope that we will eventually be able to link our work with longer-term strategies. But most of our organizations have been pushed, whether they like it or not, into the shortest of short terms.

Action learning is faced with a dilemma here. It is one of the most flexible approaches to learning that one could imagine. It can even adapt itself to the short-term expedient, by recognizing that we can learn from any experience of getting something done, even if what is done is done in a great hurry. But the key values of action learning prepare us for the long haul. Fortunately, a growing recognition of the limitations of 'short termism' is favouring the long haul, seeing it as by far the better investment, even for hard-pressed enterprises.

THREE ESSENTIALS OF ACTION LEARNING

What then is action learning? It is a form of 'learning by doing' that has three essential characteristics. First, it insists that the action being taken is a real challenge, needing hard work in decision and implementation. Second, it requires the learning to be brought to consciousness, through careful and thoughtful questioning, and full consideration of alternatives. In this way, what is learned is clearly understood by the person who has gone through the experience of learning, and is therefore available both to the person and for passing on to others. Third, these two objectives – involvement in challenging action and a commitment to learning from that involvement – are ensured by enabling each learner to take full part in a small, intimate group of fellow learners – a learning 'set'. The set must be small enough to allow high trust and detailed knowledge of one's colleagues. At the same time, it must be big enough to provide opportunities for challenge and support for each member during the process of learning from one's own actions.

The simplicity and clarity of these three fundamental requirements constitute an important strength of action learning, but this very simplicity can be misleading. People often say that it is nothing but learning by doing, or that it clearly dispenses with reflection or planning in its eagerness to rush into action. It may be useful, therefore, to discuss these essentials in rather more detail, before describing some of the lessons that have been drawn from very extensive practice.

However, it would be Hamlet without the Prince of Denmark if action learning were to be discussed without first introducing its most effective and dedicated champion – Professor Reg Revans, now well into his eighties, and a prime example of one who practises what he teaches. A remarkable leader, and a genuine pioneer, he started his working life as a research worker in physics at the Rutherford Laboratory, became a student of Einstein in Berlin, an Olympic and Commonwealth Games athlete, and for eight years the Director of Education and Training for the National Coal Board. He developed early forms of action learning with colliery managers, and engaged in a notable initiative with ten leading London hospitals in the Hospital Internal Communications Project. Between 1965 and 1975 he was managing director of a programme in Belgium which had a significant effect on leading enterprises in the public and private sectors. He returned to Britain and initiated, with Lord Weinstock, a programme for GEC companies (Pearce and Casey, 1977). Since then he has witnessed and actively supported the growing recognition worldwide of action learning as a powerful approach to achieving organizational effectiveness.

An encouraging sign that action learning is being taken seriously for the 'long haul' is the establishment of programmes in higher education. In Britain, several universities and polytechnics are now offering higher degrees which use action learning as their principal approach. The International Management Centres, whose European centre is in Buckingham, have based their whole educational strategy on action learning. The International Foundation for Action Learning has been developing a network of practitioners, and providing support for those who are seeking information and guidance. Furthermore, ten years ago, a study of 'Action Learning Around the World' (Pedler, 1983) referred to university programmes in Sweden, Saudi Arabia, Eire, France, Egypt, and Australia. These achievements are a tribute to the power of the ideas guiding the approach, as well as to the dedication and energy of Professor Revans as 'project champion'. *525*

Not least, they indicate the growing support given by hardheaded directors and managers, impatient of fads and fashions, and wishing to ground their developmental work in enduring values. Their leadership, as sponsors, clients and co-directors of action learning initiatives, has shown the value of bringing work and learning together, rather than letting them drift apart.

To return now to the three essential characteristics already noted. Each has a label that can give rise to endless misunderstanding, even confusion. 'Action' is not just 'doing'. 'Learning' is not to be tied to the classroom learning so familiar from our schooldays, nor to the lectures and reading associated with traditional higher education. And the 'fellowship' or 'partnership' of those who learn within a set is not to be identified with the familiar groups found in working life or in training courses. There is clearly more to be said about the meaning of these terms in action learning.

THE MEANING OF 'ACTION' IN ACTION LEARNING

The attractively simple term 'learning by doing' is unfortunately quite inadequate as a way of capturing the essential element of 'action' in action learning. 'Doing' covers an enormous range of activities, including things that we have done so many times before that they have become habits. We may still be learning from the constant repetition of a daily routine, in the sense that we are stamping the habit into ourselves even more deeply. The 'action' that we are referring to here is radically different. It is the kind of action that requires us to make up our minds: the kind that we contemplate when we say 'What on earth am I going to do now?' Or perhaps the more genial kind, when we say 'It seems like a great opportunity, but what's the best way of taking it up?' Friends may advise us, and intuitions may prompt us, but we know that there are many options, and the right one for us is by no means clear.

If the situation that we are questioning turns out to be one that an available expert has seen many times before, and can confidently deal with for us, then we would probably be unwise to engage in action learning (though experts and their characteristic confidence are quite often mistaken, because the situation turns out to be one that they are not expert in dealing with). We are speaking of situations where values and strong feelings play an important part, rather than technical expertise. A useful distinction can be made between the way we deal with a situation requiring this kind of action, and one requiring a cut-and-dried 'solution'). This is the distinction between a *process* and a *programme*. A process, in the sense used here, is a stepwise sequence of activities, based on discovery and including trial and error, rather than a smoothly competent *flow* emerging from long practice, or expert instruction. These steps are often accompanied by strong feelings: anxiety, concern, excitement, delight, disappointment. All these are very far from the cool procedures that indicate the running-off of a programme, as a set of directions or instructions for getting from A to B along a well-charted route.

526   Programmes are appropriate for routines and habits: processes are the paths,

as yet untrodden, that create our histories. We have become accustomed to looking at organizational life as a set of orderly programmes. Yet we know that the organizations in which we actually spend a substantial part of our lives are not like that at all. They have their share of programmes, of course, but these are the background of the lively dramas and rituals that constitute the real life of the people who are the organization's reality. Organizational life is an overlapping, often confusing, set of stories in progress, rather than a tidy flow of neatly interlocking programmes. This view of the 'action' has vitally important implications for the 'learning' that characterizes action learning, and makes it an achievement of human beings rather than a logical extension of a computer programme.

TWO KINDS OF LEARNING

Learning is one of the most complex activities of our lives, and cannot be contained within simple distinctions. Nevertheless, one distinction, coined by Professor Revans, gives us an excellent start (see Revans, in Mumford, 1987, for a succinct statement). Learning, he proposes, can be viewed as two distinctive activities. One is a conscious questioning of one's experience, and a continual reorganizing of that experience in the light of whatever results from that questioning. The other is an adoption of an existing answer, as it were, so that a new programme has been added to the existing store of knowledge and skill. These two forms of learning are dubbed 'P' and 'Q', and it is quickly seen that conventional education, and training in particular, is focused on P (programmed instruction). Action learning is appropriate when we are faced with a need to do something in which P is not available to provide an answer. Many forms of learning are valuable by-products of the activities we carry out in our daily lives. We know from experience that practice seldom makes perfect, but it does enable us to make much of our behaviour smoothly automatic, giving us the opportunity of giving our attention to something else. But what we may have lost is the ability to know *how* we learned from our experience. In a way, it 'just happened'.

Action learning, with its constant concern with Q (questioning), resists this unthinking procedure, and insists on carefully monitoring whatever is being done, and reflecting on it, so that the process of learning is deliberate, responsible, and accountable. In this way, change is always possible; and the energy and sense of renewed purpose that naturally arise when we see the gap between what has been intended and what we have so far achieved, drives the next phase of activity.

The two kinds of learning intertwine and overlap in practice. The more effective our questioning, the more clearly we will see where established knowledge can come to our aid, without giving us the complete answer. We continually find that even situations which admit of a cut-and-dried way of coping need an individual touch – which we may call 'style' or 'finesse' – if we are to deal with them sensitively (Morris, 1991).

Part of the problem with P and Q is that we come from a way of life in Western *527* civilization which gives much more attention to P than Q. We are back to the short-term expedient again. Time presses, and we are driven by competition and the scramble for scarce resources. All too often, we squeeze the situations we encounter into ready-made categories, and apply ready-made answers to them, which often fit very badly indeed. We pride ourselves on being masters of technique, solidly based on scientific truths. And so our precious 'P' moves masterfully from being a body of knowledge about the world to being a tool kit of confident know-how, aiming to fix the world at whatever points it has 'gone wrong': that is, where it has failed to fit our preconceptions.

THE ACTION-LEARNING SET

So we now have the two aspects of action learning which have provided its name. The third – the 'partnership' provided by the set – is the distinctive form of association that provides the necessary challenge and support to those who are learning from their own experience of action: learning at first hand, but in the good company of others who are also learning.

Small groups are a familiar feature of modern life. They occur in organizational life as work teams, working parties, task forces, and project teams. In the world of education and training, we find small groups within forms and classes, together with syndicates, study groups and, once again, project teams.

The action learning set has affinities with several of these groups, but has its own integrity, stemming from its particular task. It needs to be small – preferably between four and seven members. In this way, it can enable every member to become an important part of the set, and to know what others are thinking, feeling and doing in sufficient detail to be of help to them in the co-learning activities. Unlike many of the familiar small groups found in organizational life, the set is not provided with a hierarchy, or even a structure, other than the form it takes on from its own perceived needs.

Because it is an unusual mode of association, there is often a need for a set adviser, whose key task is to foster the capabilities of the set members to contribute to the learning of the entire set. An adequate account of the relations between a set and its set adviser would take us well beyond the scope of these notes, because the role of adviser is the only designated role in the structure of the set (see, for example, the discussions by Casey, 1983 and in Mumford, 1987). But in summary it can be noted that the set adviser is not a member of the set, but is there to enable the members to work effectively as a set, rather than to act as members of some other, more familiar kind of group. When that has been achieved, the adviser is expendable.

The position is in striking contrast to the role of the teacher or trainer in a class or a course; and it is even less like the role of the manager or supervisor of a work group. These traditional roles draw on the authority of status, and the demonstrable ability to use rewards and punishments in order to influence group members to achieve a particular objective (if not actually to control and even coerce them). Another notable difference between the action learning set and these more familiar groups, and their leading roles, is that work-groups and

528

teaching (or training) groups are usually sharply divided in purpose. Each belongs to a different milieu: the work-group to the workplace which has created it, and the teaching group to the school, college or training centre. The action learning set belongs to both worlds and to neither, since it tries to provide continuing opportunities to *learn from doing the work*. This concern is not limited to the actual work performance, but to the whole complex process of forming a purpose to do the work, planning it, doing it, and then reviewing its effectiveness in the light of the original purpose.

Trying to focus on both work and learning is a difficult task. This is why the set plays such a vitally important role in this approach. Without an alert set membership, clear in their purposes and with adequate understanding of what they are planning, the ever-changing balance between work and learning can be lost, and the process of action learning either fails or, more frequently, shifts into more familiar and well-established patterns of activity.

Some pitfalls

Adverse developments of this nature can be best illustrated by referring to some of the tendencies commonly observed in running action learning activities.

The set turns into a task force

In this case, the element of 'action' totally dominates. The set is given urgent assignments that are important to senior managers in the organization. It then tends to be quickly assimilated into the normal life of the organization, with attention to the task completely obscuring the important process of learning from what has been done.

The senior managers then take the authority that they habitually assume in their daily work. They see with delight that the action-learning set is no mere talking shop, but a group of people with time and talent to tackle issues that have been worrying the senior people. Time and resources will often be given to strengthen the effectiveness of the group. Senior managers give their own time and energy unstintingly to the project. The only omission is a sustained opportunity to reflect on what has been learned, which is left to purely intuitive impressions that quickly fade, since no attention is being paid to them. The set may be considered a great success, and its work achievements (especially its financial results) lauded. All the same, just as task forces are seldom asked what they have learned from what they have done, so the set quickly learns what kind of group it is required to be, and may be relieved to find that it is quite compatible with the dominant culture of the organization anyway.

The set becomes a short-lived discussion group

If the set starts out as a new form of education and training activity, and is based within a training centre or a management college, the pressure for it to become a course of a slightly unfamiliar kind, or even a rather exotic element in an *529* existing type of course, may be overwhelming. Signs of this happening are legion: assignments and projects are seen as 'mere vehicles' for the serious task of learning. The set is given, or even asks for, a lot of briefing and 'useful input' before it takes up the responsibility of doing some useful work. The input may take the form of a crash course (after all, this is what educators are good at) which gradually drains the life from the activity that it is supposedly serving. The ultimate *coup de grâce* comes from the post-course evaluation: the inputs are given good ratings, while the 'learning vehicles' are heavily criticized for vagueness and lack of structure. The set generates much discussion, but little action.

The set becomes an internal consultancy group

In this case, the set is recognized to be 'something different'; neither a task force nor a training course. Since it is not a real work-group or an easily recognizable training activity, the only alternative seems to be that it must be some kind of consultancy. Needless to say, the consultancy is expected to work to a clearly defined brief laid down by a senior manager, and be clearly under his control. The 'output' is likely to be a report with a statement of the brief (usually a problem), a sound analysis, a list of options and some recommendations. At this point, any action to be taken will be handed over to the proper authorities. The set may feel that is has done a good job, which has been thoroughly appreciated, but it has no claim to be an action-learning set, although it may have made an excellent start.

What we have been describing is the clear-cut division that most organizations make between working and learning. The set is concerned with learning *and* with work, and with keeping a clear and continuous association between the two. It is not a work-group as such, but its members must follow through the various stages of work, so that what is being learned by the members can be kept fresh, and members can learn from one another's current experience and not just from individual recollections of past incidents and episodes. These, then, are some of the pitfalls that beset action learning, in its constant effort to balance its commitment both to action and to a deliberate process of learning. But the emphasis on pitfalls runs the risk of contributing itself to a loss of balance. It is time to take a more constructive line, setting out some of the lessons that can be drawn from the many diverse achievements of action learning in many parts of the world.

THE LESSONS OF SUCCESS

First, one can point to a key combination of factors making for a successful initiative, drawn from the experience of Professor Revans. He has always stressed the dangers of letting action learning become trapped within the confines of an educational institution, or training centre. His preferred starting 530 point has always been to work with those who have direct responsibility for doing something about significant problems or opportunities. Three large projects that come to mind are the Belgian Inter-University Programme, the Hospital Internal Communications Project, and the Nile Project (Revans, 1980). These were all complex ventures, involving many enterprises and public sector organizations with relatively little experience of learning together. They were genuinely collaborative activities, but they needed to find opportunities for many different interests and styles of learning in order for those taking part to work together. The challenge presented by these three projects clearly improved the imagination of all those involved. In each case, Reg Revans acted as the 'learning consultant' to the whole venture. This role enabled him to support the natural leadership of the project, acting as a partner of the sponsors (those with funds and the authority to set up the project) and project leaders, advising on the appropriate forms of organization through set formation, adequate briefing, and the provision of a support infrastructure. An important part of the infrastructure has often been a resource group of senior managers.

In his long and fruitful life, Revans has become adept at communicating his vision of what action learning could become, through colourful accounts of work throughout the world. One such account, given in a British TV programme, was seen by Lord Weinstock on one of his few days away from GEC. This led to a considerable programme of work with GEC companies, each of which was left free to make its own decisions about whether to take part in the programme. A small group of set advisers formed themselves into a company (ALP – Action Learning Projects) in order to support this activity.

A further lesson has been that action learning needs institutional support for large programmes, and this can best be done by *ad hoc* institutions, rather than conventional management consultancies or business schools. Casey and Pearce (1983) give a wide-ranging account of this work with GEC, which extended over several years, and draws on the experiences of many participants. In striking contrast to this work with one large enterprise, Mike Pedler has initiated many programmes that seek to connect different educational institutions, employment agencies, and sets from different businesses. In a report published in 1981, he summarizes his experience of the diffusion of action learning under these circumstances in the following terms:

> Action learning – when it works – upsets hierarchy, order and existing systems of control; it makes a mockery of role specificity upon which vast edifices of formal authority are built; it rejects the simple machine theory of organizations in which people are passive role takers in favour of a more dynamic theory of organizing where people are active role makers. (Pedler, 1981, p.47)

This aspect of action learning is vitally important, and raises key questions of the authority of the set in choosing its work assignment, and the way it handles that assignment. It is clear that the successful handling of any real assignment (as distinct from one that is offered purely as a learning vehicle) requires consider-able political skills on the part of the members, since organizations are set up with fairly clear-cut allocation of responsibilities and authority, and any tempor-ary grouping is inevitably going to cut across established boundaries and *531* challenge entrenched interests. Such skills, it should be noted, are often significantly enhanced during the life of the set.

It is the settled organization that finds change subversive, and resists challenging questions. Organizations that are faced with radical changes reach out for help, and can find the flexible structures and processes of action learning provide just the kind of support they need. A prime example is the work that has gone on over many years at the Prudential Assurance Company (a relatively early account is given by Lewis and Marsh, in Mumford, 1987). Here is an internationally renowned, highly successful business finding itself with a need to widen the perspective of managers who are already technically able but can gain greatly from opportunities to learn from one another's ideas and experience. From modest beginnings, the work has expanded greatly, involving managers as set advisers and specialist resources to others working in interlinked sets. I attended a review session recently, and was immediately struck by the enthusiasm and active commitment of senior line managers, who had clearly developed an understanding of the complex processes of learning that they had initiated and were energetically continuing and expanding. Here, the training staff and facilities were a valued support, rather than (as so often) providers of courses in a specialized location to which busy managers were reluctantly exported at intervals.

I was reminded of the similar experience of a colleague and myself in Yorkshire Water, shortly before privatization. We worked with senior and middle-level managers on a wide range of issues that they had identified, including the imminent changes in their jobs. In a series of meetings, the sets planned, monitored and reviewed a vast mass of information, opinion and raw experience that they had brought together to illuminate the rather murky future. As a result of regular meetings (roughly once a month, spread over more than a year), they gained confidence in themselves and one another, and developed skills that equipped them to face the radical change in their situation.

A similar experience occurred in working with Bradford Council recently on an important change in organizational structure, involving significant devolution to 'service delivery units', such as libraries, swimming pools and community centres. These were encouraged to establish closer relationships with clients, and to take responsibility for the effective use of resources. The first tranche of unit managers formed sets, and were supported by advisers drawn from throughout the council training staff (including members of the corporate organizational development unit). The advisers themselves formed into sets in order to share their rapidly developing experience, and to foster their own skills in this new line of work. The whole project was led by two levels of senior management: the executive team and a steering group of senior managers. A significant difference in this case was that the project was integrated into a comprehensive strategy of change throughout the whole staff of the council. A wide range of change approaches was used, and my impression (although the work is still at an early stage) is that the sets provide a useful forum for the various experiences to be discussed, and to some extent integrated.

532   Mention was made earlier of the growing impatience in many enterprises

with the short-term expedient, which promises so much and actually delivers so little. One encouraging sign of this impatience, expressed constructively, is the rapid development of competence-based approaches to management education and development. The expedient provides packaged information or short-term conditioning in superficial skills. Competence-based approaches have to take stock of the actual knowledge and skills, together with supporting attitudes and values, that characterize competent performance. On inspection, these reveal themselves to be both complex and varied. Since management and leadership involve qualities of character, they are best fostered by continual practice, and the opportunity of gaining candid feedback from associates. Not surprisingly, this change of emphasis has led to a re-think of formal qualifications, so that practice plays a much more important role. Leading enterprises, such as Shell Chemicals (UK), have been developing a whole range of degree programmes in association with educational institutions, in which action learning plays an important part.

An important lesson to be drawn from these varied achievements is that the action-learning set is a flexible, basic learning unit that enables learning to be continually focused on *action* in all its different phases – in conception, in planning, implementation, monitoring, review and modification of objectives. Just as work teams and task forces are basic units for getting work done; and syndicates, classes and courses are basic units for education and training, so the set finds its place as the unit that connects work and learning by responding actively to both.

In order to be fully effective, however, basic units need to be linked together with larger systems. Sets can be linked together through action-learning projects or programmes. Two or three sets are readily brought together, for example, in programmes that initially meet in training centres, but can then take wing for other locations of their choice as they become groups with an identity of their own. These, in turn, are at their most effective if they are seen to be part of an even more comprehensive process of organizational change. The best form of organization for these larger activities appears to be that of the network, drawing on the initiatives and energies of the basic units.

ISSUES FOR THE FUTURE

Three issues represent particular challenges for action learning in preparing itself for emerging demands and opportunities:

1. How does it relate to the new information systems which enable 'P' as established knowledge to be presented in myriad forms, on terms set by the learner rather than the teacher or tutor?
2. How does action learning relate to associated approaches, such as self-managed learning, self-development, team development, organization development and the learning organization?
3. How can action learning become a flexible instrument of managers who wish to take increasing responsibilities for developing their staffs?

The following notes offer some initial thoughts on these issues.

Note 1

There has been a virtual revolution in knowledge in two directions. First, the knowledge *about* various aspects of the world has not only grown enormously, but has been codified, stored and made accessible in new forms; all of which aim to be 'user friendly' rather than the private possessions of 'learned persons' acting as teachers or lecturers. Second, the emphasis in the Western world on *useful* knowledge has placed great weight on moving the knowledge-base from knowing *about* things to being able to *do* things: in short, 'know-how' rather than 'knowing-about. These two revolutions in knowledge intertwine to form information and automation, with automation feeding us with information and information driving automation.

Action learning, and other approaches which seek to bring learning and doing together, can benefit greatly from these technical and conceptual advances. Most obviously, instead of starting action-learning activities by trying to bring set members 'up to speed' in some relevant area of knowledge relevant to their assignments, the emphasis can be on questioning, with information following flexibly. Instead of great chunks of 'P' having to be acquired, so that questions 'make sense', 'Q' can regain its rightful place, and drive enquiry.

Experience suggests that pertinent questions can be asked of any subject whatever by those who are genuinely curious, and feel committed to making a contribution. And there is a real danger that 'crash courses' in new subjects all too often serve to drive out enquiry rather than to stimulate it.

Note 2

We are living through a ferment of innovation in what used to be two 'worlds': the world of work, often seen by those in it as the 'real world', and the world of learning, with its international networks of schools, colleges, polytechnics and universities. Not surprisingly, innovation brings proliferation, as opportunities and problems are identified, pursued and tackled. The dust has not yet settled, and in these exciting times may do so only patchily and intermittently. As one attempts to assess the many ill-defined approaches in the 'learning by doing' arena, it seems evident that similarities are more apparent than differences (though innovators are understandably committed to demonstrating the distinctive advantages of their differences). Five approaches other than action learning are both active and successful: self-managed learning, self-development, team development, organization development, and the learning organization. (These are discussed elsewhere in this volume.) The similarities are more striking and encouraging than the differences, since they suggest that these approaches are likely to be compatible with one another, and in many ways mutually supportive. All of them insist on the importance of a complete process of learning, linking purpose, aims and objectives, planning, implementation, and review, leading to a possible revision of purpose. They increasingly emphasize the role of culture, values and attitudes in directing (and often inhibiting) the process of change. And they all seek to concentrate on important issues in life and work with full participation by those engaged in learning.

The differences arise mainly from the chosen area of attention. Self-development is concerned with changes in the individual, brought about by individual initiatives, though these frequently involve changes in relationships with others. Self-managed learning adds a valuable ingredient to action learning, by bringing out the importance of a personal learning contract, or agreement, which is developed within the set. This addition to the operations of the set is particularly useful when people are working for qualifications programmes, since these traditionally emphasize individual performance. Team development is usually concerned with work teams, and their effectiveness within the organization. Organization development focuses on significant changes in organizational structure and process. *The Learning Organization* (Garratt, 1987) brings out the possibility of developing an organizational process that would foster continuous learning, rather than going through alternating periods of change and consolidation.

Action learning, for its part, has tended to concentrate on the set as an active agent of change, through empowerment of its individual members, working on significant organizational opportunities and problems. Clearly, these differences of emphasis are important. They enable the energies of those using these approaches to be centred on realistic aims and objectives. No one approach can make claims to sovereignty. Academic subjects may fall into the error of drawing exclusive boundaries around themselves, but action engages us with the living world; and its manifold consequences (many of them unintended) move across boundaries with impunity.

Note 3

Managers in difficult times stay close to the job in hand and leave learning, especially creative, reflective learning, firmly on one side. Now they are becoming more aware of the advantages of clearing some time and emotional space to consider where they are, where they want to go (or need to go) and how they might get there. This awareness comes from looking at the conduct of successful enterprises, both private and public. These enterprises differ in many ways. But they are all hungry for information, and quick to use it to advantage.

An emerging role for the manager is as a developer for his or her staff, setting the example by demonstrable commitments to self-development, and to using relationships for effective learning as well as effective task performance. The interweaving of work teams and learning sets can be far more highly developed than it is at present, and managers will find that developing themselves as set advisers is a valuable addition to their skills as managers of change.

IN PLACE OF A CONCLUSION

In the foreword to a book on the Hospital Internal Communications Project, *535* referred to earlier, a Professor of Medicine at a big teaching hospital wrote: 'To act, one must understand; to understand, one must inquire; before acting, it pays to explain.' (W.J.H. Butterfield, in Revans, 1972). Action learning is a continuous essay in understanding and explaining one's actions, in a community of fellow learners. In a recent study of 'how the smartest companies use conflict to stay ahead' (Pascale, 1990), the focus is on the continual challenge of able people, within leading enterprises, to one another's assumptions and beliefs. We hear that the leaders of such enterprises 'grew with their jobs. Their growth was fuelled by the habit of inquiry. ... They displayed the characteristic of not just "having-the-answers" but of "living-in-the-question". They ask questions not merely to generate *answers* but to reveal *what is possible*' (Pascale, 1990, p. 262).

The context of this account of action learning has been the constant tension between the short-term expedients which busy managers feel forced to apply amid the daily rush of events, and the long haul that enables people and their organizations to develop qualities of awareness and sustained capacity, even wisdom. Action learning has many successes to its credit, due most of all to Reg Revans, who has used his wide-ranging abilities to the utmost to draw public attention to this approach. In the words of the title given to an account of the development activities at GEC, action learning is clearly 'more than management development'. It is really a way of life for everyone who wants to take responsibility for life-long learning.

As for the 'long haul', it does not have to be particularly arduous or painful, merely sustained. The common experience of those engaged in action learning is that the excitement of getting things done and learning to do things better is far greater than any frustrations and disappointments that are encountered. When we all pull together we find the load lighter and the company invigorating. And if we pull in good faith – our heads and hearts combining to guide and strengthen our hands – we may find that we are pulling alongside powerful and benign forces from the future, reaching out to help us.

FURTHER READING

Casey, David and David Pearce (1977), *More than Management Development*, Aldershot: Gower.

Garratt, Bob (1987), *The Learning Organization*, London: Fontana/Collins.

Hospital Internal Communications (1972), 'Seen from within', in Reg Revans (ed.), *Hospitals: Communications, Choice and Change*, London: Tavistock Publications.

Lawrence, Jean (1986), 'Action learning – a questioning approach', in Alan Mumford (ed.), *Handbook of Management Development*, 2nd edn, Aldershot: Gower.

McGill, I. and L. Beaty (1992), *Action Learning – a Practitioner's Guide*, London: Kogan Page.

Morris, John (1991), 'Minding our Ps and Qs', in Mike Pedler (ed.), *Action Learning in Practice*, 2nd edn, Aldershot: Gower.

Mumford, Alan (ed.) (1987), various articles on Action Learning in *Journal of Management Development*, **6**, 2.

Pascale, Richard (1990), *Managing on the Edge*, New York: Simon & Schuster.

Pearce, David (1991), 'Getting started', an appendix in Mike Pedler (ed.), *Action Learning in Practice*, 2nd edn, Aldershot: Gower.

Pedler, Mike (ed.) (1981), *The Diffusion of Action Learning*, Sheffield: Sheffield Polytechnic.

Pedler, Mike (ed.) (1991), *Action Learning in Practice*, 2nd edn, Aldershot: Gower.

Pedler, Mike and John Boutall (1992), *Action Learning for Change*, Bristol: National Health Service Training Directorate.

Revans, Reg (ed.) (1972), *Hospitals: Communication, Choice and Change*, London: Tavistock Publications.

Revans, Reg (1980), *Action Learning*, London: Blond & Briggs.

Revans, Reg (1983), *The ABC of Action Learning*, 2nd edn, Bromley: Chartwell-Bratt.

Weiland, G.F. (ed.) (1981), *Improving Health Care Management*, pt iv, 395–476, Ann Arbor, Mich.: Health Administration Press.

Other sources of information on action learning

The International Foundation for Action Learning, 26 Harcombe Road, London N16 0SA (Tel: 071 241 2132) (Contact: Krystyna Weinstein).

The International Management Centres (Tel: 0280 817222) (Contact: Professor Alan Mumford).

39 Management games and case studies

Ian Debenham

In this chapter, I shall be dealing with various forms of simulation in training. The term 'simulation' is used in the sense of simulating a part of life, ranging from driving an aeroplane and other types of machines to leading a team and running a business. Thus, included are mechanical and electronic simulators, case studies, role playing, substitute task exercises and dynamic statistical simulations because I consider that the advantages of using simulation to aid learning apply to all these methods.

SIMULATION AS AN AID TO LEARNING

When simulation is used, learning mainly takes place by trial, feedback (error) and practice. It offers a number of advantages over the real life situation.

1. Simplification   A simulated situation can be designed so that only one or two aspects of the job are dealt with at a time. For example, the supervisor of a typing pool can practice distributing workload without having to cope with any 'customer' or 'staff' problems.

2. Reduced time scale   A simulation is normally designed so that decisions are taken at much shorter intervals than in real life, thus speeding up the decision-making practice. In addition, decisions which occur at long intervals or which rarely have to be made in life, can be offered to the student for practice within the reduced time scale. For example, engine failure in flight, refitting a ship, rebuilding or refitting an hotel, or the blowout of an oil well.

3. Concentrating on individual needs   Once a simulation has been designed and established, it is possible to arrange for individuals to practise the aspects of the job at which they are weakest. For example, instrument approaches in aircraft, or dealing with finance instead of production.

4. Increased safety This can be clearly seen in physical simulators where risk to life and limb can be significantly reduced. For example, the flight simulator, and the sewing machine simulator with a fixed wire instead of a needle to give machinists practice in steering the material through the machine without the danger of a needle through their fingers. But even with statistical simulations the risk of financial loss and personal failure on a serious scale are removed and thus in both cases the interference with learning caused by fear can be significantly reduced.

5. Reduced cost Here there may be direct savings, not only from reduced training time but also from increased use of the operational equipment for productive use. For example, an international airline saved over £3.5 million in training costs by the full use of flight simulators, while, at the same time, making an additional 20,000 aircraft hours available for revenue earning. These figures show the possible savings. Admittedly they refer to pilot training where accurate costings can be obtained and where well-established standards have to be met, but this does not invalidate the example. On another front, an oil-platform simulator for a North Sea oil platform paid for itself from the improvements in design of the oil-platform systems before the simulator even came into use. With the costs of the platform running at about £100,000 per hour, the improved emergency shut-down and start-up performance by a crew trained thoroughly in all the possible emergencies does not take long to pay dividends.

Standards for managers are not so simple to set, but it would seem reasonable to suppose that similar cost benefits can be achieved in this field.

On a less dramatic scale, savings are generated by the improved learning, particularly of unusual or rare events, which can be handled safely in a simulation in a way which would not be possible on the job. Loss of customers, waste of materials and other consequential training losses can also be avoided.

6. Improved feedback Not infrequently in life, it is difficult to obtain any feedback at all on the results of one's actions, and then only after a long interval. This situation can be alleviated when using simulation by providing more immediate, more direct and more complete feedback. The more immediate feedback follows from the reduced time-scale. The more direct feedback also follows from the mechanism of the simulation which is designed with this aim in mind. The more complete feedback follows partly from the design of the mechanism, and partly from the conscious efforts of umpires and colleagues to help individuals see for themselves not only which of their decisions/actions have been more or less useful, but also how and why.

7. Freezing Particularly with the more sophisticated computer-based simulations, it is possible to 'freeze' a situation – perhaps a crisis compounded by the reactions of the people training on the simulator – so that this can be examined calmly to see how it arose, what actions made matters worse, what would have been more appropriate actions and how to get things going again. The situation can also be recorded and used as a starting point for further training of the same team or of others on another occasion.

Physical simulation in the form of the Link Trainer for instrument flying has been with us for many years and even the dynamic statistical form of simulation has been filling an important place in training programmes under the name of 'business games' for a considerable time. Case studies and role playing are also well-established aids to learning.

Unfortunately the name 'business game' sometimes arouses suspicion that a time-consuming 'play' period has been included in the programme, or is thought of simply as something which will give promising youngsters a chance to run a company. This training method has a much wider application than that of the top-level role so often associated with it. For this reason, I prefer the term 'dynamic statistical simulation'. This has the advantage of separating this type of simulation from the 'substitute task exercise' which is more appropriate to learning about such aspects of management as team-building and leadership.

Life is statistical; that is, there is a certain chance or likelihood that any particular event will occur. Thus, we do not know the future for certain but we can have a pretty shrewd idea what it will bring. Some events are more likely than others, and we can arrange to prepare for them by making plans and allowing for contingencies. The future depends on the past. From past experiences we are able to establish reasonably accurately the chances of any particular event taking place, so that we can build a 'model of life' in a business situation where the statistical chances are reasonably similar to actuality.

SIMULATION IN TRAINING: THE FIVE CATEGORIES

For the design of training it is convenient to divide simulation methods under the following five headings.

The mechanical

This covers electronic, electrical, hydraulic and pneumatic simulations. Normally, these are used for skill training and application and are rather specific to the particular piece of equipment which they simulate. The flight simulator used by airlines for pilot and crew training is probably the best known example.

Under this heading, I consider it reasonable to include some of the interactive video simulations which are available; for instance, for driving a heavy goods vehicle.

Case studies

It is helpful to consider case studies in two categories. First, the 'quickie', a short description of a situation in which the problem is fairly obvious; and second, the longer variety, as published, for instance, by Harvard University and Cranfield, many of which reach some fifty pages of print with supporting tables, diagrams and financial data.

When considering the use of case studies a number of items need to be taken into consideration: content; presentation; and handling.

Content

Depending upon the training needs of the group, the cases will need to be studied by the trainer to ensure that what is needed is contained in the material available. For example, marketing, finance, industrial relations, production, and so on. With the longer case a number of aspects of management are likely to be included together, which enhances the learning value.

The short case is more appropriate when the need is for problem handling; the longer case is used when members need to increase their understanding of certain aspects of running a business or organization. While one session lasting an hour and a half would normally be quite adequate for presenting and handling a short case, the longer case will certainly need handing out in advance, with time allowed for private study and possibly for syndicate study as well.

Presentation

Presentation is most frequently in written form, and this has the advantage of having the text available for reference and checking of interpretation. On the other hand, there have been some interesting presentations using film strip with recordings for short cases and film or video for the longer ones. These have the advantage of being more lifelike, in the sense that this is closer to the way managers normally encounter problems. There is usually a text of some sort available anyway, to sort out any differences of opinion as to what was said and so forth. A simple recording can also be used.

There are, of course, other forms of presentation, oral, model (e.g. sand table), role playing (either rehearsed or played to briefs), and the developing case study in which additional briefs are handed out as the discussion progresses. For example, 'in-tray', where the supposed contents of an in-tray have to be dealt with, and the 'incident process', where the 'incident' is presented and the group then have to question the tutor to gain more information.

Any form of presentation can be used for any type of content. However, one form of presentation may be more appropriate to the group than another, for example, a recording for problems normally received over the telephone.

Handling

Handling will, almost of necessity, require some private study, even if this is done while sitting round the table. Syndicate study in small groups may well be advantageous when a large amount of data needs to be assimilated and put together. Role playing may be appropriate to test a decision, but care is needed to ensure that the roles are based on material in the case only. Finally, some form of general discussion will be necessary to clarify and consolidate the lessons learned. Again, any type of handling will suit any type of content.

Basically, the use of case material can give practice, under critical conditions, in the following areas:

- Analysis and critical analytical thinking.
- Problem identification, selection and solution.
- Decision-making.
- Making judgements between different lines of action, and so on.
- Relating procedures/systems, and so forth, to life conditions.
- Making, using and testing deductions/inferences/assumptions.

Writing a short case

Most trainers are able to write a short case quite satisfactorily, although writing a longer case requires considerably more experience. The short case essentially clothes a problem in an interesting setting. This has the effect of arousing interest and encouraging the participant to identify with one of the individuals in the case. When writing a short case it should be remembered that one is presenting material for study and discussion, so it needs to be written in such a way that readers can make their own deductions and draw their own conclusions without any guidance from the writer.

The following points are offered in support of this.

1. Have a 'neutral' title which gives no indication of the sort of problem which might be found in the case. A title indicating a particular problem will tend to narrow thinking. For example, 'Jones Hardware', or 'Peter Black' rather than 'Corruption in the Council'. A title such as 'The Drinking Foreman' may arouse interest but one needs to be careful.
2. Use ordinary names. A telephone directory is a useful source. Using a regional or national name – McFee or O'Rourke, for example, can add flavour and invite the airing of prejudices. Do not use fabricated names, like Mr Fixit.
3. Write concisely with the use of dialogue, diagrams and charts, if appropriate, to help the reader grasp the situation quickly. A more complex or involved passage may invite different interpretations and add other dimensions to the discussion.
4. Try to avoid making the problem too one-sided, but have a reasonable problem for at least one character. This must not be too trivial nor impossible for the reader to identify with.
5. Allow the readers to make their own inferences and assumptions. For example, write that Peter's manager considered him a loyal worker or describe Peter's behaviour so that this can be inferred by the reader. Do not give as a fact from the case writer that Peter was a loyal worker.

Role playing

Many people have used role playing in their training programmes with successful results and in all probability have not thought of this method as a simulation. All the same, role playing does simulate life situations and can be a powerful aid to learning.

It is helpful to break down the possible uses of role playing to simplify analysis, as follows:

1. To demonstrate a point or a procedure.
2. To present a situation (case) for study and/or discussion:

   - Rehearsed – usually acted by training staff who have been briefed and rehearsed in their parts beforehand to ensure a reasonably accurate performance.
   - To brief – usually acted by the course members or one course member and a member of the training staff. The briefs typically outline the situation and give any necessary indication of the part to be played. Both parties will not necessarily have the same information. Multiple role playing with more than two characters is a variant of this.

3. To give practice and experience in handling a situation which involves dealing with people; for example, interviewing, instruction, and so on.
4. To give experience of the 'other man's' point of view; for example, a manager taking the role of shop steward in negotiation, or foreman in the role of employee in an interview situation.
5. To try out and check a decision; for example, during the discussion of a case study or following the study of a situation.
6. To gain feedback of the effect of one's behaviour/actions/tone of voice/ approach on others.

Clearly, role playing is not 'real life' but when carefully planned and handled it can give experience which is close enough to reality to allow useful lessons to be learned.

I have found four main problem areas in using role playing:

1. *Loss of confidence.* This can be caused by 'failure' on the part of the trainee, and can be made worse by bad handling of the feedback discussion, causing the trainee to feel embarrassed in front of colleagues.
2. *Refusal of the role.* The symptoms of this are 'clowning' and saying 'If I were ...' or 'In a situation like this ...'. It is usually caused by presenting a situation which is unrealistic to the participants, whether in context, level, difficulty, or by sheer bad briefing.
3. *Participants trying to 'win'* when there are two of them taking opposing roles; for example, a salesman taking the role of customer refusing to allow the other salesman to sell anything in the salesman role.
4. *Poor performance/embarrassment* due to being watched or recorded either on video or sound tape.

These problems can be overcome by the following means:

1. Making sure that the situations used are realistic to the training group.
2. Thorough and careful briefing of both trainees and of any training staff who may be playing a role. Train the staff members as necessary.
3. Having a member of the training staff take the role of customer, or whatever.
4. Teaching trainees how to erase tapes, and giving them the opportunity to erase the recordings of their own performances if they so wish.
5. Keeping out observers, particularly members' bosses, in the early stages until confidence has been built up.
6. Careful handling of the role playing while it is in progress to ensure that so far as possible the trainees achieve 'graduated success'; that is, they succeed as often as possible but, each time, have to work for this success.
7. If the role playing looks like getting out of hand because antagonism is being built up to flash point or clowning is occurring, it should be stopped smartly and efforts made to resume on a better footing.
8. Careful handling of the feedback session to ensure that useful lessons are learned by the trainee and the group as a whole.

It is better to get one, two or perhaps three useful points out of each role play than to examine one in detail and great depth. Balance has to be preserved between playing time, feedback time, and the lessons learned. It may be helpful to allow the group to look at or listen to the recordings made of their performances in their own time, and thus avoid taking up class time by going over each role play twice.

The substitute task exercise

'It's not what you do, it's the way that you do it'. When it is necessary that learning should take place on such aspects of management as leadership or team-working, it is difficult for this to occur in life because of the pressures to get the job done. So a simplified task can be designed which contains the key features of the real job, but which can be carried out without the same level of attention being needed. It substitutes for the real job, and enables the team or individual to examine how they set to work to do it. In the current terminology, they can concentrate on 'process' (i.e. how they are going about doing the job) rather than 'task' (i.e. how well the job is progressing).

At the same time, it is also a useful method for the study of other aspects, such as planning and controlling, communicating and organizing; thus giving experience and practice in the more abstract and less easily quantified aspects of management, as distinct from the dynamic statistical simulation.

When planning to use or design a substitute task exercise, it is important to establish the training objective. This would normally be in terms of increasing members' understanding of an activity or system, or of increasing members' skill in communication or team-building.

Having established the training objective, the next step is to analyse life
544 situations in which this activity occurs, and to extract the essential elements;

for example, forecasting, planning, communicating the plan, motivating, and so on.

When designing the task one needs to decide:

- What essentials have to be included.
- What should be the structure of the task.
- What has to be achieved by the team undertaking the task.
- How many people are needed in each group and is the number critical.
- How will they undertake and complete the task.
- What (if any) 'equipment' will be needed.
- How much time is reasonably required to complete the task.
- If it is essential that the task be completed.

Other questions which have to be answered before testing the exercise are:

- What (if any) interaction will there be between groups? For instance, are the groups to be competitive; or are they to negotiate an exchange of, perhaps, information; or some other type of interaction?
- What (if any) constraints will be imposed? A time constraint is fairly likely, since this is necessary to keep the exercise within the training period available; but another constraint might, for example, be the use of only the materials/equipment provided.
- What (if any) 'process' structure will be imposed (for example, 'leader' appointed or chosen by the group)?
- What briefing will group members need? How? Oral? Written? When should they be briefed and by whom? Would differential (briefs giving different information) make for greater learning opportunities? What should the 'leader' know if this is the case?
- What systems will be needed to give adequate feedback to the participants? Video, observers, checksheets, discussion?
- How much time should be allowed for this? Who will manage it?
- How many staff/observers will be necessary?
- What briefing/training will they need? When will they get it? Who will be responsible for this?
- What (if any) underlying theories are involved? How explicit or implicit are they? Do they need to be explained/presented to the participants?

Having clarified all these points and made the necessary decision, select or design the task and prepare any necessary handouts, notes and equipment. At this point it is as well to try out the exercise on a group of colleagues, so that any problems can be resolved before the exercise is applied to the training group proper.

During the trial run check:

- Does the exercise achieve the objective (or is it likely to)? Have the members learned the lessons required?

- Are the members able to assimilate the briefing satisfactorily, or are some alterations in the material or presentation needed?
- Can the task be satisfactorily achieved in the time allowed? If not, should the time allowed be increased or the task altered?
- Is there any vital element missing or too weak to give useful lessons? For example, there may be an element of planning in the task, but this may be insufficiently significant to show up among the other aspects, such as communication or motivation.

Following the trial run it is essential to make any changes which are shown to be needed, and if these are extensive it may be advisable to run another trial before using it on the training group. After trying out the exercise on the training group, it is still worthwhile checking whether or not your training objective was achieved. If not, why not? What changes need to be made to make it effective? Even if the objective was achieved, was it worth the time spent?

The dynamic statistical simulation

As I have said, life is statistical. That is to say, the future, although it depends on the past, is all a matter of chance – some parts of it more chancy than others.

The dynamic statistical simulation is a powerful aid for helping people to learn certain aspects of their jobs. This type of simulation is applicable for anyone who has to make decisions in life in relation to a 'statistical' input or offtake.

Senior managers are faced with these types of decision and there are a number of simulations which have been designed for them. However, there are a number of people doing jobs which entail this type of decision for whom there are few, if any, suitable simulations readily available; for example, the supervisor of a typing pool, a storekeeper, a publican, an hotel receptionist, a salesman, a machine-shop foreman, a service-station operator, or a dock manager.

For many people the simulations may well be simple but, for one reason or another, will have to be so specific that they will not have a wide application. Furthermore, there are only likely to be a few people needing training in these jobs at any one time. Both of these factors will discourage the development of dynamic statistical simulations for general publication. They should not, however, discourage the competent trainer from designing suitable simulations for his own organization.

The increase in the availability of microcomputers at reasonable prices has made it more practical to provide dynamic statistical simulations for individuals. It also increases the likelihood of a number of such simulations becoming available generally.

Simulation is dynamic

Business in general is a matter of forecasting the future as well as possible, and then planning a profitable activity to meet or take advantage of it. This is true whether it be at a senior level concerned with the whole business or at a more junior level taking care of only part of it. However, in both these cases, an individual or team have to make decisions which will interact with a statistical variable to give a result from which point they will have to make further decisions. It is quite possible to design a model of a limited section of life so that individuals can have meaningful and useful practice and experience from which to learn to do their jobs more effectively. Thus, the simulation is dynamic, because it contains interaction between the participants' decisions and other variables, and statistical because a statistical model has to be used to simulate the chance aspects of life. The dynamic statistical simulation, therefore, gives experience and practice in the quantifiable aspects of management, as distinct from the substitute task exercise which deals with the less quantifiable aspects.

There are a number of business games which offer experience and practice at the more senior levels. This leads to the general impression that this is the main, if not the only, use of this method, but, as I have already indicated, it is also valuable at the lower levels as well if suitably designed.

As with any other training activity it is necessary to start with the training objective, which, for this type of simulation, is likely to be something like increasing individuals' understanding of some aspects of their work and increasing their skill in making sound judgements and decisions on the job related to that understanding. The aim of the dynamic statistical simulation, as with other forms of simulation, is to provide feedback information to the participants on the effectiveness of their decisions and action in the given situation. To achieve this, it is essential that the simulation is reasonably realistic to the participants, and that the results of their action give a reasonably accurate reflection of real life, so ensuring that useful lessons are learned.

A model of the real life situation, or at least a viable part of it, has to be designed or selected from published material. Models can vary quite widely in complexity to suit the training objective. The simplest, typically, have only one variable parameter under the control of the members of the group. For example, the quantity of material to be ordered every period in a stock control exercise; or which of, say, five typists should be given the work in a typing pool supervisor simulation. In the stock control simulation, the stock figures resulting from the carry-forward stock figure plus the order less the offtake would be fed back before the next decision. The offtake would usually be random about a certain amount and only vary within given limits. For the typing pool example, both the work coming in and the output of each typist would vary randomly in the same way. More complex simulations will include a number of parameters which can be varied by the participants, some with limiting interaction. For example, sales would be limited by the stock and production available. Also, some interaction between teams may be included, such as the total market increasing in proportion to the total notional spending by all teams on marketing.

It is important to have the briefing and umpiring of a dynamic statistical simulation well planned and the umpiring team well prepared. With a very simple simulation one person may be able to do the briefing and do all the necessary calculating and recording, but this can very quickly get out of hand with the more complex simulations. With the present availability and reasonable *547* price of microcomputers, it is not too difficult to program the necessary calculations and have a printout for each team, but even here there may be problems, such as putting in the wrong period number and overwriting a previous period's data when saving the calculations.

In spite of the difficulties and expense, the dynamic statistical simulation is a powerful aid to learning and has application wherever an individual or group have to make decisions in relation to a varying input or offtake. There are a number available from various suppliers but, as with any 'off the peg' purchase, it is important to test it thoroughly before use and make sure that it does what is required. This is not to say that one's own design does not need thorough testing as well.

It may well be advantageous to give the participants some specific training in some aspect of the simulation; calculating stock re-order levels, or how to prepare a balance sheet, for example. It is also possible that the participants will learn how to 'play the system', but this should not prevent them learning other useful lessons. In fact, I understand that in one company where they used a simulation on their management development programme, one syndicate played the system to such good effect that the standard system used in the day-to-day work of the company was consequently changed with beneficial results.

I have found the following analysis useful when examining or designing a dynamic statistical simulation:

- *Membership.* For whom, for what level, for what function, and so on, has it been designed?
- *The training objective.* What is it?
- *Parameters.* Which can the participants vary/decide (player variable); which will vary randomly/statistically (statistical variable); which will vary as a result of the interaction of the foregoing (dependent variable)?
- *Constraints.* What constraints will be imposed – borrowing; price variance; stock size; notional length of decision period; week, month, quarter, year?
- *Umpiring.* Mechanism, decision–result–feedback–record; how will the result be fed back to the participants; oral, note on form, or printout?
- *Materials.* Will any forms, pro forma balance sheets/income statements, tables or handouts be required; availability and design?

If manually umpired, boards on which forms can be taped may well be helpful for keeping the records of each team. With a microcomputer-umpired simulation, it may be beneficial to arrange for the participants to enter their own decisions into the computer. In this way a number of people will gain hands-on experience possibly for the first time and thus overcome any inhibitions they may have in handling one.

CONCLUSION

548 One cause for hesitation may be the lack of conviction that certain lessons will be

learned, particularly before one has built up some experience of these aids to learning. This is understandable, because one is dealing with understanding which has to be allowed to grow; and it may well be that, in a session of an hour and a half, you will see only two or perhaps three 'lights come on' in different individuals. Each will have understood something, but probably something different for each individual; and very possibly something only very indirectly related to the case study, role play, substitute task or dynamic statistical simulation being discussed. Others will have gained some understanding but will not have shown any signs of it. To some extent the person in charge of the session can help the members to share their gains.

Another aspect, certainly of discussing complex case material, is that of 'minimum dosage'; that is, it is not until some four or five cases of this nature have been studied and discussed that the members begin to gain insight. To give an example both of this and of understanding being marginally connected with the material being studied: on one course, during which we had been studying a number of short and more complex cases, one of the members told me on about the fourth day that he now understood why he had had problems at a certain point in his past career. I have not found this problem so acute with substitute task exercises or other forms of simulation, but it needs to be borne in mind.

This may cause a training programme to look 'expensive' in time, but it is essential if real value is to be obtained. You may have a certain amount of difficulty selling it to management but you can always get them to have a go. In one instance, for example, the board of a company wished to find out about case studies because one had been proposed for a management meeting, and I was asked to run a case with them. We had an hour and a half set aside for this and we discussed a classic Harvard case, The Dashman Company, which in my experience had comfortably kept the group going for this length of time. Not on this occasion. They took it apart upwards, sideways and downwards in about fifty minutes. Fortunately, I had another case handy and was able to move on to that after summarizing the discussion on Dashman. This experience confirmed my conviction of the value of discussing suitable case material.

FURTHER READING

Adair, J., R. Ayres, A.I.S. Debenham and D. Despres (1978), *A Handbook of Management Training Exercises*, vol. I, London: BACIE.

Andrews, K.R. (1953), *The Case Method of Teaching Human Relations and Administration*, Boston, Mass.: Harvard University Press.

Canapis, A. (1959), *Research Techniques in Human Engineering*, Baltimore, Md: Johns Hopkins University.

Case Clearing House of Great Britain and Ireland, Cranfield Institute of Technology.

Debenham, A.I.S. (1968), *A Training Officer's Guide to Discussion Leading*, London: BACIE.

Debenham, A.I.S. (1987), *Design Your Own Business Games*, London: BACIE.

Elgood, Chris (1989), *Handbook of Management Games*, 5th edn, Aldershot: Gower.

Glover, J.D., R.M. Hower and P. Tagiuri (1973), *The Administrator*, Homewood, Ill.: Richard Irwin.

Greenlaw, P.S., C.W. Heron and R.H. Lawdon (1962), *Business Simulation*, Hemel Hempstead: Prentice Hall.

Harvard Business School International Distribution Service, Dynamic Graphics International, PO Box 25, 3950 AA, Maarn, Holland.

Singleton, R.F. and W.F. Tyndal (1974), *Games and Programs*, Oxford: Freeman.

40 Choosing resources

Michael Abrahams

It is now more important than ever that training and development budgets are used in the most cost-effective way. Some years ago many newly appointed management development specialists (MDS) were expected to learn 'on the job'. A portion of their budget was spent on 'mistakes'; it was part of the learning experience. Today, that luxury is rarely available. As value for money is uppermost in the minds of the board, and more time is expended monitoring the effectiveness of training, the choice of a supplier of development activities must be the *right* choice.

This chapter outlines resources available to an MDS and some methods that I have found to be practical in making a choice of suitable development suppliers. It will cover the following headings:

- Management consultants.
- Management consultancies.
- Business schools.
- Management colleges.
- Public training courses.
- Consortium programmes.
- Training packages.

The comments made in this chapter presume that a careful analysis of needs has been undertaken as described in Chapters 12 and 13. Choosing a course or other development activity for reasons other than need is unlikely to prove useful, but it does happen. The decision to use external resources to address training or development needs is usually taken after discussions have led to the realization that the organization does not have sufficient trained or qualified personnel capable of providing the knowledge and skills required for their total management commitment. The care taken in arriving at the decision to use external resources is often in direct contrast to the random way in which the resources are finally chosen.   *551*

There are many claims contained in mail shots from individuals, consultancies and prestigious business schools; terms such as 'new', 'unique', 'tried and tested', and so on, are all part of their marketing approach. It is of little use of initiate discussions with consultants, academic institutions, and others, solely in response to the number of colours used in their brochures or their geographical proximity. Similarly, to choose to use a resource simply because your chief executive had some 'good experiences' with it in the past may be politic but it will not be a decision based on up-to-date knowledge.

There is in the human psyche a deep desire to codify, categorize and label behaviour. The work done by psychologists to encapsulate characteristics of behaviour and personality using psychometric tests, and the willingness or organizations to buy the latest thinking in order to improve their selection or development processes, are tributes to hope rather than reality. Moreover, if the MDS administers a test to putative suppliers to check their chances of success, there is unlikely to be much correlation between forecast and outcome. Evidence of past successes – provided by the use of written material – references, and observation are more likely to be accurate. The following sections are a guide on how to obtain this evidence and suggest ways in which this information can be used to make the best choices. Sometimes the material gathered will be unclear and it will be difficult to make a decision. The choice will then be decided by the degree of affinity that exists between the MDS and the supplier, and maybe by comparative costs – a factor which has become more important recently.

SOURCES OF INFORMATION

There has been an increase in the availability and quality of management consultants and academics during the last ten years. Institutions of management teaching are far more rigorous than in the past and the growth of large training and OD consultancies have gone a long way to ensure a measure of integrity. Nevertheless, it pays to be careful and the first step should be to contact organizations who can give advice about suppliers of training and development.

The organizations shown below will supply information. Those marked with an asterisk are not without interest in supplying consultants or courses themselves, but they maintain a professional distance when asked for advice:

The Association of Management Education and Development
21 Catherine Street
London WX2B 5JS

The Institute of Management*
Management House
Cottingham Road
Corby
Northants NN17 1TT

The Institute of Personnel Management*
IPM House
Camp Road
Wimbledon
London SW19 4UW

The Institute of Training and Development
Marlow House
Institute Road
Marlow
Bucks SL7 1BD

Information concerning *individual* consultants is obtainable from the Brind Register but information is supplied to member organizations only:

Brind Register
11 Firs Avenue
Muswell Hill
London N10 3LY

The following agencies will provide data on a variety of courses in the United Kingdom, Europe and the United States:

Brickers Executive Education Service
425A Family Farm Road
Woodside
California 94026
USA

Directory of Management Training
Hoskyns Education
Hoskyns Group plc
5 Kerley Road
Bournemouth BH2 5DE

The Management Courses Index
7 Princes Street
London W1R 7RB

The experience of other management development specialists or management trainers within the public and private sectors is invaluable. Networks of MDSs exist and their knowledge and skills in choosing suppliers can be useful to an individual in the early stages. It is worthwhile making contact and soliciting advice from various professional groups, possibly by joining an organization such as the Institute of Training and Development. Initially, there may be a tendency to accept the judgement of others; you should remember, however, that a consultant who is successful in one organization could be disaster in another.   *553*

CONSULTANTS

Robert Townsend (1971), author of *Up the Organization*, describes management consultants as: 'people who borrow your watch to tell you what time it is and then walk off with it'.

The type of consultants dealt with in this section are not those who collate the collective wisdom of employees, feed it to the board in a large report, and then walk away after making a number of recommendations that everyone knew they would make. Human resource development consultants do speak to the people within the organization but usually they stay to carry out their recommendations.

Consultants can be individuals who work on their own or occasionally with other consultants; or they can be part of a consultancy group. Sometimes they are people who are encouraged to act as consultants as part of their contract at a business school, management college, or in some cases their company.

The decision to employ an external consultant is often made because an organization's own specialists are fully engaged or because they do not have the expertise. An external consultant can be an advantage because he or she will be seen as neutral, having no involvement in the internal politics of the organization. At the same time, the external consultant is likely to have greater credibility and experience to draw upon than many internal consultants. (It is well known that 'A prophet is not without honour, save in his own country, and in his own house'.)

Before contracting to employ external consultants, try to check on their work, either by seeing them in operation if they conduct courses, or by talking with the MDSs of those organizations where they have worked. Consultants will always refer an enquiring MDS to an organization where they have been successful; the secret is to find out where, if anywhere, success has not been achieved. No one likes to advertise failure, but if consultants are experienced, assured and successful, they will not wish to appear omnipotent and may, if questioned, volunteer information about a number of experiences they would not wish to repeat.

Before making a choice, an MDS should arrange to meet a number of consultants individually and, using a similar format for each one, should check the responses of each consultant. The MDS should then reflect on his or her personal reaction to each consultant, with whom they could be working closely at a future stage. Another criterion is whether the consultant will be acceptable within the culture of the organization. A training consultant who uses neuro-linguistic programming (NLP) or Gestalt may not be suitable for an organization whose managers expect training to be conducted in a strictly cognitive mode. Similarly an individual presenting him/herself wearing a bandanna and sandals to carry out research in a bank will be regarded with scepticism. It is also necessary to know what methods the consultants favour and how flexible they are within their repertoire.

Any discussion should be concerned with contracting an *individual*, and not a consultancy. Problems can occur if the MDS has built a rapport with a consultant only to find that he or she then subcontracts to someone who may not be as experienced or as acceptable to the organization.

The final points to be clarified before employing a consultant are: how much time will the consultant be able to devote to the assignment; and how much will it cost?

Time   A useful measure is to check how many projects a consultant has on his or her books at any one time – three would appear to be the maximum that an individual can handle effectively.

Cost   At the present time nearly all consultants are open to negotiation about their daily rate. As a guide, the average price for an individual consultant working at middle and senior level is about £800 per day. (However, when an independent trainer joins a consultancy, his or her daily fee can increase considerably – often by as much as 50 per cent. So reckon on a fee of £1,200 per day if the salary is to be paid by an employing consultancy.) Academics or senior consultants working in an area such as business strategy will charge up to £2,500 per day. For a management 'guru' expect to pay anything up to $35,000 per day.

After initial discussions, the consultant should be asked to send a note setting out what he or she understands to be the issue or problem in question and outlining the proposed course of action; if the consultant has understood the situation, it should be evident from the clarity of their proposal. If the outline is acceptable, with only some 'fine tuning' required, then it is likely that a working arrangement will succeed.

CONSULTANCIES

As mentioned above, I have found that a relationship with an individual consultant is more likely to prove successful than a relationship with a group of consultants. There is no guarantee that good working relationships will ensue simply because the consultancy has 'a good name'. In recent years, there has been a growth of consultancies seeing themselves more as corporations in their own right. This is manifested by the increasing size of this type of organization and the fact that many of the old established management accountancy consultancies have merged. For the MDS it will mean less choice of consultancies but possibly a greater chance of finding good people within one consultancy. Exceptions, though, are shown in the advertisements repeated in Figures 40.1 and 40.2, which reveal the calibre of consultants required by some consultancies and underline the necessity for checking the CVs of people you propose to use.

As noted previously, the cost of employing a trainer through a group of consultants can exceed the cost of an independent consultant by as much as 50 per cent.

Questions to a consultant or consultancies

1. Do you have experience of my type of organization or sector?
2. What experience have you had with the type of contract I have outlined?   *555*

The following advertisement appeared in a reputable international news journal.

OUTPLACEMENT AND CAREER COUNSELLING

THE growth business opportunity of the decade. Badly needed.
Recession driven and with tremendous growth potential. THIS is
NOT a franchise. Your once only investment of £3,750 purchases
expert coaching, training manuals, local business database, videos
and all starting and supporting material – your new business will
become self-financing and cash positive very quickly.

For full details, contact:

The XXX Group
Recruitment and Training Consultants

Figure 40.1   Consultancy advertisement (i)

The following announcement in a professional journal demonstrates the still
prevalent state of 'unconscious incompetence' present in a surprising number of
'would be' consultants.

Ms X has moved from education where she had considerable
experience working with pupils with special educational needs and in
developing in-service training courses for teachers. She is a partner
in a consultancy specializing in organizational change, training and
recruitment. Her particular strengths are in communication skills,
creativity, problem-solving, stress management and team-building.

Figure 40.2   Consultancy advertisement (ii)

3. Have you had experience working at the level of management we have in mind, and with the volume we are expecting?
4. Can you give me evidence of the results of your work in other organizations?
5. Who else in the consultancy might be working on the assignment? What evidence is there of their competence and suitability?
6. Are you willing to make modifications to the work as we proceed?
7. What method of evaluation do you recommend and will you be involved with it?
8. How many projects/assignments are you working on at the moment?
9. How much will it cost my company – broken down by consultant days and an outline of expenses charged?
10. What would the potential cancellation costs be?

BUSINESS SCHOOLS

For a given level of management, business school programmes can look similar. The objectives are almost interchangeable and the core content which accounts for something like 70 per cent of the offering is predictable. Each institution will claim that its faculty, and visiting faculty, is excellent, and in fact, excellence – in terms of genuinely wishing to provide a worthwhile educative experience – is maintained through out a wide spectrum of business schools.

The problem for an MDS lies in choosing the best programme to fit the objectives of a prospective participant and their organization. For example, a business school programme with a strong bias towards industrial marketing will not necessarily benefit an individual from a service industry such as insurance. It will be of interest, and it may be filed away for future reference, but any application of technique or knowledge may never take place because the fields of endeavour are so divergent. An appropriate programme would show that one or more members of the faculty has experience with marketing services such as banking, or preferably, in this instance, insurance. Another example of a possible mismatch between participant and programme would be where the programme shows a distinct leaning towards the behavioural sciences, with elements of personal exposure implicit in its objectives, while the participant's expectations are geared towards improving his or her financial knowledge, decision-making skills and powers of business analysis.

Some questions to be asked by an MDS before choosing to use a business school programme could include the following:

1. What does the organization require of its managers in the next 5 to 10 years that a business school programme might help to fulfil?
2. What will managers need for their development?
3. Have we undertaken a proper analysis of their individual needs?
4. Do they require an intensive educational programme or a skills programme?
5. When is the best time – this year or next?

6. How does their experience shape the type of programme to be used – are they specialists who need to know more about their specialization, or about another one?
7. Are they managers whose experience has been in a limited number of functional areas, and who therefore need exposure to a range of issues facing the organization?
8. Do any of the managers require exposure to an international faculty or participant group?

An important factor is to involve the manager in the choice of his or her programmes. This reduces the risk of the manager feeling he or she has been '*sent* on this course. . .!'

The most important consideration following any senior management business school/management college programme is the need to ensure either that the participants on their return have a different job more suited to their recent training, or that their present job is restructured in such a way that they can use at least some of the ideas learnt during the programme. I have seen many senior managers leave their nominating companies after having been on a management programme, not because they were badly briefed, debriefed or had no briefing at all, but because no allowance had been made for their 'growth' when they returned.

How to choose a business school

Having determined the specific educational requirement for an individual and decided to use a business school, the MDS may find the following series of actions and questions useful.

Collecting data by post

Brochures outlining courses are the marketing and public relations side of a business school, and their function is to sell and to give outline information. The more prestigious the school, the more the emphasis there is both on the quality and experience of the faculty, and on course structure and content, to ensure applications are from suitably high-calibre managers. Less prestigious business schools may stress uniqueness and novelty, and it is not unusual for some institutions to promote the setting of their colleges or the age of the buildings in order to establish an aura of tradition and learning.

Objectives

The course objectives will indicate whether the level of managers targeted is correct. If the stated objectives outline strategic thinking, macroeconomics, and international takeovers but suggest that the course is aimed at middle management, then the course is patently misdirected. The brochure should indicate the interrelationship between the various levels of courses offered, thereby giving clues on the thinking and house style of the school.

Content

The course content (or programme overview) will indicate the time allocated to the operational and corporate level of business. As suggested previously, the course content should match the objectives. Therefore, if the programme suggests, for example, that the objectives are to increase an individual's capacity to comprehend strategic decision, but apportions 80 per cent of its time to finance and management accounting, then those objectives are unlikely to be met.

Faculty

A list of faculty members should feature somewhere in the brochure. The list may indicate whether the faculty is full time, part time, or visiting, and should also indicate the mix of nationalities. Brief study will indicate the alma mater of each member of faculty and whether there is a preponderance of US-trained professors and lecturers or a balance between those trained in the New World, and the European – or Asian-educated faculty. A balance is particularly useful if the school is European and the intending participant is to be based in Europe. Many American managers posted to Europe are not happy about the over-emphasis placed on US-trained faculty in European business schools and the overuse of case study material from the United States. However, many European business schools, particularly INSEAD and IMD, have built up an impressive number of cases based on European and Pacific Basin organizations. Skim through the faculty list. This will give some idea of the strategic thrust of the school; for example, Durham is strong on small-business development, Chicago concentrates much of its activity on quantitative analysis, and at Darden the focus is on manufacturing.

Teaching methods

The teaching methods should also be indicated in the brochure. Some schools use case study only, following the lead given by Harvard. It has been suggested that this method is designed to teach people to analyse business problems and make theoretical decisions whilst divorcing them from reality. It must be said that the method does not suit all managers. The reading workload of sometimes 2–3 cases a day for between 14 and 70 days, depending on the length of the course, can be onerous and could therefore make learning more difficult. Equally, some schools use a high number of lectures, say 3–4 per day. This method can be numbing both to mind and rear end. Some schools have finally accepted that teaching methods need to be varied, and use case study, lectures, real-life consultancy, computers, simulation, role play and advanced audio visual presentation techniques to make their teaching points.

559

Participants

A list of recent participants will enable the MDS to assess the levels and backgrounds of the managers attending programmes. The MDS should note if a high proportion of the participants come from one sector of endeavour. If the dominant sector is, say, merchant banking, and the MDS is employed by a plastic containers producer, then the course is likely to be less than fruitful for the production manager. Similarly, if the majority of participants came from one geographical area, for example, Scandinavia or Nigeria, then the benefit of a mixed international flavour would be diluted. The level of managers attending particular programmes can usually be gauged by the job titles given, but it is worth remembering that vice presidents abound in American companies and that there appear to be a large number of senior executives in merchant banking who are disarmingly young and inexperienced! Contacting the MDS in a company shown to have had a manager as a participant on a course, or contacting that manager in order to discuss the programme, will be time well spent.

Publications

It is useful to obtain a list of recent research publications and articles. This will give the MDS an idea of the research strengths of the school and whether some of the published material might be applicable to the MDS's own organization, thus indicating the possibility of members of faculty having a close understanding of the needs of the MDS's organization.

MBA programme

If the school has an MBA programme it is useful to get information on the curriculum, the number of students, the programme demands, the average age, conditions of entry, breakdown of nationalities, drop out rate, and so on. These can form the basis of discussion on a subsequent visit to the school. Information of the type outlined above can be obtained by post.

Timing

It is not unusual for the ideal programme to be run at a less than ideal time for the prospective participant! In fact, it is probably a truism that most managers/ executives who attend business school programmes find it difficult to release themselves from their responsibilities. The organization may also find that its manpower planning has been less than effective, as it is unable to replace the individual even on a temporary basis! Detailed knowledge of the course and its likely benefits are essential for the MDS in these circumstances and can help to persuade the manager of the opportunity being offered. The MDS could also suggest that one manager's absence is an opportunity to develop the person who will act as a temporary replacement.

Geography/cost

The geographical position of a business school is a strong factor in determining its acceptability. Proximity can be a positive factor, but a programme held an appreciable distance from the prospective candidates' workplace can also be seen as a bonus. It has been said that for organizations based in the United Kingdom, a business school programme increases in its perceived value in direct proportion to its distance south of Calais or west of Cork! Hence the popularity of programmes in the United States or Europe. However, the cost of a programme is not inconsiderable and the closer to the home base, the less the overall bill.

Visiting a business school

The most effective method of choosing a business school is to visit a selection of the schools in order to build up a picture and to get an understanding of their methods and quality. There are many questions which can be asked of directors, staff faculty and participants, and various areas that can be observed, during the course of a visit, as outlined in the following sections.

Management structure

- Where are the decisions made?
- Is there an advisory board?
- What is its function?
- Who are represented?
- How is it structured?
- What is the level of independence of the faculty?
- Can they match their material to the needs of the companies represented on a particular programme?

Short courses

- What is the percentage of standard programmes (i.e. 'off the shelf') to 'in company' programmes?
- What changes in the profile of courses has taken place over the past five years?
- Which are the most supported courses and the least supported courses?
- What are the candidates' 'entry qualifications' for a particular course?
- How many applications does the school refuse?
- What is the average number of people on courses compared to the targeted number?

The last is an important question. Some schools accept too many people for a programme either because they do not wish to disappoint or because they wish to maintain income. Other courses have too few people on them and should have been cancelled.

561

MBAs

- What percentage leave for immediate employment?
- What is the percentage of 'funded' students?
- How many 'drop out' or are asked to 'drop out' during a programme?
- Is there a counsellor for the students?
- What is the pass rate?
- Is there a body of MBA alumni? How does it support the school?
- Do any of the faculty teach solely on MBA programmes?

General

- Which teaching disciplines are particularly strong?
- Which research area is particularly strong?
- What is the academic turnover rate?
- What proportion of an academic's time is given over to consultancy?
- Do any of the faculty hold directorial appointments in business?

Observation points

1. Sit in on a class and observe and listen to the level of participation. If the class is being conducted in English, note if the participants have difficulty with the language. If this is so, the question to the directing staff could be: 'What steps do you take to ensure that a candidate who has English as a second or third language is fluent?' (There are tests available: e.g. Test of English as a Foreign Language (TOEFL).)
2. Are there any 'clowns' or 'sleepers' on the course. This could indicate disaffection with either the subject or the teacher, or it might mean that the individual should not be on the programme and that the admission committee was lax.
3. Are the teaching methods appropriate to the subject? To give a lecture with no visual aids or participation on the subject of 'Capital evaluation techniques' does not bear thinking about, but it happens.
4. What 'energy level' do the participants display for the subject? Talk to a cross-section of participants and get views on the course and faculty and, where possible, comparisons with other courses that individuals have attended in their careers.
5. How many participants turn up late for class? This is often a measure of disaffection with the tutor or the programme.
6. Who does most of the talking in a case study class? If it is the tutor, then the class has not done enough work on the case or has not understood it.
7. How often does the programme director appear to have contact with participants? Little is gained if the director introduces the programme, disappears for its duration and then turns up only to take criticisms or plaudits at the end.

8. Is there a confusion between working hard and learning well? They are not necessarily one and the same thing.
9. Have the faculty talked to each other before the programme? Sometimes, unnecessary overlaps/gaps occur because some tutors have failed to discuss content.

The Principal

It is worthwhile meeting the head of the school and, if possible, posing the question; 'What in your view are the critical problems facing management education and how will the school respond?' Responses can indicate whether any actions being considered are innovative and responsive. The principal of a school can have great or little influence on the institution, and it is useful to check out their record in innovation and steering by having discussion with experienced MDSs.

Business schools are usually amenable to visits from MDSs. It is significant that, for all the organizations represented on the 'rolls of honour' as having sent participants to programmes, very few MDSs from those organizations visit programmes and talk with the faculty or directing staff. To make an investment of up to £35,000 for a senior manager to undertake a business school programme without a specialist visiting and undertaking some of the questioning and observations shown above, does not serve the interest of either the nominators or the business schools.

MANAGEMENT COLLEGES

Management colleges are mainly a UK/European phenomenon. The United States is far more geared to post-graduate/pre-experience education and therefore accreditation is more in evidence there. The situation in the United Kingdom is changing and more emphasis is being placed on the middle management MBA, possibly to the detriment of its British equivalent, the Accountancy degree.

Colleges provide short courses on general management, specific discipline and management skills essentially for post-experience managers. The work is usually sound but needs to be approached with caution if senior managers are being considered for placement. The faculty will usually have had previous management experience and/or have been management consultants. The approach recommended for business schools – that is, the questions and observation notes – apply equally to management colleges such as Ashridge or Henley.

The question about directorial appointments is particularly apposite for anyone considering a management college MBA. It is not unheard of for faculty members of some of the 'lower order' management colleges to be attending MBA programmes at business schools (as participants!) and then teaching their students directly on their return.

Management colleges in the United Kingdom have been active in linking up with their European mainland equivalents to provide an international perspective. This may be due to a lack of international faculty in the respective institutions, but the idea is positive and will do much to benefit the choice available to MDSs.

PUBLIC TRAINING COURSES

These are courses offered by profit-making organizations who offer participants the opportunity to gain expertise in a number of areas: for example, training skills, stress management, time management, and so forth. Courses associated with technical expertise, computers, textile technology, engineering, and so on, where individuals are being technically trained or updated on the 'state of the art', are not the subject of this section.

Public courses and training packages abound with 'the elixir effect' – that is, claiming to have the ultimate solution to all human resource development problems. There is no standard by which these courses can be assessed. That is not to say that there should not be such a standard, or that it would be difficult to institute one. It would make the job of choosing a suitable course very much easier and may rid the market of some less than professional operators.

Choosing a course

Some course providers are producing timetables of events covering a wide variety of subjects. It is enlightening to count the number of times a trainer's name appears at the bottom of the programme as course leader or tutor. In some instances a name appears so often that it stretches credulity for any individual to be so skilled and knowledgeable that they can teach such a wide range of subjects. Of even greater concern is when course providers fail to give any information at all about the tutors they are using. It is not unknown for jobbing trainers to be called in to run public programmes that have been over-subscribed in order that two programmes can be run in parallel, thus increasing income for the training company at the expense of any quality control.

Course objectives

What are the course objectives? What knowledge will participants gain, and/or what skills will they develop? If this is not clear, then it is likely that the content will be equally woolly.

What methods are employed? The methods should recognize that learning is not entirely a listening process but a talking, doing, practising activity as well.

The objectives, content and methods must be in harmony:

- The objectives should be limited to achievable, quantifiable behavioural or knowledge targets.
- The content must be adequate to cover the objectives but should not be

a huge list of words and phrases designed to flag the erudition of the trainer.

- The methods should be appropriate to the subject; for example, behaviour modification is not achieved by lecture, and marketing strategy analysis is unlikely to be learnt using interpersonal process recall.

The quality of the course tutor is critical. There are some very charismatic seminar leaders, particularly in the marketing field, where bravura perform-ances are applauded, but they are not necessarily good at facilitating learning. On the latter subject, the MDSs' grapevine could be consulted. The problem is, as ever, that one person's evaluation of an individual can be widely different from another and there are no agreed criteria. Price is no guide. A more expensive course means only that the course is more expensive. There are courses available, often mounted by the 'newer' universities, which are pro-fessionally tutored, well run and inexpensive.

The final check on a public course is either to send a suitable candidate whose judgement can be trusted or for the MDS to attend the course. If the candidate or MDS is satisfied that the objectives of the programme are met, that the content is appropriate, and that the course leader is able, then the course should prove worthwhile.

CONSORTIUM PROGRAMMES

The advantages of consortium programmes can best be described by an examination of the relative merits and demerits of internally run programmes and those of business schools, management colleges or public training pro-grammes.

Internal programmes

The *advantages* of internal programmes mounted by an individual organization are:

- Programme objectives will be in line with company aims.
- Content can be carefully scrutinized to ensure suitability and relevance.
- Faculty can be individually chosen for their match and skill in delivering what is required. The level is therefore more likely to be of uniform excellence.
- By negotiating with the potential faculty, and perhaps making the course non-residential, a company-focused programme will cost less.

The *disadvantages* are:

- The participants will not be able to match themselves against managers at similar levels from a variety of other organizations.

565

- There may be a 'cross-fertilization of self-ignorance'.

External programmes

The *advantages* of an external business school/management college/public course are:

- The participants will usually be drawn from a wide range of enterprises, both national and international, which increases the value of a programme.
- Managers/executives have time to reflect on their job, careers and the totality of their lives when they take structured time off the job, and often return refreshed and energized.

The *disadvantages* of this type of programme are:

- The MDS has little control over the aims and objectives of the programme.
- The faculty can vary in excellence from brilliant to awful.
- The participants can be wrongly selected, including the MDS's own participant!

The consortium programme

The approach eliminates most of the disadvantages and capitalizes on the advantage of external and internal programmes. This is done by agreeing with a variety of organizations on the objective of a programme, choosing a disinterested 'chairman', picking an ideal faculty, and making certain that the level of participants guarantees a high degree of participation and intellectual stimulation. I set up the first programme in the United Kingdom when working with Marks & Spencer. It included IBM, the Cabinet Office, Barclays Bank, Rothschilds Bank, Pilkingtons and a number of others. It is still operating at senior and middle management level.

TRAINING PACKAGES

Training packages which contain 'all a trainer needs to conduct effective training at every level' are attractive to a training department as a useful adjunct to development activities already in operation; they can form the basis of a whole range of associated activities. However, their ease can be their failing if an MDS is not concerned or knowledgeable about the underlying theoretical framework. Participants on any such programme soon recognize incompetent trainers who only mouth words from the course manual and who are not able to answer questions, think on their feet, read the group or respond to it.

Some organizations who promote training packages offer to train trainers in
566 their use but what they often fail to do is check whether the packages are

appropriate to the organization. They may claim that their training package can easily be assimilated within any current training or development activities but this claim needs careful analysis for the following reasons:

- Many packages originate in the United States and changing 'sidewalk' to 'pavement', or dubbing a Home Counties voice on a video tape, does not bridge the culture gap.
- High-pressure sales training may suit the marketing development of a floor polish company but not a firm of accountants and there is no way that the style can be altered.
- Packages which provide all materials down to flipchart pages and notes, and which do not allow the buyer any chance to 'personalize' or 'customize' them, are inflexible and show that they are not sensitive to the needs of the purchasing organization.

Computer-aided training and multi-media packages are becoming increasingly sophisticated and with the advent of reasonably priced 'expert systems' this form of training and development will grow. It may not be possible for the MDS to check with previous users on the effectiveness of the offered systems as they may be completely new. If budgets will stretch, the best way to use this medium is to have it 'built' to the organization's own specifications rather than buying a package off the shelf.

SUMMARY

In these days, when training and development budgets are closely scrutinized, and – yes – cut, and when a new management development manager is wary of trying out new approaches for fear of wasting the organization's money, it is more important than ever to be sure that the supplier of a development activity is the right one. The choice of who will supply consultancy or training/development services is often a matter of using the 'tried and tested', or is at the whim of the chief executive, or depends upon the proximity of the organization to a business school, or even rests upon previously shared experiences between the MDS and the supplier.

What I have endeavoured to outline in this chapter are some techniques and guidelines to ensure that the choice of development suppliers is informed by a degree of professional analysis. The deciding question must be: 'Will the development activity achieve positive results for the organization?' If the results achieved are positive, and observable or quantifiable by whatever means deemed appropriate, then the supplier will have been effective.

FURTHER READING

Huczynski, Andrzej (1983), *Encyclopedia of Management Development Methods*, Aldershot: Gower.

Moulton, Harper (annually), *The CER Evaluation Guide to Executive Pro-grammes*, (1987), Fairfield, Iowa: Corporate Education Resources, Inc.

Oliver, Judy (1990), *Developing Managers: A Guide to Executive Programmes in Europe and the USA*, London: *Economist* Publications.

Rogers, Jane (1988) *MBA: The Best Business Tool? A Guide to British and European Business Schools*, London: *Economist* Publications.

Steverink, Leo (annually), *European Management Education Guide*, Nederland: IMEC.

Townsend, Robert (1971), *Up the Organization*, London: Coronet.

Glossary of training terms[1]

Robert J. Kelly

Acquired behaviour
Measurable changes in patterns of human behaviour or changes in attitude demonstrated by certain skills and practices acquired as a result of training.

Activity Learning*
A general term used to indicate learning by means of active participation of the learner in such exercises as project work and group discussion, as opposed to passive means such as lectures or films.

Adaptation
Process by which a trainee becomes adjusted to a job or new environment through successful training resulting in behavioural change.

Adult training
A special approach to mature trainees, those with entrenched skills acquired through long experience and whose inclination to accept retraining or attitude change calls for specialized training skills.

Aim
A constituent part of a goal identified through the process of goal analysis to determine the overall aims and objectives which make up the goal. See goal analysis.

Algorith*
A mathematical term meaning an exact prescription, defining a computational process leading from various initial data to the desired result. In logical tree analysis its meaning has been extended to cover any rule of thumb procedure, any recipe – not necessarily mathematical – for achieving a desired outcome. In this

---

[1]Entries marked thus * are reproduced, by permission, from *Glossary of Training Terms* (HMSO, 1971). *569*

sense, a flowchart, or its list structure equivalent, provides the user with an algorithm for handling a variety of different conditions in the right way. This usage follows the procedures of computer programming. In both cases the process of decision-making is reduced to a sequence of 'Yes/No' or 'either/or' responses to specific questions, stemming usually from predetermined unambiguous statements of action.

Analogies
Association of similar situations, processes, operations and techniques in teaching and training activities which often provides a useful means of explaining and reinforcing theoretical and practical exercises and assignments.

Appraisal
A critical assessment of the relevance, feasibility and potential effectiveness of a project/programme prior to making a decision whether to undertake it.

Appreciation training
Usually of short duration, designed to give a general introduction and understanding of a particular subject area or the demonstration of a technique to enable the participants to appreciate the workings of a system or procedure. Appreciation courses are often arranged for senior managers who require some knowledge of subjects such as computers, selection, training, work study, and so on.

Aptitude*
Natural ability to acquire and utilize types of knowledge and/or skill. Tests to determine such ability are called aptitude tests.

Assessment
General term for the processes of ascertaining whether training is efficient or effective in achieving prescribed objectives. It covers both validation and evaluation.

Assessment centre
Norm-referenced method of assessing the composite-skill profile of an individual as measured against the average of a peer group or norm.

Assimilation
The ability (of a trainee) to absorb knowledge and skills as a result of effective training. Criterion tests are a means of determining whether new knowledge and skills have been assimilated as a result of training.

Assumption
An external event or action which must take place, or a condition which must exist, if a project is to succeed, over which project management has little or no control.
570 See Logical framework.

Attitude
The attitude of a learner is all-important in developing effective training. Attitudes govern the way groups react and may prevent or frustrate the learning process of an individual or members of a group. The instructor will strive to ensure that the environment is conducive to producing the best atmosphere for the development of positive attitudes that will benefit all trainees and improve their motivation towards the achievement of the training objective.

Attitude survey (climate survey)
1. Originally a technique pioneered by the National Institute of Industrial Psychology (NIIP) for discovering, by confidential non-directive interview with a sample of employees, their suggestions, criticisms and feelings about their work and related matters. The term is now used for other procedures as well as interviews including enquiry by questionnaire, and with other samples of people (e.g. customers).
2. A means of measuring the gap between desired norms and actual norms in an organization. Based on responses to a questionnaire the results of such a survey provide norm profiles of predetermined norm clusters. Norm clusters may be identified as, organization and/or work assignments; pride in the organization; personal performance; communications; leadership and supervision; integrity and security; training and HRD; innovation and change.

Attitude/knowledge/skill behaviour pattern*
The essential determinants of effective performance in terms of attitude, knowledge and skill – the attitude to perform, the knowledge required to take the right attitude and the skills necessary to do it.

Audio aids
Aids to communication, with special reference to controlled learning, which utilize the sense of hearing e.g. record players, tape recorders and (broadcast) radio. The quality of the software is more important than the type of hardware used to present it.

Audio-visual (AV) aids
Aids to communication, with special reference to controlled learning using sight and hearing. AV aids include sound film, film strip, broadcast radio and TV with closed-circuit TV recordings and video tapes. The quality of the software is more important than the hardware used to present it.

Basic knowledge
Requisite knowledge demanded as a condition for admission to a course of training.

Basic training*
The first stage of the learning process for a given task, job, occupation or group of occupations, aimed at developing the fundamental attitude/knowledge/skill *571*

behaviour pattern to specified standards. It may be given in training centres, technical colleges, or in special training workshops or training bays in organizations. In some cases it may have to be given in the production situation, but learning and not production is the primary objective.

Basic VT Year

A diagnostic period (e.g. one year) during which students are exposed to various skilled occupations with a view to assessing their personal adaptability and motivation towards a particular craft skill. In the construction sector students may rotate for six weeks' duration gaining experience of: plastering, bricklaying, painting and decorating, carpentry and joinery, plumbing and roofing. The results achieved over the whole period provide a means of assessing a student's job interest and aptitudes.

Behavioural objective

Precise statement of what a learner is expected to be able to do under predetermined conditions and to a level of performance in terms of time, accuracy and completeness of the task involved.

Benchmark data

Data required to be maintained as part of a training record to assess a trainee's progress and work performance compared with known or predetermined standards of performance for specified skills. When EWS is employed as a form of measurement, benchmark data may be defined as certain percentages of EWS at phased period of time throughout the training course.

Carrel

Individualized permanent study area or mobile unit suitably equipped and furnished to provide optimum facilities for a student or trainee in which to work. When provided with special facilities (e.g. chemistry sink with water supply and drainage) it is defined as a wet carrel as opposed to the normal dry facility.

Case study

Learning technique in which a real situation or a series of actual events is presented to trainees (either orally or by case papers issued in advance) for their analysis and consideration of possible solutions of identified problems. Their findings are normally compared with the way in which the real life situation subsequently developed.

CAT

Computer-aided training.

Circuit trainer

A mock-up of electrical circuitry allowing a variety of wiring exercises to be carried out with patented terminals and to enable fault-finding exercises to be set up and later diagnosed by the trainee. This type of training device also reduces the cost of training materials as patented terminals are used for jointing cables.

Competence*
Ability to perform a particular activity to a prescribed standard. The activity may involve the development of a variety of skills.

Concept approach
Unlike rote learning the concept approach to learning involves concept formation which encourages thought and stimulates questioning to assist trainees to arrive at a reasoned understanding and appreciation of the task(s) being studied or practised.

Control variable
To predict events and control operations statistical methods are used for comparative purposes. Data is normally considered in related pairs, one item of each pair of data being dependent on the other. Both data are considered as variables, viz. a dependent and independent variable. The independent variable is the variable which is not affected by changes in the other variable. The dependent variable is the variable which is affected by changes in the other one (e.g. sales of cars may be affected by advertising). The values of sales will invariably depend on the value of the advertising campaign. Accordingly, advertising is the independent variable and sales the dependent variable.

Corporate anorexia
The reduction in labour during periods of recession and high interest rates is often known by this term. See also Lean years.

Corporate culture
Accepted set of rules, values and attitudes, written or understood, formulated by corporate growth through behavioural change within an organized environment.

Cost-benefit analysis*
A systematic comparison between the cost of carrying out a service of activity and the value of that service or activity, quantifying as far as possible. All costs and benefits (direct and indirect, financial and social) are taken into account.

Counselling*
The direct personal relationship in which the counsellor makes available to another person his friendship, experience and knowledge to assist that person in solving his problems.

Criterion behaviour*
Used specifically in designing a programme for a target population to distinguish between present behaviour and behavioural objective – the new objective is the criterion for assessing the effectiveness of the programme.

573

Criterion test*
A test, in the appropriate written or practical form, designed to measure the level to which a learner has reached towards the attainment of the specified behavioural objective (criterion behaviour). It can also be given as a pre-test to identify individuals who need the training and to establish a benchmark from which to measure progress; and/or as a post-test to measure the effectiveness of the programme by comparing the pre-test and post-test scores.

Cross-cultural communication
Communicating with foreign nationals or ethnic minority groups with mutual empathy, sympathy and understanding of cultural differences.

Cultural change
Cultural change results from prolonged behavioural or norm changes. Climate surveys or attitude surveys and the like are proven ways of initiating change.

Curriculum
The content of a teaching programme or course of study.

Cycle
The measurement of a repetitive task.

Daily work sheets
A trainee's record of a day's work which provides a basis for supervision by the instructor and works-based training officer. It may be produced in purpose-made booklet form suitably lined and set out in columns to show the required information of tasks performed, time taken for completion of each task, target times (if any) and any appropriate codes relating to production work tasks, safety pointers and so on. If loose sheets are used the trainee should be supplied with a folder or clipboard. The record should be kept by the trainee, but subject to inspection by supervisors and/or training officers as a means of maintaining accuracy of entries and a check on work performance. If management is seen to value the document, so too will the trainee, as its daily maintenance will ensure the development of good working practices, with quality being uppermost in the working environment.

Data dictionary
Dictionary of relevant terms for computer operators using large databases.

Decision tree
See Algorithm.

Diagnostic period
See Basic VT Year.

Discovery method*
The discovery method is a means of teaching which avoids expository instruction. The trainee is presented with tasks which engage him in the search for and

574

selection of clues on how to proceed. The effectiveness of the discovery method depends on the design of these tasks which have two aims: to provide an intrinsic means for unassisted learning; and to provide the experience upon which insight into key relationships can be developed.

Donor fatigue
The point reached by a donor of development aid or assistance of any kind when the beneficiaries demonstrate a lack of interest in full co-operation and take aid for granted.

Element*
A distinct part of a specified task selected for convenience of observation, measurement and analysis. Work-study elements are normally the smallest units of analysis; training (or instructional) elements are normally greater and are selected for convenience of learning.

Evaluation*
The assessment of the total value of a training system, project or programme in social as well as financial terms. Evaluation differs from validation in that it measures the overall cost benefit of the project/programme, not just the achievement of its specified objectives. The term is also used in the general sense of the continuous monitoring of a project/programme or of the training function as a whole. See also Cost benefit analysis, Validation.

EWS*
Experienced-worker standard (EWS) is the standard of quality and output of production or services achieved by the average experienced worker over a given period of time (normally one working day at operator level). EWS is normally agreed between managers' and workers' representatives and often derives from work study or job analysis. The term is not to be confused with trained-worker standard (TWS).

Experiential learning
Learning by experience or repetition is generally regarded as the best method of practical training. However, long-term practice in itself may not always produce the desired results in today's rapidly changing world. Technical and craft practices in particular must be constantly evaluated and the results regularly and frequently fed back to allow modifications of techniques and practices to be introduced as a means of achieving zero faults in processes and perfection in the end result.

External validation (of a training programme)*
A series of tests and assessments designed to ascertain whether the behavioural objectives of an internally valid training programme were realistically based on an accurate initial identification of training needs in relation to the criteria of effectiveness adopted by the organization.

Factory training
Familiarization training carried out for the benefit of end users of plant and equipment manufactured in the factory. Factory training is often offered to familiarize maintenance workers with equipment failures and troubleshooting skills.

Feedback*
The process by which information about the results of an action are communicated to the learner. Various authorities have attributed the learning that takes place to either the informative characteristic or the reinforcing characteristic of the knowledge of results, or a combination of both.

Field training
Practical assignments conducted as training assignments on the job and usually associated with actual field work as opposed to factory-based production operations.

Film strip/loops
A series of positive photographic transparencies printed on a single length of film and projected frame by frame as still pictures. The series may be looped for recycling until the projector is switched off. Film strips/loops may illustrate a human situation, stage of process, assembly or manufacture and are often used in conjunction with a prepared script for personal delivery or by tape recorder or disc player.

Flannel board*
A visual aid comprising a board of suitable size covered with cotton, flannel, felt, wool or suede cloth, to which objects (principally drawings, pictures and signs) backed with strips of similar materials or coarse glass paper, will adhere, when pressed to it.

Flipchart*
Sheets of detachable paper used for display purposes with felt-tip pens or crayons.

Flowchart*
A diagrammatic representation of a system, in which interrelationships between its component parts are shown by various symbols and interconnecting arrows. See also Algorithm.

Flow diagram*
A diagram or model, substantially to scale, which shows the location of specific activities carried out and the routes followed by workers, materials or equipment in their execution. Process chart symbols may be embodied in the diagram.

Follow up
Actions taken or scheduled to apply information gained or lessons learned from the monitoring or evaluation process.

Function

The term 'useful function' was used to describe the smallest possible modular unit of work. It was made up of one or more learning elements, all of which required to be learned in order to acquire the necessary skills to carry out the specified useful function.

Functional analysis

A complete survey of an organization, division, department or a section may be carried out as part of a job-evaluation exercise or independently. All activities are listed and matched to the individual staff members who are responsible for each activity. See also Job analysis.

Functional classification

A complete survey of an organization, division, department or section as part of a job evaluation exercise. Activities are matched to individuals for Job analysis, q.v.

Glass ceiling

The unseen barrier met by women competing with men for (internal) promotion.

Goal

The ultimate target in a strategic plan, the final result obtained through the successful process of objectives achieved, aims attained and goal accomplished.

Goal ambiguity

Arises when goals are confused with aims or objectives and when strategic plans and policies are not precisely defined in qualitative and quantitative terms.

Goal analysis

A means of identifying the necessary aims and objectives required to accomplish the final outcome or goal.

Group dynamics*

The study of the interaction of the behaviour of individuals as members of a group and of the behaviour of groups generally.

Group norms

The type of responses, stimulated by selected stimuli, and identified as normal behaviour within an observed group.

Hays points system

A method of job evaluation by Edward Hays which identifies and assesses by points the levels of know-how, problem-solving and accountability required to perform a specified job.

Human resource development (HRD)

1. Corporate title used to unite those aspects of management traditionally *577*

regarded as belonging to the personnel function with the training function. The responsibility for the development of every employee rests with the employer, from the date of appointment of a worker until that worker's date of retirement, resignation or death. Some organizations include the whole HRD function under one head, whereas others maintain an administrative separation of the two ancillary functions.

2. A means designed to enable an individual to undertake any form of education or training experience that results in greater knowledge, higher qualifications, new skills or personal improvement that helps them towards life, and career, goals.

Independent variable
See Control variable.

Indicator
An explicit and objectively verifiable measure – either direct or indirect (proxy) – of the achievement of an objective.

Individualized training
A method which allows trainees to learn and develop at their own pace according to the individual's abilities and needs. Also known as 'Tempo training'.

Internal validation
A series of tests and assessments designed to ascertain whether a training programme has achieved the behavioural objectives specified.

In-tray exercise
In-tray exercises are normally associated with supervisory and management training. They provide a practical means of dealing with routine problems that arise in the course of a normal working day.

Incident method
Method where trainees seek relevant information to determine the facts of the incident described and its environment.

Incident training
A form of training, often based on a special incident or a case where learning is achieved 'by doing'. It incorporates group dynamics, in that the participants are normally given appropriate cases that are taken from real life situations and resemble incidents with which the group is familiar.

Induction
A training course designed to introduce an individual, or group, to a new or changed work situation and/or to familiarize new staff members to a company environment.

Job analysis
The process of examining a job in detail to identify its component tasks. The detail and approach may vary according to the purpose for which the job is being analysed (e.g. training, equipment, design, working layouts).

Job description
A statement of the purpose, scope, responsibilities and tasks which constitute a particular job.

Job evaluation
A generic term covering methods of determining the relative worth of jobs. The process enables jobs to be placed in rank order which can be used as a basis for establishing a balanced remuneration system.

Johari window
A matrix used in management-development schemes for analysing inter-personal skills and to enable participants to carry out self-appraisal assessments.

Key-result analysis
An analysis of the key tasks to be performed, the level of performance required and criteria for measuring the performance against required standards.

Key-result area*
A task or series of tasks within the compass of an individual's job where (a) excellent performance might transform the efficiency of the organization or (b) poor performance would significantly diminish its efficiency.

Keyboard
Words selected by a teacher or instructor, often used as mnemonics, to trigger recall when teaching or instructing. Keyword lesson plans prompt the teacher through the course of the lesson.

L-group
A highly flexible form of learning experience where a related group works individually and collectively to design a syllabus and work through a training system by identifying the training needs and situations required to satisfy them, by formulating behavioural objectives and maintaining active control over events and progression, combining individual ratings of personal impressions gained daily. Because of its high flexibility the organization of such learning experiences needs careful planning.

Lean years
Times of recession and high interest rates when businesses are forced into making reductions in staff levels. See also Corporate anorexia.

Learner-centred method*
A learning/teaching system in which the learner is encouraged to make, within *579*

his capability limits, his own decisions about the method and pace at which he learns.

Learning
The physical and mental processes involved in changing one's normal behavioural patterns and habits from the norm.

Learning curve*
A means of plotting the rate of progress of an individual or group in the form of a graph. Performance is plotted against time, and the rate of improvement over a period of time is clearly shown.

Learning plateau*
A temporary halt in progress in the process of learning, involving habits and skills of different orders, such as learning to play a musical instrument, to use a typewriter, to operate industrial equipment or to speak a foreign language.

Lecture
The classical form of conveying information from teacher to student. The success of the transfer rests with the ability of the lecturer. Lectures are most effective when presented with ample teaching aids combined with active participation by the whole group, which may previously be allocated to syndicated groupings for follow-up discussions on the content of the lecture.

Lecturette*
A lecture not longer than 20 minutes, normally delivered to trainees while on the shop floor. It should be related to a defined, practical aspect of the work undertaken by the trainees and cover only specific, discrete subjects.

Lesson*
A method of instruction incorporating a number of instructional techniques designed to ensure the participation of the learning group in reaching the specified behavioural objectives. The techniques used are those which give the instructor the necessary feedback to enable him to ascertain whether the material is being assimilated and where necessary to take appropriate remedial action. The lesson should not be confused with the lecture which is a straight talk or exposition, possibly using visual or other aids, but without group participation other than through questions at the conclusion.

Level of achievement
The level reached following a course of training in which the minimum level of achievement may be stated as part of the behavioural objective. Such a level must be measurable and the level of achievement attained in any test (e.g. the post-test) is compared with the required level as prescribed in the objective.

Logbook
A book maintained by a trainee, such as an apprentice log, in which is recorded

details of the work undertaken and completed satisfactorily with comments made by on-the-job supervisors, training staff, inspectors and so on. The logbook remains the property of the trainee and fulfils the need for a complete and accurate record of practical skill training.

Logical framework
Summary of project concept and design in the form of a matrix showing the components, their interrelationships and the expected consequences of successfully completing each significant stage of the project.

Magnetic board*
A sheet of steel cut to an appropriate size which may be surfaced to serve as a chalkboard. Display material is fixed to the board by small magnets or magnetic strip. Similarly, a board may be made of magnetic material to which steel display material will adhere. It is particularly useful for showing moving objects and for building up work-flow charts, organization charts, and so forth.

Management by objectives*
A philosophy for running a working organization which involves fixing specific and realistic targets for achieving greater effectiveness throughout part of or the whole of the organization. An integrated training system should be incorporated to aid the various functions to practise the philosophy.

Management development scheme*
A systematic scheme in an organization whereby a manager's performance and potential are developed by training and education. The aim is to ensure that the organization will have sufficient managers of the required calibre as they are needed to meet the demands of the business.

Manpower planning
The integration of human resources policies to ensure that the right numbers of the right people will be available for the right jobs at the right time. See Human resource development.

Microprojector*
An instrument which projects highly magnified pictures of microscopic objects on to a screen.

Model*
1. A two- or three-dimensional representation of an object or group of objects incorporated in a system; often used as a teaching aid.
2. Also relates to an abstract representation of a system such as a mathematical model of the economy or a business situation.

Modular training*
1. Modular training is the system of engineering craft training employed by the Engineering Training Authority (EnTra). A module consists of a period of training *581*

and experience in a group of related engineering craft skills. These skills, the training to be given and the standards of performance to be achieved are specified by the EnTra. Any trainee successfully completing first-year basic training and a minimum of two appropriate modules in accordance with the procedure recommended by the EnTra is awarded a certificate of craftsmanship.

2. The term is more generally used in respect of separate training programmes designed as a series to lead to a certain level of qualification, or as a related group from which programmes may be chosen according to need.

Multi-media learning*

The integrated use of various communication media (print, audio-tape, film, slide, video, computer, and so on) in the construction of a learning programme, in such a way that each part of the information being taught is carried by the most appropriate medium.

Multisensory learning aids*

Aids to communication, learning, teaching, remembering and research which utilize several senses (e.g. working models, simulators and synthetic trainers).

Objective

A precise statement predicting tangible benefits resulting from planned training efforts. A training objective may be described as 'behavioural' (q.v) when it related to a person or as an 'organizational' type when describing predicted measurable accomplishments of a structure. A programme objective is a long-term predicted outcome of an HRD programme determined by those responsible for creating it. All measurable objectives meet three criteria; each must describe: (a) the outcome (what is to be achieved?), (b) the level of achievement (how well is it to be achieved?), and (c) the conditions of evaluation, (under what conditions will it be achieved?).

Objective test*

A test or examination in which every question is set in such a way as to have only one correct answer. That is, the opinion of the examiner or marker does not enter in judging whether an answer is good or poor, acceptable or wrong; there is no subjective element involved.

Off-the-job training*

Training in the attitude/knowledge/skill/behaviour pattern required for a task, job or occupation away from the normal work situation and daily pressures. It is normally only part of the whole training programme and is usually combined with on-the-job training.

On-the-job training*

Training at work, in the skills needed to perform a task, to the satisfaction of the supervisor nominated to oversee that part of the training programme conducted *582* through work experience.

Overhead projector*

A projector which projects transparencies and solid objects (in silhouette) on to a screen located behind the operator in such a way that he can maintain visual contact with his audience. Material drawn or written with suitable crayons or felt pens on a sheet roll of transparent acetate is similarly projected. The transparencies are usually made to fit the ground glass screen on top of the overhead projector which is approximately 10 inches square. The overhead projector can be used in normal lighting conditions.

Phase testing*

A system of tests by which the attainment of approved standards is measured throughout a period of training. See also Modular training.

Planned experience*

Supervised practice and experience in the normal work situation, carefully planned as an integral part of the training programme to develop and consolidate the attitude/knowledge/skill behaviour pattern already acquired, on or off the job, or to provide the basis for further training in more specialized jobs.

Planned improvement programme (PIP)

A human-resources development programme designed for an organization to increase production, improve efficiency, introduce new methods and/or procedures, all or any of which is geared towards general improvement of the whole environment. PIPs may be conducted in a division or department only, or embrace the whole organization.

Project work*

1. A form of exercise leading to the accomplishment, within a fixed time, of a definite task, often a completion of a report containing recommendations on a problem stated, or on a particular aspect of it.
2. A planned undertaking, a unit of management, designed to achieve certain specific objectives within a given budget and within a specified period of time.

Refresher training*

The process of further training in work currently performed in order to improve job performance (e.g. quality and quantity of production or services). Also referred to as 'booster training'.

Reinforcement*

Behaviour is acquired as a result of a contingent relationship between the response of an organism and a subsequent event. Reinforcing operations are those which lead to acquisition when appropriately correlated with response occurrences. In general, reinforcement refers to any of a wide variety of conditions which may be introduced into a learning situation to increase the probability that a given response will reappear in the same situation. Operations that are reinforcing take place as a consequence of the occurrence of a response, and occur immediately after the response.

Role playing*
A learning technique in which students are presented with a situation which they are required to resolve by acting out the roles of those represented in this situation.

Sandwich course*
A course consisting of alternate periods of study in a university or an establishment of further education, and of associated industrial, professional or commercial experience at a place outside the university or establishment of further education, so organized that at least 19 weeks of each year of the course is spent in the university or establishment of further education. There are two basic patterns: the 'thin' sandwich, which consists of alternating period of six months' study and six months' experience over four years; and the 'thick; or 2:1:1 scheme, which consists of two years of study followed by one year of experience followed by one year of study. The six months' study/year is a nominal period but if it falls below 19 weeks, the course is classified as 'block release' and not as 'sandwich'.

Seminar*
A short course or conference making extensive use of participating methods and devoted to the exclusive study of one subject with the object of furthering knowledge in that area.

Sensitivity training
See T-group training.

Session assessment form*
Used in the validation of training courses. The form is designed to collect trainees' views on specific aspects of their training. Each trainee has three questions to consider at the conclusion of a session and he answers by putting a mark in the appropriate interval in each scale. For scoring purposes the intervals along each scale are numbered 1 to 7, starting from the unfavourable on the left.

T-group training*
A general term used to describe a number of similar highly participating learning methods whose purpose is to improve trainees' interpersonal skills. The terms 'sensitivity training', 'group dynamics', and 'group relations training' are sometimes used. Basically, T-group training aims to increase one's ability: (a) to appreciate how others are reacting to one's own behaviour; (b) to gauge the state of relationships between others; and (c) to carry out skilfully the behaviour required by the situation.

Target population*
The particular group or range of students for whom a particular training programme is designed.

Tempo training
584 See Individualized training.

Tracer study
Research activity aimed at locating trainees who successfully completed a training course to assess their success in practising the skills acquired during training.

Trained-worker standard*
The behavioural objectives specified for a normally off-job training programme which concentrates on those tasks which have been demonstrated by analysis to be most frequent, difficult and critical in the actual job. Trained-worker standard may differ in that although learning of these tasks may be rapid, EWS may be reached only after considerable on-the-job practice.

Training gap
The difference in a person's level of skills and the competence required to fulfil the job specification. See also Training specification.

Training manual*
A guide for the use of training staff and, where appropriate, of trainees, showing in detail the subject areas and behavioural objectives to be achieved, methods of instruction, equipment and materials to be used, the form of records to be kept and of tests to be administered.

Training objective
See Behavioural objective.

Training plan
A comprehensive statement drawn up in the context of the corporate objectives of an organization in relation to part or all of its training and providing for such matters as job and personnel specifications; conditions of eligibility; selection procedures, training objectives and strategy; programmes, timetables and syllabuses; location and method of training; training records, tests, qualifications and awards.

Training programme*
An interpretation of the training specification in terms of units of instruction or learning experience, set out in chronological sequence and showing the time allowed for each, the place, the method of instruction to be used, and the person responsible for giving it.

Training records
The process of keeping written evidence of training taking place in order that achievements can be measured against objectives and that factual information is available when required.

Training scheme*
A series of learning experiences, which may include formal courses/training *585*

programmes and off-the-job training, devised to meet the immediate and foreseeable training needs of an individual. See also Training specification.

Training specification*
A detailed statement of what a trainee needs to learn based on a comparison between the job specification and his present level of competence. See also Training scheme.

Training-within-Industry for Supervisors (TWI)
Unique term which evolved in the United States in the 1940s to denote training in supervisory functions of job instruction, job methods and job relations; subsequently practised worldwide.

Tutoring*
The act of giving additional knowledge and guidance to an individual or group of trainees in an off-the-job informal training situation.

Validation
1. Internal validation: a series of tests and assessments designed to ascertain whether a training programme has achieved the behavioural objectives specified.
2. External validation: a series of tests and assessments designed to ascertain whether the behavioural objectives of an internally valid training programme were realistically based on an accurate initial identification of learning needs in relation to the criteria of effectiveness adopted by the organization.
3. In programmed instruction, validation is the verification of a programme by means of tests which demonstrate whether the actual behaviour of a fully representative sample of the target population at the end of the training programme is commensurate with the stipulated criterion behaviour. Where it is not commensurate the programme is revised until it is shown to be effective against the criterion test.

Verifiable indicators
Developments or changes which portray evidence of a project's progress in the achievement of its aims and objectives towards the ultimate goal as described in a logical framework.

Work-experience schedule*
A booklet issued to trainees showing the total amount of experience they should gain during their training period. It can incorporate a logbook which is a record of work done and experience gained, completed by the trainee, countersigned by the supervisor and periodically checked by the training officer/manager.

Index

587

Dealing with Difference

Teresa Williams and Adrian Green

It's the first morning of the training course you've rashly agreed to run. You look round the assembled group and what do you see? Men and women, under-20s and over-60s, white faces, black faces, suits, jeans. Is there anything you can do – anything you should have already done – to make your training effective for people with perhaps widely different ways of regarding the world?

Yes, a great deal, according to Teresa Williams and Adrian Green. In this pioneering book they examine the effects of culture on the learning process and put forward a number of ideas and activities designed to help trainers take account of cultural values in the planning and delivery of their training. After examining both organizational and national cultures they look in detail at how diversity can affect every aspect of the learning event, from the initial announcement, through pre-course work and administration, to running the event itself and the subsequent debriefing and review.

The authors' approach will enable trainers to:
- design learning that acknowledges each participant's culture
- reduce prejudice and stereotyping
- run learning events that do not force participants to compromise their own culture
- achieve a better return on investment by working with the prevailing culture rather than inadvertently opposing it.

Contents

1994   216 pages   0 566 07425 7

Gower

Games for Trainers
Volumes 1, 2 and 3

Andy Kirby

Most trainers use games. And trainers who use games collect new games. Andy Kirby's three-volume compendium contain 75 games in each volume. They range from icebreakers and energizers to substantial exercises in communication. Each game is presented in a standard format which includes summary, statement of objectives, list of materials required, recommended timings and step-by-step instructions for running the event. Photocopiable masters are provided for any materials needed by participants. All the games are indexed by objectives, and Volume 1 contains an introduction analysing the different kinds of game, setting out the benefits they offer and explaining how to use games to the maximum advantage. An unusual feature of this volume is a programmed text designed to help trainers to develop their own games. Volume 2 contains an integrated index covering both volumes. Volume 3 reflects current trends in training; in particular the increased attention being paid to stress management and assertiveness. It contains an integrated index covering all three volumes.

Volume 1	1992	171 pages	0 566 07260 2
Volume 2	1992	173 pages	0 566 07290 4
Volume 3	1994	216 pages	0 566 07442 7

Gower

A Handbook for Training Strategy

Martyn Sloman

The traditional approach to training in the organization is no longer effective. That is the central theme of Martyn Sloman's challenging book. A new model is required that will reflect the complexity of organizational life, changes in the HR function and the need to involve line management. This Handbook introduces such a model and describes the practical implications not only for human resource professionals and training managers but also for line managers.

Martyn Sloman writes as an experienced training manager and his book is concerned above all with implementation. Thus his text is supported by numerous questionnaires, survey instruments and specimen documents. It also contains the findings of an illuminating survey of best training practice carried out among UK National Training Award winners.

The book is destined to make a significant impact on the current debate about how to improve organizational performance. With its thought-provoking argument and practical guidance it will be welcomed by everyone with an interest in the business of training and development.

Contents

1994   256 pages   0 566 07393 5

Gower

A Manual for Change

Terry Wilson

Change is now the only constant, as the cliché has it, and organizations who fail to master change are likely to find themselves undone by it.

In this unique manual, Terry Wilson provides the tools for planning and implementing a systematic organizational change programme. The first section enables the user to determine the scope and scale of the programme. Next, a change profile is completed based on twelve key factors. Finally, each of the factors is reviewed in the context of the user's own organization. Questionnaries and exercises are provided throughout and any manager working through these will have not only a clear understanding of the change process but also specific plans ready to put into action.

Derived from the author's experience of working with organizations at every level and in a wide range of industries, the manual will be invaluable to directors, managers, consultants and professional trainers battling to help their organizations survive and flourish in an increasingly turbulent environment.

Contents

1994   192 pages   0 566 07460 5

Gower